Americans-Discover-America Series

Walking

A Guide to Beautiful Walks and Trails in America

BY JEAN CALDER

William Morrow & Company, Inc. New York, 1977

With grateful acknowledgement to
Allan Garshman and Rita Stein

Copyright © 1977 by William Morrow and Company, Inc.

Printed in the United States of America.

1 2 3 4 5 6 7 8 9 10

Library of Congress Catalog Card Number 77-79232

ISBN 0-688-03131-5

CONTENTS

INTRODUCTION

This guide is meant to be used along with good highway maps, which should enable you to locate most of the sites listed within. However, for pinpointing trailheads, it is wise to write ahead for detailed park and forest maps. Addresses are given in the text whenever possible, and additional sources of information are listed below.

Hours are listed as accurately as possible, but because they are sometimes changed on account of weather, local events, or other circumstances, they should be rechecked locally.

Since admission charges are subject to frequent change, exact amounts are not indicated here. Instead, admission is listed as a) **free;** b) **sm adm** (a small admission charge, or where moderate admission for a car includes all occupants); or c) **adm** (moderate to expensive entry fees). **GEP** means entry is free with a Golden Eagle Passport (issued at Federal recreation areas).

TRAIL RATINGS: Trails cannot be rated precisely because paths can wash out, trail markers might not be maintained, and a trail that is easy in the fall may be treacherously wet after the spring thaw. Also, evaluation of a trail's difficulty is totally subjective. However, for your general guidance, we have rated every trail in this guide as follows:

1. **Easy walks**—These are walks on well-kept paths and involve no exertion beyond the pace and distance you set yourself. They are usually suitable for toddlers and people with minor ailments or disabilities. Examples: a walk in a city park or well-kept garden.

2. **Walks for everyone**—These paths might descend or climb somewhat, have uneven footing, or present other minor obstacles, but they are suitable for the average person in reasonably good health. Some of them are easy indeed, but are two or more miles long. Examples: forest trails or interpretive walks in parks.

3. **Hard walks**—These involve steep ascents and descents, are on poorly marked trails, are long, are on rough terrain, or are in remote areas. Examples: parts of trails such as the Appalachian, walks into canyons wilderness hikes.

HAZARDS: For your safety and comfort, acquaint yourself with seasonal weather conditions, unique local factors (such as flash floods in deserts or sudden storms in mountains), times when black flies or other annoying pests are prevalent, poisonous plants, venomous snakes—park and forest offices usually have booklets advising you of any such local dangers. Backcountry hikers should carry equipment to treat snake bites and consult hiking clubs about how to recognize and combat hypothermia (which results from exposure and exhaustion).

Hunting seasons (big game usually in late fall, but shooting can extend for months) are especially dangerous for hiking; even in parks and areas where hunting is prohibited it is wise to be alert for illegal hunters.

INFORMATION: For information on **National Park** facilities, write to any of the following Regional Offices: North Atlantic, 150 Causeway St., Boston, Mass. 02114; Mid-Atlantic, 143 South Third St., Philadelphia, Pa. 19106; Southeast (including Puerto Rico and the Virgin Islands), 3401 Whipple Ave., Atlanta, Ga. 30344; Midwest, 1709 Jackson St., Omaha, Neb. 68102; Rocky Mtn., 655 Parfet St., P.O. Box 25287, Denver, Colo. 80225; Southwest, Old Santa Fe Trail, P.O. Box 728, Santa Fe, N.M. 87501; Western (including Hawaii), 450 Golden Gate Ave., San Francisco, Calif. 94102; Pacific Northwest (including Alaska), 1424 Fourth Ave., Seattle, Wash. 98101; National Capital Parks, 1100 Ohio Dr., SW, Washington, D.C. 20242.

For information on **National Forest** facilities, write to any of the following Regional Offices: Eastern Region, 633 West Wisconsin Ave., Milwaukee, Wis. 53203 (including Ill., Ind., Mich., Minn., Mo., N.H., Ohio, Pa., Vt., W. Va., Wis.); Southern Region, 1720 Peachtree Rd., NW, Atlanta, Ga. 30309 (including Ala., Ark., Fla., Ga., Ky., La., Miss., N.C., S.C., Tenn., Tex., Va.); Rocky Mtn. Region, 11177 W. 8th Ave., Box 25127, Lakewood, Colo. 80225 (including Colo., Neb., S.D., Wyo.); Intermountain Region, 324 25th St., Ogden, Utah 84401 (Idaho, Nev., Utah, Wyo.); Northern Region, Federal Bldg., Missoula, Mont. 59801 (Idaho, Mont.); Southwestern Region, 517 Gold Ave., SW, Albuquerque, N.M. 87101 (Ariz., N.M.); California Region, 630 Sansome St., San Francisco, Calif. 94111; Pacific Northwest Region, 319 SW Pine St., P.O. Box 3623, Portland, Ore. 97208 (Ore., Wash.); Alaska Region, Federal Office Bldg., P.O. Box 1628, Juneau, Alaska 99801.

Publications and maps provided by the **Bureau of Land Management** may be obtained by writing to the appropriate Bureau of Land Management office: 555 Cordova St., Anchorage, Alaska 99501; Federal Bldg., Room 3022, Phoenix, Arizona 85025; Federal Bldg., Room E 2820, 2800 Cottage Way, Sacramento, Calif. 95825; Federal Bldg., Room 14023, 1961 Stout St., Denver, Colo. 80202; Federal Bldg., Room 334 (P.O. Box 2237), Boise,

Idaho 83702; Federal Bldg. and U.S. Courthouse, 316 N. 26th St., Billings, Montana 59101; Federal Bldg., Room 3008, 300 Booth St., Reno, Nev. 89502; Federal Bldg., South Federal Place, P.O. Box 1449, Santa Fe, New Mexico 87501; 729 N.E. Oregon St., P.O. Box 2965, Portland, Oregon 97208; 125 South State, P.O. Box 11505, Salt Lake City, Utah 84111; Courthouse Bldg., 2120 Capitol Ave., P.O. Box 1828, Cheyenne, Wyo. 82001.

The **Army Corps of Engineers** distributes booklets describing recreational facilities on Corps projects; write to the appropriate U.S. Army Engineer District: P.O. Box 2711, Los Angeles, Calif. 90053; 650 Capitol Mall, Sacramento, Calif. 95814; 100 McAllister St., San Francisco, Calif. 94102; 7410 U.S. Post Office and Court House, 215 N. 17th St., Omaha, Neb. 68102; P.O. Box 2964, Portland, Oregon 97208; 1519 Alaskan Way, South, Seattle, Wash. 98134; Bldg. 602, City-County Airport, Walla Walla, Wash. 99362; P.O. Box 1580, Albuquerque, N.M. 87103.

Other organizations that publish helpful information are: **Adirondack Mountain Club,** R.D. 1, Ridge Road, Glens Falls, N.Y. 12801, **Appalachian Mountain Club,** 5 Joy St., Boston, Mass. (information on New England); **Appalachian Trail Conference,** 1718 N Street NW, Washington, D.C. 20036; **Green Mountain Club,** 108 Merchants Row, Rutland, Vt. (information on Vermont); **Mazamas,** 909 NW 19th Ave., Portland, Ore. (information on Pacific Northwest); **The Sierra Club,** Mills Tower Bldg., San Francisco, Calif. (hiking guides to all areas); **Federation of Western Outdoors Clubs,** 201 S. Ashdale St., West Covina, Calif.; **Wilderness Society,** 729 15th St. NW, Washington, D.C. 20005 (information on wilderness throughout the U.S.).

Should your bookshop not carry the trail guides you need, write to **Trails** (P.O. Box 94, Collegeville, Pa. 19426) for their free, handy mail-order catalog.

Information listed in this guide is as accurate as possible at press time. However, some errors may have crept in and some changes will doubtless occur after publication. For these, the author apologizes.

List of Abbreviations

abt	about
adj	adjacent
BLM	Bureau of Land Management
C	century (ex: 18th C)

DST	daylight savings time
elev	elevation
exc	except
Expwy	expressway
FS	Forest Service
ft	foot/feet
GEP	Golden Eagle Passport
hq	headquarters
hwy	highway
jct	junction
m	mile
mtn	mountain
NFS	National Forest Service
NPS	National Park Service
ntl	national
SR	state road
Thnks	Thanksgiving
yrs	years

ALABAMA

BIRMINGHAM: Arlington Antebellum Home & Gardens (331 Cotton Ave. SW) has period furnishings; 6-acre grounds with 19th-C gardens, lawns, magnolias (1); open Tues.-Sat. 9-5, Sun. 1-6; closed Jan. 1, Dec. 25; adm. **Lane Park** (2612 Lane Park Rd.) has 67-acre Botanical Gardens with floral clock, large Japanese garden (open daily dawn-dusk; free) and zoo (open daily 9:30-5; adm); 1. **Rickwood Caverns State Park** (17 m N on US 31, I-65 to Warrior, then N) offers cave tours (adm), camping, swimming, picnicking, hiking trails; 1, 2; open daily 10-6; free. **Oak Mountain State Park** (16 m S on US 31) covers 9900 acres; 2 lakes, falls, gorge, demonstration farm; camping, swimming, picnicking; Visitor Center; attractive mountain trails, 1, 2.

Horton Mill Covered Bridge (38 m N on SR 79 off SR 75) is a pretty site with nature trails (1), picnic area; open daily in daylight; adm. **Talladega National Forest** is in 2 units: Talladega Division offers Pinhoti trail (2), 7 m between Coleman Lake and Pine Glen recreation areas (both N of Heflin on FS roads); here too is **Cheaha State Park** (17 m N of Lineville on SR 49) with trails (1, 2) and Cheaha Mtn, highest point in the state; 9-m Odum trail along a ridge from Cheaha Mtn to Pyriton (7 m N of Lineville) has overlooks (2, 3). Oakmulgee Division (SE of Tuscaloosa), on lower ground, has trails (1, 2) at Payne Lake Recreation Area (17 m NW of Greensboro on SR 25).

CULLMAN: Hurricane Creek Park (N on US 31); trails to the bottom of a canyon with unusual rock formations (1); swinging bridge, cable car, cave, waterfalls, picnic area; open daily sunrise-sunset; adm. **Ave Maria Grotto** (1 m E on US 278) is a landscaped garden in which miniature religious shrines have been constructed; open daily; adm.

DECATUR: Mooresville (6 m E on SR 20); many 19th-C buildings preserved; walking tour (1) available at the Post Office (open daily 6-10, 4-5; closed hols. **Point Mallard Park:** trails (1) and sports facilities on 550 acres on the Tennessee River; open daily 6:30-10; closed Dec. 25. **William B. Bankhead National Forest** (SW), in foothills of the Cumberland Plateau, has streams, picturesque rock formations; trail (1, 2) at Natural Bridge (1 m N of US 278 via Sr 63) and Sipsey River (17 m E of Haleyville via SR 195, local roads) recreation areas. Bee Branch Scenic Area (15 m

NE of Haleyville via SR 195, 243, local roads) has one of Alabama's few stands of virgin forest; trail (1, 2).

FORT PAYNE: DeSoto State Park (8 m NE) has a 23-m scenic drive skirting the rim of Little River Canyon; waterfalls, lake; swimming, picnicking; camping; 20 m of hiking trails cover the ridge tops and canyon floor; 4869-acres 1, 2. You can also picnic, camp, or stroll at **Manitou Cave** (11th St.) and **Sequoyah Caverns** (16 m N off US 11); both offer cave tours; the latter has deer and buffalo on grounds, swimming pool, trout pools; adm to both; 1.

GADSDEN: Noccalula Falls (NW between I-59 and US 431) drop some 90 ft from a limestone ledge; botanical gardens, nature trails (1), picnic area, pioneer homestead and museum. Open daily 8-sundown; free.

GULF SHORES: Fort Morgan State Park (21 m W on SR 180) offers a white-sand beach, the star-shape fort that defended Mobile Bay in 1864 (open daily 8-sunset; free), a museum of Civil War relics (open daily 8-5; closed Dec. 25; free), swimming, picnicking, on 400 acres. **Gulf State Park** (2 m E on SR 182), 6000 acres; a 2½-m beachfront and freshwater lakes; swimming; picnics; camping; 1.

GUNTERSVILLE: Guntersville Lake was formed as part of the TVA project to dam the Tennessee River; along the 76-m lake are dozens of TVA recreational sites with camping, picnic areas, swimming, and other water sports; strolling 1. **Lake Guntersville State Park** (6 m E on SR 227), on the lake, also offers swimming, camping, strolling 1. **Buck's Pocket State Park** (16 m NW via SR 227 near Groveoak) is an attractive area of the southern Appalachians; Visitor Center; swimming, camp and picnic grounds, other facilities; a map is available for the hiking trails with scenic lookouts in the 2000-acre park; 1, 2.

HORSESHOE BEND NATIONAL MILITARY PARK (12 m N of Dadeville on SR 9) commemorates Jackson's 1814 victory over the Creek Nation; Visitor Center (open daily 8-4:30; longer hrs in summer; closed Dec. 25) provides exhibits and maps for self-guiding tours of the 2000-acre battlefield; free.

HUNTSVILLE: Burritt Museum (3131 Burritt Dr.), a home built in the shape of a Maltese cross, has gardens and a pioneer homestead on grounds; open Mar.–Nov., Tues–Sun. 1-5; donation. **Monte Sano State Park** (4 m E off US 431), atop 1800-ft Monte Sano, is a scenic 2140 acres with camp and picnic sites, bridle and foot trails, **1, 2.**

MOBILE: Bienville Square is the heart of an area of fine old homes with iron balconies. **Church Street East Historic District** is a more modest residential area of 19th-C buildings; Church Street Graveyard is interesting. **Soldiers & Sailors Memorial Park** (Houston & Government St.) has lovely plantings; **1. Long Gardens** (250 Tuthill Lane in Spring Hill), 10-acre landscaped estate; is open during the festival, daily 8–5; adm; **1. Battleship Alabama Memorial Park** (E on US 90), a memorial to the state's veterans, contains the USS *Alabama* and a submarine that may be toured; open daily in daylight; adm. **Fairhope** (across the bay on US 98), on a bluff above Mobile Bay, has many artisan studios and crafts shops; nice for strolling, **1. Bellingrath Gardens & Home** (off US 90, 20 m S) is one of America's greatest gardens; 65 of the estate's 800 acres are planted to be colorful year-round (the azaleas of early spring are famous); many quiet corners, ponds, and special gardens (rock, Oriental, rose, etc.); bayou left in its natural state; self-guiding map at entrance; restaurant; house tour for an additional charge; open daily 7-dusk; adm; **1. Dauphin Island** (30 m S on SR 163 via bridge & causeway) has 10-m of sparkling beach; Ft. Gaines is open to the public; **1.**

MONROEVILLE: Claiborne Lake (16 m NW via SR 41, 17) is a Corps of Engineers impoundment on the Alabama River; recreational facilities; camping, swimming; ruins of Ft Claiborne; fossil beds; hiking trails include one marking DeSoto's route; **1, 2. Little River State Park** (25 m S on SR 21) offers swimming and walking, **1, 2.**

MONTGOMERY: Alabama State Capitol (Bainbridge Ave. between Washington & Monroe St.) is an interesting area for strolling, with the **First White House of the Confederacy** (open Mon.-Fri. 9–4:30, Sat. & Sun. 9–11:30, 12:30-4:30; closed hols; free), opposite, and other museums nearby. **Ordeman-Shaw Complex** (304 N Hull St.) consists of several antebellum houses, restored and furnished; one houses the information center for the Montgomery Chamber of Commerce; open Tues.–Sat. 9:30-4, Sun. 1:30-4; closed hols; adm. **Fort Toulouse Site** (off US 231, 12 m NE, then 3 m W), established by the French in 1714 at the confluence of the Coosa and Tallapoosa Rivers, is being restored; Indian mound; **1. Jasmine Hill Gardens** (off US 231, 5 m SE of Wetumpka), designed to be a setting for statuary, has cherry trees and reflecting pools; open daily in daylight; free; **1.**

MUSCLE SHOALS is a scenic waterway stretching across the N of the state along the Tennessee River, which has been impounded by the TVA to form several lakes—**Pickwick Lake** (at the Mississippi line), **Wilson Lake** (at Florence), **Wheeler Lake** (at Decatur); see also Guntersville. Facilities for camping and water sports have been provided along the shores; Wilson Dam powerhouse, with overlook, and Wheeler Dam lobby are open daily, free; near Wheeler Dam are **Joe Wheeler State Park** (S shore) and the state-run **Elk River Park** (15 m S of Athens on US 72); **Lucy Branch Park** (16 m SW of Athens on Snake Rd.) offers similar facilities; in all there are opportunities to walk 1; between Decatur and Huntsville is the 41,000-acre **Wheeler Refuge** for wintering waterfowl 1. A section of the Natchez Trace Parkway cuts across NW of **Cherokee**; also here are Colbert Park (on the river); Sink Holes (with nature trail past limestone formations); Rock Springs (nature trail); picnic area and hiking near the Tennessee River Bridge; 1, 2.

RUSSELLVILLE: Rock Bridge Canyon (18 m S on US 43, then W 7 m on SR 172, then NW), with waterfalls and springs, ferns, magnolias, mountain laurel (blooms in May), is open Apr.–Oct., Mon.–Sat. 8-6, Sun. noon-6; may be open additional months; adm; **1, 2. Natural Bridge** (35 m S via US 43, SR5) has winding paths below the bridge, picnic area; open 8-sunset; adm; **1, 2**

SELMA: Cahaba (9 m SW on SR 22, then 4 m S on unimproved rd) is a ghost town at the confluence of the Cahaba and Alabama Rivers; it was the state capital 1830-60; brick walls, chimneys, foundations; cemeteries; picnic area; open daily in daylight; free; 1.

TUSCALOOSA: The **University of Alabama** has a 65-acre arboretum (Loop Rd.) and several historic buildings; 1. Tuscaloosa County **Preservation Society** (Box 1665) provides historic tours in spring (usually Apr.). **Lake Lurleen State Park** (9 m NW via US 82, SR 21), with camping and other facilities, is attractive; easy walking 1. **Mound State Monument & Museum** (14 m S on SR 69), on the Black Warrior River, has 40 mounds; reconstructed temple and village; trails along the river (1); picnic area; open daily 9-5; closed Dec. 25; sm adm. The beautiful **Black Warrior River** has stunning walks at many points where fishermen have blazed trails.

STATE PARKS: Picnicking, camping, and walking are offered at these additional parks: **Blue Springs** (S of Blue Springs off SR 10), swimming, pretty walks 1. **Chattahoochee** (30 m SE of Dothan via US 84, Co. 89), with swimming and walking on 596 acres **1**. **Chewacla** (4½ m SE of Auburn off US 29) has 696 acres surrounding a swimming lake **1**, **2**. **Tannehill** (12 m SW of Bessemer off US 11 on Eastern Valley Rd.) has self-guiding trail through old iron works; nature trails; picnic and camp sites; open daily 7 am-8 pm; sm adm.

ALASKA

ANCHORAGE: Chugach National Forest contains 4.7-million acres of mountainous country on the coast; best walking is on the Kenai Peninsula, a wild, rugged, but accessible area. **Portage Glacier** (7 m SE of Portage on SR 1 & FS road), abt 50 m from Anchorage, gives you a fairly close look at one of the magnificent glaciers. Visitor Center with interpretive programs in summer; nature trail and another, ¾-m trail (**1**): picnic sites. **Resurrection Pass Trail**, from Hope S to Schooner Bend (mile 52 on Sterling Hwy, SR 1), well-maintained 35-m trail, 3- or 4-day trip; 6 cabins; 10-m side trail goes from a point near the top of the pass down Devil's Creek to SR 1, 2 m N of Tern Lake Campground; **3**. Across SR 1 from the S end of the Resurrection Pass Trail, a trail follows the **Russian River** for abt 11 m to a FS cabin on Upper Russian Lake; **3**. Nearby, a 6-m trail goes to **Crescent Lake** from Crescent Creek Campground (11 m E of Russian River on SR 1 & Quartz Creek Rd.); FS cabin; **2 to 3**. Along SR 9 N of Seward, several trails lead up toward the surrounding mtns; good area for short hikes: **Lost Lake Trail** leaves the road 5 m from Seward and climbs 7 m and 1800 ft to a beautiful alpine lake; outstanding views; **(3)** and **Ptarmigan Creek Trail** (from FS campground 23 m N of Seward to Ptarmigan Lake; **2 to 3**). A longer, more remote trail goes from the village of Moose Pass on SR 9, across a mtn pass, abt 20 m N to SR 1 near the Granite Creek Campground; FS cabin midway, at Bench Lake; **3**. The easternmost part of the Kenai Peninsula is the 600,000-acre **Nellie Juan Wilderness Study Area**, reached only by plane or boat; **3**. On the E side of Prince William Sound, there are trails and cabins near the fishing town of **Cordova**, **2 & 3**. **Information:** 121 W Fireweed Lane, Suite 205, Anchorage 99503. **Chugach State Park** (E of town) is a ½-million-acre area of mtns, glaciers, open alpine valleys; easy walks at campsites and picnic areas reached via SR 1 (**1**); longer hikes on extensive trail system; printed trail guides from Superintendent, Alaska Division of Parks, 2601 Commercial Dr., Anchorage 99501. **Kenai National Moose Range** covers 1.7-million acres of the beautiful Kenai Peninsula; mtns, glaciers, lowland forest; camping, fishing, canoe trails on its many rivers and lakes; hiking trails off SR 1; Skilak Lake area has campgrounds and several short trails (1 & 2). **Katmai National Monument** is a 4362-sq-m wilderness of volcanos, mtns, glaciers, forests, tundra, lakes, and rugged, indented coastline; Valley of 10,000 Smokes is still an active volcanic area; prime hiking time is mid-Aug. through Sept.; lodge and other facilities at Brooks River, reached by bush aircraft from King Salmon. Rangers lead hikes and nature walks from here; 5-m trail climbs **Dumpling Mtn,** with sweeping views of 40-m-long Naknek Lake (2 to 3; abt 2000-ft climb). A bus goes to **Valley of 10,000 Smokes,** where a 1½-m trail descends to volcanic deposits where Apollo astronauts trained (1 to 2).

FAIRBANKS: Elliot Highway, White Mtn Summer Trail, 23 m, leaves the road at mile 27, follows ridge tops to a BLM cabin at Beaver Creek, 2, 3. Grapefruit Rocks (mile 39) are popular for rock climbing and day hiking (2). Near Manley Hot Springs, a short trail at mile 136 leads up a creek to the former mining camp of **Eureka (1).** Just outside of town a 16-m primitive trail goes to **Tofty,** another former mining area (3). **Steese Highway,** 162 m NE to Circle City, offers good opportunities for hiking and backpacking, plus fossils, hot springs, and wilderness canoeing; **Pinnell Mtn National Recreation Trail,** maintained by BLM, runs 24 m along open ridges with views of the Brooks and Alaska ranges N and S; 3. Other trails include a 15-m trail to **Nome Creek** in the White Mtns, fron a point 43 m from Fairbanks; (3); a nature trail at the BLM's **Cripple Creek** campground, 60 m from Fairbanks (1). **McKinley National Park** (120 m S on SR 3), **Horseshoe Lake Trail** (1-m round trip) has self-guiding booklets at the trailhead (1). **Mt. Healy Overlook Trail** round trip is 5 m; strenuous (2). **Yanert Lakes Trail** runs along a ridge paralleling SR 3 for 9 m and then meets the road (3). You can make day hikes at many points along the 85-m route of the park bus (which stops on request), along tundra slopes, river bars, or ridge tops (1, 2, & 3).

HAINES: Totem Village (Port Chilkoot) features a replica of a ceremonial house, totem poles, exhibits of pelt drying, and tours of artisan workrooms; open weekdays; closed hols; adm; 1. From Haines, the historic **Dalton Trail,** used by prospectors in the 1898 Gold Rush, runs 30 m along the Chilkoot River to the Canadian border; strenuous, scenic hiking; trail restored; 3.

JUNEAU: Juneau Trail System, maintained by the state, provides excellent opportunities for day hikers in the mtns behind Juneau. **Perseverance Trail** begins at the end of Basin Rd., at the edge of town; 3 m to the site of a gold mine operated 1889–1921; **2. Mt. Juneau Trail** branches off to the left after 1½ m; 3500 ft climb; very steep, **3. Granite Creek Trail** leaves Perseverance Trail after abt 2 m and follows the creek for 1½ m; **2.** The 4-m **Mt. Roberts Trail** starts at the E end of 6th St. **Salmon Creek Trail** begins 2½ m NW of town and follows the creek 4½ m to a dam and reservoir; **2.** The road NW of Juneau also leads to Mendenhall Glacier and trails in Tongass National Forest. SE of town, the **Sheep Creek Trail** starts at Thane; first 3 m on state trail system, additional 15 m in national forest; **2 & 3. Mendenhall Glacier** (15 m N), at the edge of the huge Juneau Icefield, has hiking trails and short interpretive trails (**1 & 2**); Visitor Center with displays and summer interpretive programs; picnic areas. The road along the coast NW and SE of Juneau gives access to a number of trails into the forest; **2 & 3.** Near Ketchikan, several short trails NW of town are reached via FS 39: Ward lake has **Rain Forest Nature Trail** (**1**) and a 2½-m boardwalk trail through forest and muskeg to **Perseverance Lake** (**1 to 2**). **Talbot Lake Trail** follows the lakeshore for almost 4 m and rejoins the road (**2**). **White River Trail** runs 4 m from Lake Harriet Hunt to salt water at George Inlet (**2**). The 5-m **Deer Mtn-Blue Lake Trail** is NE of town, starting across the road from the city park; passes through muskeg and 300-400-yr-old forest; first 3 m involve a 2600-ft climb; 2 cabins can be used by free permit; **2, 3. Glacier Bay National Monument** (NW end of Alexander Archipelago), a rugged area of fjords and receding glaciers, can be reached only by boat or plane; park hq in Bartlett Cove (lodge in summer) has naturalist programs and trails; easy 1-m, round-trip **Forest Trail** (**1**) winds through evergreen forest to meet the shore; you can return along the beach. **Bartlett River Trail** (**1 to 2;** 5-m round trip) passes through forest and then parallels the river estuary, a good place to see wildlife. **Bartlett Lake Trail** (**2;** 10-m round trip), trail to **Wood Lake,** on the W side of Glacier Bay; spectacular views; **2. Information:** Box 1089, Juneau 99801.

PAXSON: Paxson Lake Campground (5 m S), run by BLM, offers hiking (**1 & 2**); **Fielding Lake Wayside** (14 m N) provides access to a 30-m wilderness trail (**3**). **Mankomen Lake Campground,** E of Paxson by chartered aircraft, is also a good base for wilderness hiking (**3**). **Denali Highway,** 135 m, is a gravel road through alpine tundra in country sculptured by glaciers; most land in this area is public; many good hiking spots; road is maintained May 15-Oct. 1; no towns, though food, lodging and sometimes gas available July-Aug. **Teardrop, 10 Mile,** and **Octopus lakes** are a short hike S of the highway 10 m from Paxson (**1**). A 3-m trail leads N from Rock Creek Bridge (mile 25) up to **Landmark Gap Lake** (**2**); a 2-day backpack can be made in the Amphitheater Mtns on a loop trail from the lake (**3**). At mile 31, a 3-m trail goes to **Glacier Lake** (**2**) and continues another 6 m N to **Sevenmile Lake** (**3**). The old settlement of **Denali,** reached by a

6-m trail (mile 79), was established abt 1907 for gold mining (3); 5-m **Hatchet Lake Trail** (2) at mile 68 and a trail to **Snodgrass Lake** just across the Susitna River at mile 79.5 (1 to 2). **Butte Lake** is reached by a 3-m trail at mile 95 (2). BLM campgrounds (miles 22 & 104) also offer hiking (1 & 2).

SITKA: Sitka National Historical Park (6 m N) interprets area history; Visitor Center (open daily 8-5; closed Jan. 1, Thnks, Dec. 25); exhibits, craftsmen, interpretive programs; picnic area; selfguiding trail to totem poles and other exhibits in forest; **1.**

SKAGWAY: This was a jumping-off point for prospectors during the Klondike Gold Rush in 1898 and still has many buildings of the period, including the headquarters of Soapy Smith, the town's best-known outlaw. **Gold Rush Graveyard** (Skagway-Carcross Rd., N of town center) contains the graves of Smith and other pioneers. **1. Dyea** (2.6 m on Skagway-Carcross Rd., then 7½ m on Dyea Rd.), now a ghost town (1). The state has restored and marked Chilkoot Trail from the Taiya River to the summit and built 2 shelters for backpackers.

TAYLOR HIGHWAY: Narrow, winding, and scenic, this 162-m road from Tetlin Junction to historic Eagle provides easy hiking and wilderness backpacking at many points: **Four Mile Lake** (at mile 5) is reached by a 1½-m trail (1); picnic area 1 m farther on road. **Mt. Fairplay** (mile 33) offers alpine hiking (1 & 2). **Walker Fork Campground**, run by BLM, has a short trail (1). **Jack Wade** (mile 90), a mining community active until 1938, is now a virtual ghost town (1). At mile 110, a short scenic trail overlooks the **Fortymile River**, popular with canoeists (1).

WRANGELL: Shakes Island (reached by footbridge) has restored totem poles, including 4 of the state's oldest, surrounding Chief Shakes' Community House; Tlingit tools and other artifacts.

STATE PARKS: Denali (130 m N of Anchorage), 282,000 mostly undeveloped acres S of Mt. McKinley with trails at the Byers Lake campground; **Katchemak Bay** (S end of Kenai Peninsula, reached by boat from Homer) a huge mountainous wilderness. The state runs about 50 "waysides" (some cover several hundred acres) with camping and picnic sites. Those with trails include: **Dewey Lakes Trails** (near Skagway) and **Pats Creek** (11 m S of Wrangell) in SE Alaska; **Eagle Trail** and **Porcupine Creek** (16 & 61 m SW of Tok on SR 1); **Finger Lake** and **Matanuska Glacier** (E of Palmer on SR 1); **Silver King** (on Kenai Peninsula, near Anchor Point on SR 1).

ARIZONA

BISBEE: Coronado National Forest, in 12 widely scattered divisions, includes most of the mtn ranges of the SE Arizona desert. **Chiricahua Wilderness** (18,000 acres, W of Portal) is rugged, with several peaks over 9000 ft; trails (**2**, mostly **3**) start from South Fork and Herb Martyr (5 & 8 m SW of Portal) in scenic Cave Creek Canyon, from Rustler Park (18 m W of Portal), or from Rucker (24 m E of Elfrida off US 666); also near Portal, nature trails (**1, 2**) are at Idlewild (2 m SW), Stewart (3 m SW), Sunny Flat (3 m SW), S Fork (5 m SW), John Hands (7 m SW), Herb Martyr, and Rustler Park; hikes (**2**) are at other recreation sites. **Galiuro Wilderness** (W of Bonita) is spectacular; rough and difficult to get to; numerous trails in this 53,000-acre area; no recreation sites; **3. Cochise Stronghold** (35 m SW of Willcox) is a rock outcropping that served as a natural fortress for the Apaches; FS campground has nature trail (**1**). In other divisions, recreation sites with nature trails (**1**) include **Lower Sabino** (14 m NE of Tucson on Sabino Canyon Rd.) and **Bog Springs** and **Roundup** (16 & 17 m SE of Green Valley in Madera Canyon). **Ghost Trail Along the Border** runs through the forest in the S, from abt 5 m N of Nogales (off SR 82) to SR 92 (W of Bisbee); full day's scenic drive of over 50 m, past vast cattle ranches, ghost towns, old mines; recreation areas; nature walks (**1**), hiking trails (**2, 3**). Nearby ghost towns are **Harshaw** (10 m SE of Patagonia), **Mowry** (15 m SE of Patagonia), **Oro Blanco** (W of Nogales on US 89); **1, 2. Coronado National Memorial** (off SR 92, 25 m W of Bisbee) commemorates Coronado's trek in 1540 in a vain search for the Golden Cities of Cibola; short trail (**1**) with interpretive exhibits from parking area to Coronado Peak (280-ft climb); from here, Joe's Canyon Trail runs 3 m down to Visitor Center and picnic area (**1, 2**); living history programs, other events; rangers on duty 8-5 daily.

Tombstone National Historic Site (26 m N on US 80) preserves the wild 1880s boomtown whose bawdy houses and saloons attracted nationwide attention; it drew an array of the famous and infamous, from Bat Masterson and the Earps to Diamond Annie and Big Nose Kate; many buildings preserved and restored (sm adm); boothill cemetery (N on US 80) with graves of outlaws; open daily in daylight; donation; **1.** Nearby ghost towns are **Charleston** (9 m SW: park at San Pedro River Bridge & walk ½ m) and **Gleeson** (14 m W on road from Tombstone to Elfrida), a turquoise mining area. **Skeleton Canyon** (28 m NE of Douglas off US 80), where Geronimo last surrendered, is also nice for exploring; **2, 3.**

9

FLAGSTAFF: Coconino National Forest, surrounding the city, is 1.8-million acres; outstanding scenery, with 12,670-ft Humphreys Peak (N in San Francisco Mtns) the state's highest. **Oak Creek Canyon** runs 16 m N of Sedona and is spectacular; FS recreation areas along US 98A provide trailheads **(1-3)**; Sedona Chamber of Commerce provides hiking maps for this and Red Rocks area. **Sycamore Canyon Wilderness (W)** is 20-m long, with multicolored canyon walls over 1000-ft high, sometimes up to 7 m apart; trails **(2, 3)**; access by FS roads off US 89A; ranger at White Horse Lake (N). **Fossil Creek Headwaters** (3 m from Strawberry) and **Wet Beaver Creek** (8 m W of Camp Verde) are also good hiking areas; 2, 3. Recreation areas with nature trails (1) include **Bonito** (18 m NE of Flagstaff on US 89, FS 545), **Dairy Springs** and **Double Springs** (28 & 29 m SE of Flagstaff on FS 90), and **Cave Springs** (12 m N of Sedona on US 89A). **Page Springs** has a national fish hatchery; 1. Information: 114 N San Francisco St., P.O. Box 1268, Flagstaff 86001.

Fort Verde State Historic Park (41 m S on I-17 in Camp Verde), original buildings of post used in 1870s by cavalry and Indian scouts; open daily 8-5:30; closed Dec. 25; sm adm. **Montezuma Castle National Monument** (N of Camp Verde on I-17), with impressive cliff dwellings up to 5 stories high, has self-guiding trails **(1, 2)**; Visitor Center with exhibits; picnic area; open daily 8-5 (longer in summer); sm adm or GEP. **Tuzigoot National Monument** (50 m SW via US 89A), with museum in Visitor Center, has a short trail **(1)** to rambling ruins of a 92-room hilltop pueblo; open daily 8-5 (longer in summer); sm adm or GEP. **Jerome** (S of Tuzigoot on US 89A) became a ghost town when the copper mines closed in the 1950s; colorful; **Jerome State Historic Park** has museum depicting life in boom days (open daily 8-5; closed Dec. 25; sm adm); **2. Mingus Mountain,** above the town, has a recreation area with picnic sites and trails **(1, 2)**. **Walnut Canyon National Monument** (7½ m E off I-40, then 3 m) contains ancient cliff dwellings in a stunning canyon; some of the houses can be seen along a rim trail **(1)**; self-guiding paved trail, ¾-m round trip, leads to 25 of the rooms after 185-ft climb **(2)**; hiking elsewhere in the canyon requires ranger permission; picnic area; open daily 8-5 (8-7 in summer), but snow can temporarily close roads in winter; sm adm or GEP. **Sunset Crater National Monument** (15 m N on US 89, 4 m E) is a cinder cone produced by a 1065 eruption and stained red and yellow; 45-minute, self-guiding Lava Flow Trail, at volcano base, takes you through a bizarre landscape of ice caves, squeeze-ups, spatter cones, and cracks more than 50-ft deep **(1)**; picnic sites; open daily 8-5 (longer in summer) exc when snow closes roads; free. **Wupatki National Monument** (30 m N off US 89, or via Sunset Crater) contains some 800 prehistoric ruins; most impressive is Wupatki, 3 stories high with over 100 rooms; nearby amphitheater and ball court; trails **(1, 2)** lead to Wuhoki, Nalakihu, Citadel, other ruins; Visitor Center open daily 8-5 (longer in summer); free.

Meteor Crater (32 m E off I-40), a 4000-ft-wide, 600-ft-deep crater formed by a giant meteorite over 20,000 yrs ago; museum at N rim explains its origin; open daily 8-sundown; adm. **Painted Desert** (114 m E on I-40) has viewing areas off the hwy. Opposite is **Petrified Forest National Park,** where thousands of rainbow-hued logs are scattered over badlands; 26-m scenic drive to S entrance (on US 180) has stops at interesting formations; interpretive trail (1) at Blue Mesa; at S end are museum, picnic area, short trail (2) to partially restored pueblo, Agate House; to hike off established trails and in wilderness areas, consult rangers; open all yr in daylight.

GILA BEND: An old Spanish experimental farm site is 6 m N of town (off US 80). **Painted Rocks State Historic Site** (14 m W on I-8, then 11 m N) offers a self-guiding tour of boulder-strewn desert with Indian petroglyphs (1); picnic sites; free. **Organ Pipe Cactus National Monument** (61 m S on SR 85), 516-sq-m desert chosen by UNESCO as a biosphere reserve; Visitor Center (open daily 8-5) has exhibits on this rare cactus and other desert life; 21-m and 51-m scenic drives with booklets for stops along the way; picnic areas. Several short trails near the campground include the self-guiding Desert View Nature Trail (1); 3.4-m round-trip Bull Pasture Trail (1, 2); 3.7-m round-trip Estes Canyon Trail (1, 2).

GRAND CANYON NATIONAL PARK: North Rim (30 m S of Jacob Lake via SR 67 to entrance, then 13 m to facilities at rim) is open mid-June-late Oct., depending on snow; ranger station, campground, lodge, inn, restaurants, camp store are on a promontory jutting out over the canyon; 23 m of trails (some paved) on the rim lead to breathtaking overlooks and range from ½-m stroll to 12-m, all-day round trips (1-3). **N Kaibab Trail** (2, 3) descends 14 m and 5840 ft to cross the river and join the S Kaibab Trail from the S rim; 2 campgrounds with water along the way (the first of these, 4½ m and 3400 ft down, can be a 1-day round-trip from the rim; 3. **South Rim** (off US 180) is open all yr, though some facilities close in winter; Grand Canyon Village provides most visitor needs; tours, raft trips, mule trips; Visitor Center with exhibits, many interpretive programs. Easiest scenic walk is paved **Rim Trail** (1), 4 m along the rim from Yavapai Museum to Maricopa Point; 1½ m is marked as a nature trail. On magnificent **Bright Angel Trail** (1-3), you can go as far as Mile-and-a-Half Resthouse (1½ m each way) or 3-Mile Resthouse (3 m each way)—both with water May-Sept.—or to Indian Gardens (4½ m each way), with water, restrooms, picnic tables, campground, ranger. Shortly beyond, a level trail to Plateau Point gives an overlook of the river 1400 ft below. Full distance to the river is 8 m; reservations necessary for campground or Phantom Ranch here. **S Kaibab Trail** (E of village, near Yaki Pt on E Rim Drive) is more rigorous (3); magnificent views; very steep; no water and little shade; not recommended in summer; it meets river near end of Bright Angel Trail. **Hermit Trail** (from Hermit Rest at W end of W Rim Dr.) is abt 10 m down to the river (**3**); day hikes (**2, 3**) can be made to Santa Maria Springs (2½ m each way) or to Dripping Springs (3 m each way). **Grandview Trail** (from Grandview Pt on E Rim Dr.) goes to Horseshoe Mesa (3 m each way); no water; **2, 3**. Other trails to the river are maintained only to minimum safety standards; in places they are so difficult to follow that rangers suggest you take along someone who has been on the trail before (**3**): 9-m **Bass Trail** (from Bass Camp, 4 m N of Pasture Wash ranger station), seasonal water; 11-m **Boucher Trail** (off upper Hermit & Dripping Springs trails); 8-m **Red Canyon Trail**, very steep, no water; 12-m **Tanner Trail. Tonto Trail** parallels the rim and the river for 72 m from Garnet Canyon E to Ted Canyon (**2, 3**).

HOPI INDIAN RESERVATION is a rough square surrounded by the Navajo reservation abt 75 m N of Flagstaff on SR 264, on 3 mesas. On the first mesa (reached by road from Polacca) is beautiful **Walpi**, a terraced pueblo begun abt 1680. On 2nd mesa are **Shongopovi, Shipaulovi**, and **Mishongnovi**. On the 3rd is **Oraibi**, the oldest continuously inhabited community in the U.S., dating from 1100, with old kivas and other ruins. Other pueblos here are **Hotevilla** and **Bacobi; 1.** Hopi Cultural Center (P.O. Box 123, Oraibi 86039) or Hopi Indian Agency (Keams Canyon on SR 264) can tell you about festivals, campsites, and other visitor facilities at New Oraibi, Keams Canyon, Second Mesa.

KINGMAN: This former gold-mining center has several nearby ghost towns: **Goldroad** (29 m SW); **Oatman** (32 m SW), still inhabited; **Mineral Park** (15 m NW); **Chloride** (24 m NW), inhabited. **Cerbat Mtns** (NW, reached via Chloride) have camping, sweeping desert panoramas, hiking (**2, 3**). **Hualapai Mtn Park** (abt 14 m SE), wooded camp and picnic site 6-8400 ft up in the Hualapai Mtns, has trails (**2, 3**). **Music Mtns** (25 m NE on US 66 to N of Hackberry), reached by dirt roads, are rugged; 6-m trail (15 m N of US 66 on Red Lake Rd.) goes to Music Mtns Geological Area (**3**). **Lake Mead National Recreation Area** (60 m NW on US 93), water sports center on Lakes Mead and Mohave, has developed areas with rangers at Katherine, Willow Beach, Temple Bar; desert mtns and canyons for hiking (**2, 3**); information: 601 Nevada Highway, Boulder City, NV 89005.

NAVAJO INDIAN RESERVATION, home of the largest Indian tribe in the nation, covers 11½-million acres in Arizona alone; good recreation, beautiful natural wonders, historic sites: **Navajo National Monument** (22 m SW of Kayenta via US 160, 9 m on SR 564) has Visitor Center describing the Anasazi people, who built and abandoned 3 cliff dwellings here 1250-1300; to protect ruins, the number of people allowed to visit is limited; **Betatakin Cliff Dwelling** can be seen from an overlook trail ½-hr walk from Visitor Center (2) but a closeup requires a 3-hr ranger-led hike (available Apr.-Oct.) **2**; **Keet Seel Cliff Dwelling** (open May-Sept.) requires advance reservation for 8-m trail on foot or horseback (too strenuous for one day; overnights permitted when a ranger is on duty), **3**. **Canyon de Chelly National Monument** (at Chinle, off SR 63), of spectacular red sandstone with green farm and grazing land down at the river, has many prehistoric ruins; 1-m trail to White House (2) is steep; trails along rim; to protect the privacy of the Navajo, you must have a guide on other trails; Visitor Center provides interpretation and guides; open daily 8-5; closed Jan. 1, Dec. 25.

Navajo Tribal Parks with camp and picnic sites are: **Kinlichee NTP** (8 m from Ganado via SR 264 E and Navajo Rte 3 N to Cross Canyon Trading Post, then 2½ m on dirt rd), self-guiding trail past ruins traces their development from 800-1300 A.D. (1). **Monument Valley NTP** (N of Kayenta off US 163), a 30,000-acre area with spectacular isolated mesas and pinnacles rising from the desert, many prehistoric ruins; Visitor Center (4 m E of US 163) provides information on self-guided or guided tours; exhibits; crafts for sale; open all yr, daily 8-6; sm adm; **1, 2, or 3**. **Little Colorado River Gorge NTP** (15 m W of Cameron off SR 64, then short side rd N) has picnic sites, spectacular view from rim; **(2)**; **Grand Falls** on the river are accessible from the S via reservation rd 70; Navajo Tribal Rangers are usually on hand at the jct of US 89 and SR 64 to give directions. **Grand Canyon NTP** (between Glen Canyon on the N and Little Colorado Canyon NTP on the S) is being developed to provide access to magnificent Marble Canyon **(2, 3)**. **Window Rock** and **Tse Bonito NTPs** are at tribal hq in Window Rock, where a museum (open daily 8-5; closed hols; free), library, zoo, and other facilities interpret the Navajo country, **1**. **Hubbel Trading Post National Historic Site** (1 m W of Ganado, near jct SR 264, 63) consists of 11 buildings on about 150 acres homesteaded by Hubbell in 1878; trader's office, rug room, crafts for sale; tours of home; open daily 8-5 (later in summer); closed Jan. 1, Thnks, Dec. 25; free; **1**. Picnic sites are along major routes (an example is at the interesting rock formation called **Elephant Feet**, N of Tuba City on US 160 near Tonalea and Red Lake trading posts). Tribal rangers and trading posts throughout the reservation are sources of information, or write tribal hq (Window Rock 86515).

PAGE: Glen Canyon National Recreation Area, surrounding the town, is over a million acres, most of it in Utah; Lake Powell has 1960 m of canyon-indented shoreline with trails at bays **(2, 3)**. Carl Hayden Visitor Center (US 89, W of town), with historical and natural history exhibits, is starting point for self-guiding tours of dam and power plant; open all yr; daily. **Wahweap** (5 m upstream from dam) is the activities center; camping; picnic sites; swimming; boat tours to explore the canyons and rivers, such as Escalante, San Juan, Dirty Devil; most popular excursion is to Rainbow Bridge National Monument (Utah); summer interpretive programs. **Lee's Ferry** (off US 89-A, N of Marble Canyon), embarkation point for river trips into Grand Canyon, has roadside exhibits interpreting the mining history of the area.

Paria Canyon Primitive Area, 35-m red-rock gorge with 1200-ft-high cliffs, can be entered only upstream (on US 89, 35 m NW of Page) or downstream (at Lee's Ferry), but you can backpack along its length; 2, 3. **Marble Canyon National Monument** (runs 50 m S to Grand Canyon), with breathtaking, sheer red cliffs, can be seen from Navajo Bridge on US 89A, but running the rapids is the best way to enjoy it; you can get in on foot via offshoot from unimproved road leading from US 89A to House Rock Valley buffalo reserve (3).

Kaibab National Forest (70 m SW via US 89, 89A), 1.7-million acres of the Kaibab Plateau, has pine, spruce, and aspen forests. Nature trail (1) at **Jacob Lake. Kanab Creek** canyon area (W) and **Saddle Mtn** (SE) are wilderness areas (2, 3). The unit S of Grand Canyon is mostly inhospitable, dry country; at the W end, a steep 11-m trail from Hualapai Hilltop descends to Havasupai Indian village in **Havasu Canyon** (a side canyon of the Grand, with spectacular falls) with lodge and campground (reservations needed; write Tourist Manager, Supai 86435); fee; 2, 3. The forest unit at **Williams** has several easily accessible recreation sites (1, 2); Kaibab Lake (N); Bill Williams Mtn (S) with stunning view from 9200-ft summit reached via unimproved 7-m road; access to Sycamore Canyon Wilderness (SE); nature trail (1) at White Horse Lake. **Information:** P.O. Box 817, 101 Bill Williams Ave., Williams 86046.

PHOENIX: Chamber of Commerce (805 N 2nd St., zip 85004) provides information on the city. **Arizona State Capitol** (17th Ave. & W Washington) is in a landscaped park. **Pueblo Grande Municipal Monument** (4619 E Washington St.) has Hohokam ruins, museum; open Mon.-Fri. 9-5, Sun. 1-5; closed hols; free. **Phoenix Garden Center** (1809 N 15th Ave.) features native flowers and a rose garden. **Tropic Gardens Zoo** (6232 N 7th St.) has pygmy and other small animals, birds; open Mon.-Sat. 9:30-5; closed Dec. 25; adm.

Papago Park (off US 60, 80, 89, E of city at Tempe city limits), the Phoenix Zoo, desert Botanical Gardens, reflecting ponds with waterfowl, picnic sites, nature trails (1 & 2), other recreational facilities; open 5:30 am to midnight. **Desert Botanical Garden** (entrances at 5800 E Van Buren or 6400 E McDowell Rd.), 150 acres of desert plants from all over the world;

self-guiding trail (1); cactus blooms Mar.-June; open daily 9-5; sm adm. **Encanto Park** (N 15th Ave. & W Encanto Blvd.), nature walks, exotic trees and flowers; waterfowl refuge; picnic sites, sports facilities (1). **Japanese Flower Gardens** (Baseline Rd. around 40th St.), an area in which Americans of Japanese descent began commercial flower raising; prettiest in early spring; free; (1). **Thunderbird Park** (59th Ave. & Deer Valley Dr.), 720-acre desert preserve; walk (1) or hike (2); camp and picnic sites; no water. **South Mtn Park** (7 m S at end of Central Ave.), 14,000 acres of desert and mtns; picnic and play areas; 40 m of hiking and bridle trails (1 & 2); lovely views, open 8 am-midnight; sm adm. **North Mtn Park** (10600 N 7th St.) and **Squaw Peak Recreation Area** (entrance at 16th St. & Squaw Peak Dr.) are smaller; trails (1). County parks suitable for hiking (mostly 2): **Buckeye Hills Semi-Regional Park** (5 m SW of Buckeye); **Cave Creek Semi-Regional Park** (2 m W of Cave Creek via New River Rd.); **McDowell Mtn Regional Park** (15 m NE of Scottsdale); **Usery Mtn Regional Park** (12 m NE of Mesa). **Estrella Mtn Regional Park** (2 m S of Goodyear) also has trails (1 & 2). **Horsethief Basin** (N off Black Canyon Hwy via Crown King), scenic; camp and picnic areas; hiking (1, 2). **Lake Pleasant Regional Park** (20 m NW via SR 69) has 2 recreational lakes, camp and picnic sites, desert flora, 1. **Pioneer Arizona** (24 m N off I-17, Pioneer Rd. exit) re-creates pioneer life in a village spread over 500 acres; open daily exc. Dec. 25, 9-sunset; adm includes tour and wagon ride; 1. **Jackson-Perkins Rose Farms** (36 m W on US 80 at Buckeye), 1200 acres with rosebushes; you can drive through; free. **Gila River Indian Community** (P.O. Box 97, Sacaton 85247) will allow you to use their land; recreational facilities (2-3); reservation is 35 m SE on SR 87. **Casa Grande Ruins National Monument** (midway to Tucson, off SR 87, 1 m N of Coolidge) contains Casa Grande, a unique 4-story building probably used as a ceremonial center, built c. 1350; remains from many ruined villages; Visitor Center provides interpretive displays, conducted tours, and leaflets for a self-guiding trail (1); open daily 7-6; sm adm or GEP.

    Tonto National Forest (NE), 3-million acres, is a magnificent area rising from desert flats to peaks over 7000 ft; **Bartlett** and **Horseshoe** (N), on the Verde River, are watersports recreation centers with trails (2, 3). **Apache Trail** (SR 88) is a scenic auto route (not all paved) from Apache Junction E through harsh desert and beautiful Superstition Mtns: many recreation areas (especially at lakes Saguaro, Canyon, Apache, Roosevelt) along the route; many trailheads (1-3); trail access to **Superstition Wilderness** (2, 3) from Canyon Lake and other points; Lost Dutchman mine area. **Tonto National Monument** (3 m E of Roosevelt) preserves 14th-C pueblo villages built in caves above the Salt River; short, steep self-guiding trail (1, 2) leads to one of these; another requires advance reservation for 3-hr hike (2); Visitor Center; picnic area; open daily 8-5; sm adm or GEP. At Roosevelt Lake, SR 88 turns SE to **Globe**, with

Besh-ba-Gowah Ruin (1 m S via Pinal Mtn Rd.), partially excavated Salado pueblo; ghost town of McMillen (10 m N on US 60); Aravaipa Canyon Primitive Area (11 m S off SR 77), a 9-m red-rock canyon with Indian paintings in caves; 1, 2. From Globe you can return to Phoenix along US 60, stopping at Superior for **Boyce Thompson Southwestern Arboretum** (3 m W); 1000 acres of native and imported cactus and other desert plants; self-guiding trails (1); picnic sites; Visitor Center; open daily exc. hols. 8-4:30; sm adm. You can stroll and rockhound on Picket Post Mtn above the arboretum, or in Queen Creek Canyon (on US 60), 2, 3. Also in the forest are: **Sierra Ancha Wilderness** (S of Young) is scenic; deep box canyons, high cliffs, and dense chaparral make cross-country travel difficult or impossible; trails lead in from SR 288 (to the W) and the FS roads off it; water is unreliable; ranger is at Reynolds Creek; information from Roosevelt Ranger District (Roosevelt 85545); 3. **Mazatzal Wilderness**, even more rugged and inaccessible, is 200,000 acres (2500-7900 ft); water is scarce; trails are rough and often hard to follow; access is from points along SR 87 (E) or from Horseshoe Lake (SW); the peaks are reached most directly from the E; hq is at 711 Main St., Payson (zip 85541); 3. Forest **information:** 230 N 1st Ave., Phoenix 85025.

PIPE SPRING NATIONAL MONUMENT (on SR 389, 14 m SW of Fredonia on the Paiute's Kaibab Indian Reservation): Mormon fort, built in 1871 and later used as a cattle ranch, is in a beautiful oasis in the desert; ranching skills demonstrated; trail (1); picnic area; open daily 8-5; sm adm. **Prescott: Ghost towns** and played-out gold and silver mines abound E of town, starting abt 17 m E on SR 69: McCabe, Humboldt, Walker, Mayer, Groom Creek (picnic area); 1. **Granite Dells** (abt 6 m N on US 89), interesting rock formations; lakes, picnic areas, hiking paths (1).

Prescott National Forest, 1 1/4-million acres, has part of Sycamore Canyon Wilderness. **Pine Mtn Wilderness**, a remote, 16,000-acre island of ponderosa-pine forest surrounded by desert mtns; rough trails, sometimes without water, run along deep canyons and up 6800-ft Pine Mtn; access from Dugas or from Verde Hot Springs (W of Strawberry on scenic unimproved road; 3; recreation sites are mostly near Prescott or Jerome; Thumb Butte (4 m W of Prescott via Gurley St.) and Lynx Lake (8 m SW of Prescott via SR 69 & Walker Rd.; sm adm) have **nature trails** (1). **Information:** 344 S Cortez, Prescott 86301.

QUARTZSITE: Kofa Game Range (S off US 95), includes the Kofa and Castle Dome Mtns; sanctuary for desert bighorn sheep. **Palm Canyon** (20 m S via US 95, then 9 m E on unimproved road), reached on a steep trail (2), is home to Arizona's only native palms; several side canyons can be reached on hiking trails (2 & 3).

SHOW LOW: Fort Apache Indian Reservation (SW on US 60), with the lovely Salt River Canyon, has public recreation areas in mtn, on lakes and streams **(1-3)**; Kinishba Ruins of a pueblo occupied 1050-1350; national fish hatchery (8 m N of Whiteriver on SR 73); information: White Mtn Apache Tribe, P.O. Box 708, Whiteriver 85941. **Concho** (NE via US 60, SR 61 to jct SR 180) is a ghost town, still inhabited, **1. Apache-Sitgreaves National Forest** stretches E to New Mexico and W to Coconino Ntl Forest. **W section**, with 6-9000-ft elevations and the magnificent **Mogollon Rim**, is accessible for hiking **(1-3)** from recreation areas and trailheads along SR 260 (between Helser and Kohls Ranch) and along SR 87 (N of Payson to Clints Wells area). **Outstanding sites:** Woodland (1 m W of Pinetop), with nature trail; Lakeside (½ m W of Lakeside on SR 173) with naturalist programs; Canyon Point (18 m SW of Heber on SR 260), with nature trail and naturalist programs; Rocky Point (26 m SW of Heber off SR 260), with nature trail. **Information:** 203 W Hopi Dr., P.O. Box 908, Holbrook 86025. **E section** is accessible off SR 260 (especially near Greer) and US 666 (Alpine area S to Clifton); here are **Mt. Baldy Wilderness** (access from Winn and Sheep Crossing campgrounds, 7 m SW of Greer on FS 87), 7000 acres of some of the most scenic country in Arizona; beautiful trails **(2, 3)**; varies from gentle forested slopes to steep, rocky canyons and 8700-11,000-ft mtns. **Blue Range Primitive Area,** 180,000 acres, with Mogollon Rim running through from E to W; rugged country; beautiful canyons; many trails, especially in the N; access is from points along US 666 to the W and near Blue in the N **(2, 3)**; nature trails **(1)** are at Greer (N of Greer) and Big Lake (20 m SW of Springerville) recreation areas. **Information:** P.O. Box 460, Federal Bldg., Springerville 85938.

TUCSON: Chamber of Commerce (420 W Congress St., zip 85701) provides very fine information on the city. Attractive places to see on city walking tours: **Old Adobe** (40 W Broadway), **Stevens Home** (155 N Main Ave.), **Otero Home** (219 S Main Ave.), **Mission in the Sun** (6300 N Swan Rd.), **University of Arizona** (University Blvd & Park Ave.). **Old Tucson** (12 m W on Tucson Mtn Park Rd.) is a movie set used for hundreds of films since 1939; over 100 adobe and frame buildings; open 9-sundown; adm; **1. Fort Lowell Park** (E Ft. Lowell & Craycroft Rds.) has ruins of Ft. Lowell, reconstructed officers' quarters, exhibits; open Tues.-Sat. 10-4, Sun. 2-4; free; **1. "A" Mountain** (one-way road from the end of W Congress St.) offers a fine view of Tucson, especially at night. **Mission San Xavier del Bac** (9 m S on Mission Rd.) has tours 9:30-4:30; replica of shrine at Lourdes is nearby; **1. Randolph Park** (Broadway & 22nd St.), landscaped grounds, sports facilities, picnic sites, zoo (open 10-6, sm adm), rose test garden **(1)**. **Tucson Mtn Park** (abt 10 m W of town) is a 30,000-acre area of desert mtns with some 17 m of foot and riding trails

(1 & 2); 35-m scenic drive, Indian pictographs, cactus forests, picnic areas, and Old Tucson. **Arizona-Sonora Desert Museum** (14 m W in Tucson Mtn Park) is a superb introduction to the plants and animals of the Sonoran Desert; tunnels allow you to see underground dens of small animals; some walk-in enclosures; botanical garden; extensive nature trails; open daily 9-sundown; adm; **1**.

Saguaro National Monument: Visitor Center (17 m E via Old Spanish Trail), at 63,360-acre **Rincon Mtn Unit**, offers a magnificent panorama over the desert studded with saguaros; ranger walks in winter; open daily 8-5. Nature trail (**1**) near the picnic area; 9-m Tanque Verde Ridge Trail (**3**) goes through grassland and open woodlands to ponderosa forest at 7050-ft Tanque Verde Peak. From Cowhead Saddle, Douglas Spring Trail goes N; another trail goes E to 8666-ft Mica Mtn; several interconnecting trails lead to 8482-ft Rincon Peak (in the S) via either an upland or a scrub-and-grassland route; campsites along these routes; **2, 3**. The lower and warmer **Tucson Mtn Unit** (16 m W of Tucson via Speedway to Kinney Rd.), 15,360 acres, has information center, picnicking, camping; no water; scenic roads provide access to nature trails (**1**), hiking trails (**2**), points of interest; 4-m Hugh Norris Trail through scrub and grassland to 4687-ft Wasson Peak connects with additional trails; Oct.-Apr. is best season; wildflowers are best in Apr.; the showy saguaro blooms in May.

Colossal Cave (22 m SE via Old Spanish Trail Rd.), once used by Hohokam Indians and as a bandit hideout, is a vast cavern not yet fully explored; colorful formations and dioramas of the cave's history can be seen on the 45-min guided tours; open daily 8-6; adm. **Pinal Pioneer Parkway** (starts 26 m N on US 80, 89 at Oracle Junction) goes 43 m N to Florence; an outstanding natural garden, lined with almost every kind of desert flora known in Arizona; rest areas; marked plants; **1**. **Picacho Peak State Park** (off I-10, 37 m N), with mtns rising abruptly from the desert floor to 3000 ft, has nature trails (**1**), hiking on 3400 acres (**2**); picnicking; historic display; free. **Tumacori National Monument** (48 m S on US 89), a typical frontier mission church, has museum; self-guiding walk; garden (cactus bloom Mar.-May); open daily 9-5; sm adm or GEP; **1**.

Ghost towns nearby are: **Mammoth** (SR 77, 48 m NW), a lusty 1880s mining camp with ruined adobe structures; **Copper Creek** (N of Mammoth 2 m on SR 77, then 7 m E on dirt road). The **Silver Bell Mtn** area (16 m N via I-10 to Rillito, then 21 m W) is a mining region where people still rockhound. **Helvetia** (30 m SE) has ruined cabins, foundations, and a copper slag heap. All (**1**).

WICKENBURG: Vulture Peak Pioneer Landmark (4 m SW on dirt road, then trail) is a 6-m round-trip hike (**2**). The **Hieroglyphic Mtns** (N & E) are favored by rockhounds; hikes **1-3**. **Blowout Mtn** (6 m NE near the Hassayampa River) is a rockhounding area; trail (**3**) to pioneer landmark. **Joshua Tree Forests** (about 12½ m N along US 93) is the state's best stand of these trees; free, **1**. Ghost towns include **Congress** (16 m N on US 89); from here an unimproved loop road about 2 m N off US 89 leads to **Octave, Stanton** (privately owned), **Weaver** (mere traces); **1, 2**. At Aguila (24 m W on US 60), **Eagle Eye Mtn** has unusual rock formations; 4 m S of town on a gravel road, a trail goes 1 m W to Eagle Eye Mtn Pioneer Landmark (**2**).

WILLCOX: Ghost Towns are **Johnson** (15 m S on I-10, 2 m N on gravel road), privately owned; **Pearce** (off US 666 abt 30 m SW); **Dos Cabezas** (abt 15 m SE on SR 186); **1, 2**. **Fort Bowie National Historic Site** (22 m S on SR 186, then E into Apache Pass), used for military operations against the Apache, has fort buildings reached by 1½-m foot trail (**2**); self-guiding booklet; open all year; free. **Chiricahua National Monument** (37 m SE, 8 m from jct SR 181, 186), called Wonderland of Rocks, is a 17-sq-m landscape of rocks in unusual formations; abt 15 m of foot and bridle trails; most are short and easy (**1, 2**), but 6- or 7-hr hikes can be made on Heart of Rocks trail (**2, 3**); Visitor Center provides displays, information, maps; open daily 8-5 (8-6 in summer); sm adm or GEP.

ARKANSAS

ARKANSAS POST NATIONAL MEMORIAL: (on SR 169, off SR 1, midway between De Witt and Dumas), site of first white settlement in the lower Mississippi Valley; visitor center; ½-m **Historic Walking Trail**; wildlife sanctuary; picnic area; open daily 8-5; closed Dec. 25; free.

ASHDOWN: Old Washington State Historical Park (20 m NE via SR 32, 73, 195 at Washington) preserves restored buildings (open Mon.-Sat. 9-4, Sun. 1-5; closed Easter, Thnks, over Christmas; adm) from the time when this was a rest stop for early 1800s settlers bound for Texas; pioneer cemetery; **1**.

FAYETTEVILLE: Prairie Grove Battlefield State Park (8 m SW on US 62) commemorates Dec. 7, 1862, Civil War battle; information in Hindman Hall Museum. Nearby is a re-created Ozark Mtn village. **Fountain Park** (28 m W on SR 16 in Siloam Springs), walkway over Sager Creek; caves; flowers; pleasant; **1. Beaver Lake** (NW of town), 315-m rugged shoreline; many public recreation areas; nature trails, shore walks, overlooks; caves; towering cliffs; **1, 2. Pea Ridge National Military Park** (22 m NE via US 62) Visitor Center provides maps and information for self-guiding tours (**1**); open daily 8-dark; closed Jan. 1, Dec. 25; free. Butterfield Overland Mail route may be followed from here to Ft. Smith. **Eureka Springs** (23 m E of Pea Ridge Ntl Military Park on US 62), Ozark resort called Little Switzerland, has streets that twist up and down hillsides; 63 free springs; many restored, ornate Victorian buildings; Historical Museum (95 S Main St.) and Carrie Nation's home, Hatchet Hall (35 Steel St.); Blue Spring (7 m NW off US 62), with blue water said to be of glacial origin, is circled by Cherokee Trail of Tears (open daily in summer, 8-7:30; adm); **1.**

FORT SMITH: Chamber of Commerce (613 Garrison St.) offers a booklet for a walking tour of 19th-C homes. **Ft. Smith National Historic Site** (Rodgers Ave. & 2nd St.), where the famous Judge Parker held forth; restored courtroom and gallows; ruts of Butterfield Overland Mail route can be traced from here to **Pea Ridge National Military Park**; open daily 8:30-5 (longer hrs in summer); closed Dec. 25; free. **Ben Geren Regional Park** (SR 59 & Massard Rd.), recreational facilities; trails (**1, 2**). **Devil's Den State Park** (toward Fayetteville, off US 71 via SR 74 or SR 170), wooded paths along streams, to caves and crevices in sandstone bluffs (**1, 2**); picnic areas. **Lake Ft. Smith State Park** (27 m N), 147 acres in Clear Creek Valley in Ozark National Forest; trail to Frog Bayou Falls; information center; swimming; picnic areas, **1.**

HEBER SPRINGS: Attractive park with 7 springs under pavilions (**1**); federal fish hatchery (5 m N on SR 25) with Visitor Center open free, daily (**1**). **Greers Ferry Lake**, in the Ozark foothills, is 50-m long and almost divided in the middle by a gorge; powerhouse and dam open weekdays; many walks from more than a dozen recreation sites; walks along Little Red River; award-winning Sugar Loaf Nature Trail (reached by boat from dock near Sugar Loaf campground) winds up Sugar Loaf Mtn, an island in the lake; **1, 2.**

HOT SPRINGS: Hot Springs National Park has 47 springs—2 on display on Promenade; Visitor Center with exhibits, information; self-guiding trail along Promenade and Bathhouse Row; many lovely wooded trails on 5 mountains; picnicking, camping; **1, 2. Lakes Catherine** and **Hamilton**

(SW of town) have many public recreational sites, dam, fish hatchery, commercial amusements; Lake Catherine State Park (on SR 171) has outstanding nature trails; summer naturalist programs; **1, 2. Lake Ouachita** (12 m NW via SR 227), lovely 975-m forested shore; recreation areas; Lake Ouachita State Park has nature trails, climb to Mill Creek Mtn (**1, 2**); Crystal Springs area is beautiful, with mtns to climb (**2, 3**); lookout tower on Hickory Mtn (**2**); dam.

Ouachita National Forest (W of town), in rolling hills, is prettiest when dogwoods and shrubs bloom (mid-Apr.) and mid-Oct. color. The 9-m **Caney Creek** trail (**2**) runs between 2 ridges in unspoiled Caney Creek Back Country (20 m SW of Mena between FS 38, 31); most scenic access is from Tall Peak, reachable by road or the 2½-m trail (**2**) from Shady Lake; a 2-m trail circles the lake (**1**). A 17-m trail (**3**) runs W from **Lake Sylvia** (30 m W of Little Rock via SR 10) to FS 132 near Crystal Mtn; crosses several FS roads; short, steep spur trails to high points. The 22-m **Crystal Trail (3)** along the length of Blue Ouachita Mtn, between SR 7 and SR 298, has an 8½-m section (**2**) near FS 107, which approaches the summit from the E. The more level, 10-m **Ouachita River trail** (**2**) connects US 270 and SR 27 near the Ouachita River. The **Rich Mtn trail** parallels the Talimena Scenic Drive along the S side of the mtn; 8 m from Rich Mtn Tower (NW of Mena) to state line (**2**) and 11 m in Oklahoma (**3**); access to road at several points. All these trails will be linked in the 300-m **Ouachita Trail System. Short trails** include: Mill Creek interpretive trail (off US 270 E of "Y" City); Tree and Old Pine interpretive trails (Crystal Recreation and Scenic areas, NE of Norman); several in the Charlton Recreation Area S of Lake Ouachita; interpretive trail at Lake Sylvia; **1**.

Outside the forest, (W end) is Mena, where **Janssen Park**—10 acres, deer, spring-fed lakes, 1851 log cabin—is open daily, free; in the forest is **Queen Wilhelmina State Park** (16 m N of Mena on SR 88).

JACKSONPORT STATE PARK (3 m NW of Newport on SR 69) preserves remains of an important White River port that became a ghost town when the railroad passed it by; steamboat; camp and picnic sites; open Tues.-Sun. 2-6; closed Jan. 1, Dec. 25; sm adm.

LITTLE ROCK: This is known as the City of Roses for the many roses in municipal and private gardens. The Historic Area is bounded by the Arkansas River (N), Fourche Creek (S), airport (E), and Quapaw Quarter (W). **Arkansas Territorial Restoration** (E 3rd at Scott) is lovely and has gardens; 13 buildings plus outbuildings, from the 19th C; open Mon.-Sat. 9:30-4:30, Sun. 1:30-4:30; closed hols; adm. **Arkansas State Capitol** (W Capitol & Woodlane) is on beautifully landscaped grounds. **Mt Holly Cemetery** (S Broadway at 12th) map at Victorian bell house; open daily in

daylight; free. **War Memorial Park** (W Markham & Fair Park Blvd),
sports grounds, swimming pool, picnic area, zoo; open daily 9:30-5:30;
closed some hols. **Burns Park** (in N Little Rock, off I-40), sports facilities,
amusement park, forests and open country for hiking, **1. Pinnacle Mtn
State Park** (just W, N of SR 10) is being left in a natural state; trails (part
of Ouachita Trail System); naturalist-led walks; **1, 2. Toltec Indian
Mounds** (10 m SE on SR 130 at Scott), 80-acre site with ceremonial mounds,
1, 2. Lonoke State Fish Hatchery (20 m E on US 70 to SR 31) is one of
the largest in the world; open daily; free; **1. DeSoto Trail** (24 m S on I-30
to Military & Carpenter Sts., Benton) is a 26-m route for hikers, horseback
riders, bicyclists, motorists; a marker commemorates DeSoto's march
here in 1541. **Toad Suck Ferry Lock & Dam** (28 m N on I-40 to Conway, 5
m W on SR 60), on Arkansas River; overlooks; camp, picnic sites;
1. Woolly Hollow State Park (39 m N on I-40, US 65; 6 m E on SR 285),
swimming, camping, picnicking; **1. Petit Jean State Park** (47 m NW on I-
40 to Morrilton, 5 m S on SR 9, 15 m W on SR 154), 4100-acre mountaintop park; 70-ft falls, canyon, rock formations crisscrossed with trails
(1, 2); Cedar Creek Trail **(1)**; picnicking, camping, swimming; naturalist
programs. Also here is **Winrock Farms**, founded by Winthrop
Rockefeller to breed Santa Gertrudis cattle; stables open daily all yr in
daylight; free.

MOUNTAIN HOME: Bull Shoals (11 m W via SR 5, 178), in Ozark mtns;
11-m shoreline; many recreation areas with trails; walking along White
River below dam; Bull Shoals State Park (SE end of lake), nature trail,
caves, crevices; **1, 2.** (Town of Bull Shoals has restored Mountain Village,
cavern tours, other attractions). **Norfork Lake** (9 m NE on US 62), 550-m
shoreline; 2 dozen recreation areas; dam (SE off SR 5 on SR 177); open
May-Sept. daily 8:30-4:30; free); self-guiding trail at national fish hatchery (open daily 8-4; free); lovely hiking, overlooks; river walks; **1, 2.**
    Buffalo National River runs 132 m in the Ozarks; intended primarily
for canoeists (services at several points between Boxley & Vellville); many
walking areas accessible only by boat. **Lost Valley** (2 m S of Ponca on SR
43) is an NPS site with camping, picnicking, stunning 4-m trail **(2, 3)** along
spring-fed Clark Creek, between limestone cliffs, up the deep gorge to
waterfalls, natural bridge, caves. **Buffalo Point** (17 m S of Yellville) has
Visitor Center, camp and picnic areas, swimming, guided walks, float
trips, 1½-m trail to springs and Indian Rock House, steep ¾-m trail to
Bat Cave **(1-3)**. **Information**: Supt. (P.O. Box 1173, Harrison 72601) or at
Buffalo Point.

RUSSELLVILLE: Lake Dardanelle (NW off US 64), 300-m shoreline;
more than 25 public recreation areas; Mt. Nebo State Park (on SR 155) on
mountaintop, sweeping views, 10 m of trails on 3783 acres, **1, 2.**

Ozark National Forest is in 4 units stretching W to Ft. Smith; oak forests, rock cliffs and gorges, pools, lakes, waterfalls, natural bridges, scenic drives, rockhounding. A popular section is **Sylamore**, bordered on the W by Buffalo River and on the E by White River. Here **Blanchard Springs Caverns** (14 m NW of Mountain View via SR 9) has a Visitor Center and 1-hr tour to underground formations and lake; short trail to scenic spring; open daily 9-4:30 (8-6 in summer); closed Jan. 1, Dec. 25; adm; **1**. Nearby lovely trail to crystal-clear **Partee Springs** and its run, **1**; huge cliffs called City Rock Bluff; rock formations at Sandstone; Sugarloaf, Green, and Matney lookouts; picnic, camp grounds; swimming; **1, 2**. Outside the forest at Mountain View (7 m S on SR 14) is wonderful **Ozark Folk Center,** 80-acre living museum of Ozark life; Visitor Center, 59 buildings; demonstrations, other activities; open daily May-Oct. 10-6 and for special events at other times. **Mt Magazine** (15 m S of Paris on SR 309), highest point in the state (2753 ft), is also scenic, with picnic and camp sites, springs, overlooks, trails to mountaintop (**1, 2**); swimming and trails (**1, 2**) are at nearby Cove Lake (just N) campground at even prettier Spring Lake (E); ranger station in Paris. The Paris Chamber of Commerce (124 N Elm St.) will give you a self-guiding tour booklet for Mt. Magazine and other attractions. The largest section of forest is NE of Mountainburg; several recreation sites offer camping, swimming, picnicking; **Artist Point** (5 m N on US 71) has scenic views of Boston Mtns and a trail to rock formations; the Sequoyah Trail to Oklahoma (**2, 3**) passes through here at Saddle Canyon near the ghost town of Schaberg. Here also is 2287-ft **White Rock Mtn** and recreation area; 94-acre primitive area at the summit; views of Grand Canyon of the Ozarks; nature trails; hiking trails (**1-3**). **Three Rocks** (W of the mtn) are towering formations reachable by trail; **Devil's Canyon** (SW of the mtn) has spectacular bluffs and **Indian Writing Ledge** has pictographs; wonderful bluffs also at **Bee Rock** (thousands of honeybees) and at **Deep Hollow**, both SE of the mtn; **Cherry Bend** (NE of the mtn) has 2 beautiful waterfalls. **Cass** (jct SR 23, 215 N of Ozark) is a center of legends; you can explore **Lost Spanish Mine** (5 m E) or enter the cave (on SR 23 N of Cass) where the fabled Tobe Hill Lost Mine is located. **Horsehead Lake campground** (N of Clarksville via SR 103, 164) has an attractive N-S trail; trails E of here (off SR 164) follow Horsehead Creek and Dry Spadra Creek; E of Ozone campground is a trail to Clifty Hollow; all **2, 3**. Long Pool Recreation Area (NE of Clarksville off SR 164) has trails along picturesque bluffs, **2**. At **Alum Cove Scenic Area** (off SR 7 N of Deer), a short trail into a beautiful canyon; natural bridge; mountain streams, **1, 2**. **Hurricane Creek Scenic Area** (S of Deer) also has a natural bridge, reached by steep 5-m trail (**2**; round-trip, **2**) off FS 1202 or easier 3-m route from Haw Creek Falls campground (**1, 2**); W are rock formations at **Sam's Throne and Pedestal Rocks, Falling Water Falls, Azalea Patch**, all E of Pelsor;

just N is **Richland Creek** (off SR 27), where a long trail follows the creek N near Pine Knob and SW to Greenhaw Mtn: campsites are at Fairview (N of Pelsor) or S at the White Oak Mtn area. **Buckeye Hollow** (near Bayou Bluff campground) has 7 waterfalls, **1, 2.** A smaller unit of the forest is W of Mountainburg; this has **Natural Dam,** where a rock barrier impounds a large pool, **1. Information:** Ozark-St. Francis National Forests, Supervisor, Box 340, Russellville 72801.

STATE PARKS: Lake Chicot (8 m N of Lake Village on SR 144), formed when the Mississippi River changed its course, is a picturesque subtropical delta area with bald cypress, water lilies, and 27 varieties of orchids; swimming pool; picnic area; natural history museum; summer naturalist programs; **1. Mammoth Spring** (on US 63 in town of Mammoth Spring) encompasses an 18-acre lake and ice-cold springs that give rise to the beautiful Spring River; restored train depot, federal fish hatchery, other attractions; picnic area; **(1);** S of the park, paved and secondary roads lead off US 63 and off SR 289 to the river and its S Fork **(1, 2). Moro Bay** (19 m NW of El Dorado on SR 15) has camping, swimming, picnicking, wooded nature trails **(1). Winthrow Springs** (8 m N of Huntsville off SR 23), surrounded by mtns; lovely spring gushes from a cave to feed a tranquil stream; swimming pool; picnic and camp sites; trails **(1, 2). Village Creek** (11 m N of Forrest City on SR 1), 6792 acres; lakes, picnic and camp grounds, Visitor Center; interpretive trail, garden **(1);** hiking trails **(1, 2).**

CALIFORNIA

BAKERSFIELD: Kern County Museum's **Pioneer Village** (3801 Chester Ave.), 12-acre restored village open Mon.-Fri. 8-3:30; Sat., Sun., hols May–late Oct. noon-5:30, late Oct.-Apr. noon-3:30; sm adm; **1.** E of Bakersfield on SR 178 are roads lined with many campsites offering numerous trails. **Sequoia National Forest,** S end of the Sierra Nevada Range, has several magnificent groves of Sierra redwoods; trail system in Seq. Natl Park's **Mineral King Valley** (reached by Mineral King Road off SR 198 at Hammond) connects with that of the natl forest and other back-country trails to the S; **(2 & 3). Domeland Wilderness** (E from SR 190 on unpaved FS roads), rough, dry 62,000-acre area of weathered granite mtns; elevs 3000-9000 ft; some good trails, other parts nearly inaccessible; information and required free permit from P.O. Box 6, Kernville 93238; **(2**

& 3). **Monarch Wilderness** (reached by trail off SR 180), in a separate division of the ntl forest to the N, is a steep, rough 36,000-acre section of the Monarch Divide with spectacular scenery; difficult trails; **3.**

BARSTOW: Calico Ghost Town Regional Park (7 m E on I-15, then 3 m N on Ghost Town Rd.) preserves buildings of a town that boomed after silver was discovered in 1881; open daily 9-6, longer in summer; closed Dec. 25; adm; **1.** The 137,000-acre BLM recreation area in the surrounding **Calico Mtns** offers desert hiking in spectacular canyons; **2 & 3. Afton Canyon** (30 m E,m 4 m S off I-15 on paved road) is a 4560-acre BLM recreation area in a scenic canyon where the Mojave River flows along the surface; **2 & 3.**

BISHOP: Inyo National Forest. At **Mammoth Lakes** (3 m from US 395 on SR 302) is a Visitor Center with self-guiding and guided walks; other programs; open daily 8-7:30 mid-June-Labor Day, 8-5 rest of yr; **1 & 2. Minarets Wilderness** (reached from June Lake on SR 158; from campgrounds and Devil's Postpile Ntl Monument on SR 203; through Yosemite), adjoining Yosemite Ntl Park on the SE, is over 109,000 acres of spectacular, rough mtn country, much of it above timberline (several peaks over 12,000 ft). The **John Muir Trail** (Pacific Crest) goes NW from Agnew Meadows across Minarets and through Yosemite, crossing SR 120; the Minarets themselves, and high passes to the W, are reached by some of the many side trails; **2 & 3;** E is easier to reach and has more trails. High areas may be snow-covered until the end of June. Information and required free Wilderness Permit from P.O. Box 148, Mammoth Lakes 93546. **John Muir Wilderness,** a magnificent section of the Sierras between Minarets and Kings Canyon Ntl Park, is the state's largest wilderness, with over 500,000 acres; N end (reached from Mammoth Lake and several campgrounds off US 395 on the E; also via SR 168 from the W) has an extensive trail system connecting with adjacent areas; includes a section of the **John Muir Trail** and other trails; **2 & 3.** The narrow strip to the S is crossed by many trails into Kings Canyon and Sequoia ntl parks (reached by roads off US 395 between Bishop and Lone Pine); Whitney Portal (13 m W of Lone Pine) is the nearest access point to the summit of 14,495-ft **Mt. Whitney (3). Ancient Bristlecone Pine Forest** (off SR 168 13 m NE of Big Pine, 9 m on unpaved road) has interpretive exhibits, picnic area, 2-m **Methuselah Walk, Devils Postpile National Monument** (41 m NW of Bishop off US 395) is named for its organ-pipe-like formations of gray lava; trail **(1).**

CASTLE CRAGS STATE PARK (6 m S of Dunsmuir on I-5): Spectacular granite crags soar 4000 ft above the beautiful upper Sacramento River in the 6186-acre park surrounded by primitive back country; evergeen and mixed forest; **River Trail** and **Indian Creek Trail** are short and easy (**1 to 2**); the **Crags** are reached on a 3-m trail from an overlook on Kettlebelly Ridge (**2 to 3**), most can be scaled only with technical equipment.

CHICO: Bidwell Park (½ m E) is a 2400-acre city park; hiking, riding, and nature trails; sports facilities; picnic sites; free; **1, 2**. **Plumas National Forest** E of town via SR 70 includes most of scenic Feather River Country between the Cascades and the Sierras; steep, rugged mtns rise to abt 8300 ft; lovely **Lakes Basin Recreation Area** (S of Blairsden) is popular with hikers; over 50 small lakes in granite pockets; a section of the **Pacific Crest Trail** goes through the area, **2 & 3**. **Feather Falls** (off Feather Falls Rd., 22 m E of Oroville), 6th highest waterfall in the world at 640 ft, is reached only by a 3-m trail; **2**. **Information:** P.O. Box 1500, Quincy 95971.

CRESCENT CITY: Redwood National Park (15 m S on US 101), a 46-m coastal strip, preserves the tallest trees on earth. Many of the redwoods here are over 300 ft tall. The dense, misty redwood forest contrasts with rocky headlands and driftwood-strewn beaches along the shore. Trails include the 1-m loop through **Lady Bird Johnson Grove** (off US 101 N of Orick on Bald Hill Rd.), half of which is a self-guiding nature trail; **1**; and the 8½-m **Redwood Creek Trail** (also off Bald Hill Rd.), a flat path to **Tall Trees Grove**, where the tallest redwood (367 ft) grows; bridges across stream removed in winter rainy season; 17-m round trip is **3**. The 4-m **Coastal Trail** winds along bluffs over the ocean from Lagoon Creek picnic area to Requa Rd.; Sitka spruce area; access to beach **1** or **2**. Also at Lagoon Creek is the ½-m **Yurok Loop** interpretive trail (**1**). **Enderts Beach** has a hike-in campground, beach access, picnic areas; guided beach walks; **1 & 2**. Within the natl park are 3 state parks: **Del Norte Coast Redwoods State Park**, particularly lovely when rhododendrons bloom, May-June; beautiful memorial redwood groves; nature and hiking trails (**1 & 2**); picnic area. **Prairie Creek Redwoods State Park**. The Redwood forest is only one of this beautiful 12,240-acre park's attractions; 8-m beach (**1**) backed by a forested bluff; the sand and rock contain gold; **Fern Canyon** (**1**) has 50-ft walls thickly covered with 5-fingered ferns; hq is the hub of a 40-m trail system (**1, 2, & 3**); **Revelation Trail** is a ¼-m self-guiding nature trail for the blind (**1**); herds of Roosevelt elk (**2**); Picnic areas at beach and hq. **Jebediah Smith Redwoods State Park**, the state's northernmost redwood park, dense groves where trees grow to 340 ft; exhibits and interpretive trails (**1**); hiking trails (**1 & 2**); picnic area. **Six Rivers National Forest** NE on US 199. Home of the legendary Big Foot; 140-m strip of forest E of Redwood National Park; hikes can be made from 15 campsites, plus more remote primitive camps; **information:** 710 "E" St., Eureka 95501.

DEATH VALLEY NATIONAL PARK (70 m E of Lone Pine via SR 136, 190), where plants and animals have had to adapt to less than 2 inches annual rainfall; best season is Nov.-Apr. The **Visitor Center** at Furnace Creek (open daily 9-5, longer in winter); displays of natural and human history, audiovisual programs, guided walks, naturalist programs in winter; trail leaflets **(1 & 2)**. At the end of the road through Wildrose Canyon a rugged 5-m trail climbs 3000 ft to 11,049-ft **Telescope Peak (3)**.

EUREKA: Fort Humboldt State Historic Park (off US 101): Constructed in 1853 to protect settlements that served as coastal supply bases for gold diggings on the Trinity River; abandoned in 1870; reconstructed buildings house historic and archaeological displays; self-guiding trail with exhibits on history of redwood logging; open daily 8-5; closed Thnks, Dec. 25; free; **1. Hoopa Valley Indian Reservation** (40 m E of Arcata on SR 299, then 12 m N on SR 96), public campground on the Trinity River where recreation opportunities include hiking **(2)**; Big Foot is reported occasionally seen in this area. **Patrick's Point State Park** (25 m N on US 101, 425-acre rocky headland covered with forest and meadow; many short trails **(1 & 1 to 2)**; sandy beach with cold and dangerous swimming; picnic areas. **Humboldt Redwoods State park** (S on US 101 between Miranda and Redcrest), 37,760-acre park; beautiful groves of coastal redwoods; largest is 9000-acre **Rockefeller Forest**, where trees reach 356 ft; camping and picnic areas near the road have short trails **(1)**; longer trails lead to more remote sections **(2)**; exhibits; naturalist programs.

FRESNO: Roeding Park and Zoo, (SR 99 & W Belmont Ave.) 150-acre landscaped park with a variety of trees, shrubs, and flowers; sports and recreational facilities; picnic areas; open daily; sm adm to zoo; **1. Forestiere Underground Gardens** (5021 W Shaw Ave.) 5 acres; stone arches and grottos, modeled on Roman catacombs, linked by courtyards and pathways; open June-Oct. daily 9:30-5:50; Apr.-May, Wed.-Sun. 10-4; Nov.-Mar. weekends & hols 10-4; closed Thnks, Dec. 25; adm; **1.**

KLAMATH NATIONAL FOREST: Mtns of the Coast Range and a spur of the volcanic Cascades characterize this 1,700,000-acre area of NW California. **Marble Mtn Wilderness** (several access points from SR 96 on the N & W), over 200,000 acres of forested country; small lakes, mtn meadows, abundant wildlife, and many moderate trails; **2 & 3. Salmon-**

Trinity Alps Primitive Area (reached from SR 299 on unpaved roads from Helena or Junction City, or from SR 3 on unpaved road from Coffee Creek), on the crest of the Klamath Mtns of the Coast Range, includes some of the wildest and roughest country in the state; 400 m of well-marked but rugged trails in well-watered forest and alpine areas; trails along the ridges provide spectacular views; **2 & 3**; campgrounds and picnic areas also offer hiking (**1 & 2**). Information and required free Wilderness Permit from 1215 S Main St., Yreka 96097.

LAKE TAHOE AREA: D.L. Bliss-Emerald Bay State Parks (at SW end of Lake Tahoe) adjoin on 6 m of shoreline; remarkable Vikingsholm, an authentic copy of a Norse fortress of abt 800 AD, reached by steep 1-m trail (**1, 2**; open July 1-Labor Day, 10-4:30; sm adm); from Vikingsholm, a short trail (**1**) goes to Eagle Falls, and 4½-m Rubicon Trail follows the lakeshore N to Calawee Cove Beach (**2**); at the N end are the ¾-m Lighthouse Trail and ½-m self-guiding Balancing Rock Nature Trail (**1**); summer interpretive programs. **Sugar Pine Point State Park** (10 m S of Tahoe City on SR 89), 1975 acres of high-country forest on the shore of Lake Tahoe; nature trails and other short paths (**1**), plus a trail that follows a mtn stream for 3 m within the park before crossing into Desolation Wilderness (**2**); ½-m sandy beach. **Tahoe National Forest**, High Sierra area N of Lake Tahoe, popular for outdoor recreation; 90 campgrounds and picnic areas; abandoned mining camps and old trails from the Gold Rush era; information from Hwy 49 & Coyote St., Nevada City 95959. **Eldorado National Forest**, bordering the S shore of Lake Tahoe; peaks up to 10,000 ft; many beautiful trails for hiking or riding; **Visitor Center** (on SR 89 W of S Lake Tahoe, 1 m beyond Camp Richardson) has self-guiding trails (**1**), guided walks, boat trips, information; open daily 9-6 late June-Labor Day; free. **Desolation Wilderness** (SW of Lake Tahoe, reached from points along SR 89 & SR 50), scenic alpine country along the crest of the Sierras; 63,000 acres; extensive trail system, with N-S trails along the crest; side trails; 6500-10,000 ft; some trailheads are: Fallen Leaf Lake, Emerald Bay, and via Sugar Pine Point State Park **2 & 3**; **Pacific Crest Trail** crosses Desolation between Tahoe Ntl Forest to the N and SR 50 to the S; also runs S beyond SR 50 **3**; information and required free Wilderness Permit: 100 Forni Rd., Placerville 95667. **Donner Memorial State Park** (E edge of Donner Lake, 2 m W of Truckee) interpretive trails and Emigrant Trail Museum recount the conquest of the Sierra Nevada by whites and the trials of the Donner Party, which in 1846 tried to take a mtn shortcut to California but was trapped by snow; open daily 10-4; sm adm to museum; (**1**).

LAVA BEDS NATIONAL MONUMENT (5 m S of Tulelake on SR 139, then 25 m W): This fascinating area near the Oregon border was flooded with molten basaltic lava centuries ago; paved road loops through the 72-square-m monument; short trails and dirt roads lead to points of interest. At park hq you can walk to and through some of the tubular caves; miles of passages, some with uneven footing; mostly 1.

LOS ANGELES: El Pueblo de Los Angeles State Historic Park is on the site where the city was founded in 1781 by settlers from Mexico; restored buildings surround Old Plaza (Sunset Blvd. & Los Angeles St.); conducted tours available Tues.-Sat.; special events. The center of the historic district is **Olvera St.**; stalls and shops re-create the atmosphere of a Mexican street market. Among the many buildings are: **Avila Adobe** (1818), the oldest dwelling in Los Angeles; **Nuestra Senora La Reina de Los Angeles** (1822), the oldest church in the city and still active; **Pico House** (1870), the city's first hotel; the **Firehouse** (1884), with old fire-fighting equipment. 1. **Griffith Park** (entrances: Los Felix Blvd. at Riverside Dr., Griffith Park Ave., Vermont & Western Aves.) covers more than 4000 acres; sports and entertainment facilities; bird sanctuary; "wilderness" area; picnic areas; **Los Angeles Zoo** on more than 100 acres; open daily 9-5; closed Dec. 25; adm; 1. **Elysian Park** has 575 landscaped acres with picnic areas and recreational facilities; open 5 am-10 pm; 1. **Exposition Park,** more developed; 7-acre rose garden, science museums, and spectator sports; picnic grounds; 1. **Botanical Gardens** (UCLA, 405 Hilgard Ave.) has booklet for self-guiding nature trail (1); open Mon.-Fri. 8-5, Sat. & Sun. 10-4; closed hols; free. **Beaches** include Cabrillo, Hermosa, Malibu, Manhattan, Marina del Rey, Ocean Park, Playa del Rey, Redondo, Santa Monica, Torrance, and Venice; 1. **Angeles National Forest:** Steep, rugged mtns characterize this 691,000-acre area N of Los Angeles; trails include Gabrielina National Recreation Trail and portion of the Pacific Crest Trail (runs E-W, roughly parallel to SR 2), **2, 3**; many shorter trails lead through canyons or along chaparral-covered slopes. The highest peak here is 10,064-ft **Mt. San Antonio (Old Baldy),** reached by a 5-m trail from Mt. Baldy Station (3) or a 2½-m trail from Mt. Baldy ski area (2), both on Mt. Baldy Rd. N of Ontario. **San Gabriel Wilderness** (trails from several points along SR 2 on the N & W, also from Coldbrook Station on SR 39) is rough, steep, and scenic; fire danger can lead to closing; trails mostly skirt the edges of the 36,000-acre wilderness **2,** bushwhacking **3;** information and free required Wilderness Permit: 150 S Los Robles, Pasadena 91101. **Will Rogers State Historic Park** (15 m W of Los Angeles Civic Center, off Sunset Blvd. in Pacific Palisades), ranch home of the Oklahoma-born cracker-barrel philosopher; Western and Indian art; cowboy mementos; hiking and riding trails, some laid out by Rogers (**1, 2**); open daily 10-5; closed Jan. 1, Thnks, Dec. 25; free. **Los Angeles State and County Arboretum** (301 N Baldwin Ave., Arcadia), once the estate of a railroad tycoon; 127 acres of gardens with plants from all over the world; historic area, greenhouses, demonstration gardens, peacocks, tram tour; open daily 8-6 in summer, 8-5 in winter; closed Dec. 25; free; **1. Forest Lawn Memorial Park** (1712 S Glendale Ave., Glendale) on several hundred acres, has a large collection of religious art, marble statues, and copies of European churches; proper dress required; open 8:30-5:30; free; **1. Mission San Fernando Rey de Espana** (15151 Mission Blvd., San Fernando), restored with church, workshops, living quarters, and monastery on 7-acre grounds; displays of historic material; open daily 9-5; closed Dec.25; adm; **1. Huntington Library, Art Gallery, & Botanical Gardens** (1151 Oxford Rd., San Marino), collections of railroad executive Henry Huntington; 200-acre gardens; plants from all over the world; arboretum; open Tues.-Sun. 1-4:30; closed hols, Oct.; free; **1. Santa Catalina Island** (by ferry or plane from Long Beach or San Pedro), 22-m long, 8-m across at its widest point, has a rocky spine rising 2000 ft; hiking, riding; Avalon is the only town; **2. John Muir National Historic Site** (jct SR 4, Alhambra Ave., S of Matinez), home of the great naturalist from 1890 until his death in 1914; tours of house and other structures; 8¼ acres of orchards and vineyards; audiovisual program on Muir's life and work; open daily 9-4:30; closed Jan. 1, Thnks, Dec. 25; sm adm; **1. Pomona, Rancho Santa Ana Botanic Gardens** (1500 N College Ave.), native plants; open daily 8-5; closed hols; free; **1. San Juan Capistrano** Chamber of Commerce (31793 Camino Capistrano, Franciscan Plaza) has maps for a self-guiding walking tour of historic sites; **Mission San Juan Capistrano**, founded in 1776, church, cloisters, gardens, ruins, and an Indian cemetery —celebrated for its swallows, which leave each year on or about Oct. 23 and return on or about Mar. 19; open daily 7-5; sm adm; **1. Starr-Viejo Regional Park** (8 m E on SR 74), 5500-acre county park in the Santa Ana Mtns; camping, hiking, horseback riding; picnic tables; trail leaflet at entrance; sm adm; **1 and 2. Tucker Wildlife Sanctuary** (15 m SE via Chapman Ave., Santiago Canyon Rd., Orange), 10 acres, noted for hummingbirds and local plant life; nature trail; museum; open daily 9-4; closed Thnks, Dec. 25; sm adm; **1.** Among the 20,000 grave sites at **Los Angeles Pet Cemetery** (Calabasas) are those of Hopalong Cassidy's circus horse Topper, May West's monkey, dogs belonging to Rudolph Valentino, Lionel Barrymore, and other celebrities; **1. Descanso Gardens** (1418 Descanso Dr., S of Foothill Blvd., La Canada), 150 acres, with redwoods and other fine trees, 100,000 camellias and 10,000 rhododendrons in bloom Nov.-May; roses, begonias, fuchsias (May through summer); lovely Japanese garden; picnic areas; open daily exc. Dec. 25, 8-5:30; free; **1. Rose Hills Memorial Park** (3900 Workman Mill Rd., Whittier), 2500 acres; 750 varieties of roses; blossoms most of the year; Japanese Garden with 2½-acre lake; open daily sunup-sunset; free; **1.**

MENDOCINO: Settled by New Englanders in 1852 and now an artists' colony, is reminiscent of the New England coast. **Mendocino Coast Botanical Gardens** (N on SR 1), 47 acres of rhododendrons (bloom Apr.-May), dahlias (July-Oct.), fuchsias, lilies, others; also rain forest; easy trails; picnic area, open daily 8-6, in winter 8:30-5; closed Jan. 1, Thnks, Dec. 25; adm; (1). **Mendocino Headlands State Park** surrounds the town; ¾ m of headlands and 200-yd beach; (1). **Russian Gulch State Park** (2 m N on SR 1), sea-carved rocky shore, sandy beach, 3 m of densely forested canyon surrounding ridges; pygmy forest; short trails in the shore area (1), plus abt 7 m of hiking trails in canyon and on ridges (1, 2); picnicking. **Van Damme State Park** (3 m S on SR 1) has a Pygmy Forest with pines and cypress dwarfed by poor soil and self-guiding interpretive trail (1); Fern Canyon, walled with ferns, has easy 3-m path (1, 2); 1¼ and 2½ m trails connect with Pygmy Forest (2); picnic area at small ocean beach. **MacKerricher State Park** (19 m N on SR 1), 1½-m black sand beach (1), 3-m trail toward Ft. Bragg (2); trail circles Cleone Lake (1). **Modoc National Forest: South Warner Wilderness** (SE from Alturas or E from Likely on gravel roads), well-developed trail system includes the 27-m **Summit Trail** between Porter Reservoir on the N and Patterson Campground on the S; most of the route is at high elevations; some peaks over 9000 ft; many beautiful side trails to the E and W.

MONTEREY: Founded by the Spanish in 1770; unique architectural style: Spanish colonial modified by New England seamen; harbor colorful with fishing boats. **Chamber of Commerce** (Monterey Fairgrounds Travelodge, 2030 Fremont Ave.) provides map of 3-m walking tour ("**Path of History**") past historic sites. Historic buildings include: **Casa Amesti** (1834), an adobe and redwood-log house; **Cooper-Molero Adobe**; **Monterey Presidio** (1770); **Royal Presidio Chapel**, in use since 1795. **Monterey State Historic Park** (on the bay, with parking beside Municipal Wharf & Fisherman's Wharf); self-guiding booklet at the Customs House. Highlights include: **Customs House**, built in 1827 and enlarged in the mid-1800s; **Larkin House**, a 2-story adobe home of the 1830s (closed Tues.); **California's First Theater**, originally an 1846 roominghouse; most buildings are open daily 9-5; closed Jan. 1, Thnks, Dec. 25; sm adm covers all houses (Customs House free); **1. Carmel:** Many art galleries, boutiques, and craft shops. **Biblical Garden** (Church of the Wayfarer, Lincoln St. & 7th Ave.) has plants and trees mentioned in the Bible; open daily; free; **1. Point Lobos State Reserve** (3 m S of Carmel on SR 1), spectacular and unspoiled rocky coast; trails wind along the shore and through the 500-acre land portion of the reserve (1 & 2); grove of rare Monterey cypress trees, tide pools, sea lion colony; picnic areas. **Pfeiffer Big Sur**

State Park (30 m S on SR 1) 810-acre park in the rugged canyon of the Big Sur River is forested with redwoods and other trees; 1-m self-guiding nature trail (1); other trails through canyon and into surrounding Los Padres National Forest (2); picnic areas. **Julia Pfeiffer Burns State Park** (37 m S of Carmel on SR 1), Big Sur coast; a short trail leads from a picnic area in a redwood grove through typical chaparral country to 100-ft cliffs above the ocean; 1.

NEEDLES: Old Woman Mtns (15 m S at Essex), a desert range with many old mines (2, 3). **Goffs** (NE of Essex off I-40) is desert country; a road going N leads to Old Fort Piute, Indian Desert, the ghost town of Hart, the Castle and New York Mtns (no road access), and petroglyphs in Lanfair Valley. **Providence Mtns State Recreation Area** (18 m N of I-40, N of Essex), in E Mojave Desert; limestone **Mitchell Caverns** open on daily guided walks; a 3rd can be explored by experienced cavers; ½-m self-guiding **Mary Beal Nature Trail** emphasizes desert plants (1); another trail climbs through a canyon to **Crystal Spring** (under 1 m round trip; 1) continues into the **Providence Mtns (2 & 3).**

PALM SPRINGS: Moorten Botanical Garden (1701 S Palm Canyon Dr.) has nature trails through 2 acres of desert plants; bird and animal sanctuary; open daily 9-5; sm adm; 1. **Tahquitz Canyon** (W Ramon Rd.) has a 1½-m trail and 60-ft waterfall (1 to 2). **Mt. San Jacinto Wilderness State Park** (reached by Palm Springs Aerial Tramway or SE on SR 74 to Idyllwild), this 13,521-acre wilderness park has 4 peaks over 10,000 ft; forested zones and Arctic-Alpine regions; extensive trail system is shared with San Jacinto Wilderness in San Bernardino National Forest (which see); primitive campgrounds along trails (2 & 3); permits, required for day hiking and backpacking, can be obtained in person or by writing to Box 308, Idyllwild 92349. **Agua Caliente Indian Reservation** (5 m S): **Andreas Canyon** has spectacular rock formations, caves once inhabited by Indians, picnic sites, trails; **Murray Canyon**, more primitive, is reached by hiking through Andreas; **Palm Canyon** is lined with 3000 native Washingtonian palms, estimated to be 1500-2000 yrs old—trails lead to the canyon floor; open Oct.-May daily 9-4; adm covers all; (2). **Living Desert Reserve** (13 m SE on SR 111 in Palm Desert at 49-900 Portola) is 370 acres; 3½ m of self-guiding trails (1); exhibits; guided tours; open Sept.-May, Tues.-Sat. 10-5, Sun. 2-5; adm. **Mecca** (39 m SE on SR 111): The **Mecca Hills** (bisected by SR 195, E of town), canyons with good hiking; **Painted Canyon** (off SR 195 near Coachella Canyon), has picnic facilities; **2 & 3. Joshua Tree National Monument** (NE, best entrance from 29 Palms, with Visitor Center; other entrances N at Joshua Tree and S off I-10, 25 m E of Indio), preserves unique high desert vegetation, including the giant yucca.

REDDING: Shasta-Trinity National Forest (NE & NW of town), 2½-million acres of rolling plateaus, deep canyons, granite peaks; parts of Salmon-Trinity Alps Primitive Area and Yolla Bolly-Middle Eel Wilderness; 14,162-ft Mt. Shasta, an extinct volcano with snowy summit and glaciers, has road to 8000-ft level; surrounding area has many trails (**2, 3**); information: 1615 Continental St., Redding 96001. **Shasta State Historic Park** (on SR 299, 6 m W) now a virtual ghost town; restored Courthouse has historical museum; interesting cemeteries; open daily 10-5; closed Jan. 1, Thnks, Dec. 25; sm adm; **1**. **Whiskeytown-Shasta-Trinity National Recreation Area** (N on I-5, W on SR 299), surrounding 3 large lakes for water sports, has 2 units in Shasta Trinity forest; **Whiskeytown Unit** (bisected by SR 299 W of Redding) has many dirt roads to mtns and pine forest of the back country; one climbs almost 5000 ft to the summit of 6209-ft Shasta Bally; **2, 3**.

Lassen National Forest (47 m E on SR 44), straddling the Cascade Mtns; 1,200,000-acres; peaks up to 10,000 ft., volcanic formations; pine and fir forest; cattle ranching; **Hat Creek Recreation Area** (along SR 89, 44 m SE of Burney), campgrounds, picnic areas, 2 self-guiding trails: One interprets the features of **Subway Cave**, a 1300-ft tube through a 2000-yr-old lava flow; flashlight needed; **1**. The 2nd, at **Panoramic Point**, also explains volcanic activity; **1**. Other hikes can be made in Hat Creek Valley; **1 & 2**. Nearby is **Thousand Lakes Wilderness** (reached from SR 89 on the E), with lakes in lava potholes, most concentrated in Thousand Lakes Valley; peaks up to 8677 ft, with elev differences of abt 4000 ft; closed by snow Oct-May; **3**. **Caribou Wilderness** (access from Silver Lake campground, off SR 44 W of Susanville), a forested alpine plateau with several lakes and volcanic formations, gentle trails; **2 & 3**. Information and required free Wilderness Permits: 707 Nevada St., Susanville 96130.

McArthur-Burney Falls Memorial State Park (63 m NE via SR 299 & 89), a beautiful area covered with dense evergreen forest; has lovely falls, 565 acres; 1-m self-guiding nature trail (**1**) and 4 m of trail along the gorge below the falls (**1, 2**); picnic areas; naturalist-led walks in summer.

Lassen Volcanic National Park (50 m E via SR 44), 100,000-acre coniferous forest; 50 wilderness lakes; **Lassen Peak**, a plug-dome volcano, erupted for more than 7 yrs, beginning in 1914; active hot springs, fumaroles, and sulphurous vents; self-guiding auto tour along SR 89 passes lakes, overlooks, areas devastated by volcanic activity, picnic areas, and several trails. Self-guiding interpretive trails at **Sulphur Works** and **Bumpass Hell** explain thermal areas (**1**); 10,457-ft **Lassen Peak** is abt a 2000-ft climb up a 2½-m trail (**2** to **3**); 150 m of trails leading to hidden lakes, waterfalls, mtn meadows, and old volcanoes and lava flows.

SACRAMENTO: California State Capitol, completed in 1874, is set in 40 acres of beautifully landscaped grounds, open daily 7 am-9 pm; free;

1. The small **Chinatown** offers the Chinese Cultural Center, contemporary buildings of Oriental design, shops and restaurants, and a memorial to Sun Yat Sen; **1. Sacramento Zoo** (in Land Park, off Freeport Blvd.) is the 2nd-largest in N California; nearby picnic area; open daily 8:30-4:30, later Sun. & hols; sm adm; **1. Del Paso Park** (NE of town between I-80 & I-880), hiking, golf, and other sports, picnic area; **1.** E of Sacramento, **Ancil Hoffman Park** (Kenneth Ave. & San Lorenzo Way in Carmichael) and **Sailor Bar Park** (Natoma Ave. & Finisterre Ct. in Fair Oaks) have hiking trails and picnic areas; **1. American River Parkway** is a 23-m greenbelt along the American River from Sacramento to Folsom; hiking, riding, and bicycle trails; **1, 2,** and **3. Folsom Lake State Recreation Area** (12 m E; N & S of Folsom), 50 m of hiking and riding trails through oak and pine woodland along lake shores and river banks (**1 & 2**); longest is the 17-m **Pioneer Express Trail** from Beal's Point (just N of Folsom) to Auburn (up to **3**). **Auburn** (16 m NE on I-80) Chamber of Commerce offers a booklet for self-guiding tours of **Old Town**, which retains many buildings from the gold-mining boom of the 1850s. Nearby **Recreation Park** has picnic sites; **1. Nevada City** (16 m NE on I-80, 30 m NE on SR 49), settled by goldminers in 1849, is picturesque, with many old buildings including the famous National Hotel (211 Broad St.); Chamber of Commerce (132 Main St.) provides self-guiding tour booklets; **1. Malakoff Diggins State Historic Park** (NW of Nevada City) is a preserved mining town; although some of the buildings are restored, emphasis is on the history of mining techniques; museum open summers Tues.-Sun. 10-5, spring and fall weekends 10-5. The 2600-acre park has trails through varied terrain—open meadows, 2nd-growth forest, chaparral-covered slopes, and deep canyons; several short trails in the town area and near the old pit mine, over 1 m long, now a lake surrounded by colorful cliffs; also 1½-m trail along Humbug Creek; **1, 2. Marshall Gold Discovery State Historical Park** (at Coloma, NE via I-S 80 and S on SR 49) is where *the* Gold Rush started; here in Jan. 1848, James Marshall found gold at Sutter's Mill on the American River; self-guiding trail includes the reconstructed Sutter's Mill; a ½-m trail climbs a hill behind the town to a bronze statue of Marshall; museum; picnic areas; buildings open daily 10-5; closed Jan. 1, Thnks, Dec. 25; sm adm; **1.**

SAN BERNARDINO: San Bernardino National Forest, 621,000 acres, dramatic contrasts in terrain, vegetation, climate; hundreds of camp and picnic sites; **Cucamonga Wilderness** (NW), 9000-acre enclave of 4000-ft mtn slopes; W boundary is along a high ridge, reached from the W by trail through Angeles Ntl Forest (from the road to Mt. Baldy), or from the E from Lytle Creek; trails are under 3 m (**2, 3**); information and permit: Box 100, Lytle Creek Star Route, Fontana 92335. **San Gorgonio Wilderness**

(trails from Camp Angelus & other points off SR 38) centers on the highest mtns in S California; rugged but well-maintained trails run along the crest of the range or climb up to it at several points through pine and oak forest; the backbone trail of the system leads from Camp Angelus abt 4 m up to 10,624-ft San Bernardino Peak and then follows the ridge 8 m E to 11,502-ft San Gorgonio Mtn; **2 & 3**; information and permit: Box 264, Route 1, Mentone 92359.

Heart Bar State Park (30 m NE of Redlands on SR 38), 4343-acre park, elevs 6600-9000 ft; several moderate trails; **2.**

SAN DIEGO: Old Town, site of San Diego's original settlement in 1769; Old Town Plaza (San Diego Ave. & Mason St.); buildings date from early-mid-19th C. **Presidio Park** (N on Mason St. to Presidio Dr.), has mounds marking the original presidio and fort, the first construction in the city; nearby Junipero Serra Museum traces the history of the city and missions. The plaza and surrounding blocks are a state park, and the **Visitor Center** (2660 Calhoun St.) has maps and information; walking tours. Visitor Center and houses under state park jurisdiction are open daily May-Sept. 10-6, Oct.-Apr. 10-5; closed Jan. 1, Thnks, Dec. 25; free. Other buildings may be closed Mon. and/or Tues. and charge sm adm; **1. Balboa Park** includes museums, formal gardens, wooded areas and hiking trails, picnic areas, and the **San Diego Zoological Garden** (one of the greatest in the world), open 9-6 July-Labor Day, 9-4 Nov.-Feb., otherwise 9-5; adm; **1. Rosecroft Begonia Gardens** (510 Silvergate Ave., Point Loma), beautifully landscaped; many rare plants; famous for begonia and fuchsia displays (June-Sept.); open daily, summer 10-5, winter 11-4; sm adm; **1. San Diego Wild Animal Park** (E on Via Rancho Pkwy, Escondido,), 1800-acre preserve, can be seen on a 5-m monorail safari; features African Village, a 15-acre complex of exhibits; open 9-6 July-Labor Day, 9-4 Nov.-Apr., 9-5 other months; adm; **1. Mission San Luis Rey de Francia** (4 m E on SR 76, at Oceanside) historical items on display; gardens; Indian cemetery; picnic sites; open Mon.-Sat. 9-4, Sun. 11:30-4; closed Thnks, Dec. 25; sm adm; **1. Silverwood Wildlife Sanctuary** (13001 Wildcat Canyon Rd., Lakeside), 207 acres; open all yr, with self-guided tours Wed. and Sun.; guided tours Sun.; **1. Cuyamaca Rancho State Park** (SR 79 between I-8 & Julian), 21,000 mountainous acres; oak and pine forest; willow-lined streams; high desert-like mesas; 100 m of well-maintained trails; 3½-m climb to Cuyamaca Peak for views of Pacific Ocean and the Colorado Desert **(2)**; other trails vary in difficulty **(1-3)**; picnic areas; museum of Indian life; rare Cuyamaca cypress trees. **Cleveland National Forest**, in 3 divisions, has a semiarid climate and mtns up to 6500 ft; camp and picnic grounds; those at Laguna (E of Pine Valley on Co S1), Palomar (off SR 76 E of Rincon Springs), and San-

ta Ana Mtn (E of San Juan Capistrano) have self-guiding nature trails
(1).

Anza-Borrego Desert State Park (on US 78, E of San Diego), with hq
just W of Borrego Springs, is a beautiful ½-million-acre area of rugged
mtns and hot lowlands; 25-m self-guided auto tour begins at Pegleg Smith
Monument (9½ m E of park hq), where you pick up an informative
booklet that suggests several short walks along the route. At hq, **Borrego
Palm Canyon** nature trail goes to a little waterfall and pool ringed by fan
palms (1). On the E side of the park, a grove of **elephant trees** is reached
by a 1½-m trail from the road to Fish Creek primitive camp area (1 to
2). A long hiking and riding trail runs from Borrego Springs abt 25 m S to
Box Canyon Primitive Area, then swings N for another 12 m before
recrossing US 78 outside the park (3).

Torrey Pines State Reserve (1 m S of Del Mar on N Torrey Pines Rd.),
1000 acre reserve; thousands of the rare Torrey Pines, trails less than 1 m
wind through groves or lead to lookout points over canyons and cliffs (one
is the **Fat Man's Misery Trail,** through a canyon barely over 1 ft wide at
some points); also 4½-m beach below the bluffs; 1.

SAN FRANCISCO: Convention and Visitors Bureau (1390 Market St. nr
Larkin) can provide general information. **Architectural walking tours** are
offered on Sun. afternoons by the Foundation for San Francisco's Architectural Heritage; fee; 1. **Fisherman's Wharf,** center of the fishing industry: restaurants, seafood stalls, shops; nearby is **Pier 43:** 1886 sailing
ship *Baclutha* and the paddlewheel tug *Eppleton Hall,* both maintained by
the San Francisco Maritime Museum (open daily 9:30 am-10 pm;
adm.). W along the waterfront are **San Francisco Maritime State Historic
Park,** with more historic ships (open daily 10-6 plus evenings in summer;
closed Dec. 25; sm adm); **Aquatic Park;** and the **Municipal Pier.** Adj to
Aquatic Park is **Ghirardelli Square,** a multilevel complex of shops,
restaurants, art galleries, and theaters housed in refurbished brick
buildings. The following areas are all close to one another in downtown
San Francisco: **Russian Hill** (between Nob Hill and Fisherman's Wharf) is
a fashionable residential area; 1; steep streets include Lombard St., with
10 hairpin turns in a single block. **Cow Hollow** (Union St. between
Russian Hill and the Presidio) was once a dairying area but now house art
galleries, boutiques, and cafes in refurbished Victorian buildings; 1. **North
Beach,** Italian district, with specialty shops, nightlife, and sidewalk
cafes; 1. **Telegraph Hill** (E of Russian Hill and N Beach, near the waterfront), a residential area once known for its artists; at the top of the hill is
a small park where Coit Tower provides views of the city and bay; 1. **Em-
barcadero Center** (between Battery St. & the Ferry Bldg.), an 8½-acre urban redevelopment complex on the waterfront, has a multilevel pedestrian
mall with plazas, promenades, shops, restaurants, fountain, sculpture,

greenery; **1.** Nearby **Jackson Square** offers antique shops, home furnishings showrooms, and boutiques in restored turn-of the-century buildings; **1. Chinatown** (bounded by Broadway, Bush, Stockton, & Kearny), the largest Chinese community outside Asia; its main street is Grant Ave., lined with restaurants and shops; **1. Union Square,** a formal park, is in the heart of the city's downtown shopping district; **1. Civic Center** (SW downtown, at Van Ness Ave., Hyde, McAllister & Grove Sts.) includes City Hall, Public Library, San Francisco Museum of Art, state and federal office buildings, and other public structures; **1. Japan Center** (just W of downtown, bounded by Geary, Fillmore, Post, & Laguna Sts.) is a 5-acre complex of shops, teahouses, tempura bars; Peace Plaza, crowned with a pagoda and landscaped with gardens and pools, is site of annual festivals; open daily 10-6; closed Jan. 1, Dec. 25; **1. Golden Gate Park** (between Lincoln Way & Fulton St., Stanyan St. & Great Hwy), 1017 landscaped acres, is the nation's most beautiful city park; 15 m of drives; more than 25 m of bridle, foot, and bicycle trails **(1, 2)**; gardens; paddock fields with deer, elk, and buffalo; lakes; concerts; picnic areas; **Japanese Tea Garden,** 3 tranquil acres with pools, pagodas, streams, bridges, torii gates, and ornamental trees and shrubs, open daily 8-sunset, free; **Strybing Arboretum & Botanical Garden** (9th Ave. entrance), 5000 native and exotic plants, self-guiding tours (conducted tours available; open Mon.-Fri. 8-4:30, weekends and hols 10-5; free); outstanding M.H. de Young Memorial Museum (art), the California Academy of Sciences museum complex, and a marvelous Victorian conservatory. **Ocean Beach** stretches for miles along the W edge of the city; no swimming; at the N end are Seal Rocks, where you can see sea lions Oct.-May, and **Lincoln Park,** a 270-acre city park with golf course and art museum; **1. San Francisco Zoological Gardens** (SW corner of the city, at Zoo Rd. & Skyline), 1000 animals and birds; aviary; Monkey Island and Gorilla Grotto; tape tours or "Elephant Train"; picnic area; open daily 10-5:30; sm adm; **1.**

Angel Island State Park (reached by ferry from Tiburon, San Francisco, and Berkeley), 740-acre mountainous island in San Francisco Bay; good views of the city; woods and grassland; foot and bike trails circle the island, climb the 780-ft summit, and lead to several small sandy beaches and to picnic areas; **1 & 2.**

Golden Gate National Recreation Area (Fort Mason): The landscaped **Golden Gate Promenade,** abt 2 m long, starts at either the parking lot of the Golden Gate Bridge toll plaza or Fort point; follows the shoreline E past Fort Point wharf, Crissy Field beach, Marina Green, and Fort Mason to Aquatic Park; guided walks and other activities are offered; **1. Alcatraz,** 12-acre island federal penitentiary (1934-63) and later a native American stronghold, is reached by ferry from Fisherman's Wharf.

Tiburon, harbor lined with outdoor cafes and seafood restaurants (boats leave from Fisherman's Wharf); **1. Sausalito,** former whaling town, now a picturesque artists' colony with waterside restaurants and boutiques; **1. Muir Woods National Monument** (17 m N on US 101 & SR 1), 500 acres of redwood forest; ¼-m nature trail along a creek; salmon and steelhead trout spawn in winter **(1)**; 6 m of other trails **(1 & 2)**; connecting trails **(2)** in Mt. Tamalpais State Park; picnic areas in state park; open daily 8-sunset; sm adm or GEP. **Samuel P. Taylor State Park** (15 m W of San Raphael on Sir Francis Drake Blvd.), 30 m of nature, riding, and hiking trails through the canyon and surrounding grassy hills **(1, 2, & 3)**; picnic areas. **Point Reyes National Seashore** (entrance at Olema, on SR 1, 27 m N), rocky coast, dunes and beaches, rolling grassy lowlands, areas of heavy forest, and a tough granite spine; you can walk Earthquake Trail along the fault or Woodpecker Nature Trail (both **1**); summer interpretive program and nature walks; picnic area. Beach hikes at several points along the roads through the 64,000-acre park and from the Visitor Center at Drakes Beach (2); beaches flooded at high tide.

University of California (at Berkeley), 1000 acres E of San Francisco Bay; Spanish-style buildings, museums of art, anthropology, and geology; Indian Nature Trail at University **Botanical Gardens** (Strawberry Canyon), open daily exc Dec. 25, 9-5; free; **1. Oakland: Lakeside Park**, 120 acres on the N shore of Lake Merritt, a saltwater lake in the city; gardens, picnic areas, playgrounds, summer concerts, and a duck-feeding area; **1. Kaiser Center** (300 Lakeside Dr.), the Kaiser Industries complex overlooking Lake Merritt, has changing art exhibits on mezzanine and mall, shops, and a 3-acre roof garden; open Mon.-Sat.; closed hols; free; **1. Jack London Square** (at harbor, foot of Broadway), the colorful waterfront around which the city grew, has been renovated and landscaped; still standing is **Heinold's First and Last Chance**, a bunkhouse for oystermen, later a saloon in which Jack London drank and wrote; restaurants, shops, convention facilities; **1. Morcom Amphitheater of Roses** (Jean St., W of Grant Ave.), 8 acres, has blooming plants most of the year; best season is Apr.-Dec.; free; **1. Knowland State Arboretum and Park** (98th Ave. at I-580); picnic area; zoo; open daily 10-5; sm adm some days; **1. Joaquin Miller Park** (Warren Frwy & Joaquin Miller Rd.) was site of the poet's home; cascades, fountains, statuary, picnic areas, summer concerts; open daily 9 am-11 pm; free; **1.**

Mt. Tamalpais State Park (6 m W of Mill Valley on Panoramic Hwy), several hiking and interpretive trails converge at park hq; 28 m of trails within park **(1 & 2)**; access to additional 170-m trail system open to public on adj watershed land of Marin Municipal Water District **(2 & 3)**; picnic areas. **Portola State Park** (off SR 35 W of Saratoga on Alpine Rd, 1700-acre park in a deep, forested basin; many short paths, including a nature trail, wind among redwood and other trees **(1)**; hikes of 2½ to 7 m can be made on trails that climb the chaparral-covered hills to the E and W **(2)**;

picnic areas; summer naturalist program. **Butano State Park** (7 m S of Pescadero on Cloverdale Rd.), redwood park in the Santa Cruz Mtns; several hiking trails plus fire trails (**1 & 2**); nature walks in summer. **Mt. Diablo State Park** (5 m E of I-680, Danville), unusual rock formations (Garden of the Jungle Gods, Devil's Slide); winding road to top of 3849-ft Mt. Diablo; 20 m of hiking and bridle trails; picnic sites; **1 & 2.**

SAN JOSE: San Jose Municipal Rose Gardens (Naglee & Dana Aves.) are best in May-June but thousands of plants bloom all year; open Mon.-Fri. 8-sunset, Sat. & Sun. 10-sunset; free; **1. Japanese Friendship Garden** (Senter Rd. & E Alma in Kelley Park), 6 acres patterned after the Koraka En Gardens of Okayama, Japan, sister city of San Jose; lakes, waterfall, bridges, and lanterns; open daily 10-sunset in summer, 8-4:30 in winter; free; **1. Henry W. Coe State Park** (S to Morgan Hill, then 14 m E on Dunne Ave.), gentle ridges covered with grassland and oak forest, plus some deep, steep-sided canyons; 30 m of hiking and riding trails (mostly **2**).

SAN LUIS OBISPO: The Chamber of Commerce (1039 Chorro St.) or the County Historical Museum (696 Monterey St.) provide a self-guiding booklet for a **Path of History** that includes the Mission San Luis Obispo de Tolosa; 1853 Dallidet Adobe; Kundert Medical Building, designed by Frank Lloyd Wright in 1956, and other points of interest; **1. Montana de Oro State Park** (7 m S of Los Osos on Pecho Rd.), 5600 acres, 1½ m of rugged coastline backed by grassy plain, wooded canyons, and 1500-ft hills; interpretive trail (**1**) and other trails (**2**). **Morro Bay State Park** (NW on SR 1), trail past salt marsh and through grass- and brush-covered hills; boat harbor, museum of natural history, other facilities; guided nature walks in summer; **1.**

SANTA BARBARA: Spanish-colonial buildings, shops, restaurants, and art galleries; Chamber of Commerce (1301 Santa Barbara St.) provides a map for a 12-block **"Red Tile Tour"** of the area. Highlights include buildings of the original **Presidio** (1782), the **County Courthouse** Spanish-Moorish-style structure built in 1927), and several early-19th-C adobe homes. **1.** Nearby **Stearn's Wharf** is a 3-block extension of State St., with shops and restaurants over the ocean; to the W is the **yacht harbor**, protected by a breakwater with a ½-m paved walkway (**1**). **Botanic Garden** (1212 Mission Canyon Rd., 1¼ m N of mission) has 3 m of easy trails through 60 acres of native California trees, shrubs, cacti, and wildflowers; open daily 8-sunset; free; **1. Andree Clark Bird Refuge** (1400 E Cabrillo Blvd.), walking and bicycle paths through gardens around a lagoon; free; **1.** The town has several small parks, lovely gardens, and miles of free public beaches. **Dos Pueblos Orchid Ranch** (8 m W of Goleta on US 101), with 20 acres of greenhouses, is the world's largest cymbidium orchid farm; open Sun.-Thurs. 8-4; free; **1**. **Los Padres National Forest** (N of town), 2-million acres in 2 units: Los Padres has 1750 m of trails, camp-grounds, picnic areas. The larger section extends E and NW inland from Santa Barbara; the N section is along the Big Sur coast. **San Rafael Wilder-ness** (reached via roads off SR 154 on the S or SR 166 on the N), 120 m of trails, **2 & 3**; **Ventana Wilderness** is reached by trail from Big Sur Station on SR 1, other points off SR 1, and from E via Carmel Valley Village.

SANTA CRUZ: Pacific Garden Mall is a tree-lined downtown shopping street; on nearby side streets are renovated Victorian and Edwardian houses; **1**. A few blocks away, the waterfront offers a ½-m **Municipal Wharf** plus a fine 1-m beach backed by a boardwalk and amusement park; **1**. **Begonia Gardens** (2545 Capitola Rd. in Capitola) flowers June-Nov., with peak bloom Aug.-Sept.; free; **1**. **Henry Cowell Redwood State Park** (5 m N on SR 9), **Redwood Grove Trail**, a self-guided interpretive path; sequoias up to 285 ft in height; 15 m of well-marked hiking trails, plus ser-vice roads closed to vehicles; trail system can be reached from main en-trance, from 2 roadside pullouts S of entrance on SR 9, and from camping area off Graham Hill Rd. E of the park; **1 & 2**. **Big Basin Redwoods State Park** (abt 20 m N on SR 9, 236), on the W slopes of the Santa Cruz Mtns, 12,000 acres of the scenic Big Basin country; redwood and Douglas fir grows in the sheltered canyons, while chaparral covers the steep slopes overlooking the ocean; 35 m of trails; round trips from park hq at Opal Creek range from the 3/5-m **Redwood Trail (1)** to a 10-m, all-day trip to **Berry Creek Falls (2 to 3)**; most are in the 3-to-5-m range **(2)**; 14-m **Skyline to the Sea Trail** follows a road NE to Castle Rock State park **(3)**.

SANTA ROSA: Luther Burbank Memorial Gardens (Santa Rosa & Sonoma Aves.) commemorates the great horticulturalist who is buried here; open daily; free; **1**. **Jack London State Historic Site** (S off SR 12), trail and fire road lead to the ruins of London's Wolf House, the mansion that burned before he could move in; 1¼-m round trip; London's grave reached by branch trail; museum with mementos; open daily 10-5; closed Jan. 1, Thnks, Dec. 25; sm adm; **1**. On the coast near Jenner **Salt Point State Park** (20 m N of Jenner on SR 1) 3.7 m of rocky shoreline with tide pools and caves, plus 3174 acres with hiking and riding trails **(1 & 2)**; picnic area. Nearby **Stillwater Cove** is a county park with hiking trails **(1 & 2)**. **Kruse Rhododendron State Reserve** (off SR 1 22½ m N of Jenner, on Plantation Rd.) is a beautiful, undeveloped area where rhododendrons and other wildflowers bloom Apr.-May; nature and hiking trails; **(1)**. **Sonoma Coast State Beach** (along SR 1 between Bodega Bay & Jenner), series of sand beaches along a 13-m strip of coast, separated by rocky bluffs; 5-m trail system in dunes area (reached by W Bay Rd., N of Bodega Bay); picnic sites; **1 & 2**. **Armstrong Redwoods State Reserve** (NW off SR 116 and 3 m N of Guerneville), canyon, shaded by thick redwood forest; self-guiding **nature trail (1)** and 2½-m trail to adjacent Austin Creek State Recreation Area **(2)**; picnic area.

SEQUOIA and KINGS CANYON NATIONAL PARKS (SR 198, 50 m E of Visalia; or SR 180, 55 m E of Fresno) are bordered on the E by the crest of the Sierra Nevada; 14,495-ft Mt. Whitney, giant sequoias, striking rock formations, mtn lakes, falls, wildflower meadows. **Giant Forest** has Visitor Center; resort village; picnic areas; short trails wind through the groves and meadows in the area; **Moro Rock**, with views of the high mtns, is reached by a 1½-m trail from the village; **Sunset Rock**, with views to the W, is ¾-m; **1, 2**. **Heather Lake Trail (2)** and **Alta Trail (3)** lead into the back country to the NE; 11,204-ft Alta Peak, abt 8 m distant, is a 5000-ft climb. **Twin Lakes Trail** goes N toward Kings Canyon (abt 20 m; **3**) and connects with many other trails to the N and E. Most direct route to the higher mtns is **High Sierra Trail (3)**, which also connects with the extensive trail system. Back-country trails can also be reached from the **South Fork** and **Atwell Mill** campgrounds in the S part of Sequoia **(2 & 3)**. In Kings Canyon Ntl Park, **Grant Grove** has giant sequoias; Visitor Center; village; picnic areas; short and easy trails **(1 & 2)**; no back-country trails exc one N into Sierra Ntl Forest **(2)**. Nearby Redwood Canyon has good trails for day hiking **(2)**. **Kings Canyon**, and its center of activity **Cedar Grove**, are less developed, exc for campgrounds and a Visitor Center; granite peaks rise to 9000 ft, 1 m above the river, on either side of the steep-walled canyon; some easy trails, including an interpretive trail in **Zumwalt Meadows (1)**.

SOLEDAD: Pinnacles National Monument (E on SR 146), the jagged pinnacles are the weathered remains of an ancient volcano on the San Andreas Fault; they are protected in a 23-square-m park designed for hikers and climbers; trails begin near the Visitor Center: **Moses Spring Trail**, the easiest, is a ¾-m self-guiding nature trail to "caves" in a canyon covered by huge boulders **(1)**. **Bear Gulch Trail** is a 1¾-m self-guiding nature trail along a stream between the Visitor Center and a campground area **(1)**. More challenging are **High Peaks** and **Condor Gulch Trails**, on which loop hikes of up to 7 m (1650-ft climb) can be made through the Pinnacles **(2)**; a self-guiding booklet is available for a 4-m geology hike. Most strenuous is the scenic 9-m round trip on **Chalone Peak Trail**, a 2150-ft climb through dense chaparral and along a ridge with sweeping views **(3)** Adm or GEP

SONORA: On what is now N Washington St. was the largest pocket mine, Big Bonanza. The Tuolumne County Chamber of Commerce (158 W Bradford St.) can supply information on historic houses and cemeteries in town and on tours of the surrounding area; **1.** In almost any direction are many old mining camps: Just W is **Shaw's Flat;** W on SR 49 is **Tuttletown;** on Jackass Hill is a replica of the cabin where Mark Twain lived 1864-5; S on SR 108 is **Jamestown,** where **Rail Town 1897** exhibits trains, depot, roundhouse, and other railroad memorabilia both outdoors and in a museum (picnic sites; open daily 9-5:30 in summer, weekends only in spring and fall; adm). Just S of Jamestown, and E of SR 108, are the sites of **Quartz Mtn and Stent camps.** Just beyond Yosemite Junction, SR 120 S goes to **Chinese Camp;** to **Groveland;** and to others. **Columbia State Historic Park** (4 m N on SR 49), gold town with a typical combination of one church and 30 saloons; preserved buildings; Fallon Theater (summer performances), Eagle Cottage boardinghouse, Wells Fargo office; most buildings open daily 8-5, longer in summer; closed Thnks, Dec. 25; some shops closed weekdays; **1. Stanislaus National Forest** (NE via SR 108) has many recreation areas, 750 m of trails through forested slopes and the alpine zone (11,000-ft mtns). **Mokelumne Wilderness** (reached from Silver Lake, Twin Lakes, Woods Lake, and other points on SR 88; also from SR 4) is 50,000 acres, bare granite peaks (up to 9332 ft), wildflowers and jewel-like small lakes; some trails quite difficult, **3;** information and permit from 100 Forni Rd., Placerville 95667. **Emigrant Basin Primitive Area** (reached from many points on SR 108, to the N & W), with elevs from 6000 to 11,575 ft, and the surrounding part of the ntl forest have spectacular beauty and many trails, **3;** information and required free Wilderness Permit: 175 S Fairview Lane, Sonora 95370. **Calaveras Big Tree State Park** (NE off SR 4, 3 m E of Arnold), 5437 acres; Sierra redwood groves; trails through the trees and in a deep canyon.

Jackson (45 m NW on SR 49). This town and surrounding ones were born during the Gold Rush and contain many camp remains. The **Emigrant Trail,** blazed by Kit Carson and followed by wagon trains, is marked for hikers and horseback riders from the highway above Red Lake to the area near Silver Lake; **2. Amador City** (N of Jackson on SR 49) has many restored gold rush buildings; **1. Indian Grinding Rock State Historic Park** (11 m NE of Jackson, 1½ m from SR 88 on Pine Grove-Volcano Rd.) has interpretive trail and exhibits; limestone slab used as a community grist mill; 1000 bedrock mortars for grinding seeds and acorns; petroglyphs; picnic sites; **1. Volcano** (adj to Indian Grinding Rock) has preserved many buildings of the gold rush period; **1.**

UKIAH: Clear Lake State Park (SE via SR 20, 29), site of a Pomo Indian village on a prehistoric village site; excavated sweat house and ceremonial lodge; self-guiding trail (1); hiking trails (1, 2); picnic area. **Mendocino National Forest** (NE) offers stretches of pine and Douglas fir forest, and peaks up to 8600 ft.

YOSEMITE NATIONAL PARK (entrances: SR 120 from Manteca; SR 34 from Merced; SR 41 from Fresno; summer-only Tioga Pass Trans-Sierra Rd. & SR 395): Granite mtns, waterfalls, forests, alpine meadows, cliff-flanked Yosemite Valley make this a stunning park. **Yosemite Village** has campgrounds, other accommodations; Visitor Center (open daily) with audiovisual programs, exhibits, living history programs, walks, talks, other programs. There are many easy paths in the valley; one to **Yosemite Falls** is less than ½ m (1). SW of the village, a more strenuous trail leaves Sunnyside Campground and joins other back-country hiking trails (2 & 3). A 4-m trail from the base of Sentinel Rock climbs abt 3200 ft to **Glacier Point**, where it meets other trails and a road (2 & 3). **Happy Isles Trail Center**, reached by shuttle bus, offers information on backpacking and hiking; open summer only. This is the N end of the **John Muir Trail**; short hikes to Vernal Fall (3-m round trip; 1 to 2) and Nevada Fall (5-m round trip; 2) from Nevada Fall, the 6-m **Panorama Trail** goes to Glacier Point (3). **Mirror Lake**, also reached by shuttle bus, is another access point to back country; (2 & 3). **Mariposa Grove** (at Wawona, near S entrance) has a system of paths among giant sequoias (1).

STATE PARKS: The system includes 900,000 acres and 700 m of trails. In addition to those covered separately above, others with trails are listed below. California has 54 state beaches; those most attractive to hikers are included. **Andrew Molera** (21 m S of Carmel on SR 1), 2141 acres in the Big Sur area; 1 & 2. **Annadel** (Channel Dr. E off Montgomery Dr., Santa Rosa), 4900 acres of rolling hills; 35 m of trails; 1 & 2. **Austin Creek State Recreation Area** (2 m N of Guerneville on Armstrong Woods Rd.), 4236 acres in the Coast Range, adj to Armstrong Redwoods State Reserve; 1 & 2. **Border Field** (15 m S of San Diego via I-5 & Monument Rd.), 372 acres; 1 & 2. **Bothe-Napa Valley** (4 m N of St. Helena on SR 29, 128), 1122 acres; interpretive trail and restored 1846 grist mill; 1 & 2. **Castle Rock** (off SR 35, 2 m S of intersection with SR 9 W of Saratoga), 1053 acres; trail to Big Basin Redwoods SP; 1, 2, & 3. **Caswell Memorial** (6 m S of Ripon on Austin Rd.), 258 acres; 1. **Clear Lake** (4 m N of Kelseyville on Soda Bay Rd.), 560-acre lakeside park with 2 interpretive trails; 1. **Folsom Lake State Recreation Area** (Folsom), in the Sierra foothills E of Sacramento; 1 & 2. **Forest of Nisene Marks** (4 m N of Aptos on Aptos Creek Rd.), 9779-acre redwood park near Monterrey Bay; 1 & 2. **Gaviota** (33 m W of Santa Barbara on US 101), 2795-acres; ocean beach; **1 & 2. Grizzly Creek Redwoods** (on SR 36, 20 m E of US 101 at Alton), 234 acres; **1. Grover Hot Springs** (3 m W of Markleeville), in Sierras S of Lake Tahoe area; **1 & 2. Hendy Woods** (10 m NW of Boonville, off SR 128), 605-acre redwood park; **1. Lake Oroville State Recreation Area** (7 m E of Oroville on SR 162); **1 & 2. Lake Perris State Recreation Area** (3 m N of Perris on US 395, then 3 m E on Ramona Expwy), 9 m of trails around lake; **1 & 2. Los Osos Oaks State Reserve** (8 m NW of US 101 on Los Osos Valley Rd., 2 m S of San Luis Obispo), hiking trails; **1. Mendocino Headlands** (surrounds Mendocino), **1. Millerton Lake State Recreation Area** (20 m NE of Fresno on SR 41 & Friant Rd.), 6551 acres; **1 & 2. Montgomery Woods State Reserve** (11 m NW of New Ukiah on Comptche Rd.), 1119-acre redwood preserve; **1 & 2. Natural Bridges State Beach** (W Cliff Dr., Santa Cruz), interpretive trail; **1. New Brighton State Beach** (4 m S of Santa Cruz on SR 1), interpretive trail; **1. Palomar Mtn** (off SR 76 E of Rincon Springs), 1886 acres on 6140-ft Palomar Mtn; **1 & 2. Picacho Peak State Recreation Area** (N of Yuma, Ariz.), rugged desert park on the lower Colorado River; best in late fall; **2 & 3. Pismo State Beach** (2 m S of Pismo Beach on SR 1), 967 acres; hiking and interpretive trails; **1 & 2. Point Mugu** (15 m S of Oxnard on SR 1), 6554 acres; **1 & 2. Robert Louis Stevenson** (10 m N of Calistoga on SR 29), 3143 acres in the Coast Range; **2. Saddleback Butte** (17 m E of Lancaster on Ave. J), 2875-acre desert park; **2. San Onofre State Beach** (3 m S of San Clemente on I-5), 2890 acres with trails; **1 & 2. San Pasqual Battlefield** (8 m S of Escondido on SR 78), 2-acre site of inconclusive 1846 battle; interpretive trail; **1. Seacliff State Beach** (5½ m S of Santa Cruz on SR 1), short trail; **1. Silverwood Lake State Recreation Area** (30 m N of San Bernardino on SR 138), 2 m of hiking trails through a canyon; **1. Standish-Hickey State Recreation Area** (1 m N of Leggett on US 101), 915 acres in redwood area; **1 & 2. Sugarloaf Ridge** (7 m E of Santa Rosa on SR 12, then 3 m N on Adobe Canyon Rd.), 2000 acres; hiking and interpretive trails; **1 & 2. Sunset State Beach** (16 m S of Santa Cruz off SR 1), **1. Tomales Bay** (4 m N of Inverness), 1018 acres adj to Point Reyes Ntl Seashore; **1 & 2. Trinidad State Beach** (19 m N of Eureka on US 101), N California beach plus short trail; **1. Woodson Bridge State Recreation Area** (6 m E of Corning on South Ave.), 414 acres on Sacramento River; interpretive trail; **1.**

COLORADO

ALAMOSA: Pike's Stockade (12 m S off US 285) is a replica, open mid-May-mid-Oct. daily 9-4:40; free. At **La Jara** (15 m S), nice reservoir and a fish hatchery, **1**. **Monte Vista** (17 m N via SR 160, 285) has a fish hatchery and national wildlife refuge (6 m S on SR 15), **1**. **Great Sand Dunes National Monument** (14 m E on US 160, 19 m N on SR 150), where desert sands have been blown into dunes 700-ft high, has a Visitor Center (open daily 8-5); ⅓-m self-guiding Montville nature trail (**1**); 3½-m trail climbs E to Mosca Pass (**2, 3**); you cut your own trail across the dunes (**2**); summer naturalist program, guided walks; camping; picnicking.

ASPEN: The **Chamber of Commerce** (Box GG, 81611) offers a list of hiking trails in the surrounding country, ranked in 3 levels of difficulty. Nearby ghost towns include **Ashcroft** (12 m S on Castle Creek Rd.), preserved by the Aspen Historical Society; **1**. **Marble** (30 m S of Carbondale on SR 133). You can also walk around pretty **Maroon Lake (SW of town).**

BOULDER: University of Colorado campus is lovely for strolling and has museums open to the public. **Boulder Reservoir** (6 m NE on SR 119) is open daily 5 am-11 pm; swimming in summer; **1**. **Chautauqua Park** (9th St. & Baseline Rd.) is one of several for strolling and picnicking. **Nederland** (17 m W on SR 119), in upper Boulder Canyon, is an old mining town that has been used as a film location; nearby ghost towns are Cardinal and Caribou City. **Arapaho Glacier** is reached by a 3½-m trail from a point in Boulder Canyon near Fourth of July Campground (**2, 3**); a public hike is conducted the 2nd Sunday in August. **Sawhill Ponds State Park** is NE of the city beyond the airport, **1, 2**. **Flagstaff Mtn** has well-marked, moderate trails (**2**). **Roosevelt National Forest:** Surrounding Rocky Mtn Ntl Park on the N, E, and S, Roosevelt contains a million acres of forest and almost as many acres of Pawnee Ntl Grasslands; mtn areas have glaciers, alpine lakes, and beautiful canyons. **Central City**—and N along SR 119, 72—offers campgrounds for easy walks or strenuous climbs to 13,000-ft peaks, plus St. Vrain Canyon (**1-3**). E of **Estes Park** (along US 34) are campsites for hiking Big Thompson Canyon or strolling at Drake's fish hatchery; **1-3**. NW

of **Ft. Collins**, SR 14 has campsites and walks **(1-3)** along Cache La
Poudre River and canyon, plus climbing to 8-11,000-ft peaks; Red Feather
Lakes (off SR 14 N of Rustic) offers easy and moderate walks **(1,
2)**. **Rawah Wilderness** (N of SR 14, 60 m W of Ft. Collins) is one of the
most beautiful areas, reached by trail from several points along a gravel
road off SR 14; 27,000 acres with about 75 m of well-marked trails, but
elevations are 9500-13,000 ft, and climbing is very tough; campsites are at
Rawah and McIntyre Lakes; season July 15-Sept. 15; **2, 3**. **Information:**
301 S Howes, Ft. Collins 80521.

CANON CITY: Five Points Recreation Site (17 m W on US 50), on the
Arkansas River; hiking in the foothills of the **Sangre de Cristo Mtns**; old
mining towns nearby; open year round; **2**.

COLORADO SPRINGS: The many mineral springs at the foot of Pike's
Peak were considered sacred by Indians. **Manitou Cliff Dwellings
Museum** (US 24 Bypass), cliff dwellings and artifacts; open daily in sum-
mer; closed Oct.-mid-May; sm adm. **U.S. Air Force Academy** (10 m N on
I-25) has a Visitor Center (S entrance) with displays and booklets for self-
guiding tours; open daily 8-5; free. **Palmer Park** (3 m N), 700 scenic acres
with trails and picnic areas, **1, 2**. **Garden of the Gods** (6 m W), 370-acre
park with dramatic red sandstone formations; picnic area; free; **1**. **Ramah
Reservoir** (45 m NE off US 24) is a state recreation area, **1, 2**. **Florissant
Fossil Beds National Monument** (35 m W via SR 24): Museum and information center; nature trail **(1)**; rich fossil area with impressions of
dragonflies, ants, butterflies, fish, birds, small mammals; open daily,
June-Aug. 8-7, Apr.-May & Sept.-Oct. 8-4:30; open Mon.-Fri. 8:30-5,
Nov.-Mar.; closed Jan. 1., Thnks, Dec. 25; free.
  Pike National Forest: Over a million acres of old mining territory between Leadville and Colorado Springs encompassing a spur of the Rockies;
800 m of streams; 800 acres of lakes; 14,109-ft **Pike's Peak** is reached via
18-m toll road from Cascade, cog railway from Manitou Springs, or hike
(3) from Colorado Springs. The scenic **Rampart range** in the E is reached
by road NE from Woodland park, and campgrounds along this road give
access to trails; the climb to **Devil's Head** fire lookout is popular **(2, 3)**.
From Lake George (on SR 24, 20 m W of Woodland Park), a road leads to
Eleven Mile Canyon Reservoir, with campsite, fish hatchery, hiking **(1-3)**.
Lost Creek Scenic Area is entered by 6-m trails at Twin Eagles picnic ground
(18 m N of Lake George via Co 77), or from a trailhead farther N at Ute
Creek; 2-m trail from Goose Creek campground (23 m N of Lake George
via FS 545); or roundabout trails (10 m is the shortest) from Lost Park
campground (20 m S of Bailey via FS 607); these trails intersect to make a
loop through the 15,000-acre area and around it; there are additional trails
through this well-used area of forest and weathered granite outcroppings;

elevations about 9000 ft. **Information:** 403 S Cascade, Colorado Springs 80907.

Cripple Creek: This gold-mining town boomed in the 1890s and boom-era buildings remain in town; information at **Cripple Creek Museum** (on SR 67), open Memorial Day-early Oct. daily 10-5:30, weekends only in winter; sm adm. You can tour the **Mollie Kathleen Gold Mine** (1 m N on SR 67), mid-May-Oct. daily 9-6; adm. **El Paso Gold Mine** (3 m SW on SR 67) gives tours in summer 10-6; adm. Nearby ghost towns are near Victor (6 m SW on SR 67): Goldfield, Bull Hill Station, Altman.

CORTEZ: Hovenweep National Monument (about 40 m W over dirt rds, or 20 m NW via US 666, then W 27 m on dirt roads) contains ruins of pueblos and cliff dwellings; **Lowry Indian Ruins** are in the same area, a bit N; check road conditions with **Cortez Chamber of Commerce** before starting out, and carry water and food.

Mesa Verde National Park (10 m E on US 160, then S on park road): Here you have a unique opportunity to follow the story of centuries of prehistoric residence, from the 7th C until the area was abandoned for mysterious reasons at the end of the 13th C. Either the **Far View Visitor Center** (summer only; daily 8-5) or the **Chapin Mesa Visitor Center** (all yr 8-5, longr in summer) offers booklets for self-guiding trails, plus ranger-led trips to **Cliff Palace** (200 rooms, 23 kivas), **Spruce Tree House** (114 rooms, 8 kivas), and other ruins. **1, 2.**

CRAIG: Chamber of Commerce (at entrance to city park) is in David Moffat's private railroad car; open business hrs; free. At Maybell (31 m W on US 40) there are: **Cross Mtn Canyon** (12 m W on US 40), 3 m N of the highway by jeep trail; scenic, steep-walled Canyon of the Yampa River; **2. Vermillion Bluffs** (30 m NW on back roads), a high ridge with beautifully colored cliffs; difficult to reach without 4-wheel drive; **3.**

DENVER: The downtown area includes the impressive **State Capitol**, with gold-leaf dome; the **Civic Center** (adj to the W), with modern and classical buildings and outdoor statuary; and **Larimer Square** (Larimer St. between 14th & 16th Sts.), a block of attractively restored buildings dating from the 1860s-1890s housing shops, art galleries, cafes; **1.** Denver has many city parks. Those with hiking trails include: **Avondale** (13th & Knox Ct.), **S Barnum** (3rd to 6th, & Grove to Julian), **Bear Creek** (Hampden at Sheridan), **Cook Memorial** (Florida & Monaco), **Crestmoor** (101 S Monaco), **Garland** (Mississippi & Holly), **Huston Lake** (Ohio & Zuni), **Observatory** (Evans & Filmore), **Rocky Mtn Lake** (46th & Hooker), **Ruby Hill** (Florida & Platte River), **Silverman** (Andrews & Titan), **Sloan Lake**

(26th & Stuart), **Valverde** (Byers & Pecos), **Washington** (Downing & Louisana), **Westwood** (Ohio & Wolff); mostly **1**. **Cheesman Park** (8th & Franklin) has the Denver Botanic Gardens and Boettcher Memorial Conservatory, which display native and tropical plants daily (exc Dec. 25) 9-5 (free); bike trails, picnic sites, other facilities; **1**. Denver also has an extensive Mtn Park System outside of the city, with over 13,000 acres in abt 50 units W & S of town; those with trails include: **Bell** (29 m W, 2 m SE of Evergreen on SR 73); **Dillon**, in the same area; **Echo Lake** (47 m W on SR 103); **O'Fallon** (23 m SW on SR 74); **1 & 2**. For more **information** contact parks office, 1445 Cleveland Place. Other scenic areas for walking include **Red Rocks Park** (W via Alameda Ave.), the state recreation area at **Cherry Creek Reservoir** (SE off SR 83), and **Golden Gate Canyon State Park** (on the road to Blackhawk), named for the canyon it spans, 3000 acres at an elevation of 8200-9000 ft, where a herd of bison is kept. The **Lariat Trail** is a scenic route leading from Golden to Denver Mtn Parks; nearest of the parks is **Lookout Mtn** (5 m W), on whose summit Buffalo Bill asked to be buried; his grave and a memorial museum (open daily 10-5, with longer hrs in summer, closed Dec. 25, free); the road continues past the Denver game preserve to the summit of Genesee Peak, Filius and Bergen parks, Evergreen, Bear Creek Canyon, Red Rocks Park, and to Denver. **Information**: Hospitality Center (225 W Colfax Ave., zip 80202). **Colorado Mountain Club** (1723 E 16th Ave.) and **Denver Alpine Club** (1455 S Easton Court, Lakewood) provide specialized information and organized trips. Excursions and instruction are also provided by commercial guide services in major centers, such as **Aspen Alpine Guides** (Aspen) or **Rocky Mountains Expeditions, Inc.** (Buena Vista).

Central City (30 m W on US 6, SR 119), built on steep **Gregory Gulch** and site of the state's first important gold strike, has drawn tourists from Walt Whitman and the Baron de Rothschild to today; it has a lively, gaudy air, and you can pan for gold, visit gold museums, tour mines, see the old opera house, hotels, and other boom-era buildings; **Nevadaville** (2 m W) was once larger than Denver; today it is a ghost town with a few buildings still standing. The area between Central City and Idaho Springs is dotted with mine dumps and old buildings scattered through the forest. At Idaho Springs (37 m W on I-70), the Colorado School of Mines gives guided tours of **Edgar Mine** (on US 40; open June-early Sept. daily 8:30-3:30; free); a nature trail featuring local plant life runs from **Blue Ribbon Tunnel** to a hilltop above a waterfall (**1**); and **St. Mary's Glacier** (12 m via I-70 & Fall River Rd. to Alice) has a ½-m trail to Alice, in a lovely setting (**1**). **Georgetown** (47 m W on I-70), uniquely preserved mining town, is part of a historic district that includes **Silver Plume** (SW on I-70); many old buildings survive, including the elaborate Hotel de Paris (open June-Sept. 9-5:30; adm) and luxurious Hammill House (open May-Sept. 9:30-6, rest of yr, Tues.-Sun. 9:30-6; adm). The nearby ghost town of **Waldorf**, high in the mtns, offers beautiful views, **1**.

Arapaho National Forest: Over ½-million acres S and W of Rocky Mtn Ntl Park; part of Gore Range-Eagle's Nest Primitive Area; 300 m of trails; **Monarch Lake** (W of Granby) has trails into back country, including the high Indian Peaks region; **2 & 3**. The upper **Williams Fork River** (reached by gravel road off US 40 W of Kremmling) is another good area for short or long hikes, **1-3**. **Bridal Veil Falls, Echo Lake, Loveland Pass**, and other areas along I-70 W of Denver are heavily used and provide easy as well as difficult walks, **1-3**. An FS booklet for a self-guiding auto tour of **Moffat Road**, a former railroad route across the Continental Divide, will give you a chance to stop off for walks **(1-3)**.

GLENWOOD SPRINGS: Gypsum Recreation Area (E on US 6), at site of extinct volcano, has lava beds, caves, trails, **2, 3**; open yr round; free. **Rifle Falls**, with fish hatchery, and **Rifle Gap** (W on I-70 to Rifle, then 15 m N via SR 789, 325) are attractive state recreation areas.

White River National Forest, 2 million acres of some of the most spectacular country in the state, with lakes that many consider the most beautiful in Colorado, is N and E of Glenwood Springs; **Glenwood Canyon** (NE on US 6) is splendid, with Hanging Lake, falls, hot springs, trails **(1, 2)**. **Flat Tops Primitive Area** (N of Glenwood Springs) is a high, 102,000-acre plateau, much of it grasslands; famous **Trappers Lake,** just outside the primitive area, with campground, is reached by primitive road off SR 132, W of Meeker; SR 132, along the White River, is extraordinarily scenic; trail around the lake; trail to a narrow, 1000-ft-high ridge called Devil's Causeway; trail to lovely Wall Lake and other parts of primitive area; also S off SR 132 are trailheads (and primitive roads leading to trailheads) for Twin Lakes, Marvine Lakes, and many other lakes; **1-3**. Access from the S generally requires either very long hikes or rough roads plus long hikes; 2 of the better roads are off the Colorado River, N of Dotsero, and lead to campgrounds at **Heart Lake** and **Sweetwater Lake**, from where trails lead to the primitive area; this section has many primitive roads and trails to small lakes; **1-3**. A popular and attractive forest recreation area is N of Rifle along **E Rifle Creek**; a few walks here **(1, 2)** but most trails are just E, from Meadow Lake campground, along **Clark Ridge** and in **Hadley Gulch, 1-3. Maroon Bells-Snowmass Wilderness** (SW of Aspen) is a 66,380-acre high-mtn area (8-14,000 ft) especially stunning when the aspens turn golden in the fall; nearly 130 m of trail range from fairly easy to technical climbs; campground at beautiful **Maroon Lake** (via road off SR 82 SW of Aspen) provides a 1.6-m walk to **Crater Lake (2)**; from here there are climbs to the 14,000-ft Maroon Peaks, 9-m trail via 12,462-ft Buckskin Pass to

Snowmass Lake, or 17-m trail via lower Willow Pass to Snowmass camp-ground; **2-3. Conundrum Hot Springs** (S end), where you can bathe and climb to 14,265-ft Castle Peak, can be reached in about 10-m hike from the S via Gothic (off SR 135 N of Crested Butte) or from the N along Conundrum Creek (from Castle Creek Rd); very popular; **2, 3.** From Snowmass campground, it's 7½ m to cliff-ringed **Snowmass Lake** (with trail up 14,092-ft mtn) via the creek, and you can also take cutoffs SE (harder) to **Crater Lake** or W (easier) to **Pierre Lakes** (9 m) and beyond; **2, 3.** Access points in the NW are from **Redstone** or **Avalanche** campgrounds (off SR 133, S of Carbondale). Campgrounds SE of **Aspen** (off SR 82) provide many additional trails, mostly along creeks; N of Aspen, the road following Fryingpan River offers trailheads plus primitive roads leading to campgrounds and other trailheads; especially popular are the **Sylvan Lake** (S of Eagle) and **Eagle River** (S of Minturn) areas, with recreation areas, trails along creeks to hidden lakes, and Sawatch Range climbs; **1-3. Gore Range-Eagle's Nest Primitive Area** (E of Vail), has more than 80 m of trail on 61,000 acres, where the peaks of the Gore Range rise over 13,000 ft. Trailheads in the E (S of Kemmling) are off SR 9, or from primitive roads and campgrounds on SR 9; closest access is from the campground at Lower Catarack Lake (on road off SR 9 at Green Mtn Reservoir); in the S, from Gore Creek campground and other nearby trailheads (E of Vail on US 6); from the W, primitive roads and trailheads mean long hikes before reaching the primitive area. **Information:** 9th & Grand, Glenwood Springs 81601.

GRAND JUNCTION: Colorado National Monument (entrances 4 & 15 m W off SR 340) has fantastic eroded rock formations and lovely canyons along the upper Colorado River; 28-sq-m area has short, self-guiding trails (Window Rock and Coke Ovens) along canyon rim (**1**); the longer Monument Canyon Trail offers hiking below the rim (**2-3**); Visitor Center; camp and picnic sites. State recreation areas are at **Highline Lake** (16 m NW off I-70), **Island Acres** (21 m NE off I-70), with a buffalo herd, and **Vega Reservoir** (24 m NE on I-70, then 30 m E via local roads), all with walking, **1-3. Mud Springs Recreation Site** (20 m SW via Glade Park) is an aspen grove with rock hunting, camp and picnic sites, hiking trails (**2-3**); open May-Oct.; free. **Miracle Rock Recreation Site** (25 m SW via Glade Park) is a scenic area with rocky, pinon-juniper canyon, natural bridges, other rock formations; waterfalls in **Little Dolores River**; picnic and camp sites; rockhounding; hiking (**1-3**); open all yr; free.

GUNNISON NATIONAL FOREST covers 1,7-million acres on the W slopes of the Rockies; 27 peaks are over 12,000 ft; streams, alpine lakes. **West Elk Primitive Area** (via gravel road NW of Gunnison) is a

62,000-acre region of dense forests, mtn meadows, and castle-like rock formations at 8-12,000 ft. From **Castle Creek** trailhead, 1-day trips can be made to Costo Lake (2 m) or farther into the wilderness on several trails **(2, 3)**, where you can walk for days. Another access for 1-day or longer hikes is from the S (N off US 50 at Blue Mesa Reservoir); camping along **Soap Creek** and at **Rainbow Lake.** (Blue Mesa Reservoir is a national recreation area outside the forest boundary, extending 17 m along US 50, that has easier walks, **(1).** From the N, **Horse Ranch Park** trailhead (across Beckwith Pass) is tougher, requiring a hard 3-m hike to the wild area boundary; many people do these trails on horseback. **La Garita Wilderness** (NE of Creede) is a 49,000-acre area on the Continental Divide shared with Rio Grande Ntl Forest; steep talus slopes; peaks over 14,000-ft; beaver dams. From Creede or just N of it, trails are at least 10 m to the wilderness area S of the Continental Divide; from then on, there's a 12-m trail across the Divide, a long trail along the perimeter of the wilderness, and shorter trails within it **(2, 3);** if you don't want to go that far, you can take the easier walks along the Creede-area creeks, **2. Stone Cellar** campground (S of Cochetopa Pass) has 8-9-m trails **(2, 3)** SW along creeks to take you around Sheep Mtn to the wilderness trail network S of the Divide. **Big Meadows** campground (E of Lake City & Los Pinos Pass) offers a 30-m loop, much of it along creeks, through the section N of the Divide **(2, 3);** a spur crosses the Divide **(3);** other spurs offer Canyon Diablo **(3)** and shorter hikes in the N **(2, 3). Crested Butte** (N of Gunnison on SR 135) is in an area of alpine vegetation, at 6000-14,000 ft, and the road N to the quaint ghost town of Gothic is noted for its columbine; alpine vegetation is preserved in the 900-acre **Gothic Natural Area (1-3).** Another area of magnificent scenery is NE of Gunnison (off SR 135) to **Taylor Park Reservoir, Spring Creek,** and ghost towns such as **Tincup;** or the **Waunita Hot Springs area** (E of Gunnison off US 50), **Gold Creek, Quartz Creek,** ghost towns such as **Ohio City,** and fish hatchery; both areas have camping and other facilities, and provide easy and moderate walks **(1, 2)** as well as mountain climbing **(3).** In the forest section near Lake City is **Slumgullion Earthflow** (W on SR 149). **Information:** Supervisor, Gunnison 81230.

LA JUNTA: Bent's Old Fort National Historic Site (on SR 194, 8 m E), a trading post erected 1833 on the Santa Fe Trail, is being restored; open daily; free.

LAKE CITY: Lake Fork Recreation Area (S & W), 80,000 acres; administered by BLM; peaks over 13,000 ft; more than 60 lakes; miles of trails; **2 & 3. Mill Creek Recreation Site** (14 m SW on county road) makes a good trailhead.

LEADVILLE: One of the most exciting mining camps in the country, Leadville started as a gold camp and then had an even bigger boom in silver; 9-m **Silver Kings Hwy** circles the old mines; **Horace Tabor Home,** the **Tabor Opera House,** and **Tabor's Matchless Mine** (E of town on E 7th St.), where Baby Doe was found frozen to death in 1935, are all open in summer daily; several other interesting buildings. Hiking trails in surrounding country, **2 & 3. Twin Lakes** (16 m S on US 24) and **Turquoise Lake** (8 m W) are pretty areas for walking.

MONTROSE: Black Canyon of the Gunnison National Monument (11 m E on US 50, SR 347) preserves 12 spectacular m of a somber, narrow, 2000-ft-deep canyon; 8-m S Rim Drive has several short trails to lookouts, and ¾-m self-guiding trail to Warner Point **(1, 2)**; from the N Rim (14 m S on gravel road from Crawford, where there is a state recreation area on Crawford Reservoir), there are more overviews and a nature trail, **(1, 2)**; the inner canyon is reachable only on foot **(2, 3)** and rangers provide maps; camping; usually open May-Oct., but snow closes the roads at other times of yr. **Sweitzer Lake** (19 m N off US 50), the fish hatchery (N of Delta via SR 65) and fishing lakes N of Delta, and **Hotchkiss** (E of Delta via SR 92, 133) all provide attractive trails for walking **(1, 2)**.

NATURITA: Paradox Valley (W on SR 145 to Vancorum, then 19 m W on SR 90) is so called because the Dolores River cuts across it rather than running through it; lovely area; **2, 3.**

PAGOSA SPRINGS: Navajo State Recreation Area (30 m SW via US 160, SR 151 near Arboles) has a visitor center with information on walks; swimming; other activities. **Echo Canyon State Recreation Area** (SE on US 84) has walking also.

Rio Grande National Forest includes a portion of La Garita Wilderness. **Upper Rio Grande Primitive Area** (W of Creede off SR 149) is spectacular mtn country (9-14,000-ft); several trails **(3)** cross the Continental Divide into San Juan forest; loop hikes **(2, 3)** can also be made; season is mid-late summer only; access is from campsites along the Rio Grande (and reservoir), reached S from Lake City or W from Creede; along the roads are a fish hatchery at Creede, lakes, reservoirs; **1-3. South Fork** area has campsites along the Rio Grande (N on SR 149) and the S Fork (SE off US 160 to Beaver Creek Reservoir or SW along US 160). **Summitville-Platoro** area (S of Del Norte along Pinos Creek road) has 11-13,000-ft peaks; most of these mtns have several trails **(2, 3)** blazed by the gold and silver miners who once combed this area; trails lead to mining camp remains, ghost towns (such as Summitville). Some of the peaks, such as 11,000-ft **Lyon**

Point or 13,189-ft **Bennett Mtn,** can also be climbed from campground SW of Monte Vista (road leads W off SR 15 below the town), **3.** **Elwood Pass** (S of Summitville) has a short trail from the road to its 11,631-ft summit for a panoramic view, and trails up its slopes; just S is a meadow, noted for columbines, that inspired the state flower and song, **1, 2.** Nearby **Lookout Mtn,** 12,448-ft, has several trails to the summit; camping at Stunner; **2, 3. Platoro** is a resort with miles of trails to streams, Platoro Reservoir, mtn lakes, mining remains, vistas, **1-3. Conejos River canyon** (S of Platoro), lined for miles with sheer cliffs, has interesting formations such as **the Pinnacles;** old road and trails **(1-3). Cat Creek Canyon** (12 m S of Monte Vista on SR 15, then W on road to Platoro), extending outside the forest, has ancient trails and wildflowers **(1, 2). Alamosa Canyon** (W of Cat Creek Canyon) has trails **(1, 2)** blazed by Indians and gold miners; campsite near **Terrace Reservoir** on the Alamosa River; many trails to remains of mining camps, **1-3. Information:** Rural Route 3, Box 21, Monte Vista 81144.

PUEBLO: El Pueblo State Historical Museum (905 S Prairie Ave.) contains a full-size replica of Fort Pueblo; other exhibits; open Tues.-Fri. 9-5, Sun. & some hols 10-5; free.

San Isabel National Forest covers over a million acres in 4 units with the highest elevation of any national forest (12 peaks over 14,000 ft); more than 40 timberline lakes, over 700 m of bridle and foot trails. The most popular section is SW of **Leadville** (along US 24, 285), where campgrounds and trailheads are on roads off to the W; in the spring the snow outlines the Angel of Shavano (near the Salida end). The stunning **Sangre de Cristo range** is reached from campgrounds near Crestone (E off SR 1) at Moffat, Westcliffe (W off SR 69), Hillside (W off SR 69), and Coaldale (W off US 50). The **Wet Mtn** section (S of Canon City) is heavily wooded and noted for wildflowers; **Lake Isabel** is a popular recreation area here. The smallest unit (SW of Walsenburg via US 160, SR 12) has trailheads off SR 12. Hq is in Pueblo.

ROCKY MOUNTAIN NATIONAL PARK: With elevations 8-14,000 ft, rugged gorges, alpine lakes and tundra, and glacier-scoured valleys, this 410-sq-m wildlife sanctuary offers some of the best hiking in the nation. The dazzling 50-m **Trail Ridge Rd,** which stays above the timberline for 11 m and reaches 12,183 ft, runs from Estes Park (E) to Grand Lake (W) entrances and gives an overall view; snow closes parts of this road as late as June and as early as Oct. The park provides campgrounds, riding, fishing, winter sports. Information: Hq at E entrance in **Estes Park** (write Supervisor, Estes Park 80517), open all yr 8-5; **Moraine Park Visitor Center** (W of hq), open mid-May-early Oct. daily 8-5; **Alpine Visitor**

Center (about midway on Trail Ridge Rd.), open June-Oct., weather permitting; a summer information center at Grand Lake; ranger stations throughout the park. These will give you schedules of the many fine interpretive programs (summer), including guided hikes; there are also self-guiding trails, roadside exhibits; auto tape tours are available in Estes Park and Grand Lake. Some 300 m of well-marked trails, at all levels of difficulty, are spread throughout the park; mileages given below are *one-way distances:* **Estes Park:** Gem Lake nature trail (2m) from Devils Gulch Rd, **2.** Other trails here (**3**) run from nearby Cow Creek to Black Canyon, Bridal Veil Falls, Mt. Dickinson, Big Thompson River, Lost Lake, Stormy Peaks, Signal Mtn, and connect to the W side of the park. **Horseshoe Park** (W of Fall River entrance, just NW of Estes Park) has a short trail to Horseshoe Falls (**1**), a mostly valley trail to Lawn Lake (6.5 m) and Crystal Lake (7.5), **2-3;** a tougher trail to Ypsilon Lake (5.5 m), **3;** and a climb to Deet Mtn that can be made from Deer Ridge, park hq, or several other trails in the area. **Rock Cut** (on Trail Ridge Rd. W of Estes Park) is a nature trail, **2. Beaver Meadows Visitor Center** has a nature trail, **1. Moraine Park** (W of Estes Park) has beautiful, easy trails to Cub Lake (2.5 m), the Pool (1 m), Fern Lake (4 m), Odessa Lake (5 m), **1-2. Bear Lake** (just S of Moraine Park) also has access to the Moraine Park trails (Fern Lake is 5 m, for example, and Odessa Lake is 4 m from here); also Bierstadt Lake (2m); Nymph Lake (½ m); Dream Lake (1 m); Emerald or Haiyaha Lakes (2 m); **1, 2.** Also trails around 12,342-ft Flattop Mtn (4.5 m); **2.** You can also cut completely across the park to Grand Lake, 16½ m via N Inlet Trail (via streambed and falls; cutoffs are possible to lakes Nokoni and Nanita or to Andrews Pass or Taylor Peak) or 19 m via Big Meadows Trail (via Ptarmigan Pass, 12,129-ft Notchtop Mtn, Sprague Glacier, Tonahutu Creek; **3. Glacier Gorge Junction** (just S of Bear Lake) has a valley trail to Mills Lake (2.5 m), **2,** that continues to Black Lake (5 m) with a cutoff to Solitude Lake; **2-3.** A harder trail goes via Loch Vale (2.5 m) and Glass Lake to Sky Pond (4.5 m), **2-3.** Most difficult of all is the trail to Boulderfield (8 m) that connects with trails from Longs Peak. **Longs Peak Campground** (S of hq on SR 7) has trail to Eugenia Mine (1.5 m), **2.** Storm Pass (2.5 m), Chasm Lake (5.5 m), Boulderfield (6 m) require considerable climbing as does the trail across the hwy to Twin Sisters (3.5 m); **2-3.** Long Peak (8 m) has several trails, all rough; **3. Wild Basin Campground** (S off SR 7) has easy road (**1**) or trail to Copeland Lake. Calypso Cascades (2 m) and Ouzel Falls (3 m) are **2,** but trail continues on to Bluebird Lake (7 m) and Thunder Lake (7.5 m), both **3.** Sandbeach Lake (4 m from Copeland Lake) isn't too tough, **2.** Finch Lake Trail (5 m) is moderately easy (**2**) but climbs beyond to Pear Reservoir (7 m), **3. Le Poudre Pass** (NW end of park) is reached via 7-m trail (**3**) from Phantom Valley; climb to 12,489-ft Specimen Mtn; trail past Long Draw Reservoir to Cache Le Poudre River (a trail follows the river S to Milner Pass) or across the Mummy Range (with cutoffs to Mirror Lake or 12,716-ft Comanche Peak); Mummy Pass Trail will take you across the N of the park to Stormy Peaks Trail and back down to the Cow Creek-Gem Lake area. This is remote country, **3**.

Phantom Valley (N of Grand Lake) has a lovely campground at Timber Creek; from parking and picnic areas above this there are trails **(2-3)** to Lulu City site (3 m), Thunder Pass (7 m), and beyond to Snow Lake and a poor road at Colorado State Forest and Routt National Forest; a popular trail goes W to Red Mtn (3 m), **2-3**. **Grand Lake** has a trail rimming the E shore that continues down the E shore of Shadow Lake, all the way around to Rainbow Bay on US 34 (hwy rims the W shores of these lakes, the most highly developed parts of the park on the W side); easy strolls are possible in this area, **1**. Also, trails to Shadow Mtn (4 m), **2-3**; Cascade Falls (2.5 m), **2**; Lakes Nokoni (9 m) and Nanita (9.5 m) involve some steep sections, **2-3**; Adams Falls (½ m), Lake Lone Pine (5.5 m), and Lake Verna (7 m) are not as steep, **2-3**. **Shadow Mtn Recreation Area** (US 34 at SW end of park) encompasses man-made lakes and has boating, fishing, hunting, camping, riding, picnicking, conducted walks and other naturalist programs, tours of the pumping plant (summer), and trails **(1, 2)** along the lake shore that connect to those in Rocky Mtn National Park.

ROUTT NATIONAL FOREST covers over a million acres in several sections around Steamboat Springs; just NW of town it straddles the Continental Divide. Here is the **Mt. Zirkel Wilderness**, with more than a dozen peaks over 12,000 ft, and more than 60 lakes; easiest entry is from the several campgrounds around **Seedhouse** (N of Steamboat Springs via Clark), from which a trail follows the Continental Divide and another is along Elk River (lovely); **2, 3**. You can also enter from the beautiful **Big Creek Lakes** (NW of Walden) and from the **Buffalo Pass area** (E of Steamboat Springs). N of this is the famous gold-mining area of **Columbine** and **Hahn's Peak**, with campgrounds; also the **Steamboat Lake State Recreation Area** of 2500 acres, with swimming and picnic sites. **Fish Creek Falls** (E of Steamboat Springs), with a 260-ft drop, is popular; picnic area; **1, 2**. **Information:** P.O. Box 1198, Steamboat Springs 80477.

SILVERTON: Many Westerns have been filmed on **Blair St.**, with its hitching posts and false-front buildings. Among the local ghost towns are **Eureka** and **Animas Forks**, both off SR 110. **1**.

San Juan National Forest covers over 2-million acres on the W slope of the Continental Divide surrounding Silverton and contains manzold mining remains; this is rugged country, with waterfalls, evergreen forests, unusual geologic formations, sheer canyon walls, and mountains so jagged they seem sliced by giant knives. The **Million Dollar Hwy** (US 550), so-called because of its goldbearing gravel, runs through part of the forest between Durango and Silverton; off the hwy, between Haviland Lake (22 m N of Durango) and Molas Divide, are 2 lovely power company sites—**Tacoma** (22 m N) and **Ames** (37 m N)—and forest campgrounds that make good starting points for walks and climbs; ranger stations on the hwy provide information. Ranger stations in **Durango** and **Mancos** (28 m W via US 160) can give you information on ancient Indian remains and other things to see from the several campgrounds in the SW section of the forest. Trailheads, campgrounds, and ranger stations are also off SR 145 S of **Telluride** (one campground gives access to 14,246-ft Mt. Wilson) and on a forest road that cuts off SR 145 to run along the Dolores River. But the most spectacular part is **San Juan Primitive Area** (N of US 160 between Durango and Pagosa Springs), where peaks in the Needles range (13-14,000 ft) pose a challenge to experienced mountain climbers; the 240 m of trail often rise from 8000 ft along canyon bottoms to 12,500 ft in 4-5 m, and snow usually prevents hiking exc mid-July-mid-Sept. Best access: **Vallecito Reservoir** (NE of Durango), ringed with campsites; from here an 8½-m trail along Vallecito Creek takes you to the heart of the primitive area and its trail system. **Pine River Campground** (off US 160 NW of Pagosa Springs): a popular trip from here is the 10-m trail N to Emerald Lake, with campsites; a trail NE along the Los Pinos River (with several campsites) and several other trails NE will also connect you with the primitive area trail system. Other access points are **Florida River** (NE of Durango on road past Lemon Dam), **Piedra River** (off US 160, 19 m W of Pagosa Springs), and several campgrounds off US 160 between Pagosa Springs and South Fork. National hiking associations often offer guided trips; packers and outfitters are in Durango and other nearby towns; **2, 3. Information**: Supervisor, Box 341, Durango 81002.

TELLURIDE: The **Historic District** preserves the 1891 **Sheridan Opera House** and other buildings, and the town is still a mining center. Nearby old mining towns are **Ophir** (8 m S via SR 145) and **Camp Bird** (4 m E via SR 145). There is hiking in the surrounding country, **2, 3**.

    Grand Mesa-Uncompahgre National Forest (write P.O. Box 138, Delta 81416) is 2 separate forests in different areas: **Grand Mesa** (E of Grand Junction via I-70 & SR 65) is the largest flattop mtn in the world, with 200 lakes, waterfalls, cliffs, canyons, wonderful panorama from Lands End (W end). **Uncompahgre** is named for a Ute word meaning red-water springs, hot springs surrounded by a red-mineral deposit (E of Ridgway). Also here are the popular **Ouray** and **Telluride Scenic Areas**, with many opportunities for easy walks. **Uncompahgre Primitive Area** surrounds Ouray (on either side of US 550), so that you can take short walks to look for wildflowers or attempt rough climbs; trailheads are also off SR 361, SW of town; the plateau rises to 9000 ft, with jagged peaks over 14,000 ft and barren, precipitous cliffs contrasting with colorful canyons; high waterfalls; lakes; camping at Ouray. **Wilson Mountains Primitive Area**, also an old mining center, boasts 14,000-ft peaks and is SW of Telluride (via SR 145); some of the trails here can be tried for a ways by average hikers, **2, 3**; other trails **(2, 3)** lead off SR 145 and US 550 S of here.

WALSENBURG: Lathrop State Park (2 m W on US 160), 1:14 acres; 2 lakes; trails with views of Spanish Peaks; camping, picnicking; buffalo herd; **1, 2**.

CONNECTICUT

BRIDGEPORT: Beardsley Park and Zoo (E Main St. & Noble Ave); 30-acre zoo open Tues.-Sun. 11-7 May 15-Sept. 15, 11-4 rest of yr; closed Jan. 1, Thnks, Dec. 25; parking fee Memorial Day-Labor Day; **1**. **Boothe Memorial Park** (6 m W on I-95 to N Main St. in Stratford), collection of odd architecture; gardens; free; **1**.

BRISTOL: Barnes Memorial Nature Center (175 Shrub Rd.), 70 acres; open Tues.-Fri. 2-6, Sat. 9-5, Sun. 2-5; closed Jan.; **1**.

CONNECTICUT BLUE TRAIL: This is a series of trails blazed in blue, throughout the state; over 500 m of trail, many in state parks and forests; information: **Connecticut Forest & Park Assoc., Inc.** P.O. Box 389, E Hartford, zip 06108.

FAIRFIELD: Larsen Sanctuary (2325 Burr St.): 5 m of trails through 150 acres of varied habitat **(1)**; hq of Conn. Audubon Society; open Tues.-Sat. 10-5, Sun. 12-5; free.

GREENWICH: Audubon Center (613 Riversville Rd.), 477 acres of self-guiding trails **(1)**, museum; open Tues.-Sat. 9-5; closed hols and hol weekends; adm.

HAMPTON: James L. Goodwin State Forest (W on SR 6) has a Conservation Center (open Wed.-Sun.) with trail maps.

HARTFORD: Constitution Plaza, a 12-acre downtown business district with a landscaped promenade, arcades, and high-rise buildings, **Charter Oak Trail,** a marked 1½-m walking route, starts here and includes many of Hartford's attractions, among them the Wadsworth Atheneum and the colonial graveyard of Center Church. **Elizabeth Park** (Prospect & Asylum Aves.) has famous rose gardens, best in late June. **Dinosaur State Park** (7 m S via I-91, SR 3, then E on SR 160), short but interesting walk past footprints of small dinosaurs; exhibits open Apr.-Nov., daily 10-5; park open daily; free; **1. Oak Grove Nature Center** (8 m W off I-86 to Oak Grove St. in Manchester) has trails **(1)** through 53 acres of woods, fields; pond; stream; open in daylight. **Roaring Brook Nature Center** (14 m W on US 44, 202 to Gracey Rd., Canton), 90 acres of wooded hills, fields, swamp; trails **(1)**. **Massacoh Plantation** (12 m NW via SR 185, 10 at Simsbury) is a complex of historic buildings; open May-Nov. daily 1-4; adm. **McLean Sanctuary** (13 m NW via SR 189 to Barndoor Hill Rd., S of Granby), 3400-acre area, many trails **(1)**; open daily in daylight; free.

LITCHFIELD: Many fine colonial houses, especially in the historic district around the green and along North and South Sts. **Litchfield Nature Center and Museum** (2½ m SW on US 202), on 4000 acres, has trails **(1 & 2)**, garden, picnic area, other facilities; open Tues.-Sat. 10-4:30, Sun. 2-5; closed hols; adm.

NEW CANAAN: New Canaan Nature Center (144 Oenoke Ridge) has many easy trails on 40 acres; open Tues.-Sat. 10-5, Sun. 1-5; free.

NEW HAVEN: On the Temple St. side of the historic **Green** are 3 Federal-period churches; N of the Green is **Grove St. Cemetery** (between Prospect & Ashmun Sts.), with graves of prominent early residents. **Yale University** bounds the Green on the W; free tours are offered from Phelps Gateway, the large Gothic structure visible from the Green; Art & Architecture Building (Chapel & York Sts.) offers schedule of architecture tours. **West Rock Park** (Wintergreen Ave., 3 m NW): 40 acres with trails **(1)**, nature center, picnic area; open daily 9-dark; free. **Balwin Pkwy** (just N of W Rock Park) is paralleled for 6 m by Regicides Trail, which you can get on or off at will, **1.**

NEW LONDON: Thames Science Center and **Connecticut Arboretum** (Conn. College campus, Williams St.): The center offers exhibits and information about the arboretum; trails **(1)** through 400 acres, half in a natural state and half cultivated with 300 kinds of shrubs and trees; center open Mon.-Sat. 9-5 (exc 8-4 Jul. & Aug.), Sun. 1-5; closed Jan. 1, Thnks, Dec. 25. Arboretum open daylight hours. Both free. **Bates Park Woods & Nature Center** (Chester St.) has 300 acres for strolling; open daily all yr, 9-dusk; free; **1. Ocean Beach Park** (Ocean Ave.) offers beach and amusement park; open summers; adm; **1.** Mystic (7 m E on I-95), one of the oldest shipbuilding and whaling ports in the nation, offers **Mystic Seaport** (Greenmanville Ave., 1 m S of I-95), a living museum with authentic homes, shops, and ships comemmorating a maritime New England village of the mid-19th C; daily in summer 9-5, in winter 9-4; closed Jan. 1, Dec. 25; adm. **Denison Pequotsepos Nature Center** (Pequotsepos Rd.) has 5 m of trails **(1)** on 125 acres; museum and programs; open Tues.-Sat. 9-5, Sun. 1-5; closed hols; sm adm.

SHARON: Sharon Audubon Center (2 m SE on SR 4) has self-guiding trails on 500 acres, herb garden; open Tues.-Sat. 9-12 & 1-5, Sun. 1-5; closed hols; adm.

STAMFORD: Stamford Museum and Nature Center (High Ridge Rd., ¾ m N of Merritt Pkwy exit 35): 108-acre nature center; working farm with daily demonstrations; miles of nature trails **(1)**; open Mon.-Sat. 9-5, Sun. & hols 2-6; closed Jan. 1, Thnks, Dec. 25; parking fee. **Bartlett Arboretum** (Brookdale Rd., off High Ridge Rd.), native and exotic trees and shrubs, self-guiding tours **(1)**, open 8:30-4:30; free.

WATERFORD: Millstone Pt. Nuclear Power Plant (off SR 156) has exhibits and grounds for strolling; open in summer daily 9-5; free. **Harkness Memorial State Park** (S off SR 213) offers Italian-style mansion (open daily 10-5 in summer, weekends in spring & fall), gardens, beach (no swimming), greenhouses (open summers, daily 8-5); adm in summer; **1.**

WESTPORT: The **Nature Center for Environmental Activities** (10 Woodside Lane), trails **(1)** through 53 acres of varied terrain; open Mon.-Sat. 9-5, Sun. 2-5; closed most hols; free.

WOODBURY: One of the loveliest of Connecticut's colonial villages. **Flanders Nature Center** (Church Hill Rd.), with trails **(1)** through 900 acres of woods and fields; beaver pond; maple-sugar making in season; open Tues., Thurs., Sat. 10-5, Sun. 1-5.

STATE PARKS: In addition to parks mentioned above, the following are nice for walking: **Bigelow Hollow** (on SR 197 in Union), in Nipmuck State Forest, 513 acres with 7-m trail around lake **(1, 2)** and forest walks **(1, 2)**. **Black Rock** (10 m N of Waterbury on SR 6), 439-acre recreation area surrounding a swimming pond; trails around pond (1); Mattatuck Trail runs across the park and connects with trails in Mattatuck State Forest; nearby is Humaston Brook (W on SR 209), for short walks (1). **Burr Pond** (NE of Torrington off SR 272), pretty; short trails on 437 acres (1); this, with John A. Minetto and Dennis Hill parks (farther N on SR 272), Haystack Mtn (on SR 272 at Norfolk), with overlook tower, and Campbell Falls (on SR 272 at the Massachusetts Line N of Norfolk), with well-worn paths along the cascades, are especially nice during fall foliage season. **Chatfield Hollow** (on SR 80 W of Killingworth), heavily wooded 356 acres; recreational facilities; short walks, but adjoins Cockaponset State Forest (along SR 9 NW of the park), where all-day hikes are possible (1, 2); the Mattabesett Trail runs NE of here (entry from Seven Falls Park on SR 9A in Haddam). **Devil's Hopyard** (S of Millington on Hopyard Rd.), 860 wooded acres; a series of trails (1, 2, 3) loop out from scenic 60-ft Chapman Falls to cover the park; Devil's Oven (with overlook) and Devil's Tombstone trails go to sites legends link with the devil. **Ft. Shantok** (on SR 2A, S of Norwich), on site of a Mohegan Indian village on Thames River; Indian burial ground; walking is across fields (1); on the opposite shore is Stoddard Hill; just E is the 10-m Pequot Trail, running from Long Society (Preston, on SR 165) S via Rose Hill to Indiantown Rd. (SW of SR 2, 214, between Lantern Hill Rd. & the E boundary of the Pequot Indian Reservation). **Gay City** (on the Hebron-Bolton town line on SR 85) was site of an 18th-C religious community; only a few stone foundations remain; 1569 forested acres; 10 short trails (1, 2) interconnect for longer hikes; swimming pond; you can also hike (2) at nearby Bolton Notch (jct US 6, 44A), with caves. **Gillette Castle** (off SR 82 N of Hadlyme), on the Connecticut River; 3 m of wooded trails surrounding the castle-like home (open summers daily 11-5; sm adm) built by actor William Hooker Gillette; park open all yr; **Hopeville Pond** (on SR 201 S of Jewett City) has wooded trails from the swimming pond across 554 wooded acres (1, 2). **Housatonic Meadows** (on US 7 N of Cornwall bridge) is a pretty 451 acres on the Housatonic River (1); **Housatonic State Forest** (just N, in 3 sections on either side of US 7) offers longer hikes (2, 3) in a lovely area. **Hurd** (off SR 151 S of Middle Haddam), on Connecticut River; wooded trails (1, 2) on 884 acres. **Indian Well** (N of Shelton), on Housatonic River; pleasant overviews; opposite is Osbornedale (on SR 34 N of Derby), and N is Kettletown (on a lake made by impounding the river), with good walking; opposite Kettletown is Paugussett State Forest, with additional trails; all, 1, 2. **Kent Falls** (on US 7 N of N Kent) has lovely walks along a stream and cascades on 275 acres (1, 2); pretty in fall color; nearby Lake Waramaug (SW via local roads toward New Preston) is only 95 acres but the lake shores are attractive for strolls. **Macedonia Brook** (off SR 341 NW of Kent), with 2300 acres of hilly, wooded land and a pretty gorge with a brook, has a section of Appalachian Trail (2) that gives overlooks from elevations of 1220-1350 ft; 9 other trails **(1-3)** connect with the AT and each other, enabling you to choose a short stroll or a strenuous hike. **Mansfield Hollow** (off SR 195 N of Willimantic), on a pine-covered bluff at the confluence of 3 rivers, has 4 easy trails **(1, 2)** in former farmlands and along the banks of an impounded lake; Nipmuck Trail **(2)** more or less parallels SR 195, crossing the hwy at Spring Hill and continuing N along the attractive Fenton River to US 44A. **Mashamoquet Brook** (5 m SW of Putnam on SR 44) contains a wolf den in which Israel Putnam shot a wolf in 1742; 780 acres with 13 very short trails **(1, 2)** and swimming. **Meshomasic State Forest** (SW of Marlborough, just before jct SR 66, 151) is especially nice at Great Hill, with a view over the pond **(2)**; the Shenipsit Trail (starts at Cobalt on SR 66) runs from here N (with breaks) to the Massachusetts line **(2, 3)**; you can also explore a cobalt mine (E of jct SR 66, 151), and Salmon River State Forest (SE of Marlborough) has hiking and the Day Pond recreation area. **Mohawk Mtn** (on SR 4, E of Cornwall Bridge) is a beautiful area where you can stroll (fall color) or climb the 1683-ft mountain for panorama; adj is Mohawk Mtn State Forest, 3300 acres of wooded hills; several short trails **(2)** lead to overlooks and bogs; trail **(1)** around Mohawk Pond; trail **(2)** along East Branch of Shepaug River; part of the Appalachian Trail runs through here—more than 50 m of the AT are in the state; it enters Connecticut near Bulls Bridge on US 7), follows the Housatonic River N (with a detour through Macedonia Brook State Park) to Mohawk; it then continues N through the Housatonic forest and Salisbury to 2316-ft Bear Mtn at the state line; this is a lovely area of the AT, with many access points **(2, 3)**. **Mt. Tom** (10 m SW of Torrington on US 202), with swimming in a spring-fed pond, has 2 trails **(2)** leading to overlook from 1291-ft Mt. Tom. **Naugatuck State Forest** (S of Naugatuck on SR 8) is best known for the beautiful Spruce Brook Ravine, with cascades **(2)**, but there are other trails too. **Pauchaug State Forest** is in 6 sections surrounding Voluntown; 24,000 acres of farmland reverting to forest; hq (on SR 49 N of jct with SR 138) is near Mt. Misery (441 ft); here the 15-m-long Pachaug Trail **(2)** and much longer Nehantic Trail **(2, 3)** meet; scenic walk **(1)** in Rhododendron Sanctuary; interconnecting are Quinnebaug Trail **(2)**, by brooks and through woodlands, Castle Trail **(2)**; Nehantic trail continues to section of forest S of SR 138, where it connects to Narraganset Trail at pretty Green Falls Pond; the latter trail, 16-m long, goes from the Rhode Island line to the ocean near Westerly (R.I.). **Penwood** (7 m NW of Hartford), 787 acres on a ridge in the Talcott Mtns; lookout tower; 10 parallel and interconnecting trails **(2)**; Metacomet Trail **(2, 3)** runs the length of the park and beyond (S to Talcott Mtn State Park) and N via Chimney Point, Manituck, Bald Knob, and other rises to the Massachusetts line). **Stratton Brook** (W off SR 167) has swimming and strolling on 145 acres. **Putnam Memorial** (jct SR 58, 107 near Redding) has wooded trails **(1)** on site of Gen. Israel Putnam's 1779 winter encampment; reconstructed buildings; museum (open summer afternoons); park open all yr; free. **Southford Falls** (on SR 188, S of jct SR 67 near Southford) has a walk to a brook, dam, and the falls **(2)**. **Squantz Pond** (off SR 39, just N of New Fairfield), 173 acres on scenic Candlewood Lake; trail **(1, 2)** around the pond, with little spurs; adj its N edge is Pootatuck State Forest for more extensive hiking **(2)**; the Housatonic Range Trail (off US 7 just S of SR 55), on the opposite side of the lake, goes S to SR 25, **2**. The area **NW of Winsted** deserves special mention; here are **American Legion, Peoples, Tunxis,** and **Algonquin State Forests** and lovely **Barkhamsted Reservoir**. Tunxis Trail goes S from the state line and is especially rewarding **(2, 3)**.

DELAWARE

DOVER: Laid out by William Penn, Dover has been the state capital since 1777; on The Green and surrounding streets are lovely 18th- and 19th-C homes; **Bureau of Travel Development** (45 The Green) explanatory map for the "Heritage Trail" **(1)**. **Bombay Hook National Wildlife Refuge** (on SR 9, 10 m NE), for migrating waterfowl; freshwater and brackish marshes, swamps, forest, upland fields; trails **(1)** and boardwalk; observation towers; auto tour routes; picnic grounds; open daily in daylight; free.

LEWES: Settled by the Dutch in 1631, this coast town has many old houses and churches. Lewes Historical Society Restorations include the **Burton-Ingram House, Cannonball House** (bearing scars from the war of 1812), **Thompson Country Store, Rabbit's Ferry House,** and a **Plank House** believed to have been built before 1700; open daily exc Sun. 11-4, summer only; sm adm; **1**. **Cape Henlopen State Park** (1 m E), 1446-acre park, at confluence of Delaware Bay and the Atlantic; nature trails; ocean beach **(1)**; Visitor Center; picnic area; swimming.

REHOBOTH BEACH: This resort, called the "Nation's Summer Capital" because of its popularity with Washington government officials, has a boardwalk and ocean beach **(1)**. **Delaware Seashore State Park** (6 m S on SR 14): You can walk 7 miles along this strip of land separating Rehoboth Bay and Indian River Bay from the Atlantic, on either the ocean beach or the calmer bay side **(1)**; picnic area; swimming.

WILMINGTON: **Brandywine Park**, designed by Frederick Law Olmstead, extends along both sides of the Brandywine River from Market St. to Augustine Bridges; cherry trees, Josephine Garden; picnicking; zoo (open 10-4); open daily sunrise-sunset; free; **1**. **Henry Francis du Pont Winterthur Museum & Gardens** (6 m NW on SR 52): 60-acre gardens; every tree, flower and shrub that will grow in Delaware. Noted for spring flowers (late April), azaleas (early May). Self-guided 2½mile trail (**1**); also tours. Open mid-Apr.-Oct., Tues.-Sun. 10-4 (Nov.-mid Apr. by appointment); closed July 4; mod adm. For details, museum hrs and fees, write: Winterthur, 19735. **Brandywine Creek State Park** (on SR 92, 4 m N of Wilmington): **Delaware Nature Education Center** here has nature trails (**1**) and programs.

DISTRICT OF COLUMBIA

Information is available at **National Visitors Center** (Union Station) and **Washington Area Convention & Visitors Bureau** (1129 20th St. NW, zip 20036); **West Potomac Park** has lovely plantings, the Lincoln and Jefferson Memorials, the Tidal Basin, adj 328-acre **East Potomac Park** has many recreational facilities; picnicking; Japanese cherry trees in these 2 parks bloom early to mid-Apr. Both **1**. **Rock Creek Park** (W of 16th St., from Colorado Ave. N to DC boundary) is the city's largest park; much of it is heavily wooded; 15 m of foot trails (**1, 2**) along the creek and its branches; bridle paths; Visitor Information Center S of Military Rd. on Beach Dr. provides maps; Rock Creek Nature Center (Military and Glover Rds.) has short interpretive trails (**1**) and conducts nature walks (open Tues.-Fri. 9:30-5 all year; Sat. & Sun. noon-6 Mar.-Nov., noon-5 in winter; closed hols; free); picnic sites; at S end is **National Zoological Park**, open daily 9-7:30 in summer, 9-5:30 in winter; entrance & buildings close 1 hr earlier; closed Jan. 1, Dec. 25; free, but fee for parking; **1**. **Theodore Roosevelt Island** is reached by footbridge from Virginia side of Potomac River; memorial to Roosevelt with a 17-ft bronze statue; 88-acres; natural area and wildlife sanctuary; 2½ m of trails lead through a swamp, marsh, and upland forest (**1**); access from northbound lane of George Washington Memorial Pkwy, N of Theodore Roosevelt Bridge; open 8-dark; free. **Meridian Hill Park** (16th & Euclid Sts. NW) has an elegant formal design with waterfalls and pools, **1**. Washington's other small parks include **Montrose Park**, between Dumbarton Oaks and Rock Creek, **1**. **Chesapeake & Ohio Canal**

National Monument (30th St. in Georgetown) runs to Cumberland, Maryland (which see); good hiking on the towpath; canal barge rides and interpretive programs. E of **Capitol Hill** is another area of restored 19th-century houses; **1. Brookside Nature Center** (11 m N via US 20, SR 97 to 1400 Glenallen Ave., Wheaton) has 500 acres with self-guiding trails; open Tues.-Sun.; **1. Meadowside Nature Center** (17 m N via US 29, SR 97 to 5100 Muncaster Mill Rd., Rockville) has trails on 250 acres; open Tues.-Sun.; closed hols; **1. Northwest Branch Fossilized Logs Area** (off Exit 25 of Capital Beltway, S on New Hampshire Ave. to 410, then left to Ager Rd.) is upstream (you must walk) from the bridge over the branch.

FLORIDA

APALACHICOLA: St. George Island (reached by toll bridge 7 m E on US 98), 20-m Gulf beach; **1 & 2.**

CEDAR KEY: Nice island for beachcombing; **Cedar Key State Museum** tells the island history (open daily 9-5; sm adm).

CORAL GABLES: Chamber of Commerce (Galiano & Aragon Ave.) or **City Hall** (Miracle Mile & Le Jeune Rd.) provides maps for self-guiding tours. This community, planned in the 1920s, built around landscaped plazas; most homes are in Spanish or Mediterranean styles, but sections incorporate Dutch, Chinese, and other styles. **Fairchild Tropical Garden** (10901 Old Cutler Rd.) has over 80 acres of tropical plants; tram tours; open daily 10-4:30; closed Dec. 25; adm; 1. Nearby **Matheson Hammock Beach & Park** (9610 Old Cutler Rd.), nature trails and a picnic area; 1. **Castellow Hammock** (22301 Southwest 162nd Ave.), conducted nature walks. **Garden of Our Lord** (110 Phoenetia Ave.), plants mentioned in the Bible; open daily in daylight; free.

CRYSTAL RIVER STATE ARCHAEOLOGICAL SITE (W off US 19, 98 at sign N of town of Crystal River), lovely site, overlooking the Crystal River; was a ceremonial center abt 200 BC-1400 AD; self-guiding trail; open 8-sundown; sm adm; 1.

DE LEON SPRINGS: Ponce de Leon Springs (Ponce de Leon Blvd off US 17), 54 acres of gardens with ancient oaks and bald cypresses; swimming; picnic grounds; sugar mill; peacocks and other uncaged birds; open daily 9-sunset; adm. **Hontoon Island State Park** (W of DeLand on SR 44 & Hontoon Rd.): Over 1000 acres of cypress swamp, savannah, hammocks; on the St. Johns River; short trail to Indian mound (1¼ m round trip); picnic area; **1.**

EVERGLADES NATIONAL PARK (main entrance on SR 27 from Florida City) is an extraordinary subtropical wilderness; spectacular sunrises and sunsets, unparalled boating, abundant wildlife. **Visitor Center** near the entrance; exhibits; excellent interpretive programs. From here a 38-m road leads to the developed center at Flamingo on Florida Bay. Along the way are: **Royal Palm** (2 m), interpretive center with the Gumbo Limbo Trail through hardwood hammock; boardwalk Anhinga Trail where you can see alligators and birds. **Long Pine Key** (4 m) with camping and an auto trail through pines (not always open, as it floods). **Pineland Trail** (6.5 m), interpretive trail through pinelands. **Pahay-okee** (12.5), observation tower; especially good at sunrise or sunset. **Mahogany Hammock** (19.5 m), interpretive boardwalk trail through mahogany forest. **Paurotis Pond** (24.5 m) with picnicking, rare palms. **Nine Mile Pond** (26.5 m) for birdlife. **West Lake** (30.5 m) boardwalk into a mangrove swamp. **Flamingo** has exhibits, motel, restaurant, camping, picnicking, marina; daily narrated boat trips; you can rent canoe, motor boat, or houseboat. Wonderful naturalist-led walks are offered; some are on dry land; on others you don sneakers and slog through the glades; some overnight trips. Two other park centers are **Shark Valley**, off the Tamiami Trail (US 41); tram for a 7-m, 2-hr, narrated trip to an observation tower and short nature trail in the interior; you may also bike this route or walk it (if you tire, the tram will pick you up); no trams during wet season (Sept.-Oct.). **Everglades City** (off US 41 via SR 29S), at the W end of the park, also runs daily naturalist-conducted boat trips; canoes and other craft may be rented; Sandfly Island (reachable only by boat) has an interpretive nature trail, **1.** The park is open daily all yr; most comfortable season is winter-spring; **information:** Supt., Box 279, Homestead 33030.

FLORIDA KEYS: Chambers of Commerce along the highway (at markers 31, 49, 54, 68, 82, 106, and at Mallory Sq. in Key West) offer information. Several roadside picnic areas offer short stretches for beachcombing. **John Pennekamp Coral Reef State Park** (off Key Largo) preserves part of the only living coral reef formation in N America; glassbottom-boat tours (fee) or rental boats; the land area has a beach and a ½-m nature trail and short catwalk through mangroves and across tidal creeks; **1. Harry Harris County Park** (2 m N of Tavernier on US 1) also offers beach, swimming, picnics. **Islamorada's Hurricane Monument** (Matecombe Methodist Church) has a short nature trail; **1. Long Key State Park** (at Layton) covers 291 acres; beach and nature trail; swimming; picnic sites, **1. Bahia Honda State Recreation Area** (on US 1, 10 m W of Marathon) has beautiful palm-fringed beaches on both the Atlantic and Gulf sides; nature trail along the shore of a lagoon; **1. National Key Deer Refuge** (SR 940, 2 m N of US 1 on Big Pine Key) is open daily 8-5; free. **Summerland Orchid Gardens** (6 m off US 1 in Summerland Key) is open 9-5 daily, mid-Nov.-mid.-Apr.; rest of yr, Fri.-Wed.; closed Jan. 1, Thnks, Dec. 25; adm. Key West walking tours include **Ernest Hemingway Home** (907 Whitehead St.) and **Audubon House** (205 Whitehead St.). **Peggy Mills Garden** (700 Simonton St.) is landscaped with tropical plants; open daily 9-5; adm; **1. Fort Jefferson National Monument** (in Dry Tortugas, reached by boat or seaplane from Key West) has interpretive programs, self-guiding tours.

FLORIDA TRAIL: Now only partly complete, this 700-m hiking trail will eventually run the length of the state; for information: Florida Trail Association, 33 SW 18th Terrace, Miami 33129; **1-3.**

FORT LAUDERDALE: Snyder Park (SW 4th Ave.) has nature trails and marked botanical specimens; picnic sites; sm adm; **1.**

FORT PIERCE: The **Savannas** (off US 1 at 200 Midway Rd.), a recreational area with swimming; botanic garden, zoo; open daily 8-sundown; adm per car. You can also walk along the beach here or on the boardwalk. **Jack Island Preserve** (off SR A1A, N), state park; 958-acre island reached by foot bridge; mostly salt marsh with mangroves; trails and picnic area; **1 & 2.**

GAINESVILLE: University of Florida Agricultural Experimental Station (US 441 & University Ave.), with experimental plots and greenhouses here, can give you addresses for branches throughout Florida; open daily; free. **Morningside Park Nature Center** (3540 E University Ave.), interpretive trails on 278 acres; open daily in daylight; closed Jan. 1, Thnks, Dec. 25; free. **O'Leno State Park** (26 m N on US 41-441), beautiful wooded park on Santa Fe River; 3 lovely short trails; one goes to the "river sink," a whirlpool where the Santa Fe disappears underground (it surfaces 3 m downstream); azaleas and magnolias are highlights of other trails; naturalist programs; picnic area; 1.

GOULDS: Monkey Jungle (14805 SW 216 ST.) has monkeys roaming free in simulated rainforest; open daily 9:30-5; adm.

GREEN COVE SPRINGS: City park (Magnolia & Walnut Sts.) has landscaped mineral springs and swimming pool; park open all yr; free (fee to swim).

HALLANDALE: Gulfstream Park (Hallandale Beach Blvd), landscaped ground with Garden of Champions honoring thoroughbreds, is open daily 10-4 exc during racing season (Mar.-Apr.); free.

HIALEAH: Hialeah Park (E 4th Ave., 21-32 Sts.) is open daily 9:30-5 exc during racing season (Jan.-Mar.); gardens, race track, aquarium, carriage exhibit; free.

HOMESTEAD: Redland Fruit & Spice Park (N on SR 27 to Redland Rd.), 20 acres of exotic plantings; guided tours available; open Mon.-Sat. 8-4:30, Sun. 9-5; free. **Orchid Jungle** (4 m NW at 26715 SW 157th St.) displays orchids from all over the world; open daily 8:30-5; closed Thnks, Dec. 25; adm.

HOMOSASSA SPRINGS: Homosassa Springs (US 19) has an underground observatory, boat cruises (to 4:30), gardens; open daily 8:30-6; adm.

JACKSONVILLE: Cummer Gallery of Art (829 Riverside Ave.) is set in beautiful gardens overlooking the St. Johns River; open Tues.-Fri. 10-4, Sat. noon-5, Sun. 2-5; closed hols; free. **St. Johns River Park** (901 Gulf Life Dr.) is on the river; fountain lit at night; open daily; free. **Jacksonville Zoological Park** (8605 Zoo Rd.) is along the banks of the Trout River; open daily 9-4:45 (longer in summer); closed Dec. 24-25; adm. **Fort Caroline National Memorial** (10 m E via SR 10, then N on Monument Rd.): Here in 1564 the French established the first European colony N of Mexico, but were driven out by the Spanish; reconstructed fort; Visitor Center; open Mon.-Fri. 8-5, Sat. & Sun. 8-6; closed Dec. 25; free.
    Fort George Island State Historic Sites (from Jacksonville on SR 105 or via ferry from Mayport to SR A1A, then N from village of Ft. George): **Kingsley Plantation State Historic Site,** oldest surviving plantation home in Florida; plantation developed in 1813 to train slaves for resale; exhibits; self-guiding tours; open Mon.-Fri. 10-noon, 2-4; Sat., Sun., hols 10-5; sm adm; **1.** Elsewhere on the island are sites of forts built as early as 1763, picturesque ruins of old tabby houses, and Confederate earthworks; all **1.** The 150-acre **John F. Rollins Bird and Plant Sanctuary** has many nature trails; live oaks, cedars, ferns, native orchids; **1.**
    Fort Clinch State Park (on SR A1A, 3 m from Fernandina Beach): 2 m of Atlantic Ocean beach; a lovely nature trail on the shore of a willow-

lined pond with alligators, and a well-preserved 1847 fort over which 8 flags have flown; picnic area; swimming; camping; 1.

Gold Head Branch State Park (30 m S on SR 21): Gold Head Branch is a spring-fed stream that flows through a ravine wooded with sweet bay, red bay, and sweet gum trees; easy trails wind through this beautiful ravine; lakes; swimming; camping; picnic area; 1.

Osceola National Forest (20 m W off I-10) is 157,000 acres; most popular spot is moss-draped **Ocean Pond** (at the S edge, off US 90); you can walk a bit along the pond at campsites and via forest route 241 C (off US 90).

KEY BISCAYNE: Crandon Park has beach, zoo, rides; open daily 9-4:30; sm adm. **Bear Cut** (Crandon Beach) has conducted nature walks.

LAKE PLACID: Plantation Paradise (4 m S on US 27) has tropical gardens; open daily 9-5; closed Dec. 25; free; 1. **Highlands Hammock State Park** (on SR 634 W of Sebring): Florida's first state park and one of its most beautiful, preserves 3800 acres of hammock with magnificent trees, cypress swamp, pine flatwoods, and marsh; 10 m of easy trails: Fern Garden, Limeberry, Wild Orange Grove, and others; Catwalk Trail, one of the most spectacular, is a ½-m boardwalk through the cypress swamp; camping; picnic area; 1.

LAKE WALES: Mountain Lake Sanctuary (3 m N off US 27A) is a quiet 117-acre landscaped park; Bok Singing Tower, a 53-bell Carillon, plays every ½ hr; picnic area; open daily 8-5:30; parking fee; 1. **Audubon Center** (8 m S on US 27A) has a nature trail on a lake; open daily in daylight; free; 1. **Masterpiece Gardens** (8 m NE off US 27) features a mosaic of "The Last Supper"; gardens; birds and animals; shows; open daily 9-6 (longer in summer); adm.

MELBOURNE: Florida Institute of Technology (off US 192 on Country Club Rd.) has a botanical garden with 200 species of palms; open daily; free.

MIAMI: Miami-Metro, Dept. of Publicity & Tourism (499 Biscayne Blvd) can provide information for walking tours. **Plymouth Congregational Church** (3429 Devon Rd.) has tropical garden with fountains; open daily; free. **U.S. Dept. of Agriculture Plant Introduction Station** (Old Cutler Rd.), which does research on tropical and subtropical plants, is open Mon.-Fri. 7:30-4; free, but you must register. **Greynolds**

Park (off W Dixie Hwy, N of 172nd St.), with picnic sites, boat rental, trails, has guided bird walks; open daily in daylight; free. **Simpson Park** (entrance on NW 17th Rd., ½ block W of S Miami Ave.) preserves a piece of subtropical jungle. **Bayfront Park** (Biscayne Blvd, NE 5- SE 2nd St.) and **Lummus Park** (NW 3rd Ave. & 3rd St.) are open 7 am-10 pm; free. **Watson Park** (off MacArthur Causeway) has a Japanese garden with waterfall and lagoon; open daily 9-6; free; **1. Vizcaya** (3251 S Miami Ave.) is a marvelous 71-room Italian Renaissance palace built 1912-17, furnished with Italian treasures; 10 acres of stunning gardens with reflecting pools, grottos, teahouse on Biscayne Bay; open daily 9:30-5:30; closed Dec. 25; sm adm for gardens, adm for house; **1. St. Bernard Monastery and Cloisters** (16711 W Dixie Hwy in N Miami Beach), engaging 12th-C Spanish monastery brought to the U.S. by William Randolph Hearst; Cloistered walkways; medieval art works; gardens; open Mon.-Sat. 10-4, Sun. noon-4; closed Jan. 1, Good Friday, Easter, Thnks, Dec. 25; adm; **1.**

NAPLES: Big Cypress Nature Center (2 m N, off US 41 on Big Cypress Rd.) has a nature trail; open 9-5 Mon.-Fri., also Sat. Oct.-May; closed hols; free; **1. Collier Seminole State Park** (on US 41, 15 m SE): This area of the Big Cypress Swamp was the last refuge of the Seminole Indians; nature trail and picnic area; camping; **1. Koreshan State Recreation Area** (N on US 41 at Estero): Site of a unique 1893 settlement of people who call themselves Koreshans; they believe that the earth is the universe and that the sun is inside the globe; beautiful nature trail along the **Estero River**, through the original organic gardens, now returning to a wild state; picnic area; camping; **1. Corkscrew Swamp Sanctuary** (NE, 16 m W of Immokalee via SR 846), largest remaining stand of bald cypress, is an Audubon sanctuary; lovely boardwalk; **1**; open daily 9-5; adm.

NEW SMYRNA BEACH: New Smyrna State Historic Site (on SR 44) has remains of old sugar mill under moss-draped trees; pretty site with short trail (**1**). **Turtle Mound State Historic Site** (9 m S) has an Indian shell mound overgrown with vegetation, short nature trails. Both open daily; free. The city also has 8 m of public beach.

OCALA: Chamber of Commerce (Box 1210, Ocala 32670) offers a map for self-guiding tours of thoroughbred farms (more than 20 welcome visitors; free.

Ocala National Forest (10 m E on SR 40) covers 366,000 acres, with sand pine forests and palms towering over clear, spring-fed streams flowing through subtropical vegetation; hundreds of lakes; of the 16 recreation areas, the most popular are: Alexander and Juniper Springs; swimming; nature trails (1) surround the springs areas and runs (popular with canoeists); at Juniper, a trail winds around the lovely Fern Hammock Spring; other trails; guided walks (1). The 64-m-long **Ocala Trail**, going N-S from Lake Oklawaha to Clearwater Lake, is part of the Florida Trail; it is crossed by all E-W roads in the forest so that you can get on and off easily; boardwalks have been constructed in swampy areas; 1. For **information**, see district rangers in Ocala or Eustis, or write: Supervisor (P.O. Box 1050, Tallahassee 32302).

Lake Griffin State Recreation Area (27 M S on US 27, 441), densely forested with live oaks and other hardwoods; ¼-m nature trail; Lake Griffin has floating islands (park rents canoes); picnic area; camping; 1.

ORLANDO: Leu Gardens (1730 N Forest Ave.): over 50 acres of azaleas, roses, camellias, other flowers and trees; open daily 9-4:30; closed Dec.25; adm; 1. **Dickson Azalea Park** (E Robinson St. near Fern Creek Ave.) has a pine-shaded walkway among shrubs; 1. **Sanlando Springs** (on SR 434, 3 m W of Longwood) offers swimming in the springs, gardens, picnic area; open daily; adm. **Fort Mellon Park** (Seminole Blvd., Sanford) has picnic areas; open daily; free. **Eola Park** (around Lake Eola) has walks, fountains. **Warren Park** (8 m SE on SR 15), on Lake Conway, has swimming and tropical gardens. These are only a few of the many municipal and county parks in or near the city; for information on others, phone 849-2283. **Rock Springs** (18 m N on US 441, SR 435) has picnic sites and nature trails; free; 1. **Debary Hall State Museum** (30 m N, 1 m W of Deltona-Debary Exit from I-4) preserves a fine colonial mansion (open Tues.-Sun. 1-5) on landscaped grounds; open daily 8-5; sm adm.

ORMOND BEACH: War Memorial Art Gallery & Garden (78 E Granada Ave.), with works by regional artists, has 4 acres of gardens; open Oct.-Aug. daily 2-5; closed Dec. 24-25; free. There is also an 18-m-long public beach. **Tomoka State Park** (via N Beach St.) is outstandingly beautiful, at the point where the Tomoka and Halifax rivers meet; intriguing statue of Indian chief Tomokie, by Fred Dana Marsh; museum of Marsh's work; wonderful walks and river overviews (1); camping, picnic sites. **Bulow Plantation State Historic Site** (8 m N off Old Dixie Hwy): Once planted in cotton and sugar cane, run by 300 slaves; museum; ¼-m trail to ruins; picnic area; 1. **Sugar Mill Gardens** (8½ m S on US 1, W of Port Orange) has ruins of 1763 mill under moss-draped oaks; open daily 9-5; closed Jan. 1, Dec. 25; free.

PALM BEACH: This famous resort of the wealthy has public beaches in midtown, but the best is **Phipps Ocean Beach** (6 m S on SR A1A).

In West Palm Beach, **Dreher Park** (Parker Ave. & W Lakewood Rd.) is a 100-acre town park with botanical garden, nature trails, museum, zoo, sports facilities; open daily 9-5; **1. Pine Jog Environmental Center** (6301 Summit Blvd), operated by Florida Atlantic University, provides guided tours of 40-acre area.

Jonathan Dickinson State Park (N of Jupiter on US 1), 9563 acres; riding, other activities; conducted nature tours on horseback or by boat; short trails along the Loxahatchee River and through pine flatwoods; swimming; camping; picnic area; **1, 2.**

Loxahatchee National Wildlife Refuge (hq on US 441, 12 m W of Delray Beach), 145,635 acres of shallow water flats and sawgrass; nature trails (1) at hq; fishing and picnicking are at recreation areas at the N & S borders; open daily in daylight.

PANAMA CITY: Beaches stretch for miles along the coast here; also beachcombing on **Shell Island** (boats leave from Anderson's Pier at Thomas Dr. & Grand Lagoon, spring to fall), or **St. Andrews State Recreation Area. Eden State Gardens** (28 m W on US 98 at Pt. Washington): 10½ acres of beautifully landscaped grounds and gardens; opulent 1895 mansion with moss-draped live oaks reflected in a large pool; open daily 9-5; sm adm to house; **1. Florida Caverns State Park** (52 m NE, 3 m N of Marianna on SR 167) offers guided tours (fee) of a network of limestone caverns; above ground are several short loop trails on the floodplain of the Chipola River; stunning springs; swimming; camping; picnic area; Visitor Center; open daily; sm adm; **1.**

PENSACOLA: Visitors Bureau (803 N Palafox St.) is open Mon.-Fri. 8-5, Sat. 9-5, Sun. (spring-fall) 9-5. **Pensacola Historical Museum** (405 S Adams St. at Zaragoza St.), in Florida's oldest church, will also give you a brochure for a self-guiding tour of the historic Seville Square district; open Tues.-Sun. 10:30-4:30; closed hols; free. **Gulf Islands National Seashore** (W from Pensacola Beach via SR 399A), lovely unspoiled beach from Ft. Walton Beach to Gulf Beach; camping, swimming; historic sites; for information write P.O. Box 100, Gulf Breeze, zip 32561. **Blackwater River State Park** (NE 3 m off US 90 near Harold); pine-covered hills, sandy river beach; stunning paths along river; swimming; picnic area; within Blackwater River State Forest, with additional hiking trails, **1.**

ST. AUGUSTINE: This city, oldest in the U.S., was established by the Spanish in 1565; a long-term restoration program has been returning the city to its Old World charm. **Visitor Information Center** (10 Castillo Dr. near the old city gate) provides maps, brochures, and information. **Restoration Complex,** centered on St. George St., includes silversmith, pottery, print, and other shops where crafts are demonstrated; buildings open daily 9-5:15; closed Dec. 25; sm adms or combination ticket. **Castillo de San Marcos National Monument** (opposite the city gate on Castillo Dr.) gives good overviews; open daily 8:30-5:30 (to 7 in summer); closed Dec. 25; sm adm or GEP. **Ft. Matanzas National Monument** (14 m S via SR A1A), pretty spot on Matanzas River; you have to take a boat to the monument from the Visitor Center (open daily 8:30-5:30; closed Dec. 25; free).

Washington Oaks State Gardens (on SR A1A 2 m S of Marineland): Beautiful gardens on 340 acres; native and exotic plants in natural settings; citrus grove, fruit trees; picnic areas; **1**.

RAVINE STATE GARDENS (1 m SE of Palatka off Moseley Ave. on Twigg St.): 182 acres landscaped in formal and informal arrangements; 5-m trail along rim of ravine, **1**; steep footpaths (**2**) into the ravine; 100,000 azaleas bloom in Mar.; picnic sites; open daily 8-5; sm adm. May-Sept.

ST. PETERSBURG: Chamber of Commerce (4th St. & 3rd Ave S) can supply maps for self-guiding tours of historic houses and museums. Ask about the many city parks—**Crisp** (Poplar St. & 35th Ave. NE), **Abercrombie** (Park St. & 38th Ave. N), and others—and beaches. **Boyd Hill Nature Park** (1101 Country Club Way S at 47th St.) is a 627-acre swamp; wildlife area with animals; guided walks available; open daily 9-6; sm adm. **Florida's Sunken Gardens** (1825 4th St. N) has aviaries, gardens, religious statues; open daily 9-sunset; adm.

SANIBEL ISLAND and **CAPTIVA ISLAND** are reached via toll road; both are beach resorts; you could walk all day in the **J.N. "Ding" Darling National Wildlife Refuge**; beachcombing for rare shells on the 14 m of Gulf shores is also popular (access roads to public beach are marked).

SARASOTA: Ringling Museums (3 m N on US 41), Ringling's Italian-style mansion, a circus museum, a museum of art (very fine), and Asolo Theater; extensive grounds overlooking the water; bldgs open Mon.-Fri. 9 am-10 pm, Sat. 9-5, Sun. 1-5; adm to bldgs. **Sarasota Jungle Gardens** (3701 Bayshore Rd.), tropical gardens with birds, animal shows; open daily 9-5; adm. **Myakka River State Park** (17 m E on SR 72) is a stunning wildlife sanctuary with subtropical vegetation; 29,000 acres of woodlands, streams, lakes; 3-m trail through hammocks of live oak and cabbage palm to a primitive camping area; scenic drive; wonderful birdwalk over Upper Myakka Lake; conducted nature tours; conducted boat rides; additional hiking in another section (**2**) requires prior registration; camping; picnic sites. **Desoto National Memorial** (on Tampa Bay, 5 m W of Bradenton off SR 64): Hernando de Soto landed here in 1539; interpretive displays; nature trail along the shore; open daily 8-5; closed Dec. 25; free; **1.**

SILVER SPRINGS: Silver Springs (on SR 40), source of the Silver River, are set in landscaped grounds that are open daily, free; adm is charged for glass-bottom boat rides, other attractions on the grounds.

SUWANNEE RIVER STATE PARK (13 m W of Live Oak on US 90), beautiful location, where the Withlacoochee River meets the Suwannee; viewing platform overlooks the meeting of the waters; natural springs enhance the loveliness of these rivers; walks across the spring runs; nature trails; remains of Confederate earthworks; camping; swimming; picnic area; **1.**

TALLAHASSEE: Chamber of Commerce, in a restored 1830 mansion called The Columns (100 N Duval St.) provides maps and information; open Mon.-Fri. 8-5. **1. Florida State University** (on US 90) provides maps for self-guiding campus tours at Information Service, room 324, Physical Science & Administration Bldg. **Lake Jackson Mounds State Archaeological Site** (off US 27 N of town at S end of Lake Jackson) is a 12-acre site with 3 mounds; open daily 8-sundown; free. **Maclay State Gardens** (5½ m N of Tallahassee on US 319, at 3540 Thomasville Rd.), 308-acre park, recreation section (with swimming) has trail on lake shore and nature trail (**1**); open all year, daily 8-5; sm adm. The beautifully landscaped gardens—camellias, azaleas, Torreya trees, rare plantings—are a separate section open Jan.-Apr. daily 8-sunset; sm adm; **1. Junior Museum** (6½ m S at Lake Bradford at 3945 Museum Dr.) is nice for adults too, with museum exhibits, restored 1880s regional homestead, nature trail with native animals; open Tues.-Sat. 9-5, Sun. 2-5; closed Jan. 1, Thnks, Easter, Dec. 25; adm. **Walkulla Springs** (15 m S on SR 61) is a wildlife refuge with boat rides, swimming; grounds are free; open daily 9:30-sunset. **St. Marks National Wildlife Refuge** (18 m S on SR 59) has self-guiding booklet at entrance; 65,000 acres of land and 31,700 acres of water provide a variety of habitats; roads and trails; open daily in daylight; free. **San Marcos De Apalache State Museum** (at confluence of the Wakulla & St. Marks Rivers; follow signs from SR 363 in St. Marks): On site of an early Spanish settlement and Civil War military post; museum; trail along a marsh and boardwalk along river (**1**); open daily 9-5; sm adm.

    Apalachicola National Forest: 557,000-acre area of forest, beautiful swamps, and streams; **Silver Lake Recreation Area** (on SR 260) self-guiding interpretive trail includes boardwalk through cypress swamp;

1. Three Rivers State Recreation Area (40 m NW off US 90, 2 m N of Sneads), nature trail on shore of Lake Seminole; swimming; camping; picnic area; **1. Torreya State Park** (44 m W on SR 20, 13 m NE of Bristol on SR 12): rare Torreya trees grow only in the 20-m surrounding area; trail to 1834 Gregory House, on a bluff overlooking Apalachicola River; other trails through the woods; camping; **1.**

TAMPA: Chamber of Commerce (801 E Kennedy Blvd) can give you information for self-guiding or guided tours; special maps for **Ybor City,** the Cuban area roughly bounded by Columbus Dr., E. Broadway, Nebraska Ave., and 22nd St., are available in cafes and shops in that district. **Bayshore Blvd.,** along the bay and lined with palms, flowers, fountains, is attractive. Banana docks are at 13th St. near Kennedy Blvd. The shrimp fleet unloads at **Hookers Point** (SR 556). **Bahia Beach** (S at Ruskin), a 200-acre waterfront park. **Ellsworth Simmons Park** (off US 41 S on Tampa Bay), 254 acres of beachfront. **Hillsborough River State Park** (15 m N off US 301), lovely 2848-acre park; many short trails along and near the Hillsborough River; sabal palms; picnic areas; camping; 1.

TARPON SPRINGS: Dodecanese Blvd., along the waterfront, is the center of this colorful town to which Greek sponge fishermen migrated in the early 1900s; sponge boats tie up here; auctions at the Exchange (Tues. and Fri. mornings); **1. A.L. Anderson Park** (US 19) has nature trails, picnic facilities; open 7:30 am-sunset; 1.

WHITE SPRINGS: Stephen Foster Memorial (on US 41), with museum, carillon tower, and short boat ride, is on the banks of the Suwannee River (Foster never saw it); attractive; **1**; special events; open daily 9:30-5:30; closed Dec. 25; adm.

WINTER HAVEN: Slocum Water Gardens (1101 Cypress Gardens Rd., SE of town off SR 540): 7 acres of tropical gardens; water-lily pools, sunken gardens, conservatories; open Mon.-Sat. 8-5; closed hols; adm; **1. Cypress Gardens** (4 m SE on SR 540), famous for waterskiing shows, has a botanical garden area; open daily sunrise-sunset; adm; 1.

WINTER PARK: Mead Botanical Garden (Maitland Ave. & Garden Dr.) has 55 acres of native plants; open daily 8-sunset; closed Dec. 25; free; **1. Rollins College** (Park & Holt Aves.) lovely campus on NW shore of Lake Virginia; Mediterranean-style buildings; Walk of Fame features stones from birthplaces of famous people; **1. Kraft Azalea Gardens** (on shore of Lake Maitland on Alabama Dr. off Palmer Ave.), azaleas, tropical shrubs and trees; **1.**

WITHLACOOCHEE STATE FOREST is in 4 units with hq at the smallest unit, KcKethan Lake (jct US 41, SR 476, SR 531); swimming, fishing, picnic and camp sites; hiking trail. For information write Brooksville (Route 2, Box 244, zip 33512).

STATE PARKS: Parks with springs (all have swimming in the springs, picnic sites) are among Florida's most outstanding: **Blue Springs Recreation Area** (off I-4 & US 17, 2 m W of Orange City), on St. Johns River; 518 acres; 2 springs to which manatee migrate in winter; nature trail around springs and the run, and along the river; camping. **Ichetucknee Springs** (off SR 137 between Branford & Fort White), where canoeists and tubers follow 3½-m spring-fed run to see alligators, otter; camping. **Manatee Springs** (1 m N of Chiefland via US 19, 98, turn W 6 m on SR 320) is exceptional; moss-draped gums and cypresses surround the spring, which feeds the Suwannee River; boardwalk to overlook on river; trails through forest and along river (1); boat rental; camping. **Wekiwa Springs** (off US 441 near Apopka), with 6348 acres of forests and sub-tropical jungle, has 6 m of frontage on Rock Springs and Wekiwa River; nature trails (1); picnic sites. (There are also springs in Florida Caverns State Park and Ocala National Forest, see above). Beachcombing is easy in Florida; many communities provide good public beaches (access is usually marked on nearby highways or streets): Clearwater, Cocoa Beach, Dania Beach, Fernandina Beach, Pompano Beach, Vero Beach, etc. But state-run beaches are as nice and sometimes nicer; the following have beach plus picnicking and swimming: **Anastasia** (S of St. Augustine on SR A1A), 1½-m of Atlantic beach backed by forest. **John C. Beasley** (1 m E of Ft. Walton Beach on US 98), 23 acres on the Gulf. **Bill Baggs Cape Florida** (S tip of Key Biscayne), 1 m of Atlantic beach and 2 m on Biscayne Bay. **Caladesi Island** (2 m off Dunedin, reachable only by boat), 3-m beach, nature trail, observation tower. **Flagler Beach** (2 m S of Flagler Beach on SR A1A), palm-fringed Atlantic beach; also on Intracoastal waterway. **Grayton Beach** (SR 30A, between Ft. Walton Beach & Panama City), on the Gulf's Miracle Strip; lake, dunes, pines; nature trail. **Hugh Taylor Beach** (on SR A1A at Ft. Lauderdale), 180-acre park with frontage on Atlantic and Intracoastal waterway; native and exotic tropical plants and trees; nature trails. **Little Talbot Island** (8 m N of Atlantic Beach on SR A1A), 4 m of Atlantic beach and Ft. George River. **Pepper Park** (N of Ft. Pierce on SR A1A), adj Jack Island Reserve. **St. Andrews** (W of Panama City on US 98 & SR 392): ¾-m of Gulf beach; nature trails through pine flatwoods; turpentine-still trail. **Sebastian Inlet** (on SR A1A between Vero Beach & Melbourne), 3 m of Atlantic beach; museum of Spanish treasure. **St. Joseph Peninsula** (SR S-30, off US 98), near St. Joe, 20-m beach. Parks with short nature trails are: **Dade Battlefield** (off US 301 near Bushnell), a historic site. **Falling Waters** (S of Chipley on SR

77A), observation platform over falls, swimming, nature trail. **Faver-Dykes** (15 m S of St. Augustine, E of jct US 1 & I-95), trail by lovely Pellicer Creek, another around an Indian mound. **Fred Gannon Rocky Bayou** (on SR 20, 5 m from Niceville), no special trail but you can walk beside the bayou or lake. **Grossman Hammock** (11 m NW of Homestead), 2 swamp nature trails; well waters channeled over a waterfall for swimming. **Ocholockonee River** (on SR 319, 4 m S of Sopchoppy), semitropical woodland on 2 rivers; creeks and ponds; scenic drive; swimming. **Oscar Scherer** (2 m S of Osprey on US 41), nature trails along the banks of S Creek.

GEORGIA

ATHENS: Chamber of Commerce (155 E Washington St.) booklet describing walking tours (**1**) through Georgia's classic city; gardens and old magnolias line the streets.

ATLANTA: Underground Atlanta (Central Ave. viaduct at Hunter St.) was the Victorian-era commercial center, abandoned when viaducts were built over it early in this century; restored to its Gay 90s appearance, with cobblestone streets, gas lamps (the sun doesn't reach here); boutiques, restaurants, galleries, historic displays; information: trolley at the entrance; open Mon.-Sat.; **Grant Park** (Boulevard SE) has miles of beautiful trails (**1 & 2**); Cyclorama; old Fort Walker, Atlanta Zoo (open daily 10-5:30 exc Dec. 25; sm adm); **1**; picnic sites. **Piedmont Park** (Piedmont Ave. & 10th St.), lake; greenhouses; garden; **1**. **Fernbank Science Center** (156 Heaton Park Dr. NW), 65-acre forest with 3 m of easy self-guiding trails (open Sun.-Fri. 2-5, Sat. 10-5); **1**; planetarium, observatory, exhibit hall, other facilities; botanical garden; closed hols; free. **Stone Mtn Park** (16 m E on US 78), a 3200-acre historic-recreational park, surrounds a huge relief carving of Robert E. Lee, Stonewall Jackson, and Jefferson Davis on horseback; observation tower on the 825-ft mountain accessible by foot (**2**) or cable car; many attractions, including an antebellum plantation (most open daily mid-June-Labor Day 10-9, rest of year 10-5:30; closed Dec 24-25); recreational facilities include 10 m of nature trails (**1**) and picnic areas; open 6 am-midnight; adm. **State Farmers' Market** (10 m S on US 41), 146 acres; 24-hr cafeteria; special events; open daily, 24 hrs; **1**. **Information** on Atlanta from Chamber of Commerce (1300 Commerce

Bldg. 30303) or Convention & Visitors Bureau (229 Peachtree St.). **Kennesaw Mtn National Battlefield Park** (14 m N off US 41), site of vain 1864 Confederate attempt to stop Sherman's march to Atlanta; Visitor Center exhibits, slide show; booklet for 2-m trail; loop trails (5, 8, 14 m) climb to run along the ridge (2, 3); picnicking; open Mon.-Fri. 8:30-5, Sat. & Sun. 8:30-6; closed Jan. 1, Dec. 25; free.

BRUNSWICK: Fort Frederica National Monument (E on St. Simons Island) preserves the most impressive British fort in the U.S.; town of English settlers prospered here; fort and town are in ruins, overhung with moss-draped live oaks, but enough remains to visualize life here; Visitor Center exhibits; self-guided walk (1); open daily 8-5 (8-6 in summer); closed Dec. 25; free. **Darien** (13 m N on US 17), unspoiled shrimp port; Welcome Center has self-guiding tour map. **Jekyll Island** (SE via SR 50 causeway) was controlled until 1946 by some of the wealthiest and most powerful families in the nation; now state owned, with 10 m of stunning beach; Jekyll Island Authority, 270 Washington St. SW, Atlanta 30334.

CARTERSVILLE: Etowah Mounds Archaeological Area (3 m S off SR 113), occupied 1000-1500 AD, has 7 mounds grouped around 2 plazas; museum; trails; open Tues.-Sat. 9-5:30, Sun. 2-5:30; closed Jan. 1, Thnks, Dec. 25; free. **Allatoona Lake** (E of town) is an impoundment with Corps of Engineers recreational sites plus **Red Top Mtn** and **George Washington Carver** state parks; you can walk on peninsulas and coves along the lake; 1, 2. **New Echota** (23 m N via I-75 on SR 225) is a restoration of the Cherokee capital (1825-38); printshop, courthouse, tavern, other buildings; open Tues.-Sat. 9-5:30, Sun. 2-5:30; closed Thnks, Dec. 25; free. **Cloudland Canyon State Park** (22 m N on I-75, 55 m NW on SR 143), 1699 acres on Lookout Mtn; rugged; 3-m trail down to swinging bridge over the gorge (1, 2); camping; picnicking.

COLUMBUS: Chamber of Commerce (1344 13th Ave.) or **Georgia Welcome Center** (Victory Dr. & 10th Ave.) provide maps for self-guiding walking tours of antebellum homes; also conducted tours. **Callaway Gardens** (30 m N on US 27), 2500-acre garden and recreation area; garden wildflowers in natural settings; 18 m of scenic drives; nature trails with marked plants; arboretum; greenhouses; seasonal displays; 13 lakes with watersports, other recreational facilities, accommodations, cafes; special events; open daily 7:20-6; adm. **Hamilton** (23 m N off US 27 at Hamilton) has restored the square area; 19th-C general store, apothecary, other shops; antique auto museum; open Mon.-Sat. 10-6, Sun. noon-6; adm; 1. **Franklin D. Roosevelt State Park** (28 m N off SR 27), 4980-acre recreation area; King's Gap with historic Creek Indian trail; nature trail

(1); picnic and camp sites. **Little White House** (37 m NE on US 27A in Warm Springs), where Franklin D. Roosevelt died in 1945 (open daily 9-5; closed some hols; adm); surrounding spa is pleasant (1).

CORDELE: Georgia Veterans Memorial State Park (9 m E on US 280) is pleasant (1), on the shore of Lake Blackshear, a Corps of Engineers impoundment of the Flint River, with Visitor Center, picnic and camp sites, swimming, hiking trails (1). **Andersonville National Historic Site** (23 m NE on US 280, N on SR 49), most notorious prison of the Civil War, has earthworks, monuments, national cemetery; open daily 8-5 (8-7 in summer); free; 1.

DAHLONEGA: This quaint town was site of America's first gold rush (1828), depicted in the museum (open Tues.-Sat. 9-5:30, Sun. 2-5; closed Thnks, Dec. 25; free); museum personnel can direct you to **Auraria** ghost town (6 m S on SR 9E) and other gold panning sites. **Blackburn State Park** (7 m SW via SR 9E), pretty forested area, walking opportunities (1, 2), old gold mine. **Amicalola Falls** (18 m W on SR 52) has lovely falls, nature trail, and 6-m access trail (2) to Appalachian Trail; 1, 2.

FORT GAINES: Kolomoki Mounds State Park (15 m SE) is an ancient site with mounds, museum; open Tues.-Sun. 10-6; closed hols; 1.

MACON: Residential areas with tree-shaded streets and lovely antebellum houses; Chamber of Commerce (640 1st St.) or Tourist Center (15 m N on I-75) can give you self-guiding maps (1) and, for a fee, arrange tours. **Macon Museum of Arts and Sciences** (4182 Forsyth Rd., NW on US 41) has nature trail and arboretum (1); open Mon.-Sat. 9-5, Sun. 2-5; closed Jan. 1, July 4, Labor Day, Thnks, Dec. 25; free. **American Camellia Society Hq.** (22 m SW on SR 49, S of Ft. Valley), large gardens, many varieties of camellias; best mid-Jan.-mid-Mar.; open daily in daylight; 1. **Oconee National Forest** (30 m NE via US 129 or US 23), with another section at Greensboro, covers 104,000 acres in the heavily forested Piedmont hills; attractive Rock Eagle Lake; eagle effigy made of stones; Piedmont wildlife refuge; camping, picnicking, swimming; walking 1-2. **Ocmulgee National Monument** (2 m E on US 80, 129) Visitor Center with archaeological museum gives tours of a ceremonial earth lodge; self-guiding trails to other mounds; pretty nature trail (1).

OKEFENOKEE NATIONAL WILDLIFE REFUGE (Waycross): Huge and fascinating freshwater swamp, with moss-draped cypresses and pure, dark-brown water that reflects as a mirror; Superintendent, Box 117, Waycross 31501. **Suwannee Canal Recreation Area** (11 m SW of

Folkston on SR 23) is best if you can spare the time; Visitor Center boat rentals (the canal goes 11 m into the swamp) and narrated boat trips; most spectacular is the 4000-ft-long boardwalk, with wayside benches, to an observation tower that offers a breathtaking view as the sun goes down—if you hurry, this walk (1) will take under 2 hours, but if you watch for birds, crocodiles, and other animals you can spend most of a day here; other paths (1, 2); picnic area; open daily in daylight; closed Dec. 25; free. **Stephen C. Foster State Park** (18 m NW of Fargo via SR 177) is on the W side; nature trail (1) and small museum; boat rental and guided tours; picnic and camp sites. **Okefenokee Swamp Park** (8 m S of Waycross), boardwalks into the swamp (1); observation tower; small zoo; interpretive center; picnic area; open daily 8-sunset; adm (includes boat trip).

SAVANNAH: With its many beautiful old buildings and peaceful squares, Savannah is ideal for walking. **Chamber of Commerce Visitor Center** (W Broad St.) presents an audiovisual program and can give you maps and tape cassettes for self-guiding walking (1) and driving tours. This gracious city was designed by Gen. James Oglethorpe, who laid out 24 green squares; these are still, with palms and moss-draped live oaks, some of the most charming corners of Savannah. **Chippewa Square** (Bull & McDonough Sts.) sports a Daniel Chester French memorial to Oglethorpe. **Colonial Park Cemetery** (E Oglethorpe & Abercorn Sts.) contains graves of many city founders. **Forsyth Park** (Bull & Gaston Sts.), with fountain, is spectacular in spring when azaleas bloom. Many 18th- and 19th-C houses have been restored; areas with concentrations of these include: **Washington Square** (Houston & Congress Sts.) and the nearby **Trustees' Garden Site** (E Broad St.); **Monterrey Square** (Bull & Wayne Sts.); **Lincoln & Jones St.** area. The waterfront was once a seamens' hangout, with River Street the city's main street; buildings here have been renovated and house shops, restaurants, and the appealing Ships of the Sea Museum. From the early 1800s until the Civil War, Savannah was a leading cotton market; **Factors Walk** (along the river bluff between Bull & Broad Sts.), named for the cotton factors, is reached via iron bridges; antique street lamps; cobblestones. At the E end is small **Emmet Park. Bonaventure Cemetery** (330 Bonaventure Rd.). **Fort McAllister** (17 m S off US 17), on the Great Ogeechee River, has restored earthworks, bombproofs, museum; open Tues.-Sat. 9-5, Sun. 2-5; closed Thnks, Dec. 25; free; 1. **Fort Pulaski National Monument** (15 m E off US 80), with fort built 1829-47, has a Visitor Center with maps for self-guiding walking tour (1); memorial to John Wesley; open daily 8:30-5:30; closed Dec. 25; sm adm or GEP.

TOCCOA: Toccoa Falls (off SR 17, NW edge of town, on grounds of Toccoa Falls Institute), 186-ft cascade produces a misty bridal veil; open daily in daylight; sm adm; **1. Traveler's Rest** (E on US 123), on the Tugaloo River, is a lovely plantation home open Tues.-Sat. 9-5, Sun. 2-5:30; closed hols; **1.** S on the river is **Tugaloo State Park**, also pretty; **1.** Farther S (28 m on SR 77) is **Hart State Park** on a Corps of Engineers impoundment; public recreation areas; **1. Chattahoochee National Forest**, 700,000 acres in mtns N of town, is striking; balds, bare of trees, often are covered with azaleas, laurel, rhododendron; **Appalachian Trail (2, 3)** runs 80 m from the state line SW to Springer Mtn (a good access here is via approach trail from Amicalola Falls) and crosses paved roads at: US 76 at Dick's Creek Gap, where Buzzard Knob is 4 m to the NW, abt 800 ft up **(2)**; SR 17 & 75 at Unicoi Gap; SR 348 at Tesnatee Gap, in the Raven Cliffs Scenic Area; US 19 & 129 at Neels Gap, where the Blood Mtn Archaeological Area is 1 m to the W, abt a 1000-ft climb **(2)**; SR 60 at Woody Gap, less than ½ m from the top of Black Mtn **(1)**. The AT also crosses secondary roads and is reached by side trails from other points. Recreation areas (picnicking, camping, other facilities) with trails are: **Andrews Cove** (6½ m N of Helen on SR 17, 75) in a small, steep-sided valley; **Anna Ruby Falls** (N off SR 17 & 75 at Robertstown, 1.3 m on Co. 56 and 3 m on paved road through Unicoi State Park); **DeSoto Falls** (19 m N of Dahlonega on US 19), near Neels Gap and adj to Desoto Falls Scenic Area; **Lake Winfield Scott** (6½ m S of US 19 & 129 on SR 180), on a small mtn lake; **Tallulah River** and **Tate Branch** (13½ and 16 m W of Clayton via US 76 & FS 70), near the beautiful Colman River Scenic Area, reached by trail from Tallulah River **(2)**; **Unicoi Gap** (9 m N of Helen on SR 17 & 75), on the AT; **Woody Gap** (15 m N of Dahlonega on SR 60), also on the AT but less rugged country; Trails also at: **Lake Blue Ridge** (4 m E of Blue Ridge on US 76 & Dry Branch Rd.); **Panther Creek** (9 m N of Clarkesville on US 441); **Warwoman Dell** (4 m NE of Clayton on Warwoman Rd.), **1-3.** Scenic Areas reached by trail: **Raven Cliffs** (5 m from Robertstown), off SR 348 at Duke's Creek, along creeks 3 m to cliffs **(2)**. **High Shoals** (11 m N of Helen on SR 17, 75, 1½ m on FS 283), a trail follows a beautiful stream **(1)**. Camping areas with **nature trails** include Rabun Beach, Lake Russell, Cooper Creek, and Dockery Lake; **1.** Also here are TVA dams and recreation areas at: **Blue Ridge** (jct US 76, SR 60), **Nottely** (N of Blairsville on US 129), **Hiawassee** (N of jct US 76, SR 75), all with walking, **1, 2.** The Visitor Center at **Brasstown Bald** (4784 ft) has an observation platform, interpretive programs; open daily May-Oct. 10-6; spring & fall, weather permitting, open weekends 10-6; closed mid-Dec.-mid-Mar.; free; nearby Tallulah Gorge, lakes, 5 waterfalls, rim nature trail, overlook at Tallulah Point **(1, 2)**. Also here: **Black Rock Mtn State Park** (3 m N of Clayton off US 23, 441), 3800-ft mtn, granite cliffs, sweeping views; paved road to the top; trails **(1, 2)**; camping, picnicking. **Fort Mtn State Park** (5 m E of Chatsworth on US 76), ruins of an ancient fortification (legend says it was built by "moon-eyed people," mysterious white tribesmen);

nature trail (1) hiking trail (2); camping; picnicking. **Information:** Super-visor's Office, U.S. Forest Service, P.O. Box 1437, Gainesville 30501.

WASHINGTON: This lovely town of old gardens and 40 white-columned antebellum homes was undamaged during the Civil War and has been well preserved; **Chamber of Commerce** (on the square) offers maps for self-guiding driving and walking tours (1). **Callaway Plantation** (5 m W on US 78) is a complex of Greek Revival and Federal style homes with out-buildings on a working farm; craft demonstrations; displays of farm equip-ment; open Apr. 15-Oct. 15, Mon.-Sat. 10-5:30, Sun. 2-5:30; free; 1.

HAWAII

HAWAII:: In Hilo, **Liliuokalani Park** (Banyan Dr. & Lilhiwai St., on the bay shore) has Japanese gardens and picnic area; 1. **Wailoa River State Recreation Area** (via Piilani St. from Manono Ave.), landscaped park with paths, picnicking; 1. **Boiling Pots** (2 m W of town on SR 20), a chain of pools on Wailuku River, reached by short, rough trail; 1. **Akaka Falls State Park** (off SR 22 abt 2 m N of Honomu), 65 acres; 420-ft waterfall; dense forest; landscaped section; trails; 1. **Mauna Kea State Park** (37 m W of Hilo on SR 20): 700 acres on 13,796-ft Mauna Kea; Pohakuloa Area has picnic tables; higher Hale Pohaku Area (9200 ft), reached by primitive road, is start of a trail to the summit that passes an old adze quarry; 2 & 3. **Pololu Valley** (in N Kohala), now uninhabited, has remains of old villages and temples; deep gorges into mtns to the SE, which rise over 5000 ft; trails 2 & 3. **Kohala Forest Reserve**, in the mtns, has a ranger station at Waimea with information on trails; 2 & 3. **City of Refuge National Historic Park** (Honaunau) preserves one of the religious sanctuaries where people could claim asylum; **Visitor Center** (open daily 7:30-5:30) provides self-guiding booklets and cultural demonstrations; restored Hale-o-Keawe, where bones of deified Kings were kept; reconstructed dwellings, royal sledding chutes, burial and shelter caves, tikis, and a konane-playing area; 1. **Hawaii Volcanos National Park** (S of Hilo on SR 11); jungle-covered active volcanos, many trails; **information:** Supt., 96718.

KAUAI: Ola Pua Botanic Garden (Kalaheo), 12 acres; jungle area; sunken garden; fine oriental plants; open daily 8:30-5; closed Jan. 1; adm; 1. **Plantation Gardens** (at Poipu Beach near Koloa), 7 acres; cacti from all over the world; also succulents, orchids, aquatic plants; open daily; adm; **1. Waimea Canyon State Park** (via SR 55 from Kehaka), trails in a magnificent colorful canyon; trailhead at overlook 12 m from Kehaka, **2;** farther up SR 55 is adj, 4640-acre **Kokee State Park**, a forested mtn; 8 m of trails; **1 & 2;** picnic sites. **Lumahai Beach** (on Hanalei Bay near Wainiha), beautiful; ½ m by trail from the road; **1.** Also on the N shore, beyond the end of the road, is the rugged Na Pali Coast, reached only by trails; **2 & 3.**

LANAI: Lanai City, town reminiscent of a New England village; **Kaunolu Village,** deserted ancient site reached by foot or jeep; top of 3370-ft Lanaihale is reached by a trail that climbs through rain forest; **1, 2.**

MAUI: Lahaina, royal capital 1802-45, also the whaling capital; **Lahaina Restoration Foundation** has preserved buildings from several periods of its history; **1. Haleakala National Park** (37 m from Kahului via SR 37 and park road), magnificent 10,023-ft dormant volcano; 30 m of trails in the 7½-x-2½-m crater, which makes up a large part of the 27-sq-m park, **2 & 3;** Seven Sacred Pools (W coast near Kipahulu), lovely spot with a short trail **1. Kula Botanical Garden** (W from Kahului on SR 37, 377 past Haleakala turnoff), beautiful native plants, waterfalls; picnic area; open daily 9-4; adm; **1. Waianapanapa State Park** (4 m N of Hana), 120 acres; several miles of trails, ancient temple, rocky coast, caves; picnic area; **1, 2. Kaumahina State Wayside** (25 m E of Kahului on SR 36) has a nature trail through the rain forest; **1. Puaa Kaa State Wayside** (10 m farther W), series of small waterfalls, short path; **1. Iao Valley State Park** (4 m W of Wailuku), short, scenic trail in a forested mtn canyon; **1.**

MOLOKAI: The E end is a forested mtn area; several rough, beautiful trails, used by hunters; **2 & 3.** At E tip is lush **Halawa Valley,** easy trail to 2 waterfalls; **1 to 2. Palaau State Park,** 34-acre preserve at the W edge of the mtn area; picnic sites; winding paths, **1;** short, steep trail down to Kalaupapa peninsula. **Kapuiwa Grove** (W of Kaunakakai), 10 acres of coconut palms; **1.**

OAHU: Honolulu: Brochure for walking tour of the historic area, Monarchy Promenade, is published by the State Parks division of the Dept. of Land and Natural Resources. Buildings here include the **Iolani Palace State Memorial** (King & Richards Sts.), the U.S.'s only royal palace, with landscaped grounds; **1. Foster Botanic Gardens** (180 N Vineyard Blvd.) is open 9-4; free; **1. Moanalua Gardens** (opposite Jct Puuloa St. & Moanalua Rd.), 26 acres, is private but open free to the public; **1. Kamehameha Schools** (Kapalama Heights) inherited the landscaped 200-acre estate of the Kamehameha dynasty; visitors welcome; **1. Paradise Park** (3737 Manoa Rd.), 15 acres; trails through jungle and bamboo forest, orchid garden, trained birds, flamingo lagoon; open daily 9:30-5:30; closed Jan. 1, Dec. 25; adm; **1. The University of Hawaii's Manoa Campus** (University Ave.), 300 acres; landscaping includes rare botanical specimens; **1. Chinatown** is centered around Nuuanu and River Sts.; **1. Kapiolani Park** (between Waikiki Beach & Diamond Head), 300-acre park; many facilities; rose gardens; picnic sites; **Honolulu Zoo** (151 Kapahulu Ave.; open daily 9-5; free); **1.**

Keaiwa Heiau State Park (off SR 72 3 m NE of Aiea), 384-acre forested mtn park; a 5-m loop trail through lush hills connects with other trails in Ewa Forest Reserve; medicinal plants; picnic sites; **2 & 3. Nuuanu Pali** (7 m NE of Honolulu on SR 61) is a mtn pass that offers beautiful views; **1. Byodo-in Temple** (47-2000 Kahekili Hwy, Kaneohe), in Valley of the Temples Memorial Park; replica of 900-yr-old temple in Japan; landscaped grounds include teahouse, graveyard, 2-acre lake; open daily 9-5; adm; **1. Haiku Gardens** (off SR 83 N of Kaneohe), 20-acre garden open daily; free; **1. Sacred Falls** (off SR 83 S of Hauula, 1½ m on dirt road) are a 1-m hike up a rocky ravine; lower falls drop almost 90 ft; **1, 2. Polynesian Cultural Center** (Laie), authentically re-created 15-acre complex of villages representing life on various Pacific islands; demonstrations, shows, other events; open Mon.-Sat. at 10:45, with varying closing hrs; adm; **1.** Nearby **Mormon Temple** has formal gardens open daily 10-4; free; **1. Waimea Valley** (off SR 83 on SR 835), recreation area; trails; **1 & 2. Wahiawa Botanical Gardens** (1396 California Ave., Wahiawa), 4 acres of trees, flowers, ferns; free; **1.**

IDAHO

ARCO: Craters of the Moon National Monument (18 m SW of Arco on US 20, 26, 93A), 83 sq m of volcanic landscape; 7-m loop drive from **Visitor Center** gives access to several trailheads; guided hikes in summer; Devils Orchard Nature Trail through cinder fields and other formations, trail across lava flow to lava-tube caves (**1**), Tree Mold Trail to lava-enveloped group of living trees (**1**).

ASHTON: State fish hatchery (**1**). **St. Anthony Scenic Sand Dunes** (S via US 191, then W), flat volcanic rock with strange 1-m-wide, 30-m-long belt of golden sand (**1**). **Targhee Ntl Forest** (N on US 20, 191), 1½-million acres, partly in Wyoming; N of Ashton is **Warm River** (NE via SR 47), with 2 lovely waterfalls on Henry's Fork of the Snake River **(1, 2)**, and hiking trails **(2, 3)**, campsites, rubber raft trips; **Island Park Reservoir** (W of Island Park on US 20, 191), beautiful area with private accomodations, FS facilities **(1)**; **Big Springs** (33 m N, then 5 m E) is source of S Fork of Snake River—water gushes from an underground cave, bridge with view of trout in clear spring, lookout tower (2 m E), **1, 2**; **Henry's Lake,** just S of Continental Divide, is stunning mtn-surrounded recreation area with swimming, camping, picnicking, strolling **(1)**. Forest extends W, offers only few isolated trails and walks around campsites. W of Ashton extensive trail systems connect to trails in Yellowstone and Grand Teton parks; best is along Teton Creek (NE of Driggs) to Alaska Basin (with campground on the way, at Teton Canyon) that connects to Grand Teton trails N and S of 11,923-ft Buck Mtn; magnificent country, **3**. S of Ashton is system of trails best reached from campsites SW and SE of Victor (on SR 31 or 33); these wind along creekbeds and canyons in Big Hole Mtns, with spurs to the peaks (9-10,000 ft); NE of **Palisades Reservoir** camp on E shore of reservoir, or N of Palisades Creek) are trails along Palisades Creek and Lakes, Dry Canyon, and over to Snake River Range in Teton Ntl Forest in Wyoming. Other sections of forest are farther W (W side of I-15): **Lemhi Range** area (along SR 28 S of Leadore) has trail at campsite at Charcoal Kilns **(1)**, plus trails farther S at Rocky Canyon and Pass Creek forks (both reached off SR 28; ranger station is at Kaufman), **2, 3**. Another forest section, where trails wind around 10-11,000-ft peaks near Continental Divide, has trails entering via primitive roads E of SR along **Willow Creek** and **Italian Canyon** (makes a loop between the two) and **Scott Canyon** (crosses forest to Crooked Creek); campground on Webber Creek is trailhead for additional walks, **2-3**. **Information:** 420 N Bridge St., Anthony 83445.

BOISE: State Capitol (8th & Jefferson Sts.) provides maps and information on the area in Dept. of Commerce (room 108), daily 8-6. **Howard Platt Gardens** (Union Pacific Depot, 1633 S Capitol Blvd) overlooks downtown area. **Julia Davis Park** (N of river at Capitol Blvd) has zoo; Pioneer Village; indoor exhibits at Idaho State Historical Museum. **Ann Morrison Park** (S of river on Americana Blvd), 150 acres with picnic area, formal gardens, fountain, reflection pool. **Lucky Peak** (10 m E via SR 21) is state recreation area with water sports on Corps of Engineers project that created 34 m of reservoirs on Boise River; **1. Black Canyon State Park** (31 m NW via SR 55, 52), 2 m E of the dam, offers water sports on a lovely reservoir; **1.** At **Nampa** (15 m W via I-80 N), **Lakeview Park** (2 m E on US 30) is 70 acres, with gardens, picnic areas, summer swimming pool (sm adm), open Mar-Oct.; **Deer Flat Ntl Wildlife Refuge** (5 m NW of Nampa off SR 55), with water sports on Lake Lowell, has trails **(1)**; **Swan**

Falls (25 m NW of Nampa), on Snake River, has hiking **(2)**. **Silver City** (S of Nampa via SR 45 to Murphy, then 23 m SW) is wonderful ghost town.

Boise National Forest (NE of town) is mostly high-mountain country (from 5000 ft near Boise to 10,000 ft in Sawtooth Mtns), with rolling meadows, forested canyons, attractive lakes. A gold rush left ghost towns; most famous is **Idaho City** (40 m NE on SR 21), with a boothill cemetery, museum (daily in summer); just N are remains of **Centerville, Pioneerville, Placerville; 1, 2.** **Moore's Creek** (N of Idaho City on SR 21) has several campgrounds with trails to Sunset Peak and N Fork of Boise River **(1, 2)**; just the other side of Wilson Peak, a trail goes N via Pine Flat and Deadwood campsites to 8374-ft Whitehawk Mtn **(2, 3)**. **Idaho Primitive Area** (NE corner), reached by trail NE from Dagger Falls (on Middle Fork of the Salmon River) or via trail 588 along Pistol Creek (off FS 635, E of Warm Lake). From **Warm Lake,** a trail goes S along the Middle Fork of Payette River to Boiling Springs **(1, 2)**; another goes via S Fork of Salmon River and cuts across FS roads to Dagger Falls, S to Bruce Meadows and Bull Trout Lake; here it branches, going SW to Loman or S along Warm Spring Creek; **2.** Most other walks here are short trails in the campgrounds (such as the popular area N of Bennett, off SR 68 N of Mountain Home), but in the E is part of **Sawtooth Wilderness** reached via dirt road to Grandjean campground in the N (off FS 824), with trail going S along fork of Payette River to Ardeth and Spangle lakes (14-17 m). Other trails to wilderness area are from campgrounds (reached via dirt roads) at Graham and Atlanta (NE of Boise via FS road along Middle Ford of Boise River); here a trail goes NE, branching N to Spangle Lakes (16½ m) or E to Alturas Lake (19½ m). Just W of Atlanta, a trail follows Queens River to the lakes; another follows Warrior Creek. **Information:** 210 Main St., Boise 83707.

BONNERS FERRY: Kaniksu National Forest, 1½ million acres, partly in Montana and Washington, with large areas surrounding town; 2000 m of trails, some not well maintained, in rugged back country of 7000-ft Selkirk Mtns; some trails lead to hidden fishing lakes; good hiking hq are campsites near Canadian border on **Moyie River** (NE via US 95), or at pretty **Moyie Falls** (E off US 2, then N). **Cabinet Mtn Wilderness** (see Montana) can be reached off US 2 E, or E of Sandpoint (via SR 200 to Clark Fork, then N). Stunning **Priest Lake** section (N on SR 57 from the town of Priest River), islands reached by boat; excellent hiking is from FS campgrounds on W shore **(1-3)**; **Upper Priest Lake Scenic Area** may be reached by boat, or by trailheads off SR 57 **(2-3)**; **Roosevelt Grove of Ancient Cedars** is off SR 57 near Upper Priest Lake.

BRUNEAU: Bruneau Dunes State Park (on SR 51, 5 m N and 2 m E of town), fascinating area of wind-blown sand dunes up to 468 ft high;

several lakes; 5½ m of trails, plus walking on dunes; camping, swimming, picnicking; **1, 2. Bruneau–Jarbridge Canyons** (15 m SE on Clover Three Creek Rd to dirt road turnoff), one of the deepest, narrowest gorges in the world—67-m long, 200-ft deep; Jarbridge Columns are rock formations rising 100 ft; walking along riverbed; **1, 2.**

CHALLIS NATIONAL FOREST: Largest section is in **Salmon River Mtns** (many peaks over 9,000 ft, many recreation areas) W of Challis (SW via US 93). **Bayhorse Lake** (just S via US 93, then W), at 8000-ft, is good base for ruins of Bayhorse ghost town or easy trails along creeks **(1, 2)**; trail system across forest to Idaho Primitive Area in NW or to Sawtooth Wilderness in SW **(2, 3)**, 9-10,000-ft peaks near campgrounds **(3)**. Excellent trails N of here, through **Camas Meadows** and lovely creeks, are not difficult **(2, 3)**, but you must backpack. This N area also reachable via dirt roads NW of Challis; especially nice is road to **Challis Creek Lakes** and 9846-ft White Mtn. Most popular area is **Sunbeam**, on Yankee Fork of Salmon River, with hot springs, easy trails **(1, 2)** or road to ghost towns of **Bonanza** and **Custer** (8 m N), where museum and other buildings are open daily in summer, free **(1)**. Campsites here (at Sunbeam and just E and W on US 93) offers trails through Salmon River Mtns; many are easy ones **(1, 2)** along creek beds, but you can also scale the peaks **(3)** or connect to trail systems N and S or hidden glacial lakes, old mining sites, and wilderness areas **(1-3)**. **White Cloud Peaks** (S of Sunbeam), where summits are often hidden in clouds and lakes are gathered in clusters, is reached via Little and Big Casino Creeks, or Rough Creek (to Casino and Rough Lakes); these trails connect with those of **Warm Springs, Slate,** and **French Creeks** to lovely rock-bound cirques in Boulder area; **2, 3. Boulder** lake area can also be reached by road off US 93 E of Clayton (a scenic camp and picnic site, where Salmon River forks, is good base for hiking here); this road also gives access to trailheads at Jimmy Lake and one along Pine Creek to 10,915-ft **Sheep Mtn;** trails also go S off this road to Lake Basin and to forks of Big Lost River. **Stanley Lake** (NW of Stanley via SR 21) gives easy access to Sawtooth Wilderness **(2, 3)**; beyond are campsites with hot springs (at Valley Creek, US 93), trails to numerous beautiful lakes, to Boise Ntl Forest, to 9419-ft Ruffneck Peak and lovely Seafoam Creek area, to Soldier Lakes, and to Idaho Primitive Area; these trails are reachable by primitive roads and enable you to climb peaks, so they can be varied **1-3** to suit your needs. **Sleeping Deer Mtn** (N section of forest, by dirt road from Challis) has a number of trails to sparkling lakes and along creeks **(1, 2)**, to Idaho Primitive Area **(2, 3)**, and a campground in a stunning area S at Loon Creek. **Big Lost River** (S via US 93A to beyond Dickey, then W) offers trails along fork in White Knob Mtns; Wild Horse or Iron Bog camps are good bases for wonderful nearby lakes and peaks, Surprise Valley, Broad Canyon, Muldoon Canyon, Iron Bog Lakes, Hurst Canyon, and lakes at base of 11,508-ft Smiley Mtn (**2, 3**); Show Lake and White Knob (N of here) are also nice (**2, 3**). **Lost River Range** (E of Challis) has towering mtns rising highest in Idaho at 12,655-ft Borah Peak; can be climbed without equipment in ½ day from Birch Spring (4 m SE of Dickey), **3**; in general, this area offers tough hiking and poorly maintained trails (**3**), but easy walks (**2**) lead off hwys to Grouse Creek, Carlson, Pass, Merriam, and Shadow Lakes. A cave and canyons reached via Pass Creek (E off Big Lost River at Leslie), and splendid canyons S of here (additional access E of Arco and W of Fallert), are terrific for exploration and wildlife (mostly **3**).

COEUR D' ALENE: This resort, ringed by mtns, is on breathtaking **Coeur d' Alene Lake,** with public beach and 104-m shoreline; Tubbs Hill Trail (foot of 3rd St.) gives lovely views, **1-2. Mineral Ridge Scenic Area** (9 m S on US 95A near Beauty Bay resort) has 3-m trail (information center after 1½ m) with outstanding lake views; gradual 700-ft climb, benches along the route; **1, 2.** Public campground at **Beauty Creek. Potlatch Forests, Inc.** (hq E of town) has opened picnic and campsites and will allow hiking on logging roads (**1, 2**), but nicest walk is at Beauty Bay. At S end of lake is **Heyburn State Park** (on SR 5), 8000 acres at St. Joe River—so quiet and full of reflections that it's called Shadowy St. Joe; boat trips to park and river offered from town in summer; several scenic lakes (with swimming, camp and picnic sites); forests; Indian Cliffs (near park hq on SR 5A) has 1-m self-guiding nature loop; 3-m loop trail (**1, 2**).

Coeur d'Alene National Forest covers 700,000 acres N and S of town; most popular is Fourth of July Canyon (E on I-90), and secondary roads N off I-90 between here and Wallace offer camping areas with trailheads (**2, 3**); good trails at **Shoshone Park** (3 m E of Mullan); **Settler's Grove of Ancient Cedars** (via road N of Wallace off I-90), easy walking (**1, 2**); you can also walk along Coeur d'Alene River, flowing through N section of forest (**1-3**); experimental forest (3 m NW on I-90, then N), open daily 9-3, free (**1**); another nursery 18 m E on I-90 (**1**). **Information:** 218 N 23rd St., zip 83814.

BLM areas with hiking are: **Crystal Lake** (St. Joe River Rd. E to Rochat Divide Rd., then 10 m S), reached via 3-m trail; **Mirror Lake** (I-90 E to Rochat Divide Rd., then 9 m S, 5 m E on Boise Peak Rd.); **Killarney Lake** (3 m S of Cataldo on SR 3 to Roselake, then 5 m W), reached via short trail; **2;**

LEWISTON: Kiwanis Park (Snake River Ave., 5-10th Aves) has camp and picnic sites on river; **1.** A **Washington Power Co.** project (3 m W) offers 12 m of shore for picnicking and strolling, **1. Mann Lake** (6 m SE on Grelle Ave.) and **Lake Waha** (18 m SE on Thain Rd) are Bureau of Reclamation sites for picnics, fishing; **1. Winchester State Park** (34 m SE via US 95, ½ m S of Winchester) is 320-acre lakeside park with 10 m of trails; picnic area; **1, 2**. Nearby **Soldier Meadow Reservoir** (10 m W of Winchester off US 95) is picnic area; **1**. **The University of Idaho** (23 m N via US 195, 95 at Moscow) has exceptionally handsome campus (maps at administration bldg) and **Shattuck Arboretum; 1**. **Nez Perce National Historical Park,** mostly on Nez Perce reservation, consists of 23 historic sites; self-guiding auto trail begins at **Mackenzie Trading Post** (in Clarkson, W of Town on US 12), many stops offer short walks; tour booklets also available in Lewiston and at Lolo Pass, and at park hq in **Spalding** (15 m E of Lewiston via US 95), daily 8-4:30 (8-dusk in summer), closed Jan. 1, Thnks, Dec. 25, and weekends Dec.-Feb. From Weippe, the **Lolo Trail**, an Indian buffalo route followed by Lewis and Clark, runs to Lolo Pass (at Montana line); historic markers; walking near Weippe, at points (N off US 12) where fire and logging roads cross it, and 100-m section accessible by car from Powell ranger station (W of Lolo Pass); **1-3.**

Nezperce National Forest (hq at 319 E Main St., Grangeville 83530) is E and S of Grangeville and bordered by Clearwater, Bitterroot, and Payette Forests. Especially good trails are **E of Grangeville** along S Fork of the Clearwater (14-17 m E of Grangeville via SR 13, 14); along Selway; in pretty Red River Hot Springs area (N off SR 14) with trail to Black Hawk Mtn; along FS 285 (N off SR 14, E of Red River) with trails to several 6-8000-ft peaks; **1-3**. **Wildhorse Lake** (Orogrande Rd, S off SR 14, W of Elk City), in Scenic Buffalo Hump country, also offers good hiking; this road continues S, with campsites offering access to Salmon River Primitive Area and River of No Return; **2, 3**. S of Grangeville is beautiful **Salmon River Canyon;** Spring Bar Camp (13 m E of Riggins) is good base for hiking in River of No Return country **(2, 3).**

Clearwater National Forest covers 1½-million acres (E of Orofino) along **Clearwater** (spring log drives on Middle and N Forks) and **Lochsa Rivers;** both provide campsites with trailheads (several also offer float trips). On the Lochsa, especially fine are Wild Goose (20 m E of Kooskia on US 12) and Jerry Johnson (75 m E), with hot springs and an elk lick. **Selway-Bitterroot Wilderness** is vast area (1¼-million acres) so rugged that most Indian trails circled around the Bitterroot divide; sparkling streams cascade down steep canyons, and sheer mtns ring stunning alpine lakes; many trails follow streambeds, often to fishing lakes, and are moderate **(2-3)**, but backpacking cross-country is so difficult that FS recommends you be experienced and count on no more than 4-5 m a day **(3)**. From Clearwater Ntl Forest (N), wilderness is easily accessible from Lochsa River along US 12; road to Selway Falls (E off US 12 at Lowell) leads to several camps and numerous lovely trails **(1-3)** plus float trips; just N, beyond Black Canyon, wilderness borders US 12, and campground near park bridge provides 2 entry trails **(2, 3)**; additional trailheads (N of hwy and S to wilderness) are off US 12 between here and information station at Lolo Pass; **2, 3.** From S, entry to wilderness is along SR 14, E and W of Nez Perce Pass; also, campsites along Selway River offer access; most of these trails are along streambeds **(2).** Additional easy access from secondary roads W off US 93 in Montana. While wilderness peaks are often 7000-10,000 ft, N of US 12 highest butte is 6600 ft, and trail system includes many easy walks along streams and lakes reached off primitive roads. **Information:** Ahsahka Rd., Orofino 83544; information station in summer at Lolo Pass.

Bitterroot National Forest is mostly in Montana; Idaho portion includes wild 217,000-acre **Salmon River Breaks Primitive Area** on N shore of River of No Return; several trails follow the river or lead to overlooks above it. Easy access is off SR 14 between Red River and Magruder Ranger Stations; several campsites here make good bases for day trips into primitive area as well as for creek walks & climbs to 6881-ft Haystack Mtn and other peaks 6-8000-ft high. Access from W via Nez Perce Ntl Forest. From E, access is difficult, with combination of poor roads and trails, from Painted Lake area of Montana (SR 473, SW of Conner) or W of Shoup in Salmon Ntl Forest. Some trailheads reachable by boat from Salmon River. A few forest hot springs are reached from Montana's Painted Lake area, or off SR 14 via S Nez Perce Trail from Nez Perce Pass. **Indian Creek** (8 m N of Magruder ranger station via narrow dirt road) and **Paradise** (another 7 m) are scenic campsites on Selway River that give access to Bitterroot Wilderness. **Information:** Hamilton, Montana 59840.

McCALL: Chamber of Commerce provides information on pack trips and recreation. **Ponderosa State Park** (2 m NE), on peninsula in lovely Payette Lake, is wonderful 900-acre park with 10 m of trails through Ponderosa pine; lookouts; camping and picnic areas; swimming; **1, 2. Packer John's Cabin** (on SR 55 W) is small historical park with picnic and camp sites, **1. Cascade Reservoir** (S on SR 55) has camp and picnic grounds, trails **(1-3)** on W shore. **Payette National Forest,** magnificent 2½-million acres in sections E and W of McCall; Salmon and Snake Rivers run through, and it has many ghost towns and abandoned mining camps; thousands of miles of hiking trails; you can fly into several areas. N of McCall, Warren Wagon Rd. skirts Payette Lake to campgrounds at **Upper Payette Lake** (17 m N); from here trails branch out in all directions; some are fairly easy, along creek beds **(1-2);** others go to small fishing lakes **(2);** by dirt road you can continue N to ghost town of **Burgdorf** and then E to **Warren** gold-mining area or W to Salmon River and Riggins (trails off this road go N to Salmon River or to mtn climbs, **2, 3**). A parallel road (W of McCall beyond Brundage Mtn ski area) goes to **Goose, Twin,** and **Hazard Lakes;** this road also offers many trails **(1-3)** to additional lakes, Salmon River, and to trail systems E and W. **S Fork of**

Salmon River has trail its entire length; can be reached by road E from McCall (road skirts N of Little Payette Lake, turns N, and then E), by primitive road from Warren, or by a better road NE from Cascade through Boise Ntl Forest—this latter road, which turns N just before Warm Lake, has several campgrounds along river offering creek trails (2) to tougher walks (3) along Indian Ridge. E of S Fork of Salmon River is **Idaho Primitive Area,** a 1¼-million-acre mtn wilderness extending S into Boise Ntl Forest and E into Salmon Ntl Forest; many lakes, streams, deep canyons; peaks up to 9800 ft; Middle Fork of Salmon River, Big Creek and Chamberlain Creek—each has a trail its length. This primitive area, with thousands of miles of trails (2-3), is reachable by road E from McCall via Yellow Pine to Stibnite, from where a trail goes to Thunder Mtn mining area and Roosevelt Lake, and beyond to network of interconnecting trails throughout area and to surrounding forests.

At spectacular **Hells Canyon-7 Devils Scenic Area,** partly in Oregon, the Snake River cut the deepest gorge in U.S.; 7 Devils Mtns is magnificent volcanic range to the E, rising abruptly more than 8000 ft above river; Oregon side has 3-4000-ft bench ranges, while Idaho side has jagged canyons and rocky peaks rising to 9393 ft at He Devil; rocky land with little timber below 4000 ft; steep, barren slopes project beyond lakes rimmed with evergreens. Easiest entry from **Cambridge** via SR 71, N along Snake River (trails parallel river, 1, 2); along this route are campsites and lookouts; at Hells Canyon Dam, the 20-m-long reservoir has water sports, camp and picnic sites; several trails (1-3) include one above river and an 18-m one along Dep Creek that crosses scenic area to Saddle Camp. Another access is to **Heavens Gate Observation Point** (via road W off US 95, just S of Riggins); on this road is Windy Saddle camp, offering best hiking; nearby are several walk-in campgrounds. From Heavens Gate there's a 9-m trail to splendid lookout from Dry Diggins Ridge. From Windy Saddle, trails (1-3) lead to more than 2 dozen lakes, from 7 Devils Lake (½ m) to several lakes 3-8-m distant, to Emerald Lake (18 m S), so you can choose magnificent trails of any length. From **Council** (SW of McCall on US 95), a road leads via Bear through historic mining district to ghost towns of Cuprum, Landore, and Helena; trails (1-3) from campgrounds along this road vary from easy walks around mining remains to climbs up 5-8000-ft peaks; NW of Helena is **Sheep Rock** campground with scenic 11-m trail to reservoir, via Kinney Creek, other trails (2, 3). **Black Lake** camp (44 m NW of Council) trails to Emerald (4 m) and Ruth (8 m) lakes, 9-m trail to Six Lake Basin (2, 3); 9-m trail to Rankin Mill (2, 3); trail NE along Rapid River to US 95 S of Riggins; 22-m trail N to Windy Saddle; most creeks in this area have trails approached by trails or primitive roads off US 95 between Council and White Bird. **Brownlee** camp (N of SR 71 near Brownlee dam) and **Mann Creek** area campgrounds (best reached via Mann Creek Rd off US 95 N of Weiser) also offer trails (1-3). Trails in forest S of **McCall** are best reached off SR 15, S to Donnelly, then W. **Information:** McCall 83638.

POCATELLO: Ross Park (S edge of city along Portneuf River) has zoo, gardens, picnic grounds, replica of Ft. Hall (open spring–fall, daily), swimming pool. **Fort Hall** (11 m N on US 191) was where the original trading post was established; the **Lander Cutoff** of the Oregon Trail has been marked from here to South Pass, Wyoming, and booklets for a self-guiding tour are at any BLM or FS office adjacent to trail. **American Falls Recreation Area** (22 m W on I-15, then N on SR 39) is lovely area for strolling, picnics, swimming; **1. Massacre Rocks State Park** (36 m W on I-15 W), 3000 acres along 5 m of Snake River, is named for purported Shoshone ambush of a wagon train on Oregon Trail; **Visitor Center** (daily mid-May–mid-Sept., 9-6); Creek Camp, where Oregon Trail travelers recorded their names on Register Rock and other rocks; camp and picnic sites; 4 m of trails; open all yr; **1. Indian Rocks State Park** (23 m SE via I-15 near McCammon) has information center, 3604 acres with camp and picnic sites, hiking; **1, 2.**

    Cache National Forest (SE via I-15, then E via US 30N or US 91) is partly in Utah (hq in Logan); campsite and trail in Emigration Canyon (W via Ovid & Sharon), **1-3**; ice cave (W of Paris), **2**; trails at Bloomington Lake (W of Bloomington), **1-3**; camping, trails, and summer cave tours (adm) at Minnetonka Cave, **1, 2**; trails at Willow Flat campground (E of Preston), **2, 3**; trail in White Canyon (on Utah border) **2, 3.**

    Caribou National Forest is in several sections. Just S are trails through Bannock Range, where peaks rise over 8000 ft; Scout Mtn camp is a good base (**2, 3**). Near **Downey** (40 m via I-15), Summit campground offers trails (**1-3**) around 9001-ft Elkhorn Peak, and Cherry Creek campground (S of Downey) has a trail running S to Deep Creek Reservoir, **2, 3**. E of Pocatello, in **Portneuf Range** (best entry from Pebble), campground near Pebble ranger station is good base for hiking interconnecting trails that wind among the 9000-ft peaks throughout this section of forest (some **2**, most **3**). Largest section of forest is on Wyoming border, E of Soda Springs, from **Montpelier** N to US 26; beautiful valleys; many peaks over 8000 ft. In S (E OF Montpelier), campgrounds at Montpelier canyon are good bases for exploring canyon, Montpelier Creek, Giveout Historical Site, and Preuss Creek, plus trails along creeks N and NE of here; **1-3**. N of here are trails around **Diamond Peak**, and a portion of pioneer **Lander Trail** cuts across from Wayan to Auburn (Wyoming), **2, 3**. **Pine Bar** camp (E of Wayan off SR 34), in Caribou Range, has a trail (**2, 3**) S along S Fork to Lander Trail. (The Lander Trail continues to Fort Hall; interpretive signs.) Another trail (**2, 3**) from Pine Bar goes N past Tincup Mtn and then offers several choices—along creeks, in Black Mtn area, and to ghost towns of **Caribou City** and **Keenan City**; all these trails (**1**) are also accessible from FS 087 NE of Gray. N section of forest, W of Palisades Reservoir, offers most extensive network of trails; campgrounds on **Bear Creek** or on reservoir make good starting points for trails along reservoir, creeks, scenic ridges, and over 7-900-ft mtns in this area; **2-3. Information:** 427 N 6th Ave., Pocatello 83201.

SALMON NATIONAL FOREST surrounds attractive town of Salmon (with forest hq). Visitor Center at **Lost Trail Pass** (44 m N on US 93) provides maps, information on river trips, pack trips, hiking. **Lewis & Clark Trail** is marked with monuments and plaques S of here along N Fork of Salmon River (along US 93); at Salmon it cuts across to follow Lemhi River (SR 28) to Sacajawea Monument (in forest 17 m SE via SR 28). Forest S of Lost Trail Pass has creek trails (**2, 3**) and climbs (**3**) in Beaverhead Mtns on the E; a trail (**3**) along Continental Divide; trails (**2-3**) between the Divide and US 93. This section of forest contains **Salmon River**, edged by a road (deteriorates toward interior) and in some places by trails; climbs to or from river are **3**; along river are historic towns such as Shoup, petroglyphs (near Panther and Lake Creeks) and many easy walks (**1, 2**); also tougher trails (**3**), such as Copper Mtn Trail (off Panther Creek). Dirt roads and trails (**2, 3**) go N from river to Divide Trail, and in a few places cross into Bitterroot Ntl Forest. **Salmon River Breaks Primitive Area** is accessible from a trail along river from Corn Creek camp, by longer trails from campsites farther E, or from lovely campgrounds at Horse Creek Hot Springs. **Idaho Primitive Area** (W end of forest, S of Salmon River) has popular Stoddard Trail (**2, 3**) running S from the river; from mountain-bound Crags camp, a trail (**3**) runs along periphery of primitive area and to mirror-like lakes, with Clear Creek (**2, 3**) and Sagebrush Lookout (**2**) spurs going to Panther Creek. S of Crags are Yellow Jacket Lake (with landing field; sometimes reachable by rough road) and Middle Fork camps, popular entries into primitive area (**3**); a much longer but easier route (**2, 3**) is along Camas Creek from Meyeres Cove. Trails E of the primitive area can be easy walks around lakes or along creeks, or climbs up 8-9000-ft mtns; popular areas are **Iron Lake** camp in the S (a good choice of trails); scenic **Williams Creek Rd** (off US 93, S of Salmon).

SANDPOINT is on beautiful **Lake Pend Oreille**, which has many bays and 111-m shoreline, and is almost surrounded by mtns of **Kanisku Ntl Forest** (hq is on Dover Hwy, W of town, or write P.O. Box 490, Sandpoint 83864). Sandpoint (**Chamber of Commerce** is at 210 S 1st Ave.; summer information booth S of town on US 95) provides a public beach E of town. A lovely 107-m drive loops around lake; many parking areas from which you can explore some 400 m of hiking trails (**1-3**); FS campgrounds also make good bases, especially **Pack River Viewpoint** (18 m E on SR 200), June—Sept.

ST. MARIES, on the **St. Joe River**, here still a working river with log booms, with a logging road following it E to the forest; water is so clear you can see trout from the banks; swimming; fall color in Oct. **St. Joe Baldy Mtn** (8 m E on St. Joe River Rd.) has a lookout; Tingley Spring; hiking **(2, 3)**. The N section of **St. Joe National Forest** (S & E of town in several sections) is also on the St. Joe, which is even prettier here; several campsites on river have trailheads for mtn hiking (6500-6900 ft), **2, 3**; a dirt road N from Avery to Wallace offers waterfalls, **1**; campsites near Montana border offer rugged hiking and climbing in Bitterroot Range, **2, 3**. Unit of forest S of town (along US 95 A) is heavily used; winter sports; trailheads from camp and picnic sites, **1-3**. **Information:** 222 7th St., St. Maries 83861. **McCroskey Memorial State Park** (on SR 95 near De Smet) has picnic site and walking trails **(1-2)**. Another attractive river is the **St. Maries** (S along SR 3), also with public camping; Hobo Cedar Grove Botanical Area is near S Butte **(2)**. **Elk Creek Falls** (S of Elk River on gravel road) is a 200-ft cascade with a 100-ft fall, **2, 3**. Primitive roads (off SR 3 & also coming N from Orofino) lead to splendid canyons of **Little N Fork** and **Clearwater** rivers **(2, 3)**, where there's an elk browsing area. A well-marked trail is on N shore of Little N Fork, between Meadow and Cedar Creek, to an overlook **(2)**; another, S of Smith Ridge lookout station, goes to Morris Saddle **(2)**; near Aquarius campground, trails lead along riverbank, up buttes, and (just E) to Black Mtn lookout tower. **Mallard-Larkins Pioneer Area** is a 30,000-acre wildlife and botanical sanctuary (S of Snow Peak). **Dworshak Dam** (N of Orofino) has created a 53-m-long reservoir; at the dam are a visitor center, overlook, fish hatchery, **1**.

SAWTOOTH NATIONAL FOREST: Majestic 6-12,000-ft mtns, sculptured to sharp pinnacles by glaciers, deep canyons, alpine vegetation, hot springs are among the beauties of this 1.8-million-acre forest that extends into Utah; largest section (bisected by US 93 N of Sun Valley) contains: **Sawtooth National Recreation Area**, with excellent Redfish Lake Visitor Center (on US 93 S of Stanley); here you can get maps, information, and free tapes for auto tours; conducted nature walks and wilderness hikes; historic sites and salmon-spawning sites (the salmon travel 800 m from Pacific Ocean to spawn and die in headwaters of Salmon River); daily in summer 9-7. Forest has about 100 developed picnic and camp areas; bike trails, bridle trails, water sports, other facilities. **Redfish Lake** has a nature walk and trails around lake (**1**); trails to Salmon River (**1, 2**), along nearby creeks (**1, 2**) and to lakes such as the Bench

Lakes at foot of 10,229-ft Heyburn Mtn (2); trails to Sawtooth Primitive Area (1-3). Also here are: a vantage point above salmon-spawning grounds (on Salmon River at Warm Springs Creek E of Stanley), nearby fishing area and mining camp remains at Bonanza; remains of Sawtooth City (off US 93 S of Stanley near lovely Alturas Lake), plus nearby Vienna, Galena, and Boulder Basin, all old mining camps; overlooks; other points of interest; 1, 2. **Stanley Lake** (NW of Stanley off SR 21) has a nature walk and beaver dams (1,2) and 10-m trail to Sawtooth Lake in the wilderness (2-3). **Wood River** Campground (N of Ketchum off US 93) has a lovely trout stream walk; 1. **Trail Creek Canyon** (NE of Sun Valley) has scenic trails, 1-3; nearby Pioneer Cabin can be reached by dirt road or trail, 1-2. Hiking is available in the **Soldier** and **Smoky Mtns** (W of Ketchum off US 93), with many easy creek trails (2, 3), and Boulder and White Cloud areas (NE of Ketchum off US 93), with some tougher trails (2, 3). **Sawtooth Wilderness** (adj to Recreation Area on the W) is a 216,000-acre area with 8-10,000-ft mtns, deep gorges, waterfalls, 4 large rivers, more than 200 alpine lakes; 300 m of trails, but many areas are designated "trailless" for the hardy; challenging mtn climbing; snow may not disappear from higher trails until mid-July. Popular entry from Redfish Lake via Iron Creek campground to rockrimmed Sawtooth Lake (27 m), 2; via Redfish Creek to Baron Lake (2) or Ardeth Lake (3), about 20 m. S of Redfish Lake off US 93 are 3 easy trails (2): Hell Roaring Creek, Yellow Belly, and Pettit Lake, all 2½-3½ m to wilderness boundary, lead to pretty lakes. From Alturas Lake, its's abt 20 m by roundabout creek trails to Spangle Lakes area (2, 3). **Information:** Supervisor, 1525 Addison Ave. E, Twin Falls 83301.

ILLINOIS

CHARLESTON: Lake Charleston (SE on SR 130) has picnic sites, boating; 1. Camp and picnic sites, walking (1, 2) are at: **Fox Ridge State Park** (S on SR 130), pretty, hilly trails on 751 rugged acres on Embarras River. **Lincoln Log Cabin State Park** (10 m SW on unnumbered rd), reconstruction of cabin built here by Lincoln's father in 1837; nature exhibit; nature trail; other walks. Nearby are **Moore Home** (1 m) and **Shiloh Cemetery** (3 m) with graves of Lincoln's father and stepmother.

CHESTER: Kaskaskia State Memorial, interesting old village to wander in, Liberty Bell of the West, other historic sites. **Ft. Kaskaskia State Park** (9 m NW on SR 3), on 236 beautiful acres overlooking the Mississippi; cemetery, Pierre Menard home; camp and picnic sites; hiking; **1. Ft. Charles State Park** (31 m NW via SR 3, 155), once site of a fort that guarded plantations, museum, interpretive programs (summer), picnicking; daily 8-5; closed hols; free. **Randolph Co. Conservation Area** (5 m N), 1031 acres with camping; **1, 2. Rock Castle Canyon** (about 10 m NE), on Mary's River, unusual rock formations; **1, 2.**

CHICAGO: The city, rebuilt quickly after its devastating Great Fire of 1871, is a living museum of urban architectural development. Walking tours sponsored by **Chicago School of Architecture Foundation** (Glessner House, 1800 S Prairie Ave.) include Prairie Ave. Historic District (surrounding Glessner House), downtown Loop area, Frank Lloyd Wright houses in Oak Park and River Forest, other landmarks; foundation supplies maps and books for self-guiding tours; **1.** Interesting areas for walking include Old Town (roughly bounded by W North Ave., Ogden Ave., N Clark St.), with restored Victorian buildings housing cafes and boutiques; Chicago Civic Center (66 W Washington St.), Chinatown (Cermak Rd. & Wentworth St.); Magnificent Mile (N Michigan Ave. near the Loop), a fancy shopping district; Humboldt Park (1000-1600 N, 2800-3200 W), with floral displays; Garfield Park & Conservatory (300 N Central Park at Madison St.), 188 acres with conservatory open daily 9-5, free; Pullman Community (104th-115th St. at Calumet Expwy), first planned company town in the nation; Riverside (between Harlem, Ogden, and 1st Aves., & 26th St.), a planned community designed in 1869 by Frederick Law Olmsted and Calvert Vaux, with homes by Wright, Sullivan, and other major architects; **Graceland Cemetery** (Irving Park & Clark St.), wonderful monuments and mausoleums (a couple designed by Sullivan) ask for map at main bldg; **1.**

The **lakefront** has been developed with parks accessible off Lake Shore Dr.; going N to S are: Lincoln Park (1600 to 5200 North), beaches, yacht harbors, picnic areas, sports facilities; Chicago Academy of Sciences, Chicago Historical Society; 35-acre zoo and Farm in the Zoo; 3-acre conservatory; **1.** Grant Park (Randolph to 14th St.), with lovely fountain, Aquarium, Planetarium, Museum of Natural History, stadium; **1.** Burnham Park (14th-56th Sts.), walks along the lake and, just W, campus of Illinois Institute of Technology (information and guided tours from 10 W 33rd St.); **1.** Jackson Park (56th-67th Sts.), with Museum of Science and Industry, bird sanctuary, Japanese gardens, bathing beaches, yacht harbor; just W are Harper Court (S side of Hyde Park) with boutiques, and University of Chicago (information and tours from 1212 E 59th St.), with Wright's Robie House (5757 S Woodlawn Ave.) and Henry Moore's sculpture "Nuclear Energy," marking site of Enrico Fermi's laboratory.

Trailside Museum (Thatcher & Chicago Aves. in River Forest); 35 acres; self-guiding trails; Fri.–Wed.; closed hols; **1. Sand Ridge Nature Center** (Paxton Ave. N of 159th St. in S Holland); self-guiding trails on 235 acres; Sat.-Thurs. all yr; **1. Brookfield Zoo** (8400 W 31st. in Brookfield), 200 acres; daily May–Sept. 10-6, Oct.-Apr. 10-5; adm exc free on Tues.; **1.** At nearby **Lisle** (11 m W via US 34), **Morton Arboretum** (1 m N on SR 53) has ponds, prairie, woods on 1500 acres; nature trails; picnic area; daily 8-5 (8-7 in summer); adm; **1. Little Red Schoolhouse Nature Center** (104th Ave. S of 95th St. in Palos Hills), 400 acres with self-guiding trails; Sat.–Thurs.; closed Jan. 1, Thnks, Dec. 25; **1.** At Lombard (16 m W via SR 64), **The Landing** (881 West St. & Charles Rd.) is 132-acre preserve with interpretive trail; **1.** At Glen Ellyn (17 m W via SR 64, then S on US 30-A), **Cantigny War Memorial Museum,** has a Georgian mansion, landscaped gardens; picnic area; daily 10-4:45; free; **1.** At Geneva (25 m W via US 30-A), **Fabyan Forest Preserve** (S Batavia Ave.), 245 acres, Frank Lloyd Wright's Riverbank house, a museum of antiques, a lighthouse, a windmill; Memorial Day–Sept., Sun. & hols 1-5; free; **1.** Walking along the Fox River. At St. Charles (29 m W via SR 64 to N 2nd Ave.), **Pottawatomie Park** on Fox River offers picnicking, strolling, boat trips, parking fee. **Crabtree Nature Center** (25 m NW via US 14 to Palatine Rd., 1 m W of Barrington Rd. in Barrington Hills), 1100-acre prairie restoration, self-guiding nature trails; closed Jan. 1, Thnks, Dec. 25; **1. Crystal Lake** (39 m NW via US 14), 140 acres with education center (330 N Main St.); closed mid-summer; **1. Pleasant Valley Farm** (46 m NW via US 14 to 13315 Pleasant Valley Rd., Woodstock), 460 acres with farm, nursery, garden; **1. Chain O'Lakes State Park** (44 m NW via US 12), 1541 acres with trails along lakefront and in woods; camp and picnic sites; **1.** Just S on river is **McHenry Dam State Park,** family recreation area; **1.** At **Evanston** (12 m N on SR 42), **Shakespeare Garden** (E on Garrett off Sheridan Rd.) contains plants mentioned in Shakespeare's works; **Ladd Arboretum** (McCormick Blvd & Emerson St.), noted for cherry trees; **Merrick Rose Garden** (Lake Ave. & Oak St.), 1000 rose bushes; free; **1. Baha'i House of Worship** (14 m N at Lindon Ave. & Sheridan Rd. in Wilmette), open to all creeds; 9-sided building surrounded by 9 peaceful gardens; fountains; open daily; free; **1.**

Illinois Prairie Path, 40-m hiking, biking, riding trail, runs W from Elmhurst to Wheaton, then branches nw to Elgin and SW to Aurora; information: P.O. Box 1086, Wheaton 60187; **1, 2.**

DANVILLE: Vermilion County Conservation District (write 703 Kimber St.), nature centers, self-guiding trails, including Willow Shores (5 m S on US 150 at Westville); **1. Kickapoo State Park** (4 m W on US 150), 1539 acres with picnic and camp sites; fishing lakes, pretty Vermilion River; deer park; **1. Forest Glen Preserve** (10 m S on US 150 at Georgetown), self-guiding trails; **1.**

DECATUR: Scovill Gardens Park (E shore of Lake Decatur), Oriental gardens, children's zoo (summer), picnic area. **Lincoln Trail Homestead State Park** (10 m W via US 36, then S), where Lincoln's family settled after leaving Kentucky; camp and picnic area; daily.

JOLIET: Old Canal Town Historic District (7 m NE via SR 171 in Lockport) preserves buildings from days when Lockport was hq for Illinois & Michigan Canal; museum; special events; **1.** State recreation sites and additional locks are S of Joliet on river; 2-acre **Channahon Pkwy State Park** (12 m SW via US 6); 6-acre **William G. Stratton State Park** (20 m S off I-80, E of Morris); **Gebhard Woods** (W edge of Morris), along canal in a 30-acre park; **Goose Prairie** (on S shore of river, E of Morris), 1971-acre area for nature interpretation; **1. Silver Springs State Park** (19 m NW via US 30, SR 126), 1250 acres on scenic Fox River; **1.**

MARION: S of the city is a region roughly 50-m long and 50-m wide, bounded by Mississippi and Ohio rivers, from prehistoric times until end of steamboat era an important crossroads; but because spectacular bluffs and rocky terrain hampered modern development, this area preserves the state's most extensive recreational lands. Much of the area has been designated **Shawnee National Forest** (hq at 317 E Poplar St., Harrisburg 62946); dozens of FS camp and picnic grounds and other facilities; state parks; county conservation areas. **Ozark Shawnee Trail** (also called Trigg Memorial Trail) cuts across this entire region from Battery Rock (on the Ohio River, NE of Cave-in-Rock) to Grand Tower (on the Mississippi, off SR 3). Remains of prehistoric stone walls are at Stonefort (SE of Marion off US 45) and NE of Cobden (one due E, another NE at Giant City State Park); large ceremonial centers are Kincaid Mounds (S of Unionville) and Millstone Knob (N of Glendale on SR 145); visits to which require ranger permission. Additional mounds, petroglyphs, and pictographs; forest rangers can pinpoint exact locations. The Cherokee Trail of Tears roughly parallels SR 146. W and SW of Marion are: **Crab Orchard National Wildlife Refuge** (hq is 5 m W on SR 13, then S on SR 148), 43,000-acre wintering ground for waterfowl; camping, swimming, boating, picnicking, fishing, spring to fall; most facilities on Crab Orchard Lake; some on smaller Little Grassy and Devils Kitchen lakes; **(1, 2)**; hq open Mon.–Fri. 8-4:30, closed hols. **Riverside Park** (14 m W on SR 13 at Murphysboro), swimming and picnic site; **1. Lake Murphysboro** (25 m W, beyond Murphysboro, on SR 149), a 904-acre state park; hiking in rough, wooded terrain **(1, 2)**; walking **(2, 3)** in nearby attractive Reed's Canyon

(W via SR 149, 3 to FS road N near Glenn). Just S at Gorham (on SR 3) is information station for forest; here are: **Fountain Bluffs Scenic Area** (S of Gorham), with trails **(2, 3)**, unusual rock formations, bluffs overlooking Mississippi River, nature trail **(2)**. **Turkey Bayou** campground area (SE of Gorham) on Big Muddy River, beautiful trails **(1-3)** to unusual rock formations, nature trail at Pomona Natural Bridge, Swallow Rock (scenic bluff), nature trail at Hickory Ridge picnic site, Horseshoe Bluff, Sinner's Harbor, Oakwood Bottoms, Clear Springs picnic area. **LaRue-Pine Hills Ecological Area** has picnic and camp sites; trails **(1-3)** in area of dramatic limestone bluffs, abundant wildlife, rare vegetation. Union County has state forest (N of jct SR 3, 143) with tree nursery and conservation area (S of jct SR 3, 143), both with picnic tables, trails **(1, 2)**. Trails also near Delta campground S of here; some go to fishing ponds; **1, 2. Horseshoe Lake** (15 m N of Cairo on SR 3), an 8000-acre waterfowl refuge on U-shape lake, mid-Mar.–mid-Oct.; camp and picnic grounds; walks **(1, 2)**. **Fort Defiance State Park** (at Cairo), magnificent view of confluence of Mississippi and Ohio rivers; picnicking; **1**.

S of Marion are: **Lake of Egypt** (9 m S via SR 37), camping, fishing, boating, picnicking on a 2300-acre lake; **1, 2. Ferne Clyffe** (14 m S of Marion on SR 37), 1073-acre state park with narrow, green gorges and canyons; many trails **(1, 2)**; scenic Draper's and Cedar bluffs and Borax Cave (S of the park); Mortar, Scout, and Horse caves, Fern Dell, Bulge Hole, Jug Hollow, Benson's Bluff (E of park); Panther Den, Lily Cave, and scenic Jim's Hill (W of park); **1-3. Giant City State Park** (10 m S of Carbondale on US 51, then E), prehistoric Indian ruins, rock formations; 2960 acres; interpretive center, naturalist programs, trails **(1-3)** through lovely canyons. Cave Hollow (W of park) is picturesque, wild area with nearby shelter bluff called Nature's Amphitheatre; Kerr Bluff (S of park) with nearby cave and Indian ruins, is also worth exploring; **2, 3. Mermet Lake** (22 m S of Marion on SR 37, 15 m SE on US 45), waterfowl refuge, picnic area; **1. Ft. Massac** (22 m S of Marion on SR 37, 39 m SE on US 45), state park, lovely walks on 1339 acres; **1, 2**.

E and SE of Marion are: **Bell Smith Springs** (N of Glendale), FS area for picnicking and camping, good base for exploring beautiful Jackson Hollow (SW), excellent trails **(2, 3)** and overlook; Teal Pond, Burden waterfall, and Blue Hole fossil beds (N); **1-3. Lake Glendale** (S of Glendale), FS camping, picnicking, lake swimming; trails **(1, 2)**; Pine and Rice hollows (SE); Reddick Hollow (E); Clarinda Hollow, waterfalls, Indian sites, Hay's Creek Canyon (shelter bluffs with swimming hole), stunning Lusk Creek Gorge, and an early trace at scenic Caroline Hollow (N). **Dixon Springs** (S of Lake Glendale on SR 146), a state park, has swimming in mineral-springs pool; camp and picnic area; hiking on 400 acres with fantastic rock formations **(1-3)**. **Pope Massac** (E off SR 145 N of jct US 45), 1150-acre conservation area in wooded hills and bottomland with picnic area; **2. Ohio River Recreation Area** (on SR 146, N of Golconda), wonderful river views from picnic and camp grounds; walking at picnic areas S of Golconda at a lock and dam on river and at Lover's Leap; **1, 2.**

Garden of the Gods Recreation Area (SE of Harrisburg off SR 34, NE of Herod), rock formations and nature trail at Pharaoh campground (**1, 2**). A nature trail is at Stone Face (N); nearby are an old buffalo lick, mining areas, old salt spring area, Civil War hideout; picnic areas on High Knob (E) and Williams Hill (W) overlooks. **Karber's Ridge** campground (SE) has a nature trail (**1**); S of here are volcanic extrusions, experimental forest, lovely Hooven Hollow, natural springs, nature trail at Illinois Iron Furnace. W of scenic Tower Rock campground (overlooking Ohio River) are 2 caves (one with underground cavern and stream) and fossil beds. **Saline Co. Conservation Area** (9 m E of Harrisburg on SR 13, 4 m SW via Equality), wooded area with trails at lake and S of it; trails also in Wildcat Hills (NE). **Old Shawneetown** (45 m E on SR 13, beyond Shawneetown), is preserved as a state memorial; bldgs open daily 8-5; free; **1. Pounds Hollow** (14 m E of Harrisburg on SR 13, 9 m on SR 1) is an unusually attractive FS recreation area with lake swimming, camping, picnic areas, and 3 nature trails (**1**) plus Rimrock Forest Trail and other walks (**2, 3**). SE (across SR 1) are Indian mounds, Battery Rock overlook over the Ohio River, a cave. **Cave-in-Rock State Park** (S of Pounds Hollow on SR 1), 64 acres on Ohio River; cave used by river pirates, short trails; **1, 2.**

NAUVOO: Site on Mississippi River developed in 1839 by Mormons led by Joseph Smith; schisms caused Mormons to abandon it, and it almost became a ghost town; 1849 site of unsuccessful attempt by French Icarians to set up utopian society; Germans then took over Icarian fruit, wine, and cheese industries that survive today. **Nauvoo Restoration, Inc. Visitors Center** (Young & Partridge Sts.), interpretive displays and map for self-guiding tour; June–Oct. daily 8 am-9 pm; Nov.–May daily 9-6. Among bldgs are an inn, offices of Mormon newspaper, homes of Brigham Young and other noted Mormons, blacksmith shop, other landmarks. **Joseph Smith Historic Center** (Main & Water Sts.) Joseph Smith's homestead and grave, a slide program, information; daily 8-5 (8-8 in summer); closed Jan. 1, Thnks, Dec. 25; free. **Nauvoo State Park** (on SR 96, S of Nauvoo), 147 acres, has restored Rheinberger Home (May–Sept.) maintained as museum; park (open all yr) camp and picnic areas, trails include one around little fishing lake; **1.**

OTTAWA: At confluence of Fox and Illinois Rivers, Ottawa has 5 municipal parks with recreational facilities along river. **Boyce Memorial** (W of town on the river) and **Boyce Scout Hiking Trail** (W) honor founder of Boy Scouts; **2.** State parks are: **Buffalo Rock** (5 m W off US 6), scenic trails on 43 acres on N bank of Illinois River; buffalo and antelope; picnicking. **Starved Rock** (6 m W on SR 71), on S bank of river; 1995 acres; camp and picnic sites, lodge; boat trips, naturalist program, other activities; trails to waterfalls, along bluffs with river views, deep canyons with rocky ledges, Horseshoe Canyon, and forests; **1, 2. Matthiessen** (8 m W on SR 71, then S off Sr 178), 175-acre nature preserve and wildlife sanctuary on Vermilion River; falls, caves, canyon trails, prehistoric stone sculpture, reconstructed pioneer blockhouse, deep pen, naturalist programs; **1, 2.**

PEORIA: Chamber of Commerce (307 First Ntl Bank Bldg, Zip 61602) has booklets for walking tours. **Ft. Creve Coeur State Park** (S edge of city on Illinois River), hiking trails on 86 acres (**1, 2**), picnicking. **Jubilee College State Park** (NW via US 150 beyond Kickapoo), walks (**1**) on flat, shaded 15 acres; camp and picnic sites. **Forest Park Nature Center** (5 m N on 5809 Forest Park Dr.), 800 acres with 3/4-m self-guiding trail, 4 m of other trails; museum; Tues.-Sat. 9-5, Sun. 1-5; closed hols; free; **1. Mineral Springs Park** (9 m S via US 24, SR 9 to Court St. & Park Ave., Pekin), swimming pool, other activities; Apr.-Oct. Along Illinois River between Pekin and Beardstown are several state conservation areas: **Chautaqua National Wildlife Refuge**, open free all yr, trails, picnc area; **Rice Lake** (25 m SW via US 24); **Spring Lake** (5 m S of Pekin on SR 29, then 7 m W), with camping and picnicking, is especially nice (and just S is Mason State Forest with trails); **Anderson** (10 m NE of Browning on SR 100); **Sanganois** (1 m NW of Browning off SR 100); similar areas N of Peoria are **Woodford** (13 m S of Lacon), **Marshall** (6 m S of Lacon), and **Sparland** (across river from Lacon). **Dickson Mounds State Park** (38 m SW via US 24, then S on SR 78, 97), burials of more than 200 prehistoric Indians; museum; remains of 950-1200 village; daily 8:30-5; closed Jan. 1, Easter, Thnks, Dec. 25; free; **1.**

ROCKFORD: Sinnissippi Park (1300-1900 N 2nd St.), lagoon, sunken gardens, greenhouse; daily; free. **Rockford Park District** (1401 N 2nd St.) operates other parks and self-guiding Aldeen Nature Trail (623 N Alpine Rd.); **1.**

SAVANNA: Old Mill Park (Chicago Ave. E on US 52), picnicking and other facilities, May-Oct. daily; free. **Mississippi Palisades State Park** (3 m N on SR 84), 1716 acres overlooking Mississippi River; interpretive center; Indian mounds; rock formations; camp and picnic sites; hiking trails; **1, 2.**

SPRINGFIELD: Convention & Tourism Commission (500 E Capitol Ave., zip 62701), maps for walking tours of the city where Lincoln practiced law, married, raised his sons, and is buried; historic buildings (especially 5-10th Sts.), **1. Lincoln Tomb State Memorial** (Oak Ridge Cemetery), daily 9-5; closed Jan. 1, Thnks, Dec. 25; free. **State Capitol** (2nd St. & Capitol Ave.). Washington Park (W Fayette Ave. & Chatham **Rd.**), carillon with 3 observation decks; extensive gardens; **1. Lake Springfield** (S on US 66), strolling, swimming (sm adm) picnic areas; **Lincoln Memorial Gardens** (on E bank), 60-acre area with native vegetation, nature center, 8 m of trails; daily, free; **1. Sangchris Lake State Park** (10 m S on US 66, then E on SR 104), 1414 acres, as picnic and camp sites, walks, **1. Riverside Park** (4 m N off I-55), 300 acres on Sangamon River with camping, picnicking, walking; **1, 2.** Lincoln's **New Salem State Park** (20 m NW off SR 97) preserves restored village where Lincoln spent 1831-7; Onstot Cooper Shop where he studied law; Rutledge Tavern where he stayed; other buildings; replica of steamboat *Talisman,* which Lincoln piloted briefly; museum; flower and vegetable gardens; picnic area; daily 9-5; free; **1.**

STATE PARKS: Virtually all have camping, picnicking, and fishing but few have swimming: **Argyle Lake** (2 m N of Colchester off US 136), 1051 acres on the E Fork of the La Moine River; lake; scenic trails; **1. Beaver Dam** (6 m SE of Carlinville), on Macoupin Creek; scenic trails on 737 acres along river and in woods; **1. Cahokia Mounds** (5½ m E of E St. Louis on US 40-Bus), 650-acre site with ruins of prehistoric city, museum, interpretive programs, daily 9-5, free; nearby **Frank Holten** (E of E St. Louis, S of SR 111, US 50), 1125 acres, hiking trails; **1. Lincoln Trail** (2 m S of Marshall off SR 1), through which Lincoln family passed after leaving Indiana; trails along river and in 162 acres of woods; **1, 2.** At Oquawka, on Mississippi River, are **Gladstone Lake** (5 m S on SR 164), 136 acres, **Delabar** (N on river road), 89 acres; just N on the river (3 m S of Keithburg) is 2324-acre **Big River State Forest; 1, 2. Pere Marquette State Park** (5 m W of Grafton on SR 100), 6064 acres, view of confluence of Mississippi and Illinois rivers; resort facilities; hiking trails; naturalist programs; **1, 2.**

INDIANA

ANGOLA: Lakes offering walks are **Crooked Lake** (2 m W on US 20, then N on I-69), **Silver Lake** (4 m W on US 20), **Otter Lake** (9 m W off US 20), **Lake George** (9 m N via SR 127, US 27). **Pokagon State Park** (6 m N on US 27), swimming, camping, picnicking on Lake James; 8 m of trails through 1173 acres of forest, marshland, sand hills; naturalist program; wildlife exhibit; **1, 2.**

BEDFORD: Avoca State Fish Hatchery (5 m NW on SR 54), waterfall and picnic area, daily 7:30-dusk. **Osborn Spring Park** (17 m NW via SR 58, 47 to Owensburg, then NW on Osborn Spring Rd.), 400-acres; log cabin, picnic and camp sites; sm adm. **Moses Fell Annex Farm** (4 m W on SR 158), experimental farm run by Purdue University; weekdays 6:30-5:30, Sun. 6:30-4; free. **Martin State Forest** (20 m SW on US 50), 6000 acres, camp and picnic sites; trails around lake, to lookout, to White River **(1, 2)**; just N is McBrides Bluff on river, and at Shoals is a rock column, Jug Rock. **Devil's Backbone** (7 m SE via Buddha), 20-ft-wide ridge above E Fork of White River, has a trail **(2, 3)**. **Spring Mill State Park** (10 m S on SR 450), 1319 acres; reconstructed pioneer village; craft demonstrations; cemetery; boat trips through caves; Visitor Center memorial to Virgil Grissom; 8 m of trails around swimming lake, to sink holes, caves, 30-acre nature preserve; camping, picnicking; **1, 2.**

    Hoosier National Forest hq is here (1615 J St., zip 47421), rolling hill country (see Bloomington); **Tecumseh Trail (1-3)** runs from Ohio River N to Morgan-Monroe State Forest via foot trails and dirt roads. **Williams Dam** (11 m SW on SR 450), pretty trails along White River; nearby covered bridge. **Tincher Pond** (SE on US 50) strolling plus climbs to Sally Hill and Bryantsville lookout; **1, 2. Hindostan Falls** (SW off US 50 at Shoals, then S & W via SR 545, 550), on E Fork of White River; impressive. **Pioneer Mothers Memorial Forest** (S of Paoli), 80-acre virgin woods; trails through forest, along Lick Creek; picnic area; **1,2. Hemlock Cliffs** (NW of Sulphur off SR 37), waterfalls drop 100 and 200 ft (in spring only); trail with wildflowers; trails lead S to W Fork overlook, Sulphur Pond, Sulphur Springs, Oriole Pond. **Indian Lake** and **Lake Celina** (W of Sulphur off US 460), 150-acre fishing lakes connected by 2½-m scenic drive and nice trail; trail spur to Fairview Ridge; **1, 2.** Just S is Tipsaw Lake. **Buzzard Roost** campground (S of Sulphur on SR 66), trail to fine overlooks over Ohio River; picnic sites; other trails along creeks and through forest connect with trails from Saddle Creek and German Ridge; **1, 2. Saddle Lake Recreation Area** (NE of Tell City on SR 37), camping, picnicking, swimming; information center; forest trail (1); trails along creeks, to fishing ponds, to Marchand lookout, to Ohio River, to Buzzard Roost and German Ridge, to Tipsaw Lake (1, 2,). **German Ridge Recreation Area** (E of Tell City on SR 66), visitor information, swimming, camping, picnicking; forest trail (1); trails to Lovers Leap, Deer Pond, Ohio River, fishing ponds, Saddle Lake, Buzzard Roost (1, 2).

BLOOMINGTON: Indiana University has a beautiful 1850-acre campus; many museums, landscaping, outdoor sculpture; maps at Memorial Union. Extensive park and forest lands E of town offer wonderful walking; information on trails from **North American Trail Complex** (P.O. Box 805, zip 47401). **Lake Monroe** (SE via SR 37 or SR 46, 446), huge flood-control project with Hoosier Ntl Forest on E shore; recreational facilities are run by state, Corps of Engineers, and FS; hiking along 150-m shoreline; good trails at Allens Creek, Fairfax, Paynetown, Fish and Game Area, Hardin Ridge (1, 2); information at Paynetown entrance (SR 446).

  Hoosier National Forest, 150,000 acres of rolling hills and sharp ridges, many lakes, ponds, and streams. SE of Bloomington a large unit extends E from Monroe Reservoir; information station at **Hardin Ridge Recreation Area** (off SR 37 via Guthrie). Trails N from Blackwell Pond to Allens Creek (1, 2), Middle Fork Wildlife Refuge, fishing ponds (1, 2), to Hickory Ridge (3) and S Fork. **Hickory Grove Pond** trails go to fishing ponds and S Fork, Mitchell Ridge, and S along streams (1, 2). **Nebo Ridge**, the most challenging hiking (2, 3); reached from Hardin Ridge on the W, Brown Co. State park on the N, or off SR 135 on the E. From SR 135 you can climb to Bald Knob lookout (2, 3). From SR 58, NE of Freetown, trails to fishing ponds (1, 2). See also Bedford.

  T.C. Steele State Memorial (10 m E on SR 46 to Belmont, 1 m E, studio of the Indiana artist (see Nashville, below); 4 trails total 14 m through rolling, wooded country; 1, 2. **Yellowwood State Forest** (7½ m E on SR 46) in several units N & S of SR 46; 22,500 acres with trails to Brown Co. State Park, Hoosier forest, Morgan-Monroe forest; trailheads at lovely Yellowwood Lake; 1, 2. **Brown County State Park** (17 m E on SR 46), 15,428 acres of beautiful hills, lakes, streams; 10-m trail system (under 1 m to 2½ m each, interconnecting for longer walks), climb to Weed Patch lookout, trail to Ogle Lake from Strahl Lake campground, trails S into Hoosier Forest; wildlife exhibit; naturalist programs; observation tower; fall color; swimming, camping, picnicking, other activities; 1, 2. **Nashville** (19 m E on SR 46) tour booklets from the many art galleries featuring Indiana artists; the Brown County Art Colony was founded here in the early 1900s. **Morgan-Monroe State Forest** (10 m N on SR 37),

25,000 acres, good hiking; beautiful trails through hilly country; Tulip Tree Trace follows old Indian, pioneer, and stagecoach trails 22 m SE to Yellowwood Lake; trail to Brown Co. State Park; picnic and camp areas; **1, 2. Grassyfork Fisheries** (21 m N on SR 37, just N of Martinsville), goldfish hatchery Mon.-Fri. 8-4, Sat. 8 am-11 pm; closed hols; free. **McCormick's Creek State Park** (12 m NW on SR 46) trails through 1750 acres of forest, along rushing creek which has cut a canyon to join White River (E end of park); other trails to ravines, sink holes, cave, natural bridge, abandoned quarry; wildlife display; naturalist program; swimming pool, camping and picnic area; Visitor Center; **1, 2.**

CONNERSVILLE: Mary Gray Bird Sanctuary (7 m S on SR 121), trails on 684 acres of woods; museum; picnicking; daily in daylight; sm adm; **1. Whitewater State Park** (12 m E on SR 44 to Liberty, then 3 m S on SR 101), beautiful swimming lake, camping, picnic sites, naturalist program, trails **(1, 2). Whitewater Canal State Memorial** (18 m S on SR 121 to US 52) parallels the hwy toward Brookville; pleasant walks along canal, lock and aqueduct; canal boat rides in summer; **1. Adnes Trail** is being developed along the lovely White River N of here, between Laurel and Cedar Grove; **1, 2.**

EVANSVILLE: Convention & Visitors Bureau (329 Main St.), brochures for walking tours of Old Evansville (Riverside Dr. & 1st St.); homes in all styles from Federal to Victorian Gothic. **Sunset Park** (411 SE Riverside Dr.), beautiful site on Ohio River; Museum of Arts & Sciences. **University of Evansville** (Lincoln & Weinbach Aves.), attractive 74-acre campus with gardens; **1. Mesker Park** (NW edge of town on Bement Ave.), fine city zoo. **Wesselman Park** (5 m E at 551 N Boeke Rd.), 400-acres; swimming pool, other facilities, picnic sites, nature center; self-guiding trails, **1. Bent Twig Outdoor Learning Environment,** on Indiana State University campus; 25-acre woods lake, nature center, trails; open daily in daylight; free; **1. Burdette Park** (6 m SW), county-run, 140-acre recreational park; **1. Muskhogen Trail** follows an old Indian trail along Ohio River to **Angel Mounds State Memorial** (on SR 662, 7 m E); ruins of a prehistoric center that covered 103 acres; temple and huts reconstructed and furnished; interpretive center; daily 9-noon, 1-5; sm adm; **1, 2. Rockport City Park** (27 m E on SR 66), 16 historic log houses, including replica of Lincoln family cabin, comprise Lincoln Pioneer Village (daily 8-5; sm adm). **New Harmony State Memorial** (25 m NW on US 460, S on SR 69), site of vain attempts by George Rapp and Robert Owen to establish utopian communities; original bldgs include homes, opera house, granary; Roofless Church; the Labyrinth, hedge maze; grave of Paul Tillich in Tillich Park. Self-guiding tour booklets at Visitor Center (E Church St.), May–Oct. daily 9-5. Grounds open daily, free. **Harmonie**

State Recreation Area (nearby on SR 69), lovely 3000 acres on the Wabash River, picnic and camp sites, trails; **1, 2. Central States Fishery Station** (25 m N via US 41, 11 m NE on SR 65), 39-acre rearing ponds; picnic sites; nature demonstrations; weekdays 7:30-4; free; **1.**

HUNTINGBURG: Lincoln Boyhood National Memorial (10 m S on US 231, then 5 m S on SR 345), a living history farm; furnished cabin, other buildings, crops, farm animals, craft demonstrations on land Lincoln's father bought in 1816; Visitor Center interpretive programs (daily 8-5, longer in summer; closed Jan. 1, Dec. 25); trail to grave of Nancy Hanks Lincoln; **1.** Adj **Lincoln State Park,** 1864 acres, swimming lake, picnic and camp grounds, attractive trails; **1.**

INDIANAPOLIS: Chamber of Commerce (320 N Meridian St.), brochures for walking tour of downtown; outstanding art museums with quiet courtyards and gardens; State Capitol on 9-acre landscaped grounds; homes of Benjamin Harrison, James Whitcomb Riley; 5-block plaza with war memorial patterned after mausoleum at Halicarnassus. **Garfield Park** (Shelby & Raymond Sts.), sunken flower gardens, conservatory, fountains, stream, recreational facilities; **1. Eagle Creek Park** (W of town off US 465), trails through woods on 1700 acres; reservoir; stream; nature center (6164 Reed Rd.); picnic areas; **1. Riverside Park** (2420 E Riverside Dr.), scenic 930 acres on White River; fish hatchery (N end); **1.** Pleasant walks along river can be taken at other parks and landscaped areas. **Indianapolis Zoo** (3120 E 30th St.) has Japanese garden and mini-farm; adm. **Butler University** (W 46th St. & Sunset Ave.), 20-acre gardens; free. **Chank-Tun-Un-Gi Trail** runs between Camp Belzer (Fall Creek Rd.) and Geist Reservoir (NE of town); **1, 2. Colonial Village** (13 m NW on US 421, W on SR 334 in Zionsville), reconstruction of 19th-C main street; museum; **1. Conner Prairie Pioneer Settlement** (18 m NE via SR 37A to Allisonville Rd., Noblesville), excellent living museum of pioneer days; trading post, workshops (demonstrations), other authentically restored bldgs; picnic area; special events; early Apr.–late Oct., Tues.–Sat. 9:30-5, Sun. 1-5; adm; **1.**

LAFAYETTE: Purdue University (in W Lafayette) Horticulture Park (W side of McCormick Rd. near State St.) with trails; daily in daylight; free; **1. Clegg Botanical Gardens** (5 m NE on county road 400E, 1 ¼ m beyond Aretz Airport), 20 acres along ridges and ravines bordering Wildcat Creek; wildflowers; fine view; daily 10-sunset; free; **1.**

MADISON: Clifty Falls State Park (1 m W on SR 56), 1200 acres, views of Ohio River; trails to deep, rocky canyon, to waterfalls; picnic and camp areas, naturalist programs; **1, 2.**

MICHIGAN CITY: Franklin Square (Franklin St.), 4-block park, fountains, landscaping; **1. Washington Park** (along lake), zoo, picnic areas; **1. Pottawattomie Park** (1½ m NE on US 12), 100-acre International Friendship Garden with plants from around world; daily late May–Oct., 9-sunset; donation; **1. Indiana Dunes National Lakeshore** (7 m SW on US 12), containing **Indiana Dunes State Park; 8000** acres of white-sand beach, dunes, bogs, marshes; 3-m beach; trails (up to 5½-m long); camp and picnic sites; unit near Gary and Pinhook Bog (off I-80, 90, E of jct US 421); Information Center (jct US 12 & Kemil Rd.), with ranger-conducted programs, daily 8-4:30 (longer in summer); **1, 2.**

NEW ALBANY: Clark State Forest (20 m N off I-65), hiking in woods, around fishing lake on 22,400 acres; camping, picnicking; **1, 2. Harrison-Crawford State Forest** (27 m W on US 460, then S on SR 462), camp and picnic sites; 24,000-acre wildlife refuge; dirt roads; lovely section on Ohio River; **1, 2. Wyandotte Caves** (31 m W off US 460) guided tours (daily exc Dec. 25, 8-5; fee); trails include Wyandotte Trail, which runs abt 12 m N to Marengo Cave (tours here also) and passes Pilot Knob; **1-3.**

RICHMOND: Glen Miller Park (E Main St. & US 40), rose garden, zoo, picnicking; **Hayes Regional Arboretum** (2 m E off US 40 at 801 Elks Rd.), 30 acre forest, fern garden, trails (Tues.–Sun. 1-5; closed hols; free); **1.**

TERRE HAUTE: City parks include Deming and Dobbs (both on SR 42 E of town) with wooded paths. **St. Mary-of-the-Woods College** (7 m NW on US 150), lovely 90-acre campus. **Forest Park** (12 m NE via SR 340 to Brazil, then S on SR 59), lovely large park; recreational facilities, log cabin, historical society, fountain; open all yr; free. **Billie Creek Village** (25 m N on US 41 in Rockville) re-creates turn-of-the-century town; late May-Oct., daily noon-5; adm; **1. Raccoon Lake State Recreation Area** (25 m N on US 41, then 9 m E on US 36) is on a Corps of Engineers impoundment; recreational facilities, naturalist program; trails **(1, 2).** Two stunning state parks are **Turkey Run** (33 m N on US 41) and **Shades** (N of Turkey Run), both on Sugar Creek; camp and picnic sites; naturalist programs; miles of trails through deep canyons, along bluffs, under cliffs, past waterfalls, to old quarry and coal mine, through woods; **1-3. Shakamak State Park** (18 m S on US 41, 150, then 8 m E on SR 48), 2 lakes; swimming; camping; picnicking; naturalist program; wildlife exhibit; hiking on 1766 acres **(1, 2).**

IOWA

CEDAR RAPIDS: Wapsipinicon State Park (17 m NE off US 151), swimming, picnic and camp sites, hiking; views from limestone bluffs along Wapsipinicon River; wildflowers; caves; **1, 2. Palisades-Kepler State Park** (12 m SE off US 30), on attractive Cedar River; lookout tower on river; cliff trail for views; Indian mounds; trails; 688 acres; picnic and camp sites; **1, 2.**

COUNCIL BLUFFS: DeSoto National Wildlife Refuge (22 m N on I-29 to Missouri Valley, then 7 m W), 7800-acre floodplain with lake; swimming, other recreation Apr. 15-Sept. 15; streamboat *Bertrand* with exhibits on history of steamboats (Apr. 15-Dec. 1; free); roads and trails; **1, 2.**

DAVENPORT: Municipal parks include **Vander Veer** (US 61 at Central Park Ave.), 2500 species of roses; **1. Wildcat Den State Park** (off SR 22, 18 m SW), 1850 gristmill (open Sun.) on Pine Creek; trails; rock formations, caves, bluffs; picnic and camping areas; **1, 2.**

DECORAH: Volga River State Park (32 m SE on SR 150), pretty, **1, 2. Bluffton Fir Stand** (NE off US 52 on unnumbered road), rare stand of balsam fir across the Upper Iowa River from Bluffton; scenic view; **1. Hayden Prairie State Preserve** (34 m W on SR 9, 4 m N) is 240 acres of natural prairie; pasque flower (blooms Apr.-June); others bloom Apr.-Sept.; **1.**

DES MOINES: State Capitol (Grand Ave., E 9-12th Sts.), in landscaped 80-acre park; riverfront also landscaped. **City parks** with picnicking: Greenwood and Ashfort (adj on Grand Ave.), sunken gardens; Union (E 9th St. & Mattern Ave.), flower gardens, waterfront; Ewing (SE McKinley & Indianola Rd.), lilac arboretum; Water Works (Locust St. & Fleur Dr.), arboretum, greenhouse; Des Moines Children's Zoo (7401 SW 9th St.; late May-end-Aug.); **1. Ledges State Park** (28 m NW via SR 141, 17), beautiful ledges are 25-75-ft high; trails overlook Des Moines River and Pease Creek; trails around Lost Lake, wildlife research station with animal exhibits, Indian mounds; camp and picnic sites; **1, 2.** Just NW of Ledges (2 m NE of Fraser) is **Barkley State Preserve**, also scenic; **1.**

DUBUQUE: Julien Dubuque Monument (end of Julien Dubuque Dr.), 18-acre park honoring the French Canadian who chose this Mississippi River site: **1. Eagle Point Park** (NE edge of city off Shiras Ave.), 162 acres on a promontory, lovely views also; sunken gardens; picnic areas; mid-May-mid-Oct. daily; free; **1. Old Shot Tower** (Tower St. at the river), produced shot for the Civil War, also river views. **Maquoketa Caves State Park** (31 m S on US 61 to Maquoketa, then 6 m NW on SR 30), beautiful; trails through 192 acres to ravine, cliff-top walks for views, 13 caves (major ones are lighted and have cement walks), balanced rock, natural bridge; wildflowers; camp and picnic sites; **1, 2.** Nearby **Joinerville County Park** (5 m W of Maquoketa, 1 ½ m N), pretty 8 acres, camping, picnicking, on S fork of Maquoketa River; **1. St. Donatus** (11 m S of Dubuque on US 52), picturesque village founded by French; **1. Bellevue State Park** (25 m S on US 52), on bluff overlooking Mississippi River, picnicking and camping; Nelson Unit, easy trail to views of river, to Indian mound site, spectacular views; Dyas Unit trial to overlooks; **1.** At **Monticello** (32 m SW via US 52, 151), Pictured Rocks and adj Indian Bluffs Wilderness Area (SE off SR 38), nearly 3500 acres along Maquoketa River; trails; **1, 2. White Pine Hollow** (26 m W to Luxemburg on US 52, then 2 m NW), **1, 2. Turkey River Mounds State Park** (36 m NW on US 52), forested ridge with Indian mounds, views of Mississippi and Turkey rivers; fish hatchery (just N) with displays (Memorial Day–Labor Day, daily 8-5; free) and Merritt Forest (SW), a virgin forest stand; **1, 2.**

FORT DODGE: Dolliver Memorial State Park (8 m S via US 169, 5 m E on SR 50), lovely 600 acres on Des Moines River; picnic, camp sites; wildflowers; lovely glen with 5 m of trails; caves, cliffs, rock formations; Boneyard Hollow where buffalo bones were unearthed; **Brushy Creek State Park** (4 m E of Lehigh off SR 50 & SE of Dolliver Park), pretty; just N is Woodman Hollow (5 m NW of Lehigh), forested ridge overlooking Des Moines River, ravine with rare plants, lovely walks; **1, 2. Kaslow Prairie** (18 m W on SR 7, 4 ½ m N, 1 m W) blooms Apr.-Sept. (blazing star in July), and **Stinson Prairie** (36 m N off US 169), are state reserves, **1.**

FORT MADISON: Shimek State Forest (20 m W on SR 2), 8000 acres, conifers; 2 camp and picnic sites; ponds; interpretive trail; other walks; **1, 2. Lacey-Keosauqua State Park** (37 m W on SR 2, then N toward Keosauqua on SR 1), attractive; 1600 acres of wooded slopes, gorges, cliffs, meadows along Des Moines River; camping; picnicking; trails along river, to Indian mounds, around 30-acre swimming lake; **1, 2. Bentonsport** (E of Keosauqua, across the Des Moines from the state park, is a ghost town, once an important steamboat port; daily Apr.-Oct.; **1.**

McGREGOR: Pikes Peak State Park (3 m SE via SR 340), on 500-ft bluff over Mississippi River; trails to Indian mounds, fossils, falls, overlooks, mouth of Wisconsin River; camping; fall color; adj McGregor Heights wildlife preserve, old cemetery; **1, 2. Effigy Mounds National Monument** (4 m N on SR 76), 191 mounds in the form of bears and birds; self-guiding trail; Mississippi overlook from bluffs; 5-m Hanging Rock Trail; guided walks; Visitor Center (daily; closed Dec. 25); **1, 2. Yellow River State Forest** (9 m NW off SR 76 or SR 364; hq off SR 76, 5 m N of jct SR 364), 3500 acres; trails along streams, along bluffs to overlooks; camping, picnicking; **1, 2.**

SIOUX CITY: Parks—**Ravine** (off I-75 at Lincoln Way) and **Grandview** (Grandview Blvd & 24th St.), rose gardens; **Chief War Eagle's Grave** (nr jct US 29, SR 12), wonderful view over Missouri River, picnicking; **Stone State Park** (NW off Memorial Dr.), 900 acres on Big Sioux River, trails from picnic area, lookout reachable by trail or car, swimming, camping, picnicking; **1, 2.**

STRAWBERRY POINT: **Backbone State park** (2 m S on SR 410), 1600 acres, unusually scenic; named for ridge over Maquoketa River; rocky staircases, caverns; swimming lake, streams, state fish hatchery, camping and picnic sites; many lovely trails along river, ridge, in woods; **1, 2.** A federal fish hatchery is SE of Manchester (17 m SE via SR 3, 13), daily; **1. Brush Creek Canyon State Park** (6 m W on SR 3, 7 m N off SR 154), several short trails wind above and through pretty gorge and scenic bluff; picnicking; **1, 2.**

STATE PARKS: Trails in: **Black Hawk** (S of Lake View), lakes, wildlife refuge; **Fish Farm Mounds** (4 m S of New Albin off SR 26), wooded terrace with Indian mounds; **Gitchie Manitou** (9 m NW of Larchwood on SR 9), prairie on Big Sioux River, Indian mounds; **Waubonsie** (4 m S of Sidney on US 275, 2 m W on SR 2, S on SR 239), 1208 acres of beautiful hills, ravines, fall color, 7 m of trails to overlooks, Indian mounds.

KANSAS

DODGE CITY: **Historic Front St.** (500 W Wyatt Earp Blvd), preserved as it appeared when this was stop on Santa Fe Trail; museum, jail, cattle baron home, other bldgs open daily; Boot Hill (Spruce St. & 5th Ave.); **1. Santa Fe Trail** is marked across Kansas paralleling US 56; Cimarron

Crossing Park (19 m NW of Elkhart on US 50 in Cimarron), Wagon Bed Springs (11 m S of Ulysses), other trail camps marked along river in Cimarron National Grasslands (map from ranger in Elkhart). Trails (2) in **Horsethief Canyon** (NE) and **Duncan Crossing** on Pawnee Creek (NE, 11 m E of Jetmore). **Meade Co. State Lake** (21 m S on US 282, 22 m SW on US 54, 13 m SW on SR 23), pheasant farm, fish hatchery, game preserve (elk, deer, buffalo); **Clark Co. State Lake** (21 m SW on US 283, 15 m E on US 54, S on SR 94), in picturesque Bluff Creek Canyon; **1.**

HAYS: Frontier Historical Park (SW edge of city) has Ft. Hays, Visitor Center, exhibits, other bldgs (open daily; closed hols; free); nearby Agricultural Experiment Station. **Cedar Bluff State Park** (24 m W on I-70, 15 m S on SR 147), fish hatchery, water sports, trails on reservoir; just W are chalk beds, fossils in Smoky Hill River Valley; **1, 2.**

LARNED: Fort Larned National Historic Site (6 m W on US 156), bldgs of 1859 fort; booklets for self-guiding tours; conducted walks; daily 8-5 (longer hrs in summer); closed Dec. 25; free; **1.**

PRATT: Kansas State Fish Hatchery (1 m S on US 281, 2 m E on SR 64), hq of state Forestry, Fish & Game Commission, museum, aquarium, ponds, small zoo, picnic and camp sites; daily 8:30-5; free; **1. Medicine Lodge** (31 m S on US 281), replica of Medicine Lodge Stockade (on US 160) built by settlers; town surrounded by Gypsum Hills, scenic area of colorful mesas, towering buttes, deep canyons with well-marked trails; **2.**

WICHITA: Chamber of Commerce (Douglas & Waco), maps for Wichita State University (bldgs by F. L. Wright), other points of interest; extraordinary city parks with lakes, gardens, recreational facilities include Riverside (jct of the rivers) with zoo, Sim Memorial (W on Arkansas River) with Cowtown, 37-bldg complex depicting Wichita in late 1800s (spring-fall daily; adm). **Cheney State Park** (20 m W on US 54, N on SR 251), reservoir, swimming, camping, picnicking; **1. Bartlett Arboretum** (19 m S off US 81, W of Belle Plaine), 20 acres, flowers, grasses, trees, shrubs (mid-Apr.-mid-Nov. daily 9-7; adm); **1.**

KENTUCKY

ASHLAND: Greenbo Lake State Resort Park (14 m W via US 23, SR 207), swimming, camping, picnicking; trail to 19th-C blast furnace ruins; other trails, **1-2. Carter Caves State Resort Park** (36 m W on US 60, then N on SR 182), guided tours of caves; beach for water sports; trails in wooded country with rock outcroppings, caves, natural arches; **1-3.**

BARDSTOWN: Visitor Information Center (Court Sq.) maps for self-guiding tours. **My Old Kentucky Home State Park** (1 m E on US 150), 235-acre memorial to Stephen Foster; tours of manor that inspired state song (adm); picnic and camp grounds; gardens; open daily; free; **1. Bernheim Forest** (13 m NW on SR 245), 10,000 acres, nature center with interpretive trails, live animal exhibits; arboretum; lakes; wildlife sanctuary; Mar. 15-Nov. 15, daily 9-sunset; free; **1, 2. Lincoln Homestead State Park** (9 m NE on US 62, 9 m SE off SR 55), 153 acres of farm owned by Lincoln's grandfather with replicas of cabin, shops, home of Nancy Hanks; bldgs open May–Labor Day, daily 8-6 (sm adm); picnic grounds May–mid-Sept. daily 8-6; free.

BEREA: Berea College (US 25) tours start at Boone Tavern; art galleries, science museums, craft demonstration center, museum of Appalachia; 1375-acre farm; 6000-acre forest has hiking trails to pinnacles; picnic area; **1, 2.**

BREAKS INTERSTATE PARK (5 m SE of Elkhorn City on SR 80), stunning, 2400-acre park surrounding largest canyon E of the Mississippi, carved by Russell Fork River; Canyon Rim Drive, spectacular overlooks: extensive facilities include lodge, camping, swimming, boating: miles of trails vary from easy walks at pretty Laurel Lake to rugged climbs on steep, forested slopes (**1-3**); Visitor Center (Apr.–Oct. daily 9-5), information and museum; write Breaks, VA 24607.

CORBIN: Levi Jackson Wilderness Road State Park (12 m N on US 26 to London, 2 m S on US 25), 815 acres; swimming, camping, picnicking; preserves part of Boone's Trace and Wilderness road; attractive Mountain Life Museum (daily 9-5 in summer, possibly other weekends; sm adm), furnished log cabins in rustic setting depicting pioneer life; reconstructed mill; **1. Pine Mountain State Resort Park** (36 m SE on US 25E), scenic drive to top of mountain, camping and recreational facilities on pretty lake surrounded by forested peaks; nature center provides maps for 12 m of trails (**1-3**). **Kentucky Ridge State Forest,** 12,000 acres surrounding Pine Mtn park; many miles of trails start from park or along SR 190 SW of it; **1-3.**

COVINGTON: Devou Park (Western Ave.), 550 acres on Ohio River, recreational facilities, museum of natural history; daily; free. **Big Bone Lick State Park** (9 m S on US 42, 127, then W on SR 338), museum and interpretive trails at salt lick; life-size replicas of mastodon and other animals; reconstructed Indian village; camp and picnic sites; open all yr; free; **1, 2.**

CUMBERLAND GAP NATIONAL HISTORICAL PARK (½ m S of Middlesboro on US 25E): A natural passage through mountains, a trail hacked by Daniel Boone and 30 axmen became Wilderness Road; 20,000 acres, some of the most beautiful and rugged land in the E; **Visitor Center** (daily 8:30-5; longer hrs in summer; closed Dec. 25), observation platform, audiovisual program, historical exhibits, conducted walks in summer; 45 m of hiking trails vary from 9-21 m; Wilderness Road, less attractive than these for walking, can be followed only in short stretches. From Visitor Center, 4-m Pinnacle Rd winds to panoramic view and short loop trail (**2**). This is a trailhead for grueling 21-m **Kentucky Ridge Trail** that follows 2500-3500-ft ridge of Cumberland Mtn across park to Ewing, Va.; in abt a mile, Ridge Trail is intercepted by Sugar Run Trail (runs N 2¼ m downhill along Sugar Run Creek to panoramic view and picnic area on park road) and, just beyond, by Lewis Hollow Trail (runs S 1¾ m downhill to Wilderness Rd campground); in the next few m, 2 spurs also lead to Wilderness campground, the steep, 2-m Woodson Gap Trail and the 5-m Gibson Gap Trail; at E end of Ridge Trail, spurs lead to **Hensley Settlement** and **Sand Cave** (a shallow 1½-acre cave, 80-ft high, with sand floor). Hensley Settlement, whose chief source of income was moonshine, is on a 508-acre flat on rugged Brush Mtn; abandoned 1951, being restored; also reachable via jeep road from Cabbage (Ky) and foot trail from Caylor (Va); interpretive tours in summer. From Visitor Center (E along US 58) are Tri-State Peak, with 4/5-m trail to summit (**2, 3**); Iron Furnace with interpretive trail (**1**) and ¼-m trail to the saddle of the gap (**2**); Cudgo Cave (privately operated tours daily; adm); Wilderness Rd camp and picnic area, with several attractive short trails (**1, 2**) plus Lewis Hollow and Gibson Gap trails to Ridge Trail (**2, 3**).

DANIEL BOONE NATIONAL FOREST, 500,000 acres of some of the state's most spectacular scenery; from Morehead, forest runs S to Tennessee line. In **Morehead** area, trails are at Triangle Tower campground (E off SR 519); Big Limestone Trail, runs N 6 m from Lockege Rock (3 m S via SR 519, 2 m W on SR 16) overlook along a ridge to Hungry Mother Creek (off US 60); **2.** Clear Creek Furnace trails (10 m W on US 60 to Salt Lick, then S off SR 211) lead to 20-m system of trails crisscrossing creeks, ridges, and meadows in the Primitive Weapons Hunting Area; **1, 2.** W of Pine Ridge is **Red River Gorge Scenic Area** with trailheads off a loop drive; **Koomer Ridge** and other recreation areas are bases for 40 m of wonderful trails past natural bridges and other formations; many trails are short but can be combined for walks of 10, 15, or more miles **(1-3)**; 1900-acre **Natural Bridge State Resort Park** (on SR 11 near Slade), recreational facilities, skylift, 12 natural bridges, short trails **(1, 2)** connecting to Koomer Ridge system. SW of **Corbin** is another spectacular area; trailheads at recreation areas at Baldrock (11 m NW of Corbin via SR 312, then S on SR 92); Bee Rock (W of Baldrock off SR 92); Mt. Victory (W of Bee Rock off SR 192; recreational facilities and interpretive nature trail at lodge **(1)**; 40 m of hiking trails; 10-m Moonbow Trail along Cumberland River (float trips available) to Mouth of Laurel recreation area **(2, 3).** **Yahoo Falls Scenic Area** (8 m NW of Stearns off US 27), spectacular high cliffs, waterfalls, rock formations; short trails at Yahoo Falls and Alum Ford campgrounds follow river and connect to other trail systems **(1-3).** **Natural Arch Scenic Area** (14 m NW of Stearns off US 27), short trails among formations and trails N along Beaver Creek and on Bowman Ridge to Little Lick camp **(1-3)**; also reachable from Alpine campground (N of Natural Arch on US 27). **Yamacraw** (W of Stearns on SR 92), **Hemlock Grove** and **Great Meadows** (S of Yamacraw off SR 1363) recreation areas offer trails among formations, along creeks, on forest slopes; **1-3. Information:** 27 Carol Rd., Winchester 40391.

DANVILLE: Constitution Square State Shrine (US 127, 150), site where state's first constitution was adopted; original post office, reconstructed log courthouse, church, jail, daily 9-5; free. **Pioneer Playhouse Village-of-the-Arts** (S on US 150), 43-acre restored pioneer village; swimming pool, camping; **1. McDowell House & Apothecary Shop** (125 S 2nd St.), garden with period wildflowers and herbs; Mar.-Oct., Mon.-Sat. 10-4, Sun. 2-4; Nov.-Feb., Tues.-Sat. 10-4, Sun. 2-4; closed hols; adm. **Herrington Lake** (5 m NE off SR 34), 333-m shoreline, recreational facilities; **1. Old Fort Harrod State Park** (9 m N on US 127 at jct US 68 in Harrodsburg), replica of a fort that was Kentucky's first white settlement; pioneer cemetery; historic displays; cabin in which Lincoln's parents were married; Mar.-Nov. daily 9-5, Dec.-Feb. weekends 9-5; sm adm; map for self-guiding **Red Arrow Tour** of Harrodsburg area, including Morgan Row House & Museum (220 S Chiles St.) and Old Mud Meetinghouse (5½ m S via US 68). **Pleasant Hill Shaker Village** (15 m NE on SR 33, 68), 27 restored buildings with exhibits demonstrating Shaker way of life; daily 9-5 spring-fall, shorter hrs in winter; closed Dec. 24-5; adm. **Perryville Battlefield State Shrine** (10 m W off US 150) was site of the Confederacy's last attempt (1862) to win Kentucky; museum, historic bldgs, monuments on 30 acres; picnic site; June–Aug. daily 9-5; spring & fall, Tues.–Sun. 9-5; sm adm.

ELIZABETHTOWN: Brown-Pusey House (128 N Main St.), garden; Mon.–Sat. 10-5; closed hols; free. **City Park** (N Miles St.), swimming; picnic sites; free. **Abraham Lincoln Birthplace National Historic Site** (11 m SE on SR 61 to Hodgenville, 3 m SE on US 31E), 116 acres surrounding pretty Sinking Spring, part of a farm owned by Lincoln's father; log cabin in which Abe Lincoln may have been born; interpretive programs and exhibits at Visitor Center; daily June–Aug. 8-6:45, Sept.–May 8-4:45; closed Dec. 25; free; **1.**

GLASGOW: Barren River Reservoir (14 m SW on US 31E), Corps of Engineers project, camping, water sports, 1799-acre Barren River Lake State Resort Park; **1, 2. Mammoth Cave National Park** (22 m NW via SR 90, 70), Visitor Center (daily 8-5 or later) exhibits and programs; cave with 150 m of passageways, 2500-yr-old human history; guided cave tours vary from ½ m to 5 m, on smooth walkways; schedules vary with season, fees vary with tour; **1, 2.** Wild Cave Tour (more limited schedule) is 5 m through rough trail with crawlways (3). On 51,000 acres above ground are naturalist-led walks; self-guiding nature trails are 1-m Cave Island walk, 1½-m walk to sinkhole, 2-m road to lovely Green River; additional trails start at Visitor Center or from campgrounds on Green River; **1-3.**

HARLAN: Little Shepherd Trail can be followed on foot or by car 32 m along ridges of Pine Mtn to **Kingdom Come State Park** (23 m NE on US 119); camp, picnic sites; dramatic formations and scenery on 1000 acres; **1-3.**

HENDERSON: John James Audubon State Park (2 m N on US 41), museum with displays on Audubon's life and work (daily June–Aug., Tues.–Sun. in spring & fall, weekends in winter; sm adm); swimming, camping; 2 lakes; 10 m easy trails on 600 acres; **1.**

HOPKINSVILLE: Jefferson Davis Monument State Shrine (11 m E on US 68), 16-acre park, picnic and camp sites; 351-ft obelisk with observation deck; replica of log house in which Davis was born; other exhibits; 9-5:30 daily June–Aug., Tues.–Sun. in spring & fall, weekends only in winter; sm adm. **Pennyrile Forest State Resort Park** (20 m NW on SR 109), pine and hardwood forest on lake; swimming, picnicking, camping; 5 m of marked trails; backcountry hiking; **1-3.**

JAMESTOWN: Picnicking, camping, water sports at Corps of Engineers impoundments: **Lake Cumberland** (12 m S on US 127), powerhouse displays (late May-early Sept. daily 9-5; rest of yr weekends only; free); on N shore is Lake Cumberland State Resort Park; beautiful trails on little bays, in vast forest; **1, 2.**

LAND BETWEEN THE LAKES (bisected by SR 49 S of Gilbertsville), 170,000-acre peninsula surrounded by lakes Barkley and Kentucky, both part of TVA project extending into Tennessee; on Lake Barkley are **Lake Barkley State Resort Park** (6 m W of Cadiz) and other recreation areas N and S; on Lake Kentucky are **Kentucky Dam Village** (S of Gilbertsville on US 62) and **Kenlake** (16 m NE of Murray on SR 94) State Resort Parks with full range of facilities, plus **Paris Landing State Park** (on SR 119 in Tenn.); **1.** **Land Between the Lakes,** camping, picnicking on fishing bays, short nature trails **(1); Environmental Education Center** (SR 49 N of jct US 68) interpretive programs (daily 9-5), Center Furnace iron-industry remains, Empire Farm with animals and Silo overlook, lovely trails 1/8- 2½-m long include audiovisual Trail of These Hills **(1, 2).** Elsewhere, 400 m of trails and roads include 17-m trail along shores of Lakes Barkley and Kentucky **(1, 2);** Long Creek Trail **(1);** 17-m trail tracing Gen. Grant's troop movements between Ft. Henry and Ft. Donelson; **1, 2. Information:** Box 27, Golden Pond 42231.

LEXINGTON: Chamber of Commerce (239 N Broadway), brochures for guided or self-guiding tours of historic sites and horse farms. Open for visits are **Henry Clay's law office** (178 N Mill St.), **Hunt-Morgan House** (201 N Mill St.), and Henry Clay's beautiful 20-acre estate, **Ashland** (E Main St. & Sycamore Rd. E of town on US 25). University of Kentucky has lovely **Landscape Garden Center** (US 27, near stadium), ornamental plants and flowers; daily 8 am-sunset; free. **Lexington Cemetery** (833 W Main St.), 170 acres, flower and sunken gardens, lily pools, flowering trees and shrubs; daily 8-5; free; **1.** Horse farms include Calumet, Darby Dan, others (some open to public); **Spindletop Farm** (7 m N on Ironworks Pike) has a saddle horse museum (inquire locally for hrs). **Kentucky State Horse Farm** (N on Ironworks Pike), dedicated to the horses of Kentucky; museum and barns of 963 acres; picnicking and riding; special events. **Waveland State Shrine** (6 m S off US 27, Higbee Mill Pike), plantation, Greek Revival mansion, other bldgs on 10 acres restored to illustrate Kentucky life before Civil War; Tues.–Sat. 9-4, Sun. 1:30-4:30; adm. **Georgetown College** (12 m N on US 25 in Georgetown), lovely campus, interesting old bldgs; **1. Blue-Licks Battlefield State Park** (35 m NE on US 68), swimming, camping, picnicking; site of last battle of Revolution (a year after Cornwallis surrendered); museum; 100 acres; closed in winter. **Fort Boonesborough State Park** (15 m S on I-75, 6 m E on SR 22), beautiful site where Daniel Boone settled on Kentucky River; reconstructed fort; museum; interpretive programs; swimming, picnicking, camping; may be closed in winter.

LOUISVILLE: Visitors Bureau (Founders Sq., 5th & Walnut Sts.), maps for walking tours that include Riverfront Plaza and River City Mall (4th St. to the river), fountains; Old Louisville (S 3rd & 4th Sts., St. James & Belgravia Courts) and Central Park (4th between Park & Magnolia); W Main St. Historic District (Main, 6-9th Sts.), cast-iron buildings; Butchertown (Story Ave.), 19th-C German area; Cave Hill Cemetery (701 Baxter Ave.), unusual plants and waterfowl; Carrie Gaulbert Cox Park (River Rd. E of Zorn Ave.), picnic sites over river; Farmington (3033 Bardstown Rd. at Watterson Expwy), home designed by Thomas Jefferson with 19th-C gardens (Tues.–Sat. 10-4:30, Sun. 1:30-4:30; adm); Zachary Taylor National Cemetery (7 m NE on US 42 to 4701 Brownsboro Rd.); **Iroquoid Park** (Taylor Blvd. & Southern Pkwy) with overlook. **Louisville Zoological Garden** (1100 Trevilian Way, 7 m SE via I-65), Tues.–Sun. 10-5 (10-6 in summer); closed Jan. 1, Dec. 25; sm adm. Metropolitan Park & Recreation Board (Box 13334, zip 40213) operates many surrounding parks, some with trails: **Forest View** (Holsclaw Hill Rd., Fairdale), 19-m Loop Ox Cart Trail (2, 3). **Playtorium Recreation Center** (Mt. Holly Rd.), 10-m trail (2); **Jefferson Co. Memorial Forest** (Mitchell Hill Rd.), 1000 acres (2); **Otter Creek Park** (30 m SW via US 31W and SR 1638), nature center with trails, swimming pool, picnic and camp sites, wildlife area. **Information** on trails from Kentucky Trails Assn. (P.O. Box 784, zip 40201). State parks are **E. P. "Tom" Sawyer** (Freys Hill Rd. off US 60 near Anchorage), 319 acres, recreational facilities; **Gen. Butler** (44 m NE off I-71, then N on SR 227), resort park with home of Butler, hero of War of 1812, Museum of Ohio River Lore (daily in summer, Tues.-Sun. in spring & fall; sm adm); nature trails; **1.**

MAYFIELD: Maplewood Cemetery (on US 45), animal monuments at grave of horse breeder Henry C. Wooldridge; daily 7 am-6 pm; free. **Columbus-Belmont Battlefield State Park** (28 m W on SR 80 to SR 123), on Mississippi River; interpretive trail through trenches; trails through 156 acres along bluffs over river; museum (June–Aug.); picnic and camp sites; **1, 2.**

PRESTONBURG: Jenny Wiley State Resort Park (2 m E on US 23, 460, then N on SR 304), 1700 acres, water sports, camping, picnicking, riding, lake cruises, sky ride; trails along mountainside, pretty lake; **1-3.**

LOUISIANA

ALEXANDRIA: Kisatchie National Forest is in several units N and W of town; 600,000 acres of pine forest and mossdraped cypress swamps; self-guiding nature trails at these recreation areas: Fullerton Lake (NE of Cravens on SR 399), Longleaf Trail Vista (off SR 119 between Derry & Gorum), Magnolia (off SR 488 SW of Alexandria), Valentine Lake (off SR 28 S of Gardner); Longleaf Scenic Area (off SR 10 S of Ft. Polk) also has trails; information at 2500 Shreveport Hwy (Pineville 71360); **1, 2.**

BATON ROUGE: Chamber of Commerce (564 Laurel St.) provides information. **State Capitol** (Riverside Mall & Boyd Ave.) and extensive gardens were built by Huey P. Long (he is buried in a sunken garden here). **Louisiana State University** & Agricultural & Mechanical College (3 m S) has information center at Memorial Tower, museums, Indian mounds, Rural Life Museum (Burden Research Center) illustrating 18–19th-C plantation life. Among nearby plantations are **Cottage** (just N on US 61) and spectacular **Rosedown** (St. Francisville) with formal gardens, live oaks, rare plantings, fountains, statuary (daily Mar.–Nov. 9-5, Dec.–Feb. 10-4; closed Dec. 24–25; adm). **Audubon Memorial State Park** (SR 965 off US 61, S), house (daily; closed hols; sm adm), 100-acre wildlife sanctuary with paths (**1**), picnic area (daily 7-7).

NATCHITOCHES: For details of historic tours of city (oldest town in Louisiana Purchase) and nearby plantations, write Box 2654 (zip 71457); early graves in American Cemetery (Jefferson St. & Cane River), aboveground tombs in Catholic Cemetery (5th St.); nearby fish hatchery; **1. El Camino Real** (SR 6), the historic trail, is marked with plaques SW of city; along route are **Los Adais Historical Park** (at Robeline), important Spanish center, and **Fort Jesup State Historic Monument** (6 m E of Many), with reconstructed bldgs (open Tues.–Sat. 8-4:30, Sun. 1-5; sm adm); **1. Hodges Gardens** (29 m W on SR 6, 15 m S on US 171) is stunningly landscaped around abandoned quarry; 4700 acres have natural and formal areas, pools, waterfalls, various levels, island with memorial to Louisiana Purchase, planted for color all year; 12 m of roads; many miles of pathways; daily 8-sunset; adm; **1, 2.**

NEW IBERIA: On lovely Bayou Teche; founded before 1800 by French, Spanish, and Acadians; **Shadows-on-the-Teche** (117 E Main St.), a townhouse (daily exc Dec. 25; adm); stroll and picnic at **City Park** (across the Teche on Marie off Bridge St.) or at recreation areas on nearby lakes and bayous; **1. Jefferson Island** (10 m W off SR 14) offers Live Oak Gardens; 20 acres with water gardens, formal and wild areas, Alhambra garden with fountains and terraces, oriental garden, glen with tropical plants, picnic area; daily 9-5; adm; **1. Avery Island** (10 m SW on SR 14) Jungle Gardens, one of pleasantest gardens in nation; spectacular oriental garden climaxed by a 1000-yr-old Buddha overlooking 2 beautiful ponds and reached on stepping-stone path; many special gardens and hidden nooks; lake with nesting waterfowl; miles of paths; daily 8:30-5; adm; **1.**

NEW ORLEANS: Visitor Information Center (334 Royal St.), daily 8:30-5, brochures for walking tours of the **Vieux Carre** (Canal St. to Esplanade, N Rampart St. to Mississippi River).

Garden District (Jackson to Louisiana Ave., Prytania to Magazine St.), homes built by aristocracy in 1800s (fine grillwork at 1239 1st St., 1331 1st St., 1331 3rd St., 1448 4th S.), beautifully landscaped with live oaks, palms, magnolias. **Audubon Park** (6400-6900 St. Charles Ave.), 249 acres; zoo; picnicking; **1. Longue Vue Gardens** (7 Bamboo Rd., off Metairie Rd.), 8-acre formal gardens with attractive Spanish Court; Tues.-Sun. 1-5; closed hols, mid-July-mid-Sept; adm; **1.**

City Park (City Park Ave. to Robert E. Lee Blvd., Bayou St. John to Orleans Ave.), 1500 acres; lagoons; rose garden; Dueling Oaks; art museum; recreational facilities; floral clock; lighted fountain; **1. Lakeshore Drive** (just N along Lake Pontchartrain) landscaped with parks, picnic areas; amusement park; beach; yacht harbor; **1.** Across Lake Pontchartrain (via 32-m, toll causeway) are **Fontainebleau State Park** (3 m E on US 190), 2700 acres on the lake; swimming; camping; picnicking; plantation ruins; alley of live oaks; nature trails; **1, 2. Fairview** Riverside State Park (4 m W on SR 22), 98 acres on Tchefuncte River; moss-draped oaks; camping; picnicking; **1. Bogue Falaya State Park** (5 m N on US 190), Tchefuncte River swimming; picnicking; **1.**

ST. MARTINVILLE: Longfellow-Evangeline State Park (on SR 31, N of town), beautiful site on bayou; 1765 home said to have belonged to Louis Arceneaux, whose romance with Emmeline Labiche inspired Longfellow's "Evangeline"; Acadian cultural displays; swimming; camping.

STATE PARK: Lake Bruin (5 m N of St. Joseph), oxbow of the Mississippi River; magnificent cypresses; camping; picnicking; trails **(1).**

MAINE

BATH: Many fine mansions, a marine museum (963 Washington St.), historic sites. **Popham State Park** (12 m S on SR 209), swimming, picnicking, tidal pools and rocky outcrops; **1, 2.** Nearby **Ft. Popham Memorial** is a semicircular fort with interpretive displays (Memorial Day–Labor Day, daily 10-6; sm adm). **Arnold Trail,** traced by Benedict Arnold in 1775 attempt to capture Quebec, is marked with interpretive signs from Ft. Popham 194 m N to Coburn Gore at Canadian border; trail can be followed on foot in some sections (other sections require canoes). **Reid State Park** (1 m E on US 1, 13 m SE on SR 127, then SE) has sand beach, dunes, marshes, ledges; swimming; picnicking; **1, 2.**

At **Brunswick** (8 m W on US 1), Bowdoin College (Main & College Sts.) and sites associated with Harriet Beecher Stowe are interesting; Thomas Point Beach (4 m E on US 1, Thomas Pt. Rd.); other beaches are on peninsulas S, such as Bailey Island (via bridge on SR 24); **1.** At **Boothbay Harbor** area (12 m W on US 1, 11 m S on SR 27), wharves are fun to walk around, public beaches; **1. Damariscotta** (18 m E on US 1), charming town with historic buildings, Ft. William Henry Memorial (13 m S via SR 129, 130, then W), Ancient Pemaquid Restoration (14 m S via SR 129, 130), Pemaquid Point Light, Damariscotta Lake State Park (12 m N via SR 213) with picnicking and swimming; **1.**

CAMDEN: Information Office (Town Landing) has brochures for walking tour of historic buildings; charming resort; landscaping. **Old Conway House Complex** (Conway Rd. & US 1), museum, farmhouse, blacksmith shop, other bldgs; summer, Tues.-Sun. 1-5; adm. **Ureneff Tuberous Begonia Garden** (8 m S on US 1 to 169 Camden St., Rockland) is a lovely sunken garden (July–late Sept., daily sunrise-5); free; **1.**

ELLSWORTH: Birdsacre Sanctuary (Bar Harbor Rd., 2 m S on SR 3) has trails (all yr), museum (mid-June–Oct.); **1. Lemoine State Park** (8 m SE on SR 184), on Frenchman's Bay, picnicking, camping, 55 acres; **1.** At **E**

State Parks: **Camden Hills** (just N on US 1), picnic and camp grounds, trail to 1380-ft Megunticook Mtn, other trails, climbs (such as Maiden's Cliff) with equipment; **1-3. Warren Island** (via ferry N at Lincolnville on US 1) is spruce-covered, picnicking, camping, hiking **(1, 2). Moose Point** (21 m N on US 1), evergreen picnic grove, views of Penobscot Bay; **1.**

Orland (12 m W on US 1), fish hatchery at Craig Brook; **1. Bucksport** (20 m W on US 1), cemetery (Main & Hicks St.) and Ft. Knox State Park (W across Waldo Hancock Bridge), 124 acres with historic display, paths, picnic areas; **1.**

Holbrook Island Sanctuary (21 m SW via SR 172, 15 at Brooksville), on Penobscot Bay, scenic; picnicking (**1, 2**). **Deer Isle** (reached by road 36 m SW) has pretty walks along waterfront and Ames Pond (at Stonington), where water lilies bloom June–Sept.; **1. Acadia National Park** (16 m S on SR 3, 198) preserves some of the best of Maine's coastal beauty; Visitor Center (3 m NW of Bar Harbor on SR 3), naturalist programs; daily May-Oct. Scenic 20-m drive, with spur to Cadillac Mtn, has magnificent views; 40 m of carriage paths to most scenic areas (**1**), 100 m of foot trails, from easy lowland paths to hikes across mtns and cliffs (**1-3**).

GREENVILLE: At the S end of Moosehead Lake; surrounded by forested hills; trails to mtns include Big Squaw (6 m NW off SR 6, 15), Big Spencer (abt 25 m NE), White Cap (17 m NE, then 9 m E); **2, 3.** On Moosehead Lake are public campgrounds, including **Lily Bay State Park** (swimming, camping, picnicking), that make good bases for trails; **1-3. Appalachian Trail** comes S around small lakes from Baxter State Park, crossing White Cap Mtn and circling S to Monson (on SR 6, 15); here it turns SW to Rangeley Lakes. **Little Wilson Stream** (SE of town) has spectacular 57-ft falls in a sheet slate canyon; **2.**

Greenville is gateway to huge wilderness and logging area with few roads (plane service available); much land owned by paper companies that provide public campsites along a private road (open to the public) going NE to Ashland; toll for N end of this road; before tollgate is access to **Allagash Wilderness Waterway** (write Dept. of Parks & Recreation, Augusta 04330), a canoe trail; for information on public access to roads and land, write Paper Industry Information Office (133 State St., Augusta 04330). Also before tollgate is access road to **Baxter State Park** (entrances: 22 m NW of Millinocket; 59 m N of Greenville; 24 m W of Patten), the finest wilderness in the NE; 200,000 acres with 46 mtn peaks and ridges (highest is 5267-ft Baxter Peak on Mt. Katahdin); 50-m unpaved perimeter road has several 2-m trails to ponds, 5.8-m trail to 4 ponds, 1½-m and longer trails to mtn peaks (**2, 3**); **Appalachian Trail** starts here on Mt. Katahdin and runs S 8.2 m to park boundary. Most trails start from campgrounds (2 of which are hike-in): **Roaring Brook** (SE), bog exploration, ½-m trail to see moose on Sandy Stream Pond, ½-m climb to overlook (**1, 2**); 2½-m loop, 2-m steep climb to S Turner overlook, 3.3-m trail to Chimney Pond, 7 m to Russell Pond. **Chimney Pond,** reached by foot 3.3 m W of Roaring Brook, is in Great Basin of Katahdin, surrounded by 2-2500-ft cliffs of Pamola (1¼ m), Hamlin Peak (2 m), Baxter Peak (several trails, 1.7-2.4 m); good base for toughest climbs in park

(3). **Abol** (SW), Abol Trail is 3 m to Thoreau Spring and connects with trails at Chimney Pond and Katahdin Stream; **2, 3. Katahdin Stream** (SW), 1 m N on AT to falls, 3½ m to Tableland, 5.2 m to Baxter Peak (**2, 3**); AT goes S 5½ m via ponds and stream to Penobscot W Branch (**2**); easy trails to ponds (**1, 2**); OJI, Doubletop, Owl, and Sentinel mtn trails (**2, 3**). **Nesowadnehunk** (W) offers Doubletop, the Brothers, other peaks (**2, 3**); 9-m trail to Russell Pond (**2, 3**). **S Branch Pond** (N), beautiful area with easy strolls to see moose (**1**), ridge trails (**2**), and climbs to over 3000 ft (**3**); 9½-m trail to Russell Pond (**3**); Traveler peak (3541 ft) for trailless climbs (**3**).

LEWISTON: Thorncrag Sanctuary (Montello St., 1½ m E on SR 126) has trails on 226 acres; daily yr round; free; **1.**

MACHIAS: Ft. O'Brien State Memorial (5 m E on SR 92), breastworks and displays of fort commissioned by Washington in 1775; open summer; free; **1. Bucks Harbor** (S of Ft. O'Brien), rockhounding; **1.** Wonderful state parks are **Quoddy Head** (25 m E on US 1, SR 189, then 4 m S), trails through evergreen forests on rocky ledges above smashing surf, picnicking; **Cobscook Bay** (20 m E on US 1), where tides rush in dramatically, tidal pools, trails along rocky coves, in woods, and in adj section of Moosehorn Ntl Wildlife Refuge, picnicking, camping; **1, 2. Reversing Salt Water Falls Park** (27 m E on US 1), with tidal view; 140 acres; picnicking; trails **1, 2.** Stunning coastline with photogenic coves, rocky beaches and headlands, lichen-covered cliffs, deep-red sand at Perry, quaint little weathered towns. **Roosevelt Campobello International Park** (29 m E via US 1, SR 189), on Campobello Island, where FDR was stricken with polio, is co-owned with Canada; 11-acre estate with beach and lake, landscaped grounds; Visitor Center; open mid-May-mid-Oct. daily 9-5; free.

PORTLAND: Chamber of Commerce (142 Free St.) has brochures for boat tours to Casco Bay Islands and walking tours of Portland History Trail, including renovated waterfront (Old Port Exchange), Wadsworth-Longfellow House (487 Congress St.), other points of interest; good views from Portland Observatory, mile-long Eastern Promenade and adj Fort Allen Park, Western Promenade. **Scarborough Marsh Nature Center** (3 m S on US 1 to Pine Point Rd., Scarborough), 2000 acres of salt marsh with easy trails; daily May–Sept.; **1.**

Many towns, parks, and promontories N & S offer wonderful **beach walks;** nicest are: Portland Headlight (4 m S off SR 77), Two Lights (9 m S on SR 77), Crescent Beach (10 m SE on SR 77) on Cape Elizabeth; Prouts Neck (off SR 77); Old Orchard Beach (12 m S on US 1), with waterfront N & S; Biddeford Pool (SE of Biddeford via SR 9, 208), and S on SR 9 to

Goose Rocks Beach, Kennebunk Beach (Kunnebunkport is charming), others. **Bradbury Mtn State Park** (15 m N on SR 9), picnic and camping areas; easy trails to mountaintop and views of Casco Bay; **1, 2. Winslow Memorial Park** (11 m N off I-95 at Staples Point) is a Freeport city park with picnic areas and camping; **1. Desert of Maine** (14 m N off I-95 on Desert Rd.) is an area of colored sands, shifting dunes; open weather permitting, mid-Apr.-Nov., daily 8-8; adm. **Audubon Wildlife Sanctuary** (16 m off I-95 to Freeport, 1½ m E on Mast Landing Rd.), self-guiding trails on 150 acres; picnic area; open daily sunrise-sunset; donation; **1. Wolf Neck State Park** (16 m N off I-95 via Freeport; follow Bow St. to Wolf Neck Rd.) is a scenic park on Casco Bay; naturalist program; trails **(1, 2)**; picnicking.

RANGELEY: Mtn center for some 40 lakes and ponds forming the Rangeley Lakes chain, which has public recreation areas including **Rangeley Lake State Park**, picnicking, swimming, camping, walking; **1, 2. Stratton** (19 m N on SR 16) is also center of vast recreation lands (much of it owned by paper companies) with public campsites along SR 16 and SR 27; SE is the Bigelow Range (peaks to 4150 ft) with the Appalachian and Bigelow trails (on Stratton Rd., off SR 27 abt 3 m N of Bigelow), other trails; **2, 3. AT** runs S of the lakes from Saddleback Mtn (off SR 4, abt 5 m S) to 4180-ft Old Speck Mtn (off SR 26) beyond Grafton Notch (scenic area with panorama from peaks reached by trails, 2 waterfalls, Moss Gardens, mtns of the Mahoosuc Range, picnicking); **2, 3.**

RUMFORD: Mount Blue State Park (4 m E via US 2, then 14 m N on SR 142), on lake, swimming, camping, picnicking; 3187-ft Mt. Blue and 3035-ft Tumbledown Mtns have trails for overlooks **(2)**; other trails **(1, 2). Maine Conservation School** at Bryant Pond (20 m S via US 2, SR 232), 200 acres with self-guiding trails **(1, 2)**; open June–Sept. Just S are Greenwood ice caves and 40-ft Snow Falls, and the gorge of the **Little Androscoggin River; 1, 2.**

YORK: York Village Information (York St. & Lindsay Rd.) offers booklets for self-guiding tours of old jail, tavern, warehouse, school, church, historic homes; good beach walks off US 1A, scenic overlook at Nubble Light at York Beach; **1. Ogunquit** (N on US 1A) has a beautiful beach and Marginal Way, a stunning walk along cliffs above the ocean; the town is fun to stroll; **1.**

MARYLAND

ANNAPOLIS: Called the most perfect Colonial city in the nation; maps for self-guiding tours at **Visitor Information Booth** (City Dock), daily in summer, weekends spring & fall; conducted tours by **Historic Annapolis, Inc.** (Old Treasury Bldg, State Circle). **Sandy Point State Park** (7 m E on US 50), 813 acres with beaches on Chesapeake Bay, crabbing, picnicking; **l.**

BALTIMORE: Visitor Information Center (102 St. Paul St.), information for self-guided or guided tours. A good place to start is Mount Vernon Place (Charles & Monument Sts.), the chicest residential area in the Gay 90s, on a cross of green parks with Washington Monument to use as a landmark; observation tower; **Historical Information Center** (Fri.-Tues. 10:30-4; closed Jan. 1, Dec. 25) for brochures on walking tours. **Interesting areas for walking** include: Tyson St. (Read St. to Park Ave), charming, tiny houses built about 1830; Seton Hill (Jasper & George Sts.), attractive, restored row houses; Harlem Park (Lafayette Ave., Franklin St., Fremont Ave., Monroe St.), urban renewal area with greenery; Bolton Hill (Druid Lake Drive, Dolphin St., Mt. Royal Terrace, Eutaw Place are the boundaries), restored town houses; Calvert St. (1000-1200 blocks), elegant bldgs; Green Mount Cemetery (above 1400 block of Greenmount Ave.), 68 acres, unusual tombstones; Charles Village (25-33rd Sts., Howard St. to Guilford Ave.), restored townhouse area; Hampden/Woodberry Stone Houses (under Jones Falls Expy, S from 41st St.), built by English immigrants of local stone; Spring Lake Way (Homeland to Belvedere Aves.), residential area with greenery, ponds, fountains; Windsor Hills (Leakin Park & Gwynns Falls Pkwy), wooded residential area; Dickeyville (E of Forest Park Ave. at Wetheredsville Rd.), picturesque old mill village; Druid Ridge Cemetery (Old Court Rd. & Park Heights Ave.), duck pond; Roland Park area (both sides of Roland Ave, Stoney Run & Falls Rd.), early planned community designed by Olmstead, concrete row houses.

S of Mt Vernon Place are: Charles Center (between Lombard, Charles, Saratoga, Liberty Sts.), renewal project; Lexington Market (400 W Lexington at Eutaw St.), indoor market since 1782, open Mon.-Sat.; SE is Peale Museum (225 Holliday St.), with a quiet garden (Tues.-Fri. 10:30-4:30, Sat. & Sun. 1-5; closed hols; free); Inner Harbor, renewal project; Federal Hill Park, good view of Inner Harbor; **Fells Point** (foot of Broadway), once the city's port area and shipbuilding center, many old buildings; **Fort McHenry National Monument** (E end of Fort Ave.), Visitor Center (daily 9-5, longer in summer; closed Dec. 25; free) and living history demonstrations; **U.S. Frigate Constellation** (Pier 1, Pratt St.), may be boarded (daily exc Jan. 1, Dec. 25; adm); Riverside Park (Randall & Covington Sts.), view of piers; **Little Italy** (S of Pratt St., around Albermarle & Fawn Sts.); **Mt. Clare Station** (Pratt & Poppleton Sts.), 1830 railroad station now a museum (Wed.–Sun. 10-4; closed hols; adm); **Westminster Churchyard** (Fayette & Green Sts.), with E. A. Poe's grave; **Union Sq.** (Lombard & Stricker) and **Franklin Sq.** (Fayette, Calhoun, Lexington, Carey), renovated townhouses.

Druid Hill Park (off I-83) has Baltimore Zoo, Museum of Natural History, conservatory, rose garden, picnic and sports areas; **Sherwood Gardens** (Greenway & Highfield Rd.), 7 acres of flowers; **Clyburn Park** (4915 Greenspring Ave.), 175 acres, 70-acre wildflower preserve, miles of pathways; **Patterson Park** (Patterson Park Ave. & Baltimore St.) has Chinese pagoda, observation tower, defenses from 1814; **Cloverland Guernsey Farm** (off Dulaney Valley Rd.), barn tours; **1. Vanderbilt Stables** (Sagamore Farms, Tufton Ave. in Worthington Valley) open Mon.–Sat. 11-3; free; **1. Three Springs Fishery** (Goldfish Center, Lily Ponds), ponds and hatchery, is open Mon.–Sat. 9-3; **1. Calvert Cliffs** (on SR 2 S of Lusby) for fossil hunting; Maryland Academy of Sciences offers tours; **2. Soldier's Delight** (off Reistertown Rd. in Owings Mills), trails for wildflowers, bird-watching; **1. Hampton National Historic Site** (8 m N at 535 Hampton Lane in Towson), late-18th-C iron plantation with mansion, outbuildings, formal gardens; Tues.–Sat. 11-5, Sun. 1-5; closed hols; sm adm; **1. Ladew Topiary Gardens** (22 m N via SR 45 to Monkton) has won Garden Club of America award; mid-April.–Oct., Mon.–Sat. 11-5, Sun. 2-6; adm; **1.**

Greenbelt Park (20 m S off Baltimore-Washington Pkwy at Greenbelt Rd.), administered by NPS; 1100-acre wooded enclave; camping, picnicking; 12 miles of trails (**1, 2**); guided walks.

Nearby state parks include: **Patapsco**, in several sections along Patapsco River W and S of Baltimore: Hilton (SW on SR 144, then S on Hilton Ave.), camping and picnicking, Patapsco Valley Historical Center with self-guiding or guided tours, dogwood glades (**1**); Orange Grove/Ilchester (S of Hilton), camping and picnicking on the river, historic sites, swinging bridge, orange grove trail (**1**), trail to Hilton (**1, 2**); Hollofield (W on US 40 at river), camping and picnic sites, trail to tower, views of river (**1**); McKeldin (W on SR 26, then S on Marriottsville Rd.), picnic sites, self-guiding nature trail, river trails, dam overlook (**1, 2**). **Gunpowder** (13 m NE via SR 150), 10,000-acre state park in several units along a 30-m stretch of Big and Little Gunpowder Rivers; strolls at swimming beach in Hammerman Area; steep, rocky trails in Hereford Area; hq off US 40 in Hammerman Area. **Deer Creek** (24 m NE on US 1 to Bel Air, 8 m N off

SR 24), scenic, boulder-strewn, wooded park with short trails to rock formations; self-guiding nature trail; picnic area; **1, 2. Susquehanna** (35 m N off I-95), on Susquehanna River, picnic area, restored gristmill, restored toll house, other historic structures in a pretty setting; **1.**

CUMBERLAND, once an outpost of the Colonies, was on the National Road, which passed through **The Narrows** (NW), a picturesque gap with Lovers Leap legend; former **Toll Gate House** (8 m W on US 40) restored (early June–Oct., Wed., Fri., Sun. 1-4; free). **Historic Washington Street** (with a museum in History House at #218), historic bldgs at City Hall Plaza, and Washington's hq in **Riverside Park** (Greene St.) are worth seeing. **Chesapeake & Ohio Canal National Monument,** preserving the canal paralleling the Potomac from Washington (184 m) and ending here, goes SE from town; towpath maintained for hikers and bicyclists; much of the canal no longer has water, but is overhung with trees and bordered with lush vegetation; many roads S of I-70 cross the Potomac or run parallel, giving access; campsites (some are walk-ins) every 5 m from Seneca to Cumberland; picnicking anywhere, tables frequently provided; hq in Sharpsburg (on SR 65); **Great Falls** (12 m NW of Washington on SR 190, then S on SR 189) has museum of canal history, information center, interpretive programs, guided walks; information from Supt., George Washington Memorial Pkwy (Turkey Run Park, McLean VA 22101), Supt., C&O Canal (Box 158, Sharpsburg MD 21782); **1-3. Constitution Park** (E end of town), pretty municipal park, **1. Dans Mountain State Park** (10 m W on US 40, 8 m S on SR 36) is scenic, views from 2898-ft Dan's Rock; other trails through 500 acres of rugged terrain **(2, 3)**; picnicking. **Savage River State Forest** (20 m W on US 40, then S), 53,000 acres surrounding a dam on beautiful Savage River; most is near-wilderness, and hardwood-covered mtns have rugged trails **(2, 3)**; **Big Run State Park** (S end), a picnic area, has easier trails **(1, 2)**; **New Germany State Park** (N end), with camping and picnicking, has easy trails around swimming lake, nature trail, guided walks, scenic trails with overviews **(1-3)**. **Casselman State Park** (24 m W on US 40) is only 5 acres but has a stone-arched bridge, pleasant picnic sites; **1, 2. Rocky Gap State Park** (10 m E on US 40), 2610 acres in a saddle between Evitts and Martin Mtns; stunning trails **(1-3)** with panoramas; nature trail **(1)**; lovely swimming lake; camping; picnicking. **Green Ridge State Forest** (21 m E on US 40), 28,000 acres with Warrior Mtn Wildlife Area in the W; Town Creek and the C&O Canal run through it, offering attractive trails **(1, 2)**; additional trails **(2, 3)** through forested mtns; camping; picnicking. On the C&O Canal E of the forest are: **Prospect Peak** (SR 9), **2, 3. Fort Tonoloway State Park** (1 m SW of Hancock), 26-acre picnic area on Little Tonoloway Creek, where archaeologists are seeking evidence of 18th-C fort. **Fort Frederick State Park** (6 m E of Hancock on I-70 to Big Pool, S on SR 56), partially restored fort dating from French & Indian War; museum; historic programs; forest plantation; picnicking; camping; self-guided nature trail; guided walks; trails to C&O Canal, Potomac River; **1, 2.**

FREDERICK: This historic city has many associations with Barbara Fritchie, Francis Scott Key (both buried in Mt. Olivet Cemetery on Market St.), and Roger Brooke Taney; information for walking tours from **Visitor Information Center** (Schifferstadt, Rosemont & 2nd Aves.), open daily 9-9 in summer, 9-5 rest of yr; closed Jan. 1, Thnks, Dec. 25; **1.**

Seneca Creek State Park (21 m S on I-70S, then W) has camp and picnic sites, hiking trails; **1. Cunningham Falls State Park** (14 m N off US 15) and **Catoctin Mountain Park** (18 m N on US 15) are served by NPS Visitor Center (off US 15 at Thurmont, 3 m W on SR 77) that provides folk-craft demonstrations, interpretive programs, guided walks, small museum; 11,000 acres in beautiful Catoctin Ridge; Presidential retreat, Camp David (not open to public); 7-m self-guiding auto tour offers panoramic views and historic sites; camping, lake swimming, picnic sites; miles of trails through forest, shaded glens, along streams, to waterfalls, to overlooks; 3 self-guiding nature trails; self-guiding trails to whisky still, former charcoal-making area, and furnace where plates for the *Monitor* and *Merrimac* were made; **1-3.**

Attractive state parks in the mtns are: **Gambrill** (6 m NW on US 40), on Catoctin Mtn; trail or road to view from 1600-ft High Knob; self-guiding nature trail; 5 m of wooded trails; guided walks, naturalist programs; pond; picnicking and camping; **1, 2. Greenbrier** (19 m NW on US 40), 42-acre lake with beaches; AT crossing a corner; 1112 scenic acres, other trails; picnic areas; **1, 2. Gathland** (10 m NW on Alt US 40, 6 m S on SR 17 to Burkittsville, 1 m W), remains of George Townsend's estate; Visitor Center; historical walking tour; AT crosses here; picnic area; **1, 2. Washington Monument** (16 m NW on Alt US 40), with stone tower, on South Mtn, a spur of Blue Ridge chain; views from summit; museum; short trails; AT; picnic area, camping; **1-3. Antietam National Battlefield Site** (18 m NW on Alt US 40, 6 m SW on SR 34), where in a bloody battle Lee failed to invade northern soil; Visitor Center with museum and interpretive programs; national cemetery; booklets for touring battlefield; daily 8:30-5; closed Jan. 1, Thnks, Dec. 25; free.

LA PLATA: Port Tobacco (3 m SW), an Indian village that became one of the earliest English settlements, has been excavated; homes, courthouse, other bldgs reconstructed; daily 9-5, free. **Smallwood State Park** (16 m W near Rison), home and grave of Revolutionary Gen. William Smallwood; interpretive programs in summer; picnic area; self-guiding nature trail; late May–Labor Day daily 10-6; weekends in spring and fall; sm adm.

OAKLAND: Deep Creek Lake State Park (10 m N off US 219), 1826 acres on a 6-sq-m swimming lake, swamp nature trail (1), 3/4-m trail to fire tower for overlook (2), naturalist programs, guided walks; picnicking; camping. **Potomac State Forest** (9 m SE off SR 560), along Potomac River; 12,500 acres of rugged terrain; logging roads, trails (1-3); camping. **Swallow Falls State Forest** (5 m NW on Co 20), 9000 acres with red pine and other demonstration areas, beautiful Appalachian region of rushing streams, waterfalls, narrow gorges, cliffs and rock outcroppings, quiet glens, wildflowers, giant trees; hiking can be tough (3), but **Swallow Falls State Park** (9 m NW of Oakland), with picnic and camp sites, offers lovely trails (1, 2) to falls along Muddy Creek and Youghiogheny River, 10 m of other trails (1-3), including swinging bridge above falls; **Herrington Manor State Park,** with 10 m of trails around swimming lake, through demonstration forests, along creek (1, 2); picnicking; camping; naturalist programs and guided walks. Hiking along trails and old logging roads along scenic Youghiogheny River N to Friendsville; of special interest is **Cranesville Subarctic Swamp,** an 8-acre area with vegetation usually found in Arctic regions; 1-3.

ST. MARY'S CITY; Historic port, state capital 1634-95; Visitor Center with brochures for self-guiding tours of restored sections; archaeological museum; replica of original state house; park with paths and nature trails; walks along St. Mary's River; 1.

SALISBURY: Chamber of Commerce (300 E Main St.) maps for historic tours of the area, which has many charming fishing villages, and historic **Princess Anne** (13 m SW via US 13), with Colonial and Federal bldgs. **Assateague Island National Seashore** (27 m E off US 50, then S on SR 611), lovely barrier island; 35-m beach and sand trails (1, 2) to dunes and salt marsh; swimming, walk-in campsites, picnicking; Visitor Center (daily 8:30-5, longer hrs in summer; closed Jan. 1, Dec. 25) with nature programs and guided walks in summer; adm or GEP. **Assateague State Park** (adj National Seashore at N end), 680 ocean-front acres, camping, swimming, picnicking, nature trails (1). **Pocomoke State Forest** (S off SR 12) 13,000 acres, stand of loblolly pine, pleasant walks (1); cypress swamps border Pocomoke River; dense foliage provided cover for slaves escaping N; 2 of their camps are now state parks: **Milburn Landing** (8 m W of Snow Hill) and **Shad Landing** (4 m SW of Snow Hill); both have camping, picnicking, hiking (1, 2); Shad Landing has swimming pool, nature center, nature trail (1).

MASSACHUSETTS

ATHOL: Pretty wooded area with gentle hills, surrounded by public lands: **Erving, Northfield,** and **Mt. Grace State Forests** (8 m W on SR 2A) adjoin, going N to state line; most facilities are at Laurel Lake (S), swimming; hills reach 1617-ft at Mt. Grace (N); many miles of dirt roads and trails **(1, 2)**; swimming, camping, picnicking. At Northfield (16 m NE), **Northeast Utilities** has recreation sites on hydroelectric facility; 20 m of hiking trails **(1, 2)**; nature walks in summer; picnic areas; information center (on SR 63) daily 9-5:30. **Otter River** and **Lake Dennison State Parks** (7 m NE) adjoin in hilly, wooded area with lake, rivers; camping, picnicking, swimming; trails **(1, 2)**. **F.W.C. State Forest** (7 m SW), picnicking and trails **(1, 2)** on wooded shores of huge Quabbin Reservoir.

ATTLEBORO: Captron Park (County St.), 68 acres, rose and other gardens, zoo, birds in tropical rain forest, waterfalls, picnicking; May.–Sept. daily 7:30-9; Oct.–Apr. 7:30-4; free; **1.** Federal **fish hatchery** (N Attleborough), 3/4-m self-guiding wildflower trail; daily 7:30-4; free; **1.**

BERKSHIRES: Beautiful mtns in W Massachusetts, abound in historic sites and public lands, charming villages, wildlife sanctuaries, parking areas and short trails at scenic points; information from **Berkshire Hills Conference** (107 South St., Pittsfield 01201); **Berkshire County Historical Society** hq (780 Holmes Rd., Pittsfield). **Appalachian Trail** comes S from Green Mtn Ntl Forest (Vermont) over 2254-ft East Mtn (NE of Williamstown) and continues E of US 7 through Mt. Greylock, October Mtn, and Beartown state areas; 6 m S of Great Barrington, it crosses US 7, via Mt. Everett, to continue S to Connecticut; total length—83 m; access via many roads across it; mostly **2. Clarksburg State Park** (2½ m N of N Adams off SR 8), camping, swimming, picnicking. **Mohawk Trail** (SR 2) is scenic 63-m route from NY line to Millers Falls on Connecticut River (near Turners Falls); marked parking areas, camping, historic sites, overlooks, side trips; **1, 2. Natural Bridge** (Eagle & Franklin Sts., N Adams) made famous by Nathaniel Hawthorne. **Mt. Greylock State Reservation** (1 m W of N Adams, then S), with 3491-ft mtn highest in state; camping; picnicking; AT **(2)** follows ridges and peaks; other trails **(1, 2)** along brooks, to overlooks. **Savoy Mtn State Forest** (10 m E on N Adams on SR 2) has trails **(1, 2)** to Tanney Falls, beaver pond, along gorge, to balanced rock, to fire tower; adj **Mohawk Trail State Forest** has trails (**1, 2**) to overlooks, along streams; camping, picnicking, swimming.

Pittsfield State Forest (NW of Pittsfield), camping, picnicking, swimming, trails (**1, 2**). **Wahconah Falls State Park** (6 m E of Pittsfield on SR 9), surrounding falls; trails (**1, 2**) along stream, in woods, to 2313-ft mtn. **Notchview Reservation** (11 m E of Pittsfield on SR 9), 300 acres; picnicking; miles of trails (**1, 2**). **Windsor State Forest** (adj Notchview on E) has pretty river paralleling road into forest; Windsor Jambs is scenic gorge with hiking (**2**) its full length (quiet pools along the way), or climbs (**3**) through Jambs. **Hawley State Forest** (E of Windsor State Forest on SR 116 at jct SR 8A) has trails (**1, 2**) along streams, to beaver pond. **Deer Hill Reservation** (20 m E on SR 9 in Cummington), 260-acre wildlife preserve and recreation area; picnicking; **1.**

Tanglewood (1½ m SW of Lenox on SR 183), site of Berkshire Music Festival (July–Aug.); 200 landscaped acres with gardens; picnicking; open daily (free exc during festival); **1. Pleasant Valley Wildlife Sanctuary** (2 m N of Lenox off US 7 at West Mtn Rd.), 12 m of self-guiding trails on 655 acres; nature museum (mid-May–mid-Oct.); yr round; sm ad; **1, 2. October Mountain State Forest** (3 m E of Lenox), 17,000 acres; camping; picnicking; miles of trails (**1, 2**); lovely scenery.

Berkshire Garden Center (jct SR 102, 183 in Stockbridge), landscaped; trees, roses, herbs; daily all yr (best May–Oct.); free; **1. Naumkeag** (Prospect Hill, 1 m N of jct US 7, SR 102, Stockbridge), Norman-style mansion; terraced gardens, pools, fountains, sculpture, Chinese temple and statuary; walks (**1**); usually open in summer; check locally for hrs; adm. **Chesterwood** (2 m NW of Stockbridge on SR 102, then S on SR 183), studio, gallery of Daniel Chester French; gardens; nature trail; Memorial Day–Oct. daily 10-5; adm; **1. Monument Mountain** (4 m S of Stockbridge on US 7) is state picnic area; **1. Beartown State Forest** (9 m SE of Great Barrington on SR 23, then N), camping, picnicking, swimming; pond; trails (**1, 2**) in woods. **Tolland-Otis State Forest** (6 m E of Great Barrington on SR 23, 5 m S on SR 8), camping, picnicking, swimming; hiking (**1, 2**). **Sandisfield State Forest** (16 m SE of Great Barrington via SR 23, 57), picnicking, swimming, hiking (**1, 2**); just S at state line is **Campbell Falls State Park**, picnicking, trails to falls, in woods (**1, 2**). Mt. Everett Reservation (12 m SW of Great Barrington), ponds, short trail to mtn (**2**); steep trail (**2**) to **Bash Bish Falls** (W) and **Mt. Washington State Forest**. **Bartholomew's Cobble** (off US 7, 1 m W of Ashley Falls), jagged outcropping over Housatonic River; rare ferns, flowers; 6 m of trails (**1, 2**); natural history museum; spring–fall daily 9-5; free.

BOSTON: Boston Common, 50-acre park in heart of city, was set aside for public use in 1634 and still honors old cattle grazing rights; lawns, trees, benches, pond, fountain, statuary, Central Burying Ground; W is Public Garden, with flowers, fountains, pond; **1.**

Booklets for 1½-m **Freedom Trail, Black Heritage Trail,** and other self-guiding tours at information centers on Common (Tremont St. side; daily 9-4; closed Jan. 1, Thnks, Dec. 25) or in State House (E Lobby; Mon.–Fri. 9-3:30); **1.** Boston's historic downtown area includes modern Government Center and market district (along Blackstone St.). Short walk on other side of JFK Expwy leads to **North End,** largely Italian section; Old North Church (193 Salem St.), Copp's Hill Burying Ground (Snowhill & Charter Sts.). Waterfront (Atlantic Ave.), wharves with freighters, fishing boats, seafood restaurants, Aquarium. **Chinatown** is S of Common (around Beach St.). **Beacon Hill,** still Boston's most fashionable area, is N of Common; steep, narrow streets, some paved with cobblestones, lined with elegant townhouses and converted stables; Charles St., W end of hill, has boutiques. In **Back Bay,** W of Public Garden, Commonwealth Ave. is handsome with townhouses.

The Fenway (Back Bay Fens) is a park at W end of Back Bay; paths and benches; river with wild ducks; rose garden; private gardens on individual plots; Museum of Fine Arts; Isabella Stuart Gardner Museum; **1. Arnold Arboretum** (jct US 1, SR 203), 7000 trees and shrubs on 265 acres; blooms 11 months; daily in daylight; free; **1. Franklin Park Zoo** (Blue Hill Ave. & Columbia Rd.), with children's zoo (sm adm), daily; free; **1. John F. Kennedy National Historic Site** (83 Beals St., Brookline), birthplace of JFK; family memorabilia; map for nearby sites associated with Kennedys; daily 9-4:45; closed Jan. 1, Dec. 25; sm adm or GEP. **Larz Anderson Park** (Goddard Ave. & Newton St., Brookline), 60 acres of open hillside; pond; picnicking; recreational facilities; daily; **1. Stony Brook Reservation** (W Roxbury & Hyde Park, nr Dedham town line), picnicking, paths; **1. Harvard University** (Harvard Sq., Cambridge), outstanding museums, historic buildings; brochure and map for 1-m self-guiding tour at information booth in square or at 1350 Massachusetts Ave.; **1. Massachusetts Institute of Technology** Information Office (77 Massachusetts Ave.; open Mon.–Fri. 9-5) has maps, guided tours. **University of Massachusetts** (240 Beaver St., Waltham), Dept. of Environmental Sciences greenhouses and gardens; daily; **1. Prospect Hill Park** (Totten Pond Rd., Waltham), one of the highest points in Boston area, wooded trails, picnicking; **1.**

N of Boston are: **Stoneham: Middlesex Fells Reservation** (extends into towns to S), 3500 acres; Skyline Trail (**1, 2**) across park from Bellevue Pond (off S Border Rd., Medford) or from entrances at Jerry Jingle (off Fellsway E in Malden) or Winchester (off S Border Rd); other trails; recreation areas with picnicking.

Saugus: Saugus Iron Works National Historic Site (10 m N, E of US 1 to 244 Central St.), reconstruction of iron-making operations begun 1643;

Ironmaster's House; museum; blast furnace, forge; tours daily Apr.–Oct. 9-5; grounds also open Nov.–Mar. 9-4; closed Jan. 1, Dec. 25; free; **1. Breakheart Reservation** (W of SR 1 via Lynn Fells Pkwy), lovely wooded area; ponds, stream; picnicking; **1.**

Salem (17 m NE via SR 107): **Salem Maritime National Historic Site** preserves historical waterfront surrounding Derby Wharf; Visitor Center (daily 8:30-5; closed Jan. 1, Thnks, Dec. 25; free) is in Custom House described in Hawthorne's *The Scarlet Letter.* **Chamber of Commerce** (18 Washington Sq.) provides map and information for Historic Trail walking tour that includes sites associated with witch trials; **Salem Common; House of the 7 Gables** (54 Turner St.; daily 10-4:30, longer hrs in summer; closed Jan. 1, Thnks, Dec. 25; adm); stunning **mansions** of prosperous sea captains and traders (between Federal, North, Broad, & Flint St., especially on Chestnut St.); Essex St. mansions, including Witch House (#310½), where accused witches were brought for pre-trial hearings (daily Mar.-Nov.; sm adm); Ropes Mansion (#318; early May-Oct., Mon.-Sat.; adm); remarkable **Essex Institute** (#132) housed in several bldgs (Tues.–Sat. 9-4:30, Sun. 2-5; closed hols; sm adm), **Peabody Museum** (#161), fabulous collections (Mon.-Sat. 9-5, Sun. & hols 1-5; closed Jan. 1, Thnks, Dec. 25; adm); **1. Burial Ground** (Charter St. & Liberty St.) has interesting tombstones; **Salem Willows Park** has beach and picnic area at harbor; **1. Pioneer Village** (Forest River Park) reproduces a 1630 settlement; crude dwellings include dugouts, wigwams, cottages; June-mid-Oct. 9:30-5, longer hrs in summer; sm adm; **1. Marblehead** (3 m E of Salem on SR 114); winding lanes; interesting bldgs; walks along harbor; picnics and good views from Lighthouse Point (Marblehead Neck). Chamber of Commerce (62 Pleasant St.) booklets describe Fort Sewell (Front St.), circular Powder House (37 Green St.), Old Burial Hill (off Orne St.), other points of interest; **1, 2. Beverly** (N across sound from Salem on SR 1A): Chamber of Commerce (219 Cabot St.) has booklets.

Ipswich River Wildlife Sanctuary (21 m N on US 1 in Topsfield), 2400-acre arboretum, wildflower garden, pond; 10 m of trails **(1, 2)**; museum; interpretive program; picnicking. **B. W. Palmer State Park** (25 m N off SR 1A), on Ipswich River, offers trails (1) and picnicking.

Ipswich: Ipswich Historical Soc. (in John Whipple House, 53 S Main St.; mid Apr.–Oct., Tues.–Sat. 10-5, Sun. 1-5; adm); Crane Beach (Argilla Rd. on Ipswich Bay), daily in summer, weekends in spring & fall; adm; **1.**

Gloucester (33 m NW via SR 128): Along harbor is wonderful sea walk with memorial to 10,000 fishermen lost at sea. Beautiful Cape Ann coast, often shrouded in fog, is splendid for walks, with colorful harbors (such as Bearskin Neck in Rockport). At **Mt Ann Park,** highest point on cape, 270-ft climb for views and picnics. **Eastern Point Sanctuary** has paths on 26 acres of woodland and marsh. **Ravenswood Park** (4 m SW, on Western

Ave. in Magnolia), 500-acre pine and hemlock forest, ocean views and wild magnolias. **Agassiz Rock** (6 m S on SR 128), 106 acres, picnicking. All **1.**

W of Boston: Wellesley College (13 m W on SR 9, S on SR 16), lovely campus, lake, greenhouses; **Cochituate State Park** (16 m W via SR 9), swimming, picnicking, walks; **Garden in the Woods** (19 m W via SR 9 to Hemenway Rd. in Framingham), 50-acre botanical garden with paths through woods and fields (summer, Mon.–Sat. sunrise-sunset; adm); **Ashland** (26 m W via SR 9, 135) and **Hopkinton** (29 m W via SR 9, 85) State Parks, with picnicking, swimming, hiking; **Case Estates** (14 m W on US 20 to Wellesley St., Weston), 120-acre experimental garden, run by Harvard, brochure for self-guiding tour (sunrise-sunset all yr); **Environmental Education Center** at Elbanobscot (19 m W via US 20, SR 27 to Weir Hill Rd. in Sudbury), 80 acres with programs and trails; **Drumlin Farm Educational Center & Wildlife Sanctuary** (13 m W on SR 2, then S to S Great Rd. in Lincoln), operated by Mass. Audubon Soc. is a demonstration farm with special programs, trails through 240 acres (Tues., Fri. 9-5; closed Jan. 1, Dec. 25; adm); **1.**

Lexington (10 m W on SR 2, 2A): **Chamber of Commerce** Visitor Center (E of the Green) has information and diorama of Battle of Lexington; Apr.–Oct. daily 9-5; rest of yr, 10-4. Nearby are restored Buckman Tavern (E of the Green), Hancock-Clarke House (35 Hancock St.), Munroe Tavern (1332 Massachusetts Ave.); Museum of Our National Heritage. **Minute Man National Historical Park** interprets Battle Road (SR 2A) between Fiske Hill (Lexington) and Meriam's Corner (Concord), where landscape and bldgs are restored to 1775 appearance; information at Battle Road Visitor Center (daily Apr.-Nov. 9-6; Dec.-Mar. 9-5), North Bridge Visitor Center (June–Aug. 8-6, Sept.–May 8-5), and Fiske Hill Information Center (daily, weather permitting, 8-sunset); all closed Jan. 1, Dec. 25. **Concord** is beautiful town to wander in; bldgs open to public (some closed in winter) include Old Manse (Monument St. at Old N Bridge), where Emerson and Hawthorne lived, Orchard House (399 Lexington Rd.) and The Wayside (½ m E on SR 2A), where the Alcotts lived, Emerson House (Lexington Rd. & Cambridge Tpke) and nearby Antiquarian Museum with Emerson and Thoreau memorabilia, Thoreau Lyceum (156 Belknap St.) with Thoreau memorabilia. **Sleepy Hollow Cemetery** (Bedford St.) contains graves of Thoreau, Emerson, Louisa May Alcott, others; **Walden Pond State Reservation** (S of town on Walden St.) has 2-m trail around pond, picnicking, cairn marking site of Thoreau's cabin; **Great Meadows National Wildlife Refuge** (2 m NE on SR 62 on Monsen Rd.) has paths and trails; all open daily, free, **1.**

S of Boston: Quincy (8 m SE via SR 3A): 27 m of waterfront with swimming beaches; on N promontory are Squaw Rock (Moon Island–Long Island Rd. in Squantum area) and Moswetuset Hummock (off Quincy

Shore Blvd) with parking areas for shore walks; Adams National Historic Site (135 Adams St.) with memorabilia of 4 generations of the family (mid-Apr.–mid-Nov. daily 9-5; sm adm or GEP); Quincy Homestead (34 Butler Rd. at Hancock St.), birthplaces of John Adams (131 Franklin St.) and John Quincy Adams (141 Franklin St.), Josiah Quincy House (20 Muirhead St., Wollaston), and Adams family graves at First Parish Church (1306 Hancock St.); 1.

Great Esker Park (11 m SE via SR 3A to 402 Essex St. in Weymouth), 138 acres with nature museum and trails (1), open in summer; World's End (14 m SE, N off SR 3A), 249 acres on a point in Hingham Bay, trails (1), views, natural and landscaped areas; Wompatuck State Park (14 m SE, S off SR 3A on Free St., Hingham), 3000 acres, birdwatching, trails (1, 2), camping, picnicking.

Blue Hills Reservation (N of SR 128 on SR 28 & SR 138) has nature and hiking trails (1, 2), nature museum, picnicking, recreational facilities. Ponkapoag Burying Ground (12 m S off SR 138 to Indian Lane, off York St. in Canton), 15 acres with trails to Indian cemetery; 1. Moosehill Wildlife Sanctuary (15 m S on US 1, E on SR 27 to Moose Hill Rd., Sharon), 260 acres with self-guiding trails; 1. Ames Nowell State Park (19 m S via SR 3, 37 near Brockton), picnicking, trails (1). Standish Museums (27 m SE via SR 3, 18 in E Bridgewater) has guided tours of 18th-C apothecary, other bldgs, historic exhibits, museum in 18th-C church (Mon.–Sat. 9-5, Sun. 1-5; adm); 1. Walpole (26 m SW on SR 1A) has a Memorial Park, Town Forest, Bird Park; 1. Rocky Woods Reservation (18 m SW off SR 109, N of Medfield on Hartford St.), trails through woods to quarry, observation tower, duck pond, picnic areas (Tues.–Sun. 10-sunset, all yr; sm adm); nearby is a wonderful Rhododendron Swamp; 1. Stony Brook Nature Center & Reservation (28 m SW via SR 109, 115 to North St., Norfolk), 200 acres with self-guiding trails; 1.

CAPE COD: Chamber of Commerce (Hyannis 02601) will send information on historic sites, oceanfront tours, attractive towns (Provincetown is the liveliest), and ocean and lake beaches. Cape Cod Canal, for bikers and walkers, accessible on N from Scusset State Park, Sagamore bridge, Bournedale's Herring Brook Fishway, Bourne Bridge (Bourne Scenic Park here has camping, picnicking, swimming, Apr.-Oct.); on S, from Sandwich Boat Basin, Pleasant St. in Sagamore, Bourne Bridge; 1.

Sandwich: Gristmill; old cemetery; state game farm and fish hatchery; Heritage Plantation (Pine St.), 76-acre landscaped estate, nature trails, rhododendron gardens, museums, other attractions, picnicking (May-Oct. daily 10-5; adm); Shawme-Crowell State Forest (US 6, S of canal), camping, short trails; Aptuxet Trading Post (S at Bourne), trading post replica, windmill, other displays (daily spring–fall; adm); Lowell Holly

Reservation (6 m S on SR 130), 500 holly trees on land jutting into Wakeby Lake, swimming, picnicking (daily); **Ashumet Wildlife Sanctuary & Holly Reservation** (off SR 151 at County & Ashumet Rds). self-guiding trails past holly, rhododendron, other plants (open daily in daylight; free); **Saconesset Homestead Museum** (15 m S on SR 28A in W Falmouth), 15-acre restoration (mid-June–mid-Oct., Mon.–Sat. 10-6; adm).

Barnstable: Sandy Neck Beach (off SR 6A), dunes, salt marsh, picnicking (daily in summer; weekends spring & fall; adm). Yarmouth Port: Historical Society of Old Yarmouth (Gate House, behind post office) offers maps for **Botanic Trails** (June–Oct. daily 10:30-5; sm adm). W Brewster: **Cape Cod Museum of Natural History** (SR 6A), exhibits, educational program, guided walks, nature trails (mid-June–Oct., Mon.–Sat. 10-5, Sun. noon-5; rest of yr. Tues.–Thurs. & Sat. 9:30-4:30, Sun. 1-4:30; sm adm). E Brewster: **Nickerson State Park** (SR 6A), swimming, camping, picnicking, trails **(1, 2)** in woods around ponds. Chatham: **Monomoy Island National Wildlife Refuge** is reached by boat from Chatham docks; catches unloaded on pier in afternoons; **Kate Gould Park** has gardens; **Chase Park** has 1797 gristmill; **1**. S Wellfleet: **Wellfleet Bay Wildlife Sanctuary** (off US 6), outstanding self-guided trails on 650 acres, beach-buggy wildlife tours in summer (open daily in daylight; adm); **1**.

Cape Cod National Seashore preserves 45 m of beach, glacial ponds, marshes, dunes, forest. **Salt Pond Visitor Center** (N of Eastham on US 6), on Nauset Marsh (daily 9-5; 8-6) in summer; interpretive displays, nature programs, guided walks; beautiful self-guiding trails **(1)**; swimming at Nauset Beach (one of best on Cape), Nauset Light and Coast Guard Beach; picnicking. **Marconi Station** (E of US 6, S of S Wellfleet), outdoor exhibit on wireless; beach. **Great Island** (W of Wellfleet off US 6), peninsula on bay; lovely 4-m trail its length **(1, 2)**. **Pilgrim Heights** (N of N Truro, E of US 6), good swimming beach; display on Pilgrims; trail **(1, 2)** down to a swamp; Pilgrim Spring; picnicking. **Province Lands Visitor Center** (Race Point Rd., Provincetown), (mid-Apr.–Labor Day 9-5; interpretive displays; bay and ocean beaches; beech forest, dune trails **(1, 2)**; picnicking.

FITCHBURG: Coggshall Park, trails, picnicking; trails around Burbank Hospital; **Leominster State Forest** (3½ m S on SR 31), wooded and hilly, pond, swimming, picnicking, trails **(1, 2)**; **Wachusett Mtn State Reservation** (just SW of state forest across SR 140), picnicking, wooded trails, mountaintop view **(1, 2)**. **Wachusett Meadows Wildlife Sanctuary** (13 m S on SR 3 to Goodnow Rd., Princeton), 960 acres of meadows, forest, 100-acre maple swamp with boardwalk, other trails **(1, 2)**, museum, picnicking; nearby Redemption Rock Reservation and **Mid-State Trail** (information from Appalachian Mtn Club). **Pearl Hill** and **Willard Brook**

State Parks (5 m N on SR 31) adjoin; pleasant hills, ponds, woods, falls; swimming, camping, picnicking; hiking (**1, 2**). **Fruitlands Museums** (14 m E on SR 2 to Prospect Hill off SR 110 in Harvard) includes Fruitlands (18th-C farmhouse of vain attempt to start a Transcendentalist community; memorabilia of Alcotts, Emerson, Thoreau); Old Shaker House (furniture, handcrafts; ask directions for old Shaker cemetery, trail to holy hill); Picture Gallery; American Indian Museum; May–Sept., Tues.–Sun. 1-5; sm adm.

MARTHA'S VINEYARD: At **Edgartown,** Dukes County Historical Society (Cooke & School Sts.) has indoor and outdoor exhibits, herb garden (June–Sept., Tues.-Sat. 10-4:30, Sun. 2-4:30; adm); public beach; old homes; Felix Neck Wildlife Sanctuary (NW), trails on 200 acres (7-sunset); **1. Chappaquiddick Island** has Cape Pogue nature preserve; **1.** In **Oak Bluffs,** colorful cottages surround Methodist open-air tabernacle; miles of public beach; lobster hatchery (Mon.-Sat. 9-12, 1-3); Crystal Lake Wildlife Preserve (N); **1. Vineyard Haven,** public beach; **1. Menemsha,** miles of dunes and beaches; Menemsha Hills Reservation (swimming); **1.** Gay Head has dramatic cliffs of colored clay, miles of public beach, fishing docks; **1.** At **W Tisbury,** 250-acre Cedar Tree Neck Sanctuary (250 acres of woods, meadows); wildflower preserve and Indian cemetery at Indian Hill Chapel (Christiantown Rd.); **1. Martha's Vineyard State Forest** (island interior), many miles of trails, woods roads, fire lanes; **1, 2.**

NANTUCKET ISLAND: Nantucket Historical Society (information at 23 Federal St.) publishes booklets for self-guiding walking tours of wonderful homes from whaling days in **Nantucket Town;** cobblestoned Main St. especially attractive; wharves; wildflowers, other flora, lectures, tours at Natural Science Museum (7 Milk St.); public beaches include The Jetties, Brant Point. Elsewhere are quaint hamlets; public **beaches** at Dionis, Madaket, Surfside, 'Sconset, Cisco; Nantucket State Forest. **Nantucket Conservation Foundation** beaches (no lifeguards), open for beachcombing at Squam, Eel Point, Head of the Plains, Tom Nevers Reservation; **1, 2.**

NEW BEDFORD: working waterfront, whaling museum (18 Johnny Cake Hill), seaman's chapel (15 Johnny Cake Hill) described in *Moby Dick;* **Buttonwood Park** (Rockdale Ave.), botanical gardens, pond, zoo, other facilities; public **beaches** here (E & W Rodney French Blvd) and at Ft. Phoenix Beach State Park (across bay at tip of Fairhaven); **1.**

NEWBURYPORT: Chamber of Commerce (21 Pleasant St.) offers booklets for walking tours of this historic seaport, great mansions built along High St. by sea captains and ship owners (several open June-Sept.,

Tues., Thurs., Sat. 1-5; sm adm); **1. Parker River National Wildlife Refuge** (5 m E), 6 m of beach and dunes; 7-m drive; trails (1), nature trail; picnicking; open daily in daylight; free. **Salisbury Beach State Park** (5 m N via US 1, SR 1A), ocean beach, camping, picnicking; **1.**

PLYMOUTH: Visitor Information Center (N Park Ave., also State Pier in summer), combination tickets to historic sites dating to 1620s, most near harbor in center of town; late May–mid-Oct. daily 9-9; mid-Apr.–late May & mid-Oct.-Thnks, weekends only 9-5. **Plimoth Plantation** (2 m S on SR 3A), a carefully researched reconstruction; replica of *Mayflower;* complete Pilgrim Village with homes and Algonquin Indian camp; people in period costumes demonstrate 17th-C skills; picnic area; July–Aug. 9-7, June & Sept–Oct. 9-5; Apr.–May & Nov. 10-5; adm. **1. Standish Monument State Park** (6 m N on SR 3A at S Duxbury), bay view from tower; picnicking; **Shurtleff Park** (S on SR 58), picnic grove; **Myles Standish State Forest** (S), 13,000 acres, spring-fed ponds with sandy beaches, swimming, camping, picnicking, hiking trails (1, 2).

SPRINGFIELD: For easy walks (1): **Museum Center** (State & Chestnut Sts.), fine arts, science, and historical museums; **Forest Park** (S, E of I-90, S of SR 21), nature museum, zoo, gardens, 21 m of nature trails (1); **Storrowton Village** (Eastern State Exposition Park, SR 147 in W Springfield), reconstructed 18th-C village (summer, Mon.–Sat. 1-5; adm); **Robinson State Park** (SR 147 in W Springfield, W of Storrowton Village), swimming, picnicking, trails; **Chicopee Memorial State Park** (NW of jct I-90, I-291, just N of city), swimming, picnicking. **Ludlow State Park** (11 m NE off SR 21), picnicking, trails; **1. Laughing Brook Wildlife Sanctuary** (7 m E via SR 21 to 789 Main St., Hampden), 100 acres, nature trails, museum, small zoo, picnicking; Tues.–Sat. 10-5, Sun. 1-5; closed Jan. 1, Thnks, Dec. 25; adm; **1. Norcross Wildlife Sanctuary** (12 m E on Wales Rd., Monson), 3000 acres, wooded hills, pretty streams, historic ruins, picnicking; **1, 2. Arcadia Wildlife Sanctuary** (8 m N on I-95, 5 m N off SR 141), 600-acre preserve on a Connecticut River oxbow; observation tower; guided walks; self-guiding trails (1); sunrise-sunset all yr; sm adm. **Childs Park** (20 m N on I-91 to Elm St., Northampton), 22 landscaped acres, and **Look Park** (2 m NW on SR 9), 210 acres with deer park, swimming pool, lake, tiny zoo, picnicking, trails; **1. Hampton Ponds** (7 m N on US 5, 4 m W on US 202), swimming, picnicking; **1. Mountain Park** (9 m N on US 5, just beyond Holyoke), zoo, picnicking, rides; **1. Mount Tom Reservation** (12 m N on US 5), lake, observation towers, small zoo (summer), picnicking, camping; nature trail, ridge trail (to 1210-ft Mt Tom), other trails (1, 2). **Rattlesnake Gutter** (26 m N on I-91, 7 m E off SR 116 at Leverett) is a steep ravine ending in 100-ft cliffs; **1, 2.**

WESTFIELD: Stanley Park (2 m W off US 20), beautiful rose and other gardens; 5-acre arboretum; lily ponds; trails (1) on 125 acres; dinosaur tracks, reconstructed mill; carillon; mid-May–mid-Oct., 8-sunset; free.

WORCESTER: Elm Park (Park Ave. & Highland St.) and **Green Hill Park** (Lincoln St., S of I-290) are attractive, the latter with reindeer, buffalo, children's zoo. **Worcester County Horticultural Society** (30 Elm St.) has seasonal flower shows. **Lake Quinsigamond** (E end of city), 7-m long, has water sports, picnicking, swimming at state park on shore. **Worcester Science Center** (222 Harrington Way) has excellent indoor exhibits, omnisphere, outdoor exhibits in 50-acre park with zoo, ponds, Botanical Gardens, streams, wooded walks (1); Mon.–Sat. 10-5, Sun. noon-5; closed hols; adm. **Goddard Memorial Park** (4 m S on SR 12 in Auburn), where Dr. Goddard's first liquid-fuel rocket was launched in 1926, has rocket models. **Edmond Hill Woods** (9 m E off I-290 at Northborough) has trails; **1. Whitehall State Park** (16 m E via SR 30, 135 in Woodville) has wooded trails (1, 2), swimming pond, picnicking. **Buck Hill Conservation & Education Center** (10 m W on SR 9 to McCormick Rd., Spencer), self-guiding trails (1) on 300 acres; open all yr. **Spencer State Forest** (10 m W on SR 9, S on SR 31), swimming, picnicking; wooded trails (1, 2). **Rutland State Park** (13 m NW on SR 122), on a large pond; camping, picnicking; trails in woods (1). **Wildwood Nature Center** (31 m NW on SR 122 to South St., Barre) has self-guiding nature trails (1) on 40 acres. Nearby **Cooke's Canyon** with trails (1, 2). **Worcester County Horticultural Society Experimental Apple Orchard** (5 m SE on SR 140 to 24 Creeper Hill Rd., Grafton), with 100 varieties on labeled trees; in May (when trees bloom) & Sept.–Oct. (when apples ripen), daily 9-5; free; **1.** Nearby **Blackstone River Valley Park** has hiking trails (1). **Purgatory Chasm State Reservation** (8 m S at Sutton) has walks (1).

MICHIGAN

BATTLE CREEK: Leila Arboretum (W Michigan Ave.), 72 acres with paths (1) and Kingman Museum of Natural History; **Oak Hill Cemetery** (South Ave. & Oak Hill Dr.), graves include Sojourner Truth's; **Willard Beach** (2 m S on Goguac Lake), landscaped beach, picnicking (daily in summer; adm); **Charles Binder Park** (7500 Division St.), picnics, camping, (June-Aug. daily; sm adm); **1. FFA Forest** (20 m S at Union City), 15-acre educational facility and wildlife sanctuary; **1. W. K. Kellogg Bird Sanc-**

tuary (13 m NW off SR 89), run by Michigan State University; woods, lake, experimental farm, interpretive center; daily 8-sunset; sm adm; **1.**

BAY CITY: Gardens in landscaped park along river. **Bay City State Park** (5 m N on SR 24), on Saginaw Bay; nature museum (summer), water sports, camping, picnicking; **1. Sleeper State Park** (56 m E on SR 25), 963 acres with water sports on Lake Huron; interpretive trail along dunes; guided walks; camp and picnic areas; **1. Port Crescent State Park** (62 m E on SR 25), similar facilities. Beach walks at **Grind Stone City** (grindstones on beach), **Huron City** (restored lumbering town with museums and Huron Lighthouse Park), other points along shore. At **Saginaw** (10 m S on SR 13) are a children's zoo (S Washington St. & Ezra Rust Dr.); **Tokushima Friendship Garden** (Ezra Rust Dr.), Japanese garden; **Saginaw Rose Garden** landscaped over city reservoir; several parks; **1.**

BENTON HARBOR: Sarett Nature Center (Benton Center Rd.), 175 acres, boardwalks over floodplain (Tues.-Sun.); **Benton Harbor Fruit Market** (2 m E on Territorial Rd.), large farmers' market (mid-May-mid-Nov., Sun.-Fri. 8-6); **Deer Forest** (2 m N off I-94 at Coloma), 30 acres, deer, picnicking (late May-Labor Day daily; adm); **1. Warren Dunes State Park** (13 m S off I-94), 1500 acres on Lake Michigan, 2-m beach, great dunes, forest; naturalist programs, guided walks; swimming, camping, picnicking; **1. Van Buren State Park** (18 m N on I-196), 343 acres on Lake Michigan, dunes, camping, picnicking, swimming; **1. Fernwood, Inc.**, (25 m SE on US 31 to 1720 Rangeline Rd., Niles), 90 acres, nature programs and trails **(1)**; Apr.-Oct., Tues.-Sun.

BIG RAPIDS: Walking **(1, 2)** and camping at **Paris Park** (6 m N in Paris), **Chippewa River State Forest** (one unit 24 m NE off US 10, another unit 10 m SE of town), **Chippewa Lake** (10 m E), and **Browers Park** (8 m S on US 131 in Stanwood).

   Manistee National Forest (W on SR 20), 481,000 acres, has trails **(1, 2)** from campgrounds in mtns (N end), at many lakes, on Lake Michigan beach, and along fishing streams and rivers (including lovely Manistee and Muskegon rivers); tree nursery (at Wellston, N end); **Loda Lake Scenic Area** with wildflowers.

CHARLEVOIX: Public beaches on Lake Michigan; water sports, camping, picnicking at **Young State Park** (SE, on N shore of Lake Charlevoix) and **Petoskey State Park** (20 m NE on US 31). **Shore Drive** (SR 131 N of Petoskey) is Michigan's most beautiful road; signs to points of interest; passes Harbor Point, a wealthy summering area where cars are prohibited. **Beaver Island** (ferry from city dock, 103 Bridge St.,

Apr.–Dec.), 14-m long, scenic beaches and roads, 7 inland lakes; S half of island is Jordan River State Forest, with campsites; **1.**

DETROIT: City map at **Dept. of Public Information** (1008 City-County Bldg., Civic Center, Woodward St. at river); **Ft. Wayne** (6053 W Jefferson Ave.), 15 acres on Detroit River with museums, restored fort buildings (Wed.–Sun. 10-5:45; closed Thnks, Dec. 25-Jan. 1; sm adm); **Detroit Zoological Park** (8450 W Ten Mile Rd. in Royal Oak), daily exc Jan. 1, Thnks, Dec. 25 (sm adm).

At Dearborn, **Greenfield Village & Henry Ford Museum** (Oakwood Blvd., ½ m S of US 12), 260 acres, consists of a re-created community demonstrating early American industry and home life in nearly 100 original homes, shops, other 17th-19th-C bldgs; fine arts, mechanical arts, other exhibits; amusements, activities; daily in summer 9-6; rest of yr, Mon.–Fri. 9-5, weekends & hols 9-6; closed Jan. 1, Thnks, Dec. 25; adm; **1.**

William P. Holliday Park (W on SR 153, then N to between Joy & Warren Rds., Westland), 500-acre wildlife sanctuary on Tonquish Creek; 12 m of trails **(1, 2)**. **Nankin Mills Nature Center** (W on SR 14 to 33175 Ann Arbor Trail, Westland), 500 acres with historic bldgs, trails **(1)**, nature programs (Tues.–Sun.; closed hols). **Franklin Historic District** (9 m NW off US 10 in Franklin) preserves early-18th-C bldgs; **1. Trinity Museum** (10 m N off I-94 to 47460 Sugar Bush Rd., Mt. Clemens), turn-of-the-century farm (Mon., Tues., Thurs. 2-8, Fri. 2-5:30, Sat. & Sun. noon-5; closed hols; donation); **1. Cranbrook** (17 m N on SR 1 to Lone Pine Rd., Bloomfield Hills), cultural and educational complex; art and science museums; 36-acre nature center; 50-acre Cranbrook Gardens with formal and informal plantings; sculpture court; cascades; paths **(1)**; daily May-Oct.; adm. **Drayton Plains Nature Center** (25 m NW on SR 1 to 2125 Denby Dr., Drayton Plains), trails on 137 acres (Tues.-Sun.; closed Jan. 1 Thnks, Dec. 25); **1. Seven Ponds Nature Center** (42 m N off SR 53 at 3854 Crawford Rd., Dryden), 200 acres, trails **(1)**, interpretive programs; daily. **For-Mar Nature Preserve & Arboretum** (63 m N on I-75 in Flint), 380 acres; nature trails; interpretive programs; Mon.–Fri. 9-6, also Sat. & Sun. noon-6 in winter; free; **1.**

Parks with walking and picnicking include: **Belle Isle** (via Macarthur Bridge), island in Detroit River, nature center, Dossin Great Lakes Museum (Wed.–Sun.; closed Thnks, Dec. 25–Jan. 1; adm), children's zoo (summer), aquarium (daily; free); conservatory (daily; free); recreational facilities; **1. Civic Center Park** (26000 Evergreen Rd.), 179 acres; 45-acre nature area with interpretive center; **1. Hudson Mills** (12½ m NW of Ann Arbor on N Territorial Rd.), 600 acres, lagoon nature trail; information on other parks on Huron River in Dexter area; **1, 2. Kensington** (33 m NW on I-96), beaches, nature trails and nature center on Kent Lake;

Lower Huron (26 m W on I-94), 1000 acres on Huron River, nature trails, water sports; **Metropolitan Beach** (22 m NE off I-94), water sports on 550 acres on Lake St. Clair; **Palmer** (8 m NW on Woodward Ave. to 800 Merrill Plaisance), sports facilities; **River Rouge** (14250 W Outer Dr.), 1200 acres with nature museum, small zoo, trails, recreational facilities; **Stony Creek** (26 m N off SR 53), beaches, nature center with trails, scenic; **Willow** (N of Flat Rock off US 25), 1000 scenic acres on Huron River, and nearby **Oakwoods Nature Center** (17845 Savage Rd.), with prairie, marsh, stone quarry on 350 acres.

At **Ann Arbor** (36 m W on I-94), University of Michigan offers information and tours from Visitor Relations Office; art, archaeology, natural history, other museums; **Nichols Arboretum** (Geddes Ave.), 125 acres (open daily in daylight); **Botanical Gardens** (5 m NE at 1800 Dixboro Rd.), 200 acres (closed hols); free; **1. Pinckney** (14 m NW of Ann Arbor via Dexter) and **Waterloo** (18 m NW of Ann Arbor via I-94) State Recreation Areas adjoin; forested hills; many small lakes; interpretive trails (1) at Silver Lake (2 m), Crooked Lake (5 m); maps for 17-m Potawatomi Trail (2); outdoor centers near Walsh and Cedar lakes; Waterloo Historical Museum (open summers); other features; swimming, camping.

ESCANABA: Ludlington Park (on SR 35), on Little Bay de Noc, has Delta County Historical Museum (mid-May–Aug. daily 1-9; sm adm), picnicking, swimming, sports facilities; **1. Bay de Noc State Forest** is in several sections N & S of town; **Menominee State Forest** (15 m S on SR 35) along Michigan lakefront; **Escanaba River State Forest** is NW; **1.**

Hiawatha National Forest (W unit—see also Sault Sts. Marie) extends E to Manistique and N to Lake Superior; **Ogontz Visitor Center** (25 m NE on US 41, 2) is start of self-guiding Ogontz Natureway, a short auto tour with stops for walking (1) at interpreted sites; lovely forest with frontage on lakes Michigan and Superior, many lakes, canoeing rivers, streams, gently rolling, forested country. Interpretive trails (1) at campgrounds at **Mormon Creek** and **Camp 7 Lake** (NE of Ogontz), **Haymeadow Creek** (NW of Ogontz), **Widewaters** (N of Ogontz); scenic picnic area (1) with Lake Michigan overlook at **Peninsula Point** (SW of Ogontz); **Bay de Noc-Grand Island Trail** (1, 2) runs 27 m N along Whitefish River bluff from Indian Trail (on US 2) to Trout Lake (E of Trenary off SR 7); **Haywire Trail** (1, 2) runs from Shingleton SE to Manistique River State Forest; **Big Island Lakes Wilderness** (NW of Steuben) is lake-dotted area, 30 m of old roads (1, 2); **Rock River Canyon** (N of Chatham off FS 2279), 1-m trail to falls, 5-m trail along stream between sheer sandstone walls (1-3); **Bay Furnace** campground (NW of Munising), on Lake Superior, scenic, historic (1). Information: Escanaba 49829.

GRAND RAPIDS: Riverside walks **(1)** at **Comstock Riverside Park** (Monroe Ave.) and **Johnson Park** (on SR 11). **Heritage Hill** (Michigan & Pleasant Sts., Union & Lafayette Aves.) has many Victorian mansions, 2 Wright homes; tours periodically; **1. John Ball Zoological Garden** (Fulton St. & Valley Ave.) open daily; **1. Blandford Nature Center** (5 m NW at 1715 Hillburn Ave.), 108 wooded acres, nature trails, interpretive center, Pioneer Heritage complex with farm and garden; Mon.–Fri. 9-5, Sun. 2-5; closed hols; free; **1. Animal Kingdom Wildlife Refuge** & Recreation Area (10 m S off US 131 on S Division Ave. in Byron Center), field and forest paths, interpretive program, small zoo, picnicking; daily May–Labor Day; adm; **1. Yankee Springs State Park** (22 m S off SR 37), 5000 acres on scenic swimming lakes; trails **(1, 2)** in glades, woods, hills; camping; picnicking; adj 13,000-acre game area. **Saugatuck Beach** (26 m S off I-196) is on Lake Michigan; **1.**

Holland (21 m SE on I-196) has Windmill Island with Dutch atmosphere, canals, windmill, tulip gardens, bird sanctuary, other attractions (May–Oct. daily; adm); Dutch Village, with Dutch atmosphere (daily; closed Jan. 1, Thnks, Dec. 25; adm); **Holland State Park** (7 m W off US 31), 142-acre beach on Lake Michigan, camping; **1.**

GRAYLING: Surrounding city are **state forests** with campsites (usually on water sports lakes or canoeing rivers) that make good bases for walking **(1, 2)**: **Kalkaska** (W), with Manistee River; **Jordan River** (NW), with branch of Sturgeon River; **Pigeon River** (NE), several rivers; **Au Sable** (E), with Au Sable branch; **Houghton Lake** (S), with stunning Higgins, Houghton, and St. Helen lakes, all with pine-fringed, sandy beaches, several streams and rivers. **State parks** with picnicking, camping: **Hartwick Pines** (7 m NE on SR 93), 9138 acres with 80-acre grove of virgin forest; interpretive trail **(1)**; logging camp bldgs and historical museum; attractive trails **(1,2)**, with 2½-m trail looping along lovely E Branch of Au Sable River. W of here (7 m beyond Frederick) are ghost lumbering town of **Deward** and Michigan Dept. of Natural Resources' unusual **pine stump preserve; 1.**

HOUGHTON: Gateway to great Keweenaw Peninsula copper mining area; mine tours at **Arcadian** copper mine (1 m E of Hancock on SR 26) daily in summer (adm); **Houghton County Historical Museum** (SR 26, 11 m NE of Hancock at Lake Linden), daily in summer (sm adm), provides background. The peninsula, a resort area, has many former mining towns (now almost ghost towns) and quaint fishing villages to explore; a typical mining village is **Calumet** (11 m N of Hancock on US 41); a good ghost town is **Central** (4 m N of Phoenix on US 41); interesting cemetery at **Eagle**

River (2 m NW of Phoenix on SR 26); SR 26 from Eagle River to Copper Harbor has several waterfalls, agate beaches, lovely scenery. **Ft. Wilkins State Park** (at Copper Harbor), 190 acres, has restored bldgs of historic army post; historic and natural history museums; bldgs open May–Oct. (sm adm); guided walks, interpretive programs; trails (1) on Lake Superior shore, in woods; camping; picnicking.

Whitehouse Nature Center (11 m N on US 41 to S Hanna St. in Albion), 87 acres; trails; all yr; **1. State parks** with swimming, picnicking, camping, and walks (1, 2) on wooded trails are: **McLain** (10 m N on SR 203), 380 scenic areas on Lake Superior and Bear Lake; **Twin Lakes** (24 m S on SR 26), sandy beaches; **Baraga** (28 m SE on US 41), rocky shore on Keweenaw Bay.

Isle Royale National Park is archipelago near Canadian border; largest island (with almost all facilities) is reached by summer boat service from Houghton or Copper Harbor (or from Grand Portage, Minn.) or by chartered boat out of season (smaller islands can be reached from large one by good canoeists, or with boat service); lodging at chief ports, Windigo (SW) and Rock Harbor (NE); campsites dot island. Interpretive programs, guided walks, self-guiding trails (1). Most of the 160 m of trail start at Windigo or Rock Harbor; toughest trail (2, 3) is **Greenstone Ridge** (highest point 1377 ft), running 42 m length of island between ports; **Minong Ridge** (2, 3), slightly lower, runs from Windigo to McCargoe Cove, where it connects to Greenstone; either takes 4-5 days (return by boat or plane) or can be lengthened by adding side trails that rise from coves to meet them. Valley trails to lakes and bogs are easier (1-2). Travel off trails is difficult because of bogs and swamps. Information: 87 N Ripley St., Houghton 49931.

IRONWOOD: Hq for **Ottawa National Forest** (E via US 2), 900,000 acres; lakes, streams; 3 sets of falls on Black River (N of Bessemer), plus picnicking and other activities at **Black River Harbor;** falls at **Agate** and **Bond** (SE of Bruce Crossing), **Sturgeon** (SW of Baraga), with hike (2) in gorge; iron and copper mine remains; many camping, picnic, swimming areas. **Little Girl's Point Park** (18 m N off US 2 on Co 505 N to Lake Superior), picnic and camp sites at beach with multicolored pebbles; Indian cemetery; **1, 2. Lake Gogebic** (27 m E on SR 28), 361 acres, sandy swimming beach on huge lake; trails (1); camping, picnicking. **Sylvania Recreation Area** (51 m SE on US 2 at Watersmeet) has Visitor Center with interpretive programs; beautiful area studded with lakes; miles of easy, winding trails (1, 2); swimming, camping, picnicking.

Porcupine Mountains Wilderness State Park (30 m E on SR 28, 18 m N on SR 64, then W), with Porcupine Mtns (highest range in Midwest) rising 1300 ft above Lake Superior; 58,000 scenic acres; cabins, shelters, camping, picnicking, swimming. The 80 m of wonderful trails (1-3) start from

SR 107, S Boundary Rd., or from camp and picnic sites; 16-m trail along rugged Lake Superior shore; trails to ridges and peaks for overlooks; 11-m trail along Little Carp River; shorter trails along streams, to lakes, mine remains, and springs, through forests; trail to falls on Presque Isle River; 2-m trail to wilderness area at Lost Lake.

JACKSON: Sparks Foundation County Park (SW end on Brown St.), 465 landscaped acres; cascades, canals, lakes (sm adm); **Ella Sharp Park** (S end, at 3225 4th St.), 530 acres, gardens, picnicking, sports, museum (sm adm); **1. Clark Lake** (10 m SE off US 127), 550 acres, beaches, woods; **1. Hayes State Park** (23 m SE via US 127, 12), on Round and Wampler's lakes; swimming, picnicking, camping, short walks **(1). Hidden Lake Gardens** (29 m SE via US 127, 12, SR 50 at Tipton), 620-acre arboretum run by Michigan State University; gardens; conservatory of tropical plants; picnic area; all yr; sm adm; **1.**

KALAMAZOO: Chamber of Commerce (500 W Crosstown Pkwy) provides information; **Bronson Park** (South St.) has walks **(1); Kalamazoo Nature Center** (7000 N Westnedge Ave.) has trails, interpretive center, farmyard, arboretum on 512 acres (Mon.-Sat. 9-5, Sun. 1-5; closed some hols, 2 weeks after Labor Day; sm adm).

LANSING: Carl G. Fenner Arboretum (2020 E Mt. Hope Ave.), nature center with animals, Indian garden, prairie and pioneer exhibit (daily; free); **Woldumar Nature Center** (5539 Lansing Rd.), 188 acres, nature trails (Mon.-Sat.), **Potter Park** (1301 S Pennsylvania Ave.), 100 acres on Red Cedar River, zoo, picnicking; **Francis Park** (Moores River Dr.), on Grand River, walks; **1. Michigan State University** (in E Lansing) has attractive 5000-acre landscaped campus with Beal-Garfield Botanical Gardens and Horticultural Gardens; **1.**

LUDINGTON: Stearns & Waterworks Parks; Lake Michigan bathing beach; **Ludington Hydroelectric Plant** (S Lakeshore Dr.), scenic overlook, picnicking; **1. Ludington State Park** (8½ m N on SR 116), 3705 acres of woodland and 3-m beach on Lake Mich; 25-m trail system **(1, 2)** through woods, along a low ridge, around lakes, or on Big Sable River; picnic and camp area; naturalist-led hikes.

MACKINAW CITY: Michilimackinac State park (S end of Mackinac Bridge) has reconstructed bldgs of Ft. Michilimackinac; historic displays; musket and cannon demonstrations in summer; mid-June-mid-Oct., daily; adm includes Mackinac Maritime Museum.

    Mackinac Island (boats from Mackinaw City or St. Ignace), a national historic landmark where autos are prohibited (bikes, carriages, horses, many hiking trails), has State Park Visitor Center (Huron St.), mid-June–Labor Day, daily 9-5; points of interest include Ft. Mackinac on bluff above harbor, blockhouses, dungeon, other original bldgs, exhibits, musket and cannon demonstrations (late May–Sept. daily; adm); American Fur Co. Trading Post (Mackinac Island village), established by John Jacob Astor in 1809; historic houses; museums; mission church; Beaumont Memorial, dedicated to medical pioneer (mid-June–Labor Day, daily 11-5; free); Marquette Park (Main St.), many varieties of lilies.

Wilderness State Park (11 m W), on Lake Mich, is 6925 acres; rocky shoreline, swimming beaches; many miles of trail include nature trail (1), trails (1, 2) through evergreen forest to wildlife refuge and Mt. Nebo; naturalist program; camping; picnicking. **Burt Lake State Park** (29 m S off I-75 at Indian River), swimming on Burt Lake, walks on 406 wooded acres; 1. At **Wolverine** (38 m S of I-75) are Game Haven (1375 Shire Rd.), a wildlife ranch (open Memorial Day-Oct. daily; adm), and a trout rearing station; 1. **Black Lake State Forest** (18 m SE off US 23), with Lake Huron frontage; on Black Lake beaches (N of Onaway on SR 211) are FS campground and **Onaway State Park** (swimming, camping, picnicking: many short, wooded trails: picnicking at falls at Ocqueoc; Huron beach and wooded trails, swimming, camping, picnicking at **P. H. Hoeft State Park** (4 m NE of Rogers City on US 23); 1.

MANISTIQUE: Manistique River State Forest (N and SW of town) has camping on creeks and on Manistique River; **Bay de Noc State Forest** (SW) has camping on Lake Michigan; **Mackinac State Forest** (NE) has camping on Lake Michigan and on large interior lakes; 1, 2. **Palms Book State Park** (12 m NW on SR 149) on Indian Lake (W shore), has the state's largest spring; free raft trips to see underwater features; picnicking; trails (1) on 308 acres. **Indian Lake** (S shore) and **W Shore** (W shore) State Parks have camping, swimming, naturalist programs; 1. **Fayette State Park** (15 m W via US 2, then 17 m S along Big Bay de Noc) preserves ghost town of Fayette, with self-guiding tour of remains of iron-smelting operations, homes, opera house (with museum) (1); Visitor Center; scenic trail (1) from Hay Barn; camping, swimming, picnicking. At **Burnt Bluff** (5 m S of Fayette) are caves once used by Indians. **Thompson State Fish Hatchery** (7 m SW of Manistique via US 2, SR 149), daily 8-5; free.

MARQUETTE: Lakeside Park, on a bluff; **Presque Isle Park** (on peninsula in Lake Superior), nature trails, small zoo, beaches, picnic area; **Prison Sunken Gardens** (S), maintained by inmates, are best July-Aug. (all yr; free); 1. **Michigamme** and **Baraga River State Forests** (W) are in several units; camping on lakes off US 41; logging roads for walking; 1. **Van Riper State Park** (24 m W on US 41), 1100 acres on conifer-rimmed lake Michigamme and Peshekee River; remains of iron mines;

3/4-m self-guiding nature trail (1), other trails (1,2); swimming, camping, picnicking.

MENOMINEE: Stephenson Island (in Menominee River; via bridge on US 41) has historic museum, picnicking; **Riverside Park** (13th St.) has displays on a Great Lakes schooner (May–Oct. daily; adm); **Henes Park** (NE off SR 35 on Henes Park Dr.) has beach, picnicking, small zoo, nature trails (1), June-Oct.; 1. **Menominee State Forest** (N off US 41 or NE on SR 35) is in several units; camping on Menominee and Big Cedar Rivers; walks (1, 2). **J. W. Wells State Park** (23 m NE on SR 35), 981 acres on Green Bay and Big Cedar River; glades; forest trails (1, 2); naturalist programs; swimming, camping, picnicking.

MIDLAND: Chippewa Nature Center (376 S Badour Rd.), 510 acres, nature trails; **Dow Gardens** (Northwood Institute campus); several city parks; 1. Camping, picnicking at **state parks: Gladwin** (22 m N on SR 30, 6 m W on SR 61), pretty trails (1) in woods and along Cedar River, river swimming; **Wilson** (41 m NW on US 10, 27), 36 acres on Budd Lake; 1. **Tittabawassee State Forest** (N & W) has camping and trails (1) at Sanford Lake (7 m NW off US 10) and Secord Pond (5 m W on US 10, 27 m N on SR 30). **Neithercut Interpretive Ecology Center** (31 m W on SR 20 in Mt. Pleasant), 252 acres, walks (1), interpretive programs.

MUNISING: Pictured Rocks National Lakeshore (NE) on Lake Superior, one of Michigan's most scenic areas; 15 m of colorful sandstone cliffs; broad 12-m sand-and-pebble beach; 5-sq-m of sand dunes; inland are thousands of acres of forest, lakes, bogs, streams; waterfalls; old logging roads, marked hiking trails (1-3); ranger-led walks in summer; campgrounds and back-country camping. **Hiawatha National Forest** (see Manistique) surrounds city and is in turn surrounded by state forests offering recreation and many trails (1, 2); attractive areas for camping bases are Laughing Fish Point (W on SR 28), where branch of Whitefish River meets Lake Superior; Anderson, Bass, and Little lakes, and Escanaba River (in Escanaba River State Forest, SW). **Grand Sable State Forest** (E) has camping near trout rearing station (36 m E on SR 28, then N on SR 77); on Fox River (36 m E on SR 28, then NW on Co. road); and at a group of pretty lakes (Gemini, Ross, Casino, others) 15-20 m E on county roads. **Lake Superior State Forest** (E off SR 77 or N off SR 28), in Two Hearted River country, is beautiful and remote; you can explore (1-3) for days from campsites on lakes, the river; rockhounding on beaches of Lake Superior; map of Luce County helpful for reaching these, or stop at Dept. of Natural Resources office in Newberry for directions. In forest is **Muskallonge Lake State Park** (26 m N of Newberry); camping on strip of land between lakes Superior and Muskallonge; swimming;

picnicking. **Tahquamenon Falls State Park** (30 m NE of Newberry on SR 123), unusually scenic, has 2 sets of spectacular falls with trail (2) between them; self-guiding nature trail (1), other roads and trails (1, 2); walks on Whitefish Bay (1, 2); naturalist-led walks; camping, canoeing, boating, swimming; day trips in summer and for fall color by riverboat from Hulbert and Soo Junction.

Seney National Wildlife Refuge (36 m E on SR 28, 5 m S on SR 77), 95,000 acres of fens and bogs; Visitor Center (daily Apr.–Oct.) exhibits and interpretive program; hq (daily exc hols); guided (summer) or self-guided (summer–fall) auto tour; 1½-m nature trail (1); observation tower; in Seney Wilderness (W end, reachable by roads off SR 28 between Shingleton and Seney), make own trail around watery areas (2, 3); camping; picnicking.

MUSKEGON: Muskegon Lake scenic walks (1), especially at **Veterans Memorial Park** (SR 120 on N shore) and **Muskegon State Park** (4 m W of N Muskegon on SR 213), which also has 3-m beach on Lake Mich, many m of interconnecting trails (1, 2) through 1125 acres of forested dunes, picnicking, naturalist-led hikes, camping.

SAULT STE. MARIE: Soo Locks are paralleled by parks; observation towers; scale model; information bldg; daily; free.

Hiawatha National Forest (E unit—see also Escanaba) is bounded by lakes Superior, Michigan, and Huron; Carp River (good canoeing) cuts across S; large lakes inland; national fish hatcheries (SW of Raco & on Whitefish Bay); laced with short but interconnecting trails (1, 2); some go into surrounding state forests; information station at **Point Aux Chenes** (10 m W of St. Ignace on US 2), with picnicking, sand dunes, marshes, interpretive trail (1). Interpretive trails (1) from campgrounds at **Brevoort Lake** (W of Point Aux Chenes); **Carp River** (11 m N of St. Ignace off I-75); **Foley Creek** (5 m N of St. Ignace off I-75); **Monocle Lake** (on Lake Superior), with scenic overlooks, miles of sandy shore.

TAWAS CITY: Tawas Point State Park (4 m NE off US 23) has lovely trails (1) on peninsula in Lake Huron, camping, swimming, picnicking; 1. **Oscoda State Forest** (15 m N on US 23), camping at Van Ettan Lake and on Au Sable River; 1. **Harrisville State Park** (32 m N on US 23), walks among white cedars, rare trees, wildflowers; Lake Huron beach walks (1).

Huron National Forest stretches W along Au Sable River, largest of 650 m of waterways (good canoeing); from **Lumberman's Monument** (12 m N on S bank of river on SR 65), history of logging interpreted on auto tour along river; Island Lake camp (off SR 33, 6 m N of Rose City) interpretive trail (1); pretty beaches on forested lake shores (1); beautiful **Michigan Hiking Trail** (see Traverse City) starts at Tawas City and, following Au Sable River, cuts across into Au Sable State Forest (1, 2); **Tuttle Marsh Wildlife Area** (N of E Tawas on US 23), dirt roads (1); camping, picnicking, swimming; information in Cadillac (zip 49601).

Ogemaw State Forest, with lakeside campgrounds, dirt roads, trails; **Rifle River Recreation Area** (20 m W on SR 55, N at Nester), 10 pretty lakes, river, streams, dirt roads, trails, guided walks, swimming, camping, picnicking; **Ogemaw Game Refuge** (12½ m W of Rose City), tame deer; 1.

TRAVERSE CITY: Clinch Park (Grandview Pkwy), beach, zoo, museum (late May–Sept.), model of Traverse City with dwarf trees; scenic drives with chances to walk along bayfront (SR 22, 37; US 31); **Traverse City State Park** (E on US 31), beach on bay; 1. Surrounding city are **Kalkaska** (E), **Fife Lake** (S), and **Betsie River** (SW) **state forests,** all with recreation areas on lakes and streams, trails (1, 2); camping, picnicking at **Interlochen State Park** (15 m SW off US 31, 180 acres between 2 lakes, sandy beaches, trails (1) in pines, guided walks; **Benzie State Park** (31 m SW via SR 72, 22), 2295 acres, on Platte River, beach on Lake Michigan; 1. From Benzie N along lake stretches beautiful **Sleeping Bear Dunes National Lakeside** (W of SR 109), which includes S and N Manitou Islands (S Manitou, with valley of stunning cedars, reached by ferry from Leland); scenic drive; dunes backed by evergreens; lakes; trails (1, 2). **D. H. Day State Park** (N tip) has 2050 acres for water sports, camping, picnicking; trails (1, 2); closed in winter.

Michigan Hiking-Riding Trail, 220-m long, cuts across the Lower Peninsula between Tawas City on Lake Huron to Traverse City on Lake Michigan; along level dirt roads through pine or hardwood forest, mostly on state or federal land; information from Chamber of Commerce (Traverse City 49684); 1, 2, 3.

MINNESOTA

AITKIN: Ak-Sar-Ben Gardens (8 m S on US 169, 3½ m W on Co 11), on Tame Fish Lake; waterfalls, fish ponds, flowers: picnic area: early June–early Oct. 9–9; adm; 1. **Wealthwood State Forest** (14 m S on US 169) is on N shore of Mille Lacs Lake (see Onamia); 1. **Rice Lake National Wildlife**

Refuge (23 m E on SR 210, S off SR 65), 18,000 acre waterfowl sanctuary with roads, trails; daily in daylight (free); camping in adj Sand Dunes State Forest, 18 m of trails; **1, 2.**

ALBERT LEA: Walks (1) at: Freeborn County Historical Museum & Village (Fairgrounds, N Bridge St.), restored 19th-C bldgs (June-Aug., Tues.-Thurs. & Sun. 2-5; Apr.-May & Sept.-Nov., Wed. & Sun. 2-5; free); Fountain Lake (NW of city), picnicking; Walnut Lake Wildlife Area (20 m W on US 16). **Helmer Myre State Park** (5 m E), 920-acre wooded island in Albert Lea Lake, wildflowers, 13 m of trails; picnic and camp sites; **1, 2.**

BAUDETTE: Lake of the Woods (12 m N on SR 172), scenic lake, partly in Canada, with 7000-m shoreline; **Northwest Angle State Forest** (on Canadian shore) accessible only by plane or boat; **Zippel Bay State Park** (20 m NW off SR 172), 2745 acres on S shore, has camping, picnicking, swimming, 10 m of trails **(1, 2.)**

BEMIDJI: Information Center (3rd St. & Bemidji Ave.) provides maps for area tours; **Lake Bemidji State Park** (6 m NE on US 71) has camp and picnic sites, swimming, 3 m of trails **(1)** on 405 acres of pine forest; surrounding city are state forests with walking **(1, 2)** and camping on wooded lakes, large rivers, streams: Buena Vista, Blackduck, and Big Fork (NE); Welsh Lake and Battleground (SE), Headwaters and Paul Bunyan (S), White Earth (SW). **Chippewa National Forest** (E on US 2), hq of the Chippewa Indians; headwaters of the Mississippi River; 2 huge reservoirs, hundreds of smaller lakes; rivers, streams; pine forests; many camp, picnic, water sports sites; miles of roads and trails **(1, 2)**; Turtle Mound Trail (off SR 35 at Cut Foot Sioux Lakes) passes prehistoric effigy mounds (nearby fish hatchery open spring-early summer, daily, free); Information: Supervisor, Cass Lake 56633. **Red Lake Indian Reservation** (26 m N via US 2, SR 89) has tours and festivals July-Aug. **Itasca State Park** (31 m SW off US 71), beautiful 30,000-acre forest; 155 lakes; 17-m scenic drive; University of Minnesota laboratories and arboretum; Indian mounds; lookout; lodging, camping, picnicking, water sports; naturalist program, guided walks; 3 m of self-guiding nature trails **(1)**, 25-m trail system **(1, 2).**

DETROIT LAKES: Surrounded by 412 small lakes; **walking (1, 2)** at: City Park (Washington St.), beach, picnicking; Hubbel Pond Wildlife Area (NE off SR 34); Tamarac National Wildlife Refuge (8 m E on SR 34, 10 m N), 47,000-acre waterfowl refuge, picnicking (daily in daylight, free); state forests.

DULUTH: Walking (1, 2) at: Minnesota Park Point Recreation Area; Leif Erikson Park (11th Ave. & London Rd.), on the lake, rose gardens, replica of Erikson's ship; Fairmont Park (72nd Ave. W & Grand Ave.) with zoo; 27-m skyline Pkway, on bluffs overlooking city, passes 4 city parks, university, other points of interest; Fond du Lac Park (jct SR 23, 210), on St. Louis River, historic interest; Jay Cooke State Park (jct SR 23, 210), 8920 acres on St. Louis River gorge, camping, picnicking, 14 m of trails. State parks with camping, picnicking are: **Moose Lake** (33 m SW on I-35), 965 acres, 2 lakes, 8 m of trails; **Banning** (53 m SW on I-35), 3355 acres, trails in scenic gorge of Kettle River; **1, 2.** Just S of Banning, at **Sandstone**, are 535-acre Northwoods Audubon Center and Sandstone National Wildlife Refuge; **1, 2.** On scenic **North Shore Dive** (US 61 NE), are state parks (see also Grand Marais): **Flood Bay** (21 m NE at Two Harbors), lovely beach **(1)**; **Gooseberry Falls** (34 m NE), 740 acres, rocky lake shore, river cascades, camping, picnicking, 6 m of trails **(1, 2)**; **Split Rock Lighthouse** (39 m NE), 1-m trail to bluff on Lake Superior **(1)**.

GRAND MARAIS: Grand Portage National Monument (38 m NE on US 61) has restored and reconstructed bldgs where voyageurs gathered for rendezvous (open summer-early fall daily); 9-m portage trail (used to bypass falls) from stockade to Ft. Charlotte (camping) on Pigeon River **(2)**. **Grand Portage State Forest** (12 m N on US 61) has walks **(1)** off roads to lakes; Good Harbor Bay (5 m S on US 61) has rockhounding **(1)**. State parks with picnicking on scenic US 61: **Kodonce River** (8½ m NE) nature trail **(1)**; **Judge C.R. Magney** (14 m NE), 4195 acres, scenic, falls, boiling rapids, camping, 3 m of trails **(1, 2)**; **Cascade River** (10 m SW), 2815 acres, camping, rocky shore on Lake Superior, narrow gorge on river, 5 m of trails **(1, 2)**; **Ray Berglund** (22 m SW), camping, trail **(1)** to cascades on Onion River; **Temperance River** (23 m SW), rock formations, rocky gorge, 5 m of trails **(1, 2)**, camping; **Cross River** (25 m SW), 600 acres, gorge trail **(1, 2)** to cascades and falls; **Caribou Falls** (33 m SW), 90 acres with gorge trail **(1)**: **George H. Crosby-Manitou** (43 m SW, 10 m NW off SR 1), 4790 rugged acres on beautiful Manitou River, camping, 9 m of trails **(1, 2)**; **Baptism River** (44 m SW), 705 acres, gorge, waterfalls, 2-m trail **(1)**.

GRAND RAPIDS: Chamber of Commerce Welcome House (jct US 2, 169) can advise you on public recreation on 4 lakes witin city limits and hundreds of surrounding lakes; city parks on the Mississippi River are Izaak Walton and Riverside; University of Minnesota Experiment Station (on US 169) offers free weekday tours of forestry and agriculture research facility; Sugar Hills (14 m SW on US 169), 1000 acres of lakes and forests, has all-year recreational facilities; state forests with lakeside campsites, walks **(1, 2)** include George Washington and Sturgeon River (NE), Savanna, Hill River (S), Land O'Lakes and Remer (SW). **Chippewa National Forest** (see Bemidji) and **Mud Goose Wildlife Area** are W. State Parks with camping, picnicking, walks **(1,2)** are: **Scenic** (40 m N off SR 38), 1300 acres, pine forests, 5 lakes, swimming, 8 m of trails; **McCarthy Beach** (20 m NW of Hibbing on Co 5), 2000 acres of pine forests, 2 swimming lakes, 11 m of trails; Savanna Portage (19 m SE on US 2, 29 m S off SR 65), 15,000 acres surrounding a historic portage linking Mississippi and St. Louis Rivers, swimming, 16 m of trails.

INTERNATIONAL FALLS: Walking (1) at Rainy River, Rainy Lake (E on SR 11), City Beach (E on SR 11). Walking **(1, 2)** at state forests: **Smokey Bear** (14 m SW off SR 11); **Pine Island** and **Koochiching** (29 m SW on US 71), with lovely campsites along Big Fork River; **Kabetogama** (25 m SE on US 53), with camping on beautiful forest-rimmed lakes. Much land in this area is owned by Boise Cascade Corp. (Midwest Woodlands Div., International Falls 56649; information office also at Effie), which provides camping and other facilities.

Voyageurs National Park (P. O. Box 50, International Falls 56649), 219,400 acres (80,000 acres of it water), still being developed, preserves part of the trade route canoed by French-Canadian voyageurs. Most of the park is on Kabetogama Peninsula (bounded by Rainy, Kabetogama, and Namakan lakes), heavily forested in evergreens; trails **(1-3)** from many campsites (most reachable by boat; check for completion of road and trail access); trails **(1, 2)** to interior lakes; bogs, sand beaches, cliffs, coves, mainland portions (along Kabetogama, Namakan, and Sand Point Lakes) are reached from country roads E off US 53 (7 & 10 m SE of Ray; E of Orr; E of Cook) and roads N from Superior National Forest; camping.

MANKATO: Tourtelotte Park (Mabel St.); **Sibley Park** (Park Lane), zoo; **Minneopa State Park** (4 m W off US 169), falls, historic site, 3½-m trail in scenic gorge, picnicking; **1. Traverse des Sioux State Park** (13 m N on US 169), historic site, 2-m trail **(1)**, picnicking. **Sakatah Lake State Park** (25 m E on SR 60), 745-acre forest, 3 m of trail **(1)**, swimming, camping, picnicking. **New Ulm** (24 m NW on SR 68), settled by Germans; historic monuments; Hermann Heights Park with observation tower, picnicking; Riverside Park (Front St.), picnics; Schell Garden & Deer Park (2 m S off SR 15), gardens, deer herd on landscaped grounds of Schell Brewery (open daily; free); **1. Flandrau State Park** (1 m S on SR 15), 836 acres, bluffs above Cottonwood River, 7-m of trails **(1, 2)**, swimming, picnicking, camping.

MINNEAPOLIS-ST. PAUL: Minneapolis Tourism Commission (15 S 5th St.) and **St. Paul Visitor Information Center** (51 E 8th St.), maps for walking tours. In Minneapolis, **walking (1)** at tree-lined Nicollet Mall, colorful downtown shopping street with sidewalk cafes, flowers, fountains, special events, contemporary architecture: immediate area is interconnected by skyways, enclosed passageways at 2nd-story level. **University of Minnesota** campus extends on either side of the Mississippi (N of I-94). Fine park system (Minneapolis Park & Recreation Board, 250 S 4th St.), 152 parks, 22 lakes, includes: **St. Anthony Falls** (Main St. SE & Central Ave.). overlooks Mississippi; **Minnehaha** (Minnehaha Pkwy & Hiawatha Ave. S), on Mississippi, with falls described in Longfellow's "Hiawatha"; adjoining **Hiawatha** and **Nokomis** (Minnehaha Pkwy & Cedar Ave.), large lakes; **Powderhorn** (35th St. W of Cedar Ave.), lake; **Loring** (Hennepin Ave. & Harmon Pl.), lake with swans; **Lyndale Park** with rose gardens on Lake Harriet.

In **St. Paul,** walking (1) from landscaped State Capitol (University & Park Aves.) to Harriet Island Park (W on Wabasha St. Bridge) on Mississippi River; Arts & Science Center (30 E 10th St.); Minnesota Historical Society (690 Cedar St.); sculpture at Dayton Plaza (7th & Cedar), Wabasha Ct. (6th & Wabasha), Garden Plaza (370 Wabasha); from St. Paul Cathedral (239 Selby at Summit) along Summit Ave. and nearby streets, with dozens of fine 19th-C homes. **Thomas Irvine Dodge Nature Center** (1668 Delaware Ave.), 185 acres, self-guiding trails, interpretive programs; open Mon.-Sat.; closed hols. **Warner Nature Center** (30 E 10th St.), 350 acres, inquire for programs. **City parks** include: Smith (6th & Sibley); Cherokee (Cherokee Ave.), city overlook; Como (N Lexington & Como Aves.). lake, formal gardens, waterfalls, exhibits in conservatory (open daily, free), zoo, amusement park; Indian Mounds (Mounds Blvd & Earl St.); Battle Creek (E off US 61); Phalen (off US 61 at Larpenteur Ave.), 2 large lakes, woods. **Gibbs Farm Museum** (2097 W Larpenteur Ave.), restored 19th-C farm, craft demonstrations; May-Dec.; adm. **Ft. Snelling State Park** (6 m SW at jct SR 5, 55), interesting 2000-acre restoration of frontier fort on bluff at confluence at Mississippi and Minnesota rivers; demonstrations of frontier life; cemetery, gardens, boat landing; 18 m of trails; open daily May-Oct.; adm; **1, 2. Carlos Avery Wildlife Area** (25 m N on I-35 at Wyoming); at N end is Sunrise Nature Center (W of Stacy on Co 19), self-guiding trails on 60 acres, project of St. Paul Science Museum.

Nearby parks with walking **(1, 2): Coon Rapids Dam** (10 m N on SR 1), on Mississippi; **Elm Creek** (14 m NW off SR 152), 5000 acres, lakes, nature center, trails, picnicking; **Morris Baker** (18 m W on US 12) and **Rebecca Lake** (23 m W on US 12, then N), reserves, lakes, swimming, camping, picnicking; University of Minnesota **Landscape Arboretum** (16 m W on SR 7, S on SR 41 to jct SR 5), 525 acres, self-guiding trails (May-Oct. daily): **Carver Reserve** (19 m W on SR 7), lakes, nature center; **Wood Lake** (7 m S on I-35 W to 735 Lake Shore Dr., Richfield), 150 acres, nature center; **Highland Lake Park** (10 m SW off US 169 on E Bushlake Rd.), lakes, picnicking, nature center.

The **St. Croix River** is being preserved as part of the National Wild & Scenic Rivers system. From Stillwater (15 m NE on SR 212), St. Croix

Scenic Hwy (SR 95) runs 30 m N to Taylors Falls; along this route are: **St. Croix Islands Scenic Reserve**, 40 acres, trails; **William O'Brien State Park** (near Copas), 530 acres, camping, picnicking, swimming, trails; **Interstate State Park** (1 m S of Taylors Falls), 165 acres, camping, picnicking, river boat trips, museum, rock formations, 5 m of trails; **St. Croix Wild River** (off US 95, 12 m NW of Taylors Falls). N of here the river is partially bordered by state forests reached via roads E off I-35, and by **St. Croix State Park** 15 m E on Hinckley on I-35 via SR 48)—30,000-acre forest, swimming, camping, picnicking, boating, 3 m of nature trails, 124 m of hiking trails (some connect to 21-m trail system of St. Croix State Forest adj on N).

MONTEVIDEO: Pioneer Village (jct SR 7, US 59), reconstructed 19th-C town, open summers (sm adm); **Lagoon Park** (SR 7) on Chippewa River; **1. Upper Sioux Agency State Park** (16 m S on US 212, SR 67), interpretive center, camping, picnicking, 7 m of trails **(1, 2)** on Minnesota River. **Lower Sioux Agency** (S on river at Morton), interpretive center; Birch Coulee State Park (2 m NE of Morton), 1-m trail on site of Sioux uprising, picnicking; **Ft. Ridgely State Park** (18 m S of Morton via SR 19, **4**), on river, fort and museum of Sioux uprising (May-Sept. daily 9-5; sm adm), camping, picnicking, 15 m of trails on 315 acres; **1, 2.**

ONAMIA: Mille Lacs Lake (4 m N on US 169), Mille Lacs Indian Reservation, Indian Museum (SW shore), 150-m shoreline, 1000 Indian mounds; on the lake are state parks with swimming, camping, picnicking, walking **(1).**

PIPESTONE: Pipestone National Monument (1 m N), sacred quarries, stone still mined for peace pipes; Visitor Center and Upper Midwest Indian Culture Center (closed Dec. 25); 3/4-m trail **(2)** past quarries, lake, falls; daily 8-5 (8-9 in summer); free. State parks with picnicking, camping, swimming; **Split Rock Creek** (8 m SW on SR 23), 1-m trail **(1)**. **Blue Mounds** (20 m SE off US 75), 3-m bluff used as buffalo trap, buffalo, 4 m of trails **(1, 2)**; **Lake Shetek**, 4-m trails, 13-m Casey Jones Trail to Slayton (continues 24 m to Pipestone), **1-3; Camden** (34 m NE on SR 23), 1100 acres, 10 m of trails **(1, 2).**

ROCHESTER: Mayo Institutions (200 1st St. SW) tours Mon.-Fri. 10, 2; closed hols; free; open Mon.-Fri.; free. **Quarry Hill Nature Center** (701 Silver Creek Rd., NE), trails on 212 acres; closed weekends & mid-July-mid-Aug.; **1. Douglas Trail** (starts at golf course W of US 52 at 55th St.), 13 m along abandoned railroad right-of-way to Pine Island; **1, 2. Oxbow Park** (8 m W on US 14, 3½ m N on Co 5), 570 acres, hiking along Zumbro River, zoo, picnicking, other facilities; May-Oct. daily; **1. Mantorville** (13 m W via US 14, N on SR 57), restored to 1880s appearance; self-guiding tour maps. State Parks with camping, picnicking: **Rice Lake** (26 m W on US 14, then N), swimming, 4 m of trails **(1)** in 285-acre forest; **Carley** (11 m E on US 14, N off SR 42), 3-m trail **(1)** in 210-acre river valley, adj wildlife area; **Whitewater** (20 m E on US 14, 7 m N on SR 74), swimming, 13 m of trail **(1, 2)** in 960-acre forest, Whitewater River gorge; **Forestville** (24 m S on US 63, 9 m SE off US 16), 1940 acres on Root River, abandoned 19th-C town (daily in summer; sm adm), 10 m of trails **(1, 2)**.

ROSEAU: Walking (1, 2) at Roseau River Wildlife Area (20 m NW via SR 11, 89), 65,000 acres; Hayes Lake State Park (22 m SE via US 89) on Roseau River, 2680 wooded acres and prairie; Thief Lake Wildlife Area (25 m S on US 89, then W) and Agassiz National Wildlife Refuge (40 m S on US 89, then W) are on lakes along Thief River; Twin Lakes Wildlife Area (32 m SW on SR 11) and Lake Bronson State Park (15 m NW on country roads), swimming, camping, picnicking, 10 m of trails on 1130 acres.

ST. CLOUD: Walking (1) at city parks: Riverside (Riverside Dr. SE), gardens, and Wilson (Riverside Dr. NE), both on Mississippi; Hester (6th Ave. N), terraced, overlooks Mississippi; St. Johns University (10 m W on US 52 in Collegeville), bldgs by Marcel Breuer. **Lake Maria State Park** (15 m SE off I-94), 1070 acres, 2 lakes, picnicking, 3 m of trails; **1.** At **Little Falls,** (31 m N on US 10), Primeval Pine Grove (W on SR 27) is a city park with zoo, virgin pines, picnicking; Charles A. Lindbergh State Memorial Park (SW), 295 acres on W bank of Mississippi, aviator's home, interpretive center (May-Oct), camping, picnicking; **1.**

SUPERIOR NATIONAL FOREST: Voyageur Visitor Center (¼ m E on SR 169), open May 15-Labor Day, daily 6 am-10 pm (closed hols); interpretive trail **(1)**; information on history and facilities in 3-million-acre forest (or write Box 338, Duluth 55801), 5000 lakes, dense evergreens, sand beaches, pretty islands, agate hunting, camping, swimming, picnicking, boating; nation's best wilderness canoeing in **Boundary Waters Canoe Area** (continuing in Canada as the Quetico Wilderness), where many hiking trails are reachable only by canoe. **Gunflint Trail,** auto route N from Grand Marais, winds through BWCA to scenic views: interpretive trails **(1, 2)** at E Bearskin and Flour Lake campgrounds; near Magnetic Rock are short trails **(2)**, 38-m-long Kekekabic Trail (starts as **2** in hilly forest but becomes **3** in wetlands W) across BWCA to Fernberg Rd. at Kawishiwi River; interpretive trail **(2)** at Trail's End campsite. Interpretive trail **(1)** at Two Island Lake camp (N of Grand Marais); nearby 3-m trail to Eagle Mtn (2301 ft, highest point in state), continues 6-m to Brule Lake lookout tower.

Sawbill Trail auto route (off US 61 at Tofte), trail (2) to 927-ft Carlton peak, interpretive trails (1) at Blister Rust research area and Sawbill Lake campground.

Echo Trail auto route (runs NW from Ely to Buyck); interpretive trail (1) at Fenske Lake campground; short spurs (1, 2) to lakes; 12-m La Croix Trail (2, 3) fairly easy to Stuart Lake but difficult forks beyond; from Meander Lake campsite, trail (2) to Ramsherd Lake, 27-m Sioux Hustler Trail (3) loops through pretty lake region; from Lake Jeanette camp, interpretive trail (1), 8-m Norway trail (2, 3) to Trout Lake. From Ely, a trail (2, 3) goes SW via lakes in Iron Range and Bear Head State Park (4110 acres, swimming, picnicking, camping, 10 m of trails) to Vermilion Lake—40-m long, wooded shores, several islands (one large enough to have its own lake)—and Tower Soudan State Park (982 acres, historic mine tours, self-guiding trails, picnicking, visitor center). Interpretive trails (1) at Pfeifer Lake campground and W of Leander Lake (SW of Tower), at Whiteface Reservoir (S of Hoyt Lakes).

WINONA: Winona Co. Historical Soc. (160 Johnson St.), country store, other displays (Sun.-Fri. 12:30-4:30), maintains steamboat Museum (Levee Park), Arches Branch Museum (11 m NW on US 14 near Lewiston), pioneer homestead; 1. City parks: Lake (Main & Lake Sts); Garvin Heights (S off Lake Blvd.) overlooks Mississippi River from bluff, trails, picnicking; Prairie Island (3 m N of US 61 via Prairie Island Rd); 1. O.L. Kipp State Park (17 m S off US 61) has wonderful views of Mississippi River, trails (1, 2). Minnesota Memorial Hardwood State Forest surrounds the city, running W to Mantorville, S to state line, N to Hastings; trails (1, 2) along many trout streams and canoeing rivers. State parks with picnicking, camping: John A. Latsch (10 m N on US 61), 2-m trail, views of Mississippi; Frontenac (40 m N on US 61), 6 m of trail on 905 acres on Lake Pepin; Beaver Creek Valley (40 m SW via US 61, SR 44, then W of Caledonia), 615 acres with steep bluffs, spring-fed stream, 7 m of trail; 1, 2.

MISSISSIPPI

COLUMBUS: Chamber of Commerce (318 7th St. N), information on 100 antebellum mansions (some open all yr, some only during spring pilgrimage); many are between the river and 5th St. (2nd-8th Ave. S), 7th-9th Sts. (3rd-7th Aves.). Waverley Plantation (10 m NW off SR 50 near W

Point), with gardens; daily in daylight; adm. **Lake Lowndes State Park** (7 m SW on SR 69), swimming, camping, picnicking **(1)**. **Noxubee National Wildlife Refuge** (25 m W on US 82, S on SR 25), 46,000 acres, lake, picnicking; walks **(1)**; all yr; free. **Tombigbee National Forest** (25 m W on US 82, 13 m S on SR 25), nature trail **(1)** at scenic Choctaw Lake campground; swimming; picnicking.

GREENVILLE: Winterville Mounds Historic Site State Park (7 m N on SR 1), ceremonial center; museum; picnicking; Tues.-Sat. 9-6, Sun. 1-6; closed Dec. 25; sm adm; **1**. **Leroy Percy State Park** (15 m S on SR 1, E on SR 12), lovely, lush vegetation along stream; alligators; swimming; camping; picnicking; **1**.

GREENWOOD: Florewood River Plantation (2 m SW on US 82), with 21 buildings, is a living history park illustrating an 1850s plantation; formal garden; adm. **Carrollton** (14 m E via US 82) has more than 20 antebellum homes (open on spring pilgrimage), old jail, courthouse, cemetery. **Wisteria Gardens** (30 m S on SR 7 at Belzoni), 14 acres; formal and informal plantings; roses, other flowers; best in Apr.; daily 6-6; free; **1**.

GULFPORT: Public beach stretches 26 m here; Tuxachanie Lake (N on US 49) with hiking trail **(1)**; fish hatchery (7 m N on US 49 at Lyman); **1**. **Pass Christian** (7 m W on US 90) has recreational facilities at War Memorial and Harbor Parks. **Buccaneer State Park** (17 m W on US 90), water sports on Gulf; **1**. **Gulf Islands National Seashore**, picnic and camp area at Davis Bayou (Ocean Spring, 17 m E off US 90), 4 stunning islands offshore; Ship Island **(1)**, with camping and Ft. Massachusetts, reached by boat from Biloxi or Gulfport (daily in summer, less frequently in spring & fall); other islands **(1, 2)** reachable by private boats.

HATTIESBURG: Paul B. Johnson State Park (16 m S on US 49), 805 acres on spring-fed lake; water sports; walks **(1)**. **De Soto National Forest** (NE & SE), ½-million acres; **Thompson Creek** camp (38 m E off SR 42) has lovely trails on creek; beautiful **Black Creek** (12 m S on US 49, then E) has float trips, tree nursery, trail **(1)** at Ashe Lake camp, trails **(1, 2)** at Moody's Landing and other creek-access campgrounds; **Airey Lake** camp (40 m S on US 49, then SE) is on 10-m **Tuxachanie Trail** (runs from US 49 to POW camp) through lush vegetation past fire tower, wildlife waterhole, experimental plots **(1, 2)**.

JACKSON: Chamber of Commerce (208 Lamar Life Bldg., 317 E Capitol St.) sponsors spring pilgrimage and has information on sites open all yr; **Battlefield Park** (Terry Rd. & US 49) has Civil War relics; **zoo** (2918

W Capitol St.), daily all yr; **Riverside Park** (jct I-25, SR 25), on Pearl River, has 4-m nature trail **(1, 2)**, swinging bridges, boardwalk, picnicking. **Mynelle Gardens** (W of town at 4738 Clinton Blvd), 10 acres with azaleas, magnolias, other flowering trees and shrubs; Japanese, bog, medical gardens; antebellum home; fountains and pools, summerhouse; daily in daylight; adm; **1. Ross Barnett Reservoir** (7 m N on I-55, 3 m E on Natchez Trace Pkwy) has walks **(1)** at public campgrounds. **Petrified Forest** (20 m NW off US 49 at Flora), trail among giant stone logs; museum; picnicking, camping; daily 9-5; closed Dec. 25; adm; **1. Roosevelt State Park** (30 m E off I-20), swimming, camping, picnicking, nature trails **(1)**. **Bienville National Forest** (30 m E on I-20), 177,000 acres; Shongelo campsite (N of Raleigh on SR 35) has trail **(1)** beside swimming lake; Marathon Lake camp (8 m E of Homewood off SR 35), trails **(1, 2)** beside swimming lake, on old railroad beds, along creek; Bienville Pines Scenic Area (2 m SE of Forest on SR 501), trail **(1)**.

NATCHEZ: Chamber of Commerce (300 N Commerce St.) or **Stanton Hall** (Pearl & High Sts.) provide maps for self-guiding tours in this showplace of antebellum mansions; most are between Mississippi River and Union St., Washington to High Sts.; all are landscaped, some have outstanding gardens.

NATCHEZ TRACE PARKWAY, paralleling the original Natchez Trace, will run 450 m from Natchez to Nashville (Tenn.); 300 m have been completed by NPS. Originally an Indian trail, it was most heavily traveled road in Old Southwest. Parkway preserves sections of original trace (in places worn so deep that the tree-lined banks rise above your head) and interprets its history. From Natchez N are: **Emerald Mound** (Mile 11), 8-acre ceremonial mound, Turpin Creek nature trail **(1)**, picnic area; **Loess Bluff** (Mile 12.5) geological area **(2)**; **Mt. Locust** (Mile 15.5), restored 1717 inn that served travelers on the trace **(1)**, **Old Trace Drive,** hiking trail **(2)**; **Coles Creek** (Mile 17.5) picnic area **(1)**; **Bullen Creek** (Mile 18.5) nature trail **(1)**; **Magnum Mound** (Mile 43), Indian burial mound **(1)**, walking on Old Trace, hiking **(1, 2)**; **Rocky Springs Park** (Mile 54), campground, nature trail **(1)**, remains of a once-prosperous town; **Dean's Stand** (Mile 77) picnic area **(1)**; **Ridgeland** (Mile 103), museum; **Boyd Mound** (Mile 107), Indian mounds **(1)**; Ross Barnett Reservoir (Mile 112), see Jackson; **Cypress Swamp** (Mile 123), boardwalk trail **(1)**, picnicking (1½ m N) overlooking bend in Pearl River; **Southern Pines** (Mile 128), nature trail **(1)**; **Yockanookany** (Mile 129) picnic area **(1)**; **Beaverdam** (Mile 145), trails over beaver dams and canals **(1, 2)**, exhibits; **Holly Hill** (Mile 150) picnic area **(1)**; **Hurricane Creek** (Mile 165) nature trail **(1)**; **Cole Creek** (Mile 176) nature trail **(1)**; **Bethel Mission** site (Mile 182) and **Yowani** (Mile 188.5) picnic areas; **Jeff Busby Park** (Mile 194.5), camp and picnic sites, nature walk and trails to rock formations, springs, 600-ft overlook **(1, 2)**; **Old Trace** (Mile 222), walking, picnicking **(1, 2)**; **Witch Dance** (Mile 231.3), picnicking, bridle paths, Bynum Mound, fossil exhibit **(1, 2)**; **Davis Lake** (Mile 243), camping, water sports, hiking in Tombigbee Ntl Forest **(1, 2)**; **Tockshish** (Mile 249), picnicking; **Chickasaw Village** site (Mile 260) with interpretive markers, nature trail featuring plants used by Indians **(1)**.

Tupelo Visitor Center & hq (5 m N of Tupelo at jct pkwy & US 45), maps, exhibits, film; working farm; craft demonstrations; nature trails **(1)**; daily; closed Dec. 25; free. N of here the pkwy is unfinished. A small section (S of Tishomingo, jct SR 25, 30) has **Bear Creek Mound** (Indian temple mound), trail to caves at **Cave Springs, Tishomingo State Park** (1400 acres; rock formations, swinging bridge; beautiful nature trails; camping; picnicking; cottages; lovely swimming lake); **1, 2**.

OXFORD: Antebellum mansions open on spring pilgrimage. University of Mississippi has a handsome campus; museums; William Faulkner's home. **Holly Springs** (30 m N on SR 7) has antebellum mansions open on spring pilgrimage. **Wall Doxey State Park** (23 m N on SR 7), 855 acres, with swimming on spring-fed lake, camping, picnicking, trails **(1, 2)**. **Holly Springs National Forest**, 143,570 acres, has recreation at Puskus Lake (8 m NE on SR 30) and Chewalla Lake (7 m SE of Holly Springs), with camping, swimming, picnicking; hiking **(1, 2)**; Indian mound; another unit (19 m SE on SR 7) has similar facilities on Tillatoba Lake.

VICKSBURG: Hospitality House (Monroe & Clay Sts.), tapes, guide service, map for self-guiding tours including antebellum homes; *Sprague,* largest sternwheeler ever built (foot of China St.); Vicksburg Bluffs views of Mississippi. Beautifully landscaped **Vicksburg National Military Park,** curving NE around the city, preserves 9 major Confederate forts, 12 Union trenches, parapets, other remains of Battle of Vicksburg; Visitor Center (off US 80; daily 8-5; closed Dec. 25; free) offers exhibits and brochures; park open daily; free; **1, 2.**

MISSOURI

CAPE GIRARDEAU: Landscaped **Cape Rock Dr.** circles the city (which sits on a rocky promontory on the Mississippi), ending at Cape Rock, site of original settlement and trading post. **Capaha Park** (Parkview Dr.), with Rose Display Garden, is open daily in daylight; free. **Trail of Tears State Park** (10 m N on SR 177), 3268 acres on bluffs over the Mississippi, commemorates Cherokee Trail of Tears; picnics; camping; nature and other trails; **1, 2.**

CHILLICOTHE: State parks with camping, picnics, trails **(1): Pershing** (25 m E off US 36), 1836 acres; **Crowder** (22 m N on US 65, 4 m W on SR 6, N on SR 128), 674 acres. **Swan Lake Ntl Wildlife Refuge** (2 m S on US 65, 19 m E on US 36, 13 m S on SR 139), observation tower, trails **(1, 2)**; Mar.–Sept.; free.

COLUMBIA: University of Missouri (Elm & 8th Sts.), maps for campus walking tours, including Botany Greenhouses, Learning Garden; 1028-acre **Strip Mine State Park; Rock Bridge State Park** (S), trails on 1385 acres, picnicking; **1, 2. Boonville** (22 m W on US 40), camping, picnicking and Indian mounds in Harley Park (Parkway Dr.) on bluffs above Missouri River, plus Boone's Lick State Historic Site (9 m NW on SR 87, W on SR 187); **1, 2. Arrow Rock State Historic Site** (28 m W on I-70, 10 m N on SR 41) preserves a once-bustling frontier town on Santa Fe Trail; homes, tavern, jail, other restored bldgs open Tues.-Sat. 10-4, Sun. noon-5; closed Jan. 1, Easter, Thnks, Dec. 25; sm adm. **Van Meter State Park** (22 m W of Arrow Rock on SR 41, SR 122), archaeological site; camping, picnicking, trails on 794 acres; **1.**

FARMINGTON: State parks with camping, picnicking, walking **(1, 2): Hawn** (13 m E off SR 32), 2257 acres of pine forest, wild azaleas; **St. Francois** (14 m N on US 67), 2403 riverside acres, swimming; **Washington** (18 m W on SR 8, 11 m N on SR 21), 1101 riverside acres, hundreds of petroglyphs, museum, swimming; **Johnson Shut-ins** (29 m SW on county roads) on rugged Black River Fork Canyon between Bell and Proflit Mtns, 2386 acres with trails in park and to surrounding 1700-ft summits. **Elephant Rocks** (5 m NW of Graniteville on SR 21), picnic area, trails through rock formations, **1, 2.**

KANSAS CITY: Convention & Visitors Bureau (1221 Baltimore), maps for walking tours including 85-acre landscaped Crown Center (opposite Union Station); Country Club Plaza (47th & Main), landscaped shopping area with Loose Park rose gardens; Civic Center (11-15th Sts., Holmes-McGee Sts.); River Quay (Delaware St.), restored waterfront; City Market (3rd-5th Sts., Main & Walnut Sts.), Mon.-Sat., closed hols; Stockyards (12-23rd Sts., Genesee St. to Kansas River). Outstanding city parks include **Swope** (Meyer Blvd & Swope Pkwy), 2 lakes, zoo, sports facilities, picnicking on 1705 acres; **Penn Valley** (W of Main, N of 31st St.), wooded, statues. **Harry S. Truman Museum** and grave (US 24 & Delaware St., Independence), daily 9-5; closed Jan. 1, Thnks, Dec. 25; sm adm. **Ft. Osage** (11 m NE of Independence on US 24, then N to Sibley), restored 1808 trading post; daily 8-5; closed Jan. 1, Thnks, Dec. 25; free. **Battle of Lexington State Park** (30 m E on US 24 at Lexington), historic displays (Mon.-Sat. 10-4, Sun. noon-5, closed hols; sm adm), camping, picnics. **Knob Noster State Park** (60 m SE off US 50 on SR 132), 3511 wooded acres, lakes, streams; swimming, camping, picnics; trails **1, 2. Fleming Park** (17 m SW on US 40 in Blue Springs), 4400 acres on Lake Jacomo, animal exhibits; self-guiding trails; Missouri Town 1885, recreated typical mid-19th-C town (daily 9-5, in summer 9-7; closed Jan. 1, Thnks, Dec. 25); park open daily yr round; free; **1.**

ROLLA: Hq (P.O. Box 937, zip 65401) for **Clark National Forest,** 791,000 acres SW and SE; forested hills, flowering trees, fall color, rivers, streams for float trips and fishing; campsites are mostly on riverbanks; trails along logging roads, waterways, and to Ozark Mtn summits (1772 ft is highest, near Pilot Knob). **Maramec Springs** (8 m E on US 66 to St. James, 6 m SE on SR 8), used to power furnace and gristmill, ironworks remains, museum, observation tower; picnicking; daily in daylight; parking fee. **Montauk State Park** (35 m S on US 63, 2 m S on SR 137, then E), 1096 acres; springs give rise to Current River (see Van Buren); camping, picnicking; naturalist programs; fish hatchery; trails **(1).**

ST. JOSEPH: Pony Express Stables Museum (914 Penn St.), terminus of Oregon Trail and Pony Express, displays historic route maps, other exhibits; May-mid Sept., Mon.-Sat. 9-5, Sun. & hols 2-5; free. **City parks (1):** Krug (N end, W of St. Joseph Ave.), Hyde (4th & Hyde Park Ave.). **Lewis & Clark State Park** (19 m SW off US 59 on SR 45, 138), 35 acres on lake, swimming, camping, picnicking; **1. Squaw Creek Ntl Wildlife Refuge** (36 m NW via US 59, off SR 111), 10-m Wild Goose Trail; **1, 2.**

ST. LOUIS: St. Louis Tourist Board (911 Locust St.), brochures for self-guiding walking tours. **St. Louis Chapter, American Institute of Ar-**

chitects (107 N 7th St.), brochures on historic sites; frequently conducts walking tours. At the waterfront is **St. Louis Visitor Center** on restored riverboat *Becky Thatcher;* other museum and cruise ships; Jefferson National Expansion Memorial with Gateway Arch and Visitor Center (daily exc. Jan. 1, Thnks, Dec. 25); Old Courthouse (daily exc. Jan. 1, Thnks, Dec. 25; free), historic exhibits; other historic sites. **Sovlard Farmers Market** (Lafayette Ave. & 7th Blvd), open Tues.-Sat. **Forest Park** (between Lindell, Skinner, & Kings highway Blvds), 1374 acres; St. Louis Art Museum; Jewel Box Floral Conservatory; Municipal Opera; Missouri Historical Society; 83-acre St. Louis Zoo; Planetarium; sport facilities; statuary, fountains; walks; picnicking; **1. Missouri Botanical Garden** (Tower Grove Ave. at Flora Pl.), 70 acres; rose garden; arboretum; flower shows; greenhouse; daily exc Dec. 25, 9-dusk; adm; **1. Hanley House** (7600 Westmoreland at Clayton), city restoration of 19th-C farm; bldgs; native plants; Fri.-Sun. 1-5; sm adm. **Grant's Farm** (Grant & Gravois Rds.), 280-acre wildlife preserve; birds, animals, Ulysses S. Grant cabin, other attractions; open for free tours by advance reservation (write Grant's Farm Tours, St. Louis 63123), mid-Apr.–mid-Oct. **Gen. Daniel Bissell House** (10225 Bellfontaine Rd.), attractive gardens; Wed.–Sat. 8-5, Sun. 1-5; sm adm; **1.**

Jefferson Barracks Historical Park (10 m S on SR 231 to 10000 S Broadway), 413-acre historic site, on the Mississippi, museums, restored bldgs, picnics; daily in summer, rest of yr Wed.-Sun.; closed Jan. 1, Dec. 25; free. **Ste. Genevieve** (50 m S via I-55, US 61), oldest permanent settlement in Missouri; French Creole homes, other historic sites; information at Historical Museum (Du Bourg Pl. & Merchant St.), Apr.–Oct. daily 9-4; Nov.–Mar., Thurs.–Tues. noon-4; closed hols; sm adm; **1. Black Madonna Shrine & Grottos** (8 m SW via I-44 to Eureka), chapel, hand-built grottos (Apr.-Oct.; parking fee). **Mermac State Park** (52 m SW on I-44, SE on SR 185), scenic 7153 acres, on Mermac River; 20 caves (tours), nature museum, game refuge, many springs; camping, picnics, swimming; trails; **1, 2. Dr. E. A. Balder Memorial State Park** (25 m W on SR 100, N on SR 109), 2445 acres, interpretive center, camping, picnicking, trails; **1. August A. Busch Memorial Wildlife Area** (15 m W at jct US 40, SR 94), 7000 acres, open under restrictions; write Manager, Route 2, Weldon Spring, St. Charles 63303. Missouri Botanical Garden's **Arboretum** (2 m W off I-44 at Gray Summit), 1800 acres, trails, open yr round; **1. Rockwoods Reservation** (12 m W on I-44, N on SR 109 to Glencoe), 1885 acres, small zoo, trails (1); all yr; closed Jan. 1, Dec. 25.

SPRINGFIELD: Historic sites include **National Cemetery; Drury College** (Benton Ave. at Central St.), Indian mounds, Civil War trenches, museums; **Wilson's Creek National Battlefield** (13 m SW via US 60, SR

22), information booth for self-guiding map (open summers), grounds open daily, free. **George Washington Carver National Monument** (60 m W on I-44, 7 m S off US 71A), farm on which Carver was born; Visitor Center open daily 8:30-5, closed Dec. 25; free.

Springfield is gateway to the Ozarks, cave tours, float trips, riding, other recreation; **School of the Ozarks** (36 m S on US 65 near Hollister), campus tours from Friendship House; **Shepherd of the Hills Farm** (7 m W of Branson on SR 76), based on writings of Harold Bell Wright, free, daily, Apr.-Nov. 15; **Silver Dollar City** (9 m W of Branson on SR 76), an 1880 Ozark mining town, demonstrations (daily in summer, inquire for spring & fall schedule; adm); **1.**

Mark Twain National Forest, 622,000 acres; unit SW of Van Buren; unit S of **Cabool** (on SR 181), hot springs, large lake, White River, hills to 1376 ft, camping, picnicking; unit at **Bradleyville** (28 m SE of Springfield), Hercules Glades (wildflowers) in S, Beaver Creek; walking **(1, 2)** mostly on logging roads. Unit 45 m S of Springfield (via US 160, SR 13) surrounds huge Corps of Engineers impoundment, Table Rock Lake, many public sites for camping, fishing, water sports, including **Table Rock State Park** (naturalist programs, nature trails); at W edge of forest, **Roaring River State Park,** 3500 acres; camping, picnicking, swimming, trout hatchery, naturalist program, nature trails; **1, 2.**

State park with swimming, camping, picnicking: **Bennett Spring** (33 m N on US 66, 12 m NW on Co roads), 1228 acres, large spring, stream, nature center, trout hatchery, nature trails **(1).**

VAN BUREN: Ozark National Scenic Riverways, along Current and Jacks Fork rivers (write Supt., P. O. Box 448, Van Buren 63965); information, guided walks, float trips, interpretive programs at **Powder Mill Visitor Center** (10 m W of Ellington on SR 106) and **Alley Spring Visitor Center** (5 m W of Eminence on SR 106), both open Memorial Day–Oct. daily (free); both have trails (1), camping. Trail also at Akers access and campsite.

Clark National Forest (see Rolla) unit E of here; Black and St. Francis rivers, springs, streams; Lake Wappapello (E end), swimming, camping, picnicking in state park; Mingo National Wildlife Refuge (NE of Wappapello), 672 acres of swamplands, trails, guided tours; **1, 2. Sam A. Baker State Park** (7 m E on US 60, 30 m E on SR 34, N on SR 143), 5148 acres, riverside trails **(1, 2),** camping, picnics.

STATE PARKS: Also for picnicking, walking: **Big Oak Tree** (10 m S of E Prairie on SR 102), 1004-acre virgin forest **(1); Thousand Hills** (4 m W of Kirksville), 3192 acres, water sports, camping, naturalist program, petroglyphs **(1, 2).**

MONTANA

BILLINGS: Chamber of Commerce (N 27th St. & Montana Ave.), information; Chief Black Otter Trail, scenic drive above valley N of city, passes Boothill cemetery, other points of interest. **Indian Caves** (5 m SW off US 212), weathered pictographs, picnicking; **1, 2. Cooney State Recreation Area** (42 m SW off US 212), water sports, camping, picnicking on reservoir; **1. Crow Indian Reservation** stretches S to Wyoming; at W end (35 m SE at Pryor), Chief Plenty Coups State Monument (195 acres; Visitor Center; graves; camping, picnicking; walks, **1**); at E end are: Crow Agency (61 m SE on I-90), cultural exhibits at Crow Indian Heritage village, camping, recreation; **1, 2. Custer Battlefield National Monument** (65 m SE on I-90, US 212), on Little Big Horn River, site of Custer's defeat by Sioux and Cheyenne; Visitor Center, exhibits, interpretive programs; 4-m road or self-guiding Entrenchment Trail **(2)** to historic sites; open daily 8-4:30 (longer spring-fall); closed Jan. 1, Thnks, Dec. 25; free.

Bighorn Canyon National Recreation Area (46 m E on I-90 to Hardin, 44 m S on SR 313), thrilling area where prairies meet foothills of Rockies; Visitor Center at Yellowtail Dam; Bighorn Lake, colorful cliffs, green canyons; water sports, camping; historic Bozeman Trail; creek, lakeside walks **(1, 2). Big Horn Mtns** (E of canyon, 12 m E of Lovell, Wyoming, on US 14A), mtn meadows, canyons, subalpine forests, streams, falls; from road (gradually deteriorates) to John Blue Canyon are trails along Cottonwood Creek, to Little Mtn, to overlook over magnificent Devils Canyon, to 3 caves; **1-3.** Campgrounds off US 14A give access to: Bald Mtn trails **(2, 3)**; trail from Medicine Wheel across Little Mtn to Devils Canyon overlook and caves **(2, 3)**; beautiful trail **(2, 3)** along Porcupine Creek to falls and beyond; road E of Porcupine Creek, trailheads **(2, 3)** to Trout and Deer Creeks. **Pryor Mtns** (W of canyon), partly in Custer National Forest, many primitive roads and trails, scenic views, wildflower meadows; S of them is colorful desert, barren red buttes, sparse vegetation; access from Sage Creek campground (E off US 310 S of Bridger), Helt Rd. (E off US 310 at Warren), or—from Wyoming—E of Frannie, N of Cowley, or NE of Lovell (off US 14A); unforgettable are primitive road and trail **(1-3)** along Crooked Creek through vivid Vermilion Canyon and 30,000-acre Wild Horse Range (access also from Sykes Ridge Rd. on E or Britton Springs in S); other trails **(1-3)** to overlooks, ice caves, springs, peaks, along waterways, to Yellowtail Wildlife area; camping, swimming, picnicking.

Red Lodge (59 m SW on US 212) Zoo (1 m S on US 212), prairie dogs, other native animals and birds on landscaped grounds (open May-Sept. daily 8-dark; adm). **Beartooth Hwy** (US 212; closed in winter), runs SW to Yellowstone Ntl Park, views of glaciers, mtns, canyons, lakes, wildflowers. **Custer National Forest** camping in a Pryor Mtn unit (W of Bighorn Canyon, which see). Larger unit is SW of Red Lodge; majestic, 230,000-acre **Beartooth Primitive Area**—wild country (often snowed in exc July-Aug.), 26 peaks over 12,000 ft, treeless plateaus, forests, alpine meadows, lakes, waterfalls—reached from campsites and rugged trails **(2-3)** along Beartooth Hwy (or off SR 307 NW of Red Lodge); at Cooke City, 14-m trail (you can rent a horse or jeep), to Grasshopper Glacier, where grasshopper are frozen into an ice cliff. Easier trails **(1, 2)** plus mtn climbs **(3)**, at campgrounds off SR 477 (W of Red Lodge), SR 425 (S of Fishtail to Mystic Lake & E Rosebud Lake), SR 419 (S from Nye along Stillwater River and to Emerald Lake). **Information:** 2602 1st Ave. N, Billings 59103.

BOZEMAN: Montana State University has an Agricultural Field Complex (College St.), livestock; open daily 8-5; closed hols & school vacations; free. **Madison Buffalo Jump State Monument** (25 m W on SR 289, N toward Logan), picnicking at interpreted site where Indians trapped buffalo. **Bear Trap Canyon Primitive Area** (30 m W on SR 289), 3639 acres, trails **(2, 3)** along river or rim of 9-m scenic Madison River Gorge; easiest access at Red Mtn campground (N end); access at S and from Montana Power Co. plant N of Ennis Lake. **Virginia City** (36 m W on SR 289, 26 m SW off US 287 on SR 287), site of Montana's 2nd biggest gold strike, restored with museums of gold-boom days, opera house, brewery, false-front buildings; gold panning, other attractions; similarly restored is Nevada City (1½ m W on SR 287); Vigilante Trail, marked from Virginia City to Bannack (see Butte). **National Fish Hatchery** (36 m W on SR 289, 28 m S off US 287) for rainbow trout is open daily 8-5; free; BLM camping (S on US 287), access to Madison River. **Missouri River Headwater State Monument** (31 m NW on I-90), lovely camping, picnicking, walks **(1,2)** at confluence of Jefferson, Madison, Gallatin rivers.

Gallatin National Forest (N & S of town; write Federal Bldg, Bozeman 59715), 1.7 million acres, snowclad peaks, 11 outstanding waterfalls, 200 lakes, trout streams. **Hood Creek** campsite (S off SR 345), lake, walks **(1, 2)**, climbs **(3)**. Scenic **Gallatin Canyon** (S on US 191), campsites with trails **(2, 3)** to perpetually snow-capped **Spanish Peaks Primitive Area** (6-11,000 ft); mtn lakes, alpine meadows, streams, craggy peaks and ridges; access also from Big Sky (off US 191) in S and via tougher trails from Ennis Lake area (off US 287) in W. **Visitor Center** (8 m N of W Yellowstone on US 191, 22 m W on US 287), maps, exhibits, interpretive programs on Madison River Canyon Earthquake Area, booklets for self-guiding tours and trails off US 287 or from many campsites in the area (open daily, free, Memorial Day–Labor Day). Camp and picnic sites along Yellowstone River (off US 89, SR 540 S of Livingston), river access **(1, 2)**; hot springs, ghost towns **(1, 2)** of Chico, Yellowstone City, and other mining remains in Emigrant Gulch (37 m S off US 89); tough wilderness climbs **(3)**. **Absaroka Primitive Area** (60-80 m S on US 89), 64,000 acres of spectacular, remote mtns with most access trails over 5-m long; access via FS road and trail **(2, 3)** E from Jardine, trails **(3)** N from Yellowstone Ntl Park, trails W from Silver Gate **(2, 3)** and Cooke City **(3)**, S from Boulder Canyon **(3)**; information: Gardiner 59030. Beautiful **Boulder Canyon** (S of Big Timber on SR 298), camp and picnic sites, riverside walks **(1, 2)** and climbs **(3)** among 10-11,000-ft peaks; access **(3)** to Absaroka Primitive Area. **Bridger Mtn** unit (N off SR 293), walks **(1,2)** at Fairy Lake, other campsites, climbs **(3)** in 9000-ft peaks. **Crazy Mtn** unit (off US 191 N of Big Timber), climbs **(3)** in 10,000-ft peaks.

BUTTE: Chamber of Commerce (100 E Broadway at Wyoming), arranges free mine tours; attractions include Copper King Mansion (219 W Granite St.); World Museum of Mining (W Park St.), reconstructed mining camp & museum displays at site of Orphan Girl Mine (open June-Sept. daily 9-9; Oct.-May, Tues.-Sun. 10-5; free). **Anaconda** (7 m W on US 10A), fish hatchery, gardens, picnicking in Washoe Park (NW edge of town); wild Daly Hotel; **1. Humbug Spires Primitive Area** (18 m S off US 91), 7000 acres of ponderosa forests surrounding white granite spires; easy paths **(1, 2)**, rock climbing from beginner to experienced **(2, 3)**. **Big Hole National Battlefield** (62 m SW of Butte on SR 43, W of Wisdom), 655-acre site of 1877 attack by U.S. Army on Nez Perce Indians attempting to escape to Canada; self-guiding battlefield trail, walks along Big Hole River; Visitor Center; open daily 8-5 (8-7 in summer); free; **1. Grant-Kohrs Ranch National Historic Site** (34 m N on US 10, I-90 to Deer Lodge), interpretive center on Montana ranching. **Lewis & Clark Caverns State Park** (47 m E on US 10), 3/4-m guided cave tour (daily May-Sept., adm); nearby picnic & camp sites; **1.**

Deerlodge National Forest (Federal Bldg, Box 400, Butte 59701) surrounds Butte: Flint Creek Range (W of Anaconda on US 10A), camping at Georgetown Lake, many trails **(1-3)** including access to rockhounding, ghost towns, and Anaconda-Pintlar Wilderness; other lakes, creeks **(1, 2)**; Lost Creek State Park (6 m NE of Anaconda off US 10A & SR 274), falls in limestone canyon, camping, picnicking, walks **(1-3)**. Unit N of Butte, many campsites along US 91 and on Boulder River; mining remains; 8000-ft peaks; walks **(1-3)**; rockhounding E of Butte **(1, 2)**.

Beaverhead National Forest (hq at Skihi St. & US 91, Dillon 59725), 2.1-million acres in several units: **Pioneer Mtn Range** (19 m S on US 91, 10 m W on SR 43), booklets on self-guiding auto tours; lovely road along Wise River, camping, rockhounding, hot springs, many trails (1-3); trails (2, 3) S of Melrose to Lidden Mtn lakes; mtn trail (3) E of Wisdom. **Bannack State Monument** (S off SR 278, 25 m SW of Dillon), first territorial capitol, is a ghost town; camping, picnicking; **1,2.** A large section of forest runs along Continental Divide: In N is **Anaconda-Pintlar Wilderness** (20 m S of Anaconda on SR 274), 158,000 acres; climbs to 5-10,000-ft peaks from meadows, forests, barren alpine regions; 45-m trail along Divide (3); many trails (2, 3) approach or cross Divide; access from W at campsites S of Georgetown Lake or N of Sula (E Fork Reservoir, Copper Creek, Martin Creek; access from E from primitive roads off SR 274, 43), including camps at Lower Seymour Lake, Mussigbrod Lake. Hiking also from campsites at: Twin Lakes (W off SR 278 S of Wisdom), trail (3) across Divide; Miner Lakes (W off SR 278 at Jackson), creek, lake, Divide trails (1-3); Sacajawea, historic interest, trails across and along Divide (1-3); trails (1-3) off primitive road around Tendoy Mtns and Clark Canyon Reservoir (78 m S of Butte on I-15, US 91), state recreation area with camping, picnicking, water sports. **Tobacco Root Mtn** unit, camping at Potosi Hot Springs (S of Cardwell off SR 359), and at Mill Creek (N of Virginia City) for exploring mining camp remains (1-3); primitive roads off SR 287 (S of Whitehall), mtn trails (2, 3). **Madison Range** and **Gravelly Range** units (S of Ennis along US 287), self-guiding auto tours; campsites along Madison River; trails to lakes, in mtns to 10,000 ft (1-3); access to Spanish Peaks (E of Ennis); a primitive road along Ruby River (off SR 287, W of Virginia City), from Robbers Roost mining area, rockhounding (1, 2); Red Rock Lakes Ntl Wildlife Refuge (roads usually open May-Oct.) at S end.

EKALAKA: Medicine Rocks State Park (NE on SR 7), 220 acres, camp and picnic sites, caves and fantastic rock formations (1-3); Chalk Buttes and sections of Custer National Forest are S of town.

GLACIER NATIONAL PARK (hq entry, 32 m NE of Kalispell on US 2 to W Glacier), 1600 sq m bisected by Continental Divide, one of the most spectacular places in the world; precipitous mtns, 60 living glaciers, 200 alpine lakes, wildflower meadows, plentiful wildlife; on N it adjoins Waterton Lakes National Park in Canada; most of the park can be reached only on the 700-m trail system; park has lodges, campgrounds, saddle horses, tape tours, boat tours, many excellent naturalist programs and guided hikes, other activities. **Going-to-the-Sun Road,** only auto route across park, glorious experience; 51 m from hq in W Glacier across Divide to St. Mary on US 89; closed by snow mid-Oct.-early June; on road are: **Fish Creek** campground (S end Lake McDonald), picnicking, lakeside trail (1); **Sprague Creek** (E shore of lake), camp and picnic grounds, lodge, trails to Lincoln Creek (2); connects to Middle Fork Trail (2, 3), lookout tower (2), Sperry Glacier (2-3; continues across the Divide, (3); **Avalanche Creek** (N of lake), camp and picnic area, nature trail (1), 2-m hike to stunning falls in deep gorge (2-3), other trails (1-3) including one to Camas Lake; **Granite Park Chalets,** extensive trail system to Logan Pass, along and across Divide, to glaciers, to other park centers (some 2, most 3); **Logan Pass** (6664 ft), Visitor Center (late June-mid-Sept.), magnificent views, nature trail (1), trail to Granite Park and beyond (2-3); beautiful **St. Mary Lake,** camp and picnic sites, nature trail (1), choice of trails (1-3) on Red Eagle Creek to Continental Divide, to glaciers, Gunsight Pass across Divide, and to Many Glacier trail system. St. Mary has Visitor Center (late June–mid-Oct.), programs, exhibits. Other areas: From hq, trail (2, 3) goes S along Middle Fork of **Flathead River** to Walton campground (at Essex on US 2); off this, side trails follow creeks (2) up to Divide and across it (3). W of hq, road along N fork of Flathead River leads to several campsites with creek trails (2), to lakes, other trails (3) to glaciers and across the Divide. **Two Medicine** camp (NW of E Glacier off SR 49), lake in deep valley, can be reached by road or trail; trails (1-3) include steep ones along and across the Divide; also trail (3) to Cut Bank campground (just N) and St. Mary Lake. **Many Glacier** (9 m N of St. Mary off US 89 at Babb), camp and picnic grounds, hotel, greatest number of trails; nature and easy trails (1), creek and lake trails (2), trails to glaciers (2-3), across the divide (3), and into Canada (3). **Belly River,** trail (2, 3) leading to lakes and interior trail system. **Goat Haunt** ranger station and trail shelter in center of park near its highest peak (10,448-ft Mt Cleveland), reachable only by trail (also by trail from Canadian hq). **Information:** Supt., W Glacier 59936.

GLASGOW: Ft. Peck Dam & Lake (20 M SE on SR 24 on the Missouri River), information center, exhibits on area geology and wildlife, powerplant tours (June-early Sept., daily 9:30-5:30; free); dam has created enormous lake with federal and state camp and picnic sites for swimming, other water sports, walking (1-3): **Ft. Peck** (at Ft. Peck), **The Pines** (N shore, W of Ft. Peck), **Downstream** (off SR 24, N of dam), **Bear Creek** and **Rock Creek** (E shore, off SR 24), **Hell Creek** (S shore, N of Jordan); the last is good fossil and rock hunting area. **Charles M. Russell National Wildlife Area** surrounds the Missouri W of recreation area; display ponds and pasture at Devils Creek Recreation Area (NW of Jordan); also accessible via dirt roads (off SR 200, 19, US 191, 2); 1, 2.

GLENDIVE: Makoshika State Park (3 m S off I-94), most striking when sunrise or sunset plays up stark beauty of the badlands; camping; picnicking; many miles of trail (1-3), popular for fossil hunting, rockhounding (including moss agates) here, along Yellowstone River, and off roads in mtns W of the river.

GREAT FALLS: Visitor Center (10th Ave. S. at 47th St. S), map for self-guiding tour that includes drive along Missouri River: Gibson Park (gardens, lagoon, picnicking), Riverside Park (picnicking, birdwatching), Black Eagle Falls, Giant Springs (picnicking, fish hatchery open daily), Rainbow Falls; **1, 2.**

Lewis & Clark National Forest, 1.8-million acres in several scenic mtn areas (hq Federal Bldg, Great Falls 59401); unit NW along Continental Divide has part of Bob Marshall Wilderness (see Kalispell); lovely Teton River (NW of Choteau off US 89), camping, walks (1-3); lovely Sun River (SW of Choteau off US 287), camping and walks (1,2) to Pishkun, Willow Creek, Gibson, and Nilan reservoirs, Wood Lake, and climbs (3) to Divide and wilderness areas. Unit in **Little Belt Mtns** (40 m SE on US 89), campsites along US 89, good bases for exploring (1, 2) old mining remains, trails (2, 3) to 7-9000-ft mtns; camping and walks (1, 2) on lovely Judith River (on SR 239 W of Hobson); camping and ghost town (1, 2) of Castle (6 m E of White Sulphur Springs on US 12, 15 m S of FS road).

HELENA: Main St. runs through Last Chance Gulch, where gold was struck in 1864; from State Capitol (6th Ave & Montana) and Montana Historical Society (225 N Roberts), trackless train runs in summer to points of interest, including old brick row bldgs in Reeder's Alley (S end), Pioneer Cabin (208 S Park Ave); **1. Frontier Town** (17 m W on US 12), reconstructed pioneer village; open Apr.-Nov.; adm; **1.** Nearby ghost towns include Marysville (7 m N on I-15, W off SR 279); **1. Canyon Ferry State Recreation Area** (10 m NE via US 12, SR 284), historical museum (May-mid-Oct. daily 9-9; free), water sports, camping, picnicking; **1. Missouri River, Wolf Creek Canyon,** and **Beartooth Recreation Areas** (36 m N off I-15), clustered near Holter Lake on Missouri River; scenic; camping; picnicking; walks 1-3.

Helena National Forest surrounds the city; scenic drives, ghost towns, fishing streams. **Gates of the Mtns** (16 m N off I-15), gorge on Missouri River where cliffs rise 1200 ft; best views are on summer boat trips up the Canyon from Helena; green gorge and rugged cliff wilderness; trailheads (1-3) are at campsites on the river (reached by boat from Upper Holter Lake), off road S from Holter Lake, and off road along Beaver Creek (N of York); nearby trails in Big Belt Mtns (2, 3). **Eldorado Bar** here is open May-Sept. for hunting sapphires (fee). **Scapegoat Wilderness** (45 m NW, reached via trails N off SR 200 near Lincoln), in Continental Divide; peaks rise to 9185-ft and are snowclad most of yr; hiking tends to be steep, rough

(2, 3); easier trails **(1-2)** are S of Blackfoot River, at FS camps and Hooper State Recreation Area. **Information:** 616 Helena Ave. zip 59601.

KALISPELL: Fort Kalispell (E on US 2), replica of frontier town (open mid-Apr.–mid-Oct. daily; free exc for activities); **Woodland Park** (2nd St. E), 37 acres, lagoon, flower and rock gardens, birds, summer pool, picnicking, other facilities; **Lawrence Park** (off N Main St.), attractive.

With snow-capped mtns and deep-blue lakes, scenery here is spectacular. Most of the surrounding land is part of 2.3-million-acre **Flathead National Forest,** hanging valleys, jagged mtns, glaciers, scores of glacial lakes. **Bob Marshall Wilderness** (SE), 950,000 acres of rugged mtns; 15-m-long vertical cliffs called Chinese Wall and 60 m of Continental Divide; access on W is from campsites along SR 209 (S of Swan Lake) at Swan Lake (with wildlife refuge), Swan River State Forest, Holland Lake; from S, trails come up through Scapegoat Wilderness from camps at Upsata, Coopers, and Snowbank lakes; entry is harder from E, off US 287 to Benchmark (Wood Lake) or other remote campgrounds; access trails may be **2,** but miles of interconnecting trails within wilderness are mostly **3. Mission Mtns Primitive Area,** also reached from Holland Lake and other camps along SR 209, and from Kicking Horse Reservoir and Crow Creek camps off US 93; marked trails **(1-3)**, in S lakes area and in N, but much of this is trailless, challenging hiking **(3). Jewel Basin Hiking Area** (20 m SE off SR 35), 15,000 acres, trails **(1-3)** from Echo Lake; interior mostly **3. Information:** 290 N Main St., Kalispell 59901.

Kalispell is ringed with state and national recreation areas; camping and picnicking; all have easy trails **(1, 2)**, access to wilderness and climbs to 3-9000 ft **(3)**; major sites are: **Ashley Lake** (15 m SW on US 2, then N), swimming; **Bitterroot Lake** (23 m W off US 2), swimming; **Whitefish Lake** (14 m N on US 93), swimming. **Hungry Horse Dam** (19 m NE on US 2), Visitor Center (mid-May-late Sept. daily 9 am-9 pm), exhibits; scenic drive; self-guiding tours; information on Flathead Ntl Forest; trails **(1-3)** include access to Bob Marshall Wilderness.

LEWISTOWN: Picnicking and walks **(1)** at **Big Springs Creek; Lewistown Fisheries Station** (7 m S on Co. 466; open daily 8-5; free); **Warm Springs** (13 m NW via US 191, SR 235). **Maiden Canyon** (10 m N on US 191, 6 m E), scenic canyon, forested hillsides in Judith Mtns is BLM land, mining remains including Maiden ghost town; other ghost towns: Kendall (16 m N on US 191, 6 m W); Gilt Edge (14 m E on US 87, 6 m N). **James Kip State Park** (31 m E on US 87, 40 m N on SR 19, US 191), S of Missouri River in Charles M. Russell National Wildlife Refuge; swimming, camping, picnicking, walking **(1, 2). Missouri River Breaks** stretch 150 m W along river to Ft. Benton; best seen by boat, but some dirt roads penetrate badlands; camping; **1-3**. **Little Rockies** area (N on SR 19, US 191 across the Missouri), rough, scenic roads, prairie views, public campsites (Camp Creek and Montana Gulch) from which to explore old mining camps including Zortman (off US 191) and Landusky (off SR 376). **Big Snowy Mtns** unit (SW off US 87) of Lewis & Clark Ntl Forest (see Great Falls), camping, walks **(1, 2)** at beautiful Crystal Lake; back packing **(3)**.

LIBBY: Kootenai National Forest surrounds the city; 1.8-million acres; magnificent scenery; Yaak River (31 m NW on US 2, N on SR 508), scenic, campsites on river and Kilbrennan Lake, trails **(2, 3)** to 6500-ft peaks, access **(3)** to Northwest Peak (7700-ft) Scenic Area. **Libby Dam** (12 m E on SR 37), a Corps of Engineers project, Visitor Center (Apr.-Oct. daily), camping, water sports on 90-m-long Lake Koocanusa **(1, 2)** and hiking **(1-3)** in Kootenai River canyon (N on SR 37); road S of dam has access to lovely Fisher River **(1-3)**; Ten Lakes Scenic Area (N of dam on SR 37 to Eureka) trailheads **(1-3)** at campsites. **Ross Creek Scenic Area** (15 m W on US 2, S on SR 202), trailheads **(1-3)** at campgrounds on Bull Lake; also stunning self-guiding Giant Cedars Trail **(1)**, Spar Lake **(1)**, access to Cabinet Mtn wilderness **(2, 3)**. **Cabinet Mtn Wilderness** (S of Libby), 94,000 acres; snowclad peaks rise to 8712-ft Snowshoe Peak; waterfalls; glacial lakes; reached on E by dirt roads and creek trails **(2, 3)** from Libby, Howard Lake and Pleasant Valley (S on US 2) campsites; on W (SR 202) trails **(2, 3)** go in from campsites at Ross Creek, Bull River, Noxon Reservoir; on S, trails **(1-3)** go N from dirt roads that follow Thompson River between Logan (off US 2) and Thompson Falls (off SR 200) Recreation Areas (these 2 areas have other trails, **1-3**). **Information:** 418 Mineral Ave., Libby 59923.

MISSOULA: University of Montana (University & Arthur Aves.), campus tours. **Aerial Fire Depot** (7 m W on I-90), Visitor Center (open June 15–July 3, Mon.–Fri. 8-5; July 5–Labor Day daily 8-5; free), exhibits; smoke jumpers lead tours of their training loft; information on area forests; **1**. Walks along Blackfoot (E) and Bitterroot (S) rivers, Clark Fork (W); **1, 2**.

    Lolo and **Bitterroot National Forests** surround city; beautiful country, wildflowers, hot springs, foot trails to a hundred lakes and peaks. **Lewis & Clark Hwy** (US 12 W of Lolo) has Sawmill Gulch trail to 6435-ft Blue Mtn **(2, 3)**, campsites at Lolo Hot Springs and Lee Creek giving access to trails **(1-3)** S into Bitterroot Mtns, other trails **(1-3)**. **Selway-Bitterroot Wilderness**, reached by roads & trails W of US 93 (S of Lolo); among good camping bases are: Charles Waters Memorial, Larry Creek, Lake Como **(1-3)**; **Painted Rocks Lake Recreation Area** (62 m S on US 93, SW on SR 473), swimming, camping, wonderful variety of trails **(1-3)**, some leading into Idaho forests. **Ravalli National Wildlife Refuge** (20 m S off US 93), Sleeping Child Hot Springs (49 m S on US 93, SE on SR 501), and especially Medicine Springs (S on US 93 near Sula) have hikes **1-3**. **Seeley Lake** (42 m NE via SR 200, 209), camping, trails along streams & lakes, mtn climbs **(1-3)**. **Garnet Range** (W of town between SR 100 & I-90), scenic, recreation areas; Garnet, Bearmouth, other ghost towns; many trails **(1-3)**. **Beavertail Hill Recreation Area** (18 m E on I-90), many trails & mtn climbs **(1-3)**, walks on Rock Creek (more campsites and old mining remains farther S along the road paralleling it). Information: Lolo, 2801 Russell, Missoula 59801; Bitterroot, 316 N 3rd St., Hamilton 59840.

NEBRASKA

BROWNVILLE: Indian Cave State Park (S off SR 67), bordering 3 m of Missouri River; most of the 3000 acres can be reached only on foot, and hiking **(2, 3)** is through wooded bluff lands often without well-marked trails; points of interest include an old cemetery; camping; picnic sites.

CRAWFORD: Crawford City Park (Main St.) has Crazy Horse Museum (open summer weekends, free), swimming pool (summer, sm adm), picnic and camp sites, fish hatchery; all yr; free. **Fort Robinson State Park** (4 m W on US 20), fort buildings, including guardhouse in which Crazy Horse was killed; museum (Apr.-Nov. daily 8-5 or longer); trailside nature museum, hiking **(1, 2, 3)**; swimming, other facilities; free. **Nebraska National Forest** (8 m S on SR 2), grassland with only a few of marked trails; most recreational sites are S of Chadron, along with **Chadron State Park** (23 m E on US 20 to Chadron, then 9 m S on US 385)—hiking trails are along brooks and beside a lagoon **(2)**, Ponderosa pine; camping, cabins, swimming pool, picnic sites. **Oglala National Grasslands** (N on SR 2) covers the NW corner of the state; picnicking at Toadstool Park (23 m NW off SR 2); **1**.

HOMESTEAD NATIONAL MONUMENT (off SR 4, 4 m NW of Beatrice), cabin and other structures of first person to file under the Homestead Act; Visitor Center; 1½-m trail to cabin with spurs to graves and other sites; daily 8-5 (8-7 in summer); closed Jan. 1, Thnks, Dec. 25; free; **1**.

KEARNEY: Fort Kearney Museum (311 S Central), boatrides, fossils, guns, armor, other collections; summer daily 9-9; adm. **Fort Kearny State Historical Park** (4 m S, 4 m E via SR 10), restored buildings of fort that protected emigrants on the Oregon Trail; 40-acre site with camping, swimming, picnic tables, and walking trails (1); free. **Harold Warp Pioneer Village** (20 m SE via SR 44, US 6, 34) displays historical items in 25 furnished homes, shops, other buildings, museum, outdoor exhibits; daily 8-sundown; adm. **Kearney State Recreation Area** (NE of town), swimming, picnic sites, camping (1).

LINCOLN: Chamber of Commerce (US 34 & 10th St.), maps for self-guiding tours. City parks include: **Pioneers** (½ m S of jct Burlington Ave & Van Dorn St.), zoo, picnic sites, other activities, and self-guiding tours from Chet Ager Nature Center (daily; free); **Holmes** (70th & Van Dorn Sts.) boat rental and picnic sites; Wood (33rd & J Sts.) a rose garden, swimming pool, picnic sites. **Antelope** (23rd & M Sts.), a sunken garden, swimming pool, zoo (May-Aug.), other activities. State recreation areas with hiking, camping, picnic sites: **Pawnee** (8 m W on US 80), also swimming; **Conestoga** (6 m W on US 6, 3 m S via SR 55A); **Branched Oak Lake** (13 m NW via US 34, SR 79), also swimming; **Bluestem** (13 m SW via US 77, SR 33).

NEBRASKA CITY: Arbor Lodge State Historical Park (NW of town on US 73, 75), 65-acre wooded estate with gardens designed by Olmsted; mansion (mid-June-mid-Sept., Mon.-Sat. 10-5:30, Sun. 1-5:30; possibly other times; sm adm); park open daily; free; 1.

NEBRASKA NATIONAL FOREST (16 m SE of Thedford via SR 2, spur 202), 3-m self-guiding tour of Bessey Nursery; lookout tower; camp and picnic sites; swimming and wading pools; 1. (See also Crawford.)

NIOBRARA STATE PARK (1½ m W of Niobrara on SR 12), on Lewis and Clark Trail along the Missouri River; hiking through hardwood forest (2, 3); camping; swimming pool; picnicking.

NORTH PLATTE: Buffalo Bill Ranch State Historical Park (1 m N on Buffalo Bill Ave.) preserves winter quarters of William F. Cody's Wild West Show; open daily in summer 8 am-9 pm, possibly at other times; 1. **Cody Park** (N on US 83), wildlife refuge with swimming pool (summer), camping, picnicking, other activities; daily; free; 1.

OGALLALA: Front Street (519 E 1st St.), pioneer buildings with exhibits; shows in summer; late-Apr.-Sept. daily 8-midnight; 1. **Ash Hollow State**

Historical Park (27½ m NW on US 26), excavation of prehistoric cave dwelling, museum.

OMAHA: Chamber of Commerce (1620 Dodge St.), maps and information. Among city parks (1) are **Levi Carter** (N of Carter Lake), a strip created when the Missouri River changed course, picnic sites. **Riverview Park & Zoo** (Deer Park Blvd & 10th St.), zoo open Apr.-Oct. daily 10-5 (sm adm); picnic sites. **Fontenelle Forest** (9 m SE via US 73, 75 to 1111 Bellevue Blvd N in Bellevue), 1200-acre preserve with 16 m of hiking trails (1, 2) through floodplain, prairie, marsh; nature center offers animal exhibits, guided walks, lectures; daily 8 am-6 pm; closed Jan. 1, Thnks, Dec. 25; sm adm.

SCOTTSBLUFF: Scottsbluff-Gering Chamber of Commerce (information booth open on US 26 E of town in summer), information for self-guiding tours on foot or by car; routes of the Oregon Trail, Mormon Trail and Pony Express marked on map. **Scotts Bluff National Monument** (3 m S on SR 71 to Gering, then 2 m W on SR 92), landmark on Oregon Trail; museum (open daily, 7 am-8:30 pm in summer; rest of yr, 8:30-4:30; closed Dec. 25); from the Visitor Center a road leads to a parking area from which short trails (1) lead to N and S overlooks; trail to summit (2); fourth trail (3) leads directly from Visitor Center to summit; sm adm or GEP. S of Visitor Center, Oregon Trail, worn down by passage of emigrants, is marked. **North Platte Valley Museum** is just S (1349 10th St., Gering), open in summer Mon.-Sat. 9-5, Sun. 1-5; rest of yr, Tues. & Thurs. 9-5; closed hols; sm adm. Trail ruts and monuments to pioneers are near **Robidoux Pass** (8 m W). **Wildcat Hills Game Reserve** (S on SR 71), herds of buffalo, elk, and deer; camping; scenic views; hiking, 1. N of the river is **Riverside Park & Zoo** (W Overland Dr.), camping and picnic areas; 1. **Lake Minatare State Recreation Area** (8 m NE), camping, swimming, boating and hiking trails, 2. **Agate Fossil Beds National Monument** (9 m NW on US 26 to Mitchell, then 30 m N on SR 29), exposed Miocene fossil mammal bones; Visitor Center open daily 8:30-4:30 in summer; rest of yr, weekends or by contacting ranger; closed hols in winter; free; 1.

VALENTINE: Swimming, camping, picnicking, walks (1) at: **City Park** (½ m N off Main St.); state recreation areas at **Big Alkali Lake** (17 m S on US 83, 3 m W on SR 483) and **Merritt Reservoir** (25 m SW on local rds). **Snake River Falls** (23 m SW), popular with trout fishermen. **Ft. Niobrara National Wildlife Refuge** (5 m NE on SR 12), on Niobrara River fed by falls; plains area; buffalo and elk, prairie dog town; museum of natural history; Fort Falls; self-guiding nature trails (1); picnic tables; open daily in daylight; free. **Valentine National Wildlife Refuge** (17 m S on US 83, 13 m W on SR 16B), marshes, rolling hills, 9 lakes for waterfowl migration.

NEVADA

AUSTIN: Colorful silver boom town in the 1860s; **Historic District** includes old courthouse, 3 churches, newspaper office, and ruined "castle." Ghost towns and mining camps are along SR 21 NE of town, such as **Mineral Hill** (50 m, then E), **Cortez** (58 m, then E), **Tenabo** (70 m, then W). **Hickison Petroglyph Recreation Site** (20 m E on US 50), Indian rock art, camping, picnic sites, and hiking (2); Apr.-Oct. daily; free.

Toiyabe National Forest (in 3 sections between Austin and Tonopah) is laced with trails that are unusually scenic and of historic interest; many begin at the end of canyons and require approach via four-wheel drive from the highways; marked nature trail (1) from Big Creek campground (12 m S of Austin) is one of the easiest, and Toiyabe Summit Trail (running 100 m the length of the Toiyabe range) is one of the toughest; information from District Ranger, Austin Ranger District (Austin 89310) or Tonopah Ranger District (Tonopah 89049). In forest is **Berlin-Ichthyosaur State Park** (8 m SW via US 50, SR 2; 58 m S on SR 21, 4 m E), fossil shelter with exhibits; ranger programs; interpretive signs in Union Canyon; colorful ghost town of Berlin; 1, 2.

BAKER: Lehman Caves National Monument (5 m W on SR 74), 640 acres in pinyon pine and juniper country; wildflowers; 1½-hr tour of caves given yr round (sm adm); write Supt. (Baker 89311). Surrounding the monument is the Snake Division of **Humboldt National Forest;** campgrounds at Lehman Creek (2 m N), Baker Creek (2½ m S), Wheeler Peak (12 m W), and Snake Creek (15 m S) give access to **Wheeler Peak Scenic Area,** with lakes, streams, ancient bristlecone pines (2, 3).

CALIENTE: Signs of ancient habitation include petroglyphs at **Pine Canyon** (27 m E) and **White River** (25 m W). Mining ruins around **Pioche** (25 m N on US 93) include **Bristol** and **Monarch** mines (just N of Pioche, W of US 93), **Bullionville** (W off US 93, just S of town), other camps. **Beaver Dam State Park** (4 m N on US 93, then 31 m E on dirt road), 2032 acres, swimming, camping, boating; hiking in beautiful pine-clad mtns, cliffs towering over stream and lake (1-3). **Kershaw-Ryan Recreational Area** (3 m S on dirt road), 240 acres, scenic cliffs and canyons; spring water; camping, swimming; picnic tables; hiking trails (1-3). **Cathedral Gorge State Park** (2 m N of Panaca off US 93), high, tan-colored walls have eroded into interesting spires, other formations; camp and picnic sites; hiking trails **(1-3)**. **Panaca Charcoal Kilns** (12 m E of Panaca, then N off SR 25), short walk, **2**. **Echo Canyon Recreation Area** (13 m N on US 93, then 5 m E on SR 25, 5 m N), 320 acres in pinon-juniper country, camping, boating, swimming; hiking trail **(1-3)**. **Meadow Valley Camp** (17 m E of Pioche on gravel road via Ursine, then 2½ m NE), less developed camping area, rockhounding; Apr.-Dec. **Eagle Valley Reservoir Recreation Area** (18 m E of Pioche on SR 85), camping, swimming, boating, hiking trails **(1-3)**, 350 acres.

CARSON CITY: Named for Kit Carson, this was a trading post that prospered as a stop on the Pony Express, Overland Trail, and other early routes. **Chamber of Commerce** (1191 S Carson St.), in a caboose, provides information on the many homes built during the silver boom (Bowers Mansion, 10 m N on US 395, is open mid-May-Oct. daily; sm adm), and on other attractions in the city and area. **Mormon Station Historic State Monument** (11 m S on US 395, then 4 m W at Genoa), oldest permanent white settlement in the state; reconstructed trading post with historic displays; daily all year 9-5 (museum open May-Sept. daily 9-7). **Virginia City National Historic Landmark** (15 m NE via US 50, SR 17), the Queen on the Comstock Lode, fun to walk around in; Visitors Bureau (C St.) shows a film on the city's history and provides maps, schedules of hours for attractions, and information on special events; Ophir Open Pit and Old Chollar Mine offer tours; opera house and saloons open all yr; mansions, church, school, other restored buildings, generally open daily during Easter Week and Memorial Day-Oct.; **1.** Nearby ghost towns are **Dayton** (10 m E on US 50), **Washoe City** (15 m N on US 395), **Gold Hill, Silver City, Como** (all S of Virginia City on SR 17).

ELKO: Chamber of Commerce provides information on rockhounding sites and ghost towns including **Tuscarora** (28 m N on SR 51, 18 m N on SR 11, 8 m W), **Midas** (40 m W along same rd), **Metropolis** (46 m E on I-80, then 4 m N); **1. Wildhorse Reservoir** (74 m N on SR 51), open Apr.-Dec., offers camping, fishing, and short walks **(1)**. **Humboldt National Forest** (Supervisor, 976 Mountain City Hwy, Elko 89801) contains the spectacular Ruby Mtn Range; 40,720 acres are designated **Ruby Mtn Scenic Area** (extends from Verdi Peak in N to Overland Lake in S) that includes 11,000-ft Ruby Dome. **Lamoille Canyon** (25 m SE off SR 46) is the major recreation area; camping also at Thomas Canyon; extensive trail system **1-3**. Stunning Ruby Crest Trail (mostly **3**, some sections **2**) runs N-S through the scenic area; Overland Trail **(2, 3)** crosses the scenic area E-W in the S; other trails generally run E-W, following creek beds (this is true of most trails outside the scenic area too); many of the trails lead to lovely lakes or to historic sites such as abandoned mines. **Angel Lake** (13 m SE of Wells), especially scenic forest-rimmed lake, has trails **(1-3)** including 4-

m Angel Trail-Pole Canyon Trail to Gray's Lake.   Also beautiful is **Ruby Valley** area; picnicking, camping, hiking **(1-3)** at Ruby Marsh (50 m S via SR 46; 3 m beyond Jiggs turn E on gravel rd 25 m over Harrison Pass to Ruby Valley); walks **(1, 2)** also at nearby Ruby Lake fish hatchery and Ruby Lake National Wildlife Refuge. **Humboldt Division** (N via SR 51) has wonderful trails **(2, 3)**, ghost town remains, camping, but the magnet for experienced hikers **(3)** is **Jarbridge Wilderness** with tough trails in exhilarating scenery among 10,000-ft peaks.

ELY: Ward Charcoal Ovens (5 m SE on US 6, 50, 93, then 10 m S), 6 stone ovens used for making charcoal during the 1870 mining boom; near-by ruins of Ward mining camp; camping; picnic sites; hiking trails **(1-3)**. **White Pine County Chamber of Commerce** can give you information on reaching the many ghost towns in the area, including **Osceola** (35 m E off US 6, 50), **Cherry Creek** (48 m N on US 93, then 9 m W on SR 35), **Hamilton** (35 m W on US 50, then 10 m S), and Eureka (78 m W on US 50). **Garnet Hill** (NW of town off US 50), popular for rockhounding. SW of town volcanic area with cinder cones and **Lunar Crater** (US 6 between Black Rock and Sandy Summits). **Bristlecone Natural Area** (15½ m NW via Butte Valley Rd.), scenic area of ancient pines at elevations of 10,000 ft or higher; 3/4-m hike from end of road **(2)**. Several sections of **Humboldt National Forest** are in this area: Ward Mtn (just SE), recreation area and a few trails **(2, 3)**. White Pine (37 m W on US 50), several campgrounds, trails **(2, 3)**; several trails in the area of Hamilton ghost town lead to other historic and mining sites. Longer hikes are possible in the **Quinn Canyon Division,** 2 campgrounds; remote area, elevations from 5000-11,000-ft, for the experienced only **(3)**. Most developed trails **(2, 3)** are in **Schell Creek Division** (E off US 93, 50); trailheads usually near camp-grounds. Write Supervisor (976 Mountain City Hwy, Elko 89801).

LAKE MEAD NATIONAL RECREATION AREA (4 m E of Boulder City on US 93, 466), 2-million acres of colorful canyons and deserts extends 240 m along the Colorado River from Bullhead City, Az., to Grand Canyon National Monument; **Boulder Beach Visitor Center,** information on naturalist programs and other activities; Boulder Beach, most developed area, swimming, water sports, campsites, lodging, restaurants, other facilities.

LAS VEGAS: Chamber of Commerce (2301 E Sahara Ave.), information and maps. Walking The Strip (Las Vegas Blvd. S of town) is fun; gambling casinos, flamboyant hotels (many with landscaping); behind-the-scenes tour of gambling is offered by Mint Hotel (100 Fremont St.) for adults (over 21), daily, free. **Red Rock Canyon** Recreation Area (14 m W via Charleston Blvd. & Red Rock Front Dr.), interpretive material on ancient pueblo-like structures and the nearby Willow Springs petroglyphs; lovely area for walking (1, 2) and rockhounding; other archaeological sites and a nearby sandstone quarry; picnic sites; drinking water. **Toiyabe National Forest** (17 m NW on US 95 to SR 39 or 14 m beyond to SR 52), off scenic drive between Kyle and Lee canyons are campgrounds and short trails (1, 2) to Fletcher Canyon and spring, Cathedral Rock (an overlook), Mary Jane Falls, Robbers Roost Cave, and others. From Cathedral Rock campground South Loop Trail (2, 3) connects to Charleston Peak Trail (11,918 ft), with a spur to Peak Spring; you can continue along North Loop to Deer Creek Trail; the latter has terminals near Deer Creek campground and Mary Jane Falls campground, making the total trip about 17 m. Lee Canyon (used for winter sports) has another long trail that goes via 10,000-ft peaks to Whiskey Spring in the N part of the forest; inquire for condition; 3. Campgrounds (at elevations of 8000 ft) are open May-Nov. For details: Supervisor (111 N Virginia St., Reno 89501). **Desert National Wildlife Range** (28 m NW on US 95), desert bighorn sheep; daily 8-5; free. **Valley of Fire State Park** (55 m NE via I-15, SR 40), impressive formations of red Jurassic sandstone; Visitor Center; Atlatl Rocks petroglyphs and other formations near the campground and Visitor Center easily reached (1) and most have picnic sites, ¼-m Petroglyph Canyon Trail (1); from Rainbow Vista, a 1½-m trail goes to Fire Canyon View (2) but you can go farther (3), and a 3½-m one-way trail with a spur to White Domes goes to Dead End (3); open daily (museum 9-5) free.

RENO: Chamber of Commerce Hospitality Center (150 S Virginia St.), information on the city and area; tapes and escorted tours available to Mother Lode country; **University of Nevada** campus (9th & N Virginia Sts.), landscaped and pleasant to stroll, and **Casino Row** (Virginia St.) is fun too; **Washoe County Library** (Center & Ralston Sts.), open daily, planned as a garden, interior landscaping. **Pyramid Lake** (36 m N on SR 33), on the Paiute Indian Reservation, deep blue and 28 m long; Anahoe Island is a sanctuary for white pelicans; Washoe County Park on the W shore at Warrior Point offers camping and swimming. **Davis Creek Park** (17 m S off US 395), all-yr campground with trailheads for lovely trails (1, 2, 3); information: Washoe County Parks & Recreation Dept. (1205 Mill St., Reno 89502). **Lake Tahoe State Park** (35 m SE via US 395, SR 27, 28), 12,000 acres of beautiful country, 3 m of shoreline, swimming beach.

WINNEMUCCA: This was a supply center for wagon trains and later for mining; best preserved ghost town is **Paradise Valley** (22 m N on US 95, 19 m N on SR 8B). **Humboldt National Forest** (N via US 95 or SR 88) has an especially lovely drive via Indian Creek to Hinkey Summit, with outstanding views; several trails (2, 3) branch out from here and there are 2 campgrounds. Summit Trail in the S end of the forest also offers wonderful panoramas (3),

NEW HAMPSHIRE

ALLENSTOWN: Bear Brook State Park (2 m E off SR 28), 9300 forested acres with swimming, picnic and campgrounds; 18 m of well-marked trails (**1, 2**); an Audubon nature center operates Tues.-Sun. 10-5 (sm adm), with self-guiding trail, exhibits, field trips, other activities.

COLEBROOK: Coleman State Park (7 m E on SR 26, then 5 m N), 1685 acres on pretty pond; camp and picnic sites; state fish hatchery (1 m E on SR 26) is open daily, free, **1. Beaver Brook Falls** (2 m N on SR 145) is scenic; **1.**

FITZWILLIAM: Rhododendron State Park (NW off SR 119) has 16 acres in bloom in July; pretty trails in glen and for overlooks (**1, 2**); picnic grove.

HOLDERNESS: Squam Lakes Science Center (on US 3), a 280-acre preserve of meadows, ponds, woods, offers daily interpretive programs in summer; 2-m nature trail with exhibits of animals, blacksmith shop, sugar house, sawmill; picnic area; July-Labor Day, Mon.-Sat. 10-5, Sun. 1-5; adm; **1.**

JAFFREY: Monadnock State Park (2 m W off SR 124) has a 30-m network of well-maintained trails to the 3165-ft mtn summit (**2, 3**); camping; picnicking, early May-mid-Oct.

PORTSMOUTH: Chamber of Commerce (78 Congress St.) provides general information. **Historic Information Center** !143 Pleasant St.) offers information on the surrounding area, with many 17-19th-C buildings.
  Strawbery Banke Restoration (Hancock & Marcy Sts.), 10-acre site with more than 30 restored bldgs of 1630 settlement that became Portsmouth; exhibits; demonstrations of boat-building, crafts; special events; May-Oct., daily 9:30-5; adm. **Prescott Park** (Marcy St.), on the Piscataque River; 1705 Sheafe Warehouse and 1812 Shaw Warehouse with local folk art and maritime relics (May-Sept. daily; free), early burying ground, gardens, fountains; daily; free. **Odiorne Point State Park** (on SR 1A, 3½ m S), nature preserve of 137 acres with tidal marsh, 2 ponds, trails (**1**); daily in summer 10-7.

WASHINGTON: Pillsbury State Park (5 m N on SR 31), 3702-acre wilderness area and bird sanctuary; 5 large ponds; walking **(1, 2)**; hiking to nearby mtns **(2)**.

WHITE MOUNTAINS NATIONAL FOREST, 700,000 acres, includes Presidential Range and most of the White Mountains; 39 lakes, ponds, 650 m of streams, 1000 m of hiking trails. Most scenic route is 34-m-long-**Kancamagus Hwy** between Lincoln and Conway; the **Passaconaway Information Center** (late May-mid-Oct. daily 9-5), midway between the 2 towns, has a short nature trail **(1)**. Also off the highway are **Greeley Ponds Scenic Area** (½-day hike with overnight shelters, **2, 3**); **Sabbaday Falls,** short stroll along brook, **1**; **Sawyer Pond Scenic Area** (½-day's hike, shelters, **2, 3**); **Rocky Gorge Scenic Area,** reached via a short walk, **2**; **Covered Bridge Interpretive Trail, 1.** Other sites include several covered bridges; historic exhibits at **Dolly Copp** (5 m S of Gorham on SR 16) and **Stone Iron Furnace** (Franconia Village on SR 18, 116); **Glen Ellis Falls** (on SR 16 N of Jackson), **Silver Cascade** (N end of Crawford Notch) and 3 m N, Flume Cascade; **Arethusa Falls** (6 m N of Bartlett); other waterfalls; fish hatcheries (on SR 25 S of Warren and at York Pond in the N section of the forest); **1.**

The **Appalachian Trail** cuts through some of the loveliest areas; in the N it enters near Shelburne, cuts through a corner of the Great Gulf Wilderness (with access to other trails here), then through Franconia Notch, and exits at SE end near Glencliff; **2, 3.**

Mt. Washington (10 m SW of Gorham on SR 16), highest point in NE (6288 ft) has attractive Alpine Garden **(1)**; you can get up by auto (rd starts in Pinkham Notch on SR 16), cog railway (station 6 m E of US 302), or by hiking (from Pinkham Notch.

Great Gulf Wilderness (2, 3) is nicest reached through Snyder Brook Scenic Area (off US 2, SW of Randolph); more than half a dozen trails here interconnect. Just S is **Pinkham Notch Scenic Area** with Tuckerman Ravine (a ski area), reached from Pinkham Notch. Other **Scenic Areas** include Lincoln Woods, Nancy Brook, Gibbs Brook, Lafayette Brook.

The forest is laced with trails too numerous to describe here **(1-3)**; trail information and maps are available at **Appalachian Mountain Club** in Pinkham Notch (they also have a guided hike program). Rangers at Conway and Gorham also provide information. The Carroll Reed Shop (Main St., N Conway) often provides all-day, guided hikes, free. For information: Supervisor, Laconia 03246.

Within the forest are several resorts and: **Crawford Notch State Park** (12 m N of Bartlett on US 302), picnic and camp sites, small zoo, waterfalls, historic house, trails leading to the forest network; late May-mid-Oct. **Echo Lake State Park** (N Conway), a scenic lake with swimming and picnicking. **Franconia Notch State Park** (on US 3), in a deep valley of

6440 acres between towering peaks; many trails (1-3), some of the more scenic ones graded and provided with boardwalks for easy walking; the Appalachian Trail cuts through here; beautiful Profile Lake; aerial tramway to summit of 4100-ft Cannon Mtn, with several trails around the summit (2, 3); 800-ft Flume Gorge; many other natural features. Below the park is **Lost River Reservation** (5 m W of N Woodstock on SR 112), a chasm in which a river disappears to reemerge in falls; museum; gardens; picnic sites; mid-May-Oct. daily 9-6; adm.

STATE PARKS: In addition to parks mentioned above, the following have walks: **Cardigan** (4½ m E of Canaan off US 4 & SR 118), with a road leading to picnic area on Cardigan Mtn; trails (2) to 3100-ft summit for overlook. **Miller** (4 m E of Peterborough on SR 101) on 2288-ft mtn; picnic sites; trails around summit (2). **Moose Brook** (2 m W of Gorham on US 2), 755 acres in beautiful area with good views; swimming; picnic and camp sites. **Mt. Sunapee** (6 m S of Sunapee on SR 103), attractive 2175-acre park with gondola to summit, picnic sites, swimming, hiking trails (1-3). **Weeks** (3 m S of Lancaster on US 3), a mountaintop (2058 ft) park with observation tower, picnic sites, museum (open summer-early fall), easy walks (1, 2). **Wellington** (4 m NW of Bristol off SR 3A) has a swimming lake, picnic sites, bird sanctuary, and scenic trails around the 183-acre peninsula. **White Lake** (6 m N of Center Ossipee on SR 16), 603 acres in pretty area on forested swimming lake; picnic area; trails (1, 2). **Winslow** (Wilmot Flat off SR 11) has views from road up N slope of 2937-ft Mt. Kearsarge, picnic sites, steep 1-m trail to summit (2, 3); **Rollins** (off SR 103 at Warner) is up the S slope of Mt. Kearsarge, with ½-m trail to summit (2).

NEW JERSEY

ALLAIRE STATE PARK (off SR 547 between Farmingdale & Lakewood) preserves **Historic Howell Works,** a bog-ore furnace established 1822; worker houses, shops, bakery; nature trails (1); bldgs open Apr.-Oct. daily 10-5; Nov.-Mar., weekends only; sm adm.

BATONA HIKING TRAIL: Marked, 29.8-m trail from Carpenter Spring in Lebanon State Forest S to Batsto fire tower in Wharton State Forest; pine barrens; roads intersect at many points; map free from Lebanon or Wharton forest rangers; mostly easy walking on sandy roads; **1, 2.**

BATSTO STATE HISTORIC SITE (7 m NE of Hammonton on SR 542), delightful restoration of village that grew up around 18th-C bog-iron furnace; ironmaster's home (adm), blacksmith and other shops, cottages; craft demonstrations; daily exc Jan. 1, Dec. 25; free; **1.**

CAPE MAY COURT HOUSE: Cape May County Historical Museum (on US 9 in center of town) or **Chamber of Commerce** (Crest Haven Rd. & Garden State Pkwy), information on historic houses. Beachcombing for Cape May diamonds (quartz polished by the sea) along Delaware Bay.

DELAWARE WATER GAP: Both sides of the Gap are being developed for recreation; 19th-C villages of Slateford Farm, Millbrook Village, and Peters Valley being restored, craft displays; Appalachian Trail runs through Worthington State Forest to Pennsylvania; hiking trails; information office (I-80 just before Gap) open daily May-mid-Oct. 9-5; also weekends before and after; or write hq in Columbia (NJ 07832).

GREAT SWAMP NATIONAL WILDLIFE REFUGE (on Long Hill Rd., N of Meyersville), 5800-acre sanctuary, boardwalk loops through swamp and forest; blinds; booklets at entrance; open daily in daylight; free.

ISLAND BEACH STATE PARK (S of Seaside Park), barrier beach, stunning maritime vegetation; nature center with 1/8-m nature trail; additional walks conducted by naturalists (scheduled frequently in summer); you can walk along beach; swimming; daily 8-8 all yr; sm adm.

MILLBURN: South Mountain Reservation (just N of town), 2000-acre park with hiking trails **(2)**, picnic sites; open all yr; free. **Cora Hartshorn Arboretum & Bird Sanctuary** (2 m W to Forest Drive, Short Hills), nature trails, nature museum, guided walks; open daily; free; **1.**

MORRISTOWN: Morristown National Historical Park consists of 3 units, sites of Washington's winter encampments in 1777, 1779-80: Ford Mansion (230 Morris St.) with museum (sm adm). Ft. Nonsense (Washington St. & Western Ave.). Jockey Hollow (3 m SW on Jockey Hollow Rd.) with reconstructed soldiers' huts, field hospital, 1750 Wick House and garden; living history programs; nature trail **(1, 2)**; daily exc Jan. 1, Thnks, Dec. 25; free.

RINGWOOD STATE PARK (Sloatsburg Rd., Ringwood) has ironmaster's mansion set on landscaped grounds **(1)**; nearby Skylands Manor is also set in gardens and has wooded trails **(1, 2)**; May-Oct., Tues.-Sun.; sm adm.

SANDY HOOK: Gateway National Recreation Area, swimming and beachcombing along 6 m of beach; booklets for self-guiding walks; guided walks; Information Center open in summer, daily 8-6, variable hrs in winter; park open daily all year.

SCOTCH PLAINS: Watchung Reservation (1 m NE) offers Trailside Nature Science Center (Coles Ave. & New Providence Rd. in Mountainside); write Union County Park Comm. (Box 275, Elizabeth 07207), which operates other nearby parks.

SOMERVILLE: Duke Gardens (on US 206 at Dukes Pkwy E), former Doris Duke estate, gardens covering an acre under glass; 1-hr conducted tours by appointment (Duke Gardens Foundation, Inc., Rte 206 S, zip 08876); adm; usually open Oct.-mid-June.

WASHINGTON CROSSING STATE PARK (on SR 546, 579 on the Delaware River N of Trenton), has section in Pennsylvania; **McKonkey Ferry Museum** (Tues.-Sat. 10-noon, 1-5, Sun. 2-5; closed Jan. 1, Thnks, Dec. 25; sm adm); nature center with trails and bird blind (1); open all yr.

STATE FORESTS: Stokes (on US 206 NW of Branchville), on Kittatinny Ridge, best mtn scenery in state; 14,843-acre forest with camping, swimming lake; 45-minute walk in Tillman Ravine, overhung with hemlocks (2); 9 m of Appalachian Trail runs up to scenic lookout on Sunrise Mtn; 17 other trails; 6 easy walks (1) include 1½-m Blue Mtn, .8-m Steam Mill, 1.8-m Stephen; moderate trails (2) include 1.3-m Coursen and .7-m Stoll, where laurel and rhododendron bloom June-July; 2-m Criss Trail (2, 3) is rocky; .7-m Stony Brook Trail (2, 3) goes up Sunrise Mtn; maps and trail descriptions from hq (on US 206). **Wharton** (US 206 near Atsion), 99,000-acre pine barren preserve; cedar swamps, canoeing streams; nature trail in Batsto Nature Atea (1); part of Batona Trail (1, 2); walking (1) on wide sand roads; camping; swimming.

STATE PARKS: High Point (on SR 23 N of Sussex) adj Stokes State Forest on Kittatinny Ridge; state's highest point (1803 ft); Appalachian Trail follows stony crests (2, 3); trail (1) circles attractive Kuser swamp; 9 other trails: pretty Ayer's (1), 1-m past abandoned farm between Sawmill Rd. & Ridge Rd.; ½-m stony, slippery Blue Dot (3) runs from campsite 34 on Sawmill Lake to Appalachian Trail; 4-m Iris (2) through forest between SR 23 & Deckertown Pike; ½-m Life (1), from group campsite to Ridge Rd.; 1½-m Mashipacong (1, 2) goes by abandoned farm between Ridge & Mashipacong Rds to Sawmill Rd; 3½-m Monument Trail (2, 3), loop from monument to Kuser swamp and back; ½-m Old Trail (1), near bear pen; 1-m Parker (2, 3), with wet and rocky portions, runs from Ridge Rd. to Stokes forest; 3/4-m Steenykill (1, 2) at Lake Steenykill (on SR 23) beaver area, climbs to meet Monument Trail.

NEW MEXICO

ALAMOGORDO: White Sands National Monument (15 m SW via US 70, 82), 146,535 acres, has glistening dunes of white gypsum; Visitor Center offers guided walks in summer, occasional auto caravans; 8-m scenic drive; 1-m Big Dune Trail (2) takes 1 hr (carry water); daily 7 am-6 pm (to 10 in summer); closed Dec. 25; sm adm. **Three Rivers Petroglyph Site** (29 m N on US 54, 5 m S) has 1400-yard trail to representative examples; hundreds more are scattered along the ridge; picnicking (no water); **2. Mescalero Apache Reservation** (30 m NE via US 54, 70) has a trading post and national fish hatchery at Mescalero; hiking from recreation areas on the reservation (1-3): Eagle Creek (5 m W of Ruidoso via SR 37) and Ruidoso Creek (W of Ruidoso on Rio Ruidoso), open May-Sept.; Apache Summit (12 m S of Ruidoso on US 70) and Silver Spring (20 m N of Cloudcraft via SR 24), open all yr. **Lincoln National Forest** (E on US 82) has stunning trails (2,3) at recreation sites; guided walks; nature trail (2) at Karr Canyon (US 82 & FS 63); information: Federal Bldg., Alamogordo 88310.

ALBUQUERQUE: Chamber of Commerce (Civic Center, 401 2nd St.) provides maps for surrounding area, dates of local festivals; **Old Town** (N of Central Ave. at Rio Grande Blvd) is nice for strolling; **Rio Grande Zoological Park** (903 10th St. SW) is open daily (sm adm); **1.** Nearby pueblos are: **Santa Ana** (18 m N via I-25 to SR 44, then 10 m N), usually open feast days, no photography; **Zia** (8 m NW of Santa Ana off SR 44), nearby reservoir for picnics; **Jemez** (6 m N of Zia via SR 44, then 5 m NE on SR 4), plus picnics at Holy Ghost Spring (19 m N via SR 44) with permit (obtainable at San Isidro store at jct SR 4, 44). **Jemez State Monument** (10 m N of Jemez Pueblo on SR 4), ruins of mission, museum, Visitor Center (Wed.-Sun. 9-5; free). **Isleta** (13 m S off US 85), old mission, adj recreation ares. See also Grants.

   Coronado State Monument (18 m N via I-25, W on SR 44, follow signs), ruins of pueblos with 1200 ground-level rooms, painted kiva, museum;

Fri.-Tues. 9-5; sm adm; **1. Indian Petroglyph State Park** (9 m W on Atrisco Rd.) is open daily 9-5 (7-7 Apr.-Sept.); closed hols; sm adm; **2. Sandia Crest Drive** (15 m E on US 66, 6½ m N on SR 14, follow signs), extraordinarily scenic route in Cibola Ntl Forest; trail maps at campgrounds or on drive; well-marked but high-altitude trails **(2,3)**; information: P.O. Box 1826, Albuquerque 87103.

AZTEC: Aztec Ruins National Monument (1 m N off US 550), ruins of one of largest pueblos in SW; Visitor Center; self-guiding trail **(1,2)**; daily 8-5 (8-6 in summer); closed Jan. 1, Memorial Day, Dec. 25; sm adm or GEP. **Riverside Park** (S off US 550 on S Light Plant Rd.), city park, camping, picnicking; open daily; free. **Navajo Lake State Park** (26 m E via SR 173, 511), water sports, camping, picnicking at huge reservoir; dam overlook; Visitor Centers at Pine River and Arboles. **Farmington** (7 m SW on US 550) has swimming, picnicking, other facilities at Brookside (1701 N Dustin) and Lions (405 N Wall Ave.) parks. **Salmon Ruins** (7 m S via SR 44 to Bloomfield, 2 m W), 11th-C pueblo with 700 rooms, museum, picnicking; daily 9-5; closed Dec. 25; sm adm; **1,2.**
Huerfano Overlook (27 m SE on SR 44), picnic site with fine views; **1. Angel Peak Recreation Area** (42 m SE on SR 44), beautiful badlands; camping, picnicking, no water; easy trails **(1)**, trails **(2,3)** to 6988-ft Angels Peak.
Bandelier National Monument (12 m S of Los Alamos, off SR 4), extensive pueblo ruins; self-guiding trail **(2)** from Frijoles Canyon Visitor Center to view of masonry structures built in front of caves for 2 m along cliffs; trail climbs to 400-room Tyuonyi pueblo; guided walks, campfire programs; camping; 60 m of glorious trails to cave dwellings, pueblo ruins, kivas, petroglyphs; climb in and out of canyons and altitude (7000 ft) makes them strenuous **(2,3)**, so you must register with ranger for these; daily 8-5 (8-7 in summer); closed Dec. 25; sm adm or GEP. A separate unit, **Tsankawi** (11 m N on SR 4), 35-room, unexcavated ruin atop a mesa has views of Rio Grande Valley; 2-m self-guiding loop trail **(2)**, past cave structures and petroglyphs, follows a centuries-old Indian trail worn as deep as 18 inches.

CARLSBAD: Carlsbad Caverns National Park (20 m SW via US 62, 180, then 7 m W on SR 7) has exhibits, guided walks, cave tours, observation tower at Visitor Center; tours of main cavern daily (7-6 in summer, 8-4 rest of yr; adm). Complete tour is strenuous 3-m, 3½-hr descent of 800 ft to lunchrooms and restrooms, then 1¼-m, 1½-hr trail; return by elevator; **2.** A shorter tour (both ways by elevator) goes to 14-acre Big Room **(1)**. Tours of **New Cave** (23 m SW) by reservation only (phone 785-2233 at least 1 day in advance), usually daily in summer, weekends rest of yr; 3½-m trip (1¼ m in cave, 2½ m to and from parking lot); hiking boots or tennis shoes, long pants, water, flashlight required. **Walnut Canyon Loop Drive** (9-m primitive road) with picnic sites; Desert Nature Trail **(1)**; Oak Springs Trail **(1)**; Bat Flight Program (late spring-autumn, dates vary). Hiking in 46,735-acre park is limited only by how much water you can carry; maps are essential as some trails are not well marked; no campgounds but you can camp on the trail; registry with rangers required.

Lake Carlsbad Recreation Area (E end of Church St.), on Pecos River; swimming, picnicking, other activities; city-run Jim White Campground (off US 62, 180), on E bank of Pecos; **1. Zoological Botanical State Park of the Southwest** (1½ m NW off US 285), 360-acre cactus garden, animal display (daily 8-5:30; adm); adj is city-run park for picnicking, recreation. **Lincoln National Forest** (12 m N on US 285, 39 m SW on SR 137) has a beautiful recreation area at Sitting Bull Falls; hiking **(3)** in Guadalupe Mtns; information: Supervisor, Federal Bldg., Alamogordo 88310.

CARRIZOZO: White Oaks (3 m N via US 54, then 9 m E on SR 349), ghost town. **Valley of Fires State Park** (3 m W on US 380), strange badlands with 60-m-long lava field, overlook, camping, picnicking.

CHACO CANYON (on SR 57, 23 m S of Blanco or 64 m N of Thoreau): Visitor Center (S entrance) offers conducted walks, evening programs; campsites with water; beautiful canyon with 12 large and 400 small Anasazi ruins; auto loop has self-guiding trails to Pueblo Bonito (largest ruin, 800 rooms), Chettro Kettle, Casa Rinconada **(2)**; trails **(2,3)** to other ruins; daily 8-5 (8-9 in summer); closed Jan. 1, Dec. 25; free.

CIMARRON: Historic town, in beautiful country, on the Santa Fe Trail (which went N past Raton and S to Ft. Union); information at **St. James Hotel Museum** (open daily in summer, weekends in spring & fall; adm) or **Old Mill Museum** (May-Sept., Fri.-Wed. 9-5; sm adm). **Philmont Scout Camp & Explorer Base** (6 m S on SR 21) contains Kit Carson Museum and Ernest Thompson Seton Museum; daily in summer 7-7; rest of yr, Mon.-Fri. 8-5; closed hols; free. **Cimarron Canyon** (US 64 W toward Eagle Nest), scenic area with palisades; camping, picnicking. **Elizabethtown** (on SR 38, 5 m N of Eagle Nest) is a ghost town.

DEMING: State parks with camping, picnicking **(1)**: **Rock Hound** (14 m SE via SR 11), 250 acres in volcanic hills and mtns for rockhounding; views. **City of Rock** (29 m NW of Deming via US 180, SR 61) has clumped rock formations giving the appearance of a city; up close, they resemble houses crowded on narrow streets; cactus garden. **Pancho Villa** (35 m S on SR 11 to SW edge of Columbus) commemorates Villa's 1916 raid into U.S. territory; historic markers; lovely botanical garden on Villa Hill (views); open daily; free. **Massacre Peak** (13 m NE on SR 26) is a BLM site with petroglyphs, caves (2,3); ruins of **Ft. Cummings** (17 m NE on SR 26, then marked road 7 m), 2.

DULCE: Jicarilla Apache Indian Reservation (US 64), beautiful 750,000 acres; campgrounds on several mtn lakes; riding, special events, guides; trails (2,3) to cliff dwellings, other ruins; information: Jicarilla Tourist Dept., P.O. Box 147, Dulce 87528.

GALLUP: Chamber of Commerce (103 W 66th Ave.) information on the town, festivals, and surrounding Indian reservations. **Zuni Indian Reservation** (17 m S on SR 32) has lovely campsites as bases for exploring (permits at Governor's Office) in Zuni Pueblo (on SR 53, 6 m W of jct SR 32). **El Morro National Monument** (58 m SE of Gallup via SR 32 & 33), sandstone monolith with petroglyphs and inscriptions left by Conquistadores, pioneers, other travelers; from Visitor Center a self-guiding trail leads around base of the cliff and to top of mesa, where there are pueblo ruins (1, 2); camping; picnicking; daily 8-5 (8-8 in summer); sm adm or GEP. **Cibola National Forest** (12 m E on I-40, 10 m S on SR 400) has 2 nice recreation areas here, nature trail at McGaffey campground, other trails (1-3); district ranger is in Gallup. **Navajo Indian Reservation** (N on US 666), chief center is Shiprock (camping, picnicking in Community park; annual fair in Oct.), but for information write tribal hq in Window Rock (see Arizona); camping, trails (3) at **Bowl Canyon** Tribal Park (NE of town of Navajo, 43 m NW of Gallup via US 666, SR 264, tribal rds), a bowl-shaped canyon dominated by sandstone bluffs; camp and picnic sites also at **Asaayi Lake** (11 m E of Navajo), **Berland Lake** (13 m N of Crystal), **Capt. Tom Reservoir** (4 m N of Newcomb off US 666), **Cutter Dam** (8 m S of Blanco off US 64), **Mariano Lake** (near Mariano Lake School), **Morgan Lake** (near Four Corners Power Plant), **Todacheene Lake** (1 m N of Washington Pass), **Washington Pass** (5 m E of Crystal), **W Mexican Springs** (5 m W of Mexican Springs); 2,3.

GRANTS: Much of the Malpais Lava Beds (S on SR 53) is public land; lava flows, grassy valleys, wooded hills, cliffs, mesas; ice cave tours. **Acoma Pueblo** (26 m E via I-40, 13 m S), with picnicking at Acomita Lake (Acomita exit of I-40) Mar-Dec. (tribal permit at store on lake); **Laguna Pueblo** (33 m E off US 66), with Paguate Reservoir (on SR 279) open all yr for picnics (permit from Laguna police). **Bluewater Lake State Park** (21 m W via I-40, SR 412), colorful rock formations, water sports, camping, picnicking; lakeside (1) or overview (2,3) trails.

LAS CRUCES: Chamber of Commerce (760 W Picacho Ave.) provides information on ghost towns. **La Mesilla State Monument** (2 m SW), once the Confederate capital of the territory, has preserved bldgs on the old plaza; picnic area; **1**. **Ft. Selden & Leasburg State Parks** (14 m NW off I-25), on the Rio Grande; former has ruins of 1865 army post; overlooks; cemetery; **1,2**. **San Augustin Pass Overlook** (12 m E via US 70), magnificent view; **3**. **Aguirre Spring Recreation Area** (17 m NE via US 70 & local rd), camping, picnicking, walks, **1**.

LAS VEGAS: Chamber of Commerce (721 Grand Ave.) offers maps for self-guiding tours. **Villanueva State Park** (31 m SW via I-25 & SR 3), near charming village of Villanueva, on Pecos River, has camping; trails through juniper and pinon up the mesas above the river **(2,3)**, or through cottonwoods near the water; caves; open May-Nov. **Ft. Union National Monument** (20 m NE via I-25, 8 m NW on SR 477), ruins of fort established on Santa Fe Trail; wagon ruts; Visitor Center displays, living history programs in summer; picnicking; self-guiding trail through ruins **(1)**, trail **(2)** to Turkey Mtns; daily 8-4:30 (8-7 in summer); closed Dec. 25; sm adm or GEP. **Storrie Lake State Park** (6 m N on SR 3) and **Las Vegas Ntl Wildlife Refuge** (2 m E on SR 104, 4 m S on SR 281), both with camping, picnicking, walks **(1,2)**. **Gallinas River Canyon** (N of town), also pretty for walks; **2**.

MOUNTAINAIR: Abo State Monument (11 m SW off US 60) and **Quarai State Monument** (6 m N off SR 14), unexcavated ruins of pueblos; Abo is open daily 9-5; Quarai has Visitor Center, picnic tables, and is open Wed.-Sun. 9-5; free; **2**. **Gran Quivira National Monument** (26 m SE on SR 14), ruin tracing human habitation from pithouses to 17th-C; Visitor Center; self-guiding trail through ruins of pueblo and Spanish mission; picnicking; daily 8-5 (longer in summer); closed Dec. 25; free; **1**. **Manzano State Park** (13 m NW via SR 14) has camping, picnicking, walks **1-3**.

RATON: Capulin Mountain National Monument (29 m E via US 64, 87 to Capulin, 3½ m N on SR 325), extinct volcano; Visitor Center exhibits and audiovisual program; road partway up, then trails **(2)** to summit; wonderful 1-m Crater Rim Trail **(1)** with views of Folsom Man Site (closed to public); ¼-m trail to crater bottom; picnicking: daily 8-4:30 (longer in summer); sm adm. **Sugarite Canyon Park** (10 m NE on SR 72), 9000 acres with camping and picnicking; nice walks **(1,2)**; adm per car. **Maxwell National Wildlife Refuge** (25 m S to Maxwell via I-25, 4 m NW) offers trails **(1,2)**; daily all yr; free.

ROSWELL: Bottomless Lakes State Park (16 m SE via US 380, SR 409), 6 lovely lakes with dark-green moss on bottoms giving appearance of great depth; swimming; 35-m scenic loop from Roswell with overlooks, picnicking; rockhounding; camping; riding; walks **1-3**. **Dexter National Fish Hatchery** (15 m SE at Dexter) is open daily; free; **1**. **Bitter Lake National Wildlife Refuge** (13 m NE off US 70), walks (**1,2**), picnics; daily; free.

SANTA FE: The Plaza (at Lincoln between Palace Ave & San Francisco St.), hub of the old city, is start of walking tour; **Chamber of Commerce** (SE corner of plaza in La Fonda Hotel) offers maps: Palace of the Governors (N side), Delgado House (W side), Sena and Prince Plazas (E side), Oldest House (215 E DeVargas St.), San Miguel Mission (Old Santa Fe Trail & DeVargas St.), State Capitol (DeVargas St., W of Old Santa Fe Trail), and excellent museums; **1**. **Santa Fe River Park** (Delgado to Shelby Sts.) along the river; strolling; picnics. **Canyon Road,** originally an Indian trail, is now lined with studios and shops (plus Cristo Rey Church at Camino Cabra). **Camino del Monte Sol** is also charming.

Nearby pueblos include: **Tesuque** (8 m N on US 84), with camping, picnicking, swimming pool, other facilities at Camel Rock (2 m beyond); **Nambe** (20 m NE via US 84, SR 4), with Nambe Falls (7 m E of Pajoaque via SR 4) open Mar.-Dec. for picnicking, camping; **San Ildefonso** (22 m NW via US 84, SR 4); **Santa Clara** (27 m NW via US 84, SR 5), with picnicking, camping, other facilities (open Apr.-Nov.; obtain permit from ranger) at Puye Cliffs (on SR 5) and Santa Clara Creek (5 m beyond Puye Cliffs on SR 5); **San Juan** (28 m N via US 84, 285); **Cochiti** (30 m SW off US 85); **Santo Domingo** (31 m SW off US 85 on SR 22); **San Felipe** (34 m SW off US 85).

Pecos National Monument (25 m SE off I-25), ruins of one of the largest Anasazi settlements; 650 rooms, 22 kivas; self-guiding trail through ruins (**1,2**); daily 8-5 (8-7 in summer); closed Jan. 1, Dec. 25; free.

Hyde Memorial State Park (35 m NE via SR 475), 350 acres heavily forested with evergreens; 5 trails (**2,3**) tend to be steep (2 connect to Santa Fe Ntl Forest trail system); fall color. **Santa Cruz Lake Recreation Area** (30 m N via US 285, SR 4, 76), open spring-fall with camping, picnicking; trails around lake (**1,2**), to dam; trails to Santa Cruz overlook and Vista Valle trails (**2,3**) that climb above the lake for overlooks; free.

Santa Fe National Forest (E & W) is magnificent—lakes, streams, 100-ft waterfall, springs, stunning scenery. **Pecos Wilderness** (E), 167,000 acres, above headwaters of Pecos River at S end of Sangre de Cristo Mtns, is partly in Carson forest; SR 75 and a dirt road along Santa Fe River lead to a cluster of campsites (open May-Oct.) at trailheads (**2, 3**); nature trail (**2**) at Aspen Vista. **Glorieta** picnic area with trail (**2,3**) is reached on good-weather road 12 m W of Pecos (via SR 50, then 12 m NW on FS rd). **N of Pecos** (via SR 63) is a state fish hatchery and a series of campsites giving access to easy trails along creeks and closest access to the most rugged and remote areas **(1-3)**; Fair Tract, Holy Ghost, Windsor Creek, and Panchuela have naturalist programs; Jack's Creek has self-guiding trail **(1, 2)**. **On the E,** SR 65 from Las Vegas leads to another cluster of campsites; good local hiking **(2,3)** but trails do not connect to the wilderness area. Additional wilderness access is off rough peripheral roads. **Anton Chico Section** is reached by rough road from Bernal; the road makes a loop through the forest and has a cutoff to the Pecos River; **2,3.** W of Santa Fe is the 41,000-acre **San Pedro Parks Wilderness** (averages 10,000 ft), a plateau green with spruce and mtn meadows reached via rough roads from Cuba and Coyote, or from SR 4 in the S (where most of the campsites are); Rodondo and San Antonio offer nature trails **(2).** Information: P.O. Box 1689. Santa Fe 87501.

SILVER CITY: Splendid **Gila National Forest** (301 W College Ave., Silver City 88601) surrounds the city; 1200 m of trails **(1-3)** are through floodplains, deep canyons, flat mesas, magnificent mtns. **Gila Cliff Dwellings National Monument** (47 m N via SR 15), excavations of dwellings constructed inside cliffside caves AD 100-1400; Visitor Center (daily 8-5; closed Jan. 1, Dec. 25) has trail information; steep ½-m trail to cliff dwellings **(2)**; trails to Gila Wilderness start here and at nearby Scorpion campground (also nature trail, **1**). **Gila Wilderness** (access via Cliff Dwellings or from Glenwood-Snow Lake area), with the highest mtns (9000-10, 892 ft), attractive rivers; 22 entry points **(2,3)** off US 180, SR 78, 61, or 15. The 75-m **Inner Loop Drive** (N via SR 15 to SR 35; SW via even more spectacular 235-m **Outer Loop Drive** (US 180 N to beyond Glenwood; SR 78 to SR 61; S to Santa Rita on SR 90; W to Silver City) give good views of the area; wonderful optional route off Outer Loop between Willow Creek campground (via Snow Lake) and Beaverhead ranger station. **Cherry Creek** (N on SR 15) camp and picnic area has wildflowers. **Black Range Primitive Area** (37 m E on SR 90) has camping and picnicking on pretty streams; campsites with trailheads to the Black Range are Emory Pass (SR 90 near Kingston), and Black Canyon and Rocky Canyon (SR 61), which also lead to the Gila; district ranger at 405 Main St., Truth or Consequences. **Gila Primitive Area** (between SR 15 and SR 61 N of SR 35) has campgrounds on the periphery, the highest mtns, attractive waters; trailheads are off SR 15 (N of jct SR 35), off SR 61 (N of jct SR 35), or from Lake Roberts. **Lake Roberts** (25 m N on SR 15, then E on SR 35), attractive fishing lake at 6000 ft, has 3 campsites with trailheads to the Gila **(2,3)**; Lake Roberts camp also has picnicking, nature trail **(1)**, trail to Indian ruins **(2)**; Upper End camp has nature trail **(2)**. **The Catwalk** (62 m via US 180 to Glenwood, 5 m on FS road) is a trail on metal grillwork that hangs you off the cliffs above Whitewater Canyon. The area between **Glenwood** and **Snow Lake** has Mogolon ghost town (on SR 78), campsites with trailheads to Gila Wilderness (these start at high elevations, eliminating climbs out of deep valleys); old mining areas are at Kingston, Hillsboro, Pinos Altos.

Kwilleylekia Ruins (30 m NW via US 180 to Cliff, 1 m N), of a Salado pueblo, has Visitor Center, guided tours, observation of excavations; Apr.-Nov. daily 8-6; sm adm.

TAOS: Colorful town in 3 sections—Don Fernando de Taos, around Spanish plaza; Ranchos de Taos (4 m S on US 64), adobe homes, old church; Taos Pueblo (2½ m N on Pueblo Rd.). **Kit Carson Memorial State Park,** with picnicking, is near Kit Carson Home & Museum (E Kit Carson Rd. on US 64). **D. H. Lawrence Ranch & Shrine** (15 m N on SR 3, 5 m E on gravel rd) is open daily in daylight; free. **Picuris Pueblo** (San Lorenzo, 16 m S via US 64) has archaeological excavations, picnicking (May-Oct.) on 2 lakes and river; **1.**

Carson National Forest (hq on Cruz Alta Rd., S of town: write FS bldg, P.O. Box 587, Taos 87571), a million acres in beautiful country E and W of Taos and Santa Fe. E unit, in Sangre de Cristo Mtns, has recreational sites and **Wheeler Park Wilderness (1-3).** **Pecos Wilderness** is accessible from Santa Barbara (7 m E of Rodarte on FS rd) and Trampas Canyon (17 m S of Penasco on SR 76, FS 207) campsites. Between Penasco and Tres Ritos on US 3 are campsites with hiking **(2,3)**; campsites with trails **(1-3)** on US 64 **SE of Taos** and **N of Taos** via SR 3, 150 (Twining camp offers trails to wilderness); in N, camps and trailheads are E of Questa off SR 38. **Rio Grande** is being preserved as a wild river; a bridge crosses the gorge 8 m NW of Taos (on SR 111), observation decks, picnicking; many campsites at beautiful area where Red River and Rio Grande meet, overlooks, trails **(2,3)** include one over Cebolla Mesa; trails at Cedar Springs camp, Bear Crossing, Chieflo camp, Sheep Crossing. Forest section **W of Taos** has nature trail **(1)** at Echo Amphitheater (15 m SW of Canjilon on US 84), short trail at other recreation sites **(2,3)**. **Ghost Ranch Museum** (US 84, 17 m NW of Abiquiu) has exhibits, animals, small-scale forest, picnicking. Forest unit **SE of Dulce** (on US 64) offers backcountry hiking from ranger station.

TRUTH OR CONSEQUENCES: Elephant Butte Lake State Park (5 m E of I-25) has walks **(1)** near dam, spectacular views from ridge walks **(2)** near hq **(3** m N at Lions Beach), fossils in McRae Canyon **(2)**. **Caballo Lake State Park** (14 m S on I-25) has camping, picnicking, walks **(1,2)**; also at Percha Dam. **Cibola National Forest** has 3 units NW, with Datil Well Recreation Site (off US 60) offering the best hiking **(2,3)**; camping, picnicking. **Bosque del Apache** (off I-25 on Rio Grande) is a national wildlife refuge; **1.**

NEW YORK

ADIRONDACK PARK: Although boundaries of this preserve were established in 1883 to include 5.6-million acres, only 2.4-million acres is public land; here is the state's grandest scenery; 5 mtn ranges include 42 peaks over 4000 ft (5344-ft Mt. Marcy is the state's highest); chains of stunning lakes are often so closely connected that 100-m canoe trips can be made with short portages; scenic drives; historic sites; other attractions; dozens of camp and picnic sites plus leantos on foot trails; the trail system is so extensive that separate booklets are available for each region; write to: **Dept. of Environmental Conservation** (Albany 12201). **Adirondack Mtn Club, Inc.** (RD 1, Ridge Rd., Glens Falls, N.Y. 12801) also offers information, publications.

Northville-Lake Placid Trail runs over 100 m S from Lake Placid (closest camping is Meadowbrook, 5 m W on SR 86) to Long Lake, across Blue Ridge and a series of small lakes to Piseco Lake, and ends at Northhampton Beach campsite on Sacandaga Lake; this is to be part of the Long Path to the George Washington Bridge (see New York City); campsites and leantos along the way; trail booklet available.

Blue Mtn Lake: Adirondack Museum (SR 30) houses area exhibits in 20 bldgs; open summer-early fall daily; adm; **1. Blue Mtn Trail**, 5 m, to observation tower; parking fee; **2.** Trail booklets for several short trails (**1,2**) available from state or Blue Mtn Lake Assn. Camping at Lake Eaton (11 m N off SR 30), sand beach, 2-m trail (**2**) to Owlhead Mtn; Forked Lake (N off SR 30 at Deerland); Lake Durant (S on SR 30), on Northville-Placid Trail; Golden Beach & Tioga Pt (10 m SW on SR 28), lovely beaches on Raquette Lake; Brown Tract Pond (14 m SW on SR 28), Eighth Lake (18 m SW on SR 28) have trails (**1-3**). Just S is **Old Forge**, year-round resort with public beach, 125-m canoe trip to Saranac Lake area, lake cruises, chair lift, park campgrounds with good trails (trail booklets available for Old Forge-Big Moose area and Moose River), **1-3**.

Elizabethtown: Adirondack Center Museum & Colonial Garden has exhibits on area life; mid-May-mid-Oct. daily; adm; **1. Poke-O-Moonshine camp** (13 m N on US 9), trail (**2**), to 2162-ft Poke-O-Moonshine Mtn for views of Lake Champlain.

Lake George: Beautiful lake extends 50 m N to Ticonderoga; village at S end has amusement areas; lake cruises; public swimming beach; Ft. William Henry (Canada St.), reconstructed 1755 fort, Indian Village, film, exhibits, demonstrations (daily; adm); Lake George Battlefield Park (off US 9), fort ruins, camping, picnicking, state-run, 2 trails to views from 2100-ft Prospect Mtn (open summers); Prospect Mt. State Pkwy (toll road off US 9), 5½-m scenic route with free bus to summit from parking lot (Memorial Day-mid-Oct. daily 9-6); **1. Hearthstone Pt.** campsite (2 m N on SR 9N), swimming in Lake George, near system of beautiful trails (booklet available) that run along Tongue Mtn Peninsula on W shore (hiking boots advised because of large timber rattlers); these trails also reachable by boat from campsites on islands in the lake (boat rental and ferrying of camping equipment from Bolton or Huletts Landings); **1-3. Schroon Lake** (23 m N on I-87), commercial attractions, cave tours, hiking **(1-3)** from Eagle Pt. campground (booklet available) on trails ½-11-m long. At **Pottersville** (23 m N off I-87), Natural Stone Bridge & Caves, waterfalls, nature trails, picnicking (May-Oct.; adm); **1,2.**

Lake Placid: This and Lake Saranac (10 m W) are yr-round resorts; lake cruises; **John Brown Farm State Historic Site** (3 m S off SR 73 on Hogn Brown Rd.), home and grave of abolitionist (open daily; closed Jan. 1, Easter, Thnks, Dec. 25; free); **Uihlein-Cornell Sugar House** (Bear Cub Rd.), Cornell University maple sugar demonstration facility (late-Mar.-Apr. for sap boiling, July-Labor Day, & in fall foliage season; free); zoo (SR 86 open spring-fall; adm); start of Northville-Lake Placid Trail.

Mt. Marcy (trail booklet available) lies in a wilderness of peaks, stunning rivers, where few roads penetrate; perimeter paved roads provide access to an extensive system of wonderful trails where you can wander for days. From N, best access is via Northville-Lake Placid Trail or from unpaved road from N Elba (S of Lake Placid on SR 73) penetrating to Heart Lake. From S, Lake Harris campground (off SR 28N E of Newcomb), has trailheads, and unpaved road E (penetrating to Henderson Lake) has additional trails. Unpaved road to private resort of Elk Lake (off I-87 at Blue Ridge, 5 m W), magnificent trails **(1-3)**; some such as 3815-ft Boreas Peak, can be ½-day round trips; Mt. Marcy requires 2-3 overnights.

Speculator: Campgrounds here provide excellent trails **(1-3): Moffit Beach** (2 m W off SR 8), on Sacandaga Lake, has trails up Kunjamuk Creek, nearby lakes, Pillsbury Mtn, and connection to Indian Lake Trails **(1-3); Indian Lake** and **Lewey Lake** (12 m N off SR 30), good trails up Jessup River, to 3903-ft Snowy Mtn, 7-m Sucker Brook Trail to Cedar River (1 m more to Northville-Placid Trail), and trails off Indian Lake bays (some reachable by boat) to wilderness ponds **1-3; Poplar Pt, Little Sand Pt.**, and **Pt. Comfort** (all 8 m S on SR 8, then W), on Piseco Lake, offer scenic trail over lake **(2)**, 5½-m trail (from Poplar Pt.) to beautiful T Lake Falls **(2,3)**, trails to 2750-3250-ft summits **(2,3).**

Ticonderoga: Ft. Ticonderoga (2 m E on SR 73), built 1755 by French to guard waterway, is reconstructed; museums; demonstrations, special activities; open mid-May-mid-Oct. daily; adm; **1.** Good views from Ft. Mount Hope (½ m E on Burgoyne Rd.) and Historic Mt. Defiance (1 m

SE via toll road), both open late May-mid-Oct. daily; 1. **Skenesborough Museum** (26 m SE on SR 22 to Whitehall), early shipbuilding and railroad exhibits, picnicking; summers daily; adm; 1. **Penfield Homestead** (5 m W via SR 74, then N to Ironville), self-guiding trail through 500-acre ironwork ruins, picnicking; mid-May-mid-Oct., Tues.-Sun.; adm; 1. Nearby campsites with swimming, picnicking: **Rogers Rock** (6 m S on SR 9N) on Lake George, access to Tongue Mtn. Trails (2,3); **Crown Pt.** (13 m N off SR 9N), ruins of French and English forts, museums, nearby lighthouse (1); **Putnam Pond** (6 m W off SR 74), trails (1,2) to lovely trout ponds, climbs (2) to mtns; **Paradox Lake** (15 m W off SR 74), stunning, trails to ponds (1,2), 2557-ft Pharoah Mtn (2), trails (2) across lake (by boat) to pond and overlook (ask for Schroon Lake trail booklet).

Tupper Lake: Yr-round resort; walking (1,2) to many fishing ponds (camping N on SR 30 at Fish Creek and Rollins ponds). **Cranberry Lake** campsite (28 m W on SR 3), bathing beach on lovely lake, start of beautiful ½–16-m hiking trails (1-3) and canoe trips into wilderness; trail booklet available. **Meacham Lake** campsite (31 m N via SR 30), swimming beach; trails E of lake include one to 3305-ft Debar Mtn; 1,2.

Wilmington: Gateway to **Whiteface Mtn Memorial Hwy** (3-m W on SR 431), 5-m toll road (weather permitting, late May-mid-Oct., daily 9-5) to parking area; 4867-ft summit reached by trail (2) or elevator. Aerial Lifts operate (summer-early fall; adm) to 2-m summit of Little Whiteface. Whiteface can be climbed (3) from Wilmington Notch campground (3 m SE on SR 86) in a beautiful narrow defile; **Wilmington Recreation Area** (½ m SW on SR 86) has beach on Ausable River. **High Falls Gorge** (4 m SE on SR 86), carved by Ausable River, has falls, wildflowers, observation platforms, scenic trails on steel walks and bridges (2), museum, picnicking; early May-late Oct. daily; adm. See also Plattsburgh.

ALBANY: Chamber of Commerce (510 Broadway), maps for walking tours including State Capitol, Mall with museums and government bldgs, old Dutch houses, other historic sites, State University (guided tours weekdays from Campus Center Information Desk; free); 1. **Capitalland Natural Science Center** (Livingston Jr. High School, Northern Blvd.), 82 acres with guided, self-guiding tours; 1. **Five Rivers Environmental Center** (S to Game Farm Rd. in Delmar), 260 acres, self-guiding trails, state-run; free; 1.

ALEXANDRIA BAY: Gateway to thousand islands resort area shared with Canada—1700 islands from rock dots to islands over 10-m long; boat cruises (spring-fall) usually stop ½-hr on **Heart Island** for self-guiding tours of Boldt Castle (adm). **State parks,** most with camping, water sports, picnicking, short walks (1) include: Keewaydin (1 m SW on SR 12),

Grass Pt. (4 m SW on SR 12); Wellesley Island (2 m N of bridge), Waterson Pt. and DeWolf Pt. (4 m N of bridge).

AMSTERDAM: Erie Canal (4 m W on SR 5S at Ft. Hunter) preserves 3 sections of original canal; 1. **George Landis Arboretum** (15 m S via SR 30 to US 20), 50 acres of rare plantings, gardens; picnics; Apr.-Oct.; free; 1. **William W. Badgley Historical Complex** (24 m S on SR 30 in Schoharie) has museums, carriage house, church (open daily in summer, Tues.-Sun. in spring & fall; closed hols; adm); 1. Camping, picnicking, walks (1) at **Toe Path Mtn** (35 m S on SR 30) and **Mine Kill** (44 m S on SR 30) state parks.

BUFFALO: Convention & Visitors Bureau (164 Franklin St.), information on historic sites; **Zoological Gardens** (Amherst & Parkside Aves.), 23 acres (open daily; closed Thnks, Dec. 25; adm); **Delaware Park** (Lincoln Pkwy) designed by Olmstead; 1. **South Park Botanical Gardens** (4 m SE off S Park Ave.), exotic plants, seasonal display; daily 9-4; free; 1. State Parks with picnicking, walks (1): **Beaver Island** (S end of Grand Island), swimming beach; **Buckhorn Island** (N end of Grand Island), 896-acre wildlife sanctuary; **Darien Lakes** (20 m E on US 20), swimming, camping; **Evangola** (21 m SW on SR 5), swimming, camping; **Lake Erie** (37 m SW on I-90, 7 m SW on SR 5), swimming, camping. **Niagara County Historical Center** (20 m NE via SR 263, 78 in Lockport), complex of 19th-C bldgs, exhibits, canal locks (free); 1. **Griffis Sculpture Park** (45 m SE off US 219), 400-acre park with sculpture, picnicking, cultural events, nature trails; June-Oct. daily; 1.

ERIE CANAL: Cutting 363 m across the state from Waterford to Tonawanda on Niagara River, canal follows the Mohawk River to Frankfort; then a land-cut channel to New London; Wood Creek, Oneida Lake and River, Seneca and Clyde rivers to Lyons; from here it is a land-cut channel to Tonawanda. Feeder systems include 24-m Oswego Canal (to Lake Ontario) and 92-m Cayuga-Seneca Canal to Ithaca and Watkins Glen. Pleasure boats are allowed on all sections. **Canal parks** with picnicking, overlooks, interpretive trails (1) are being constructed and include sites at Locks #4 (Stillwater), #9 (Rotterdam Junction), #20 (Whitesboro), #23 (Brewerton), #30 (Macedon), #32 (Pittsford). Trails are being marked with interpretive signs; completed sections are Lockport to Rochester, Pittsford to Fairport, section at Canastota. **Information:** State Office of Parks & Recreation (S Mall, Albany 12223) or at canal museums (See Rome, Syracuse).

FINGER LAKES: (write Finger Lakes Assn., 309 Lake St., Penn Yan 14527), 6 large and 5 small, finger-shape lakes running N-S between

Syracuse and Rochester; all have resort facilities, most have municipal and state recreation areas; best walking (1,2).

Owasco Lake: Hoopes Park (in Auburn, N end of lake, on US 20), rose gardens; **Emerson Co. Park** (E shore, on SR 38A), swimming, recreation, Owasco Indian Village (open summers); **Fillmore Glen State Park** (5 m S of lake on SR 38), swimming, camping, picnicking, trails; **1.**

Cayuga Lake: Montezuma National Wildlife Refuge (5 m NE of Seneca Falls on US 20), open daily, free **1,2.** Swimming, camping, picnicking at state parks—**Cayuga Lake** (3 m S of Seneca Falls on SR 89), strolls; **Long Point** (2 m S of Aurora on SR 90), strolls; **Taughannock Falls** (8 m N of Ithaca on SR 89), trails to 215-ft falls, in woods; **Buttermilk Falls** (2 m S of Ithaca on SR 13), 675 acres, trails; **Robert H. Treman** (5 m S of Ithaca on SR 13), strolls. In **Ithaca, Ithaca College** campus (on SR 96B) overlooks the lake; **Stewart Park** (Cayuga St.), small zoo; **Cornell University** offers guided tours or maps for self-guiding tours at Visitor Information Center (Edmund Ezra Day Hall on East Ave.; Mon.-Fri. 8:30-4:30), test gardens and plantations (along Plantation Rd.; open daily in daylight; free), and wonderful 250-acre bird sanctuary at Laboratory of Ornithology (Sapsucker Woods; open daily, free).

Seneca Lake: In **Geneva, Rose Hill Mansion** (E on SR 96A) overlooks lake (May-Oct., daily; adm). Swimming and picnicking at **Seneca Lake** (E of Geneva on US 20, SR 5) and **Sampson** (12 m SE of Geneva on SR 96A) state parks. **Blueberry Patch** (8 m N of Watkins Glen off SR 414), camping, picnicking, good trails. **Watkins Glen State Park** (S shore), 19 waterfalls in 2-m rocky gorge; narrow trail with steps and bridges; many people taxi to top and walk down; gorge lit at night; camping, summer pool, picnicking.   Town of **Watkins Glen** has municipal parks on lake. **Montour Falls** (2 m S of Watkins Glen on SR 14), 156-ft falls, Catherine Creek, 7 glens including Havana Glen with trails to Eagle Cliff Falls; **1,2.**

Keuka Lake: Penn Yan has municipal parks on lake. **Keuka Lake State Park** (6 m SW off SR 54A), swimming, camping, picnicking. **Hammondsport** (S end of lake), winery tours. **Bath** (7 m S of lake), walks, picnics, in Mossy Bank Park; state fish hatchery.

Canandaigua Lake: In **Canandaigua** (N shore), **Granger Homestead** (295 N Main St.; open Tues.-Sun; closed hols; adm) with carriage museum (open summers); **Sonnenberg Gardens** (Howell & Charlotte Sts.), Japanese, Italian, 8 other gardens on 50 acres (mid-May-Oct. daily; adm). In **Naples** (S of lake), **Grimes Glen** has camping, picnicking; **Cumming Nature Centure** is run by Rochester Museum; **Widmer's Wine Cellar** tours are given summer-early fall; **Ontario Co. Park** has picnicking, trails; **1.**

FingerLakes Trail will eventually form a 650-m link between the Appalachian Trail and Canada's Bruce Trail; more than half is completed between Syracuse and Letchworth State Park along S end of Finger Lakes;

300 m of branch trails will parallel the lakes; access from Buttermilk Falls, Watkins Glen, many roads; for list of sectional maps, send stamped, self-addressed, #10 envelope to P.O. Box 4054, Brighton Station, Rochester 14610.

JAMESTOWN: On **Lake Chautauqua** are: **Long Point State Park** (10m N on SR 17), picnicking, swimming. **Chautauqua Institution** (16 m N on SR 394), 700 acres with educational and recreational facilities, outdoor model of Holy Land; open (adm) July-Aug. daily (for information: Box 1095, Chautauqua 14722); **1. Panama Rocks** (13 m W on SR 474), caves, rock formations, picnics (open summers; adm); **1.**

KINGSTON: Free walking tours of 2 dozen 17-18th-C homes are conducted at 2 pm on 3rd Thurs. of each month from **Gov. Clinton Hotel** (1 Albany Ave.); tours also on Stone House Day (July) in Hurley (2 m S on US 209); Senate House & Museum (312 Fair St.), boxwood garden (Wed.-Sat. 9-5, Sun. 1-5; closed hols; free). **Seamon Memorial Park** (10 m N on US 9W), spectacular chrysanthemum displays (Oct.); **1. Bronck House Museum** (27 m N on US 9W), stone houses, barns, cemetery, picnicking; mid-June-late Sept., daily; adm; **1. Ashokan Reservoir** (5 m NW on SR 28, 28A), aeration basin with 2000 fountains; **1. Slabsides** (8 m S on US 9W to West Park, 1 m W), 175-acre sanctuary with cabin of John Burroughs is open by appt. (write caretaker, Slabsides, W Park 12493). **Huguenot Historical Society Old Stone Houses** (15 m S on I-87 to Huguenot St., New Paltz), 17-18th-C church and homes, museum; some bldgs open mid-May-mid-Oct., others open all yr, Wed.-Sun. 10-4:30; closed hols; adm; **1.**

Lake Mohonk and **Lake Minnewaska** (15 m S on I-87, W on SR 299, watch for signs), 17,000 acres surrounding stunning lakes in beautiful Shawangunk Mtns, were preserved by a conservation-minded family; both have Victorian hotels and areas reserved for overnight guests; most of land is open to public use. Mohonk has 60 m of wonderful carriage roads and trails, observation tower, picnicking, map at entrance (adm); Minnewaska has 50 m of carriage roads and trails, falls, map at entrance (adm); between the 2 is the Trapps, an incredible cliff offering the finest rock climbing in NE; for information write Lake Mohonk Mtn House or Lake Minnewaska Mtn House, New Paltz 12561; **1-3. Lake Awosting** (off US 44) may be open for day use as part of Minnewaska State Park; trails **1,2. Sam's Point** (via Lake Awosting or via Cragmoor), self-guiding tour of ice caves, rock formations, overlooks, falls, picnicking, nature trail, other trails (adm); **1,2.**

Catskill Park (W on SR 28), 250,000 acres with 34 forested summits over 3500-ft high, lake streams; camps at Beaverkill, Little Pond, Mongaup (off SR 17 N of Livingston Manor) are handy to Neversink, Red

Hill, other trails (1-3), trailless summit climbs (2,3), fish hatchery at DeBruce (1); Woodland Valley camp (off SR 28 SW of Phoenicia) has access to Slide Mtn. popularized by John Burroughs (his grave, W of the park at Roxbury, open spring-fall daily), Long Path, and other trails that are among the prettiest in the park (2,3); Devil's Tombstone camp (off SR 214 S of Hunter) is at trailheads for Hunter Mtn, Hunter Mtn Range Trail, and many side trails (1-3); N Lake camp (off SR 23A, NE of Haines Falls) is on cliff-and-ledge Escarpment Trail that runs 24 m across Blackhead Mtn, and on Long Path (2,3). Also in the park are: Catskill Game Farm (12 m W of Catskill on SR 32), picnicking (mid-Apr.-mid-Nov. daily; adm); Bellayre Mtn Chair Lift (on SR 28 W of Pine Hill), operates daily in summer, weekends for fall foliage, picnicking on summit (adm); chair lift at Hunter Mtn ski area also operates for fall color. **Information:** Div. of Lands & Forests, State Campus, Albany 12226.

LONG ISLAND: Fishing docks nice for walks in many areas (Montauk Pt. is best); vestiges of old whaling ports remain (especially at Sag Harbor and Southampton); access to town and private beaches usually effectively blocked in summer; state park beaches (adm spring-fall), among the best on the island, are wonderful for yr-round walks (some, such as Jones, Robert Moses, and Sunken Meadow, have all-yr cafes), all have picnicking; **1.**

Along N shore (E from NYC line) are: **Old Westbury Gardens** (Old Westbury Rd. in Old Westbury), patterned after 18th-C English parks; Georgian-style mansion (adm); Italian, sunken, other gardens; early May-late Oct., Wed.-Sun. & hols 10-5; adm. **Garvies Pt.** Museum & Preserve (follow signs from Glen Cove Rd., Glen Cove), 70 acres, interesting museum (closed Jan. 1, Thnks, Dec. 25), nature trails open daily in daylight; sm adm. **Muttontown Preserve** (S of SR 25A at E Norwich on SR 106), trails on former estates. **Planting Fields Arboretum** (off SR 25A via Wolves Hollow, Chicken Valley, & Planting Fields roads), run by the state university, daily 10-5; closed Dec. 25; adm. **Mill Neck Preserve** (NW of Oyster Bay at Mill Neck railroad station), trails. **Theodore Roosevelt Memorial Sanctuary** (Oyster Bay Cove Rd. off SR 27A, Oyster Bay), open to Audubon members only, but Roosevelt's grave is in a pretty cemetery open daily. **Sagamore Hill National Historic Site** (3 m NE of Oyster Bay on Cove Neck Rd.), Theodore Roosevelt's home, landscaped grounds; daily 9-5; closed Jan. 1, Thnks, Dec. 25; sm adm or GEP. **State Fish Hatchery** (SR 25A at jct SR 108, Cold Spring Harbor), daily, free. **Vanderbilt Museum—Eagles Nest** (2 m N of SR 25A on Little Neck Rd., Centerport), rambling mansion, natural history museum, grounds; May-Oct. daily; sm adm. **Heckscher Park** (SR 25A & Prime Ave., Huntington), museum, paths; open Tues.-Sun.; closed hols; free. **Sunken Meadow State Park** (SR 25A N of Kings Park), 1232 acres, swimming and walking on sound beach, boardwalk, walks around sound inlet. **Nissequogue River State Park** (jct SR 25, SR 25A at Smithtown), woods, lake, stream, trails, adj is lovely lake trail on Weld Estate Preserve. **Cathedral Pines Forest Preserve** (S off SR 25 on Yaphank-Rocky Pt. Rd. in Middle Island), 30 acres of white pines. **Peconic River Co. Park** (N off LI Expwy at exit 69), ponds, streams, trails. **Wildwood State Park** (off SR 25A at Wading River), 503 acres, sound swimming beach with bluffs, wooded camping area. **Oysterponds Historical Society** (Village Lane, Orient), restored several bldgs, exhibits; July-Oct., Tues., Thurs., Sat., Sun. 2-5; sm adm. **Orient Beach State Park** (SR 25), beautiful 357 acres on bays, swimming, picnicking; bird sanctuary; outstanding.

Along S shore (E from NYC line) are: **Valley Stream State Park** (Southern State Pkwy off Corona Ave), 100 acres, trail, pond. **Hempstead Lake State Park** (jct Southern State Pkwy & Peninsula Blvd), 867 acres, lakeside walks, duck pond, swamp; adj on S is Tanglewood Preserve (Ocean Ave. & Peninsula Blvd), 10 acres, pond. **Wantagh Park** (on Merrick Rd. & Wantagh State Pkwy), trails. **Tackapausha Preserve** (on SR 27, 1 m E of Seaford railroad station), 80 acres, 3 nature trails, museum; daily in daylight. **Old Bethpage Village Restoration** (Round Swamp Rd., 1 m S of L.I. Expwy in Bethpage), 2 dozen bldgs depicting pre-Civil War community; open daily; closed Jan. 1, Thnks, Dec. 25; adm. **Bethpage State Park** (S of the restoration), bridle trails, wooded paths around golf course; Massapequa Preserve (just S on Bethpage State Pkwy), lake, trails. **Belmont Lake State Park** (Southern State Pkwy & Belmont Ave.), 459 acres, nature trail, bridle path, other trails, lake, pond, stream. **Jones Beach State Park** (toll via Meadowbrook or Wantagh State Pkwys or Robert Moses Causeway), 2413-acre swimming beach, sports fields, other facilities; **JFK Memorial Wildlife Sanctuary** (E on Ocean Pkwy at Tobay Beach) requires free permit (write Town Clerk, Oyster Bay L.I.) for trail use. **Captree State Park** (15 m E of Jones Beach or via toll Robert Moses Causeway), 298 acres, charter boat docks, beach walks. **Robert Moses State Park** (S off SR 27A via toll Robert Moses Causeway), swimming at W end of Fire Island, good sand beach, short boardwalk. **Heckscher State Park** (off SR 27 E in E Islip), on Great South Bay, swimming, beach, marsh, good wood trails near hq and deer-feeding area. **Bayard Cutting Arboretum** (SR 27A, ½ m E of Great River railroad station), 690 acres on Connetquot River, bird feeders, pond, wildflowers, 5 nature trails (Wed.-Sun. & hols 10-5:30; closed Dec. 25; adm); on NE adjoins Connetquot River State Park, with trails. **Fire Island National Seashore** is intended to preserve the 32-m-long barrier island off the S coast of LI; much of the land is still privately owned; walking (on sand) between the separate units is possible but impractical; road access only at E (Robert Moses State Park) and W ends;

ferries run spring-fall; **Great S Beach** (reached via ferry from Bay Shore) consists chiefly of private resort communities; **Sailor's Haven** (via ferry from Sayville), lovely swimming beach, attractive Sunken Forest nature walk, naturalist programs; **Watch Hill** (via Ferry from Patchogue), good beach, marshes, camping, self-guiding trails, naturalist programs; **Smith Point** (by car via toll William Floyd Pkwy), marshes and beaches, miles of self-guiding trails, special activities; **information:** hq, 65 Oak St., Box 229, Patchogue 11772. **Smith Pt. County Park** (off SR 27 via toll Wm Floyd Pkwy), 512-acre beach. **Southaven County Park** (exit 67 L.I. Expwy), woods, trails, on Carmans River. **Wertheim National Wildlife Refuge,** S on the Carmans River and Bellport Bay, 2149 acres, trails. **Old Mastic Ranger Station** (on Moriches Bay, Mastic), fields, salt marsh, bogs. **Quogue Wildlife Refuge** (N off SR 27 via Old Main Rd. in Quogue to S County Rd.), 200 acres, nature trail. **Elizabeth Morton National Wildlife Refuge** (W of Sag Harbor on Noyack Rd., Noyack), pretty 202-acre peninsula in Peconic Bay, swimming permitted; trails on beach, in woods; duck pond. **Cedar Point Co. Park** (NE of Sag Harbor on Gardiners Bay), 600 acres, wood trails beach walk. **The Nature Trail** (E off Main St. in E Hampton via Davids Lane), 17-acre bird and wildflower sanctuary. **Hither Hills State Park** (on SR 27 between Amagansett and Montauk Village), 1755 acres for day-long walks; beaches, dunes, woods; camping, swimming; pretty. **Montauk Point State Park** (tip of L.I.), 700 acres, rich bird life, good walks.

MASSENA: St. Lawrence Seaway units may be seen from: **Robert Moses State Park** (NE off SR 37 on Barnhart Island), swimming, camping, picnicking; visitor gallery, exhibits, dams open spring-fall; nearby Eisenhower Lock has observation platform, picnicking; **1.**

MONROE: Museum Village of Smith's Cove (Museum Village Rd.), 19th-C village, more than 30 bldgs, museums, demonstrations; mid-May-Oct. daily 10-5; adm. **Schunemunk Mtn** (NW on SR 208 to Mtn Rd., then to Seven Springs Rd.) is a ridge running N to Salisbury Mills with trail access also at Mountain Lodge; 8-m Jessup Trail along crest; shorter trails intersect; trail connections to Black Rock Forest; **1-3. Sterling Forest Gardens** (SE via SR 17M, 17, then W on 17A), gardens, forest paths, animal shows; May-Oct. daily; adm; **1.**

NEW YORK CITY: Convention & Visitors Bureau (90 E 42nd St.) and **Information Center** (on Times Sq.), general information. Guided walking tours are sponsored by **Museum of the City of New York** (5th Ave. & 104th St., zip 10029) and other organizations, and are often announced in *The New York Times, The Village Voice,* other local publications; guided nature walks are sponsored by the **American Museum of Natural History**

(Central Park W at 79th St., zip 10024); area hikes are conducted by **New York-New Jersey Trail Conference** (GPO Box 2250, zip 10001), which sponsors the *New York Walk Book* and other publications. Suggestions for self-guiding walks (1) are listed below; paperback guides available in bookshops offer greater detail; **Landmarks Preservation Comm.** (305 Broadway, zip 10007), issues free booklets on historic districts; **N.Y. Parks, Recreation & Cultural Affairs Admin.** (830 5th Ave., zip 10020), issues free booklet to city facilities.

Manhattan: Downtown area has: Statue of Liberty (boats leave daily from Battery Park at S tip of island); Castle Clinton National Monument (Battery Park), open daily (closed Jan., Dec. 25; adm); Old U.S. Customs House (S side of Bowling Green); Fraunces Tavern Museum (54 Pearl St.); Federal Hall National Memorial (Wall & Nassau Sts.); New York Stock Exchange (20 Broad St.); Trinity Church (Broadway & Wall St.), old cemetery; old skyscrapers with ornamentation on upper stories, new skyscrapers with ground-level plazas. **South St. Seaport** (museum and information at 16 Fulton St.) is restoring several blocks important in city's maritime history; schooners and other ships at Seaport Pier (Fulton St. & East River); other bldgs, special events. **Chinatown** (on Mott, Pell, & Doyers Sts., N of Worth St.); the **Bowery** (N from Chinatown to Cooper Sq); Orchard St. Market (Sun.); **Little Italy** (Mulberry and adj sts., between Chinatown and Greenwich Village); **Soho** (Canal St. N to Greenwich Village), artist quarter. **Greenwich Village** (between Broadway & Hudson River, W Houston St. to 13th St.) with Washington Sq. (S end of 5th Ave.), Washington Mews (N of Washington Sq. off 5th Ave.), MacDougal Alley (N of Washington Sq. off MacDougal St.), other quaint streets and historic bldgs; guidebooks for sale in the area bookshops. **Gramercy Park Historic District** (Irving Place at 21st St.), Murray Hill (E 35-39th Sts., Madison to 3rd Aves.) has J.P. Morgan House (231 Madison Ave.), Morgan Library (29-33 E 36th St.), charming Sniffen Court (150-158 E 36th St.), other historic bldgs. **United Nations** (1st Ave., 42-48th Sts.), information desk in General Assembly Bldg (daily 9-4:45; closed Jan. 1, Dec. 25). **Rockefeller Center** (W of 5th Ave., 48-51st Sts.), street level walks and underground concourses.

Riverside walks at Battery Park, East River Park (S of 14th St. along E River), Carl Schurz Park (84-89th Sts., East End Ave. to E River), Ward's Island (pedestrian bridge at W 103rd St. & E River), Randall's Island (by foot or car from E 125th St. & E River); Riverside Park (72-129th Sts. on Hudson River); Ft. Washington Park (N from 145th St. along Hudson River) goes N to Ft. Tryon and Inwood Hill parks. **Central Park** (59-110th Sts., 5th Ave.-Central Park W), designed by Olmsted and Vaux; 840 acres; zoo, children's zoo, lakes, reservoir, model yacht pond, bird sanctuary, miles of paths. **Ft. Tryon Park** (off Riverside Dr. just S of Dyckman St.), on bluffs above the Hudson River, contains the magnificent

Cloisters (Tues.-Sat. 10-5, Sun. & hols 1-5; adm); paths, some descending to river; good views; **1,2**. **Inwood Hill Park** (off Riverside Dr. N of Dyckman St.) also has views; trails, Indian rock shelters; **1,2**.

Bronx: Bronx Park (E. 180th St to Burke Ave., Southern Blvd. to Bronx Park E), 721 acres, contains 252-acre New York Zoological Park; special exhibits of birds and nocturnal animals (open daily; adm); sports facilities; 250-acre New York Botanical Garden with formal plantings, 40-acre hemlock forest, river, rose and rock gardens, many paths and trails **(1,2)**, snuff mill, museum, conservatory (open daily; free; parking fee). **Hall of Fame for Great Americans** (W 181st St. & University Ave.), open-air colonnade with busts; information at N Gate; open daily exc hols; free. **Wave Hill Center for Environmental Studies** (675 W 252nd St.), 28 acres overlooking Hudson River, 2 restored mansions, nature center, gardens, outdoor sculpture, greenhouses; open daily (bldgs open Apr.-Nov.); sm adm. **Van Cortlandt Park** (between Broadway & Jerome Ave, N from 242nd St. to city line), 1150 acres, varied terrain, trails **(1,2)**, Van Cortlandt House (Tues.-Sun.; closed Feb., hols; sm adm); bird sanctuary (E of Parade Grounds); open daily; free. **Pelham Bay Park** (E off Hutchinson River Pkwy), 2000 acres; paths along Hutchinson River and salt marshes in Thomas Pell Wildlife Refuge; Hunter Island area with great trees, rocky outcroppings, marshes, trail; Barstow Mansion (Tues., Fri., Sun. noon-5; sm adm); open daily, free; **1,2**.

Brooklyn: Brooklyn Heights and **Cobble Hill** are historic districts along the waterfront near Brooklyn Bridge (W of Fulton St.); Pierrepont, Montague, Remsen Sts, plus river walk at foot of Montague St; mews of converted stables on Hunt's Lane, Grace Court (Remsen St.); area ends at Atlantic Ave., with Near East shops. **Green-Wood Cemetery** (5th Ave. & 25th St.), 478 acres, has ornate tombs of many famous New Yorkers; open daily. **Prospect Park** (jct Flatbush Ave. & Eastern Pkwy), 526 acres, zoo, lake, Quaker cemetery, Lefferts Homestead, many hilly paths; adj. (across Flatbush Ave.), Brooklyn Botanic Gardens, 50 acres, Japanese, rose, other gardens, conservatory, open daily. **Coney Island** (Surf Ave., Ocean Pkwy to 37th St.), boardwalk, amusement area, aquarium (W 8th St. & Boardwalk).

Queens: Walking **(1)** at series of parks joined by park corridors along L.I. Expwy: 1258-acre **Flushing Meadows** (11th St.), museum, zoo; 35-acre **Botanical Gardens** (43-50 Main St.); 234-acre **Kissena** (164th St); 335-acre **Cunningham** (Francis Lewis Blvd); 550-acre **Alley Pond** (Douglaston Pkwy) with path along Cross Island Pkwy on W side of Little Neck Bay. Also at 538-acre **Forest** (off Woodhaven Blvd. & Myrtle Ave.) and **Highland** (3½ m S on Jamaica Ave.). **Jamaica Bay Wildlife Refuge** (on Cross Bay Blvd.), 2 large ponds, marshes, upland areas; this is part of Gateway National Recreation Area (write Floyd Bennet Field, Brooklyn,

N.Y. 11234) being developed also on Rockaway Peninsula, Staten Island, and in New Jersey.

Staten Island: Reached by ferry (from Battery Park) or Verrazano Bridge; St. George ferry terminal has maps of bus routes; **Staten Island Institutes of Arts & Sciences** (2 blocks from ferry at 75 Stuyvesant Pl.; Tues.-Sat. 10-4, Sun. 2-5; closed hols) sponsors walking tours and sells guidebooks. On S shore, **Woodland Beach** and **Great Kills Park** (off Hylan Blvd.), part of Gateway National Recreation Area (see Queens); just S is **Wolfe's Pond Park**; all have good walks, beach, marshes, woodland; **1. Conference House** (7455 Hylan Blvd.), on a hill with views of Raritan Bay, was site of vain 1776 peace conference (Tues.-Sun. 1-4; sm adm). **High Rock Park** (off Richmond Rd. on Nevada Ave.), 72-acre unit of S.I. Institute of Arts & Sciences; visitor center, trails (daily exc Dec. 25); nearby is pretty Moravian Cemetery. **Jacques Marchais Center of Tibetan Art** (336 Lighthouse Ave. between Richmondtown & New Dorp), meditation gardens (June-Aug., Tues., Thurs., Sat., Sun. 2-5; Apr.-May & Sept.-Nov., Sat. & Sun. 2-5; closed hols; sm adm). **Richmondtown** (Richmond & Arthur Kill Rd.), several dozen bldgs of restored 1600s settlement; museum (Tues.-Sat. 10-5, Sun. 2-5; closed Jan. 1, Thnks, Dec. 25; sm adm); grounds free, sm adm to some bldgs (open in summer; inquire for other hrs.). **La Tourette Park** (W of Richmondtown on Richmond Hill Rd.) continues S along Richmond and Main Creeks to Fresh Kills Park, W.T. Davis Wildlife Refuge (Victory Blvd. to Travis Ave.), and Willowbrook Park, forming an almost complete circle of parklands with short trails. Walking also at **Silver Lake Park** (Victory Blvd & Clove Rd.), lakes and woods, and **Staten Island Zoo** (Clove Rd.), famous snake collection.

Walks N of city: (see also Peekskill): **The Long Path** is a blue-blazed trail from New York City (from the George Washington Bridge) to the Adirondacks (Whiteface Mtn); sections are complete through Palisades, Catskills, and Adirondacks parks, as well as outside park lands; information: New York-New Jersey Trail Conference (G.P.O. Box 2250, New York City 10001).

Palisades Interstate Park is in several units on W side of Hudson River; from George Washington Bridge, trails (1,2) follow the clifftops (parallels Palisades Interstate Hwy) or the shore for abt 12 m; **Tallman Mtn** unit (S of Piermont on US 9W), swimming, picnicking on Hudson shore (1); **Blauvelt** (2 m N of Piermont off US 9W), 200 acres inland, has trails (1,2); **Nyack Beach, Rockland Lake,** and **Hook Mtn** units (2-4 m N of Nyack on US 9W), on river; swimming, picnicking, other facilities, trails (1,2; best at Hook Mtn); **High Tor** (2 m E of Mt. Ivy via US 202), swimming, picnicking, trails (1,2); trails to be part of Long Path run outside the park, connecting some of these units. The largest units are adj 5000-acre **Bear**

Mtn and 46,000-acre **Harrison** parks (N end of Palisades Interstate Hwy); 12-1300-ft mtns, lakes; swimming, camping, lodging, small zoo, nature museum, many other activities; Perkins Memorial Drive (sm toll) to observation tower on Bear Mtn; the AT crosses the park from Bear Mtn Bridge to SR 17 (S of Arden), connecting to the park trail system; although the parks are heavily used, hundreds of m of trails enable hikers to find solitude; trails **(1-3)** vary from ½-m strolls to over 20 m and are too numerous to describe here; maps and information from Palisades Interstate Park Commission, Box 155, Alpine, N.J. 07620. **Storm King** (7 m N of Bear Mtn Bridge), another unit of Palisades Interstate Park, on Hudson River with fine views from heights but no marked trails; marked trails **(1,2)** from short pond walks to 7½-m Scenic Trail and 10½-m Stillman Trail are in adj Black Rock Forest (across 9W).

Also in this area are: **Stony Point Battlefield** (7½ m S of Bear Mtn Bridge off US 9W), earthworks, museum, lighthouse, picnics; May-Oct. daily 9-5; free; **1. West Point,** U.S. Military Academy (3 m N of Bear Mtn Bridge off US 9W), museum, chapels, monuments; maps for self-guiding tours at Visitor Center (mid-Apr.-mid-Nov., Mon.-Sat. 9-5, Sun. & hols 11-5) at Thayer Gate or at West Point Museum (daily 10:30-4:15; closed Jan. 1, Dec. 25; free) on Cullum Rd; **1. Washington's Hq** (17 m N of Bear Mtn Bridge on US 9W to 84 Liberty St., Newburgh), museum, Hudson River views (Wed.-Sat. 9-4:30, Sun. 1-4:30; closed Jan. 1, Easter, Thnks, Dec. 25; free); **1. New Windsor Cantonment** (from Kingston, 4 m SW off SR 32, 1 m N of Vails Gate on Temple Hill Rd.), reconstructed military village of 1782 on pretty hill, exhibits, demonstrations; mid-Apr.-Oct., Wed.-Sun. 9-4:30; free. **1.**

NIAGARA FALLS: Niagara Reservation State Park (Foot of Falls St.), overlooks, information on American and Canadian falls, schedules of activities; boat trips, mini-train tours spring-fall; in Prospect Park are overlooks, elevator to gorge, Schoellkopf Geological Museum (open daily in summer; Wed.-Sun. rest of yr; closed Jan. 1, Thnks, Dec. 25), exhibits, rock garden, trail to gorge; on Goat Island (between American and Canadian falls), walks on 70 acres, picnicking, elevator to guided tours through spray of American falls; **1,2.**

OLEAN: Picnicking, walks **(1,2)** at **Rock City Park** (5 m S on SR 16), scenic overlooks, trail between rock formations (adm); **Cuba Reservation** (8 m N on SR 16, 10 m N on W Fire Mile Rd.), swimming. **Allegany State Park** (12 m W on SR 17), 60,000 acres of lovely forested hills on Allegany River; camping, picnicking, swimming; 55 m of trails **(1-3)**; maps from Allegany State Park Comm., Salamanca 14779.

PEEKSKILL: Appalachian Trail enters the state at Webatuck and comes SW to cross the Hudson at Bear Mtn Bridge just N of town. **Clarence Fahnstock State Park** (jct SR 301 & Taconic Pkwy), 6000 acres with low mtns, ponds, swamps, mtn laurel (blooms in June); camp and picnic sites; AT crosses the park, with access from Canopus Lake, and side trails (2). **Heights** (along SR 9D) N of town rise to 885 ft above Hudson River and are laced with trails (1,2), some of which connect with the AT; much of this is private land but owners have traditionally allowed hikers; trails are not marked but well worn and easily followed; access also off SR 403, 301; **Three Notch Trail** (10 m N on SR 9D to Mountain Ave. in Cold Spring) follows ridges for 8 m to Beacon for Hudson River views, with several trails off this (1-3); **Breakneck Ridge** (off SR 9D at Storm King) is toughest (2,3). **Blue Mtn Reservation** (S edge of town via Welcher Ave.), 1600 acres, a swimming pond, 15 m of hiking and bridle trails (1,2) for views from 560-680-ft hills; sm adm in summer, spring-fall weekends & hols. **George's Island, Oscawana,** and **Croton Pt.** (SW of town off SR 9A) parks are on the Hudson River; 1. **Croton Reservoir** (5 m S on US 9 to Croton-on-Hudson, 2 m E on SR 129 to Croton Dam Rd.), scenic trails (1,2); **Kitchawan Woods** and **Teatown Lake** (1½ m SE of Croton Dam to Spring Valley Rd.), run by Brooklyn Botanic Garden, have trails (1,2), picnicking. **Mohansic State Park** (4½ m E on SR 35, US 202), 828 acres with swimming, picnicking on 2 ponds; 1. **Hammond Museum** (15 m E on SR 35, 7 m N on SR 121 to Deveau Rd., N. Salem), 3½-acre Oriental Stroll Gardens, lake, reflecting pool (mid-May-late Oct., Wed.-Sun. & hols 11-5; adm; 1. **Ward Pound Ridge Reservation** (15 m E on SR 35 to Cross River; entrance just S on SR 121), 4172 acres, nature museum, picnicking; 35 m of trails (1,2) through wooded hills; map at entrance. Nearby **Mianus River Gorge** (off SR 22 SE of Bedford Village on Mianus River Rd.), 200-acre nature preserve; trail map at entrance; 1,2.

PLATTSBURGH: Walking (1) on beaches on **Lake Champlain** and **Ausable Bay**; with picnicking at **Cumberland Bay State Park** (1 m N on SR 314); picnicking, swimming at **Ausable Bay State Park. Macomb Reservation** (6 m W), lovely, on Salmon River; water sports, camping, picnics; 1,2. **Ausable Chasm** is a beautiful gorge only 20-50-ft wide and 1½-m long, rock formations, falls and rapids on the river; walks on bridges across the gorge, along stream; boat rides through flume (early May-mid-Oct. daily; adm).

POUGHKEEPSIE: Lovely walks (1) above Hudson River at: **Franklin D. Roosevelt National Historic Site** (5 m N on US 9), museum, home, library, graves (daily 9-5; closed Dec. 25; sm adm); **Vanderbilt Mansion**

National Historic Site (7 m N on US 9), lavish mansion (daily 9-5; closed Jan. 1, Dec. 25; sm adm); **Norrie State Park** (10 m N on US 9), camping, picnicking; **Mills Memorial State Park** (12 m N on US 9), mansion (mid-Apr.-mid-Nov. daily; rest of yr, weekends & hols; closed mid-Dec.-Jan. 1; sm adm), picnicking; **Clermont** (28 m N on US 9, SR 9G), picnicking. **James Baird State Park** (9 m E on SR 55, 1 m N on Taconic Pkwy), summer pool, picnicking; **1. Innisfree Garden** (15 m NE off US 44 at Tyrell Rd., Millbrook), Eastern design motifs; May-Oct., Wed.-Fri. 10-4; Sat., Sun., hols 11-5; adm); **1. Stissing Mtn** (12 m NE on US 44, 13 m N on Taconic Pkwy, N on SR 199 to Lake Rd., then S), with Thompson Pond at its base, preserved in a wild state by private groups; 1¾-m loop to summit, other short trails; **1,2. Ancram Opera House & Garden** (38 m NE on SR 82 in Ancram), open Thurs.-Sun. 1-5 in summer, Sat. & Sun. 1-5 in spring & fall; adm; **1.** Swimming, camping, picnicking at: **Lake Taghkanic State Park** (12 m NE on US 44, 25 m N on Taconic Pkwy, E off SR 82), 1691 wooded, hilly acres; attractive trails **(1,2)**. **Taconic State Park** (28 m E on US 44, 9 m N on SR 22), 4686 splendid acres on ridges along the state line; from Copake Falls campground, 1.8-m trail to North Mtn, 5-m loop trail **(2)**; from SR 344 (E of campground), 3/4-m trail to Bash Bish Falls (in Mass.), trail to Cedar Mtn **(2)**; other trails, old roads **(1-3)**, some connecting to AT and other trail systems across the state line.

ROCHESTER: Chamber of Commerce (55 St. Paul St.), information on industrial and winery tours, historic sites, museums; Rochester Museum (657 East Ave.), colonial rose and herb garden open June-Sept. daily (free); **International Museum of Photography** (900 East Ave.), 10-acre garden open daily (free); **University of Rochester** campus is at S edge of town on Genesee River; **1.** City and county parks are noted for flower displays, especially lilacs (late May): **Highland** (Highland Ave.), many gardens surrounding reservoir, conservatory; **Genesee Valley** (S of Elmwood Ave.), on Genesee River; **Maplewood** (on the river at SR 104), rose gardens; **Seneca** (N edge of city on St. Paul Blvd), on Genesee River, zoo, swimming; **Mendon Ponds Park** (S of city via Clover St.), beach on small lake, beautiful nature area, guided walks, crafts demonstrations; **Powder Mills Fish Hatchery** (S of city via I-490); **Durand-Eastman** (N of city on Kings Hwy), rhododendrons, Japanese cherry gardens; **Ontario Beach** (N via Ontario State Hwy), on Lake Ontario; for others write Monroe Co. Park Bureau (375 Westfall Rd., Rochester 14620).

Letchworth State Park (30 m SW via US 15, 20A to Mt. Morris or Perry entrances), stunning, 14,000-acre wildlife sanctuary surrounding the 17-m-long Genesee River gorge; forested canyon walls rise 500 ft over dramatic cascades; scenic drive, historic sites, museum (mid-May-Oct., Tues.-Sun.; free), camping, lodging, swimming pools, ponds; 60 m of trails **(1-3)** include views of gorge, rainbow; information: hq, Castile 14427.

ROME: Fort Stanwix National Monument (in city center), site of 1758 fort being restored through excavation; Visitor Center open daily in summer, free; **1. Roscoe Conkling Park** (Steele Hill Rd.), zoo; **1. Oriskany Battlefield** (5 m E on SR 69), site of 1777 battle, visitor center, picnicking; free; **1. Erie Canal-Ft. Bull Tourism Project** (1½ m W off SR 49), restored section of Erie Canal (which see), 19th-C village, packet boat (open spring-fall; inquire locally for hrs); **1. At Canastota** (18 m SW via SR 365, I-90), **Canal Town Museum** (open spring-fall; free) and **Old Erie Canal State Park** (30 m of canal with restored features, hiking trails, other activities); **1. Baron von Steuben Memorial** (15 m E on SR 365, N on SR 12 to Remsen, W on Starr Hill Rd.), grave, replica of his cabin; open mid-May-mid-Oct., Tues.-Sun; free; **1.** State parks with picnicking, walks **(1,2): Verona Beach** (20 m W via SR 49, 13), 1335 acres with swimming on E shore of Oneida Lake; **Delta Lake** (6 m N off SR 45), swimming, state fish hatchery (off SR 46 on Fish Hatchery Rd.) open daily, free; **Pixley Falls** (18 m N off SR 46), camping, pretty.

SARATOGA SPRINGS: Once-chic resort called Queen of the Spas is attractive for walks **(1): Chamber of Commerce** (358 Broadway), maps for area historic sites; Casino (Congress Park) houses historic collections (daily May-Oct.; adm); National Museum of Racing (Union Ave. & Ludlow St.); Yaddo (2 m SE on Union Ave.), a 500-acre estate for working writers and artists, is private but rose gardens are open spring-fall; Saratoga Lake (3 m E on SR 9P), water sports, picnics, amusements; Petrified Gardens (3 m W on SR 29), excavated reefs of petrified plants, potholes, crevices, outdoor sundial museum, deer park, picnic and recreation areas (late May-mid-Oct. daily; adm). **Saratoga Spa State Park** (3 m S on US 9), 2200 acres, performing arts center, mineral baths, springs, swimming, picnicking (fee per car plus fees for some activities); **1. Saratoga National Historical Park** (11 m SE on SR 32 & US 4), Visitor Center with interpretive programs (open daily; closed Jan. 1, Thnks, Dec. 25; free); 9-m tour road with interpretive signs (open, weather permitting, Apr.-Nov.); **1. Moreau Lake State Park** (12 m N on US 9), pretty swimming pond, camping, picnicking; **1,2.**

SYRACUSE: Chamber of Commerce (1700 Mony Plaza), maps for **Syracuse University**, other sites; **Thornden Park** (S Beech St. off E Genesee St.), rose gardens; **Burnet Park** (Coleridge Ave.), zoo; **Beaver Lake Nature Center** (8477 E Mud Lake Rd. off SR 370 in Baldwinsville), 500 acres, self-guiding and guided tours; **Onondaga Lake Park** (NW on Onondaga Lake Pkwy in Liverpool), along lakefront, salt spring, salt museum, fort replica (daily mid-Apr.-mid-Nov; free); **Canal Museum** (Erie Blvd. & Montgomery St.), exhibits on Erie Canal life and history, information on restored sections of canal (closed Mon; hols; free); **1. Clark**

Reservation (2 m SE on Rock Cut Rd.), picnicking, lake, trails; **1,2. Marcellus Park** (10 m W via SR 175, 174), trails, **1. Carpenters Brook Fish Hatchery** (16 m W on SR 5 at Elbridge), nature trails, **1. Fort Ontario** (35 m N to E. 7th St., Oswego), restored fort on a hill over Lake Ontario; Visitor Center with interpretive programs, self-guiding tour booklets; Apr.-Oct. daily, possibly other hrs; closed hols; free. State parks with swimming, camping, picnicking: **Selkirk Shores** (17 m NE of Oswego on SR 104B), **Fair Haven Beach** (15 m SW of Oswego off SR 104A), both on Lake Ontario; **Green Lakes** (13 m E off SR 5); **1. Chittenango Falls State Park** (11 m E on SR 173, 4 m S on SR 13), picnicking, camping; **1,2.**

NORTH CAROLINA

ALBEMARLE: Morrow Mtn State Park (7 m E off SR 740), 4425 acres, is an attractive forested area on Lake Tillery; swimming pool; picnic and camp sites; natural history museum; nature trails, hiking; **1,2. Town Creek Indian Mound State Historic Site** (10 m S on US 52, then 5½ m E): reconstructed stockade and temple of 15th-C Indian ceremonial center; Visitor Center with exhibits; Tues-Sat. 9-5, Sun. 1-5; closed Thnks, Dec. 25; free; **1. High Rock Lake** (10 m N via US 52, SR 8) is popular for watersports; 400-m shoreline; **1. Uwharrie National Forest** (8 m E on SR 24), 43,826 acres in a hilly area where peaks rise 650-1050 ft, borders Badin Lake; trails have been blazed chiefly by hunters, some are not well marked; **2,3.**

ASHEVILLE: Carolina Mtn Club (PO Box 68, zip 28802) sells excellent trail guides for the state and leads hikes. **University of N Carolina** (University Heights), 10-acre botanical garden of S Appalachian plants; pioneer log cabin; daily in daylight; free.

Zebulon B. Vance Birthplace State Historic Site (9 m N on US 23, then 6 m E on Reems Creek Rd to Weaverville): reconstructed pioneer homestead with slavehouse, smokehouse, other bldgs; Visitor Center; Tues.-Sat. 9-5, Sun. 1-5; closed Thnks, Dec. 25; free. **Biltmore House & Gardens** (2 m S on US 25), the 250-room chateau built by George W. Vanderbilt and furnished with grand European art works, has a magnificent 4-acre English walled garden, rose garden, pool, overlooks, greenhouses, dairy herd, forests; daily 9-5; closed Thnks, Dec. 16-Jan.; adm. **Asheville**

Municipal Zoo (3 m E on SR 81), in Recreation Park, has museum, petting area; Mon.-Sat. 10-dark, Sun. 1-dark; sm adm. **Chimney Rock Park** (25 m SE on US 74), with a giant rock monolith offering views of Lake Lure, is a commercial park with cave, rock formations, hiking trails to scenic overlooks; daily 8-4:30 (longer in summer); closed Dec.-Feb.; adm. **Pearson's Falls** (46 m SE off I-26 in Tryon) is a pretty cascade with a glen developed as a botanical sanctuary.

BLUE RIDGE PARKWAY: See Virginia; the first stop in NC is **Cumberland Knob** (Mile 217.5). In addition to Pkwy facilities, the following are nearby: **Stone Mountain** (S off Pkwy near Mile 228 via US 21 toward Roaring Gap) and **Mount Jefferson** (N off Pkwy near Mile 260 via SR 16 toward Jefferson) are state parks with beautiful picnic areas and trails (1-3). **Blowing Rock** (S off Pkwy near Mile 291 via US 321), with gorge and mtn views; May-Nov. daily 9-5; adm.

CHAPEL HILL: University of N Carolina has a lovely campus with art center, museums, planetarium, theaters; **Coker Arboretum** (Cameron Ave. & Raleigh St.), 5 acres. **N Carolina Botanical Gardens** (Laurel Hill Rd. & US 15) has nature trails through 329 acres featuring vegetation of the SE, wildflowers; trails daily 8-5; free.

CHARLOTTE: University of N Carolina (N on SR 49) has a rhododendron garden (blooms Apr.-May); free. **Charlotte Nature Museum** (1658 Sterling Rd), on 29 acres, features an electronic nature trail; Mon.-Sat. 9-5, Sun. 2-5; closed hols; free.

DURHAM: Duke University has E and W campuses covering 8000 acres; W campus is especially attractive, with 55-acre Sarah P. Duke gardens offering year-round displays, cherry and crabapple trees, rock garden (daily 8-8; free); maps at Office of Information Services. **N Carolina Museum of Arts & Sciences** (433 Murray Ave.) has indoor and some outdoor exhibits (including nature trail and prehistoric nature trail); Tues.-Sat. 10-5, Sun. 2-5; sm adm.

GREAT SMOKY MOUNTAINS NATIONAL PARK, half in Tennessee, named for the haze over its forested peaks, is one of the most popular parks in the nation; as a result, overnight backcountry permits (apply after arrival) are required, and overnight use of the Appalachian and several other trails is rationed; wildflowers are best Apr.-June, rhododendron June-July, fall color late Oct.; auto tape tours are available along US 411 in Cherokee and Gatlinburg (Tenn.). **Ocanaluftee Visitor Center** (2 m N of Cherokee on US 441) offers information and a pioneer museum; daily June-Oct. 8-7:30, Nov.-March. 8-4:30; closed Dec. 25. **Newfound Gap**

Hwy winds across the park to the Tennessee side; a scenic spur at the state line goes to 6642-ft. **Clingmans Dome,** highest point in the park, with a ½-m trail to lookout tower **(2)**; from here trails go S to Smokemont, Deep Creek, and Forney Creek areas, or N to Elmont and Mt LeConte areas **(2,3)**; Buckeye and Big Locust nature trails are on the hwy N of the gap; **1,2.** Park hq is at **Sugarlands Visitor Center** (2½ m SW of Gatlinburg), daily 8-4:30 (longer in summer); closed Dec. 25; exhibits, nature trail **(1)**. The **Appalachian Trail** crosses the park for 68 m from Davenport Gap campground (off I-40) in the NE via Clingmans Dome to Fontana Dam (off SR 28 in the SW); it follows the main ridge (also the state line), with elevations above 5000 ft, most of the way; many other trails climb to the AT along streambeds or lesser ridges.

Smokemont campground (N of Oconaluftee) has nature trail **(1)**; trail N to popular Kephart Prong **(2)** and beyond to AT **(2,3)**; trails W to Deep Creek camp, Thomas Divide, Noland Divide, and the AT **(2,3)**. **Balsam Mtn camp** (E off Smokemont, N off Blue Ridge Pkwy) has nature trail **(2)**. **Twentymile Creek** (off SR 28 W of Fontana Dam) has trail N to popular Moore Spring area **(2)** and Cades Cove **(3)**, E to the AT, Eagle Creek and Hazel Creek **(2,3)**. Between Twentymile Creek and Deep Creek are trails along Hazel Creek and Forney Creek (to the AT), and along Fontana Lake.

Elmont camp (4 m SW of Sugarlands) has a nature trail **(1)**; trails to Cucumber and Husky gaps **(2)**, to Chimney Tops and AT **(2,3)**, along Little River to AT **(2,3)**; trail to Laurel Falls **(2)**. **Cades Cove** (25 m W of Sugarlands) is a mountain settlement being preserved as a living museum; an 11-m, one-way auto route circles this pretty area; 2 nature trails **(1)**; trail to Abrams Falls **(2)** continues to Look Rock camp (NE of Tallassee), with nature trail **(1)**; trail to AT **(2,3)**; permits for backcountry hiking from ranger at campground. Mt Leconte area (SE of Sugarlands) is about the most scenic and popular for hiking; hike-in cabins; trails lead to waterfalls, Alum Cave Bluffs, and the AT **(1-3)**. Just E are creek trails including one to lovely Ramsay Cascade **(2)**. Cosby camp (off SR 73 S of Cosby) has trails along Big Creek, to popular Laurel Gap, to the AT, easier creek walks, and climb to 5835-ft Mt Sterling **(1-3)**; these trails are also reached from Cataloochee Camp (NE of Balsam Mtn). **Information:** Supt. Gatlinburg TN 37738.

GREENSBORO: Greensboro Country Park (5½ m N at 4301 Lawndale Dr.) has picnicking and strolling; Natural Science Center (Mon-Sat. 9-5, Sun. 2-5; closed Easter, Thnks, Dec. 25) has indoor and outdoor exhibits, petting zoo (sm adm), trails; free; **1. Guilford Courthouse National Military Park** (6 m NW on US 220), where Cornwallis won a Pyrrhic victory in 1781, has interpretive trails and monuments through 220-acre battlefield; exhibits in Visitor Center (daily 8:30-5; closed Jan. 1, Dec. 25);

free; **1. Chinqua-Penn Plantation** (19 m N off US 29 to Reidsville, then 3 m NW off US 29 Bypass to Wentworth Rd.) has tours of a mansion with rare art objects; self-guiding tour of large rose and formal gardens with large pagoda; Mar.-Dec., Wed.-Sat. 10-4, Sun. 1-4; closed July 4, Thnks; adm. **Hagan-Stone Park** (10 m S off SR 22) offers camping, picnicking, museum, boat rides, nature walks; open in daylight all year; sm adm in summer; for information write Parks Dept., Greensboro 27402. **N Carolina Zoological Park** (20½ m S off US 220) is open daily 9-6; adm.

NANTAHALA NATIONAL FOREST (along US 19, 441 SW of Cherokee) was named "land of the noonday sun" by Indians because its deep, narrow valleys receive sun only at midday. Some 81 m of Appalachian Trail wind S from Fontana Dam, following the many peaks (elevations reach 5000 ft) to the Georgia line (S of Rainbow Springs); several roads cross the AT, giving access; trails join it from recreation areas such as Santeetlah Lakes, Apple Tree (easy trails), Nantahala Lake, Wayah Crest, Arrowwood, Standing Indian (many good trails). S of Fontana Lake, walks **(1,2)** are available from Cable Cove and Tsali campgrounds; free, daily incline railway to Fontana Dam, **Joyce Kilmer Memorial Forest** (15 m NW of Robbinsville off US 129) is a 3800-acre area with 100 species of native trees; wonderful trails from the picnic area vary from short loops to a 7-m climb to 5341-ft Stratton Bald. Campgrounds on Santeetlah Lake (S of here) are good bases for lovely 1-10-m trails that can be connected for longer hikes in the Snowbird Creek area (especially nice is 6-m Big Snowbird Trail with spurs to waterfalls) and into Snowbird Mtns; the trail to Big Stamp lookout (reachable from Murphy ranger station) is also well marked; **1-3.** Additional trails **(1-2)** are N of Kilmer Forest around Slickrock and Deep creeks (several 1-3-m trails can be connected for longer hikes). Ammons picnic area, Van Hook Glade and Cliffside Lake campgrounds (SE of Franklin on SR 28), are good bases for a lovely region with **Glenn Falls Scenic Area** (on SR 106 SW of Highlands), **Whitewater Falls Scenic Area** (E of Highlands via US 64, SR 107 S, waterfalls (at Dry Falls, a footpath takes you behind the falls), lakes, and knob overlooks; trails are mostly short and easy **(1, 2)** but you can connect to systems in surrounding forests **(3)**. Rockhounding areas are N of Franklin off SR 28; wildflowers are best mid-Apr-May; rhododendron/mtn laurel season is June-July; fall color starts mid-Oct. **Information:** District Ranger in Murphy (P.O. Box 577, zip 28906), Robbinsville (Route 1, Box 16A, zip 28771), Franklin (zip 28734), Highlands (P.O. Box 749, zip 28741).

NEW BERN: Chamber of Commerce (608 Broad St.), maps for self-guiding tours of this interesting town settled 1710 by Germans and Swiss; most historic sites are in the area bounded by the Trent River, Johnson St.,

Neuse River, George St.; many pretty gardens here. **New Bern Historical Society** (511 Broad St.) conducts occasional tours; Tues.-Sat. 2:30-5; closed hols. **Cedar Grove Cemetery** (Queen St.) has a coquina arch; "weep" water said to doom anyone on whom it drops. **Tryon Palace Restoration** (S end of George St.) is magnificent; elegant mansion built by Royal Governor William Tryon is shown by guided tour, and afterward you can walk in the 18th-C English-style gardens, planted to be colorful spring-fall; Tues.-Sat. 9:30-4, Sun. 1:30-4; closed Jan. 1, Thnks, Dec. 24-26; adm.

Morehead City (35 m SE on US 70) has remains of early-19th-C fortifications. **Fort Macon State Park** (S to Bogue Island, then 3 m E of Atlantic Beach), with restored dungeons, gun emplacements from Civil War, museum, is nice for swimming and picnicking. Nearby Beaufort was once a whaling center; **Beaufort Restoration** June-mid-Sept., Mon.-Sat. 9-5, Sun. 2-5) is restoring the Turner St. area to its 18th-C appearance and sponsors tours and special events in summer; here are a jail, several homes, museum, and interesting Old Burying Ground.

Croatan National Forest (S via US 70 or US 71, SR 58), 150,000 acres with 40 m of streams and 4300 acres of lakes, has large areas of swamp that are impenetrable on foot; swimming, camping, picnicking, fishing; trails are at Island Creek (Island Creek Rd., SW of the city); at Neuse River campground (E of Croatan off US 70), also known as Flanner Beach, short trails; Pinecliff campground (on the Neuse River off US 70 E of Havelock) with short trails in the area and Neusiok Trail going S to Mill Creek on the Newport River; short trails at Cedar Swamp (W of Newport), and Patsy Pond (off Sr 24 E of ocean), and Cedar Point camp (off SR 24 W of ocean); 1, 2. Information: District Ranger, 435 Thurman Rd., New Bern 28560. **Hammocks Beach State Park** (on island off the SW edge of the forest; free ferry in summer from Swansboro) is nice for beachcombing; swimming, picnicking.

OUTER BANKS: Wright Bros. National Memorial (2 m S of Kitty Hawk on US 158 Bypass), marks sites where successful 1903 flight took off and landed; Visitor Center exhibits, including replica of the plans; daily 8:30-4:30 (8-8 in summer); closed Dec. 25; free; **1. Fort Raleigh National Historic Site** (on Roanoke Island, 3 m N of Manteo off US 64), site of the first English colony in America (1585), has reconstructed fort, excavations, nature trail that loops through woods to Roanoke Sound, Visitor Center with interpretation; daily 8-4:30 (9-8:15 in summer); closed Dec. 25; free. Adjacent is pretty **Elizabeth Garden,** with ornaments from England, established as a memorial to the colonists; lawns, sunken garden, herb garden, other areas; daily 9-5 (plus evenings when the outdoor drama, *The Lost Colony,* is playing in summer); closed mid-Dec.-early Jan.; adm; 1.

Cape Hatteras National Seashore extends S from Whalebone Junction to Ocracoke Inlet; within its boundary is private land, including 8 resort villages; the hwy runs to Hatteras and from there all-yr ferries across Hatteras Inlet (free) and Ocracoke-Cedar Island (toll) make daily crossings (reservations advised). At **Bodie Island,** a Visitor Center offers exhibits and information (May-Sept. daily 9-6); nature trail and bird observation platform near lighthouse; miles of beaches and dunes; wildflowers; **1.** You can buy a map showing the 500+ ships sunk off the coast here, called The Graveyard of the Atlantic, and NPS maps pinpoint wrecks you can see along the beaches. Just S is **Pea Island National Wildlife Refuge,** with trails around ponds and to the sound; **1-2.** Additional miles of beach to **Buxton;** live oak and loblolly pine; lighthouse with museum (open daily 9-5); camping and other facilities; nature trail; Visitor Center; **1.** At **Ocracoke** is a Visitor Center (daily 8-5; closed Dec. 25), camping, beach. Information: Supt. Box 457, Manteo 27954. **Cape Lookout National Seashore** (just S) will be left in a wild state; reachable only by boat; for information write Supt., Box 690, Beaufort 28516.

PISGAH NATIONAL FOREST covers 482,000 acres of stunning, rugged country surrounding the Blue Ridge Pkwy and extends S on Asheville to Nantahala Ntl Forest; 6684-ft Mt. Mitchell is the highest point in the E, and 17 other peaks rise over 6000 ft. **Cradle of Forestry Visitor Center** (NW of Brevard on US 276) is open daily in summer 9-6; the nation's first forestry school was established here; forest demonstration area, historic exhibits. The area around White Pines and Coontree Creek campsites (just S) is laced with trails (many easy ones 1½-3-m long, some over 10 m) and gives access to Looking Glass Falls (where white water drops a vertical 60-ft into a pool), Looking Glass Rock (glistening from water seeping from the forest above; nearly vertical 400-ft wall on N side; 3-m winding trail **(2)** up S side from Davidson River Rd.), fish hatchery (Davidson River Rd.), Sliding Rock Falls (a 60-ft-long rock covered with water on which you can slide to a pool below); **1-3. Art Loeb Trail (3)** comes 24-m S from Shining Rock Wilderness to Pilot and Chestnut Mtns, to end on US 64 (S of jct US 276), and intersects with many 2-5 m-long trails **(1-2).** Pink Beds campground (N of Cradle of Forestry) has 4-m Thompson Ridge-Pilot Rock loop **(2-3).**

Shining Rock Wilderness, 13,000 acres in the Balsam Mtns, is reached by trails that meet in the center to circle the outcrops of white quartz for which Shining Rock was named; waterfalls, streams, meadows, flowering trees and shrubs. Art Loeb Trail (from milemarker 420.2 on Blue Ridge Pkwy) runs 5 m N to Shining Rock **(2),** then turns E 3 m along Shining Creek to Big East Fork camp (on US 276, NW of Cradle of Forestry) and connects to trail systems outside the wilderness area; a spur at Shining Rock continues 3-m N to Deep Gap camp or another m to Cold Mtn **(3);**

Deep Gap camp has exit trails 2½ m E (to road along Crawford Creek to US 276) and 4 m W (along Sorrell Creek to SR 215). **Sunburst Recreation Area** (on SR 215) is a good base for the Sorrell Creek Trail (**2, 3**), for 5½-m Little East Fork Trail to Shining Rock (**2, 3**), and for 6-m Fork Mtn Trail (**3**) that follows a high ridge along the wilderness border to Art Loeb Trail 12½ m from Blue Ridge Pkwy; Sunburst is also convenient for half a dozen trails 1½-3-m long (**1, 2**), plus 5-7-m trails (**2, 3**) outside the wilderness area. **Bridges Camp Gap** (on Blue Ridge Pkwy) has a 4-m trail (**2**) along E Fork of the Pigeon River to Big E Fork camp; here you can join the Art Loeb Trail W to Shining Rock or take tougher 3½-m Butt Knob Trail (**2, 3**) along Chestnut Ridge (over 5500 ft) to Shining Rock. **Mt. Pisgah** area (N of Cradle of Forestry) has 1-m trail to summit of Mt. Pisgah, 8½-m Laurel Mtn Trail (off Blue Ridge Pkwy); **2, 3**. N Mills River and Lake Powhatan campsites (surrounded by Bent Creek Experimental Forest), have several easy trails (**1, 2**) plus access to longer ridge climbs (**2, 3**).

Harmon Den Campsite (off I-40 just N of Great Smoky Mtn Ntl Park) has an 8-m trail along Pigeon River to Hurricane Ridge (**2, 3**); shorter trails are N at Rocky Bluff Camp (S of Hot Springs), **1, 2.**

Mt Mitchell area (off Blue Ridge Pkwy N of Black Mountain) has more than 50 m of trails; most trailheads are near Black Mtns FS campground or Mt Mitchell State Park; trails up Mt Mitchell (**2, 3**); beautiful 6½-m Black Mtn Trail (**3**); other trails 2-8-m long (**1-3**); Visitor Center at Craggy Gardens (**1, 2**) can inform you on trails to 950-acre Craggy Mtn Scenic Area (**3**). **Roan Mountain** (13 m N of Bakersville via SR 261) has picnic areas and trails (**1, 2**) in a 5000-acres, high-mountain area that becomes spectacular when rhododendron blooms (last 2 weeks of June) against a background of evergreens.

Linville Gorge Wilderness (at town of Linville Falls), 7600 acres where the gorge encloses the river for 12 m, has a spectacular panorama from Wiseman's View; cascades; odd rock formations; Pine Gap Trail (off SR 105, S of jct SR 183) goes S 2½ m to meet the scenic 3½-m Linville Gorge Trail (**2**) along the river (ranger permit required, as hiking is rationed); 6 short, steep trails (**2, 3**) come down for campsites and gravel roads E & W of the gorge to meet the gorge trail; additional trails are along the rim (**2, 3**); Pinch-in Trail descends steeply 1 m from the rim to the river at the S end (**3**). **Grandfather Mountain** (2 m NE of Linville off US 221) has a Visitor Center (Apr.-mid-Nov. daily 8-7); bear pen; mile-high swinging bridge; cave; picnic and camp sites; adm.

The Appalachian Trail follows the Tennessee state line for 60 ridgecrest m, much of it over 5000 ft; it enters the forest near Elk Park and runs S to Davenport Gap in Great Smoky Ntl Park; it is accessible from dozens of major and dirt roads, and by trail from forest recreation areas and little towns.

SOUTHERN PINES: Weymouth Woods-Sandhills Nature Preserve 1½ m SE on Ft. Bragg-Aberdeen Rd.) has nature trails along pine-covered sandridges; museum; Tues.-Sat. 9-5, Sun. noon-5; free; **1, 2. Claredon Gardens** (3 m W on Linden Rd. 1 m from Pinehurst) is famous for 300 varieties of holly; also azaleas, camellias; lake; nursery; **1.**

WILMINGTON: This was capital of the colony, an important port, and a center of rebellion against England; during The Civil War it was an important blockade-running port for the Confederacy; maps for self-guiding tours of the city and The Cape Fear Trail are available at Chamber of Commerce (P.O. Box 330, zip 28401). **Greenfield Gardens** (2½ m S on US 421), a stunning municipal park, covers 185 acres; 5-m scenic drive; zoo; lake with boat rides; rose garden; bald-cypress swamp; picnicking; open daily; free; **1. Airlie Gardens** (7 m E on US 17, 2 m S) has lawns, lakes, live oaks, flowers; Mar.-Sept. daily; adm; **1. Masonboro State Park** (15 m S on US 421) has camping, picnicking on Intracoastal Waterway; **1.** Walking (1) also at Carolina Beach. **Ft. Fisher** (20 m S on US 421), with earthworks used to keep Wilmington open to blockade runners during Civil War, has interpretive exhibits at Visitor Center (Tues.-Sat. 9-5, Sun. 1-5; closed Thnks, Dec. 25); picnicking; free; **1. Moores Creek National Military Park** (17 m N on US 421, then 3 m W on SR 210) also has Visitor Center (daily 8-5; closed Jan. 1, Dec. 25); free; **1. USS N Carolina Battleship Memorial** (W bank of Cape Fear River) may be toured; museum; daily 8-sunset; adm; **1. Orton Plantation** (18 m S off SR 133), on the Cape Fear River, is magnificent; gardens under moss-draped oaks are reflected in pools and lagoons; one of the showplaces of the nation, where you'll be tempted to linger all day; Feb.-Sept. daily 8-6; Oct.-Jan. daily 8-5; closed Dec. 24-27; adm; **1. Brunswick Town-Ft. Anderson State Historic Site** (abt 1 m S) is a ghost town on Cape Fear River.

WINSTON-SALEM: Old Salem (S off I-40, W off US 52), founded by German Moravians in 1766, is still inhabited and is charming for strolling; Reception Center (Mon.-Sat. 9:30-4:30, Sun. 1:30-4:30; closed Dec. 25) provides background, exhibits, tours, and sells tickets to some of the bldgs (some bldgs are free); **1. Bethabara Park** (2147 Bethabara Rd.), site of original settlement by the Moravians in 1753; reconstructed bldgs include pottery and brewery; Easter-Nov.; Mon.-Fri. 9:30-4:30, Sat. & Sun. 1:30-4:30; free; **1. Reynolda House** (2 m NW on SR 67, Reynolda Rd.), with fine arts; 125 acres of wooded grounds (daily 7:30-5; free) with 4 acres of formal gardens. **Tanglewood Park** (12 m SW off I-40 in Clemmons), former Reynolds estate, 1117 acres; swimming, camping, picnicking, other facilities; lake, deer park, arboretum with fragrance garden, rose garden; daily Mar. 15-Nov. 15; sm adm.

NORTH DAKOTA

BISMARK: Walks (1) at: **State Capitol** (N 6th St.), landscaped grounds; **Sertoma-Riverside Park** (Riverside Park Dr. & Bowen Ave.), **Dakota Zoo** (May-Sept. daily; sm adm), picnicking; **Camp Hancock Museum** (Main & 1st Sts.), original townsite, restored bldgs, museum (mid-May-mid Sept., daily exc hols; free).

    Missouri River sites include campgrounds 4 m S on Washington St., 9 m S on SR 1804, 30 m S on SR 1804 near Livona, and on Big Beaver Creek (off US 83 at Linton); in Mandan N at city line on Heart River and at 3rd St. & 2nd Ave. SE; **1. Ft. Lincoln State Park** (3 m S of Mandan on SR 1806), historic site from which Custer set out for Battle of Little Big Horn; reconstructed blockhouses; restored Slant Indian Village; interpretive center, trails; camping, picnicking; May-Oct. daily; sm adm; **1,2. Ft. Rice Historic Site** (22 m S of Mandan on SR 1806), restored blockhouses, interpretive signs; **1. Knife River Indian Villages National Historic Site** (14 m W of Washburn via SR 200A to N of Stanton) is being developed; **1.** At Riverdale, **Garrison Dam** (SR 200) has impounded the Missouri to form Lake Sakakawea (see also Williston); displays in powerhouse, summer guided tours; many camp and picnic areas for water sports along shores include **Lake Sakakawea** (1 m N of Pick City) and **Ft. Stevenson** (2 m S of Garrison) state parks; S of dam is national fish hatchery and aquarium (mid-Apr.-mid-Oct. daily; free); E of lake is **Audubon National Wildlife Refuge** with 5-m self-guiding auto tour (daily in daylight; free); **1.**

CAVALIER: Camping, picnicking, walks (1,2) at state parks: **Icelandic** (4 m W on SR 5), swimming lake with forested shores; trails include self-guiding walk through 200-acre Gunlogson Arboretum with pioneer homestead.

FARGO: City parks on Red River of the North are **Lindenwood** (5th St. & 17th Ave.), camping, picnicking; **Island** (4th St., S of Main), pool; **Oak Grove** (foot of 7th Ave.), picnicking; **1. Bonanzaville** (on US 10 on Cass Co. Fairgrounds), re-creates Red River Valley farming community; museum; demonstrations; special events; daily in summer; check locally for spring and fall schedules; adm; **1. Ft. Abercrombie State Historic Site** (30 m S on US 81), reconstructed blockhouses, original guardhouse, on Red River; museum (May-Sept. daily); picnicking; site open all yr; sm adm; **1. Chahinkapa Park** (47 m S on US 75 to 1st St. & 7th Ave. N in Wahpeton), lovely riverside park, lagoons, gardens, zoo, historic museum (summer-early fall), camping, picnicking; **1. Woodland Park** (37 m N off I-29 at Hillsboro), picnicking on Goose River (Apr.-Oct. daily).

Sheyenne River (SW) is scenic; runs through Sheyenne National Grassland (19 m W on I-94, 35 m S on SR 18, then W); fish hatchery (**1**) on river NW of Lisbon (10 m W of Grasslands on SR 27); **Ft. Ransom Historic Site** (12 m W of Lisbon on SR 27, then N), pretty site, camping, picnicking, remains of earthworks of former fort on the river, nearby Indian mounds (**1,2**); N of Ft. Ransom is **Little Yellowstone State Park** (reachable 15 m W of Enderlin off SR 46), beautiful, camping, picnicking, walks (**1,2**) in sand hills.

GRAND FORKS: Turtle River State Park (22 m W on US 2), 486 lovely forested acres, camping, picnicking, swimming, horse rental, nature trails; **1,2. Homme Reservoir** (39 m N on US 81, 24 m W on SR 17), Corps of Engineers lake with water sports, camping, picnicking; wooded trails; beautiful Pioneer Memorial Gardens; bird sanctuary; Apr.-Oct.; sm adm; **1.**

MEDORA: Chateau de Mores Historic Site (1 m SW off I-94), chateau and packing house ruins, remains of estate of French marquis who intended to build an empire; Visitor Center; daily (weather permitting); sm adm.

Theodore Roosevelt National Memorial Park (Supt., Medora 58645), 70,000 acres of spectacular badlands in 3 Units surrounded by Little Missouri River National Grasslands (extend N to Lake Sakakawea). **Visitor Center** (daily all yr) in Medora offers audiovisual program, exhibits; summer interpretive programs, guided walks, adj. is Roosevelt's Maltese Cross Cabin. From here, 38-m **Scenic Loop Drive** through S Unit passes overlooks, buffalo herds, prairie dog colonies; self-guiding Wind Canyon nature trail (**2**) to oxbow of Little Missouri; short trails (**2**) to burning lignite vein, 2855-ft Buck Hill overlook; 3-m Jones Creek Trail (**2**); 12-m Petrified Forest Trail (**3**); extensive system of backcountry trails extends to N unit (free permit required); camping, picnicking; rental horses and guided tours. **Painted Canyon** (7 m E off I-94), overlook, picnicking; **1,2. Elkhorn Ranch Site** is a separate unit on Little Missouri River midway between N & S units; reached by rough dirt roads; ranger permit required. N unit (20 m E on I-94, 50 m N on US 85) has ranger station, 13-m scenic drive to dead-end Sperati Pt. overlook, longhorn herd; self-guiding 3/4-m Caprock Coulee and ½-m Squaw Creek nature trails (**2**). Best season is May-Sept.; sm adm or GEP.

Camping, picnicking in national grasslands at **Sully Creek State Park** (2½ m S on E River Rd), S at **Burning Coal Vein** (10 m NW of Amidon) with nearby columnar junipers, N at **Sather Reservoir** (16 m SW of Alexander); **1-3.**

MINOT: Walks (1) at: **Theodore Roosevelt Park** (1215 4th Ave. SE), 28 acres, sunken gardens, zoo, picnicking, camping, sports.

National Wildlife Refuges cover thousands of acres of lowland meadows, prairie, timbered sandhills, and bottomlands along rivers and lakes NE and NW of town: **Lostwood** (40 m NW on US 52, 22 m W on SR 50), 3 large lakes. **Des Lacs** (45 m N on US 52) extends along Des Lacs River and Lower, Middle, and Upper Des Lacs lakes beyond Kenmare (hq ½ m W of town, open weekdays) to Canadian border. **Upper Souris** extends along Souris River NW of town to N of SR 5; hq (18 m NW on US 52 to Foxholm, 7 m N) has observation tower on Lake Darling, maps for other access points. **J. Clark Salyer** (20 m N on US 83, 31 m E to Bantry, 7 m N on SR 14 to Upham, 2 m N to hq), 60,000 acres along Souris River to Canadian border; lakes, canoe trails; self-guiding auto tour (May-Aug.). All have picnicking, trails; **1,2.**

RUGBY: Geographical Center of N America (NW) has monument, museum, reconstructed pioneer village (May-Sept. daily; adm); **1. International Peace Garden** (46 m N on US 281, SR 3), 2300 beautifully landscaped acres partly in Canada, formal gardens, picnicking, camping (all yr; free); **Lake Metigoshe State Park** (12 m W of gardens off SR 43), beautiful lake set in wooded hills, water sports, camping, picnicking, 8 m of trails; **1,2.**

WILLISTON: Spring Lake Park (3 m N on US 2, 85), handsomely landscaped, lagoons, zoo, hiking trail (1,2), picnicking (daily; free); adj on W is Frontier Museum & Village with furnished bldgs, displays (summer; adm). **Ft. Union Trading Post National Historic Site** (5 m W on US 2, then follow signs), most important fort on the Missouri, is being reconstructed on original foundations; interpretive signs; guided tours in summer; mid-May-Oct. daily; free. **Ft. Buford Historic Site** (5 m W on US 2, 17 m SW), officers' hq, powder magazine, museum exhibits; picnicking; Apr.-Sept. daily; sm adm. **Lewis & Clark Museum** (19 m S on US 85 in Alexander), general store, saddle shop, blacksmith, other bldgs; guided tours; daily in summer; adm. **Divide Co. Pioneer Village** (50 m N on US 85, 14 m E on SR 5 in Crosby), frontier displays in school, church, other bldgs; spring-fall; closed Sun., hols; sm adm; **1. Writing Rock Historic Site** (12 m W on US 2, 40 m N to Alkabo), pictographs on large boulders; interpretive signs; picnicking; daily; free; **1,2. Lake Sakakawea,** a 200-m Corps of Engineers project on the Missouri River; among state and federal camp and picnic sites for water sports are: **Lewis & Clark** (12 m E on SR 1804, then SE); **Tobacco Garden Creek** (3 m E of Watford City on SR 23,

20 m NE); **1.** At **New Town,** hq for Berthold Indian Reservation, sites are on either shore; **Four Bears Memorial Park** (2 m W on SR 23) is an Indian-owned complex with museum, lodging, trail rides available; S of reservation, at confluence of Little Missouri, is **Little Missouri Bay State Park** (45 m SW via SR 23, 22), 6000 acres of rugged badlands with camping, picnicking, beautiful trails **(2,3);** at E end of reservation in **Deep Water Creek** camp (16 m S of Parshall off SR 37); for E end of lake see Bismarck.

OHIO

AKRON: Chamber of Commerce (137 S Main St.) provides information on metropolitan parks, of which **Virginia Kendall Park** is the largest; **Sand Run Park** (1828 Smith Rd), 1039 acres; 10-acre **F. A. Seiberling Nature Center** with self-guiding trails **(1),** guided walks (open all yr; closed some hols). **Summit County Historical Soc.** (550 Copley Rd.) includes Perkins Mansion on 10 landscaped acres and John Brown's house; Tues.-Sun. 1-5; closed hols; sm adm. **Stan Hywet Hall & Gardens** (1½ m N of jct SR 18 at 714 N Portage Path), a Tudor Revival mansion; 70 acres of gardens famous for tulips in spring, chrysanthemums in fall; rose, sunken, Japanese gardens; Tues.-Sun.; closed hols; adm; **1. Jonathan Hale Homestead & Western Reserve Village** (10 m N at 2686 Oak Hill Rd., Bath) consists of 6 furnished, authentic buildings; May-Dec., Tues.-Sun. noon-5; closed hols; adm. **Adell Durbin Park & Arboretum** (N to 3300 Darrow Rd., Stow), 34 acres; rose and other gardens; self-guiding trails; **1. Cuyahoga River Gorge Reservation** (3 m N of Main & Market Sts.) has a cave; **2.** In Kent (7 m NW on SR 261, then 2 m S on SR 43), **Wolcott Lilac Gardens** (450 W Main St.), 100 varieties of lilacs, other flowers; **1.**

BELLEFONTAINE: Piatt Castles (7 m S on US 68 to W Liberty, 1 m E on SR 245), 2 Norman-style, 19th-C chateaux; tours Apr.-Nov. daily; closed Thnks, adm; **1. Kiser Lake State Park** (9 m W on SR 47, 15 m S on SR 235), 840 acres, trails **1,2. Zane Caverns** (6 m E on SR 540) offers cave tours; 100 acres of lovely canyon, forest; camping, picnicking; mid-Apr.-Oct. daily 10-5; adm. **Indian Lake State Park** (12 m NW off US 33), 6448 acres; swimming, camping, picnicking; nature programs; hiking trails **(1,2). Buckeye Trail** is 478-m long and winds NE across the state from the Ohio River at Cincinnati to Headlands Beach State Park (NE of Cleveland at Fairport Harbor); much of it is easy (along canal towpaths, through metropolitan parks, forest and park lands, historic sites), in gently rolling hill country; for information: Buckeye Trail Assoc., Inc. (P.O. Box 8746, Columbus 43216); **1-3.**

CANALS: Ohio's extensive 19th-C canal system is being preserved in many areas, with hiking **(1,2)** along towpaths: **Ohio-Erie Canal** ran from Cleveland to Portsmouth; 8-m section (along US 21 just S of Canal Fulton) is a public park; most colorfully preserved at Coshocton (which see); 42-m segment with 15 locks is along Tuscarawas River (from Bolivar S via New Philadelphia to Tuscarawas and Newcomerstown), with best access in Bolivar-Zoar area and along SR 416 near Tuscarawas; Deep Lock Quarry Metropolitan Park (11 m N of Akron on SR 8, just S of SR 303 in Peninsula); Canal Road (SR 631) in Cleveland runs S along Cuyahoga River to Northfield area; locks in a county park at Lockville; 5-m section at Circleville; see also Marietta, Beaver Creek State Park. **Miami-Erie Canal** ran between Toledo and Cincinnati; Rentschler Forest Preserve (N of Cincinnati between Hamilton & Middletown) preserves sections; towpath hiking at Delphos; Side Cut Metropolitan Park (on US 24 S of Maumee) has 3 locks; see also Dayton, Defiance, Piqua.

CANTON: Central Plaza provides information; **Canton Garden Center** (Stadium Park) has Japanese garden, year-round floral displays (daily; free); **West Creek** (6th St. SW-30th St. NW) has several parks on its banks; **Nimisilla Park** (12th St NE & Mahoning Rd. NE) has zoo and botanical gardens (daily 10-4; free); **1.**

CINCINNATI: Convention & Visitors Bureau (208 W 5th St.), at Fountain Square, offers brochures for self-guiding city tours, guided walking tours (fee), tours of special areas (such as Dayton St.), river cruises, other attractions.

Good walking areas include **Public Landing** (foot of Broadway), where settlers landed to establish a river port and where the *Delta Queen* now docks; **Riverside Drive** (across the river), with charming restored homes; **Mt. Adams** (via Ida St. bridge), with winding, hilly streets, old homes, boutiques, bars; **Auburn Ave.**, where century-old residences include William Howard Taft National Historic Site (daily 8-5 in summer, weekdays in winter; closed Jan. 1, Dec. 25; free); several interesting churches along **Madison Rd.** and old homes on nearby streets such as **Dexter Place; Findlay Market** (Elder between Race & Elm), open Wed., Fri., Sat. at dawn; **Historic Dayton St.**, the 1890s Millionaire's Row, with some of the finest 19th-C townhouses in the nation; **Spring Grove Cemetery** (4521 Spring Grove Ave.), with map of graves and catalog of arboretum plantings available in office; **Clifton** area (along upper Clifton & Lafayette

Aves.), with Victorian mansions and gas lamps; **Mt. Storm Park** (end of Lafayette Ave.), 66 acres with a Temple of Love, gardens, views of Millcreek Valley; **Cincinnati Zoo** (3400 Vine St.), one of the nation's finest, with landscaped areas, pioneer log cabin, picnicking (daily 9-5; adm); **1.**

Eden Park (between US 50 & SR 3), 184 acres; art and natural history museums; Elsinore Arch; Playhouse; old water tower; Twin Lakes, with overlooks for views of Ohio River; cherry trees; pretty walks; Krohn Conservatory (Mon.-Sat. 10-5, Sun. 10-6; free) with tropical and desert plants, orchids; daily 6 am-10 pm; free; **1. Sooty Acres Botanic Gardens,** Greater Cincinnati Garden Center (2715 Reading Rd.), has seasonal exhibits, herb garden, roses, evergreens; daily; free. Trailside Nature Center, **Burnet Woods** (Clifton Ave., Clifton), nature center; trails; Mon.-Sat. 10-5, Sun. 2-5; **1. Mt. Echo Park** (W at Elberon Ave. off US 50), with panoramic view of city, Millcreek Valley, Ohio River; **1. Mt. Airy Forest** (8 m NW on US 27 at 5083 Colerain Ave.), 1476 acres; Mt. Airy Arboretum with azaleas, rare plants (6 am-dark); Green Garden of ground covers; rhododendrons; Garden of the States; nature trails (1); picnic areas; daily 6 am-10 pm; free. **Fleischmann Gardens** (Forest & Washington Ave.) is open daily; free; **1. Cincinnati Nature Center** (4949 Tealtown Rd. in Milford), 750 acres with nature trails; Mon.-Sat. 7:30-dusk; **1. Adult Park** (8 m E at Principio & Observatory Rd., Hyde Park) has rose garden, formal gardens, dahlia trail; daily 8 am-11 pm; free; **1.**

John Rankin House (53 m SE on US 52 to Liberty Hill, Ripley), home of abolitionist; good views of Ohio River; path slaves used escaping from South; Apr.-Oct., Tues.-Sun. 9:30-5; sm adm; **1. Fort Ancient State Memorial** (18 m NE on I-71, then 4 m E on SR 350), 3½ m of earthern walls enclosing 100 acres dotted with Indian mounds; museum; nature trails; Mar.-Nov., Tues.-Sun. 9:30-5; closed Thnks; sm adm; **1.**

CHILLICOTHE: First capital of the Northwest Territory and of Ohio, this city has many interesting historic sites; information from Chamber of Commerce or **Ross County Historical Soc.** (45 W 5th St.), open Feb.-Nov., Tues.-Sun. 1-4. **Yoctangee Park** (Yoctangee Blvd & Riverside St.), small lake, picnic area; daily; free; **1. Adena State Memorial** (W end of Allen Ave. off SR 104), 19th-C mansion set on 300-acre estate overlooking Scioto River valley; formal gardens, pond, pastures; open Apr.-Oct., Tues.-Sun. 10-5; adm. Nearby sites for walking **(1,2)** include: **Mound City Group National Monument** (4 m N on SR 104 on W bank of Scioto River), 13 acres with 23 Indian mounds, Visitor Center (daily 8-5; closed Jan. 1, Dec. 25), guided tours (summer), free; **Tarlton Cross Mound** (19 m N on SR 159 in Tarlton), cross-shape earthwork in 17-acre park, 1-m nature trail (daily in daylight; free); **Scioto Trail State Forest** (9 m S on US 23, N on SR 372), 248 acres with good trails in gentle hills and in state park (camping); **Lake White State Park** (18 m S off US 23 via SR 220), lakeside strolls; **Seip Mound State Memorial** (17 m SW on US 50), ceremonial mounds, museum (Apr.-Oct., Tues.-Sun. 9-5, paths (daily in daylight; free); **Pike State Forest** (20 m SW on US 50 to Bainbridge, 7 m S), trails in pine-covered hills and in state park with camping, picnicking, swimming lake, wildlife display, 1-m and 2-m nature trails; **Fort Hill State Memorial** (20 m SW on US 50, 10 m S on SR 41), 2000-ft trail to Indian earthworks on hilltop, 16 m of trails to scenic gorges and woodlands, museum (Mar.-Nov., Tues.-Sun. 9:30-5; closed Thnks; sm adm), picnicking (daily in daylight; sm adm); **Serpent Mound State Memorial** (20 m S on US 50, 20 m S on SR 41, 3 m W on SR 73), 61-acre Adena site with 1335-ft-long, snake-shape earthwork, observation tower, museum (Apr.-Oct. daily 9-dark), scenic gorge, short nature trail, picnicking (daily in daylight; free); **Seven Caves** (24 m SW on US 50 in Bainbridge), rugged area of deep gorges with waterfalls, trails, picnicking, self-guiding tours of 7 lit caves (mid-Mar.-mid-Nov. daily 8-6; adm); **Paint Creek State Park** (off Paint Valley Skyline), with loops past cascades, chasms, gorges, grottoes; **Rocky Fork State Park** (30 m SW on US 50, 1 m S on SR 753), 4667 scenic acres on wooded swimming lake, camping, picnicking, lakeside and other trails; **Tar Hollow State Forest** (10 m E on US 50, then N on SR 327), lovely area, state park with camping, swimming, naturalist programs, trails including Buckeye Trail; **Leo Petroglyph State Memorial** (18 m SE off SR 35 on Co 28) in scenic gorge with nature trail (daily in daylight; free); **Lake Alma** (NW of Wellston off SR 93), 231 acres with swimming, camping, hiking; **Buckeye Furnace State Memorial** (31 m S on US 35, 5 m NE on SR 124, then E), on Little Raccoon Creek, is a reconstruction of Hanging Rock charcoal iron furnace with ironmaster's home, company store, other bldgs (Apr.-Oct., Tues.-Sun. 9:30-5; adm), with paths in the complex and trails to the surrounding Jackson County Wilderness Area.

CLEVELAND: Convention & Visitors Bureau (511 Terminal Tower, Public Square) can give you a map, information on walking tours. **Public Square** is center of the business district; here are Soldiers & Sailors' Monument; statues; the Mall, with fountain, courthouse, library; nearby are Cleveland Arcade (401 Euclid Ave.), a 19th-C promenade.

On W Side: Edgewater Park and **Lakewood Park** (Lake Ave.) on the lakefront. **Brookside Park** (off I-71 at Denison Ave. & Fulton Rd.), 157 acres; swimming pool and Cleveland Zoo. **Rocky River Reservation** follows the Rocky River from Lake Erie S; museum; swimming; many trails **(1,2)**; this reservation is part of a green belt ringing the city that continues S (beyond Berea & Strongsville), along Royalton-Brecksville Pkwy to Brecksville Reservation (at Brecksville on SR 21), which has a museum and many trails **(1,2)**; for information on other sections, guided walks, consult Cleveland Metropolitan Park District (2000 Standard Bldg, zip

44113). **Lake Erie Junior Nature & Science Center** (28728 Wolf Rd.), planetarium, indoor exhibits, trails (1) on 825 acres.

On E Side: Western Reserve Historical Society Museum (10825 East Blvd at University Circle) is a historical complex that includes many displays and 2 Italian Renaissance-style residences; Tues.-Sat. 10-5, Sun. 2-5; closed hols; adm. This is an attractive area with a chain of parks nice for picnics and walks (1); near **Wade Park** (Euclid Ave. at University Circle near 107th St.), an 88-acre area with lake and gardens, are museums of art and natural history (both at University Circle), the health museum (8911 Euclid Ave.); museum of medicine (11000 Euclid Ave., 3rd floor); Lakeview Cemetery (12316 Euclid Ave. at 123rd St.) with graves of James A. Garfield, Mark Hanna, others; Case Western Reserve University. **Ambler Park** (along Fairfield Rd., S of the university) and **Shaker Heights Park** (just S) have lakes, gardens. N of the museum complex is **Rockefeller Park** (between Wade Park & Gordon Park along Liberty Blvd) with tropical plants in greenhouse, Japanese gardens, Shakespeare & Cultural Gardens (string of sculpture gardens dedicated to various ethnic groups); daily; free. **Gordon Park** (just N) is on the lakefront; aquarium.

Gardenview Horticultural Park (10 m SW on US 42, 1½ m S of SR 82 at 1671 Pearl Rd., Strongsville), 16 acres; gardens with flowering crab apples (bloom in May), bulbs; early Mar.-Oct., Sat. & Sun. in daylight; adm; 1.

At **Mentor** (23 m E via I-90, SR 615) are: **Holden Arboretum** (5 m S of jct I-90, SR 306; follow signs from Kirtland-Chardon Rd.), beautiful 2400-acre wildlife sanctuary with many trails (1,2); lakes, picnic sites; May-Oct., Tues.-Sun. 10-7; rest of yr, Tues.-Sun. 10-4; closed Jan. 1, Dec. 25; adm. **Mentor Beach Park** (7779 Lake Shore Blvd, 5 m NW), on the lake, picnicking, swimming; open all yr; sm adm. **Wayside Gardens** (8605 Mentor Ave., US 20), nursery with rare plants, blooms July-late fall; open Mon.-Sat; 1. **Mentor Marsh Preserve** (Corduroy Rd.) requires reservations through Natural Science Museum (10600 E Blvd., Cleveland 44106.

State parks E of the city include: **Headlands Beach** (27 m E on I-90, N toward Fairport Harbor on SR 44), on Lake Erie (1); **Big Creek** (16 m E on I-90, 13 m E on US 6 beyond Chardon), 1; **Punderson** (29 m E on SR 87, S on SR 44), trails on lake, 2½-m hiking trail (1,2); **Tinkers Creek** (N of Aurora on SR 306), 1143 acres with hiking (1,2); **Nelson-Kennedy Ledges** (SR 282 N of Nelson), 167 acres with trails (1-3) on rocky ledges, along streams, caves. **Findley** (36 m SW via SR 10, US 20, then 11 m S on SR 58), 931 acres on swimming lake; naturalist programs; several miles of trails around lake, in woods (1,2).

COLUMBUS: Chamber of Commerce (50 W Broad St., zip 43216) provides map and information. Along the Scioto River, parks are being developed with walkways; **Griggs Reservoir** (6½ m N on Riverside Dr.), falls, overlook picnicking, trails (1); **Riverside Park** (16 m N on Riverside Dr.), adj to O'Shaughnessy Dam, has Columbus Zoo (daily; adm), picnicking, trails (1,2); **Lower Scioto** (Whittier St.) and **Southview** (Greenlawn & Deckenback) have trails (1,2). **State Capitol** is in a landscaped park (High, Broad, State, & 3rd Sts.) with statues. **Ohio Historical Center** (off I-71 at 17th Ave.), a modern complex with indoor exhibits (Mon.-Sat. 9-5, Sun. & hols 1-5; closed Jan. 1, Dec. 25); adj Ohio Village (Wed.-Sun. 10-6), a reconstructed 19th-C town with many bldgs, craft demonstrations; adm; **1. Ohio State University** (N High St. & W 15th Ave.) has an extensive campus; **1. German Village** (Livingston Ave., Blackberry Alley, Nursery Lane, Pearl Alley), 233-acre restored historic section with brick homes, cobblestone streets, Old World charm; Beck Sq. with picnic sites; many special events.

Columbus parks are outstanding, with recreational facilities, special programs; many are along waterways such as Alum and Walnut Creeks; best for walks (1,2) are: **Big Run** (Clime & Demarest Rds.), 277 acres; **Big Walnut** (Livingston Ave.), 122 acres on Walnut Creek; **Blendon Woods** (8 m NE via I-71, SR 161), nature trails, wildlife observation blinds; **Blacklick Woods** (13 m E via I-70, SR 256 near Reynoldsburg), nature center, live animal exhibits; **Cherrybottom** (Cherrybottom Rd.), 47 acres; **Clinton** (Pacemont & Weber), 19 acres, flower gardens; **Darby Creek** (10 m NW on US 40, 1 m S on Keebel-Suydam Rd. near Georgesville); **Forest Park** (1711 Penworth Dr.), 400 acres; **Franklin** (1500-1800 E Broad), with conservatory (daily 9-4, free) of exotic plants, special displays, flower garden; **Glen Echo** (Parkview & Cliffside), 4 acres with nature trail; **Goodale** (W Goodale & W Park), 32 acres with flower gardens; **Hoover Reservoir** (Sunbury Rd.), 4707 acres, with flower garden, good trails; **Linden Park** (Myrtle & Republican), 21 acres, with flower garden; **McKinley** (McKinley & Central), 7 acres, flower garden; **Schiller** (Reinhart & City Park), 23 acres, flower garden; **Sharon Woods Reservation** (9 m N on I-71, then 1½ m E near Westerville); **Sunshine** (Sandusky & Sullivant), 11 acres, flower garden; **Westgate** (Westgate & Wicklow), 45 acres, flower gardens; **Wheeler** (Neil & Collins), 4 acres, flower gardens; **Whetstone** (N high & Acton), also known as Park of Roses, is 161 acres with 35,000 rose bushes in bloom June-Sept. (open Memorial Day-Late Oct. daily); **Wolfe** (E Broad & Nelson), 43 acres. For complete information, contact Columbus Div. of Parks & Forestry (in Franklin Park) or write Metropolitan Park District (Box 72, Westerville, 43081).

COSHOCTON: Roscoe Village Restoration (on SR 16, NW of town), once a busy Erie Canal port, restored; canal boat rides, historic bldgs; booklets for self-guiding tours; guided tours (fee); Visitor Center (daily May-Sept. 10-6, Oct.-Apr. 11-5; closed Jan. 1, Thnks, Dec. 25).

DAYTON: James M. Cox., Jr. Arboretum (6733 Springboro Pike, SR 741), 130-acre former farm displaying trees, shrubs, vines; **1. Dayton Museum of Natural History** (2629 Ridge Ave.), on 17 acres overlooking Stillwater River, is open Mon.-Sat. 9-6, Sun. 2-6; closed hols; sm adm; **1. Carillon Park** (2 m S off I-75 at 2001 E Patterson Blvd), 60-acre site with indoor and outdoor displays on Wright brothers, transportation and aircraft; section of Miami-Erie Canal; historic bldgs include Wright Cycle Shop; May-Oct., Tues.-Sat. 10-8:30, Sun. 1-8:30; free; **1.**

Aullwood Audubon Center (10 m NW on SR 48 to SR 40 at Englewood Dam, 1000 Aullwood Rd.) is a 70-acre wildlife refuge with restored tall-grass prairie, museum, nature trails **(1)**; Mon.-Sat., Apr.-Oct. 7 am-8 pm, Nov.-Mar. 9-5; closed hols; adm. Audubon Society also maintains 120-acre Aullwood Farm (9101 Frederick Rd.), with demonstrations of farm skills; Tues.-Sat. 9-5, Sun. 1-5; closed hols; adm; **1. Ft. St. Clair State Memorial** (25 m W on US 35, SR 122), 89-acre scenic nature preserve with pretty trails **(1,2)**; historic monuments; site of 1792 fort; daily in daylight; free.

DEFIANCE: Au Glaize Village (5 m SW off US 24 on Krouse Rd.), restored and reproduced bldgs of 1860-90; cider mill, canal lockkeeper's house, railroad station; museum exhibits; adj 19th-C Black Swamp Farm with nature trails **(1,2)**; craft demonstrations; Memorial Day-Labor Day, daily 10-6; May & Sept.-Oct., Sat. & Sun. 10-6; adm. **Fort Defiance Park** (E edge of town), with swimming, picnicking; earthworks built by Gen. Anthony Wayne in 1794; **1. Independence Dam State Park** (3 m E on SR 281 to Independence), 606 acres on Maumee River; canal locks; camping, swimming, trails; **1.**

LIMA: Swinging Bridge Nature Preserve (15 m N off I-75 at Bluffton), on Bluffton College campus; 100 acres with trails for guided or self-guiding walks; open all year; **1.**

LOGAN: Hocking Hills State Park (SW via US 33, SR 180, 374, 664, 678) includes 6 separate sites, all scenic areas of evergreen forests, wildflowers, ferns, spectacular cliffs; summer naturalist programs; the most spectacular hiking in Ohio: **Cantwell Cliffs** (SR 374) is a rugged area with trails **2,3**; **Rock House** (SR 374), also rugged, interesting rock formations in a sandstone cliff, picnicking. **Conkle's Hollow** (SR 374) has rim trails **(2,3)** that connect S to Old Man's Cave and Buckeye Trail; also a long loop **(3)** N to Cedar Falls. **Old Man's Cave** (SR 374, 664) has camping, overnight lodging, swimming, other facilities; gorges, caves; nearby Cedar Falls with trail and Buckeye Trail **(2,3)**. **Ash Cave** (SR 56) has picnicking, cave with sometime waterfall, a rim trail, Chief Leatherlips Trail, part of Buckeye Trail **(1-3)**. **Lake Logan State Park** (3 m W via US 33, SR

664), water sports, lakeside walks; **1. Wahkeena** (15 m NW on US 33) is a sandstone area nature preserve with trails (1); adm by permit (write Ohio Historical Society, Columbus 43211).

MANSFIELD: Kingwood Center & Gardens (1 m W on SR 430 to 900 Park Ave. W), industrialist's mansion (Tues.-Sat. 8-5; Easter-Oct., Sun. 1:30-4:30; closed hols; free); 47 landscaped acres, gardens, greenhouses, nature trail, wildlife area; daily 8-sundown; free; **1. Louis Bromfield Malabar Farm** (12 m SE on SR 39, S on SR 603 to Pleasant Valley Rd., Lucas), tours of home of conservationist; 47 acres beautifully landscaped, flower displays (lilacs bloom in May); pheasant, waterfowl in gardens; picnicking; daily 9-5; closed Sun. in Dec.-Mar., Jan. 1, Thnks, Dec. 25; adm; **1.**

Mohican State Park (SE of Pleasant Hill, 2 m S of Loudonville on SR 3), 1875 acres; Johnny Appleseed planted tree nurseries here and carved his name on wall of Lyons Falls; nature center with programs, guided hikes; self-guided nature trails; trails along river and lake, to falls and other attractions; camping, water sports, canoeing; **1,2.**

MARIETTA: Chamber of Commerce (308 Front St.) offers maps for self-guiding tours of historic sites.

Wayne National Forest is in 4 extensive units in SE Ohio; SR 26 E parallels Little Muskingum River through the forest; SR 7 along E boundary parallels Ohio River; between the 2 is pretty **Archers Fork Creek** (E of Dart); a few trails **(1,2)**. At Athens (E off US 50), best walking **(1,2)** is in **Strouds Run State Park**, with swimming, camping, picnicking, naturalist programs; W of Athens are marked trails **(1,2)**; **Burr Oak Lake** (11 m SW of McConnelsville) has FS camping and a state park with swimming, camping, other facilities, naturalist programs, 3-m trail around lake, 1-m ravine trail, 1-m cave trail **(1,2)**.

MASSILLON: Parks are **Sippo** (Lincoln Way E) and **Lincoln** (17th St. NW off Lincoln Way W); **1. Canal Fulton** (6 m NW on US 21, 1 m NE on SR 93), 8 m of Ohio-Erie Canal preserved as public park; museum; summer canal boat rides; festivals; walks **(1,2)**. **Stark Wilderness Center** (8 m SW on SR 241, 4 m E on US 250), 409-acre preserve with interpretive bldg (open weekends 1-5); 7 m of loop trails **(1,2)**; Sigrist woods with ancient trees; daily in daylight; free.

NEWARK: Newark Earthworks are scattered remains of what was once a huge Hopewell cultural area: **Mound Builders State Memorial** (S of city on SR 79) has Great Circle (earthern walls enclosing 26 acres); **Wright State Memorial** (James & Waldo Sts.), remains of walls; **Octagon State Memorial** (N 30th & Parkview), earthworks enclosing 70 acres with small mounds; all open daily in daylight; free. Interpretation at Museum of

Ohio Indian Art (SR 79), open Mar.-Nov., Tues.-Sun. 9:30-5; sm adm. **Flint Ridge State Memorial** (5 m E on SR 16, then 5 m S), 515 acres with flint quarry used in prehistoric times; museum; nature trails; **(1,2)**; Mar.-Nov., Tues.-Sun. 9:30-5; sm adm. **Dawes Arboretum** (6 m S on SR 13), 325 acres; Japanese and special gardens; self-guiding trails; daily in daylight; free. **Buckeye Lake State Park** (12 m S on SR 79), 3310 acres with lake swimming; sphagnum bog; walks **(1,2)**.

NEW PHILADELPHIA: Zoar Village State Memorial (3 m NW on SR 416, 5 m NE on SR 800, N on SR 212), site of communal society founded 1817 by German Separatists; maintained as living museum with demonstrations in blacksmith, tinsmith, other shops and bldgs; museum; garden (open daily) based on description of New Jerusalem in Book of Revelations; Apr.-Oct., Tues.-Sun. 9:30-5; adm. **Schoenbrunn Village State Memorial** (3 m SE off US 250), reconstruction of village built 1772 by Indians supervised by Moravian missionaries; booklets for self-guided tours; museum; craft demonstrations; cemetery; pretty glen for picnics; May-Oct. daily 9-dark; Mar.-Apr. & Oct.-Nov. daily 9-5; adm; **1**. **Ft. Laurens State Memorial** (14 m N on SR 39, I-77, SR 212, then ¼ m S of Bolivar), site of 1778 fort; museum with audiovisual program; 81 acres for walks **(1)**; Apr.-Oct., Tues.-Sun. 9:30-5; sm adm. **Gnadenhutten Memorial** (9½ m S on SR 416), site where Indians were massacred, is interpreted at Gnadenhutten Historical Soc. Museum (on US 36), open in summer 9-5; free. From here signs direct you to **Devil's Den Park**, with caves, waterfalls, swimming, camping, hiking **(1,2)**; daily Mar.-Sept.; adm.

Muskingum Conservatory District (1319 3rd St. NW, zip 44663) is a widespread E Ohio flood control project that has created 10 lakes with recreational facilities (camping, lodging, boat rental, picnicking, swimming) and hiking **(1,2)**; summers daily 8 am-9 pm, winters 8-5 or 6; sm adm usually charged: **Leesville** (12 m E on SR 39, S on SR 212), walks on 2600 acres. **Atwood** (12 m E on SR 39, N via SR 212), fine trails, campfire programs. **Beach City** (12 m NW via I-77, US 250), strolls on 930 acres. **Tappan** (25 m SE on US 250), 4800 acres, good trails, nature walks, wildlife display. **Wills Creek** (12 m S of Coshocton), 2830 acres. **Seneca Lake** (E of Senecaville on SR 313), national fish hatchery, good trails on 4000 acres. **Piedmont** (26 m NE of Cambridge on US 22), strolls at lakeside on 4000 acres. **Clendening** (15 m N of Piedmont Lake via SR 800, 799), lakeside and forest walks on 4780 acres.

PIQUA: Piqua Historical Area (3½ m NW on SR 66), on the Great Miami River, a trading crossroads since prehistoric times; museum (Apr.-Oct., Tues.-Sun. 10-5; adm); Indian agent's home, other bldgs; a section of Miami-Erie Canal with trail, canal boat rides in summer; **1**.

PORTSMOUTH: Horseshoe Mound (Mound Park, 17th St. & Hutchins Ave.) and **Tremper Mound** (SR 73, NW of town) are unexcavated; **1. Wayne National Forest** (NE), 147,000 acres, hardwood forest; **Lake Vesuvius Recreation Area** (29 m SE on US 52, 7 m N off SR 93) has camp and picnic grounds with interpretive trail **(1,2)** to iron furnace ruins, whiskey still, other attractions; short lakeside trail **(1)**; 16-m trail through forest to Kimble fire tower with cutoffs for 9-m and 12-m loops **(2,3)**. **Shawnee State Forest** (SW), 60,000 acres, 6 lakes; naturalist program; **Shawnee State Park** (7 m SW on US 52, W off SR 125) with swimming, camping, naturalist program, picnicking on lake, hiking **(1,2)**; FS 17 (N of Buena Vista) connects with other roads to circle a lovely wilderness area with short hikes or climb to Twin Creek fire tower **(1,2)**; other trailheads **(2,3)** are W of Friendship along SR 125, which also has Shawnee Backpack Trail loops; hq in Friendship. **Bush Creek State Forest** (just N of Shawnee forest) has several small units bounded by SR 32, US 23, SR 348, 73; trails **(2,3)**. **Davis Nature Preserve** (30 m W via SR 73, 348, 781) has trails through prairie, forest; cave; **1,2**.

SANDUSKY: Battery Park (Water St.) overlooks Lake Erie and piers, picnic tables; **Cedar Point** (toll causeway off US 6), a peninsula in the lake, has swimming beach, amusement park (adm); **1.** Excursions and car ferries operate from here (also from Port Clinton, Catawba Island, Marblehead) to islands in the lake: **Kellys Island**, with Glacial Grooves State Memorial (W shore) outdoor interpretive displays; Kelleys Island State Park (N shore), with camping, swimming, trails **(1,2)**, naturalist programs; Inscription Rock State Memorial (S shore) with petroglyphs. **S Bass Island**, with Perry's Victory & International Peace Memorial (Put-in-Bay), open daily in summer, free; Perry's Cave and Crystal Cave (tours in summer; adm); S Bass Island State Park, with camping, swimming, naturalist program, trails **(1)**.

Blue Hole (7 m SW on SR 12, 101 to 502 N Washington St. in Castalia), deep spring, picnicking, trout stream; daily June-Aug. 9-dusk; spring & fall 10-5; adm; **1.** Nearby Lagoon Deer Park (on SR 269), open Apr.-Oct. daily 9-dark; adm; **1. Galpin Wildlife & Bird Sanctuary** (13 m S on US 250 to Milan, ½ m SE on Edison Dr.), birdwatching, wildflowers; open all yr; free; **1.**

Marblehead Peninsula (W via SR 2) is a resort area with roadside parking for walks, overlooks; town parks; E Harbor State Park (N of jct SR 163, 269), 1600 acres with swimming, camping, naturalist programs, trails **(1)**; Catawba Island State Park (SR 53), 9 acres for picnics **(1)**; walking **(1)** at lake beach at Port Clinton.

SPRINGFIELD: Chamber of Commerce (102 E Main St.) provides maps, information on historic home tours. **Snyder Park** (W along Buck Creek &

Mad River), 225 acres for strolls, picnics; **1. George Rogers Clark State Memorial** (3½ m W on I-70), interpretive signs, picnicking, nature trail; daily 7:30-dark; free; **1. Cedar Bog Nature Preserve** (N on US 68, midway to Urbana) is an unusual area preserving ice-age vegetation; 2-m boardwalk; entry is limited (permit from Ohio Historical Society, Columbus 43211). **John Bryan State Park** (9½ m S on US 68, 3 m SE via SR 343, 370), 881 acres on Little Miami River's scenic gorge; remains of stage route; swimming pool, camping, picnicking, 12 nature and hiking trails **(1,2)** in gorge or along rim.

TOLEDO: Chamber of Commerce (218 Huron St.) provides brochures for touring the port (observation deck on St. Lawrence Dr.) on the Maumee River. **Toledo Zoological Gardens** (4 m S on US 24) has animals plus lily, rose, other gardens; daily 9-5; adm; **1. University of Toledo** arboretum (Sylvania & Corey Rd.); **1.**

Toledo has a fine park system of over 100 parks with recreational facilities and walking: **Bay View** (3900 Summit St.), 219 acres on the river; **George P. Crosby Park** gardens (5403 Elmer Dr.), 50 acres; **Ottawa** (Bancroft & Parkside Sts.), 305 acres; **Oak Openings** (W on SR 2 near airport), 3300 acres, especially attractive, with only "live" sand dunes in the state; **Secor** (Berkey), 500 acres with arboretum; **Swan Creek** (4102 Glendale Ave.), 412 acres; for information: Toledo Metropolitan Park District (911 Madison Ave., zip 43624).

Ft. Meigs State Memorial (across Maumee River, SW of jct US 20, SR 65), 10-acre restoration of War of 1812 fort; interpretive programs; picnicking; Apr.-Oct., Tues.-Sun. 10-5; sm adm.; **1.**

STATE PARKS: Adams Lake (SR 41 N of W Union), 96 acres, picnicking; **1,3. A. W. Marion** (4 m E of Circleville off US 22), 412 acres in gentle hills; self-guiding trails around scenic 5-m lakeshore **(1,2)**. **Barkcamp** (SR 149 at Belmont), 1121 acres; 2-m trail **(2)**, bridle trail, on lake. **Beaver Creek** (9 m N of E Liverpool via US 30, SR 7, then E), 2405 acres, trails **(1,2)**, naturalist programs, old mill, lock of Sandy & Beaver Canal; pretty; **1,2. Cowan** (6 m SW of Wilmington via US 68), 1775 acres; swimming lake; naturalist programs; several miles of trails near campgrounds N of lake. **Forked Run** (3 m S of Reedsville on SR 124), 794 acres; camping, swimming; naturalist programs; 1½-m trail on lake **(1)**; trails **(2,3)** connect with trails through forests, steep gorges, on ridges in surrounding 2400-acre Shade River State Forest. **Geneva** (10 m W of Ashtabula on SR 531), 682 acres; walks **(1)** on Lake Erie, in woods. **Grand Lake-St. Marys State Park** (S & E of Celina), 14,000 acres on huge lake; water sports, camping; nature programs; trails **(1,2)**. **Hueston Woods** (4½ m N of Oxford on SR 732), 3584 acres; camping, swimming, nature center programs; scenic overlooks, Pioneer Farm Museum.

OKLAHOMA

ARDMORE: Lake Murray State Park (8 m SE via SR 77S), 12,000 acres on lake, water sports, camping; Tucker Tower geologic museum (Tues.-Sun.; free); walks, **1, 2. Turner Falls** (19 m N on US 77), privately owned (adm) cascade, swimming pool, trails (**1, 2**); adj Devil's Den rock formation. **Platt National Park** (25 m N on US 77, 9 m E on SR 7 to Sulphur, 1 m S off US 177), 912-acre woodland; Buffalo, Antelope, 29 other sulphur and mineral springs; camping, picnicking; Travertine Nature Center (daily exc Dec. 25) has naturalist programs, guided walks; self-guiding nature trails (many wildflowers), trails to springs and around bison range; **1, 2.**

   Lake Texoma (E on I-35 at Texas border), with 580-m shoreline, is a huge water sports center on a Corps of Engineers impoundment; dozens of campgrounds, swimming beaches, Lake Texoma State Park (on US 70 SE of Madill); shore walks, rockhounding, back trails (**1, 2**); at N end of lake are: Univ. of Oklahoma Biological Laboratory at Willis (S of Madill on SR 99). **Tishomingo Ntl Wildlife Refuge** (14 m N of Madill on SR 99), **Chickasaw National Capital** in Tishomingo, trails along **Blue River** (NE of Tishomingo) and along scenic, crystal-clear **Pennington Creek** (flows past Tishomingo into lake at wildlife refuge.

BARTLESVILLE: City parks include **Frontier** (300 block of S Virginia), **Sooner** (3 m E on Madison Blvd.). **Woolaroc Museum** (14 m SW on SR 123), 3500-acre ranch with buffalo, Japanese deer, other animals; museum on history of man, Western art; National Y Indian Guide Center with audiovisual programs, exhibits; open daily 10-5; free; **1.**

BOISE CITY; Attractive area with streams in green valley, and abrupt rocky buttes; Santa Fe Trail ruts (8½ m N on US 287, 385); Ft. Nichols Site (W to Wheeless, then 2½ m N), scenic. **Black Mesa State Park** (22 m W, 8 m N), water sports, camping, picnicking on lake; winter goose refuge; trails to lava formations, Indian pictographs, petrified wood, dinosaur tracks and excavation site; also hikes in surrounding rock formations, cave exploration; **1-3.**

BROKEN BOW: Beavers Bend (7 m N on US 259, 3 m E on SR 259A), 5000-acre park with camping, water sports on stunning Broken Bow Reservoir; wooded islands dot the lake, shores heavily forested with evergreens; lovely Mtn Fork River cuts through to bayou country below; spring flowers, fall color; nature, hiking trails (1, 2); magnificent Wilderness at upper reaches of lake may be entered only on guided tour (offered in summer) or be experienced hikers with permission for day trips. **Weyerhauser Paper Co.** (Craig Plant, Broken Bow 74728) will grant permission for hikes on their logging roads in the area; some roads give access to scenic Glover River. **Ouachita National Forest** (12 m SW via US 70, E on SR 3) has lakeside walks (1) at Kulli campsite (W of Haworth) and Ward Lake (W of Tom); stream walks at Bokhoma camp, other sites, climbs to 3 fire towers (2, 3); hiking maps from ranger in Idabel.

GRANITE: Granite quarries may be toured; Boot Hill, old epitaphs; Custer's Cave near Balanced Rock. **Quartz Mtn State Park** (13 m via SR 6, 44 to E shore of Lake Altus), water sports, camping, other facilities on reservoir; sited among rugged granite buttes, scenic; lakeside walks (1); trail to 1950-ft Granite Rock (2) for overlook; trail to Devil's Canyon (2, 3); rugged climbs on buttes (2, 3).

LAWTON: Wichita Mountains Wildlife Refuge (hq 15 m W on US 62, 12 m NW on SR 115), 59,000 acres primarily for elk, buffalo, other big game, also has prairie dogs; outstanding native grassland, impressive scenery; 50 m of paved and gravel roads to scenic areas, 20 lakes, camp and picnic areas, swimming beaches; splendid view from 2467-ft Mt. Scott; N Mtn Wilderness and Buffer Zone closed to public; from hq at French Lake are short nature trail, 5-m hiking trail (1, 2); other trails (1-3) to Charon Gardens Wilderness (one trail goes through it to Treasure and Post Oak Lakes), short trail from Sunset camp to Elk Mtn, trails at lakes.

MUSKOGEE: **Honor Heights Park** (3 m NW on Honor Heights Dr.), 100 landscaped acres, roses (May-Oct.), azaleas (Apr.); Five Civilized Tribes Museum (daily; closed Dec. 25; sm adm); picnicking, swimming; daily; free; 1. **Ft. Gibson Stockade** (9 m NE on US 62, SR 80), 55-acre reconstruction of 1824 post, exhibits, national cemetery; daily; closed Dec. 25; free; 1. **Ft. Gibson Reservoir** (11 m NE on US 62, SR 80), Corps of Engineers project with water recreation, camping, other facilities.

OKLAHOMA CITY: Chamber of Commerce (1 Santa Fe Plaza) maps for walking tours of renewals including Oklahoma Theatre Center (N Walker & Sheridan), Penn Square and other shopping malls; Heritage Hills (NW 14-21st Sts., Walker to Robinson), preserved early homes; stockyards; Oklahoma City University (NW 23rd & Blackwelder) with gardens on campus; **Fair Park** (NW 10th St. & N May Ave.), with Art Center, Science & Arts Foundation, Planetarium; parks such as **Trosper** (SE 29th & Eastern), **Canyon** (N Santa Fe & NE 50th), **Lincoln** (NE 50th & N

Eastern) with zoo and lake; lakes **Stanley Draper** (S of SE 74th & E of Midwest Blvd), **Hefner** (7 m NW off NW expwy), **Overholser** (8 m W on US 66); **1. Will Rogers Park** (I-240 at NW 36th & Portland Ave.), swimming, sports, aquatic center (summers; sm adm), rose garden, Garden Exhibition Bldg (weekdays; closed hols), Horticulture Gardens with arboretum, conservatory, flower gardens; free; **1.**

At **El Reno** are **Lake El Reno** (W); **Old Ft. Reno** (5 m W on I-40, 1½ m N), pamphlet for self-guiding tours of 19th-C bldgs, prairie dog colony, livestock research station (open daily; free); **State Game Farm** (7½ m NW via US 81) for game birds (daily; closed hols; free); **Red Rock Canyon State Park** (17 m W on I-40, 4½ m S on US 281), lush oasis towered over by impressive red cliffs, swimming, camping, picnicking, hiking **(1-3).**

Roman Nose State Park (39 m N on SR 8, US 81; 27 m W on SR 33, 8 m N), camping, lake swimming, other facilities in canyon of white and red shale bluffs; trails to springs, lakes, wildlife sanctuary, canyon; **1-3.**

TULSA: Chamber of Commerce (616 S Boston Ave.) has maps for self-guiding auto tour. Walking **(1)** at **Philbrook Art Center** (2727 S Rockford Rd.), collections in ornate Italian villa on 23 acres with formal gardens; **Tulsa Garden Center** (2435 S Peoria Ave.), arboretum, conservatory, chrysanthemum test gardens (Sept.-Oct.), rose gardens (Mon.-Fri.; weekends during shows; closed hols; free); **Mohawk Park** (6 m NE on US 169 at E 36th St. N & N Yale Ave.), zoo, picnicking, lake; **Nature Preserve of Redbud Valley** (on Bird Creek, N edge of twon), floodplain nature walk, pond, woods, rock climbing, cave exploration **(1-3).**

Will Rogers Memorial (21 m N via US 66 to Will Rogers Blvd., Claremore), exhibits, grave (daily; free); **1. Pawnee Bill Museum & Park** (on US 64), home of Gordon W. Lillie, exhibits, herds of buffalo and longhorns (daily; free); **1.** Corps of Engineers projects have created large lakes with water sports, camping, other facilities: **Keystone** (14 m W via US 64), winding lake in rolling hills, 330-m shoreline for walks **(1, 2);** walks **(1, 2)** at state parks, 715-acre **Keystone** (SR 51), 1429-acre **Walnut Creek** (US 64), 140-acre **Feyodi Creek** (US 64 W of Walnut Creek); 1-m Washington Irving Scenic Nature Trail begins at Washington Irving Cove (N off US 64 via SR 151), winds along bluffs with 7 scenic stops **(1, 2).**

WOODWARD: Alabaster Caverns (9 m E on SR 34C, 50B; 18 m N on SR 50, 50A), cave tours daily (adm); trails **(2,3)** into beautiful Cedar Canyon and over Natural Bridge.

OREGON

ASTORIA: On the Columbia River mouth, one of the oldest towns in Oregon; **Astoria Column** (marked route to Coxcomb Hill), memorial to Lewis & Clark Expedition, observation tower, summer information booth; superb Columbia Maritime Museum in Astoria Maritime Park (16th & Exchange Sts.), restored Astor trading post, Ft. Astoria (14th & Exchange Sts.), historical museum (441 8th St.), all open daily in aummer, Tues.-Sun. in winter, closed hols, sm adm; **1. Ft. Clatsop National Memorial** (4½ m SW on US 101A), replica of Lewis & Clark winter camp, Visitor Center, living history demonstrations; daily; closed Jan. 1, Thnks, Dec. 25; free; **1. Ft. Stevens State Park** (5 m W on US 101, 5 m N), swimming, clamming, camping, picnicking, wreck of 1906 ship; **1,2. Seaside** (18 m S on US 101), scenic 8000-ft ocean promenade; **1. Cannon Beach** (23 m S on US 101), 7-m swimming beach, beachcombing; **1.** State parks: **Ecola** (2 m N of Cannon Beach on US 101), spectacular (1), sea lion and bird rocks, clam digging, trails with mtn, ocean views (2); **Saddle Mtn** (9 m E of Ecola on US 26, then N), camping at foot of trail (2) to 3287-ft summit; **Oswald West** (10 m S of Cannon Beach on US 101), walk-in last ¼ m from road on mtn slopes above the sea, scenic trails (2); **Nehalem Bay** (6 m S of Oswald on US 101), sheltered beach (1).

BAKER: Chamber of Commerce (Box 69), information on many ghost towns in this area; a few are Sumpter (6 m S on SR 7, 20 m W on SR 220), Bourne (6 m N of Sumpter), Granite (15 m W of Sumpter), Greenhorn (6 m S of Granite).

    Wallowa-Whitman National Forest (NE & W), 2.2-million acres, snowcapped peaks, glaciers, alpine meadows and wildflowers; easy trails **(1, 2)** along lovely **Imnaha River** (especially at Indian Crossing campsite, 40 m SE of Joseph), **Eagle Creek** (especially at Two Color camp, 14 m E of Medical Springs, with wilderness access), other fishing areas. **Eagle Cap Wilderness,** 220,000 acres of glacial moraine dotted with lakes, streams; 9845-ft Sacajawea and Lesser peaks can be climbed (3) without equipment from campsites on **Hurricane Creek Rd.** (off SR 82 S of Enterprise), from campsites along **Lostine River Rd.** (off SR 82 S of Lostine), from beautiful **Wallowa Lake State Park** (on SR 82 S of Joseph), from **Kettle Creek** campground (off SR 203, 25 m E of Medical Spring); all of these have magnificent scenery and easier trails **(1, 2).** Another splendid area is

Anthony Lakes (21 m W of N Powder off US 30), with camping, picnicking, rockhounding, many trails **(1-3)**. Information: P.O. Box 471, Baker 97814.

BEND: City parks include **Drake** (Riverside Blvd) and **Pioneer** (Hill St.), both on Deschutes River; **Pilot Butte** (1 m E on US 20), wonderful view; **La Pine State Recreation Area** (22 m S on US 97, 4 m W), in ponderosa pine forest on Deschutes River, picnicking, swimming; **Petersen's Rock Gardens** (10 m N off US 97, then W), small rock castles and mansions, bridges, lagoon with water lilies, flower gardens, peacocks, picnicking (open daily; donation); **Sawyer State Park** (1 m NW on US 20), trails, picnicking; **1. Smith Rock** (23 m N on US 97) and **Ogden Scenic Wayside** (25 m N on US 97) are canyon picnic areas, beautiful trails **(1, 2)**. **Cline Falls** (16 m N on US 97, 4 m W on SR 126), swimming, picnicking on Deschutes River; **1. Cove Palisades State Park** (36 m N off US 97), on Lake Chinook; swimming, camping, picnicking; observatory and museum on Round Butte; **1, 2**. At **Prineville** (16 m N on US 97, 19 m E on SR 126), Chamber of Commerce provides map for rockhounding; camping, water sports, rockhounding at state parks **Ochoco Lake** (7 m E on US 26) and **Prineville Reservoir** (17 m SE off US 26); rockhounding and picnics at **Chimney Rock** (20 m SE off SR 27); camping, picnicking, rockhounding in **Ochoco National Forest** (E on US 26), best trails at Wildcat camp (19 m NE); **1, 2**.

Deschutes National Forest (W) borders Mt. Jefferson, Mt. Washington, Three Sisters, and Diamond Peak wildernesses (see Eugene); easier trails **(1, 2)** are at camp and picnic sites along the chain of lakes and reservoirs running N off SR 58 from **Crescent, Odell,** and **Summit** lakes to Davis, Wickiup, Crane Prairie, Cultus, Lava, Elk, and Sparks lakes; many also have access to climbs **(3)**. Scenic trails **(1, 2)** at **Tumalo Falls** (12 m W of Bend) and at the lava area (10 m S of Bend on US 97) with **Lava Butte Visitor Center,** Lava River Caves, Lava Cast Forest Geological Area, Arnold ice cave, with camping at Cinder Hill, nature trail on East Lake, picnicking at Paulina Lake. **Suttle Lake** area (34 m NW on US 20), many recreation sites on the lake and on Metolius River (N) with scenic trails **(1-3)**. Information: 211 E Revere, Bend 97701.

BURNS: Vast cattle raising country and high deserts with few towns, much remote public land for backcountry hiking **(3)**; walks **(1, 2)** at Buchanan Springs picnic site (24 m E on US 20), Delintment Lake (48 m NW) campground in Ochoco National Forest. **Malheur Ntl Wildlife Refuge** (hq 32 m S on SR 205), 181,000 acres, museum, trails **(1-3)**, guided tours, display pool, fire tower overlook; information: Box 113, Burns 97220. **Steens Mtn** (59 m S on SR 205) loop Summit Road climbs to 9500 ft from Frenchglen (usually snow-free July-Oct.); grand scooped gorges, beautiful hidden lakes with forested shores; rockhounding; camping at Page Springs (3 m), Fish Lake (10 m), Jackman Park (17 m), Blitzen Crossing (25 m), all with trails (2, 3).

CANYON CITY: Chamber of Commerce (240 S Canyon Blvd), maps, information on historic sites, old gold camps and ghost towns, rockhounding, fossil hunting. **Clyde Holliday State Park** (on US 26, 7 m W of John DAy), camping. **Thomas Condon-John Day Fossil Beds State Park** (41 m W of John Day), 4000 acres of fossil beds; trails (1-3) start at Foree Camp (8½ m S of Kimberly on SR 19), Turtle Cove (3 m N of jct US 26, SR 19); Picture Gorge with petroglyphs (jct US 26, SR 19); picnicking; other fossil beds on road N of Kimberly (via Monument & Hamilton) to Long Creek, then S on US 395.

Malheur National Forest surrounds the city; ponderosa pine, wildflowers and flowering bushes, mtns. **Strawberry Mtn Wilderness** (SE), 33,000 acres with 5 glacial lakes, 9044-ft mtn, alpine and subalpine flora; easiest entry from beautiful Strawberry Lake (off US 26, 12 m S of Prairie City), camping, many trails (1-3) from ½-m to 18-m Skyline Trail connecting to extensive trail system; roads S off US 395 give trail access from Wickiup, Canyon Meadows, Big Creek camps; also Trout Farm and Crescent camp (off US 26, 16 & 18 m SE of Prairie City); 2, 3. Hiking (1-3) elsewhere from campgrounds at **Parish Cabin** (off US 395, 11 m E on Seneca); on river at **Elk Creek** and **N Fork Malheur** (32 & 35 m SE of Prairie City); **Dixie** (8 m NE of Prairie City); **Magone Lake** (26 m N of John Day); **Beech Creek** (25 m NW of John Day on US 395). Off US 395 are trails at **Star** (14 m), **Rock Spring** (6 m E of Silvies), **Joaquin Miller** (18 m N of Burns), **Idlewild** (16 m N of Burns), **Yellowjacket** (23 m NW of Burns). **Separating Corrals** picnic area (off US 26, 20 m SE of Dayville) also has trails (1, 2). Information: 139 NE Dayton St., John Day 97845.

COOS BAY: The 400-m Oregon coast is the most scenic in the nation—crashing surf, sheltered sand beaches, dunes, rocky headlands, clamming, rockhounding, bird and sea mammal watching, inland lakes—all backed by green hills and mtns, and dotted with public recreation areas; information from **Chamber of Commerce** (400 N Bayshore Dr.); **Sea Lion Cave Tours** (49 m N on US 101 are daily exc Dec. 25 (adm). **Marine Science Center** of Oregon State Univ. (83 m N off US 101 on Marine Science Dr., Newport), daily exc Dec. 25 (free); 1. Picnicking and scenic trails (1, 2) at state parks S: **Sunset Bay** (12 m on Cape Arago Hwy), camping, swimming; **Shore Acres** (13 m on Cape Arago Hwy), observation shelter; **Cape Arago** (14 m on Cape Arago Hwy), promontory with 2 beaches; **Bullards Beach** (22 m S on US 101), swimming on ocean beach, camping, Coquille River; **Bandon** (27 m S on US 101), dunes, swimming beach. **Trout hatchery** at Bandon (23 m S on

US 101, E on SR 42) is open daily, free; **1. Oregon Dunes National Recreation Area** (N on US 101), 32,000 acres between Coos and Siuslaw rivers, has the most spectacular sand dunes; swimming, camping, pcinicking; rhododendrons bloom May-June; trails **(1, 2)** at Umpqua Lighthouse, Honeyman, other units. Of more than a dozen state parks N of Florence (off US 101), most with picnicking and swimming beaches **(1)**, many with camping, those with the most scenic trails **(2)** are: **Devils Elbow** with marine gardens at Heceta Head, **Washburne, Patterson, Beverly Beach, Rocky Creek, Fogarty Creek.**

Siuslaw National Forest stretches N along US 101 in several units to Tillamook. **Cape Perpetua Visitor Center** (2 m S of Newport) offers information, films, exhibits, 22-m self-guiding auto tour; interpretive trails **(1, 2)** to beach, tidepools, views, Indian shell mounds, giant-spruce forest, fern-lined stream. Many picnic and camp sites on beach **(1, 2)**, with especially scenic trails **(2)** at Devils Churn (3 m S of Yachats), Ocean Beach and Rock Creek (10 m S of Yachats), Sutton Lake and creek (6 m N of Florence)—with nearby Darlingtonia Botanical Wayside—Siltcoos (7 m S of Florence), Carter Lake (9 m S of Forence), Eel Creek (15 m N of N Benf), Bluebill Lake (3 m NW of N Bend on FS 2431). Good inland trails **(2, 3)** are along **Alsea River** and **Missouri Bend** (E of Waldport on SR 34), **Canal Creek** (4½ m S off SR 34 on SR 1462), and **Marys Peak** (NW off SR 34, N of Alsea). Near **Mapleton,** camping, hiking **(2)** at Turner Creek (7 m E on SR 126), Whittaker Creek (14 m SE on Whittaker Creek Rd.), Clay Creek (28½ m SE on Siuslaw Rd.). **Smith River Falls** and **Vincent Creek** (30 and 35 m E of Gardiner on Smith River Rd.), picnicking and hiking **(2)**. Information: P.O. Box 1148, Corvallis 97330.

Hiking **(1, 2)** at BLM sites near Coquille: **Park Creek** (26 m E on Middle Creek Rd.), swimming, camping; **Cherry Creek** (27 m E on Cherry Creek Rd.), picnics; **Burnt Mtn** (30 m E on Burnt Mtn Rd.), camping. Along Coquille River S of Myrtle Point are **Coquilee Myrtle Grove State Park** and **China Flat Recreation Area** (trails in scenic gorge). **Golden & Silver Falls** (24 m NE on river), falls, trails **(1, 2)**.

EUGENE: University of Oregon museums of open daily, free (closed hols); views from **Skinners Butte Park** (via High St.); rhododendron gardens (late May-early June) in **Hendricks Park** (24th St.); roses (late June-early July) in **Owen Municipal Rose Gardens** (N Jefferson St.).

Willamette National Forest, 1½-million heavily timbered acres, lakes, waterfalls, hot springs, snowcapped peaks of the stunning Cascade Range. **Pacific Crest Trail (3)** is generally rough here, high in Cascades, through wilderness areas, the rough Belknap lava flow, the lake district down to Crater Lake; road access on US 20 at Santiam Pass, SR 242 at Mckenzie Pass, from a cluster of campsites between SR 242 and SR 58, from campsites just S of SR 58. Hiking trails are so numerous that

detailed guides should be bought; hardest trails and rock climbing are in:
Three Sisters Wilderness (W on SR 126, 242), 250 m of trails to stunning
lakes; climbs to 10,000-ft N, Middle, and S Sister peaks; glaciers (Collier,
between N & Middle Sister, is largest in state); streams; lava flow, cinder
cones; 40 m of Pacific Crest Trail cuts N to S; access: from camps on N at
Scott Lake, frog, Alder Springs (on SR 242); on W at Frissell Crossing,
Skookum Creek, Roaring River (31-33 m SE of Blue River on FS 163); on
S at Cultus Lake (N off SR 58); on E at Lava Lake, Elk Lake, Soda Creek,
others SW of Bend. **Mt. Jefferson Wilderness** (SE of Detroit) has 10,497-
ft Mt. Jefferson and tough 7841-ft Three Fingered Jack; Pacific Crest
Trail cuts N to S; trailheads on W on SR 22 SE of Detroit, on S along US
20, on E from Jack Lake and other camps N off US 20; climbing is tough
(3) but some of these entry trails are 2 for a while. **Mt. Washington
Wilderness** (between US 20 and SR 242) is rugged; lava beds; 7802-ft Mt.
Washington has sheer rock faces, a difficult ascent (3); Pacific Crest Trail
cuts N-S; trail (2) from Big Lake (off US 20) goes S to Patjens Lakes; trails
(3) from Scott Lake cut across S end. **Diamond Peak Wilderness** (S of SR
58), cut through by Pacific Crest Trail, has rock climbs (3) at 7100-ft Mt.
Yoran (from Salt Creek Falls camp, 25 m SE of Oakridge), 8744-ft
Diamond Peak (from Summit Lake camp, 12 m W of Crescent Lake);
trails (2,3) also from Tandy Bay (30 m W of Crescent off SR 58) and
Trapper Creek (30 m NW of Crescent Lake off SR 58) camps. Other trails
at campgrounds at: **Breitenbush** (off SR 22, 10 m NE of Detroit), hot
springs (1,3); **Marion Forks** (off SR 22, 16 m SE of Detroit), 2,3; **Fern-
view** (11 m E of Cascadia on US 20), **Lost Lake** (2 m E of jct US 20, SR 22),
Big Lake (off US 20, S of Santiam Pass), 1-3; **Horse Creek** and **McKenzie
Bridge** (US 126, 1-1½ m W of McKenzie Bridge), **Paradise** (US 126,
4 m W of McKenzie Bridge), with hot springs, **Alder Springs** (SR 242,
15 m E of McKenzie Bridge), **Frog** (SR 242, 20 m NE of McKenzie Bridge),
1-3; SE of **Blue River** are Echo picnic area, French Pete camp, Frissell
Crossing, 1-3; **Broken Bowl** picnic area (off SR 58, 12 m NE of Lowell),
Blair Lake camp (off SR 58, 17 m NE of Oakridge), **Gold Lake** (off
SR 58, 26 m SE of Oakridge) and many nearby camps N of SR 58 on
Waldo and other pretty lakes with walks 1-3. Easy walks (1, 2) with
chances for hikes and rockclimbing (3) also at handsome area of **Opal,
Indigo,** and **Timpanogas** lakes (42 m SE of Oakridge). Information:
P.O. Box 1272, Eugene 97401.

GOLD BEACH: Beautiful trails at **Cape Sebastian State Park** (7 m S on
US 101), wildflowers (1); **Boardman Wayside** (26 m S on US 101), views,
clamming (1); **Harris Beach State Park** (30 m S on US 101), beach and
wildflower walks (1, 2), camping; **Azalea State Park** (30 m S off US 101),
beautiful displays (1); **Loeb State Park** (30 m S on US 101, 8 m NE), camping on Chetco River in myrtle trees (1); **Palmer Butte** (30 m S on US 101,

11 m NE), overlooks (2); **Humbug Mtn State Park** (24 m N on US 101), beach, 1750-ft peak (1, 2), camping; **Battle rock** (30 m N on US 101), swimming beach (1); **Cape Blanco** (34 m N on US 101, then W), scenic trails (1, 2), swimming beach, camping, lighthouse, Coast Guard station; **Sixes River** (34 m N on US 101, then E), trails (1, 2).

GRANTS PASS: Chamber of Commerce (131 NE "E" St.), information on Rogue River trips, gold panning sites. **Valley of the Rogue State Park** (12 m E on I-5), swimming, camping, walks (1). **Rogue River,** a national wild and scenic river; recreational areas reachable by road E from Gold Beach (to Illahe) or NW from Grants Pass (to Grave Creek), both of which supply whitewater and other boat tours; a 40-m foot trail runs along the N bank of the river between Illahe and Grave Creek, with camping along the way; agate hunting at river mouth (2 m N of Gold Beach). **Siskiyou National Forest** (W & SW), 1-million acres; rare trees and wildflowers; gentle peaks (not much over 5000 ft) in W provide good hiking (3) in-**Kalmiopsis Wilderness,** with easiest access from campgrounds along Chetco River (NE of Brookings); trails (2, 3) from **Fairview** (20 m NE off US 101 via Pistol River Rd.), **Elko** camp (18 m SE of Golf Beach via Wildhorse Rd.), **Wildhorse** camp (26 m E of Gold Beach off Wildhorse Rd.), **Big Pine** picnic area (34 m W of Grants Pass off Galicie Rd.); **Illinois Falls** (off US 199 W of Selma). Unit SW on US 199 contains **Oregon Caves National Monument** (20 m E of Cave Junction on SR 46), cave tours (strenuous, 2, 3; adm) daily (raincoats and overshoes for rent, as caves are wet) and trails (2, 3); **Smokejumper Base** (4 m S of Cave Junction on US 199), open daily (closed hols), free; hiking (2, 3) from **Elk Valley** (on US 199 on Calif. line). Information: P.O. Box 440, Grants Pass 97526.

KLAMATH FALLS: Walking (1) at **Moore Park** (Lakeshore Dr. on upper Klamath Lake), zoo, picnicking, nature trail; **Collier Memorial State Park** (30 m N on US 97), extensive logging museum and pioneer village, picnicking, camping; **Kimball State Park** (40 m N on US 97, SR 62), on Wood River, picnics, camping; **Gerber Reservoir** (40 m E via SR 140, 70).
    Winema National Forest (N), 909,000 acres of former Klamath tribal lands with historic sites, wildlife sanctuaries (NW end of upper Klamath Lake; 47 m NW on US 97, then E; 12 m E of Bly on SR 140); **Mtn Lakes Wilderness,** with stunning lakes and peaks over 7500 ft, is easily reached from trailheads on SR 140 (NW of town), campsites at Lake of the Woods, and trail N off SR 66 along Clover Creek (2, 3); **Pacific Crest Trail** (2, 3) comes down from Crater Lake; **Spruce** and **Cold Spring** campgrounds (33 & 40 m NW on SR 140) have trails (2, 3); **Cold Spring** (38 m NW on SR 140, 11 m NW on FS 358), trails (2, 3). **Digit Point** (73 m N on US 97, NW), with water sports on Miller Lake, has trails (1-3).
    Crater Lake National Park (47 m N on US 97, SR 62), deepest and

possibly most beautiful lake in U.S., is rimmed with 500-2000-ft walls; 2 small islands; 33-m scenic drive circles rim; exhibit bldg and Sinnott Memorial outlook open daily late-June-Labor Day with interpretive programs, guided walks; picnic and campsites; boat trips; self-guiding wildflower garden (hq) and Godfrey Glen (near Mazama camp) trails (1, 2); other trails are 1.7-m Garfield Peak (E of lodge) for views (2), 1.5-m Discovery for views (1), .8-m Watchman for views (2), 1.1-m Cleetwood (only access to lake, descending 760 ft in 1.1 m; 2), 2.5-m Mt. Scott (8926 ft) for views (2); 4-m Lightning Springs trail connects rim to Pacific Crest Trail (runs 25 m through park on W side of lake with no views of it); permit required for backcountry hiking; trails usually closed by snow Oct.-July; information: supt., Crater Lake, 97604.

LAKEVIEW: Volcanic area; geysers and hot springs (3 m N on US 395); **Albert Rim** (NE on US 395), a fault block; Indian artifacts on shores of **Lake Albert** (25 m NE on US 395); **Paisley** (45 m N on SR 31), picturesque Western town; water sports, camping, on **Goose Lake** (S on US 395); **Hart Mtn Antelope Refuge** (NW off SR 140); 1, 2. **Fremont National Forest** surrounds the city; 1.2-million acres; 19,000-acre **Gearhart Wilderness**, with volcanic domes over 8000 ft and strange rock formations, has a 14-m trail (3) running N-S (reached from campsites near Blue Lake on FS 340 NW of Lakeview or from trailheads off road NE of Bly ranger station); campsites are grouped at SE end of wilderness on streams (1-3); other forest areas have low hills, campsites on valley creeks or lakes, easy walking (1) on flat roads; information: P.O. Box 551, Lakeview 97630.

MEDFORD: Chamber of Commerce (304 S Central Ave.), information on rockhounding sites and ghost towns. **Jacksonville** (4 m W on sr 238), beautifully preserved gold boom town; 70 bldgs; maps for self-guiding tours at Jacksonville Museum (206 N 5th St.), open daily in summer, Tues.-Sat. in winter; free; 1. **Cantrall-Buckley** (8 m SW of Jacksonville off SR 238) and **Little Applegate** (16-19 m SE of Jacksonville off 38, 238) have swimming, trails (2). **Lithia Park** (15 m S on I-5 to Ashland City Plaza), 100 acres, ponds, woods, nature trails (1); **Surveyor Camp** (33 m E of Ashland via Keno Rd.), trails (2); **Emigrant** (5 m SE of Ashland off SR 66) trails (2). **Tou Velle** (3 m NE on I-5, 6 m N on Table Rock Rd.), pretty swimming, picnic site on Rogue River; **Gold Nugget** (14 m NE on I-5, 2 m N on SR 234), pretty picnic site; 1.

Rogue River National Forest (N & S), ½-million acres. **Pacific Crest Trail** comes S from Crater Lake through 7000-ft elevations (3) to easier terrain (2, 3) near scenic Lake of the Woods campsites; Pacific Trail access also at Howard Prairie (25 m NE of Ashland) camps. Good trails (2, 3) at campsites at **Beaver Dam** and **Daley Creek** (30 m NE of Ashland on FS 3706), **Whiskey Springs** (10 m E of Butte Falls on FS 3317), **Abbott Creek-** (off SR 62 N of Prospect); waterfalls at **Prospect.**

ONTARIO: Chamber of Commerce (Moore Hotel Bldg lobby, 125 S Oregon St.), maps for rockhounding, petroglyphs, Indian artifacts; river flows in an arc around Jordan Crater lava beds to scenic **Lake Owyhee** (22 m S on SR 201, 26 m SW), with state park camping, picnicking; S of the park the river is designated a scenic waterway.

PENDLETON: Walks (1), picnics at state parks: **Emigrant Springs** (26 m SE off I-80 N), camping; on river at Hilgard Junction campsite (45 m SE of I-80 N) and **Red Bridge** (5 m SW of Hilgard on SR 244); **Battle Mtn** (40 m S on US 395); **Ukiah-Dale** (50 m S on US 395), camping on John Day River, canyon walks (2, 3). McNary Lock & Dam (32 m N on US 395 to Umatilla, 2 m E on US 730), self-guiding tours of powerplant, fish ladders (daily in daylight; free); water sports on lake; 1.

Umatilla National Forest (NE & S), 1.3-million acres partly in Washington; spectacular Kendall-Skyline Forest Rd. along summit of Blue Mtns. Trails (1-3) and rockhounding off US 30 at **Umatilla Forks** (31 m E), **Elk** picnic ground (35 m E); also off SR 204 from **Tollgate:** Woodward (½ m W), Alpine Spring (7 m SE), Target Meadows (3 m N, Dusty Spring (9 m E), Luger Spring (17 m E), scenic Bear Canyon (26 m E), Jubilee Lake (12 m NE), Mottet (14 m NE), Timothy Spring (17 m NE), Squaw Springs (20 m NE), Deduck Springs (23 m NE), Indian (27 m NE), Goodman (37 m NE). From **Dayton** (Wash.) via SR 12, trails (1-3), rockhounding at: Tucannon (20 m SE), Teepee (32 m SE); from **Pomeroy** (Wash.) via SR 12, at Pataha picnic ground (15 m S), Teal Spring (30 m S), Sprice Spring (32 m S); from **Anatone** (Wash.) via SR 3, Wickiup (21 m SW). From **Troy** on SR 204, trails (1-3), rockhounding at: Mosier Spring (16 m), Elk Flats (21 m W). Trails (1, 2) at campsites at **Big Creek** (23 m SE of Ukiah off SR 244), **N Fork John Day River** (off SR 7, 220); **Olive Lake** (27 m SE of Dale off US 395) picnic area. Trails (1, 2) at **Bull Prairie Lake** camp (17 m N of Spray off SR 207). Information: 2517 SW Hailey Ave., Pendleton 97801.

PORTLAND: Visitor Information Center (824 SW 5th Ave.), information on fine museums, architectural landmarks including cast-iron facades, pedestrian malls at Lloyd Center (Broadway, 2 blocks E of Union Ave.), cascades at Auditorium Forecourt (SW 3rd Ave. & Clay St.); **Washington Park** (via Canyon Rd. or W Burnside St.), 59 hilltop acres, city views outstanding Rose Test, 5½-acre Japanese (spring-fall, Tues.-Sun.; adm), and Shakespeare Gardens, picnicking; **Portland Zoological Gardens** (4001 SW Canyon Rd.), daily, sm adm; **Hoyt Arboretum** (4000 SW Fairview Blvd), self-guiding trails on 214 acres, picnicking (daily, free); **Pittock Acres Park** (off W Burnside St.), mansion, 46 landscaped acres, views (Wed.-Sun. 1-5, longer hrs in summer; closed hols, Jan. 1-15; adm); **Council Crest Park** (SW Greenway Ave.), views; **Peninsula Park** (N

Portland Blvd & Albina Ave.), sunken rose garden; **American Rhododendron Soc. Gardens** (Crystal Springs Island, SE 28th Ave.), in forested setting (open daily; free); **Mt. Tabor Park** (off SE 60th Ave.), picnicking, views, on extinct volcano; **Sanctuary of Our Sorrowful Mother** (SANDY Blvd & NE 85th Ave.), beautifully landscaped 58 acres on 2 levels (elevator) on cliff overlooking Columbia River, grotto, gardens, religious statuary (daily; free); **1. Bybee-Howell House** (12 m N off US 30 to Howell Park Rd., Sauvie Island), 120 acres, restored 19th-C home (open May-Oct. daily; adm); **1.**

Portland General Electric Co. project on Clackamas River (SR 224) provides **River Mill** picnic site (30 m S); **N Fork** Fish Ladder viewing gallery (36 m S) open salmon and steelhead spawning season; **Promontory Park** (37 m S), water sports and camping; **Austin Hot Springs** (65 m S), picnic area with springs, bathing; **1. Aurora Colony Historical Soc.** (23 m S on I-5, 3 m S off SR 214 to 2nd & Liberty Sts., Aurora) preserved bldgs of 19th-C German colonists; open Wed.-Sun.; closed hols; adm. **Champoeg State Park** (20 m SW on SR 99W, 7 m SE of SR 219), on pretty Willamette River; site of village destroyed by floods; museums; camping, picnicking, botanical garden; **1. Butteville** (20 m SW on SR 99W, E on Wilsonville Rd.), ghost town, cemetery. Walks **(1, 2)** at **Milo McIver State Park** (20 m SE via SR 211, 5 m W of Estacada), swimming, camping; **N Fork Eagle Creek** (8 n NE of Estacada on Co. Rd.), camping; **Little Bend** (32 m NW off US 26 on EFork Dairy Creek Rd.), picnics; **Scaponia** (37 m NW off US 37 on Veronia-Scappoose Co. Rd.), camping. **Trojan Nuclear Plant** (42 m NW via US 30), landscaped and wooded 635 acres on Columbia River; Visitor Center exhibits; swimming, picnicking; whistling swan lagoon; nature trails **(1)**; daily exc hols; free.

Mt. Hood Loop (from Visitor Information Center) is a marked, 171-m auto tour (E along I-80N)to the spectacular Columbia River gorge and Mt. Hood; stops at scenic, historic, and recreational sites. Thrilling **waterfalls** include Latourelle (29 m), sheer 250-ft drop; Bridal Veil (31.3 m); Coopey (32.5 m); Mist (34.3 m), 2 cataracts; Wahkeena (34.5 m), picnicking, trails; Multnomah (35 m), stunning, trails, picnics, cafe; Oneonta (37.3 m), beautiful but slippery trail through narrow fern-lined gorge; Horsetail (37.5 m). State parks (picnicking): **Lewis & Clark** (17.2 m), camping, swimming; **Dabney** (20.1 m), camping, swimming; **Rooster Rock** (23.7 m), swimming; **Portland Women's Forum** (25.6 m), views; **Crown Point** (26.8 m), view, cafe; **Guy Talbot** (28.8 m), trails; **Benson** (29.5 m), swimming; **Shepperd's Dell** (30.3 m), rock formations, falls, trails; **Ainsworth** (38.1 m), camping, trails; **John B. Yeon** (42.7 m) falls, views, trails. **Booneville Dam** (44 m), hydroelectric project; self-guiding powerhouse tours, walkway displays, fish ladders, salmon hatchery; daily in daylight; free; **1. Cascade Locks Park** (E off I-80N), museum (May-Oct.), camping; **1.**

Mt. Hood National Forest (W), 1-million acres surrounding 11,235-ft, snow-capped mtn; waterfalls, glaciers, lakes, hot springs, flowered alpine meadows; winter sports, camping, picnicking, riding, other activities. **Pacific Crest Trail** enters at Columbia Gorge Work Center (information; camping 2 m S) and follows Pacific slopes of the Cascades along the W forest border to Mt. Jefferson Wilderness; **3. Mt. Hood Wilderness** is usually reached from Timberline Lodge (6000 ft) or adj Alpine campground, via road N from Government camp; 38-m trail circles mtn, 9 routes to summit (3); access on E from Cloud Cap picnic area and Tilly Jane campsite (33 m S of Hood River off SR 35), with trails (2, 3). **Larch Mtn** (26 m E off I-80 N, 13 m S), extraordinarily beautiful picnic area, huckleberry picking (mid-Aug.-mid-Sept.), trails (1-3) here and at Rainy Lake. **Eagle Creek** (43 m E via I-80 N), with nearby Wy'East (4½ m), Tenas (4½ m), Seven & One-Half Mile (7½ m) camps with lovely trails 1-3; fish hatchery. **Lava beds** (25 m S of Hood River, off SR 35 near Parkdale); **2.** Scenic trails (1-3) at camps at **Wahtum** and **Lost** lakes (20 & 28 m SW of Hood River off SR 35), the latter reflecting Mt. Hood; Hood River Meadows (37 m S of Hood River on SR 35), nearby falls; Bonney Meadows (18 m E of Government Camp off SR 35) and nearby Lower Twin Lake (off SR 26). **Clackamas** and **Timothy** lakes (18-20 m SE of Government Camp on Skyline Rd.) have camp and picnic areas with trails (1, 2), access to Pacific Crest (3). Beautiful **Mirror Lake** (off US 26, 3 m W of Government Camp) is picnic area reached by 1-m trail (2). **Green Canyon** camp (off US 26, 5 m S of Zigzag on SALMON River Rd.), exceptionally scenic trails (1-3); also at McNeil camp (7 m N of Zigzag), Wildwood (1 m E of Zigzag). Scenic trails (1-3) at **Little Fan Creek**, King Fisher, Bagby Hot Springs, Pegleg Falls camp and picnic areas (35-43 m SE of Estacadea on SR 224); at camps at **Hambone Springs** (43 m SE of Estacada on Abbott Rd.), **Little Crater** (Abbott Rd.). At **Olallie** and **Horseshoe** Lakes (27 m NE of Detroit) are trails (1, 2), access to Pacific Crest (3).

ROSEBURG: Scenic trails (2) at **Cavitt Creek Falls** (18 m E on SR 138, 8 m S) swimming, camping; **Wolf Creek Falls** (18 m E on SR 138, 10 m SE); **Millpond** and **Rock Creek** camps (24 m E on SR 138, 4-5 m NE on Rock Creek Rd.), swimming, camping; **Susan Creek Falls** (29 m E on SR 138), picnics.

Umpqua National Forest (E on SR 138), 984,000 acres, spectacular waterfalls, lakes, mtns 5-6000-ft; beautiful trails (2) at **Steamboat Falls** camp (32 m E on SR 138, 4 m N), Scaredman Creek (5 m N of Steamboat), Horseshoe Bend camp (6 m SE of Steamboat), Weeping rock picnic area (13 m SE of Steamboat), Eagle Rock camp (14 m SE of Steamboat), Boulder Flat camp (17 m SE of Steamboat), Toketee Lake camp (2 m E of Toketee), Watson Falls picnic area (2 m SE of Toketee), Lake Creek picnic area (7 m NW of Diamond Lake), lovely Diamond Lake (with Mt.

Thielsen, **3**), Broken Arrow (S end of Diamond Lake), Poole Creek and
Inlet camps (15 m N of Diamond Lake on Lemolo Lake). On **Little River
Rd.** are pretty trails (**2**) at Coolwater Camp and White Creek Picnic
Ground (16 & 17 m E of Glide), Hemlock Lake campground (32 m SE of
Glide), Big Twin Lakes camp (40 m E of Glide, 2 m on trail). On **S Ump-
qua Rd.** are attractive trails (**2**) at Camp Comfort, Cliff Lake, Fish Lake
camps. **Devils Flat** camp (18 m E of Azalia), scenic trails (**2**). **Bohemia
Gold Mining District** may be seen by guided tour (from Cottage Grove
Village Green) or with self-guiding tour booklets (FS office or Chamber of
Commerce in Cottage Grove). Other trails (**1,2**): **Bear Creek** camp (33 m
W on SR 42), swimming; **Gunter-Smith River** (34 m via I-5 to Drain, on
river 15 m NW), camping; **Tyee** camp (10 m N of Roseburg off I- I-5),
swimming. Information: P.O. Box 1008, Roseburg 97470.

SALEM: Walks (1) at State Capitol (Court & Summer Sts.); Bush Park
(600 Mission St. SE), Victorian mansion; Thomas Kay Historical Park
(12th & Ferry Sts.), 19th-C bldgs (open late May-early Sept.). **Silver Falls
State Park** (20 m SE via SR 22, 214), 8337 acres, 2 beautiful canyons, 14
splendid waterfalls (5 over 100 ft); picnicking, camping; many trails (**1-3**)
include 2 behind falls.

THE DALLES: Chamber of Commerce (404 W 2nd St.), maps for ghost
towns and emigrant landmarks along the Oregon Trail and Barlow Rd.
(can be followed on Mt. Hood FS road). **The Dalles Dam** offers train
tours (May-Sept., Thurs.-Mon.), fish counting station; water recreation
on reservoir; daily in daylight; **1. John Day Dam** (30 m E on I-80 N at
Biggs), powerhouse, fish-viewing station, lock open daily in daylight;
wildlife refuge on Lake Umatilla; **1. Memaloose** and **Mayer State Parks**
(10 & 11 m W on I-80 N), short walks, views; **1. Deschutes River State
Park** (17 m E off I-80 N), camping, fishing, trails; river can also be
reached from SR 216 and Maupin, where Deschutes River Rd. runs 25 m N
along the E bank; scenic camping areas at Beavertail, Macks Canyon,
other sites, offer trails (**1-3**), rockhounding.

TILLAMOOK: Stunning drive W (via Bay Ocean Rd.) to **Cape Meares,**
sand dunes, beach combing, clamming, sea lion and bird refuges, trails (**1-
3**); drive continues S to **Cape Lookout State Park** (10 m SW on Netarts
Rd.), camping on a swimming and clamming beach surrounded by spruce
forests, (trail to headland), a unit of **Siuslaw Ntl. Forest** with camping at
fishing streams (**1, 2**) and trails (**2**) at Hebo Lake (5 m E of Hebo), Mt.
Hebo (10 m E of Hebo), South Lake (12 m E of Hebo), Alder Glen (20 m E
of Hebo), N Creek (off US 101, 20 m SE of Neskowin on Drift Creek
Rd.), and **Devil's Lake State Park** (off US 101 at Lincoln City) with
lakeside camping (**1**).

PENNSYLVANIA

ALLENTOWN: Allentown-Lehigh Co. Tourist Bureau (462 Walnut St., zip 18105) and **Bethlehem Chamber of Commerce** (11 W Market St. zip 18018), information. City parks include **Trexler Memorial** (W at Cedar Crest Blvd.), greenhouses, and adj Cedar Creek with rose garden; **Little Lehigh** (SR 309 E of Cedar Crest Blvd.), trout nursery; **1. Bethlehem Historic Area** (5 m E on US 22, S on SR 378 to Lehigh River), settled by Moravians in 1741, has preserved bldgs surrounding Central Moravian Church (Church & Main St.); museum (Gemein Haus, 66 Church St: Tues.-Sat.; closed hols, Jan.; adm), residences, other bldgs; interesting cemetery (Heckewelder Pl.); early factories (foot of Church St.); **1, 2. Trexler-Lehigh Co. Game Preserve** (2 m W on US 22, 7 m N on US 309), 1100 acres in pretty area; herds of bison, elk; other animals; children's zoo; usually open afternoons—July-Aug. daily, weekends & hols in spring & fall—but check locally; adm; **1, 2. Hawk Mtn Sanctuary** (22 m W on I-78, 8 m N on SR 61, 895, then E), 2110 acres, bird feeders; trails (1) include hawk lookouts; major lookout with naturalist explanations (Aug.-Nov.) reached via steep trail (2); museum; daily; sm adm. **Blue Rocks** (17 m W on I-78, 2 m N on SR 143), boulder field, museum, picnicking (May-Oct. daily, weekends in spring & fall; adm). State parks with picnicking: **Beltzville** (22 m N on Tnpk Ext, E on US 209), swimming on large lake, fossil exhibit (1,2); at nearby **Jim Thorpe** (6 m NW on US 209) are Asa Packer Mansion (Packer Rd.) and Flagstaff Mtn Park (½ m S) with observation platform for view of Lehigh Valley. **Tuscarora** (8 m W on I-78, 31 m N on SR 309, then W), 1100 wooded acres on lake, swimming, trails; SW is **Locust Lake,** 1144 wooded acres, camping, trails; **1, 2.**

Hugh Moore Park (13 m E on I-78 to 200 S Delaware Dr., Easton), at Forks of the Delaware, preserves section of Lehigh Canal; locktender's home; 3½-m Towpath Trail, 2½-m River Trail (1, 2); picnicking; daily; free. In park is **Canal Museum** (Tues.-Sun.; closed hols; sm adm) with exhibits and literature on canals and their hiking trails. One detailed guide covers **Roosevelt State Park,** a thin strip of land preserving the Delaware Canal towpath from Eaton 50 m S via New Hope, Yardley, Morrisville to Grundy Park in Bristol; mostly easy walking (1, 2).

ALTOONA: Wopsononock Mtn (6 m NW on Juniata Gap Rd.), 2580 ft, fine view; accessible by car or trail. State parks with swimming, picnicking: **Prince Gallitzen** (10 m NW on SR 36, 8 m NW off SR 53), 6600 acres, camping, large lake (1); **Curwensville** (12 m N on US 220, 30 m NW on SR 453), camping, on W branch of Susquehanna River impoundment (1); **Blue Knob** (14 m S on US 220, 6 m W), 4422 acres, camping, many beautiful trails (1, 2) include climb to 3146-ft peak; **Shawnee** (19 m S of Blue Knob on SR 486, 96), 3800 acres, camping, trails, around large lake, forest trails (1, 2). **Canoe Creek** (4 m S on SR 36, 7 m E off US 22), picnicking on fishing stream (1). **Allegheny Portage Railroad National Historic Site** (4 m S on US 220, 10 m W on US 22), a series of inclined planes linking 19th-C railroad across mtns; Visitor Center in Lemon House, former rest stop; interpretive signs at restored railroad features; summer guided tours, craft demonstrations; picnicking; interpretive trails at summit, inclines 6 & 8 (1, 2); daily exc Jan. 1, Thnks, Dec. 25; free. **Raystown Reservoir** (27 m E on US 22, S on SR 26), 27-m-long impoundment with camping, water sports; on SE shore is **Trough Creek State Park**, camping, swimming, picnicking, ice mine, balanced rock, gorge overlooks, trails (1, 2) include scenic Abbott Run Trail with waterfalls and foot bridges across ravine; S of reservoir is **Warrior's Path** picnic area on a peninsula bounded by Juniata River; 1, 2.

CHAMBERSBURG: Cowans Gap State Park (14 m W on US 30, 5 m N off SR 75), water sports on lake, camping, picnicking; stream; forest trails, 6-m fire trail to tower, part of Tuscarora Trail; 1, 2.

DOYLESTOWN: Mercer Mile connects 3 castle-like bldgs constructed by Dr. Henry Chapman Mercer: **Mercer Museum** (S Pine & E Ashland Sts.), with 30,000 tools used in hand-made crafts; **Moravian Pottery & Tile Works** (Swamp Rd. & E Court St.), in a bldg patterned after Spanish mission churches and decorated with tiles produced here, guided and self-guided tours; **Fonthill** (E Court St., behind the pottery), Mercer's home, also decorated with tiles, guided tours; Mar.-Dec., Tues.-Sun.; closed Thnks, Dec. 25; adm; 1. **Newtown** (4 m E on US 202, 10 m S on SR 413), many pre-Revolutionary houses; map from Historic Assn in Court Inn; 1. **Green Hills Farm** (6 m N on SR 313 in Dublin), 60-acre estate of Pearl Buck (closed hols; adm). **New Hope** (11 m E on US 202), charming old canal town on Delaware River now an artist center; hiking (1, 2) on canal towpath (see Easton). **Washington Crossing State Park** is in 2 units (see also New Jersey): **Bowman's Hill** (2 m S of New Hope on SR 32), historic farmhouse (daily), memorial; observation tower (daily); Nature Education Center with weekend programs and bird banding; 100-acre wildflower preserve with 22 trails (1, 2); picnicking. **Washington Crossing** (7 m S of New Hope on SR 32), monuments, memorial, old ferry house, information at hq in Taylor House (daily), picnicking, 1.

GETTYSBURG: Gettysburg National Military Park (S on US 15-Bus) has Visitor Center (daily exc Jan. 1, Dec. 25) with ½-hr electric-map program for battle orientation; guided walks, living history programs, museum exhibits; 15-m self-guiding auto tour through battlefield; easy walks in many areas, 1-m High Water Mark trail (1) through area where Pickett's charge was repulsed, self-guiding nature trail (1) at Big Round Top, 10-m trail (1, 2) from McMillan Woods; free. State parks (picnicking) connected by Appalachian Trail are: **Pine Grove Furnace** (15 m W on US 30, 23 m N on SR 233), 637 acres, 2 lakes, streams, camping, water sports (1, 2); **Caledonia** (15 m W on US 30), 1444 acres, swimming, camping, nature trails (1, 2), nature center; **Old Forge** (NE of Waynesboro), on stream (1).

HARRISBURG: Walking (1) at: **Capitol** (3rd & State Sts.), in 13-acre landscaped park; **River Parkway** with 4-m promenade along Susquehanna River; **Reservoir Park** (off State St. at N 19th St.), views; **Italian Lake** (N 3rd & Division Sts.), flowers; **Wildwood Park** (S of I-81), lake, stream; **Ft. Hunter Museum** (6 m N at 5300 N River Rd.), colonial home, other bldgs (spring-fall, Tues.-Sun.; adm). **Hershey** (12 m E on US 322), information center, amusement park (summer; adm), museum (Feb.-Nov., Tues.-Sun.; adm), ride through display of simulated chocolate production (daily exc Jan. 1, Thnks, Dec. 25; free); Rose Gardens & Arboretum, 23 acres, flowers best Apr.-Sept., daily (adm mid-Apr.-Nov.); **Carlisle Barracks** (12 m W on US 11), with museum in Hessian Guard House (May-Sept. weekends; free); **Huntsdale Fish Hatchery** (25 m SW off SR 174 in Huntsdale), aquarium, springs, streams (daily; free); 1. State parks with picnicking, swimming: **Col. Denning** (30 m W on SR 944, 2 m N on SR 233), camping, lake, streams, 2½-m trail (2) to overlook, part of Tuscarora Trail; **Little Buffalo** (12 m W on SR 944, 15 m N off SR 34), lake, streams, gristmill, covered bridge (1). **Tuscarora Trail** starts from Appalachian Trail E of Sterretts Gap (15 m W on SR 944) and runs SW via Col. Denning and Cowans Gap state parks to state line just E of SR 456; 2.

JOHNSTOWN: Johnstown Flood National Historical Memorial (10 m NE on US 219, SR 869) commemorates 1889 disaster after South Fork Dam broke; Visitor Center exhibits, audiovisual programs, summer guided walks, booklets for self-guiding walks; daily exc Jan. 1, Thnks, Dec. 25; free; 1, 2. **Grandview Cemetery** (1 m W via SR 271 to Westmont) contains graves of many flood victims. **Yellow Creek State Park** (19 m N on SR 56, 5 m NE off SR 259), 2800 acres, lake, swimming, trails (1, 2).

Laurel Ridge State Park (write Supt., Rt. 3, Rockwood 1555) is a beautiful 15,000-acre preserve composed of state park, forest, game and conservation lands running from Conemaugh Gorge (W end of city) S through Laurel Highlands to the state line; 80-m **Laurel Highlands Hiking Trail** (1, 2) links all segments, with parking areas at major hwy crossings and overnight shelters; largest segments include state parks with picnicking: **Linn Run** (10 m NW of Somerset) with adj Laurel Mtn ski area, 1500 acres, falls, streams, Laurel Summit; **Kooser** (9 m NW on SR 31), 170 acres, swimming lake, stream, camping, trail (1); **Laurel Hill** (10 m W of Somerset), 4100 acres on swimming lake, camping, stream, many trails (1, 2); **Ohiopyle** (W of Confluence off SR 281), 18,463 acres surrounding 14 m of beautiful Youghiogheny Gorge with several waterfalls, overlooks, camping, canoeing, trail following river, 100-acre Ferncliff Natural Area (in a great horseshoe bend in the river) with nature trails (1, 2). Just N of Ohiopyle (on SR 381) are 1500-acre **Bear Run Nature Reserve** (write RD 1, Box 97, Mill Run 15464) and **Fallingwater,** the Frank Lloyd Wright-designed home built over a waterfall and set in woodland (tours Apr.-mid-Nov., Tues.-Sun.; adm). SW of Ohiopyle are **Ft. Necessity National Battlefield** (on US 40 W of Farmington) with Visitor Center (daily mid-Apr.-mid-Oct; weekends rest of yr; closed hols), Mt. Washington Tavern, monuments, picnicking; **Lick Hollow** picnic area (7 m W of Ft. Necessity on US 40); 1, 2. SE of Ohiopyle are **Youghiogheny Reservoir** with Corps of Engineers camping, water sports facilities, trails S along river; 3213-ft- **Mt. Davis** (W of reservoir); 1, 2.

LANCASTER: Pennsylvania Dutch Tourist Bureau Visitor Center (US 30 at Hempstead Rd. Interchange; or write 1800 Hempstead Rd., zip 17601), maps, exhibits, film, tour counselors to aid in planning day or overnight trips among the plain and fancy Pennsylvania Dutch (daily exc Jan. 1, Thnks, Dec. 25). Similar services from **Mennonite Information Center** (4 m E via US 30 to 2215 Mill Stream Rd.), Mon.-Sat.; closed Thnks, Dec. 25. **Ephrata Cloister** (13 m N off US 222 at 632 W Main St., Ephrata), austere bldgs reflect life of community of German recluses founded 1732; chapel; printshop; residences, other bldgs; serene site on stream for quiet walks; daily exc hols; sm adm; 1.

LEBANON: Walks (1) at: **Coleman Memorial Park** (W Maple St., N on SR 72), 100 acres, swimming, picnicking (free); **Cornwall Furnace** (5 m S on SR 72, 2 m E), stone houses, museum (daily exc hols; sm adm); **Historic Schaefferstown** (5 m S on SR 72, 7 m E on SR 419), Swiss-built village green with log and stone houses; **Memorial Lake State Park** (5 m W on US 422, 12 m N on SR 934), picnicking.

LOCK HAVEN: Bucktail State Park runs 75 m NW along SR 120 via Renovo to Emporium, with outstanding scenery, trails (1,2) along Sinnemahoning Creek and many side streams, and state park recreation areas with picnicking: **Hyner Run** (22 m NW on US 120), swimming, with adj stunning overlook over Susquehanna River at Hyner View; **Jesse Hall** (W of Renovo); **Kettle Creek** (7 m W of Renovo, 7 m N), camping, water sports on lake, overlook; **Sinnemahoning** (8 m N off US 120 on SR 872), water sports, camping on large lake, trails into adj Elk State Forest with elk herd (at Hicks Run); **Wayside Memorial** picnic area (S of Emporium); **Sizerville** (7 m N of Emporium on SR 155), camping, swimming, creeks, many trails. Other state parks with camping, picnicking: **Parker Dam** (34 m S of Emporium via SR 120, 255; 4 m SE), 895 wooded acres on lake, water sports, naturalist program, guided walks, historic logging exhibit, trails **(1,2)**; **S.B.Elliot** (10 m S of Parker Dam on SR 153), mountain laurel **(1)**.

MEADVILLE: Walks **(1)** at **Woodcock Creek Lake** (5 m NE off SR 86), camping; **Erie National Wildlife Refuge** (11 m E off SR 27); **Linesville State Fish Hatchery** (14 m W on US 6, 1 m S), Visitor Center, ponds (daily; free); **Pymatuning State Park** (17 m SW via US 322), camping, water sports on 17-m reservoir; waterfowl museum and refuge. **Shenango River Lake** (28 m SW via US 322, SR 18), Corps of Engineers camping, water sports. **The Ohio Extension Canal**, which ran from Beaver on the Ohio River N to Lake Erie, came through here via Sharon and Sharpsville, curved around to New Hamburg, and continued N via Shenango and Greenville; traces of the towpath can be followed in sections, and 18-m segment has been restored; **1,2. Maurice K. Goddard State Park** (16 m S on US 19), waterfowl and deer management area on impoundment, observation tower.

PHILADELPHIA: Tourist Center (jct Franklin Pkwy, 16th St., JFK Blvd), brochures for self-guiding or guided walking tours **(1)** of historic sites, 150-m Liberty Trail auto tour, other tours, special events (daily exc Dec. 25); most attractions surround Independence Hall or are along route of Culture Loop Bus (daily; sm fee enables you to get on and off all day) that runs from Independence Mall along Franklin Pkwy to zoo.

Independence National Historical Park (2nd-6th Sts., Chestnut to Walnut Sts.), maps, information, schedules of programs at Visitor Center (3rd & Chestnut Sts.), open daily, free: Liberty Bell (Independence Mall); Independence Hall (Chestnut & 5th Sts.); Congress Hall and Old City Hall (Chestnut & 6th Sts.); Carpenter's Hall (Chestnut & 4th Sts.); First Bank (Chestnut & 3rd Sts.); Philadelphia Exchange (313 Walnut St.); Pennsylvania Horticultural Society (325 Walnut St.), 18th-C garden (weekdays; free); Todd House (Walnut & 4th Sts.); Christ Church (2nd St. between Market & Arch Sts.); Christ Church Burial Ground (5th & Arch Sts.); Arch St. Friends Meeting House (4th & Arch Sts.); Betsy Ross House (239 Arch St.); Elfreth's Alley (between 2nd & Front St., off Arch); Penn's Landing, the renovated Delaware River waterfront with *USS Olympia* (Dewey's flagship during the Battle of Manila) and *Gazela Primeiro* (Portuguese square-rigged fishing vessel); **1.** Other areas for walks **(1): Society Hill** (SW of Independence Mall and Washington Sq.),

25-block, 18th-C residential district with Man Full of Trouble Tavern (127 Spruce), other historic bldgs; **Southwark** (S of Society Hill), settled by Swedes, with Old Swedes Church National Historic Site (Delaware Ave. & Christian St.) and American-Swedish Historical Museum (1900 Pattison Ave.); **Congregation Mikveh Israel Cemetery** (8th & Spruce); Chinatown (Race & 10th Sts.); **Franklin Pkwy** (from Logan Circle NW) with Academy of Natural Sciences, Free Library, Franklin Institute, Rodin Museum, Philadelphia Museum of Art. **Germantown** (E of Fairmount Park), with Cliveden (6401 Germantown Ave.; daily exc Dec. 25; adm), Deshler-Morris House (5442 Germantown Ave.; Tues.-Sun.; closed hols; sm adm), other historic bldgs; information at Germantown Historical Society (5214 Germantown Ave.).

Fairmount Park (NW of Philadelphia Museum of Art), on Schuylkill River and Wissahickon Creek, 4000 acres; handsome 18th-C mansions (brochures and schedules at Park Houses Office in Philadelphia Museum of Art); **Bartram's Garden** (54th & Elmwood Ave.), 11 acres, first botanical gardens in nation, home of nation's first botanist (daily exc hols; sm adm); **Japanese Exhibition House** (Lansdowne Dr. & Belmont Ave.) with garden, waterfall, pool, interpretive tea ceremony (daily in summer; check other hrs locally; sm adm); **Zoological Garden** (34th St. & Girard Ave.), 42 acres, 5-acre African Plains exhibit, 10 bldgs, wolf woods, waterfowl, picnicking (daily exc Jan. 1, Thnks, Dec. 24, 25; adm); sports facilities, picnicking, fountains; theaters; **Boathouse Row** (E River Dr. on Schuylkill River), crew competitions; **Grant's Cabin** (Girard Ave. bridge); **Morris Arboretum** (101 Hillcrest Ave; at N end via US 422), 170 acres, exotic and native trees, rose and other gardens (daily exc Dec. 25; free); **1,2. Schuylkill Valley Nature Center** (Hagy's Mill Rd., Roxborough), 360 acres, wildlife, trails, nature programs (daily; adm); **1,2. Tinicum Wildlife Preserve** (S 84th St. & Darby Creek), bird watching, observation bldg; daily; free. **Pennypack Park** (US 1 & Pennypack Creek), environmental center, scenic trails, **1.**

Andalusia (E on US 13 to just S of SR 63), impressive home on Delaware River; open by appointment (write Reservations, 6401 Germantown Ave., zip 19144). **Neshaminy State Park** (E off I-95 at SR 132), on Delaware, Neshaminy Creek, 333 acres, picnicking, swimming, **1. Silver Lake Outdoor Education Center** (8 m E on US 13 to Bath Rd., Bristol), 45 acres, trails (1); Wed.-Sun.; closed hols; **1. Pennsbury Manor** (8 m E on US 13 to Bristol, then follow signs 5 m NE), re-creation of William Penn's estate on Delaware; home, outbuildings, livestock on 40 acres (Mon.-Sat.; closed hols; sm adm); **1.**

Churchville Outdoor Education Center (22 m N on SR 232 to 501 Churchville Lane, Southampton), 50 acres, trails, nature programs (all yr; closed Mon., Tues., hols); **Briar Bush Nature Center** (15 m N on SR 611 to 1212 Edge Hill Rd., Abington), 20 acres, all yr, and nearby **Crosswicks**

Wildlife Sanctuary (Delene & Crosswicks Rd.); **Graeme Park** (19 m N on SR 611, just N of Horsham), charming 1722 home on pond (Tues.-Sun.; closed hols; sm adm); **Curtis Arboretum** (N of city line on Bethlehem Pike to Greenwood Ave. & Church Rd., Wyncote), ponds (daily); **Hope Lodge** (13 m N at 555 Bethlehem Pike, Whitemarsh), historic Georgian manor (Tues.-Sun.; closed hols; sm adm); **1. Ft. Washington State Park** (14 m N on Bethlehem Pike) consists of 3 units: Ft. Hill Historic Site (N of Tpke), Clifton House (473 Bethlehem Pike) with museum, earth redoubt, picnicking, overlook; Militia Hill (S of Tpke), wooded trails, overlook, picnicking; Flourtown (S of Militia Hill), creek, picnicking; **1. Four Mills Nature Reserve** (25 m N on Bethlehem Pike, W on Butler Pike to Morris Rd., Ambler), 50 acres, trails; **1. Mill Grove** (23 m NW on I-76 to SR 363, 5½ m N to Egypt Rd., 2 m W on Pawlings Rd.), 120 acres, former John James Audubon estate, wildlife sanctuary; 6 m of trails along Perkiomen Creek and in woods; house open Tues.-Sun.; grounds open daily in daylight; closed Jan. 1, Thnks, Dec. 25; free; **1,2. Valley Forge State Park** (23 m NW on I-76, N on SR 363), 2000 acres; Reception Center (Apr.-Oct. daily) with information, auto tape tours; observation tower; Washington's hq; museum (daily exc Dec. 25; free); parade ground; reconstructed soldiers' huts, field hospital; other bldgs, monuments; picnicking; daily exc Dec. 25; free; **1.** From here, **Horse Shoe Trail** runs through pretty countryside 120 m NW across the state to meet the Appalachian Trail at Rattling Run Gap near Harrisburg Reservoir (NE of Harrisburg); access at many crossroads; most sections can be walked by the average person, information: Horse Shoe Trail Club (51 Revere Rd., Drexel Hill, PA 19026.

Ridley Creek State Park (16 m W off SR 3), 2489 acres, meadows, stream, woodland, remains of 18th-C village, Visitor Center, exhibits, nature programs, trails **(1,2)**, picnicking; just S is **John J. Tyler Arboretum** (515 Painter Rd. off SR 352), 711 acres, labeled trees, trails **(1)**. **Brandywine River Museum** (23 m W on US 1 to Hoffman's Mill Rd., Chadds Ford), nature trail (daily exc Dec. 25; adm) and nearby Brandywine Battlefield (jct US 202, 322), a state historical park with interpretive markers, picnicking; **1. Longwood Gardens** (29 m W on US 1 to jct SR 52), 1000-acre estate of Pierre S. du Pont, finest gardens in NE; 4 acres of conservatories; fountain garden, Italian water garden; waterlily pools; wildflower, rose, other flower gardens; arboretum; plays, concerts, other events; daily; adm. **Conrad-Pyle Rose Gardens** (38 m W on US 1 at West Grove), 40 acres of roses bloom July-Oct; free; **1. Gov. Printz Park** (12 m SW off SR 291 in Essington), Tinicum Island, site of state's earliest settlement (1638); daily in daylight; free; **1. Caleb Pusey House** (15 m SW on SR 291 to Chester, 2 m N to 15 Race St., Upland), home of William Penn's mill manager, 11-acre plantation restored to illustrate 17th-C way of life; museum; other bldgs; Tues.-Sun. 1-5; closed Jan. 1, Thnks, Dec.

25; sm adm; **1**. Also in Chester is **Taylor Memorial Arboretum**, 28 acres, heathers, azaleas, hollies; **1**.

PITTSBURGH: Visitor Information Center (300 Jenkins Arcade in Gateway Center), information, maps, film and brochures for walking tour of **Golden Triangle** (daily exc hols); nearby fountains and flowers at Equitable Plaza, also at Mellon Square (6th Ave. at Smithfield). Walking **(1): Point State Park** (foot of Duquesne & Ft. Pitt Blvds), where Allegheny and Monongahela rivers join to form the Ohio; riverfront promenade; fountain; Ft. Pitt Blockhouse (Tues.-Sun.); museum (daily exc hols; sm adm). **Pittsburgh History & Landmarks Foundation** (Old Post Office Museum, 701 Allegheny Sq. W), exhibits, information on landmarks (such as Syria Mosque, via Bigelow Blvd in Oakland Civic Center) and modern architecture (Tues.-Sun.; closed hols; adm). **University of Pittsburgh** (Bigelow Blvd & 5th Ave.) offers campus maps, film, student guides from Commons Room in 42-story Cathedral of Learning (36th-floor overlook, 19 nationality classrooms; Mon.-Sat.; closed hols; free). **Mt. Washington** (Grandview Ave.) has walkways to city overlooks. City parks: **Conservatory-Aviary** (W Ohio & Arch Sts.), exotic and domestic birds in habitat settings (daily; sm adm); **Riverview** (2 m N on US 19), 240 acres, observatory, sports and picnic facilities; **Highland** (Washington Blvd & Butler St.), zoo (includes aqua zoo, nocturnal section, children's zoo; daily; adm), picnicking, sports facilities, swimming, reservoirs (parking fee); **Schenley** (Forbes Ave., Oakland Civic Center), 456 acres, nature museum with live exhibits (daily; free), stunning Phipps Conservatory with yr-round displays (daily; free exc for shows), picnicking, sports; **Frick** (Beechwood Blvd & English Lane), 499 acres, nature museum, nature trails in natural areas with hills and ravines, picnicking (daily; free); **Kennywood** (4800 Kennywood Blvd in W Mifflin), gardens, picnicking, amusement rides; **1**. **Allegheny Co. parks** (phone 355-4241 or write County Office Bldg, zip 15222) include: **North** (14 m N on SR 19), 3000 acres on lakes, observation tower, walks **(1)**, sports, picnics; **South** (12 m S on SR 88), sports, picnics, museum, walking and bridle trails **(1,2)**; **Round Hill** (20 m S off SR 51) with Exhibit Farm, picnics **(1)**.

Old Economy Village (17 m NW on SR 65 to Great House Sq., NW of Ambridge), charming restored village with cobblestone streets, established by Harmonists in 1825; 17 bldgs, artifacts; Grotto in the Gardens for meditation; daily exc hols; sm adm; **1**.

State parks with swimming, camping, picnicking: **Raccoon Creek** (23 m W on US 30), 8000 acres on lake; several trails **(1,2)** include one to springs formerly site of a spa. **Ryerson Station** (5 m W on O-279, 41 m S on I-79, 19 m W on SR 21), 1104 acres on lake; 4 nature trails **(1,2)**. **Keystone** (18 m E on US 22, 119; then SE), 1200 acres; nature trail on lake; trails in

woods (1,2). **Crooked Creek** (20 m NE via SR 56, 66), 2480 acres; walks
(1) on extensive lakeshore; part of Baker Trail (1,2); Traders Path parallels
Baker Trail but runs S of the park, between Shelocta and the Allegheny
River. **Moraine** (41 m N via US 19, I-79, SR 488), 15,767 acres on huge
lake, streams, swamp, many trails (1,2); just NE is **Jennings Nature Reserve**
(off SR 173 toward Slippery Rock), 383 acres, operated by Slippery Rock
State College, noted for blazing star (open daily Feb.-Nov.; weekends
Dec.-Jan.). **McConnells Mill** (41 m N via US 19, I-79; 5 m W on US 422;
then S) is a state picnic site in a spectacular gorge on Slippery Rock Creek;
restored gristmill; trails (1-3).
    Pittsburgh Council, AYH (6300 5th Ave., zip 15232), information on
Baker and other trails.

READING: The Pagoda (on Mt. Penn, via Skyline Blvd), observation
tower (daily), flowers; **Penn's Common** (Penn at 11th Sts.), 50 acres,
flowers; **Reading Public Museum** (500 Museum Rd.), 25 acres, arboretum,
streams, pond (free); **Daniel Boone Homestead** (7 m E on US 422 to
Baumstown, N on Boone Rd.), 600 acres, 18 bldgs restored to reflect 18th-
C frontier life (daily exc hols), trails (1), camping, picnicking (sm adm).
Hopewell Village National Historic Site (7 m E on US 422, 7 m S on SR
345), restored ironmaking community of 1770-1883; Visitor Center with
exhibits, summer living history programs; self-guiding trail to homes,
company store, other bldgs, iron-making operation (daily exc Jan. 1, Dec.
25; free); **1.** Surrounding Hopewell Village is 6000-acre **French Creek
State Park,** with camping, water sports, picnicking, 3 lakes; mining
remains; part of Horse Shoe Trail; other trails; **1, 2. Ringing Rocks Park**
(16 m E to Pottstown, 3 m N off SR 663), rock formations, picnicking,
trails; free; **1. Nolde Forest State Park** (2 m S on SR 625), 644 acres
devoted to environmental education; nature center; streams; 40 m of interconnecting trails with exhibits; **1, 2.**

SCRANTON: Nay Aug Park (Arthur Ave. & Mulberry St. in E Scranton), waterfalls, conservatory, zoo, swimming pool, model coal mine
(summer, Tues.-Sun.), museum of natural history and art (Tues.-Sun.;
closed hols), pioneer memorials; **1.**
    At **Wilkes-Barre** (18 m S on I-81), walks (1) at 35-acre **River Common**
(River St., N to S Sts.) with Japanese cherry trees; **Kirby Park** (across river
S of Market St.) with nature center; **Harveys Lake** (12 m N on SR 415).
Ricketts Glen State Park (24 m W of Wilkes-Barre via SR 309, 118), scenic
13,000 acres, 33 waterfalls; trails (2) follow 2 branches of Kitchen Creek to
Waters Meet, then trail follows combined waters flowing 2 m through
giant hemlocks of Ricketts Glen; Evergreen Trail (1) at S end has falls
overlook; waling (1) also at N end, with water sports and camping at Lake
Jean; trails (2) to Mt. Spring Lake, fire tower, creeks.

State parks with picnicking, walks: **Lackawanna** (10 m N via I-81, SR 524), lake swimming; **Prompton** (27 m NE on US 6, 7 m N), swimming; **Archbald Pothole** (7 m NE on US 6), 38-ft-deep, 24-42-ft-wide pothole; **1. Promised Land** (28 m E via SR 348, I-84, SR 390), pretty 2300 acres in Poconos; 2 lakes; swimming, camping; 20 m of trails **(1, 2)** to Bruce Lake Natural Area, Balsam Swamp, Egypt Meadow Lake, other attractive areas. **Shohola** (32 m E on I-84 to Lords Valley, 7 m NE), lake; **1. Gouldsboro-Tobyhanna** (14 m S on I-380, E on SR 507), 4000 acres, swimming, camping, 3 lakes, many trails **(1, 2)**.

STATE COLLEGE: Boal Mansion (4 m E on US 322 in Boalsburg) has interesting indoor and outdoor exhibits (including Christopher Columbus family chapel), picnicking; daily May-Oct; adm; **1. Pennsylvania State University,** on attractive 4900-acre campus; museums of art, earth sciences College of Agriculture (Ag Hill) with dairy (daily) and flower gardens (July-Sept.); **Outing Club** publishes maps for 55-m Mid-State Trail and is a source of information for Tuscarora Trail and many other beautiful trails in the attractive mtns and ridges through the central part of the state. Among the larger state parks with camping, picnicking that make good bases for walkers: **Bald Eagle** (22 m NW on SR 26), on large reservoir **(1)**; **Black Moshannon** (9 m NW on US 322, 7 m NW), 3450 acres on (N of R. B. Winter), on stream; **Sand Bridge** (E of R.B. Winter on SR 192), on stream; **Hairy Johns** (3 m E of Woodward off SR 45); **Poe Valley** (8 m SE of Woodward), swimming, camping, plus camping at nearby Poe Paddy; **Reeds Gap, Bear Gap, Ulsh Gap,** and **Snyder-Middleswarth** (named a National Natural Area for its original growth big timber), with woods and streams, are on road between Reedsville and Troxelville; **Alan Seeger** and **Penn-Roosevelt,** with Detweiler Run Natural Area, are on road N from McAlevys Ft. (at jct SR 26, 305); **Colerain** (20 m S on SR 26, 45), on stream; **Karl B. Guss** and **County Line,** on streams, on road along E Licking Creek S of Mifflin; **Kansas Valley, Fowlers Hollow, Hemlocks, Big Spring,** all on streams, off SR 274 S of Blain; see also Altoona, Chambersburg. **Stone Valley Recreation Center** (20 m S via SR 26, 305 at Petersburg), 600 acres, has programs run by Pennsylvania State University; just N is Pine Hill picnic site on Mid-State Trail; **1,2.**

STROUDSBURG: Pocono Mtns Vacation Bureau (1004 Main St., zip 18360) and state travel office at Delaware Water Gap (3 m E on I-80) provide information. **Delaware Water Gap National Recreation Area,** being developed on both sides of the river, has an extensive trail system **(1-3)**; trails on the Pennsylvania side climb above the Gap for views or are in woods. **Appalachian Trail** enters the state at Delaware Water Gap and follows Blue Mtn ridges to Susquehanna River at Clarks Ferry (13 m N of Harrisburg); across the river it turns S through valley farmlands to Pine

Grove Furnace, Caledonia, and Old Forge state parks; total of 225 m to state line (5 m E of Waynesboro); **2, 3.**

Waterfalls (N off US 209) include Winona 5 Falls (5 falls, picnicking), Bushkill (several falls in scenic gorge, picnicking, animals, Dingmans (rhododendrons, picnicking), Raymondskill (picnicking, animals), also Buck Hills (14½ m N on SR 447), most open Apr.-Nov. (adm). State picnic sites: **George W. Childs** (23 m N on US 209, to Dingmans Ferry, then W), with Stillwater fishing area just W **(1)**; **Pecks Pond** (22 m N on US 209, SR 402), in state forest **(1, 2)**; **Snow Hill** (12 m N on SR 447, then E), in state forest **(1, 2)**; **Big Poccno** (8 m W off SR 611, W of Tannersville), 1200 acres, fire tower and other views, 10 m of trails **(1,2)**; **Hickory Run** (22 m W on I-80, 8 m SW on SR 115, 903, 534), scenic 15,000 acres, camping, swimming, 23-acre boulder field, 13 trails **(1, 2)**.

WARREN: Allegheny National Forest, 495,000 acres in Allegheny Plateau Country, one of the prettiest areas of the state; 150 m of canoe streams; scenic drives; water sports, camping, picnicking. **Information Center** at Kinzua Pt. (10 m E on SR 59); overlooks over Allegheny Reservoir, dam, fish hatchery; interpretive trails **(1)** at **Jakes Rocks, Old State Road,** and **Rimrock** picnic areas. **North Country Trail (2)** runs S from Willow Bay campground along E shore of reservoir; also accessible from Tracy Ridge camp, where 3-m Tracy Run and Johnnycake Run trails **(2)** intercept it; continues S along Kinzua Bay past Big Rock Overflow Area and Tionesta Scenic Area to Nansen (7 m S of Kane on SR 66); here it turns W to Seldom Seen Corners, Guitonville, Muzette, and ends at landing field near Vowinckel. At **Tionesta Scenic & Natural Area** (S of Ludlow), 4000 acres of virgin timber, N Country Trail and **Tanbark Trail** meet; Tanbark **(2)** runs W via Minister Valley and Hearts Content to the Allegheny River N of Slater (US 62). **Minister Valley Backcountry** (4 m NE of Mayburg) has campsites, swimming, interpretive trail. **Hearts Content Scenic Area** (12 m W of Sheffield), 120 acres of thick woods with virgin trees, has camp and picnic sites, several short trails **(1, 2)**. **Twin Lakes Trail (2)** runs from Twin Lakes campground (also has nature trail, **(1)** W to Nansen, where it meets N Country Trail. Interpretive trails **(1, 2)** also at camp and picnic grounds near Marienville: **Amsler Spring** (W), **Beaver Meadows** and **Blue Jay Spring** (N), **Loleta** (S), **Kelly Pines** and **Hill Farm Spring** (E).

State parks with camping, picnicking, water sports are: **Chapman** (S on US 6, W of Clarendon in the forest), large lake, trails **(1, 2)** continuing into forest. **Clear Creek** (S of forest on SR 949 N of Sigel), nature museum, naturalist programs and guided walks in summer, fire towers for overviews, 11 m of trails **(1, 2)**. **Cook Forest** (S of forest on SR 36 NW of Sigel), 8000 acres on lovely river, virgin timber; summer naturalist programs; fire tower; 27 m of beautiful trails **(1, 2)**; 130-m **Baker Trail (2,**

3) starts here and runs S via Mahoning Creek Lake to Crooked Creek State Park and the Allegheny River.

WELLSBORO: Chamber of Commerce (Box 733, zip 16901), self-guiding tour maps of this area; a million acres of state lands with recreational facilities stretch W to Coudersport and Emporium, S beyond the Susquehanna River, E beyond Laporte; see also Williamsport, Lock Haven. State parks with picnicking: **Stony Fork** (1 m W on SR 660, 20 m S), on stream. **Pine Creek Gorge,** the 47-m-long, heavily forested "Grand Canyon of Pennsylvania," is accessible via **Leonard Harrison** (10 m SW on SR 660), on E rim, and **Colton Point** (8 m W on SR 660, 362 to Ansonia; 5 m S), on W rim, both with camping; beautiful overlooks, cascades, waterfalls, fall color; many trails **(1-3)** include Turkey Path, a 1-m steep descent from E rim and an even more precipitous descent from W rim; gorge becomes deeper and wider S of the parks and can be reached at **Bradley Wales** picnic area (via Leetonia); throughout this area the state has marked scenic routes with red, yellow, and white arrows. **Asaph** (15 m NW off US 6), on stream. **Lyman Run** (23 m W on US 6, 8 m SW), camping and swimming on lake; creek; trails **(1, 2)**; access to Susquehannock Trail. **Ole Bull** (23 m W on US 6, 16 m S on SR 144), on Kettle Creek, historic site where Norwegian violinist Bomeman Bull attempted to colonize "New Norway"; swimming, camping; trails **(1-3)**; Susquehannock Trail (can be followed N, or in a loop SW and then N, to Denton Hill); 40-m **Black Forest Trail (2, 3)** loops SE to deep canyons and is also accessible on SR 44 or on road W of Slate Run (on SR 414). **Cherry Springs** (23 m W on US 6, 10 m S on SR 44, 8 m W on SR 44), camping, **Patterson** (6 m W of Cherry Springs on SR 44), and **Prouty** (8 m SW of Cherry Springs off SR 44) are also near Susquehannock Trail. **Denton Hill,** developed for skiing, is beginning and end of 85-m **Susquehannock Trail (2, 3)** that loops S via Patterson to East Fork and Kettle Creek (at Cross Fork), turns E to meet Black Forest Trail and join it N to Ole Bull, and returns N to Denton Hill; also here is **Pennsylvania Lumber Museum.**

WILLIAMSPORT: State parks with picnicking, walks **(1, 2)** are: **Susquehanna** (SW edge of town), walks along Susquehanna River; **Ravensburg** (18 m SW via SR 654, 44, 880), creek, picnicking; **Little Pine** (14 m W on US 220, 14 m N off SR 44), camping; **Upper Pine Bottom** (14 m W on US 220, 13 m N on SR 44), creek. From N of Loyalsockville (7 m E on US 220, 5 m N on SR 87), **Loyalsock Trail (2, 3)** runs 48 m NE via Kettlecreek Gorge (and Dry Run picnic area) to Eagles Mere (High Knob Natural Area just W), World's End State Park, and E along Layalsock Creek to US 220 N of Laporte. **World's End State Park** (on SR 154 W of Laporte), 780 acres in a beautiful gorge; swimming, camping; Mineral Springs Trail **(2)** to Canyon Vista; other trails **(1, 2)**.

RHODE ISLAND

BLOCK ISLAND: Block Island Historical Soc. (Old Town Rd. & Ocean Ave.) sponsors walks; maps from **Chamber of Commerce** (Box D, ZIP 02807).

BRISTOL: Maps for **walking tours (1)** of historic sites from Bristol Historical and Preservation Society (Court St.) or Chamber of Commerce (Town Hall); many well-preserved 17-19th-C homes, especially along **Hope St.; Colt State Park** (2½ m NW off SR 114), restored 18th-C Coggeshall Farm (summers; sm adm), picnicking; town **beaches** (end Asylum Rd., Juniper Trail on E, off SR 114 near Wanen); **Llys-Yr-Rhosyn Rose Garden** (4½ m NW off SR 114 at 93 Rumstick Rd., Barrington), 11-acre rose garden, wildflower garden (mid-May until frost, daily, free); **Brickyard Pond** (off Nayatt Rd., Barrington); **Haines Memorial State Park** (off Washington Rd., Barrington), 101 acres on Bullocks Cove, brook, woods picnicking. Ferries leave from here for **Providence Island,** with swimming beach NW of Homestead and 450-acre tract belonging to Heritage Foundation of R.I.; **1.**

CHEPACHET: Walks **(1, 2)** at: **Black Hut Management Area** (4 m N off SR 102), Spring Lake (W) with swimming, streams, trails; **Round Top Fishing Area** (7 m N via SR 100, 98, 96), lake, pond, streams; **Buck Hill Management Area** (7 m NW on SR 100, 2 m W on Buck Hill Rd.); **George Washington** and **Casimir Pulaski Memorial** state parks adj (5 m W on US 44), 7000 acres, lakes, ponds, streams, swimming, camping, picnicking, extensive trail system extends into Conn. parks and includes 8.2-m Walk-About Nature Trail marked by Australians; **Ponagansett Public Fishing Area** (5 m S on SR 102, 3 m W on SR 101, then S), on Ponagansett River; **George B. Parker Woodland** (13 m S on SR 102), 450-acre Audubon sanctuary.

HOPE VALLEY: Wooded area with much public land **(1, 2): Meadowbrook Herb Garden** (SR 138, 1 m E of I-95), formal gardens, greenhouses; daily. **Carolina State Forest** (2 m S on Hope Valley Rd.), 1434 wooded acres, pond, trails; **Rockville Public Fishing Area** (1½ m S on SR 3, NW on Canonchet Rd.) with trails around Ashville Pond leading N via Wincheck and Yawgood ponds W to Connecticut and N to Beach Pond State Park; **Locustville** and **Moscow** ponds (W), **Wyoming Pond** (N) public fishing areas; **Dawley Memorial, Arcadia,** and **Beach Pond** (N of town between I-95 and W to state line along SR 165), swimming, camping, picnicking, fish hatchery, extensive trail system.

JAMESTOWN: Jamestown Historical Soc. (Narragansett Ave.), exhibits, information on historic sites on Conanicut Island (usually open Wed.-Sun. afternoons in summer; sm adm). Walks (1) at **Seaside Beach** (N of Jamestown Bridge), off E Shore Rd., **Marsh Meadows Wildlife Preserve** (North Rd. W of Newport Bridge), **Ft. Wetherill State Park** (S of Jamestown Harbor), **Mackerel Cove** (W on Beaver Tail Rd.), **Beaver Tail** (end of Beaver Tail Rd.).

KINGSTON: Main St. has many 18-19th-C homes; Pattaquamscutt Historical Soc. and Helme House (Kingstown Rd.), and Fayerweather House (SR 138) may be visited; Univ. of Rhode Island (NW) has museums, flower gardens; Pettaquamscutt Rock (4 m E on SR 138, S on Tower Hill Rd.) historic site, views. Walks (1) at: **Narragansett Pier** (5 m E on SR 138, 5 m S on Scenic 1A) and S to **Scarborough State Beach** (Ocean Rd.) **Pt. Judith** Coast Guard Station and lighthouse (S end of Ocean Rd.), **Sand Hill Cove State Beach** (W of Pt. Judith), fishing villages of **Galilee** and **Jerusalem** (W of Pt. Judith) on opposite sides of Pt. Judith Pond outlet, **Fishermen's Memorial State Park** (NW of Pt. Judith on Old Pt. Judith Rd.) with camping and picnicking, **Galilee Bird Sanctuary** (S of Galilee Rd.). **Great Swamp Wildlife Reservation** (2¼ m W on SR 138, then S), 2793 acres, is best when rhododendron blooms (June); ponds on S and E; Indian battlefield site (W); trails, **1, 2.**

NEWPORT: Visitor Bureau (93 Thames St.) has maps for self-guiding tours; **Preservation Soc. of Newport Co.** (Washington Sq.) sells combination tickets to mansions. Walks (1) include: **Bowen's Wharf** with cobblestone streets, 18-19th-C wharf bldgs, *H.M.S. Rose* (King's Dock, foot of America's Cup Ave.); **Washington Square** with Brick Market, Hunter House, Colony House; **Touro Synagogue** (85 Touro St.); many nearby historic homes, churches, museums; **Touro Park** (Bellevue Ave. & Mill St.) with Old Stone Mill (free); **Casino** (194 Bellevue Ave.; mid-May-late-Oct.; adm). Newport mansions, all with extensive landscaped grounds, may be seen from 3-m **Cliff Walk,** a stunning promenade between the mansions and the sea; most of the mansions are open daily in summer, and many are open at least weekends in spring and fall (adm). Walks (1) at: **Ft. Adams State Park** (off Harrison Ave.), one of largest forts ever built, picnicking (guided tours in summer; sm adm); **Castle Hill Coast Guard Station** (Ocean Dr.) open afternoons; **Brenton Point** (S tip) with fishing, picnicking. **Purgatory Chasm** (E of Cliff Walk), scenic cleft in rock ledges; adj are 3 bathing beaches and Norman Bird Sanctuary (3rd Beach Rd.), a 450-acre refuge with museum, trails, pond (Wed.-Sun.; closed Jan. 1, Dec. 25; adm). **Whitehall Museum House** (3 m NE on Berkeley Ave. in Middletown) has garden (daily in summer; adm); **1. Portsmouth** (7½ m NE on SR 138) has **Lehigh State Picnic Grove** (on SR 114), said to be haunted; **Green Animals** (Cory's Lane), topiary gardens with trees and shrubs sculpted into animal forms, pet cemetery, formal flower displays, other gardens (daily in summer; weekends in spring and fall; adm).

PROVIDENCE: Chamber of Commerce (Howard Bldg, 10 Dorrance St., Zip 02903) provides maps for many interesting historic sites **(1): Market Square** (Main St. at river), focal point since settlement, historic markers; **business district** (W of Market Sq.) along Weybosset, Westminster, Washington Sts. from river to Weybosset Hill, with many notable bldgs including Arcade (between Westminster & Weybosset Sts.), Beneficent Congregational Meeting House (Weybosset at Empire); **Kennedy Plaza** (N of Market Sq.) with government bldgs. **College Hill** (E of Market Sq.), more than 200 beautifully restored 17-19th-C homes surround Brown Univ. along Benefit St. and adj streets (river to Hope St., Transit to Star Sts.); many museums, fine collections; **Prospect Terrace** (a block E of Benefit at Congdon & Cushing St.), view, Roger Williams Memorial; **Roger Williams Spring** (N Main at Alamo Lane), small park, site of original settlement; **N Burying Ground** (1 m N on Main St. from Market Sq.), graves of settlers. **Swan Point Cemetery** (585 Blackstone Blvd.) is landscaped. **Roger Williams Park** (3 m S on Elmwood Ave.), 450 acres, 10 m of drives, lakes, miles of paths, gardens, Betsy Williams Cottage (limited hrs; free), Museum of Natural History (daily exc Jan. 1, Dec. 25) with planetarium, zoo (daily) and children's contact area; **1.** *Providence Sunday Journal* lists guided tours by Hikers Club of R.I., Yankee Trailers Hiking Club, Audubon Society, and local historic groups.

TIVERTON: Walks **(1)** at 4 public **beaches: Nanaquaket** (S), **Stafford** (E) ponds; **Ft. Barton** (Highland Rd.), Revolutionary War redoubt; **Sin and Flesh Brook** (S); **Ruecker** (off SR 77, N of Sapowet Ave.) and **Sapowet Marsh** (off SR 77, S of Sapowet Ave.) wildlife refuges.

WESTERLY: Walking **(1)** at: **Watch Hill** (6 m S on Beach St.), beach, Victorian homes, 1850 carousel. Public beaches stretch 15 m along Block Island Sound, including **Misquamicut** (5 m SE), **Weekapaug** (8 m SE), **Ninigret** (E of Quonochontaug) with camping, **Charlestown Breachway** (S of Charlestown) with camping, **E Matunuck** (3 m SE of Perryville).

S. CAROLINA

ALLENDALE: State parks: **River Bridge** (15 m E off SR 641), 390 acres, swimming, camp and picnic sites; site of a Civil War skirmish; museum, breastworks, nature trails; **1. Barnwell** (17 m N on US 278, 7 m NE on SR 3) 307 acres; camping, swimming, picnicking, nature trail; nearby fish hatchery; **Healing Springs** (6 m N of Barnwell State Park on SR 3), 1 acre, spring; **1.**

BEAUFORT: **Chamber of Commerce** (1006 Bay St.), pamphlets for self-guiding tours of this historic port; several houses and museums open to public. **Hunting Island State Park** (16 m SE on US 21), semitropical barrier island shaded with palms; camping, picnic sites, swimming; beautiful beach, nature trails; **1, 2. Hilton Head Island** (20 m SW via SR 170, 12 m E on US 278), yr-round resort; **Chamber of Commerce** maps for self-guiding tours and facilities.

CAMDEN: **Historic Camden** (S Broad St.), colonial restoration; Visitor Center; museum, information for walking tours; June-Labor Day, Tues.-Sat. 10-6, Sun. 1-6; rest of yr, Tues.-Fri. 10-4, Sat. 10-5; closed Thnks, Dec. 25; adm. **Hampton Park** (Lyttleton St.) and nearby **Rectory Square** are restful. **Hanging Rock** (29 m NW off US 521), picnic area, historic exhibits. **1.**

CHARLESTON: **Visitor Information Center** (Arch Bldg, 85 Calhoun St.), maps for walking tours and information on conducted tours; daily 8:30-5:30; closed Jan. 1, Thnks, Dec. 25. **Old Charleston** (N from White Point Gardens at E Battery & Murray Blvd.), on peninsula between 2 great rivers, one of the most beautiful urban areas in the nation; walks along riverfront at tip of peninsula; streets running N from here to about Calhoun St., and streets running E & W, are overhung with trees and lined with magnificent homes (most with lovely gardens), fascinating museums, lovely churches, interesting cemeteries, outdoor market (Market St. off E Bay St.); to explore this section could occupy several days. **Hampton Park** (adj the Citadel at Moultrie St. & Elmwood Ave.), flower displays, sunken garden, reflecting pool, pavilions, rose-bordered walks, aviary, zoo, picnic areas; daily; free. **Charles Towne Landing** (1500 Old Town Rd., SR 171), 200 acres on site of first permanent settlement in the state, exhibits pavilion, reconstructed fortifications, gardens, experimental crop area, barnyard, animal forest, boat rental, picnic areas; daily; closed Dec. 25; adm. **Ft. Sumter National Monument** (on an island in the harbor accessible by boats from Municipal Marina on Lockwood Blvd.), brochures for selfguided walking tours, guided tours, museum; daily; closed Dec. 25; free. **Ft. Moultrie** (US 17 N, then SR 703 to W Middle St., Sullivan's Island), interpretive displays (daily; free); nearby are Sullivan Island Lighthouse (Atlantic Ave.) and miles of beach.

Magnolia Gardens (12 m NW off SR 61), peaceful, moss-draped live oaks and cypresses; camellias, magnolias, azaleas; Feb. 15-May 1, daily 8-sundown; adm. **Middleton Place Gardens** (14 m NW on SR 61), world-renowned masterwork begun in 1741; camellias brought from the Old World; gardens stretch along terraces above the Ashley River, reflected in artificial pools and ponds; views across expanses of water edged with magnificent shows of blooms are incomparable; sunken gardens, secret gardens, cypress lake, bamboo grove, formal and wooded acres, garden ornaments; adj is Plantation Stableyards, domestic animals and fowl, slave cemetery, plantation shops, demonstrations, other events; picnic areas; daily 9-5; adm. **Old Dorchester State Park** (19 m NW on SR 61), ruins of an early settlement on Ashley River; daily; free. At **Summerville** (26 m NW on SR 61, Alt US 17), azalea gardens (Mar.-Apr.) on Main St. **Givhans Ferry State Park** (34 m NW on SR 61), camp & picnic sites, swimming, nature trails; **1. Cypress Gardens** (24 m N off US 52), 160 acres, masses of floral displays reflected in black waters of cypress lagoons; Feb. 15-May 1, daily; adm. **Edisto Beach State Park** (26 m SW on US 17, 22 m S on SR 174), wonderful beach; camping, swimming, picnicking; nature trails; **1. Boone Hall Plantation** (8 m N off US 17 on Long Point Rd., Mt. Pleasant), 738-acre estate, manor, avenue of live oaks; slave cabins, gin house, pecan grove; Mon.-Sat. 9-5, Sun. 1-5; closed Thnks, Dec. 25; adm. **Bull Island** (15 m N off US 17), part of Cape Romain Wildlife Refuge, reached by boats that leave daily at 8:30 am from Moore's Landing (return in late afternoon); beachcombing; **1.**

Francis Marion National Forest (NE via US 17, 52 or SR 41), 246,000 acres, remains of colonial settlements and plantations; black swamps; (short walks possible at half a dozen camp and picnic sites. **Buck Hall Recreation Area** (on US 17 N of Awendaw), shaded by moss-draped live oaks and evergreens, walks to Intracoastal Waterway overlooking wildlife refuge; inland is **Little Awendaw Swamp Scenic Area**; S off US 17 is **Sewee Indian Shell Mound**; **1, 2. Elwood** campground (off US 17 on SR 857 at N end), hikes to fishing creeks, and **Waterhorn Historic Area** on Santee River; **2. Huger Creek** campground (SR 41 N of Huger), on lovely creek overhung with moss-draped gums and cypresses, walks to historic sites; **2. Guillard Lake Scenic Area** (off SR 41 E of Jamestown), beautiful area of red cypresses on Santee River; camp and picnic sites; trails **1, 2. Bonneau** campsite (US 52 at Bonneau), nearby fish hatchery. **Tarpit**

Recreation Area (E of Bonneau on FS roads), at site of pre-Revolutionary tar kiln and tar pit; **1. Santee Coastal Reserve** (adj forest on N), 14 m of oceanfront bisected by the Intracoastal Waterway, is a 25,000 acre bird sanctuary.

CHERAW: Heritage Beauty Trail marked through residential areas; flowers best in Apr. **Cheraw State Park** (4 m SW on US 1) over 7000 acres in rolling sandhills, shaded picnic and camp sites; swimming; self-guiding nature trails, other walks (**1, 2**); national fish hatchery (1 m S on US 1, daily 8-5, free. Walking along the **Pee Dee River** and at **Lake Wallace** (15 m SE off SR 9 on Country Club Dr., Bennettsville).

CLEMSON: Clemson University campus, trial gardens (Feb.-Oct.), greenhouses, ornamental gardens (daily 8-5; free); **Ft. Hill**, John Calhoun's plantation home, other attractions; information from Public Relations office. **Lake Keowee** (NW of town), hill-circled boating area; exhibits on energy, picnic area at **Toxaway Visitor Center** (14 m NW on SR 130, 183; daily; closed hols; free;). **Hartwell Reservoir** (S of town), Corps of Engineers project on Savannah River; water sports and camping areas, including **Sadlers Creek State Park** (13 m SW off US 29), walks; **1, 2.**

   Sumter National Forest, Pickens District (20 m NW on SR 28), beautiful Blue Ridge Mtn region: **Stumphouse Mtn Tunnel** (20 m NW on SR 28) was an abortive 1852 attempt to drill through mtn to connect ports of Charleston with Midwest; you can walk 1600 ft in (tunnel is lit); nearby camping and picnic area; Isaqueena Falls; several easy trails (**1**) to nearby lakes and other points of interest; daily; free. S of here (off SR 290) are many trails along creeks (**1, 2**), and W (off SR 196) are trails connecting to Chattahoochee Ntl Forest in Georgia. **Oconee State Park** (on SR 107 just N of jct SR 28), lovely lake, picnic and camp grounds; self-guiding nature trail (**1**); other trails go S to Mountain Lake and up mtn slopes (**2**); just N of park boundary is a FS lookout tower on Long Mtn, beginning of the 18-m **Foothills Trail** via Cherry Hill and Burrells Ford campgrounds and Chattooga River (where part of *Deliverance* was filmed) to Ellicott Rock (tri-state view), **3. Cherry Hill Campground** is accessible to other trails (**1-3**), the longest going S along Pigpen Brook. **Chattooga Recreation Area** (N of Cherry Hill on SR 107) has short walks at Walhalla National Fish Hatchery (**1**) and a 2½-m trail W along the E fork of the Chattooga, through Ellicott Rock Scenic Area, to Chattooga River; from here it's 2 m along river to Ellicott Rock.

COLUMBIA: State House (Main & Gervais Sts.), landscaped grounds; Columbia Garden Trail starts here; Mon.-Fri. 9-5; closed hols; free. **Trinity Church** (1100 Sumter St.), interesting cemetery. **University of**

South Carolina has Memorial Garden (behind Library on Horseshoe Dr.) and another through a doorway in the old brick wall on Pendleton St. (between Marion & Bull); both free all yr. Nearby **Maxcy Gregg Park** (Blossom St.), garden noted for roses; azaleas in spring; free all yr. Small, restful gardens at **Columbia Museum of Art & Science** (1112 Bull St.), free; **Hampton-Preston House** (1615 Blanding St.), sm adm; **Robert Mills Historic House & Park** (1616 Blanding St.), adm; **Woodrow Wilson's Boyhood Home** (1705 Hampton St.), sm adm to home, gardens free; all open Tues.-Sat., Sun. aft., closed hols. **Memorial Gardens** (Lincoln & Calhoun Sts.), formal plantings with fountain, statues, summer houses; Sun. 1-5:30; free. **Riverbanks Park** (off I-26 at Greystone Blvd exit), zoo and 2 botanical gardesn; daily 10:30-6; adm. **Downunder** (entrances Main & Washington Sts.), underground area of cafes and boutiques. **Sesquicentennial State Park** (13 m NE on US 1), pioneer log house, camping, swimming, picnic areas, interpretive center and nature trail, other walks.

FLORENCE: Florence Beauty Trail (best early Apr.), 12-m tour past gardens. **Timrod Park** (Timrod Park Dr. & S Coit St.), shrine to Henry Timrod, Poet Laureate of the Confederacy; museum; old schoolhouse; picnic areas; rose gardens; azaleas; daily; free; **1. Lucas Park** (Santee Dr. & Azalea Lane), fountain, rose gardesn, azaleas, camellias; **1. Williamson Park** (6 m NW off US 52 to Spring St. in Darlington), planted with hundreds of flowering shrubs and flowers; daily; free; **1. Kalmia Gardens** (6 m NW on US 52, then 14 m NW off SR 151 to W side of Hartsville on Carolina Ave.), belonging to Coker College, named for mountain laurel; beautiful glen with 24-acre arboretum; daily; free. **Lee State Park** (23 m W off I-20 near Bishopville), 2800 acres on Lynches River, camp and picnic sites, swimming, nature trail (1). **Little Pee Dee State Park** (22 m NE on US 76 to Marion, 12 m NE on SR 41A), similar facilities, hiking (1).

GEORGETOWN: Chamber of Commerce (Front St.), maps for self-guiding tours of historic sites and information on plantation tours; nearby Rice Museum, open daily exc hols; **Hopsewee Plantation** (12 m S on US 17), on the N Santee River, example of local rice plantations (Tues.-Fri. 10-5; closed hols; grounds open daily in daylight; adm). **Belle Isle Gardens** (5 m S off US 17), former rice plantation now planted with azaleas and other flowers; Nov.-Aug daily 9-5; closed Dec. 25; adm; **1. Fluitt-Nelson Memorial Park** (36 m W on US 521, then 6 m N on SR 377 in Kingstree), 1749 mansion Thornhill, gardens; **1. Wedgefield Plantation** (2 m N off SR 701), 618-acre estate on Black River, lovely manor house, gardens; Mon., Sun. 10-5; adm; **1. Brookgreen Gardens** (18 m N on US 17), created as a showcase for sculpture on a former rice and indigo plantation; beautifully landscaped; zoo; game sanctuary; picnic area; daily 9:30-4:45;

closed Dec. 25; adm; **1. Huntington Beach** (17 m N on US 17) and **Myrtle Beach** (26 m N on US 17) are state parks with wonderful Atlantic beach backed by shaded areas with trails (**1**); both have camping, picnicking, swimming.

GREENVILLE: A Dogwood Trail (at peak in Apr.), marked through residential areas. **Cleveland Park** (1200 block of E Washington St.), rose garden, zoo, picnic sites; daily; free. **Paris Mountain** (9 m N off US 25), 3 lakes and self-guiding nature trail on 1275 acres, and **Pleasant Ridge** (23 m N off US 25) are state parks with camp and picnic grounds, swimming, hiking; **1, 2. Table Rock State Park** (20 m N on US 25, 15 m W on SR 11) surrounds mountain swimming lake; picnic and camp sites; nature center with interpretive trails; trails to Table Rock and summit of Pinnacle Mtn; **1, 2. Sassafras Mountain** (18 m W on US 123, 25 m N off US 178), 3548 ft, highest point in state, lookout tower; 2-m trail leads to 3483-ft Hickory Nut Mtn (**2**); open yr round; free. **Williamston City Gardens** (17 m S on US 29 at Williamston), mineral spring, azaleas, camellias, other flowers; Christmas display; daily; free.

GREENWOOD: Park Seed Co. Gardens, test gardens and floral displays yr round, Mon.-Fri. 9:4:30; closed hols; free. **Star Fort & Ninety Six** (11 m E on SR 34 to Ninety Six, 2 m S on SR 248), ruins of starshape earthen fort; **1. Greenwood State Park** (17 m E on SR 34, 702), picnicking, camping, swimming, hiking on Lake Greenwood; **1. Cokesbury Historic District** (6 m N on SR 254) preserves 8 of 54 mansions of a cotton-producing area; **1.**

    Sumter National Forest, Long Cane Division (S on SR 10), is too riddled with creeks for good hiking; most walking is on roads, occasional short trails scattered throughout forest, paths to old cemeteries and churches, or around campsite area; Long Cane Scenic Area has 28-m bridle trail; best hiking at Parsons Mtn Lake camp, where trails go up mtn and to lookout tower (**2**); at the Georgia border, the forest edges Clark Hill Reservoir, with Corps of Engineers recreational areas, **Baker Creek** and **Hickory Knob** state parks, with nature trails and lakeside walks (**1**); district ranger is Edgefield. **Enoree Division** (29 m NE on SR 72) is chiefly for hunters, with most trails in viocinity of hunting camps and rifle ranges; **Buncombe Trail** (SE of Whitmire on SR 66) runs to I-26, but is also used by horses and motorcycles (**2**); **Rose Hill State Park** (9 m SW on Union on US 176) contains federal-style mansion named for extensive rose gardens, picnic area, **1.**

ORANGEBURG: Edisto Gardens (S on US 301), along N Edisto River, city-owned park, cypresses, flowering trees and shrubs, azaleas (Apr.), thousands of roses (Apr.-Oct.), other blooms yr-round; picnic area; daily;

free; **1. National Fish Hatchery** (427 Lakeview Dr.), aquarium, picnic area; daily; free; **1.** At **Santee** (26 m E via US 301) is **Ft. Watson Battle Site** (N on Lake Marion) with Indian mound; **Santee State Park** (N on Lake Marion, camp and picnic sites, swimming, interpretive center, self-guiding nature trail, other walks; **Eutaw Springs Battlefield Site** (12 m SE on Lake Marion); **1.**

ROCK HILL: Glencairn Gardens (725 Crest St.), city-owned has fountain, reflection pool, terraced lawns, formal flower beds on 6 acres; best in Apr.; daily, all yr; free; **1. Andrew Jackson Historical State Park** (14 m SE on SR 5) where 7th President was born, museum (Tues.-Sat. 9-5:30, Sun. 1-5:30), camping picnicking, free; **1. Chester State Park** (23 m SW on SR 72, 121), recreational facilities, nature trails (**1, 2**). **Lake Wylie** (N on SR 274) is a power company project, water sports; **1.**

SPARTANBURG: Pine Street is landscaped all yr, special shows in spring. **Kings Mountain National Military Park** (29 m NE off I-85) preserves site of 1780 battle; Visitor Center (daily; closed Dec. 25; free); maps for self-guiding tour of major battlefield sites (**1**); also here is Kings Mtn State Park, 2 lakes, camping, swimming, other recreation, plus 1½-m nature trail and 2¼-m trail to Ntl Park hq; **1, 2. Cowpens National Battlefield Site** (9 m NE on I-85, then 6 m N on SR 110), open daily, free; interpretive booklets at Kings Mtn; **1. Croft State Park** (3 m SE on SR 56), attractive 7000 acres, camp and picnic sites, walks (**1, 2**). **Walnut Grove Plantation** (8 m SE off US 221), home of Revolutionary War heroine Kate Barry; cemetery, formal gardens; Apr.-Oct., Tues.-Sun.; Nov.-Mar., Sun.; closed hols; adm; **1.**

SUMTER: Swan Lake Gardens (W Liberty St.), named for swans living on lake, has Japanese irises (late spring), flower beds; picnic area; daily 8-8; free. **Poinsett State Park** (18 m SW via SR 763, 261), 1000 acres of hilly and swampy terrain, camping, water sports, picnicking, nature trail, other walks; **1, 2.**

SOUTH DAKOTA

HOT SPRINGS: Wind Cave National Park (11 m N on US 385), 44-sq-m prairie; wildflowers; low fees for several cave tours (**2, 3**) from 1-1 3/4-hrs, spelunking (by advance reservation; involves crawling), from Apr.-Oct.; visitor center (daily) exhibits, naturalist programs (summer); camping (spring-fall); picnicking; prairie dog, buffalo, antelope exhibits; short, self-guiding Rankin Ridge and Elk Mtn trails (**1, 2**); backcountry, trailless hiking (**2, 3**) by permit information: Supt., Hot Springs 57747.

RAPID CITY: Chamber of Commerce (Box 747, Zip 57701), maps for Red Carpet Tour of city. Walks (**1**): campus of **S Dakota School of Mines & Technology** (St. Joseph St.) with fine museums; **Halley Park** (St. Joseph St.) with Sioux Indian Museum, Minnilusa Historical Museum; **Dinosaur Park** (Skyline Dr., life-size dinosaur models on hillside (daily; free); **Sioux Park** (Canyon Lake Dr.), picnicking, children's storybook forest, swimming; **Canyon Lake Park** (Canyon Lake Dr.), picnicking; **Stave Church** (5 m W on SR 44 & Chapel Lane), Norwegian-style church, reception center (May-Oct. daily), sunken garden (all yr), free; **State Fish Hatchery** (7 m W on SR 44), huge hatchery with many pools (daily; free).

　　Rockerville Ghost Town (8 m S on US 16 in Rockerville), museum; mid-May-Sept. daily; free; **1. Big Thunder Gold Mine** (18 m S off US 16A at Keystone) tours mid-May-mid-Sept. daily; adm; **1. Hill City** (24 m SW on US 16), old mining town; museum; **1. Mt. Rushmore National Memorial** (22 m S off US 16A), visitor center with interpretive programs; **Four Presidents Trail** consists of 4 trails (**2, 3**), each 10-m long, that converge here; daily; free; **1. Crazy Horse Memorial** (38 m SW on US 16, 385), daily; adm; **1. Custer** (43 m SW on US 16, 385), old mining town with gold rush bldgs, museums; Chamber of Commerce (31 S 5th St.) has brochure for historic sites. **Jewel Cave National Monument** (57 m SW on US 16), 1275 acres of ponderosa forest with small cave opening in Hell Canyon; visitor center (Apr.-Oct. daily); summer guided tours (adm); 1½-hr **scenic tour,** on paved trail, requires uphill walking, step climbing (**2**); 1½-hr **historic tour,** unimproved trail, ladders, requires climbing, bending, crawling (**2**). **Spelunking tours** (4-hr, 3000-ft trip; 6-hr, 6000-ft trip), by advance reservation, have special clothing and health requirements (phone 605-673-2288 or write hq at Custer, zip 57730), and invoice crawling. **Custer State Park** (29 m S via SR 79, 36—scenic route is 40 m SW via US

16, 16A), beautiful 72,000-acre game preserve and recreational park in Black Hills; hq (on SR 16A) with nearby historical and natural history museum, pioneer monument, pioneer stockade, doll museum, cabin of poet Badger Clark, zoo, other attractions; scenic 14-m **Needles Hwy** (SR 87 between Sylvan & Legion Lakes) with spire-like rock formations; scenic 18-m **Wildlife Loop Trail** (S off SR 16A, 8-m gravel section) for free-ranging animals and buffalo corral; trails **(1, 2)** at **Sylvan** (3-m trail to Harney Peak), **Center, Legion, Stockade** lakes, **Coolidge** and **Blue Bell** areas (all with camping, picnicking); **French Creek Wilderness** has no marked trails (average hike in and out is 10 m) and requires registration at hq **(3)**; spectacular 1.9-m **Sunday Gulch Trail (1, 2)** from Sylvan Lake through a stone ravine, over water on wooden bridges, in evergreen forest; information: Hermosa SD 57744.

Old Ft. Meade Cavalry & Pioneer Museum (30 m W on US 14 to Sturgis, 1 m NE on SR 34, 79), on site of fort to which remains of 7th Cavalry, and horse Comanche, came after Little Big Horn; museum; cemetery; daily in summer; sm adm. **Bear Butte State Park** (6 m NE of Sturgis on SR 79), 1500 acres around core of extinct volcano that rises from plains; visitor center (daily in summer) exhibits on Cheyenne, natural history; camping, picnicking, swimming; 3.5-m trail to summit **(2, 3)**; trails **(2, 3)** to caves, formations; all yr. **Deadwood** (43 m W via I-90, US 14A), picturesque gold rush city in canyon; restored bldgs, museum (Sherman & Deadwood Sts. open all yr), cemetery; recreation area (105 Sherman St.) for swimming, picnicking; 1. **Lead** (4 m S), hilltop gold town; Sinking Gardens (Main St.), 13-acre park (spring-fall; free); **Rockford** (17 m S on Lead on FS road) and **Tinton** (8 m S on US 85, 2 m N off US 14A) are ghost towns.

Black Hills National Forest (Supt., Custer 57730), 1¼-million acres of magnificent forests, canyons, manmade lakes, waterfalls; historic sites; swimming; miles of marked trails and primitive roads, trailless walks. Good hiking bases with camping, picnicking are: **Pactola Reservoir** (25 m W of Rapid City via SR 44), visitor center; trails **(1-3)** to 5000-ft peaks, 5922-ft Seth Bullock lookout, Silver City and other mining areas, Sheridan Lake. **Sheridan Lake** (7 m S of Pactola Reservoir on US 385), trails **(1-3)** to 5000-ft mtns, Five Points, mining remains, several gulches W (an extensive trail system reachable also from Newton Lake camp, 3-m NW of Hill City), Horse Thief Lake, Mt. Rushmore. **Horse Thief Lake** (2 m W of Mt.Rushmore) with trails **(1-3)** from lake and nearby Palmer Gulch to Elkhorn Mtn, Pine Creek Natural Area, 7242-ft Harney Peak (several trails), Sylvan Lake, Cathedral Spires, Grizzly Creek Valley, Grizzly Mine and other mining remains, Mt. Rushmore; access to these trails also from Iron Mtn and other camps S and E of Mt. Rushmore, and from Custer State Park. **Deerfield Lake** (NW of Hill City) has easy trails **(1)** and climbs to mtns over 5000-ft including 6779-ft Hat Mtn (S), 6358-ft

Castle Peak (N); N of Castle Peak are many trails (1, 2) between
Moonshine Gulch (NE) and **Black Fox** (NW) campgrounds; **Roubaix Lake**
(16 m S of Deadwood off US 385) has many trails (1-3) to creeks, experimental forest, lookout on 6804-ft Custer Park; trails from all 4 camps
interconnect, with some trails (3) running N to **Hanna** camp (2 m S of
Cheyenne Crossing off US 85); Hanna camp is a good base for the lookout
on 7077-ft Terry Peak (also accessible by road to 200 ft of summit) and
trails to Lead. **Roughlock Falls** (W of Savoy) and nearby **Timon** camps
have creek and gulch trails (1, 2), climbs (3) to nearby peaks and lookouts,
Cement Ridge, access to Terry Peak area and Spearfish Canyon trails
(3). **Spearfish Fisheries Center** (321 S Canyon St. in Spearfish) and
McNenny National Fish Hatchery (14 m W of Spearfish on US 14) are
open daily in daylight; free; 1. **Boxelder** (E of Nemo near the Boy Scout
camp) is on 55-m **Silver Arrow Trail** (3) S to Pactola and Sheridan lakes,
over Harney Peak to Mt. Rushmore; shorter trails (1, 2) are just N from
Dalton camp to Stagebarn (E), Wonderland (N) and Bethlehem (N) cave
areas. In the S, **Flynn Creek** (SE of Custer) has climbs (2, 3) to 6166-ft
Cicero Peak. **Rifle Pit** camp (E of Pringle off US 385) has trails E into
Wind Cave National Park and N to Bowman Ridge and old mine remains
(2. 3); the proposed 150-m **Paha Sapa Trail** (with feeder trails) would run
from here N across Harney Peak to Sheridan and Pactola Lakes, Spearfish
Canyon, to Devil's Tower National Monument (Wyo.), but only unlinked
sections in most popular areas are complete; **Battle Mtn** (E of Hot Springs)
has trail (2). **Cascade** (9 m S of Hot Springs) is a ghost town on hot
springs (1). In the W, best hiking camps: **Moon** (via unpaved rds SW of
Deerfield Lake or N off US 16 at State line), with trails (1, 2) to springs,
caves, Summit Ridge and lookout (3); **Tepee** camp (W of Jewel Cave on
US 16) with 5662-ft Elk Mtn, springs (1, 2); **Comanche** camp (E of Jewel
Cave on US 16), springs, creeks, mining remains, N to 7166-ft Bear Mtn
(1-3).

   Smithville (37 m E to Wasta, 17 m N, 8 m E), ghost town at jct Elk
Creek and Rapid River; 1. **Badlands National Monument** (62 m E via I-
90, US 16A) has strange, colorful formations with spires and sawtooth
ridges that resemble stone castles and villages; junipers in protected coves,
yucca in valleys, islands of cottonwoods and wild rose; at **Cedar Pass** are
visitor center (daily exc Jan. 1, Dec. 25) with audiovisual program and
exhibits, cabins and camping (summer-early fall); summer naturalist
programs, guided trips; 40 m of road with wayside exhibits, picnicking,
prairie dog town; short Cliff Shelf, Door, and Window trails (1) among
junipers, panoramic views (1); ¼-m Fossil Exhibit Trail (1); 3-m (2) and 8-
m (3) loops on Prairie Break Trail; information: Interior, SD 57750.

SIOUX FALLS: Chamber of Commerce (101 W 9th St., zip 57101; summer booth at jct I-90, US 77) has maps for city circle tour including

Pettigrew Museum (131 N Duluth) and collections at **Sioux Falls** (marker for Yankton wagon trail, ruts still visible, to Flandreau) and **Augustana** colleges; **Stockyards** (Rice St. & Cliff Ave.); **Falls Park** (Rice St., W of Cliff Ave.); **Terrace Park** (Menlo Ave. & W Madison St.), lake, pool, picnicking; **Sherman Park** (Kiwanis Ave., 12-22nd Sts.) with Battleship *South Dakota* Memorial (summer, daily; free), zoo (daily; sm adm), children's Dennis the Menace park, Indian mounds; **1. Dells of the Sioux** (15 m N off I-29), craggy cliffs of Big Sioux River, native grasses, prairie flowers, picnicking; **1, 2. South Dakota State University** (41 m N on I-29 in Brookings) has a summer visitor center at Coughlin Campanile (rest of yr, in room 304, Admin. Bldg.), museums, medicinal herb garden, agricultural plots, 700-acre agricultural experiment station on Medary Ave; McCrory Gardens (6th St. & 20th Ave.), native trees and flowers. **Prairie Village** (28 m N on I-29, 21 m W on SR 34), reconstructed frontier town of 50 bldgs including opera house; 1893 carousel; special events (daily spring-fall; adm); adj **Lake Herman State Park** has swimming, camping, picnicking, historic markers, pioneer cabin; **Madison Waterfowl Production Area** (3 m S of Madison on SR 19), interpretive center, observation point, picnicking, nature trail. State parks with camping, picnicking, walks **(1, 2): Newton Hills** (22 m SE on SR 11), 948 wooded acres on hills on Big Sioux River; visitor center, swimming lake; caves; lookout tower. **Union County** (37 m S off I-29), 276 acres on hill above Brule Creek; arboretum; overlook; fossils in gravel pits; nature trails. **Palisades** (6 m E on I-90, 8 m N on SR 11), on Split Rock Creek with sheer, towering walls; caves; many trails. **Lake Vermillion** (18 m W on US 16), swimming.

SISSETON: State park with picnicking, camping: **Sieche Hollow** (12 m NW), also called Sica Hollow, beautiful wildlife sanctuary; Trail of the Spirits **(2)** circles a bog area said to be haunted; other trails **(1, 2)** to overlooks, old cemetery.

YANKTON: Chamber of Commerce (104 E 4th St.) provides maps for historic sites in this former steamboat port, once capital of the Dakota territory. **Milltown** (39 m N on US 81, 14 m W on SR 44), ghost town with picnicking on James River; **1.** Missouri River has been impounded by **Gavins Pt. Dam** (5 m W on SR 52) to form Lewis & Clark Lake; dam has visitor center (May-Sept. daily) with historic and natural history exhibits; powerhouse tours (summer); fort replica; maps for Lewis & Clark campsites, ghost towns, old cemeteries, other historic sites on river.

TENNESSEE

CHATTANOOGA: Convention & Visitors Bureau (399 McCallie Ave.), maps for self-guiding tours, information on guided tours. **Lookout Mtn,** 2000 ft above city, is reachable by road (S via Ochs Hwy & Scenic Hwy) or incline (3917 St. Elmo Ave.; daily; adm); on mtn are: **Point Park** (see below); museums; **Reflection Riding** (Garden Rd.), 3-m scenic auto route, reflecting pools, flowers, historic sites (daily; sm adm); **Rock City** (off SR 58), 10 acres, trails (**1, 2**), views, rock formations, caves, swinging bridge, amusements for children (daily; adm); **Ruby Falls-Lookout Mtn Caverns** (Scenic Hwy), tours of caves, falls (dialy; adm). **Chickamauga & Chattanooga National Military Park** (Supt., Ft. Oglethorpe, GA 30741) preserves numerous sites associated with Civil War battles for control of Chattanooga; information at **Point Park** (1101 E Brow Rd. on Lookout Mtn), with museum, overlooks (**1,2**), monuments, Bluff Trail (**2**) running length of park with many spurs to scenic and historic sites, maps for reaching other units, picnicking; daily exc Dec. 25; free.

Bowaters Southern Paper Corp. (Public Relations Dept., Calhoun 37303) provides maps for scenic areas set aside as "Pocket Wilderness" picnic and camp sites with nature trails (**1**); included are: **Aetna Mtn** (18 m W on I-24), 6-m road to summit picnic area overlooking Nickajack Lake, short trail (**2**). **Wolf Creek** (24 m W on US 41 to Jasper, 10 m NW to Townley, 6½ m W), camping, nature trail (**1, 2**) adj Wolf Creek State Game Management Area. **Wooten Place** (32 m N on US 11 to Charleston, 6.8 m W on Lower River Rd., follow signs 1.8 m SW), picnicking (**1**). **Laurel-Snow** (41 m N on US 27 to 3 m N of Dayton, then W), beautiful, rugged 710 acres with 2½-m trail between bluffs up Richland Creek; trail branches 1½-m W to Morgan Creek and Laurel Falls, both with 900-ft climbs to bluffs, 1–2-m spurs to overlooks, caves; **2, 3.** **Piney River Tree Farm** (54 m N on US 27 to Spring City, 2 m W via SR 68, Shut-In Gap Rd.) has booklets for 2½-m Twin Rocks nature trail (**2**) that loops between 2 picnic sites on Piney River; 4 m beyond is Stinging Fork, a pocket wilderness with 3-m loop (**2**) to 30-ft waterfalls; 2 m beyond is a primitive camp at Newby Branch; the 3 areas connect by trail (**2, 3**) or road.

COOKEVILLE: Corps of Engineers projects have created water recreation, camping, picnicking at: **Center Hill Lake** (13 m W on I-40, then S), trails (**1,2**), waterfalls in **Rock Island State Park. Dale Hollow Lake** (20 m N via SR 136), partly in Kentucky; national fish hatchery (off SR 53 below dam), daily, free. **Standing Stone State Park** (17 m N via SR 136), 11,000 acres, swimming, camping, picnicking, extensive system of forested trails; **1,2.** **Pickett State Park & Forest** (21 m N on SR 42, 29 m E on SR 52, 10 m NE via SR 154), 10,000 acres in Cumberland Mtns; caves, rock formations; swimming, camping, picnicking; 60-m trail system **(1-3)** includes scenic path to home and gristmill of WWI hero Alvin York.

GREENEVILLE: Walks (1) at: **Davy Crockett Birthplace State Park** (9 m E off US 11 E), 15 acres on Nolichucky River, visitor center, replica of log cabin birthplace, picnicking; Apr.-Nov. daily; free. **Davy Crockett Lake** (6 m S on SR 70), TVA project on Nolichucky River.

KINGSPORT: Netherland Inn Complex (2155 Netherland Inn Rd.), Boatyard Historic District, landscaped Church Circle, mansions including Allandale (5 m W on US 11 W). **Bays Mtn Park** (5 m S of Kingsport off SR 93), 1300-acre wildlife and botanical sanctuary, nature education center, water ecology teaching station, planetarium, small zoo, observation tower, 25 m of trails **(1,2)**; all yr exc Jan. 1, Dec. 25, but days & hrs vary; sm adm.

KNOXVILLE: **Chamber of Commerce** (705 S Gray, zip 37902) or **Tourist Bureau** (811 Henley; P.O. Box 237, zip 37901) provide information on this attractive city, capital of Territory S of River Ohio (1792-6) and State Capital (1796-1811, 1817), with interesting historic sites **(1)**: **Gen. James White Home & Fort** (205 E Hill Ave.) with 18th-C garden, **Gov. William Blount Mansion** (200 W Hill Ave.) with 18th-C garden, **Craighead-Jackson Home** (1000 State St.); **pioneer graves** at First Presbyterian Church (620 State St.) and Courthouse lawn (Main & Gray Sts.); **Dulin Gallery of Art** and **Confederate Memorial Hall** (3100 & 3148 Kingston Pike) in mansions; **Ramsey House** (6 m NE on Thorngrove Pike) with family graves nearby on Tennessee River; **University of Tennessee** (W Cumberland Ave.) with museums, gardens; **Marble Springs** (5½ m S via US 441, SR 33 to Neubert Springs Rd.), reconstructed log trading post complex with visitor center exhibits (daily, mid-Mar.-mid-Nov.; sm adm). **Chilhowee Park** (2½ m E on Magnolia Ave.), zoo (Tues.-Sun.; adm); **Sharp Ridge Memorial Park** (n on US 441, W on Ludlow St.), trails; **Ijams Nature Park** (2915 Island Home Ave.), wildflowers, spring flowers, nature trails; **Ivan Racheff Gardens** (1943 Tennessee Ave.), rock gardens, flowers, pond; **1, 2.**
    TVA projects (Information Office, New Sprankle bldg. zip 37902) provide large lakes in this area (see also Oak Ridge) with TVA, state and county park facilities for water sports, camping, picnicking: **Norris Lake** (23 m NW on US 441), visitor lobby at dam (daily), overlooks, nature trails **(1, 2)**, forestry-fisheries laboratory (weekdays); **state forest** with

trails (1, 2) on peninsula W of Sharps Chapel; **Norris Dam State Park** (W end, 4 m NW of Norris on US 441), 4000 forested acres, operating gristmill, museum, overlooks, nature trails (1, 2); **Cove Lake State Park** (30 m N on I-75, NW off US 25W), on N finger of Norris Lake, wooded mtn setting, goose refuge, scenic trails (1, 2); **Big Ridge State Park** (S shore; 11 m NE of Norris on SR 61), 3600 wooded acres, visitor center, nature exhibits, pioneer sites and cemeteries, many trails (including 2-m Indian Hollow and 6-m Dark Hollow) may be combined for long hikes; **Museum of Appalachia** (SW of Norris on SR 61), restored blacksmith and other shops, cabins, broom and rope factory, molasses mill, museum exhibits (mid-Feb.-mid-Nov. daily; adm). **Douglas Lake** (28 m SE on US 25W), visitor lobby (daily), overlooks; 1. **Cherokee Lake** (25 m E on US 11E, N on SR 92) extends NE beyond Morristown, visitor lobby (daily); **Panther Creek State Park** (6 m W of Morristown), visitor center, pretty trails, (1, 2); N of lake near Treadway are Elrod Falls on Flat Gap Creek (off SR 31), reached via ¼-m trail (2).

Cherokee National Forest (Supervisor, P.O. Box 400, Cleveland 37311), 615,000 acres in 2 units NE and SW of Great Smoky Mtns National Park; rugged mtns, scenic gorges, streams, waterfalls; wildflowers, fall color; camp and picnic sites; summer interpretive programs and guided walks at major recreation centers. **Appalachian Trail** enters from Virginia near Damascus and parallels SR 133, 91 to Watauga Lake; here it turns SE via Roan Mtn to follow the state line S to Great Smoky Mtns. S portion of forest is rugged, with most remote sections in the Tellico area; N section has broad valleys, with many areas privately owned. **S section: Indian Boundary** and especially **Double Camp** (off SR 68 NE of Tellico Plains) are excellent campsite bases for hiking; both have nature trails (1); many trails 2½–8-m long to Citico Creek and its forks and tributaries, other creeks, Pinestand Ridge, 3600-ft Brush Mtn, Falls Branch Scenic Area, other trails (2, 3); several 3–5-m access trails (2, 3) to 16-m Fodderstack Trail (3) following W slopes and ridges along state line to Bob Bald in N Carolina (spurs connect to Nantahala Forest trail system). **North River, Holly Flats,** and other campsites E of Tellico Plains are also good bases; 5-m trail (2, 3) from Holly Flats along Bald River to Tellico River and Bald River Falls recreation area; 6 trails (2, 3) along creeks run 2½–4-m N of Tellico River (off FS 210); 5 trails (2, 3) run 3-6 m S of the river. **Coker Creek** (S of Tellico Plains on SR 68), site of placer gold mining; 6-m trail (3) to Unicoi Mtn (off FS 311). **Quinn Springs** campground (NW of Reliance on SR 30), on Hiwassee River, has nature trail (1), trails (2, 3) S to Oswald Dome and N to Chestnut Mtn and Gee Creek Wilderness; John Muir Trail (2) runs 3 m along river bluffs on N shore of Hiwassee River (there are plans to extend this NW via TVA lands and Frozen Head and Pickett state parks). **Ocoee River** has dam at parksville that forms-Parksville Lake; campgrounds here have fine trails (1-3); Chilhowee (N of lake) has trails (1, 2), 3-m trail (2) to Benton Falls that can be continued up Rock Creek Scenic Area (has 11 falls); trails go N (1, 2) along Ocoee River and creeks, to mtn summits, trails (2) at Thunder Rock campground; trails S of river include nature trail (1) at Sylco camp and many 1–8-m trails (1-3) with many spurs around 4200-ft Big Frog Mtn (these trails also accessible from Tumbling Creek camp). **N section: Holston Lake** (6 m SE of Bristol on US 421), TVA project with visitor information at dam, overlook, camping, water sports; from E shore, many short trails (1, 2) and climbs to 4000-ft overlooks, AT, 12-m Holston Trail, 20-m Iron Mtn Trail (access in N from Backbone Rock Camp or town of Laurel Bloomery; in S connects to AT). **Watauga Lake** (8 m SE of Elizabethton via US 19E, SR 67), TVA project, overlook, water sports, camping; several camp and picnic areas have 1–8-m trails (1-3) to AT, Watauga Scenic Area, Little Pond Mtn (W of Elk Mills). **Laurel Fork** (SE of Elizabethton off US 19E) has waterfalls, 6-m Laurel Fork Trail (from Dennis Cove camp), access to AT, Doe River Gorge; **Roan Mtn** (32 m E of Elizabethton on US 19E) with spectacular rhododendron (June) and state park facilities, has trails (1-3) that include easy paths and the AT. **Rock Creek** camp (E of Erwin) has trails (2,3) to Unaka Mtn Scenic Area, 4½-m trail from Stamping Ground to Limestone Cove camp, access to fish hatchery (US 23 N of Erwin), 5-m Patty Ridge Trail (3 m NW of Erwin off SR 81) with cave and iron furnace remains, trail S to Temple Hill. **Old Forge** and **Horse Creek** camps (E of Greeneville off SR 107), attractive trails (1, 2), access to AT. **Paint Creek** camp (S of Greeneville vis SR 70, 107) has trails (1-3) to Andrew Johnson Wildlife Management Area, along creek, to AT and Pisgah Forest (N Carolina). **Houston Valley** camp (10 m E of Newport on US 25, 70; N on SR 107), scenic area with easy valley trails (1), climb ((2) to Meadow Creek lookout and 15-m Meadow Creek Mtn trail (3); SE are trails (2, 3) at Rand Mtn camp; S near Hartford (W off I-40) is 4½-m Stone Mtn Trail (2, 3) and shorter Greene Mtn Trail (2), plus access to Great Smoky Mtns Trails.

McMINNVILLE: Chamber of Commerce (Box 574, ZIP 37110) has maps for caves, other attractions. **Great Falls Lake** (12 m NE off US 70S), TVA dam, water sports; 1, 2. Swimming, camping, picnicking at **Fall Creek Falls State Park** (30 m E via Sr 30, then S), 16,000 acres, beautiful scenery, cascades, 256-ft waterfalls, canyons, virgin timber, nature center, 8 nature trails plus hiking (1-3); **Bledsoe State Forest** (N across hwy on SR 101), trails (2). **Virgin Falls** (27 m NE on US 70S, 6 m E on US 70 to DeRossett, 8 m S), beautiful 317-acre pocket wilderness of Bowaters paper company (see Chattanooga); 2-m trail to Big Laurel Falls (2) may be continued on 7-m loop (3) via old moonshine stills to Sheep Cave and Virgin Falls, and return via Caney Fork River.

MEMPHIS: Chamber of Commerce (Union & 2nd Sts.), maps for walking tours (1): **Beale St. Historic District** and **Handy Park, Front Street** cotton market. **Mississippi Riverfront** with riverboat cruises, Tom Lee Park (foot of Beale St.), Ashburn Park (S on Riverside), DeSoto Park (S of Memphis-Arkansas Bridge), Jefferson Davis Park (N of riverboat docks). **Court Square** (off Main St.), fountain and nearby Confederate Park; Victorian Village (600 block of Adams) and surrounding streets, preserved Victorian homes. **Overton Sq.** (Madison & Cooper), lively shops, cafes. **Southwestern at Memphis** (N Parkway), attractive, shaded campus. **Fairgrounds** area (E Parkway at Central) with amusement park, stadium, coliseum, Memphis Belle, college, Spanish Memorial Park, nearby Memphis Park Palace Museum (Central at 232 Tilton Ave.). Parks **(1,2)** include: **Forrest** (Union & Dunlap), **Overton** (N Parkway to Poplar Ave., E Parkway) with zoo and aquarium (daily exc Thnks, Dec. 24, 25), Brooks Memorial Art Gallery (Tues.-Sun.; closed Jan. 1, Thnks, Dec. 25; free). **Audubon** (Park Ave. & Goodlett St.) with Memphis Botanical Garden, gardens, arboretum, Japanese garden, wildflowers, exotic plants (daily; free). **Memphis Memorial** (US 72, E of I-240), lovely gardens, religious displays in caverns, underground exhibits.

State parks with swimming, camping, picnicking: **T.O. Fuller** (5 m S on US 61, 4 m W on Mitchell Rd.), 1000 acres, nature trail; Chucalissa Indian Village (Tues.-Sun.; closed Jan. 1, Thnks, 3 weeks late Dec.), Memphis State Univ. excavation of village inhabited 900-1600, reconstructed houses, interpretive programs, museum, burials; nature trails; **1. Meeman-Shelby Forest** (10 m NW on US 51, then follow signs), lovely 12,500 acres on Mississippi; lakes; nature center; other attractions; many miles of trails **(1,2)**.

NASHVILLE: Chamber of Commerce (161 4th Ave. N), brochures for walking tours here, at hotels, or from Historical Commission of Metropolitan Nashville & Davidson County (Room 329, Stahlman Bldg, zip 37201).

The Hermitage (13 m E on US 70), 625 acres with Andrew Jackson's stunning mansion; tomb of Rachel and Andrew Jackson; Tulip Grove Mansion; Old Hermitage Church; museum; many other bldgs; cemetery; garden; arboretum of local trees; daily exc Dec. 25; adm; **1. Cragfont** (29 m E on US 31, E, 5 m E on SR 25 in Castalian Springs), 1798 mansion (mid-Apr.-Oct., Tues.-Sun.; adm), landscaped, and nearby **Wynnewood** (4 m E on SR 25) at site of mineral spring (daily exc hols; adm); camping, picnicking at **Bledsoe Creek State Park** (S off SR 25); **1. Cheekwood** (7 m W on Cheek Rd. off SR 100), 55 acres; 1930 mansion with art works (Tues.-Sun.; closed Jan. 1, Thnks, Dec. 24, 25, 31; adm); **Tennessee**

Botanical Gardens with formal gardens, greenhouses, splendid boxwood gardens, nature trails, pools, fountains, daily in daylight; **1. Tennessee Game Farm** (18 m N off US 41 A), on 170 wooded, hilly acres with native and exotic species (daily Mar.-Nov.; weekends in winter; adm).

Natchez Trace Parkway (see Mississippi) runs N from Alabama line at Cypress Inn to Gordonsburg and eventually will be completed to Nashville; **Old Trace** (mile 350), section of original trace **(1)**; **Sweetwater Branch** (mile 363) nature trail and Glen Rock (1 m N) picnic area **(1)**; **David Crockett State Park** (16 m E of Trace on US 64), 1000 acres on banks of Shoal Creek, swimming, camping, picnicking, trails **(1, 2)**; **Old Trace Loop Drive** (mile 376), 2½ m over original trace **(1)**; **Jack's Branch** (mile 382) picnic area **(1)**; **Metal Ford** and **Napier Mine** (mile 381-382.5), early iron ore mining and smelting site **(1)**; **Meriwether Lewis Park** (mile 386), camping, picnicking, nature trail **(1)**, grave of the Louisiana Territory explorer who died on the Natchez Trace, picnicking, museum, walks **(1, 2)** on trace.

State parks with swimming, camping, picnicking, nature trails **(1)** plus other trails **(2)** that continue into surrounding state forests: **Montgomery Bell** (34 m W on US 70), 5000 acres in rolling hills, 2 lakes, streams; **Cedars of Lebanon** (10 m E on I-40, 12 m SE), 9000-acre red cedar forest, limestone caverns and sinks. Corps of Engineers projects in the Cumberland River Basin have created numerous lakes with public water sports, camping, picnicking: **Cheatham** (30 m NW on SR 12), ruins of old navigational locks, trails; **Old Hickory** (15 m NE on US 31E, 70), nature trails, blinds for wildlife watching, trails; **J. Percy Priest** (11 m E off I-40), visitor center (daily) near dam with beautiful overlook, forested; **1, 2**.

OAK RIDGE: Chamber of Commerce (1400 Turnpike, zip 37830) provides maps showing greenbelts, scattered wooded parks, and 7½-m **North Ridge Trail**—access from several points on Outer Drive between Endicott Lane (E) and near Louisiana Ave. (W)—a wooded corridor with streams, wildflowers **(1, 2)**. **Univ. of Tennessee** arboretum (Kerr Hollow Rd., SR 62), 250 acres, weekdays; **1**.

Cumberland Mtn State Park (30 m W opn I-40, 8 m SW off US 70 on US 127), 1400 acres on Cumberland Plateau, lake, swimming, camping, picnicking, walks **(1, 2)**. **Crab Orchard Gap** (30 m W off I-40), 1660 ft, and other heights in area are popular for climbs **(2, 3)**; trails not always well marked.

Cumberland Trail (starts at Oliver Springs, 3 m NW on SR 62) follows Walden Ridge 20 m NE to Lake City **(3)**; when completed, this trail is to run NE to Cumberland Gap and SW to Georgia via Prentice-Cooper State Forest on Nickajack Lake. **Frozen Head State Park** (12 m NW on SR 62), 10,000 acres surrounding 3324-ft Frozen Head Mtn; 35-m Boundary Trail (from the campground) circles the park, following ridges and peaks for overviews (entire loop **3**, but many sections **2**); many other trails (**1, 2**) from ½-m to 9-m cross interior of the park to Garden Spot, ridge and peak overlooks, springs, streams, glades, scenic areas, and to connect with Boundary Trail. **Rugby Restoration** (22 m NW on SR 62, 21 m N on US 27, 5 m W on SR 52), 17 restored bldgs of abortive attempt to start a school and colony in 1880; spring-fall, Tues.-Sun.; sm adm; **1. Honey Creek** (22 m NW on SR 62, 21 m N on US 27 to Elgin, 8 m NW off SR 52) is a beautiful Pocket Wilderness of Bowaters paper company (see Chattanooga) at jct of Honey Creek and Big S Fork River; rugged 5-m loop (**3**) has a shortcut (**2**) midway enabling you to do 2½ or 3 m loops; overlooks from bluffs, rock shelters used by Indians, small waterfalls. Nearby **Paint Rock Creek** (9 m N of Elgin to Huntsville, then S) is a scenic, rocky area where you can walk along an unimproved road with little traffic; **2.**

PARIS: TVA projects on the Tennessee River have created recreation areas including **Kentucky Lake;** many boat docks; water sports, camping, picnicking at **Paris Landing State Park** (17 m NE on US 79), nature trail, hiking trails, nearby access to trails in Land Between the Lakes (see Kentucky). **Ft. Donelson National Military Park** (30 m NE on US 79), site of the Union's first major Civil War victory; visitor center (daily exc Dec. 25) with audiovisual programs, exhibits, observation platform; 8½-m self-guiding auto trail to earthworks and other remains on battlefield; Dover Hotel, site of surrender; cemetery; short walks on battlefield (**1**); historic trail (**1, 2**) continues into Land Between the Lakes; free. S on Kentucky Lake are: **Tennessee National Wildlife Refuge** (N of Big Sandy via Lick Creek Rd.), on peninsula between lake and Big Sandy River; other sections S off US 70, E of Camden, N off SR 20, 100, E of Parsons; **1, 2. Nathan B. Forrest State Park** (8 m NE of Camden at end of Eva Rd.), 840 acres at site where Confederates destroyed 30 Union vessels; Pilot Knob observation point; other historic sites across lake at New Trace Creek; museum; picnicking, camping; trails (**1, 2**).

SAVANNAH: Shiloh National Military Park (10 m SW on SR 22), site of bitter Civil War battle in 1862; visitor center (daily exc Dec. 25; free); film, exhibits, booklets for 10-m self-guiding tour including log cabin, cemetery, rebuilt Shiloh Church; Indian mounds; **1.**

UNION CITY: Reelfoot Lake (9 m S on US 51, 13 m W on SR 21), beautiful lake created by 1811 earthquakes; cypresses, water lilies, partially submerged forests; national wildlife refuge; state park (S shore) with swimming, camping, picnicking, boat cruises, museum of natural history and Indian artifacts; Apr.-Oct. daily; sm adm; **1, 2.**

TEXAS

ABILENE: Burro Alley (S 1st St. & Willis), re-created Mexican village with shops (Mon.-Sat.; closed hols; free); 11 city parks including **Nelson** (3 m E on SR 36) with zoo; **Old Abilene Town** (4 m NE on I-20), frontier town replica, museum, amusements (daily exc Dec. 25; adm); **Ft. Phantom Hill** (10 m N on FM 600), fort ruins, lake for water sports, camping; **1**. State parks with camping, swimming, picnicking: **Abilene** (15 m SW on FM 89), 507 acres, pecan grove; **Ft. Griffin** (33 m NE on SR 351, US 180 to Albany, 14 m N off US 283), 503 acres on Clear Fork of Brazos River, ruins of 1867 Cavalry post; Longhorn herd; **1**.

ALPINE: Walks **(1, 2)** at: **Museum of the Big Bend** (Sul Ross State Univ., E of town), exhibits, general store, workshops (Tues.-Sun.; closed hols; sm adm). **Ft. Davis National Historic Site** (25 m NW on SR 118), impressive ruins and restored bldgs of 1854 fort named for Jefferson Davis; Visitor Center with interpretive programs; daily; sm adm or GEP. **Davis Mtns State Park** (6 m W of Ft. Davis via SR 118), scenic 1869 acres; swimming, camping, picnicking; interpretive center (summer); wildlife watering station; trails **(1, 2)**. **Ghost towns** are Study Butte (77 m S on SR 118); Terlingua (77 m S on SR 118, 5 m W on SR 170), mine tour; Shafter (26 m W on US 90 to Marfa, 39 m S on US 67).

Big Bend National Park, 707,000-acre wilderness; desert; stunning canyons; mtns over 7000 ft; cactus and wildflowers bloom Mar.-Oct.; bordered on 3 sides by Big Bend of Rio Grande; hq at **Panther Junction** (103 m S of Alpine on SR 118 or 68 m S of Marathon on US 385), information, gas, grocery, interpretive trail **(1,2)**, trailer sites (daily); from here are: **The Basin** (5 m W, 11 m S), at 5400 ft in Chisos Mtns; information, lodging, camping, cafe, picnicking, horse rental; Lost Mine Trail (4 m round trip; **2, 3**) to overlook at head of Juniper Canyon, even better overlooks from ridge; 14-m trail **(3** on foot; can be done on horseback) to South Rim; other trails **(2, 3)**; nearby are dirt roads, 8-m to Grapevine Hills, 3½ m to Paint Gap Hills, ½ m to Croton Spring **(1-3)**. **Santa Elena** (35 m SW via scenic road with viewpoints), ranger, camping, picnicking, gas, grocery; historic sites; self-guiding trail (8 m W) to Santa Elena Canyon **(1-3)**, to overlook, along river, picnicking; 49-m, unpaved, scenic road through S end of park has spurs to mine ruins, Juniper and Pine canyons, other attractions, and loops to either hq or Rio Grande Village.

Rio Grand Village (20 m SE), camping, trailer sites, picnicking, information, gas, grocery; self-guiding trail (2, 3) to beautiful 25-m-long Boquillas Canyon; other trails (2, 3); unpaved 27-m road to Dagger Flat. Walks (1-3) also at Dugout Wells picnic site (6 m SE) with trails (2, 3); Fossil Bone Exhibit (9 m N); 7-m interpretive auto trail at Dagger Flat (12 m N), spectacular in spring cactus bloom; Persimmon Gap (29 m N), ranger, picnicking. Permission required for backcountry hiking or for rockclimbing; guides to trails and backcountry sold; information: Supt., TX 79834.

AMARILLO: Amarillo Tourist Center (I-40 at Nelson St.), at Helium Monument (open daily 10-6; closed hols); city has 34 parks (write Parks Comm., Box 1971, Municipal Bldg., zip 79105), including Thompson (NE 24th St. at US 87) with zoo; Amarillo Medical Center (5 m W via I-40) has 51-acre park with floral displays, picnicking; 1. Boys Ranch (40 m NW on FM 1061, 2 m N on US 385), self-guiding tours; Tascosa ghost town with cemetery, museum (daily exc Dec. 24-Jan. 1; free). Palo Duro Canyon State Park (15 m S to Canyon, 15 m E on SR 217), brilliant formations; camping, picnicking; trails 1-3. Tule Canyon (28 m E on US 287, 45 m S on SR 207) is also colorful; 2, 3. Buffalo Lake Ntl Wildlife Refuge (28 m SW on US 60, 2 m S on FM 168), camping, picnicking, trails (1, 2); daily. Lake Meredith Recreation Area (33 m N on SR 136), camping, picnicking, water sports; Alibates National Monument (S shore), prehistoric flint quarries (guided tours daily in summer from Bates canyon); McBride Canyon Environmental Study Area trails (1, 2); hiking (3); information: Box 325, Sanford 79078.

AUSTIN: Old Bakery (1006 Congress Ave.), restored 19th-C ovens, cafe offers information on Congress Ave. historic sites and other attractions (Mon.-Sat. 9-4; closed hols; free). State Capitol (N end Congress Ave.) on 46 landscaped acres, has Tourist Information Center (daily 8-5; closed Dec. 25). Walking (1) at University of Texas (San Jacinto Blvd & Guadalupe St., 19-26th Sts.), museums observation tower, Visitor Information Center (Sid Richardson Hall; daily 9-5; closed Dec. 25); Mt. Bonnell (via W 35th St. & Old Bull Creek Rd.), hilltop view of city; State Cemetery (7th & Comal); scenic Hike & Bike Trails along Shoal Creek, Blunn Creek; 8 city parks (hq 1500 W Riverside Dr.). Highland Lakes, created by a series of dams across Colorado River, run 150 m NW (map from Chamber of Commerce, 901 W Riverside Dr.); on Town Lake (center) are Fiesta Gardens with lagoons, flowers, and Zilker Park with springs, flower gardens, Japanese gardens, swimming; Decker Lake (10 m NE on Blue Bluff Rd.), boating; Lake Austin (W end via Buss Creek Rd.), city park with swimming, boating, picnicking, camping; Lake Travis (23 m NW off SR 71); **Marble Falls Lake** (43 m NW off SR 71, US 281) and adj **L.B.J. Lake,** with nearby **Longhorn Cavern State Park** (off US 281 N of SR 71), cave tours (daily; adm), museum, picnicking, nature trails.

State parks, camping, picnicking, walks **(1): Bastrop** (20 m SE on SR 71), 2100 acres, swimming, trails through lost Pines of Texas, 15-m scenic drive to **Buescher** (35 m SE on SR 71), 1730 acres, live oaks with Spanish moss, nature trails; **Lockhart** (23 m S on US 183).

Walks **(1):** At Burnet (20 m N on US 183, 23 m W on SR 29), **Ft. Croghan Museum** with several bldgs reconstructing 1848 fort, museum (summers, Wed.-Sun. 1-5; sm adm) and abandoned Old Mormon Colony (S Pierce St. to Mormon Mill Rd.), mill, cemetery, Indian mounds. At Lampasas (54 m NW on US 183), **Hancock Park** with springs, picnicking, swimming. At Georgetown (27 m N off I-35), **San Gabriel Park** with swimming, picnicking, show barns, events. At Wimberley (20 m W on US 290, 13 m S on FM 12), **Pioneer Town** (River Rd.), re-created 1880s town, entertainment (daily in summer, other hrs, sm adm); Devils Backbone scenic drive E to San Marcos. At **San Marcos** (29 m S on I-35), city park on river, wildlife park with cave tour and observation tower (daily; adm), Aquarena Springs with gardens, boat rides, submarine theater (daily exc Dec. 25; adm).

BROWNSVILLE: short walks **(1)** at **Ft. Brown** (S end of Elizabeth St.) bldgs, now part of Texas Southmost College, marked with plaques, and nearby **International Friendship Garden; Palo Alto Battlefield** (5½ m N on FM 1847); **Palmito Hill Battlefield** (12 m E on SR 4); **Port Brownsville** (6 m NE on International Blvd.), shrimp boat harbor; **Dean Porter Park** (Camille Dr.), picnicking, sports, outstanding 26-acre Gladys Porter Zoo (daily; adm); **Brazos Island State Park** (24 m E on SR 4), Gulf beach walks, swimming, camping, picnicking; **Port Isabel Lighthouse State Historic Site** (21 m E on SR 48 on SR 100); **S Padre Island** (24 m E on SR 48), beachcombing, county parks, turtle kraal (4 m N on Park 100). **Laguna Atascosa Ntl Wildlife Refuge** (15 m N on US 77, 25 m NE of jct FM 106, 1847), on Laguna Madre, drives, walks, maps at hq; **1, 2.**

BRYAN: Texas A & M University (S at College Station), 5200-acre campus; audiovisual programs and information at visitor center; **1. Washington-on-the-Brazos State Park** (26 m S on SR 6 to Navasota, 3 m SW off SR 90), reconstruction of first capital of Texas; information, guided tours, audiovisual programs at Independence Hall (daily; free); Star of the Republic of Texas Museum (daily in summer; Wed.-Sun. rest of yr; free); other bldgs; picnicking; **1.**

CORPUS CHRISTI: Chamber of Commerce (1201 N Shoreline Blvd.), information on recreation, 10 city parks. **Corpus Christi Marina** (bay front), fishing and charter boat piers; dock walks also at Aransas Pass (15 m NE on US 181, SR 35), Port Aransas (E via JFK causeway, then N); **Lake Corpus Christi State Park** (19 m NW on I-37), 14,000 acres on large lake, water sports, camping, picnicking; **1. Padre Island National Seashore** (3 m SE via JFK causeway), stunning 80-m-long barrier island; roads at private development and county parks at N & S ends, and for 14-m at N end of park, remainder reachable by four-wheel drive or hiking; at N end are camping, water sports, picnicking, observation tower, ¾-m nature trail, interpretive programs; exceptional beachcombing; hiking **(2, 3)**, allowed on entire island, is on soft sand and arduous; information: P.O. Box 8560, Corpus Christi 78412. **King Ranch** may be viewed from 12-m loop drive (34 m S on US 77 to Kingsville, then W off SR 141); **Kleberg Park** on creek in Kingsville for picnics; **Kleberg Co. Park** (16 m S of Kingsville on US 77, E on FM 628), water sports on Baffin Bay; **1.** At **Rockport** (31 m N on SR 35), beaches, docks; Texas Parks & Wildlife Marine Laboratory (boat basin), aquarium, other displays (daily exc hols; free); **Copano Bay Causeway State Park** (5 m N on SR 35), fishing; **Goose Island State Park** (10 m N off SR 35), water sports, camping, picnicking; **Aransas Ntl Wildlife Refuge** (23 m N of Rockport on SR 35, 9 m E on Fm 774, 6 m SE on FM 2040), 54,000 acres on peninsula, is wintering ground for whooping cranes; observation tower; loop road, trails; daily; free; **1, 2.**

DALLAS–FT. WORTH: Dallas Convention & Visitors Bureau (1507 Pacific Ave.), information. Walks **(1)** at **Dallas Market Center International Sculpture Gardens** (2700 Stemmons Frwy); **State Fair Park** (2 m E off I-20, I-30), the major museums, Midway amusement area with picnicking (grounds free), Dallas Garden Center (lush tropical gardens, catwalk at treetop level, subterranean window for aquatic plants, lagoons); Old City Park (St. Paul & Ervay Sts.), bldgs and exhibits tracing city's history comprise **Dallas Heritage Center** (Tues.-Sun.; closed Dec. 24, 31, Sept. 3; adm); **Marsalis Park** (621 E Claredon Dr., Oak Cliff), zoo (daily exc Dec. 25; sm adm); **White Rock Lake Park** (Garland Rd.), boating, picnics. **Heard Natural Science Museum & Wildlife Sanctuary** (28 m N on SR 5 at McKinney), indoor displays, 265 acres on Wilson Creek, nature trails; Tues.-Sat. 9-5, Sun. 1-5; closed hols; free. **Greenville** (46 m NE on I-30), picnicking, small zoo, historic house, swimming at N City Park, prairie dog town at S City Park.

Ft. **Worth Chamber of Commerce** (700 Throckmorton at 6th St.), open weekdays 8:30-5; closed hols. Walking **(1)** at 5000 acres of fine municipal parks, including landscaped banks of Clear Fork of **Trinity River** (S from Lancaster St. along University Dr.) with **Civic Center** (major museums, nearby Van Zandt Cottage); **Trinity Park** with Botanic Garden (daily; free) and Japanese Garden (Tues.-Sun.; adm); **Forest Park** with zoo (daily; adm) and Log Cabin Village (daily; sm adm) of restored pioneer homes. **Lake Worth** (9 m NW via SR 199), with city park picnicking, scenic drive, has 3900-acre Greer Island Nature Center (daily 8-5; closed hols; free) a wildlife refuge with observation tower, nature trails; **1.**

State parks: **Acton** (25 m SW off US 377), grave of Davy Crockett's second wife; **Cleburne** (36 m SW via I-35W, SR 174, US 67), water sports, camping, picnicking, lake, trails (**1**) on 498 acres; **Dinosaur Valley** (27 m S on I-35W, 40 m SW on US 67), 1204-acre scenic park on Paluxy River, dinosaur tracks, swimming, camping, picnicking, nature trails (**1, 2**); **Ft. Richardson** (60 m NW on SR 199, US 281 at SW edge of Jacksboro), original bldgs of 19th-C cavalry post, museum, camping, picnicking, pond, nature trails (**1**); **Possum Kingdom** (77 m W on US 180, park rd. 33), 28,000 acres on huge lake, water sports, camping, picnicking, Longhorn herd, walks (**1**), nearby fish hatchery, observation point, prairie dog colony.

DEL RIO: Moore Park (jct US 90E, 277), lush oasis around San Felipe Springs, spring-fed swimming pool; **1. Whitehead Memorial Museum** (1308 S Main St.), in former trading post; on grounds are graves of Judge Roy Bean and his son (Mon.-Sat.; sm adm). **Judge Roy Bean Visitor Center** (60 m NW on US 90 in Langtry), state tourist facility; Bean's preserved saloon and exhibits on his life; impressive cactus garden; daily; free; **1. Amistad Recreation Area** (10 m NW on US 90), international project impounding the Rio Grande; Visitor Center at US end of dam; camping, water sports; pictographs; nature trail (**1**); at N end of reservoir is awesome Pecos River Canyon; **1-3.**

EL PASO: Chamber of Commerce (1 Civic Center Plaza), information for El Paso Walking Tour to 32 historic sites; 1000 acres of city parks, including beautiful McKelligon Canyon; Scenic Drive and Rim Rd. on Mt. Franklin; tours of Juarez; Aerial Tramway (Alabama & McKinley Ave.) to observation deck on Ranger Peak. Walks (**1**) include **Chamizal National Memorial** (via Delta Dr.), commemorating peaceful settlement of boundary dispute—museum, bilingual programs, monuments (daily; free); **University of Texas** (NW end of town), museum exhibits, lovely grounds with bldgs of Bhutanese design, gardens; **Ft. Bliss Replica** (N of Montana Ave. on Pleasanton Rd. at Ft. Bliss), adobe bldgs of 1848 post, museum (daily exc Jan. 1, Easter, Thnks, Dec. 25; free); **Sierra de Cristo** (3 m W), mtn topped with statue of Christ, 4-m trail (**2**) with Stations of the Cross. **Ysleta Mission** (11 m SE on I-10, 2 m SW on FM 659), museum (Tues.-Sun.; adm); **Socorro Mission** (3 m SE of Ysleta on FM 258); **San Elizario** Presidio Chapel (5 m S on FM 258), nearby arcade; **1. Hueco Tanks State Historic Park** (28 m E on US 62, 180; 7 m N), rock formations that trap water, pictographs; camping, picnicking; daily; sm adm; **1,2.**

Guadalupe Mountains National Park (110 m E on US 62, 180), 77,500 acres; forested mtns rising (to 8751-ft Guadalupe Peak) above desert; colorful canyons; 2000-ft sheer cliff, Capitan Reef (most extensive fossil reef on record); caves (exploration by permission only); historic features; mtn climbing (registration required); Information Office at Pine Springs (open daily) or Dog Canyon ranger station (N end); guided walks in summer and fall. Trails include: **Frijoles Historic Site** (at Information Office), ½-m trail to early Texas ranch bldgs (2), 1½ m to Smith Spring (3), 1-m to Butterfield Stage Stop Historic Site (3); from nearby **Pine Canyon** campground, trail (2) continues as Devil's Hallway (304), a 3-m trip up the scenic, narrow canyon on a rocky trail to backcountry trails. **McKittrick Canyon,** with rare vegetation, disappearing stream, fossils, may be reached by shuttle van from Information Station or high-clearance vehicle; 4-m canyon trail (1,2) later climbs ridge (2,3) to join backcountry trails. From **Dog Canyon,** 3-m scenic but tough trail (3) to 7834-ft Lost Peak and access to backcountry trails. **Guadalupe Peak** (4 m to 8751 ft), reached by rocky, difficult trail (3) SW of Pine Canyon (off US 62, 180). **West Side** (SW of Pine Canyon off US 62, 180) has 7-m primitive road to Williams Ranch Historic Site, day use only, 2-hrs minimum for round trip; 1.

FREDERICKSBURG: Chamber of Commerce (Pioneer Plaza off Main St.), in Vereins Kirche (open Mon.-Fri.), provides maps for self-guiding tours of museums and historic sites, including charming mini-homes called Sunday Houses; **Lady Bird Johnson Park** (3 m S on SR 16), picnicking, camping, sports, trails; 1. **Enchanted Rock** (20 m N off RM 965), picnicking on formation revered by Indians. **Lyndon B. Johnson National Historic Site** consists of Birthplace (17 m E on US 290), with grave, plus Boyhood Home and Johnson Settlement (30 m E on US 290 at Johnson City), with exhibits, demonstrations; all open daily; closed Dec. 25; free. **LBJ State Park** (16 m E on US 290), Visitor Center (daily 9-6) interpreting Texas Hill Country, free bus tours to LBJ sites, exhibits on Johnson family, pioneers; swimming, picnicking; wildlife exhibits; wildflower displays; nature trails; 1. **Pedernales Falls State Scenic Park** (38 m E via US 290, FM 2766), swimming, picnicking; waterfalls; wonderful trails (1-3) on 4800 acres (backcountry campsites).

HOUSTON: Convention & Visitors Council (Suite 1101, 1006 Main St.), maps for walking tours (1): **Sam Houston Historical Park** (Bagby & Lamar), replica of early Houston; **Holcombe Civic Center** (Smith & Rusk), with music halls, Alley Theatre, National Space Hall of Fame; **Old Market Square** (Preston to Commerce on Travis), old commercial center revitalized; **Allen's Landing Historical Park** (Main & Commerce); **Buffalo Bayou** Hike & Bike Trails (bayou banks along Allen Pkwy, Sabine to

Shepherd); **Memorial Park** (Memorial Dr. at Crestwood); 260-acre
McAshan Botanical Hall & Arboretum (4501 Woodway), trails,
wildflowers, ferns, greenhouse, exhibit hall (daily; free); **River Oaks
Scenic Drive** (Allen Pkwy onto Kirby), mansions, azaleas (Mar.-Apr.);
Rothko Chapel (Yupon & Branard); **Port of Houston** (Gate 8 on Clinton
Dr.), boat tours, observation tower. **Hermann Park** (3 m S on Main St.),
Houston Zoological Gardens (daily; free), Museum of Natural Science
(daily; closed hols; free), Houston Garden Center with rose trails (daily;
free), picnicking, sports, hiking trails; **1. Texas Medical Center** (Fannin
between Holcombe & Outer Dr.), tours available; **Rice University** (S Main
& Sunset Blvd), lovely campus with Mediterranean-style bldgs, live oaks,
museums; **Astrodomain** (6 m S on Kirby Dr. & S Loop 610), Astrodome,
entertainment and amusement complex; **1. Busch Bird Park** (9 m E on
I-10 to 775 Gellborn Dr.), landscaped, walk-through aviary, waterfowl
lake, fountains, bird shows (daily exc Jan. 1, Thnks, Dec. 24-25; free); adj
brewery tours. **San Jacinto Battleground** (6 m SE on US 75, I-45; 12 m E
on SR 225, 4 m N on SR 134), monument, observation deck; picnicking
(daily; free); **Battleship Texas**, exhibits, memorial (daily; adm). **Sylvan
Beach** (21 m E on SR 225 to La Porte), county park, boating, picnicking
on bay; **1. NASA Lyndon B. Johnson Space Center** (21 m SE on I-45, 5 m
E on FM 528, Nasa 1), Visitor Orientation Center; booklets for self-
guiding tours; daily exc Dec. 25; free; **1.** At the opposite side of Clear
Lake is **Kemah** (MSR 146) with colorful shrimp fleet; **1.**

 Lake Houston (NW edge via S Lake Houston Pkwy), camping, water
sports; **1. Sam Houston National Forest** (28 m N), 158,000 acres, has 30
m of trails from **Stubblefield** camp (W of New Waverly) on Lake Conroe,
15 m from **Evergreen** to Four Notch lookout, 10 m from **Double Lake**
camp (SE of Evergreen) through Big Thicket Scenic Area; **Huntsville State
Park** (8 m S of Huntsville), camping, water sports on lake, botany trail; **1,
2. Sam Houston Memorial Park** (51 m N on I-45 to Lake Ave., Huntsville), home, house in which he died, museum (daily; closed Thnks, Dec.
25; donation); signs to nearby grave. **Stephen F. Austin State Park** (41 m
W on I-10, 2½ m N on FM 1458 at San Felipe), 664 acres; at old ferry
crossing on Brazos River, country store museum (open weekends & hols;
adm), Austin home; swimming, camping, picnicking, nature trail, river
walks; **1.**

 Galveston (50 m SE on I-45), an island-city with 10-m seawall; information on self-guiding tours to many historic sites from Tourist Information
Center (Seawall Blvd & 23rd St.): 32 m of beaches; free fishing piers;
shrimp fleet; wharves (9-41st Sts.); Bishop's Palace (1402 Broadway);
Powhatan House (3427 Ave. at 35th St.), Garden Center; **The Strand** (20-
25th St.), former commercial bldgs restored as cafes and boutiques; old
waterfront district (The Strand to Sealy Ave.); **Lafitte's Grove** (11 Mile &
Stewart Rds.), supposed site of buried treasure; **Texas A & M University**

has Marine Science labs and display (Ft. Crockett campus) open afternoons (free) and training vessel *Texas Clipper* (moored off Pelican Is.)
open weekends Oct.-May (free); **Seawolf Park** (Pelican Is.), submarine,
other displays, picnicking, fishing pier (daily; adm); **Galveston Island
State Recreation Area** (6 m SW on FM 3003), water sports, camping and
walks on beach; **1.**

LAREDO: Historic bldgs include **Capitol** (1000 Zaragoza St.), capitol
1839-41 of independent Republic of Rio Grande; old plaza with San
Agustin church (214 San Agustin Ave.); bldgs of Ft. McIntosh on university campus (on Rio Grande, foot of Washington St.). **Cactus Gardens**
(3209 San Bernardo Ave.), nursery of cactus and succulents; daily; free;
1. **Falcon Reservoir** (along Rio Grande from Zapata, 49 m S, to Falcon
State Park, 89 m S) has public water sports and camping areas; **1.**

LUBBOCK: Texas Tech University (University Ave. & Broadway), attractive 1800-acre campus; museums; Ranch Hq., restoration illustrating
development of ranching in Texas (Tues.-Sun.); tours of archaeological
site at Lubbock Lake (N on SR 289 & Indiana Ave.). Water sports, camping, picnicking at state parks: **MacKenzie** (E Broadway), 549 acres,
prairie dogs, amusement area; **Buffalo Springs** (5 m SE on FM 835), 2000
acres; **1.** **Blanco Canyon Roadside Park** (38 m E on US 82) has picnicking,
trails along White River; **1, 2.** **Muleshoe Ntl Wildlife Refuge** (36 m NW
on US 84, 28 m W via SR 54, 37, SR 214), waterfowl, prairie dogs; daily;
free; **1,2.**

LUFKIN: Ellen Trout Park (N on Lake St.), zoo, lake, picnicking (daily;
free). **Forestry Museum** (1903 Atkinson Dr.), Texas Forestry Assn. hq, has
exhibits; also information on scenic Woodlands Trails (1)—examples
are: 1½-m **Bull Creek** (8½ m W of Corrigan on US 287); ½-m **Griff Ross**
(2.2 m E of Mt. Enterprise on US 84); 1½-m **Dogwood** (3 m E of Woodville, just off US 190), on pretty creek; 2-m **Longleaf Pine** (3 m E of
Camden on FM 62); **Massey Lake** (5.6 m S of Silsbee, E of US 96); ½-m
and 1½-m **Moscow** (1 m S of Moscow on US 59), on creek; 1-m **Oil Springs**
(5 m SE of Woden on FM 226, 4 m E); 2½-m **Old Carter** (12 m E of
Livingston on FM 1276 off US 190); 1½-m **Old River** (off US 190 SE of
Jasper, 3.3-m on FM 1747, then 2.9 m W) to area of bog flowers on
Angelina River; ½-m **Sylvan** (4 m SE of Newton off US 190 opposite
roadside park); 1-m **Yellow Poplar** (8½ m N of Jefferson on US 59 opposite roadside park); several lovely trails in **Wild Azalea Canyons** (4.4 m
N of Newton on SR 87, 6.7 m E of FM 1414, 1.8 m on dirt roads).
   Angelina National Forest (SE), 155,000 acres of pine and hardwood
forests, rolling sandy hills, surrounds huge Sam Rayburn Reservoir; water
sports; trails (1, 2) at DAR and Magnolia Memorial Forests (SE off SR 63

toward Caney Creek campground), Bouton Lake and Boykin Springs camps (S off SR 63 S of Zavalla), Sandy Creek and Letney camps (N off SR 63 S of Zavalla), Townsend and Harvey Creek camps (25 m E on SR 103, then S). **Davy Crockett National Forest** (18 m W on SR 103), 162,000 acres, loblolly pines, hardwoods; water sports; Ratcliff Lake campsite (off SR 103) has trails, demonstration forest; just N is Big Slough Wilderness with canoe trail and 3 hiking trails (2); Neches Bluff camp (on SR 21, SW of Alto), has trails plus trails (camping, picnics) at nearby Mission Tejas State Park (W).

ODESSA: Meteorite Museum (5 m W on US 80; 2 m S), on site of craters formed by meteorite showers 20,000 yrs ago (Thurs.-Mon.; closed Dec. 25; sm adm); **1. Monahans Sandhills State Park** (28 m W on US 80, I-20), 4000 acres of sand dunes (sand buggy rides) with miniature trees; museum of natural history (daily); picnicking, camping; self-guiding nature trail (1, 2).

PECOS: West-of-the-Pecos Museum (US 285 & 1st St.) in Orient Hotel & Saloon, has exhibits, information on historic sites (Tues.-Sun; closed Jan. 1, Dec. 25; sm adm). **Municipal Park** (S at I-20, Cothrun St.), cactus and flower gardens; prairie dogs, buffalo, other animals; swimming, sports; **1.**

SAN ANGELO: Walks (1, 2) at: **Ft. Concho Preservation** (along Burges St. & Aves. C & D), barracks, chapel, other restored stone bldgs; museum (daily, exc hols; sm adm). **Ft. McKavett State Historic Site** (18 m S on US 277, 28 m SE on FM 2084, 20 m SE off SR 29), barracks, guardhouse, stables, other ruins of 1852 fort being restored; museum (daily exc hols). **Hayrick** ghost town (32 m N on SR 208 to Robert Lee, 8 m NE; ask directions locally), in ruins. **Caverns of Sonora** (67 m S on US 277, 8 m W on I-10, 7 m S on FM 1989), tours (daily; adm), camping, picnicking. **Real Presidio de San Saba Ruins** (45 m SE on US 87, 21 m S on US 83 to county park 2 m W of Menard off SR 29), remains of Spanish fort.

SAN ANTONIO: Convention & Visitors Bureau (602 HemisFair Plaza Way), maps for walking tours of this unusually handsome city: **Paseo del Rio**, landscaped riverside walk in center, lovely; **The Alamo** (Alamo Plaza) open daily (exc Dec. 24-25), free; **HemisFair Plaza** (200 S Alamo St.), observation tower, fine museums, waterways, flowers, shaded walks; **La Villita** (S. Presa, Alamo, Nueva Sts. & Paseo del Rio), walled enclosure with historic bldgs; **Military Plaza** with Spanish Governor's Palace and Cathedral; **Mexican Market** (W Commerce St), colorful shops; **King William St. Historic District,** with ornate homes built by Germans in late 19th-C. **Mission Trail** is marked S along the river (all open daily; sm

adm): Mission Concepcion (807 Mission Rd.), still in use; San Jose
Mission (6539 San Jose Dr.), national historic site; Mission San Francisco
(9800 Espada Rd.), friary and chapel restored; Mission San Juan
Capistrano (off US 181 at Bergs Mill), church still in use. **Brackenridge
Park** (2 m N of the Alamo via US 81 to N Broadway), 343-acre showplace
on San Antonio River (banks lined with ancient live oaks), stables, sky
ride, mini-train ride, wonderful zoo (daily; sm adm), alligator gardens
(daily; sm adm), Oriental sunken gardens (daily; free), Witte Memorial
Museum (daily; sm adm) with 4 restored historic bldgs on grounds, picnicking; **1.**

Palmetto State Park (57 m E on I-10), 5 m S off US 183), 178 acres on
San Marcos River; camping, swimming, picnicking; booklets for trails
through rare vegetation, wild orchids, ferns, moss-draped trees, quaking
bogs; lovely; **1. Garner State Park** (61 m W on US 90; 25 m NW on SR
127, US 83), camping, water sports, picnicking, hiking on 630 acres on
scenic Frio River; Frio River Canyon (N along US 83, FM 336) is
beautiful; **1-3. Natural Bridge Caverns** (13 m N off I-35, exit at FM 1604),
tours (daily exc hols; adm), picnicking, nature trails.

Walking tours (**1**) at: **New Braunfels** (33 m NE on I-35), founded by
Germans in 1845; interesting history, museums; maps from Chamber of
Commerce; exceptionally pretty Landa Park on natural springs feeding
Comal River, camping, picnicking, swimming, trails. **Seguin** (37 m E on
I-10), also settled by Germans; Chamber of Commerce (Central Park, W
Court St.) maps for historic sites; attractive Max Starcke Park (SR 123, N
of river), sports, picnics. **Castroville** (20 m W on US 90), Historic District
with bldgs erected by Alsatian settlers; museum in Landmark Inn (Florence
St.); cemetery (W end of town). **Helena** (50 m S on US 181, 8 m E from
jct SR 123), ghost town with historic markers.

TYLER: Walks (**1**) at **Tyler Rose Gardens** (Fairgrounds, W on SR 31 to W
Front & Boone ST.), 35,000 roses (Apr.-Oct.), camellias, other gardens,
greenhouses on 20 acres (daily exc Dec. 25; free); **Children's Zoo** (W Bow
& Lincoln Sts.) open free spring-fall; **Tyler State park** (8 m N off FM 14),
camping, swimming, nature trails; **Gov. Hogg Shrine** (22 m N on US 69,
10 m N on SR 37 to 518 S Main St., Quitman), museum (Tues.-Sun.), picnicking; **Jim Hogg State Historic Park** (42 m S to Rusk on US 69, 2 m NE
off US 84), restored bldg, picnicking, with nearby 2.6-m New Birmingham
Trail (S of Rusk off US 69 to FM 343); **Community Forest** (47 m SW on
SR 155 to Palestine, 2 m NW on US 287), 1000 acres, trails, picnics.
Harmony Hill (33 m SE on SR 64 to Henderson, 18 m NE on SR 43),
ghost town; bldgs, cemetery.

VICTORIA: Riverside Park (Red River & Bluff Sts.), 400 acres on
Guadalupe River, picnicking, zoo; **1. Fannin Battleground** (16 m W on

US 59, then S), state historic park commemorates Col. James Fannin and 342 men massacred by Mexicans, picnicking; 1. **Presidio La Bahia** (22 m W on US 59 to Goliad, 2 m S off US 183), where Fannin and his men are buried, has restored bldgs, museum (daily exc Good Friday, Dec. 25; sm adm); nearby are memorial to Gen Ignacio Zaragoza, Goliad State Park (restored Mission Espiritu Santo, museum, camping, picnicking), ruins of Mission Rosario; 1. Water sports, camping, picnicking at **Port Lavaca State Park** (24 m SE off US 87); **Indianola Co. Historical Park** (S of Port Lavaca on SR 316), site of historic town destroyed by 1886 hurricane; 1.

WACO: Ft. Fisher Park (I-35 & University Dr.) on Brazos River; water sports, camping, picnicking; replica of Texas Ranger fort with displays (daily; closed Dec. 25; sm adm); Tourist Information Center with schedules of hrs and fees for several 19th-C homes; 1. **Cameron Park** (N 4th St. & Herring Ave.), pretty 680 acres at confluence of Brazos and Bosque rivers; camping, other facilities; 1. **Old Ft. Parker State Historic Site** (40 m E on SR 164 to Groesbeck, 4 m N off SR 14), restored stockade and blockhouses of 1834 fort, museum; open daily; sm adm; 1. **Marlin** (29 m SE on SR 6) has mineral springs and Brazos River Falls (2 m W); 1. State park camping, picnicking at **Mother Neff** (34 m SW via US 84, SR 317, FM 3671, SR 236), 259 acres on Leon River, bird watching, trails (1, 2); **Meridian** (23 m NW off SR 6 on SR 22), on creek, lake, swimming, trails (1). Corps of Engineers lakes with camping, picnicking, water sports: **Waco** (2 m NW off FM 1637) with nearby children's zoo; **Whitney** (35 m NW via FM 933, 2114) with state park; **Navarro Mills** (39 m NE on SR 31), with nearby ghost town of Dresden and cemetery; **Belton** (35 m S on I-35, NW off SR 36); **Stillhouse Hollow** (39 m S on I-35, W off US 190), with one of Temple's 21 municipal parks; 1.

WOODVILLE: Heritage Garden Village (W on US 190), 26 restored bldgs illustrating 19th-C life in Texas; daily exc Jan. 1, Dec. 25; adm. **Alabama-Coushatta Indian Reservation** (16 m W on US 190), museum, Indian village, dances, Big Thicket tour, other attractions; camping, swimming; daily exc Dec. 25; adm; 1. Water sports, camping, picnicking at **Lake Tejas** (12 m NE on US 69, FM 256) and **B. A. Steinhagen Lake** (18 m E on US 190) with Martin Dies, Jr. State Park; 1. **Big Thicket,** a dark area of dense vegetation with bogs, cypress swamps, wildflowers, rare plants, runs S to Beaumont, E to N Neches River, W to Sam Houston National Forest (see Houston); will include 87,000 acres but many sections are still privately owned; scenic drives; Big Thicket Assn (Saratoga, zip 77585) offers museum, information, nature trail in Rosier Park; from Saratoga, 8-m scenic Ghost Rd. for cars or hikes (1-3); logging roads (1,2).

UTAH

CEDAR CITY: Cedar Breaks National Monument (21 m E off SR 14), gigantic, multicolored natural amphitheater with fantastic formations; surrounded by evergreen forests; Visitor Center (early June-Labor Day daily) with exhibits; camping, picnicking; 5-m Rim Drive for panoramic views and 3 short trails **(1,2)** to pond, wildflowers, pines, overlooks; no trails into amphitheater; consult rangers about climbs and backcountry hikes; information: Box 749, Cedar City 84720.

Dixie National Forest (hq at 500 S Main), 2-million acres in 4 sections: **Cedar Canyon** campground (12 m E on SR 14) is near trail **(3)** N to Sugarloaf Mtn and trail **(2,3)** N across the Desert (E of Cedar Breaks Ntl. Mon.); walks **(1,2)** at nearby Navajo Lake campground; Panguitch Lake camp (SW of Panguitch) has walks **(1,2)**, lava flows; Bear Valley Guard Station has trails **(2,3)** S and E; excellent view of Cedar Breaks from 11,307-ft Brian Head, reachable by car. Section **E of Panguitch** also has 10-11,000-ft peaks; several trails **(2,3)** near Jones Corral Guard Station (SW of Antimony) and S near Adams Head; SE of Alton are trailheads for Paunsaugunt Plateau and Pink Cliffs **(3)**. Section **N of Escalante** has 10,000-ft peaks, lakes, campsites **(1)**; trails **(2,3)** near Aquarius Guard Station and SW at Boulder Mtn and Boulder Creek; campgrounds near Wildcat Guard Station have overlooks of Wayne Wonderland, several trails **(1-3)**; long trail **(3)** S of here skirts Deer Mtn, crosses Boulder Creek and goes W to near Jacobs Reservoir; Blue Spruce camp is near Hells Backbone Ridge **(3)**; interconnecting trails **(1-3)** at Cyclone Lake and Barker Reservoir run N to Pollywog Lake area; trail from Barker Hollow to 10,577-ft Barney Top **(3)**; trail S to 9196-ft Canaan Peak **(3)**, trails **(1,2)** W at Pine Lake. Section **SW of Cedar City** has many trails **(1-3)** in Pine Valley Mtns, accessible from Pine Valley campsite; walks **(1)** at ghost towns of Old Irontown (17 m W on SR 56, 3 m S) and Pinto (2 m S), Hamblin and Mtn Meadow historic sites (S of Enterprise on SR 18); several trails **(1,2)** between SR 18 and Enterprise Reservoir. **Red Cliffs Recreation Site** (20 m NW of St. George on I-15, then W) has 1/8-m trail to ghost town of Silver Reef **(1)**, ½-m self-guiding trail through desert vegetation; camping, picnicking.

HANKSVILLE: Capitol Reef National Monument (29 m W on SR 24), 397 sq m of eroded formations; archaeological remains, petrified forest, natural arches; Visitor Center (daily exc Thnks, Dec. 25); campfire programs, guided walks; camping, picnicking; 10-m scenic drive to formations, petroglyphs, site of abandoned Mormon settlement of Fruita; jeep roads and trails (2,3) cut across stunning Cathedral Valley (N) desert and go S paralleling Waterpocket Fold; information: Supt., Torrey 84775. BLM sites (information: 850 N Main St., Richfield 84701): **McMillan Spring** and **Lonesome Beaver** campgrounds (18 m S on SR 95, 7 m W), open June-Nov.; buffalo range, historic sites, rockhounding (N & W), 1-3. **Hog Springs** (36 m SE off SR 95) picnicking at pictograph site; **1,2. Starr Springs** (29 m S on SR 95, 21 m SW off SR 276), picnicking, camping, rockhounding, nature trail; **1,2. Goblin Valley State Park** (20 m N on SR 24, 11 m SE), chocolate-colored formations, camping, picnicking, trails (1-3); San Rafael Reef and Swell are N of here on BLM lands.

LOGAN: **Walking (1)** at Mormon Tabernacle (Main & Center Sts.), Mormon Temple grounds (175 N 3 E); Man & His Bread Museum & Historical Farm (5 m S on US 89, 91), illustrating development of agriculture (daily in summer; free); water sports, camping at state parks on **Hyrum Lake** (12 m S off SR 163) in Cache Valley (1), **Bear Lake** (40 m NE on US 89) with trails (1-3).

Wasatch National Forest unit (information at Federal Bldg; see also Ogden, Salt Lake City) has most campsites and trailheads along beautiful Logan Canyon (E on US 89); trails (1-3) follow Logan River, streams, side canyons, climb to 8-9000-ft peaks, and interconnect for long hikes N & S; **Jardine Juniper** trail (15 m E on US 89) is steep 1½-m climb (2) to 3000-yr-old tree; Hatties Grove campground is near pretty **Ricks Spring (1,2)**; from **Red Bank** campground trails go NW to Mt Magog, Tony Grove and White Pine lakes, and via stream trails to Idaho section of forest (also reachable from High Creek recreation area). Also scenic is **Blacksmith Fork** area (SE via SR 165, 101), camping; trails (1-3) including 2 to Logan Canyon; elk herd fed in winter.

MOAB: **Canyonlands National Park**, 337,000 acres with spectacular, colorful formations surrounding canyons of the Green and Colorado rivers; Supt. in Moab (sip 84532), ranger stations on entry roads: **N entrance** (12 m N on US 163, 24 m SW on oiled road) leads to **Island in the Sky**; camping, picnicking; overlooks to vast expanses of canyons, spires, buttes, and rivers 2000 ft below; short trails (2); 100-m White Rim Trail and connecting Shafer Trail, suitable for four-wheel drive, spur to Lathrop Canyon, can be walked at any point (1-3). Just before N entrance is **Dead Horse Point State Park**, breathtaking views of Colorado River, Visitor Center, museum, camping, picnicking; 1-3. **S entrance** (40 m S on US 163, 38 m W) leads to **The Needles** formations; cars can go as far as campground near Elephant Hill; miles of trail through The Needles, Chesler Park, to Druid Arch, at Cave Spring, along Salt Creek (1-3); jeep roads to Horse Canyon (with Tower Ruin), Salt Creek (S to Angel Arch, N to Colorado River overlook), to The Grabens (trail to overlook of confluence of Green and Colorado rivers, trail to Colorado River), and others also offer walks (1-3). W entrance (jeep roads off SR 24 S of Green River) leads to **The Maze**; roads poor (even for four-wheel drives); miles of trail (3); consult ranger before hiking in this remote area.

Arches National Park (5 m NW on US 163), 53 sq m of red sandstone eroded into more arches (89), windows, and spires than in any other section of the nation; Visitor Center (daily), interpretive programs, guided hikes, camping, picnicking; 18-m paved road (with short spurs) runs N-S, with overlooks, also some unpaved roads, but best viewpoints are from trails in 7 sections N of Visitor Center: **Courthouse Towers** (1½ m N) with 1-m Park Avenue trail (1,2), a narrow corridor between spires resembling skyscrapers; **Windows** (9.2 m N, 3m E), 8 large arvhes, many windows, spires, passageways, coves; from **Balanced Rock** (9.2 m N) picnic area, four-wheel drive roads W through Herdina Park can be walked (1-3); **Delicate Arch** (12 m N, 1½ m E on unpaved road), 1½-m trail (2) to arch, also viewpoints; **Fiery Furnace** (15 m N), fabulous walk through narrow passages between immense walls that glow in the setting sun; **Devils Garden** (18 m N), trails (1-3) to 2 large arches (1 m), 4 other large arches (2 m), additional arches; **Klondike Bluffs** (8 m from Devils Garden on unpaved road), 1-m trail to arch, other trails (2,3); backcountry hikers and rock climbers must register; information: Supt., Moab UT 84532.

Fisher Towers (25 m NE on SR 128, 2 m E), BLM picnic area; 2.2-m trail (2) around base of dramatic formations to overlook over Colorado River. **Sego Canyon Petroglyphs** (30 m N on US 163, 6 m E on I-70 to Thompson, 4 m N) extend along red Book Cliffs; ruins of Sego ghost town; 1-3. **Manti-LaSal National Forest**, Moab Section (SE off US 163; ranger in Moab), has short trails (1-3) near Lake Oowah campground; long trails (2,3) from Pack Creek; tough backcountry hiking (3).

MONTICELLO: San Juan Co. Travel Council (Box 425, zip 84535) or **Chamber of Commerce** in Blanding (21 m S on US 163) offer maps for this area where virtually all the land (exc for Indian reservations and a few private enclaves) is public; primitive roads and scattered trails (1-3); BLM maps from Monticello district office (284 S 1st W, zip 84535).

Manti-LaSal National Forest (ranger station on access road W of town; also accessible off US 163 S of town) has primitive road and trails (2,3) to 11,360-ft Abajo peak, nearby campsites, W is Indian Creek Trail (1-3); from Indian Creek guard station, 12-25-m trails (2,3); at Round Mtn, S Cottonwood Creek Trail (1-3) can be walked a short way or S to near Blanding; from Big Notch, trails (2,3) go for miles NW and SE; long trail (2,3) near Little Notch; short trail (1,2) at Chippeau Spring; other primitive roads (1), trails (2), tough backcountry hiking (3).

Indian Creek State Park (14 m N on US 163, 10 m W on SR 211) contains Newspaper Rock (cliff with ancient rock art), petroglyphs in canyon; camping, picnicking; 1-3. **Edge of the Cedars State Historic Site** (22 m S, just NW of Blanding) and **Westwater Ruins** (just SW of Blanding), Anasazi dwellings, rock art (1,2); canyon trail from Westwater (2,3). **Natural Bridges National Monument** (4 m S of Blanding on US 163, 40 m W on SR 95), 200 Anasazi sites dot mesas and canyons in brilliantly colored landscape; from Visitor Center (information, exhibits, audiovisual program), 8-m loop drive gives spectacular views and has trailheads for rocky walks (2) to 3 natural bridges; Sipapu and Kachina bridges are connected by trail (2,3) passing cliff dwellings; open all yr, but bad weather may close roads in winter; sm adm or GEP. **Grand Gulch** (34 m W of Blanding on SR 95, 2 m S on SR 261), reached via trail from Cane Gulch, is a lovely canyon with archaeological remains, nearby camping (2,3). **Valley of the Gods** (NW of Bluff), striking formations; 1-3. **Great Goosenecks of the San Juan** (6 m N of Mexican Hat on US 163, SR 261; 4 m SW), state scenic preserve with deep gorge; camping, picnicking (no potable water); trails 1-3. **Monument Valley** (15 m S of Mexican Hat via US 163), see Arizona. **Navajo Indian Reservation** (22 m S of Blanding on US 163) has public recreational facilities, trails; for information, contact tribal hq (see Arizona); on the reservation is **Hovenweep National Monument** (via seasonal road E of Hatch Trading Post), self-guiding trails to unexcavated, scattered ruins of cliff dwellings (2,3). **Glen Canyon National Recreation Area** (see Arizona) has facilities in Utah at **Hall's Crossing** (98 m SW of Blanding via SR 95, 263), **Hite** (40 m SE of Hanksville on SR 95), **Bullfrog Basin** (57 m SE of Hanksville via SR 95, 276); **Hole-in-the-Rock** (via seasonal roads SE of Escalante), trails (3) and primitive roads (2). **Rainbow Bridge National Monument** (S shore of Lake Powell), brilliant red in afternoon sun; springs with wildflowers, ferns at base; all-day excursions from Page (Arizona); steep 1-m trail (2); also accessible via 24-m pack trail (3) from Navajo Mtn Trading Post or 13-m trail (3) from Rainbow Lodge ruins (NE of Tonalea) on the Navajo reservation, but check trail conditions before starting.

OGDEN: Walking (1) at landscaped Temple Square; Weber State College campus with museums; 5-acre Municipal Gardens (Municipal Bldg), paths, picnicking. **Willard Bay State Park** (10 m N off US 89), camping, water sports, picnicking, waterfowl refuge; Apr.-Nov.; 1. **Bear River Migratory Bird Refuge** (23 m N on I-15, 15 m W), 64,000-acre federal refuge, 12-m self-guiding road, observation tower; Apr.-Dec.; 1. **Utah**

State University Agricultural Station (16 m S on US 89), 25 acres with flowers (daily 8-6); free; 1.

PANGUITCH: Bryce Canyon National Park (26 m SW on US 89, SR 12), 56 sq m, has a golden glow, with most of the formations (often resembling cities from the rim) in pinks, reds, oranges, and yellows; Visitor Center (daily) has maps, trail leaflets, information; naturalist programs, displays at overlooks, guided walks, camping, picnicking; 17-m rim drive passes 12 amphitheaters (in winter, a shorter tour to 4 major viewpoints is open). Rim Trail, 5½ m between Fairyland and Bryce Point, is level between Sunset Pt. and N Campground (2); all other trails require steep climbs back out of the canyon: From Sunset Pt., 1½-m self-guiding Queen's Garden is easiest trail (2), with 320-ft ascent; 1½-m Navajo Loop (2) is more strenuous, ascending 521 ft; 5-m Navajo-Peekaboo Loop has rest area with water (2-3). From Bryce Store, Tower Bridge trail (3-m round trip) can be linked to 5½-m Fairyland trail (3). Under-the-Rim Trail (3) is 22 m from Bryce Pt. to Rainbow Pt. (4 exits along the way) and can be continued 28 m to Yovimpa Pass. Information: Supt., Bryce Canyon 84717.

Much of the area between Dixie Ntl Forest (see Cedar City) and Glen Canyon (see Monticello) is public land with walking opportunities in colorful canyons, some reachable on jeep or seasonal roads: In Kanab area (67 m S on US 89) are Coral Pink Sand Dunes (7 m N of Kanab on US 89), scenic state preserve with hiking (2), camping among colorful sandhills; pink dunes outside the state preserve are BLM land; Johnson Canyon (9 m E of Kanab on US 89, then N) and Cottonwood Canyon (40 m E of Kanab on US89, then N) are also colorful (2,3); latter road continues N to SR 12 (E of Bryce Canyon), with Paria ghost town, Grosvenor Arch, and Kodachrome Basin State Park (vivid sandstone spires, gray buttes, camping, picnicking, hiking 1-3); Paria Canyon Primitive Area (43 m E of Kanab on US 89, then S) has Indian petroglyphs, caves, vivid formations and small arches, trails (2,3) and jeep roads (obtain map and information, as some areas are hazardous); dinosaur tracks, petrified wood, arches, movie sets, and archaeological sites are scattered in the Vermilion Cliffs area (consult BLM maps). Escalante area (60 m E of Panguitch on SR 12) also has natural arches, archaeological and historic sites, many reachable on jeep or seasonal roads (best one runs SE to Hole-in-the-Rock at Glen Canyon—with rockhounding 15 m S of Escalante, W of Barney's Reservoir) and trails E for tough hikes (3) along Escalante River; Calf Creek (15 m E of Escalante off SR 12), a BLM camp and picnic site, has petroglyphs, 2 3/4-m trail (2) to Lower Falls; Upper Calf Creek Falls (2½ m N) are reachable by difficult 1-m trail (3) off SR 12; Wolverine Petrified Wood area (via dirt road 12 m E from Boulder, then 9 m to Horse Canyon), BLM site; Waterpocket Fold (43 m E of Boulder on graded road), BLM site, is 80-m section of Capitol Reef formation running along W side of Hall's Creek, with 36-m Burr Trail (3) a jeep road running E to Capitol Reef. **BLM maps** for Kanab and Escalante sections from district office (320 N 1st E, Kanab 84741).

State sites near Escalante are: **Anasazi Indian Village** (NE of Boulder in Dixie Forest), camping, picnicking trails (1,2), excavated historic site, museum (Apr.-Oct. daily; sm adm); **Escalante Petrified Forest** (off SR 12, W of town), trails (1,2).

PRICE: Chamber of Commerce (Municipal Bldg), maps for self-guiding tours of area; outlaw hideouts; **Nine Mile Canyon** (US 6, 50, S) with petroglyphs, historic relics. **Cleveland-Lloyd Dinosaur Quarry** (20 m S on SR 10, E off SR 155), interpretive center at BLM picnic site (Apr.-Nov.); **Cedar Mtn** and **San Rafael Bridge** (16 & 25 m SE of Cleveland on dirt road), BLM picnic and camp areas, nearby pictographs (Apr.-Nov.); **Buckhorn Draw** (30 m S on SR 10 to Castle Dale, then E), pictographs, other Indian remains; **1,2**. **Price Canyon** (15 m N on US 6, 50; 2½ m SW), BLM camping, hiking (1,2) area; ghost towns of Rains, Lathuda, Standardville just S. State Parks with water sports, camping, fishing: **Scofield** (22 m N on US 6, 50; 10 m SW on SR 96), 40 m of scenic drives around lake, walks (1,2), abandoned coal mining towns; **Huntington Lake** (21 m S off SR 10), walks (1); scenic **Millsite Lake** (38 m S on SR 10 to Ferron, 4 m W), trails (1-3) around lake, in forest; **Green River** (59 m SE on US 6, 50; E off I-70), float trips, beautiful cliffhugged river.

Manti-LaSal National Forest (W of town): Unpaved, scenic **Skyline Drive** runs length of forest from Thistle (N) to Fishlake Ntl Forest (S); many access roads off US89 on W. Trails at Dry Creek (1,2) near **Smiths Reservoir** (SE of Thistle; along **Price River** (1-3) from Fish Creek campground (NW of Scofield); **Gooseberry** camp (1) area (NE of Fairview) and at lakes and reservoirs S of here (reachable also by trail from Huntington Canyon and Forks of Huntington campgrounds); Black Canyon trail (2,3), N of **Seely Reservoir**; long trail (1-3) from **Ferron Canyon** camp (W of Ferron), with nearby access to trails (1-3) in Nelson Mtn area; campsites near **Ferron Reservoir** (SW of Manti have easy walks (1,2) at nearby lakes, streams, and **Aspen Giants Scenic Area**, plus longer trails and trailless hiking (3) in Wasatch Range (W); walking (1,2) also on many primitive roads, fishing streams; backcountry hiking (3).

PROVO: Brigham Young University, with many fine museums, Botany Garden (8N & 5E), tours from Herald R. Clark Bldg; Pioneer Museum (500 N, 500 W), relics, pioneer village (June-Sept.), memorial rose garden (free).

Uinta National Forest (information at Tourist Bureau, Pioneer Bldg), 797,000 acres of mtns rising 8-12,000 ft above desert, 200 m of streams, lakes, deep canyons with waterfalls; 1000 m of dirt roads and 1000 m of trails. **Timpanogos Scenic Area** (NE via US 189, Alpine Scenic Hwy) has 6-m trail **(2,3)** via Emerald Lake to 11,750-ft Mt Timpanogos (communal hike held in July); Indian Trail **(2,3)** and others SW of mtn; from campsites on Alpine Scenic Hwy and lovely American Fork Canyon, trails **(2,3)** go N to Wasatch Forest and W to Dry Creek Canyon. Scenic **Provo Canyon** (6 m NE on US 189) has river trails, waterfalls (a mtn railway trip to Bridal Veil Falls cuts through the forest from Heber Springs); S of Bridal Veil Falls, a scenic drive (check condition before starting) with overlooks, Rock Canyon campground trails **(2,3)** across Cascade Mtn to Spring and Water Hollows (trails from latter go S to Dry and Bartholomew canyons on Left Fork Hobble Creek). Road through beautiful **Hobble Creek Canyon** (E of Springville) loops to Diamond Canyon; many campsites, trails **(2,3)**; trail **(2,3)** from Cottonwood Canyon can be followed E to Ashley forest, with many spurs along the way. **Mill Hollow** campground (E of Heber City) is also a good base for extensive trail system **(1-3)** into Ashley forest. **Nebo Loop Road** (S of Payson), also spectacular (climbs 9000 ft), can be taken W via Santaquin Canyon or S via vivid Devils Kitchen and Mt. Nebo; camp and picnic sites; trails marked on the route for short or extended hikes **(1-3)**. **San Pitch Mtns** unit (E of Levan) has trails and primitive roads that interconnect for hikes **(1-3)** the entire length; Maple Canyon camp is a good base.

State parks with water sports, camping, picnicking: **Utah Lake** (5 m W on Center St. with visitor center; **Deer Creek Lake** (23 m NE on US 189), trails on Provo River, nearby state fish hatchery (on SR 113) open free, daily; **Wasatch Mtn** (W of Deer Creek Lake), 22,000 acres in lush valley; **1,2.**

Eureka area (17 m S on I-15, 22 m W on US 6, 50) has rockhounding; **ghost town** remains include Homansville (1 m E), Dividend (5 m E on US 6, 50; 1 m S), Silver City (4 m S on US 6, 50), Ironton (5 m SW), Diamond City (6 m SE), Mosida (6 m W on SR 36); **Little Sahara** (15 m S on US 6, 50; then W), sand dunes; **2. Camp Floyd & Stagecoach Inn State Historic Monuments** are at Fairfield (on SR 73, W of Utah Lake), commissary and cemetery of 19th-C army camp, restored inn that served Overland Stage and Pony Express, camping, picnicking (Apr.-Oct. daily; free). From here the **Pony Express** route, with stations 8–15-m apart, has been marked along a graded and dirt road via Faust, Simpson Springs (camping), Fish Springs (national wildlife refuge), Callao, to Deep Springs; station remains, cemeteries, rockhounding, historic markers, many chances for walks along the route; **2,3.**

RICHFIELD: Big Rock Candy Mtn (24 m S on US 89); **1,2.** State parks with water sports, camping, picnicking: **Piute Lake** (37 m S on US 89); **Otter Creek Lake** (46 m S on US 89, 13 m E on SR 62); **Palisade Lake** (42 m N on US 89), pretty trails; **1,2.**

Fishlake National Forest (hq in Richfield), 1½-million acres of high plateau E, W, and S of town; camping, picnicking, trails, walks on logging and prospecting roads. Most popular section is **Fish Lake** (32 m SE on SR 119, 24; NE on SR 25), camping; trails **(1-3)** to Fishlake Mtns, nearby lakes, Fremont River, many creeks, to 11,527-ft Hilgard Mtn (N), Limestone Cliffs (E); trails **(1-3)** also near Elkhorn camp in scenic Thousand Lake Mtn area (SE), Wayne Wonderland, Paradise Flats, Cathedral Valley (E of forest). **Monkey Flat Ridge** (13 m SE via Monroe) has trails **(2,3)**, nearby camp, lakes N and S **(1,2)**. Many trails in unit **W of Richfield** include: City Creek camp (NW of Junction) **2**; group of campsites in Little Reservoir area (E of Beaver) have Beaver River walks, trails to lakes, climbs to 10–11,000-ft peaks, **1-3**; Castle Rock camp (W of Sevier) has many trails **(1-3)** along creeks, in Gold Mtn mine area, along Fish Creek (S to North Creek) with spurs, N to the beautiful Pavant Range; campsites E of Kanosh, Meadow, and Fillmore are also good bases for the Pavant Range and trails along streams **(1-3)**; Maple Hollow camp (E of Holden) trails connect to Pioneer and other canyon trails and N through the Pavant Range **(1-3)**; by walking sections of dirt and primitive roads, you can hike the entire distance of this unit from Circleville Mtn (S near Circleville) to Noon Rock Peak (N near Scipio). **Canyon Mtn** section has many trails **(1-3)**; Plantation Flat and Oak Creek camps (SE of Oak City) are good bases.

ST. GEORGE: Visitor Center (daily exc Thnks, Dec. 25) at the Temple (400 S 300 E) provides films, tours, information; **Dixie State Park** (2N, 1W), winter home of Brigham Young (daily exc Thnks, Dec. 25; free). Ghost town of **Grafton** (7 m NE on I-15, 24 m NE on SR 15), a former Mormon settlement, has been used as a movie set; access is via road across Virgin River from Rockville; **1**. State parks with camping, picnicking: **Snow Canyon** (7 m NW on SR 18), vermillion cliffs rise above flatbottom gorge, black lava fields; **Gunlock Lake** (15 m NW via Shivwits), water sports in desert setting, trails; rockhounding; **1,2**.

Zion National Park (42 m NE on SR 15), 147,000 acres of incomparable beauty; massive, multicolor formations rise vertically above the Virgin River; many vivid side canyons; pinyon-juniper woodlands on canyon ledges, evergreens in high country; Visitor Center (daily), near S entrance, offers maps, trail trips and guided walks; scenic 12-m of SR 15 cuts through park, with spur to Temple of Sinawava; camping, picnicking. NW corner of park may be reached off **I-15**, S of Cedar City; ranger station; picnicking; 12-m foot and horse trail **(3)** but no car access to other sections of park. **Kolob Reservoir Rd.** (N off SR 15 at Virgin to SR 14 E of Cedar City) is winding, unimproved; access to other park areas by long, strenuous trails **(3)**. Stunning trails (round trip) from: **S campground**, 2 m to Canyon overlooks **(2)**; **tunnel** parking area, 1 m to Great

Arch for views (1); **Court of the Patriarchs,** 3½ m, canyon and formation views (2); **Zion Lodge** or Grotto Picnic Area, 2-m trail across river on foot bridges to pools, waterfalls (2); **Grotto** picnic area, 5-m trail with 280-ft climb to Angels Landing (3), 12-m trail to W Rim (3); **Weeping Rock,** ½-m self-guiding trail with hanging gardens, 2-m trail to quiet Hidden Canyon (2), 7-m trail with tough climb to E Rim (3); **Temple of Sinawava,** 2-m trail with trailside exhibit (2); free permits, trail maps, suggestions for backcountry hiking (3) from hq. Information: Springdale 84767.

SALT LAKE CITY: Temple Square (Main & Temple Sts.), hq of LDS, is walled, landscaped 10 acres (daily) with Visitor Center offering exhibits and tours; Tabernacle, Temple, other bldgs, monuments. **Walking tours** (1) include several museums; Brigham Young Monument (Main & S Temple Sts.); Brigham Young grave (1st Ave. between N State & A sts.); State Capitol (Capitol Hill) on landscaped grounds; Memory Grove (E of Capitol), park dedicated to war dead; Arrow Press Square (W Temple, 1-2 S), renovated bldgs with cafes, boutiques; Municipal Rose Gardens (S Temple at 11th E); University of Utah (1-5 S, E from University St.) with museums, recreational areas; Ft. Douglas (E of University) with cemetery; Utah Pioneer Village (2998 Connor St.), 35-bldg complex illustrating pioneer life (Apr.-Sept. daily; adm); Trolley Square (5th S, 7th E), renovated bldgs with boutiques. **This Is The Place Monument** (E on Sunnyside Ave. to Emigrant Canyon), monument, Visitor Center (daily exc hols; free). An exceptional park system of more than 50 recreation areas includes: **Liberty Park** (10th S, 6th E), arboretum, picnicking, 1852 log cabin, museum, flower displays, 11-acre Tracy Aviary (free); 52-acre **Hogle Zoological Garden** (daily exc Jan. 1, Dec. 25; adm); **Jordan Park** (1060 S 8th W), picnicking, sports, beautiful International Peace Gardens (May-Sept.; free).

Great Salt Lake (17 m W via US 40, I-80), camping and picnicking at Silver Sands and Sand Pebble beaches; Antelope Island (26 m N on I-15, 14 m W on SR 127), via causeway, has buffalo herd, waterfowl, state park with water sports, camping, picnicking, trails (1,2); waterfowl refuge on SE shore (NW of Bountiful). State parks with water sports, camping: **East Canyon** (14 m E on I-80, 15 m N on SR 65), on reservoir at 5700-ft (1-3); **Rockport Lake** (30 m E via I-80, SR 150), in valley (1,2). **Timpanogos Cave National Monument** (26 m S on I-15, 10 m E on SR 80) has scenic 1½-m self-guiding trail (2) to caves with colorful formations for 3-hr guided tours (daily; closed Nov.-Apr.; sm adm); Visitor Center exhibits and summer interpretive programs (closed Jan. 1, Dec. 25); picnicking; 1½-4-m trails (2,3) to FS campgrounds and picnic areas.

Wasatch National Forest (hq 4438 Federal Bldg, 125 S State St., zip 84111) is in several units (see also Ogden, Logan). Six canyons edging Salt Lake City cut through the forest, offering picnicking, hiking at state and federal sites: **City Creek** (N off State St.), picnicking **(1); Emigration** (E off Sunnyside Ave.), stream, historic markers, Rotary Glen park **(1,2); Parleys** (E off I-80), stream, at George Washington Grove, reservoir, historic markers **(1,2); Mill Creek** (off Wasatch Blvd.), sports, stream, short trails to lakes, mtns **(1-3); Big Cottonwood** (off Wasatch Blvd. at 70th S), beautiful canyon with park, trails **(1-3),** camping, sports, creek, lakes; **Little Cottonwood** (E via 94th S), park, camping, sports, waterfalls, wooded slopes, mining remains, rock climbing **(3),** trails to lakes and peaks **(1-3).** Camping, picnicking, mtn trails **(1-3)** in unit N of city (21-m **Bountiful Peak Scenic Drive** open May-Oct.), and in desert W at **Stansbury Mtn** unit (SW of Grantsville) and **Sheeprock Mtn** unit (S of Vernon). Large, attractive unit is in **Uinta Mtns** (29 m E on I-80, 20 m SE on SR 150), adj Ashley Forest and sharing **High Uintas Primitive Area; Pine Valley** camp has trails **(1-3)** on Beaver Creek, along Shingle Creek to hidden lakes and Smith Reservoir, mtn peaks; especially lovely is lake-dotted area in **Mirror Lake** region, with mahy campsites, trails **(1-3)** to lakes, primitive area, climbs to 12,000-ft peaks. **Christmas Meadow** camp (S of Lily Lake) has trails (start **2,** then **3**) S via Amethyst and other lakes to primitive area; trail **(2-3)** from **Lily Lake** E to E Fork-Blacks Fork ranger station is intercepted by N-S trails (all to primitive area) from Scout Camp, Lyman Lake camp, Smiths Fork Creek; excellent trails **(2,3)** from campsites at **Bridger Lake** (S of Robertson, Wyo.) S to nearby lakes and to primitive area, E to Henrys Fork, Island Lake, Hoop Lake camp, Fish Lake, and into Ashley Forest trail system.

At **Tooele** (22 m W on I-80, 11 m S on SR 36), Chamber of Commerce (City Hall) has information on rockhounding, historic sites; Mormon grist mill (9 m N on SR 36); ghost towns **(1,2)** include Stockton (7 m S on SR 36), well-preserved Ophir (19 m S on SR 36, 4 m E on SR 73, then NE), Mercur (4 m SE of Ophir on SR 73); prospecting trails in Oquirrh Mtns **(2,3).** At Wendover (127 m W on I-80), **Danger Cave State Historical Monument** (1 m NE), 60×120-ft cave occupied in prehistoric times (daily; free); **2.**

VERNAL: Natural History State Park (235 E Main St.), with Utah Field House of Natural History (daily; free), camping, picnicking, life-size replicas of dinosaurs; **Uintah Co. Park** (7 m NW on Red Cloud Loop), picnicking, Indian petroglyphs in Dry Fork Canyon; **Steinaker Lake State Park** (6 m N on SR 44, 2 m SW), water sports, camping, picnicking; **1.**

Dinosaur National Monument, 326 sq m; the green Yampa and Green rivers contrast with rugged yellow canyons; 4 road entrances that do not connect: **Quarry Visitor Center** (13 m E on US 40, 7 m N on SR 149), exhibits, naturalist programs, technicians excavating fossils (daily); 3-m scenic drive to Split Mtn Gorge with campgrounds, nature trail **(2),** boat ramp. **Monument Hq** (on US 40, 2 m E of Dinosaur, Colorado) interpretive programs and displays (daily in summer; closed weekends & hols Nov.-Mar.); scenic 30-m Harpers Corner Rd. dead-ends in heart of canyon country; overlooks, nature trail (2), picnic sites, spur to Sand Canyon overlook picnic area; 1-m trail (2) to spectacular view of Echo Park. Beautiful, unpaved, 13-m **Echo Park Rd.** descends steeply (2000 ft) from Harpers Corner Rd. past canyons, formations, petroglyphs, to campground at rivers confluence; outlet on US 40 (E of Elk Springs, Colo.). **Gates of Lodore** (NW of Maybell, Colo. off SR 318), at beautiful canyon; camping, nature trail (2), boating. Other unpaved roads lead to 9006-ft **Zenobia Peak** fire lookout (W of Maybell off SR 318) and to Indian rock art at **Island Park** (off SR 44 N of Vernal); hiking below rim is strenuous (3) and rangers should be consulted first; float trips also provide hiking opportunities (2,3). Information: Box 101, Artesia, CO 81610.

    Ashley National Forest (hq 437 E Main, zip 84078), 1.4-million acres in the Uinta Mtns (only major E-W range in the nation) rising from sagebrush benchland at Green River to 13,528-ft Kings Peak; 680 m of streams; sapphire mtn lakes; many recreation areas. Via **Drive Through the Ages** (SR 44), interpretive auto route, are spectacular gorges and Flaming Gorge National Recreation Area; **Flaming Gorge Dam & Visitor Center** (40 m N on SR 44, 260) and **Red Canyon Visitor Center** (44 m N & W on SR 44), open all yr, offer exhibits, overlooks, campsites, float trips, other recreation, trails (1-3); **Sheep Creek Geological Area** (10 m SW of Manila), earth fault, mammoth rock spires and cliffs. **High Uintas Primitive Area**, with 100 lakes, glacial moraines, scenic basins, mtns over 13,000 ft, wildflower meadows, conifer forests; many trails N-S interconnect with E-W trails for extensive hikes; easiest access (1-3) from Moon Lake campground (N of Mtn Home), access to Brown Duck Basin lakes; longer trails (2,3) from camps on Yellowstone Creek (NE of Mtn Home), access to 2 basins with many lakes; access (2,3) from camps on Rock Creek (NW of Mtn Home) or from camps on Duchesne River (N of Hanna) to Grandaddy Lake basin and 3 other lake basins (also reachable off SR 150 in Wasatch Ntl Forest). Also scenic are gorges of **Ashley Creek** (NW of Vernal), difficult access; **Brush Creek** (N of Vernal), with picnicking at Iron Springs and campsite at Oak Park Reservoir (good trails N); campsites at **Browne Lake** (S of Sheep Creek Canyon), **Spirit Lake** (SW of Sheep Creek Canyon), **Hacking Lake** (W of Oak Park Reservoir), **Paradise Park** Reservoir (N of Lapoint) are good bases for extensive trails (1-3), beautiful lakes.

VERMONT

BARRE: Center for granite quarries; sculpted granite headstones in **Barre Cemetery; Rock of Ages Quarry** (1 m S on SR 14, then follow signs 3 m SE), observation deck, artisan demonstrations, tours, visitor center (May-Oct. daily; free). **Groton State Forest** (5 m N on SR 14, 11 m E on US 2), lovely 20,000 acres, 7 ponds, camping, picnicking, swimming, extensive trail system (**1-3**); nearby wildlife management area. State parks with camping, picnicking: **Allis** (17 m S on SR 14, 2 m W), 487 acres on stream (**1**); **Elmore** (20 m N on SR 12), 709 acres on swimming lake, trails (**1,2**) include climb to 2608-ft Elmore Mtn.

BENNINGTON: Tourist Information Booth (507 Main St.) has information on museum, lovely colonial homes in Old Bennington (2 m W), historic bldgs; Green Mtn National Forest (see Rutland) recreation. Also attractive are **Manchester** (24 m N on US 7) with toll road up 3816-ft Equinox Mtn; garden and botany trail at S Vermont Art Center (N via West Rd.; early-June-mid-Oct., Tues.-Sun; sm adm); town of **Dorset** (5 m N on SR 30); **1.**

BRATTLEBORO: Chamber of Commerce (180 Main St.), area maps. **Living Memorial Park** (W end of town, S of SR 9), sports areas, swimming, picnicking (**1**). Walks (**1**) at **Steamtown, USA** (25 m N off I-91), open spring-fall (adm), **Adams Grist Mill** (25 m N on US 5 to Mill St., Bellows Falls), open summers (sm adm); cemetery of **Rockingham Meeting House** (25 m N on I-91, 3 m W on SR 103), interesting carvings, epitaphs (daily in summer; sm adm). New England Electric System picnicking, walks (**1,2**) at **Vernon** (6 m S on SR 142), dam on Connecticut River; **Bellows Falls** (21 m N on US 5), dam, old grist mill with museum. State parks with picnicking: **Ft. Dummer** (2 m S off US 5), 217 acres, camping, trails (**1,2**); **Molly Stark** (15 m W on SR 9), 158 acres, camping, many trails (**1,2**) to 2438-ft Mt. Olga, other nearby mtns; **Dutton Pines** (5 m N on US 5), 13 acres (**1**); **Townshend** (18 m NW on SR 30), 856-acre forest, camping, trails (**1,2**), swimming at dam recreation area (just N on river), 2500-acre West River Valley Greenway conservation area.

BURLINGTON: On **Lake Champlain**; swimming beach, camping, picnicking on Institute Rd. (off SR 127); views from campus of **University of**

Vermont, landscaping, museum; **Battery Park** (SR 127 & Pearl St.); **Ethan Allen Park** (N on Ethan Allen Pkwy), picnicking; **1.** Exceptional **Shelburne Museum** (7 m S on US 7), 35 colonial bldgs on 45 acres; fine collections of folk art, vehicles, unusual items; covered bridge, pond, picnicking; **1.** State parks: **Mt. Philo** (13 m S off US 7), 163 acres on 980-ft mtn, camping, picnicking, scenic trails **(1,2)**. **Sand Bar** (15 m NW off US 2), picnicking and adj wildlife area (S), and **Grand Isle** (20 m NW off US 2), camping, swimming on Lake Champlain; **1. Mt. Mansfield State Forest**, 27, 377 acres surrounding 4393-ft Mt. Mansfield (toll road to summit) and other rugged peaks, has recreation areas at: **Underhill** (20 m E off SR 15), camping, picnicking, trails **(1-3)**; scenic **Smuggler's Notch** (on US 108 between Jeffersonville & Stowe), camping, trails **(1-3)** include 3668-ft Madonna and 3715-ft Whiteface peaks; **Little River** (23 m E, then N off US 2), less rugged area on reservoir, camping, swimming, trails **(1-3)**; **Long Trail (2,3)** runs length of forest from Whiteface Mtn S over major summits to Camels Hump. **Camels Hump State Park** (S of I-89 from Mt. Mansfield Forest), rugged hiking preserve **(2,3)**; access on Long Trail in N (E of Jonesville on US 2) or S (at Appalachian Gap, 7 m W of Irasville on SR 17); access also from primitive roads and trails off periphery roads, especially in Camels Hump area; bird sanctuary **(1,2)** on river at Huntington (W of park).

MIDDLEBURY: Middlebury College (W on SR 125) has museums, historic bldgs, and administers Robert Frost Cabin with woodland trail (4 m SE on US 7, 4 m E on SR 125 at Ripton); **1. Morgan Horse Farm** (2½ m NW off US 7), University of Vermont breeding and training farm; tours; picnicking; May-Oct. daily; Nov.-Apr., Mon.-Fri; closed Jan. 1, Dec. 25; adm; **1.** State parks with camping, picnicking, swimming: **Branbury** (10 m SE via US 7, SR 53), 96 acres on Lake Dunmore, access to Green Mtn. Forest trails, trails **(1,2)** to Silver Lake (SE), fish hatchery (NW); **D.A.R.** (15 m W on SR 125), 70 acres, Lake Champlain beach **(1)**; **Button Bay** (13 m NW on US 7 to Vergennes, 6 m W), 236 acres on bluffs over Lake Champlain, natural area **(1)**.

NEWPORT: Lake Memphremagog (extends N into Canada), swimming, camping **(1)**; **Big Falls** (11 m W on SR 105) on Missisquoi River **(1,2) Jay Peak State Forest** (15 m W on SR 105, 5 m S on SR 242) with Long Trail **(2,3)**; charming village of **Derby Line** (7 m NE on US 5); **Crystal Lake State Park** (15 m S off US 5), 16-acre woods, swimming, picnicking **(1)**; **Willoughby State Forest** (7 m E of Crystal Lake at Westmore), beautiful lake, 2500-3300-ft mtns, Mt. Pisgah Hiking Trail **(2)** at S end, fish hatchery S near Newark; **Brighton State Park** (21 m SE on SR 111, 4 m S on SR 105), 152 acres, camping, picnicking, swimming, nearby ponds and streams with public access **(1)**, good trails **(1,2)**.

RUTLAND: Wilson Castle (2½ m W on US 4, 1 m N on W Proctor Rd.), 115-acre estate with furnished mansion, 15 other bldgs, picnicking (daily mid-May-late Oct.; adm); **1. Marble Exhibit** (2 m W on US 4, 4 m N on SR 3 to 61 Main St., Proctor), exhibits, demonstrations (late May-mid-Oct. daily; sm adm); **1. Hubbardton Battlefield** (11 m W on US 4, 7 m N), visitor center exhibits; late May-mid-Oct. daily; sm adm; **1. National Fish Hatchery** (12 m N off US 7 at Holden), daily; free; **1. Middleton Springs** (9 m S on US 7, 9 m W on SR 140) has landscaped springs; **1.** State parks with camping, picnicking: **Gifford Woods** (11 m NE on US 4, 2 m N on SR 100), 114 acres adj Green Mt. Forest; Trails include Appalachian which joins Long Trail (just W) and continues S via Killington resort area (gondola to Killington Peak with nature walk) and Bear Mtn to S section of Green Mtn Forest; access to AT also E of N Clarendon, E of E Clarendon, E of Wallingford. **Bomoseen** (17 m NW via US 4, Town Rd. to W shore of Lake Bomoseen), 2795 acres, lake, ponds, swimming, many trails **(1,2)**. **Lake St. Catherine** (9 m S on US 7, 16 m W on SR 140 to E Poultney, 3 m S on SR 30), 117 acres, swimming **(1)**. **Okemo State Forest** (24 m SE on SR 103, then W) surrounds 3372-ft Mt. Okemo; road plus ½-m trail **(2)** to summit views; other trails **(1-3)**.

Green Mountain National Forest (Supervisor, Box 519, 05701), 240,000 acres in units N and S of town along Green Mtn range (highest peak is 4135-ft Mt. Ellen); 30 lakes and ponds; 400 m of streams; spectacular fall color; historic sites; camping, picnicking; miles of trails **(1-3)**. **Long Trail** runs from Canadian line near Jay Peak (see Newport) 260 m S to Mass. line (E of Pownal); most of it is in Green Mtn Forest and state lands; 95 m of S section is also the Appalachian Trail; Long Trail and other trail guides from **Green Mountain Club** (Box 94, 05701). Many trails connect with Long Trail; trails in N unit include: **Lincoln Gap** and 4052-ft **Abraham** (E of Bristol) and **Bristol Cliffs** (S of Bristol); **2,3. Moss Glen Falls** and stunning **Granville Gulf** area (N of Granville); **1-3. Texas Falls**, Sugar Hill Lake, Robert Frost Wayside, other sites along SR 125 between Hancock and Ripton, with Moosalamoo a handy camp; **1-3**. Trails **1-3** near **Brandon Brook** and **Chittenden Brook** recreation sites (W of Talcville on SR 73), Chittenden Reservoir (10 m NE of Rutland) with nearby ponds. Trails **(1-3)** in S unit include: **White Rocks** camp (SE of Wallingford); **Little Stone Pond** (E from S Wallingford or N from Black Branch camp); **Devils Den** (E of Black Branch camp); **Greendale camp** (NW of Weston) on pretty brook; **Emerald Lake State Park** and Forest (N Dorset), camping, swimming, picnicking, trails on N to Peru Peak and Griffith Lake, trails on S (from E Dorset) along Mad Tom Brook; **Hapgood Pond** campsite (N of Peru), swimming, picnicking, brook and mtn trails; **Lye Brook Backwoods Area**, reached by brook trail near airport E of Manchester, from Long Trail, or from trail N from Branch Pond (E of Arlington); **Daniel Webster Monument** trails to Stratton Mtn and Stratton Pond, and

Somerset Reservoir with picnicking (S); **Red Mill Brook** camp (SR 9 W of Wilmington) has brook and mtn trails, trails NE in ski areas of Haystack Mtn and Mt. Snow, trails S to Dutch Hill ski area (trail turns W to Stamford stream), and SW to **Woodford State Park** with swimming, camping, picnicking on Adams Reservoir.

ST. ALBANS: Walks (1) on brooks; **Greenwood Cemetery** (S Main St.) with Brainerd Monument; **Missisquoi National Wildlife Refuge** (11 m N on US 7, SR 78), on Missisquoi River and Bay; **Chester Arthur Homestead** (8 m E on SR 36 to Fairfield, follow signs 5 m NW), home in 35-acre park, picnicking (spring-fall); **Fairfax** (10 m S on SR 104), century-old fieldstone homes, museum, waterfalls. State parks with picnicking, swimming, walks (1): **St. Albans Bay** (3 m W on SR 36), ½-m beach on Lake Champlain; **Burton Island** (5 m W on SR 36, 3 m SW to ferry landing), camping on 253-acre island in lake; **N Hero** (11 m NW on US 7, SR 78; 5 m S on US 2, then E), camping, 399 acres on Lake Champlain; **Lake Carmi** (15 m NE on SR 105 to N Sheldon, 2 m N), 4820 acres, camping, 2-m lakefront.

ST. JOHNSBURY: Walks (1) at: **Fairbanks Museum of Natural History** (83 Main St.), small zoo in garden in summer (daily; free); **Maple Museum** (E on US 2), sugar house, museum, demonstrations (early June-late Oct. daily; free); beautiful town of **Peacham** (6 m W on US 2, 6 m S); pretty area at **Barnet** (9 m S on US 5), McIndoe Falls, with Roy Mtn wildlife management area (S to Ryegate). Concord area (9 m E on US 2) has public access at **Miles Pond, Shadow Lake;** mtns over 2000 ft with trails (2); **Victory State Forest** and wildlife management area (N of N Concord) with trails (1, 2), plus camping, picnicking, good trails (1, 2), conducted hikes up Burke Mtn on Sun. in adj. 2041-acre **Darling State Park** (also accessible off SR 114).

WHITE RIVER JUNCTION: White and Connecticult Rivers meet here, with sites for picnics, walks (1, 2). Walks (1)at: **Woodstock** (13 m W on US 4), beautiful town with historic museum, riverside paths, 57-acre environmental center of Vermont Institute of Natural Sciences. **Appalachian Trail** enters state at Norwich (5 m N on US 5) and runs W to join Long Trail at Green Mtn National Forest (W of Sherburne Center); 2. State Parks with camping, picnicking: **Quechee Gorge** (7 m W on US 4), 76 acres in beautiful canyon on Ottauquechee River, trails (1,2); **Silver Lake** (13 m W on US 4, 10 m NW on SR 12), 34 acres, swimming (1); **Thetford Hill** (16 m N via US 5, SR 132), 262 acres on pretty river with Union Dam Recreation Area (S), hilly trails (1,2); **Ascutney** (15 m S off US 5 & Brownsville Rd.), 1984 acres at 3144-ft Mt. Ascutney, scenic trails (1,2); **Wilgus** (21 m S off US 5), 100 acres on Connecticut River, trails (1).

VIRGINIA

ALEXANDRIA: Walking tours of Old Town, settled in the late 1600s, start at **Ramsay House Visitor Center** (221 King St. at Fairfax St.); film, brochures, guided tours; daily 10-4:30; closed Jan. 1, Thnks, Dec. 25; **1**.

Gunston Hall (18 m S on US 1, then 4 m E on SR 242 in Lorton), former estate of George Mason, daily 9:30-5; closed Dec. 25; adm; gardens, picnic tables. **Occoquan** (20 m S on US 1, then 1 m on SR 123) is a charming village; information at the Mill House; **1. Pohick Bay Regional Park** (10651-A Gunston Rd. in Lorton), 1000-acre, overlooks, picnic and recreational facilities, short beach trail; adm per car; **1. Prince William Forest Park** (18 m S on I-95, ¼ m W of Triangle on SR 619), 12, 290 acres; picnicking, camping; hq at Turkey Run Ridge nature center has exhibits, naturalist programs, conducted walks, interpretive trail, trail maps; self-guiding nature trails at Oak Ridge and Travel Trailer Village; 35 m of other trails and fire roads; **1, 2.**

ARLINGTON: Arlington National Cemetery, Visitor Center (Apr.-Oct. daily 8 am-7 pm; Nov.-Mar. daily 8-5; free); Tomb of the Unknowns; Arlington House. **Great Falls Park** (12 m N off SR 193 on Old Dominion Dr.) has Visitor Center exhibits, booklets for self-guiding walks; conducted walks to historic and natural features; 4 m of trails and roads include short walks near Visitor Center to overlooks at Potomac River and gorge, to remains of canal town of Matildaville and Potowmack Canal; River Trail, rough in parts, follows the gorge for over ½ m; Old Carriage Rd. borders a swamp; Ridge Trail is the longest and hardest; **1, 2;** free all yr in daylight. Nearby parks in Fairfax are: **Bull Run Regional Park** (on SR 621), 1800 acres, swimming pool, picnic tables, other facilities; nature trail, **1;** daily; adm. **Burke Lake County Park** (on SR 123 in Fairfax Station), **Lake Fairfax County Park** (on SR 606 in Vienna), and others also have recreational facilities and adm charges; write to Fairfax County Park Authority (Box 236, Annandale, VA 22003). At **Leesburg,** Loudon Co. Museum & Visitor Information Center (16 W Loudon St.) has exhibits, booklets for 45-minute walking tour (daily; free); **Morven Park** (N on Old Waterford Rd.), 1200-acre estate with mansion, boxwood gardens, 2 self-guiding nature trails (Apr.-Oct., Tues.-Sun.; adm); **Waterford Restoration** (3 m NW on SR 7, 3 m on SR 9, 662), pre-Revolutionary bldgs, Waterford Mill craft demonstrations (summer weekends), house tours (Oct.); **Oatlands** (6 m S on US 15), mansion, 261 acres with formal gardens (Apr.-Oct. daily; adm); **1.**

Sully Plantation (19 m W on US 50, N on SR 28, Sully Rd.) has house tours daily 10-5; closed Dec. 25; sm adm. **Reston** (11 m NW on SR 7, W on SR 606), a new town, offers maps for walking tours at Information Center (Lake Anne Center, off SR 606); daily; **1. Manassas (Bull Run) National Battlefield Park** (25 m SW off I-66 at SR 234), site of 2 major Civil War battles in which 28,000 men were killed or wounded; Visitor Center, on Henry Hill, overlooks battlefield and offers museum, audiovisual program (daily exc Dec. 25; free); 5-m self-guiding auto trail of First Manassas and 9-m trail of Second Manassas have stops for walks; picnicking; **1, 2.**

George Washington Memorial Highway is landscaped along the Potomac for 17 m S to Mt. Vernon; walks along the Potomac; waterfowl sanctuary, picnic areas, overlooks, historic sites; **1. Mount Vernon** (10 m S off US 1), George Washington's home, village-like grouping of service bldgs; graves; daily; adm; **1. Woodlawn Plantation** (3 m W of Mt. Vernon on SR 235), home of Nelly Custis, gardens (daily exc Dec. 25; adm); on grounds is Frank Lloyd Wright's Pope-Leighey House (Mar.-Nov. weekends; adm); nearby is George Washington Grist Mill Historical Park, with rebuilt mill on site of original, audiovisual exhibits (summers; daily; sm adm); **1.**

ASSATEAGUE ISLAND NATIONAL SEASHORE (via causeway from Chincoteague), 37-m-long barrier island includes Chincoteague Ntl Wildlife Refuge; Visitor Center (daily) with naturalist programs; Sika deer, wild ponies, birds; boat trips, water sports, hike-in campsites, picnicking; beach walks, wildlife trails **(1, 2)**; adm.

BLUE RIDGE PARKWAY: The parkway runs S from the Skyline Drive 451 to the Great Smoky Mtns, through rugged, stunning landscape. Mile markers (numbered from N to S) are keyed to maps indicating facilities. **Visitor Centers** are: Humpback Rocks (Mile 5.8); James River (Mile 63.6); Peaks of Otter (Mile 86); Mabry Mill (Mile 176.1); Cone Memorial Park (Mile 294.1); Craggy Gardens (Mile 364.6); open May-Oct. daily 9-5 (some may be open later). The park is especially beautiful after mountain flowers bloom in May and through October color; in winter, some parts closed by snow; elevations reach over 6000 feet at the S end; most facilities open May-Oct., with full programs June-Labor Day. **Appalachian Trail** roughly parallels the parkway from Rockfish Gap (Mile 0) to Mile 103; **2,3.** Short easy trails (1): **Humpback Rocks** trails to mtn homestead, to hump-shape rocks; self-guiding forest trail (Mile 8.8); **Yankee Horse** (Mile 34.4); **Otter Creek** (Mile 58), trail to Otter Lake (Mile 63.1), James River &

Kanawha Canal display (Mile 63.6); **Thunder Ridge** (Mile 74.7) to overlook where rhododendron blooms in June; **Onion Mtn** (Mile 79.7) short loop for rhododendron, mtn laurel; **Fallingwater** (Mile 83.4) loop to cascades; **Peaks of Otter** (Mile 84) with nature trail, trail to restored farm, tougher hiking trails; **Roanoke River Gorge** (Mile 114.9) to overlook; **Roanoke Mtn** (Mile 120.4), several trails; **Smart View** (Mile 154.5), several trails; **Rocky Knob** (Mile 167), nature trail, tougher trails; **Mabry Mill** (Mile 176.1) mtn industry display; **Groundhog Mtn** (Mile 188.8) stroll; **Puckett Cabin** (Mile 189.8) stroll; **Cumberland Knob** (Mile 217.5), several trails; **Fox Hunters Paradise** (Mile 218.6), short trail; **Doughton Park** (Mile 238.5), stroll to Brinegar Cabin, trails (**2**), hikes to Bluff Mtn, Wildcat Rocks (**3**); **Jumpin-Off Rocks** (Mile 260.6) to overlook; **E.B. Jeffress Park** (Mile 272) to cascades; **Cone Memorial Park** (Mile 292.7), 25 m of easy trails (**1, 2**); **Julian Price Memorial Park** (Mile 295.1), 2½-m Price Lake loop, 2½-m nature trail at Sims Pond, 5-m Boone Fork loop (all **1, 2**), plus access to trailheads for long hikes (**2, 3**); **Flat Rock** (Mile 308.3) to overlook; **Linville Falls** (Mile 316.3) to falls and gorge (**1,2**); **Chestoa** (Mile 320.7) to overlook; **Crabtree Meadows** (Mile 339.5) to falls, also strolls; **Mt. Mitchell State Park** (off at Mile 355.4 to SR 128), with many walks and hikes to summit, observation tower, other trails (**1-3**); **Craggy Gardens** (Mile 363.4) with self-guiding nature trail, trail to Craggy Pinnacle, other trails (**1-3**); **Mt. Pisgah** (Mile 408.6), several forested trails, access to tough hikes; **Devils Courthouse** (Mile 422.4), 40-minute walk to overlook; **Richard Balsam** (Mile 431) evergreen trail; **Waterrock Knob** (Mile 451.2) loop to overlooks; **Heintooga Ridge** (Mile 458.2), easy trails, overlook trail, access to Great Smoky trail system. **Information:** Supt., Box 7606, Asheville, NC 28807.

CHARLOTTESVILLE: Chamber of Commerce (100 Citizen Commonwealth Center), maps for self-guiding walking tours. Some buildings designed by Jefferson—such as Albemarle County Court House (Court Sq.) and University of Virginia (W end of Main St.)—are open all yr; others are open Historic Garden Week (late Apr.-May). **Historic Michie Tavern** (2 m SE on SR 53), daily 9-5; closed Jan. 1, Dec. 25; adm. **Monticello** (3 m SE on SR 53), Mar.-Oct. daily 8-5; Nov.-Feb. daily 9-4:30; closed Dec. 25; free.

FREDERICKSBURG: Brochures for self-guiding tours from **Information Center** (2800 Princess Anne St. at US 1 N of town): Mary Washington House (1200 Charles St.); Old Slave Block (William & Charles St.); James Monroe Museum (908 Charles St.); cemetery of St. George's Episcopal Church (George & Princess Anne Sts.); Masonic Lodge 4 (803 Princess Anne St.); Hugh Mercer Apothecary Shop (1020 Caroline St.); Rising Sun Tavern (1306 Caroline St.); Stoner's Store

Museum (1202 Prince Edward St.); beautiful Kenmore (1201 Washington Ave.); Historic Fredericksburg Museum (818 Sophia St.) with audiovisual programs, exhibits on city history; all open daily (some closed hols); **1. Fredericksburg & Spotsylvania National Military Park** preserves sites of 4 major Civil War battles; **Fredericksburg Visitor Center** (Lafayette Blvd & Sunken Rd) offers brochures for self-guiding tours of all battle sites (all with picnicking), summer living history programs, museum with exhibits, nearby national cemetery; **Chancellorsville Visitor Center** (9 m W on SR 3) offers exhibits, film; both open daily (closed Jan. 1, Dec. 25); free. **Stonewall Jackson Memorial Shrine** (12 m S on I-95, 5 m E on SR 606 in Guinea), plantation outbuilding where Jackson died; picnicking; daily in summer, Thurs.-Mon. spring & fall, Fri.-Sun. in winter; free.

George Washington Birthplace National Monument (38 m SE off SR 3) illustrates life of 18th-C Tidewater planters; house, surrounding Colonial Living Farm with livestock, crops; Colonial Garden; Washington family graveyard (1 m NW); interpretive booklets; walk through grove of ancient cedars at Burnt House Point for views of Popes Creek; loop trail from picnic area; daily; closed Jan. 1, Dec. 25; sm adm or GEP; **1. Stratford Hall Plantation** (43 m SE on SR 3), birthplace of 4 generations of Lees; Great House; 1200-acre operating plantation; Reception Center with audiovisual program, exhibits; open daily; closed Dec. 25; adm; **1. Westmoreland State Park** (on SR 3 between Washington's Birthplace & Stratford Hall), 1302-acre preserve with nature center, guided walks, bird watching; swimming, picnicking, camping; interpretive Big Meadows Trail through swamp, marsh, forest; 4 m of other trails; walks along Potomac; **1.**

HARRISONBURG: New Market Battlefield Park (19 m N off I-81), Civil War museum, self-guided tour of 160-acre, 19th-C Bushong Farm; overlooks over river and Shenandoah Valley; daily; closed Dec. 25; adm.; **1. Natural Chimneys Regional Park** (15 m SW off SR 42 in Mt. Solon), interesting rock formations, swimming pool, other facilities; interpretive trail; self-guiding nature trails with overlooks; daily; closed Jan. 1, Dec. 25; adm.

George Washington National Forest (hq in Federal Bldg, Harrisonburg 22801), rugged 1-million acres in Blue Ridge and Shenandoah Mtns; camping, picnicking; **Massanutten Visitor Center** (US 211 between Luray & New Market), audiovisual and other programs, nature trail (**1**), open daily spring-fall. Lovely trail (**3**) overlooking Shenandoah River accessible from **Elizabeth Furnace** (10 m W of Front Royal off SR 55) with interpretive trail (**1**) and climb to Signal Knob (**3**), from **Camp Roosevelt** (8 m NW of Luray via US 340, SR 675) with tough climb (**3**) to Kennedy Peak, or from **Hazard Mill** (on FS 236 between Elizabeth Furnace and Roosevelt). Near Little Fort unit (S of Woodstock) is **Woodstock Tower**, stunning views of Shenandoah. Through Pedlar Range district (S of

Waynesboro) are 70 m of **Appalachian Trail (2, 3); Sherando Lake,** with swimming, nature trails (2), nearby Mt Torry furnace ruins, Montebello fish hatchery, lovely trail to Crabtree Falls In large forest section bordering W Va, **Hawk** and **Wolf Gap** units (in N) give access to rugged Big Blue Trail (2, 3) to Elizabeth Furnace; from Wolf Gap, the trail climbs to rock outcropping, Big Schloss (2,3); nearby Trout Pond has easier hike (2). From **Brandywine Lake** and **Hone Quarry** (W of Harrisonburg), backpacking along 4000-ft crests (3); just S, Todd Lake and N River units have short trails (3); just S, Todd Lake and N River units have short trails (2) and are near trailheads for long climbs to Reddish Knob (4397 ft). **Mountain House** (W of Staunton on US 250) has lovely Ramseys Draft (forest route; 2), tougher Jerry Run (2, 3), easy walk (1) among Confederate breastworks. Trails (2) at **Blowing Springs** (9 m W of Warm Springs) and **Longdale** (E of Clifton Forge).

LEXINGTON: Visitor Information Center (107 E Washington St.) has maps for self-guiding walking tours; conducted tours in summer. Stonewall Jackson House (8 E Washington St.); Lexington Presbyterian Cemetery (Main St.) with Jackson's grave; Washington & Lee University (W Washington St.), beautiful campus, Lee Chapel with Lee family crypt (daily exc Jan. 1, Thnks, Dec. 25; free); Virginia Military Institute (off US 11); Natural Bridge (13 m S on US 11) open daily in daylight (adm). **Douthat State Park** (32 m W on US 60 to Clifton Forge, 5 m NE via SR 629), outstanding mtn scenery, swimming lake, camping, picnicking; nature center with summer naturalist programs, trail maps; trails (1, 2) lace the 4493 acres, interconnecting for walks of any length.

LYNCHBURG: Appomattox Court House National Historical Park (20 m E on US 460, 3 m NE of Appomattox on SR 24), site of Robert E. Lee's surrender; 900 acres with restored village of Appomattox Court House (daily exc Dec. 25; adm per car); Visitor Center with museum, audiovisual programs; self-guiding tour booklets; 1. **Holliday Lake State Park** (9 m NE of Appomattox on SR 24, 6 m SE on SR 626, 692), 250 acres, water sports, camping, picnicking; trail around lake; trails in surrounding Buckingham-Appomattox State Forest; 1, 2.

MARION: Saltville (10 m W on I-81, 8 m N on SR 107), Chamber of Commerce brochures for self-guiding tour of museum, salt mine, salt furnaces, other historic sites; 1. **Abingdon** (28 m W on I-81), Washington Co. Chamber of Commerce (127 W Main St.) brochure for walking tour of historic sites, including Barter Theatre; 1. State parks with picnicking: **Hungry Mother** (3 m N on SR 16), swimming, camping; 2180 acres; lovely country; 12 m trails (1, 2) interconnect E of lake; climb to Molly Knob view; trail maps at nature center. **Grayson Highlands** (24 m S on SR 16, 5 m W on US 58), beautiful country; summer crafts demonstrations; scenic trails (2, 3), one to summit of Haw Orchard Mtn.

NORFOLK: Norfolk Tour Information Center (475 St. Paul's Blvd) has booklets for self-guiding auto and walking tours. Information also at **Gardens-by-the-Sea** (8 m E on Airport Rd., adj to airport), observation tower, film on city and gardens (summers), narrated boat and train tours (Apr.-Oct., weather permitting), extensive gardens; daily; sm adm. **Hermitage Foundation Museum** (7637 N Shore Rd.), art works in elegant Tudor-style mansion, landscaped grounds; daily exc Dec. 25; sm adm. **Lafayette Park** (35th & Granby Sts.), greenhouses, biological conservatory (daily exc Dec. 25), zoo (daily exc Dec. 25; sm adm), picnicking; **1.** Swimming and beach walks at **Community Beach** (foot on Granby St., N edge of town), **Virginia Beach** (19 m E on US 58) with 28-block boardwalk; **1. Seashore State Park** (on US 60, 4½ m E of jct with US 13, in Virginia Beach) is unique and lovely; campgrounds, swimming, beachcombing on Atlantic; across the hwy is a preserve of several ecological zones with unusually varied plant and animal life, nature center, 40 m of easy trails, 1-m interpretive Bald Cypress Trail with boardwalk across swamps; **1, 2.**

PETERSBURG: Historic Petersburg Information Center (400 E Washington St.), booklets for self-guiding walking tours of historic bldgs, including Old Blandford Church (319 S Crater Rd.) with audiovisual program and cemetery (daily exc Jan. 1, Dec. 25; free), Farmers Bank (23 Bollingbrook St.) with audiovisual program (daily exc Jan. 1, Dec. 25; free). **Petersburg National Battlefield** has Visitor Center with exhibits, living history programs (daily in summer), guided hikes, picnicking (daily exc Jan. 1, Dec. 25); 4-m auto tour with intrepretive signs and foot trails; **1. Lee Memorial Park** (S end, off Johnson Rd.), bird sanctuary, lake, picnicking; **1.**

RICHMOND: Greater Richmond **Chamber of Commerce** (616 E Franklin St., zip 23219) or **Visitor Information Center** (420 N 6th St.) provide information on city, nearby historic sites, James River plantations, guided tours. During **Historic Garden Week** (Apr.), private homes and gardens throughout the state are opened; for schedule write 12 E Franklin St.

Walking tours **(1)** start at **State Capitol** (Capitol Sq.), with nearby City Hall, Governor's Mansion, bell tower, monuments; St. Paul's Church (9th & Grace St.), Robert E. Lee House (707 E Franklin St.), Museum of the Confederacy (1201 E Clay St.), Valentine Museum (1015 E Clay St.), John Marshall House (818 E Marshall St.); Edgar Allan Poe Museum (1914 E Main St.). **Church Hill,** once a fashionable residential area, is being restored by Historic Richmond Foundation (Elmira Shelton Houe, 2407 E

Grace St.) which opens some houses on special tours—area includes
Carrington Square (2300 block of E Grace St.) with The Mews, Carrington
Row (2307-11 E Broad St.), 2300 block of E Church St., 2600-2700 blocks
of E Franklin St., St. John's Church (24th & Broad Sts.) with cemetery.
Monument Avenue (between Lombardy St. & Belmont Ave.) has
monuments to Confederate heros, attractive townhouses; just S is the **Fan
District**, with restored Victorian homes. **Hollywood Cemetery** (412 S
Cherry St. at Albermarle St.) has graves of Jefferson Davis, James
Monroe, others (daily; free). **Battle Abbey**, Virginia Historical Society
(428 N Blvd.), with superb collections (open daily) has lovely gardens;
adm. **Maymont Park** (Hampton St. & Pennsylvania Ave.) contains
Dooley Mansion (Tues.-Sun.), nature center, children's farm, wildlife
exhibit, Italian gardens, Chinese gardens, landscaped grounds; free.
Virginia House (off SR 147 at 4301 Sulgrave Rd., Windsor Farms), a
Tudor bldg reconstructed from an English priory, has extensive gardens
(Tues.-Sun.; closed hols; adm); adj is **Agecroft Hall** (4305 Sulgrave Rd.),
reconstructed Tudor manor (daily; closed hols; adm) with gardens. **Bryan
Park** (Westbrook Ave. & Hermitage Rd.), 279 acres, extensive azalea garden (best late Apr.-mid-May), picnicking; free. **William Byrd Park**
(Boulevard & Idlewood Ave.), 300 acres, woods, lakes, carillon tower.
James River Park (W 22nd St. & Riverside Dr.), wildlife sanctuary
overlooking James River; trails; information office; **1. Richmond
National Battlefield Park** preserves battleground in 10 sections of the city;
hq **Visitor Center** (in Chimborazo Park, 3215 E Broad St.), exhibits,
audiovisual program (Apr.-Nov. daily; Dec.-Mar. weekdays; closed Jan.
1, Dec. 25; free), marked auto tour at **Cold Harbor** (16 m E on SR 156)
and **Ft. Harrison** (10 m SE on SR 5), the latter with living history program
in summer (daily exc Jan. 1, Dec. 25; free); interesting walks in all sections, but special hiking trails at Watt House, Ft. Harrison (picnicking),
Ft. Brady, and Drewry's Bluff; **1. Historic James River Plantations** (see
also Surry, Williamsburg) have extensive grounds, gardens, river
overlooks (adm); **Shirley Plantation** (20 m SE on SR 5), daily exc Dec. 25;
Berkeley Plantation (23 m SE on SR 5), daily; **Westover** (24 m SE on SR
5), grounds open daily; **Brandon Plantation** (20 m SE on SR 5, 3 m S on
SR 156, 9 m S on SR 10 to Borrowsville, then toward river), grounds open
daily; **1.**
    Sayler's Creek Battlefield State Park (48 m SW on US 360, 7 m W on SR
307, 2 m N on SR 617), site of 1865 battle 3 days before Lee's surrender;
museum (Tues.-Sun. in summer); all yr; free; **1.** State parks with water
sports, camping, picnicking: **Pocahontas** (7 m SW off US 360, 4 m S),
pretty, 3 lakes, nature center, hiking in surrounding Pocahontas State
Forest (2); **Bear Creek** (47 m W on US 60), 5 m of trails (1) plus hiking in
surrounding Cumberland Ntl Forest (2), conducted walks in summer;
Goodwin Lake and **Prince Edward** (59 m SW on US 360), trail around lake

(1), short interpretive trail (1), hiking in surrounding Prince Edward State Forest (2).

ROANOKE: Wasena Park (Wiley Dr. & Winchester St.) has indoor and outdoor exhibits of Transportation Museum (daily in summer; sm adm); **1. Mill Mtn Children's Zoo** (off SR 220), atop 2000-ft mtn with city views, zoo (daily in summer; sm adm), picnicking; **1. Booker T. Washington National Monument** (18 m S on SR 116 to Burnt Chimney, 5 m E on SR 122), 224 acres of small tobacco plantation where Booker (he had no surname and chose "Washington" later) was born; Visitor Center; self-guiding trail across fields to reconstructed farm with period crops, livestock, bldgs and slave cabins; picnicking; daily exc Dec. 25; free; **1.**

Jefferson National Forest (hq in Roanoke), 600,000 acres in beautiful Blue Ridge Mtns; many recreation areas. **Appalachian Trail** enters at James River near Snowden and continues S to Mt. Rogers National recreation Area to Tennessee line; this and other trails following crests 4-5000-ft high are stunning but can be rough; **2,3.** Easy trails **(1,2)** at **Cave Mtn Lake** (7 m S of Natural Bridge), **Cave Springs** (NE of Dryden), **High Knob** (4 m E of Pembroke); **Mt Rogers** section has the beautiful but rugged Iron Mtn Trail **(2, 3)**; short interpretive trails **(1, 2)** at **Grindstone Recreation Area** (SR 603 W of Troutdale); other trails **(2, 3)** at **Bear Tree, Comers Rock, Hurricane, Raccoon Branch,** and **Skulls Gap** units. Trailheads in other sections at **Fallingwater Falls** (off SR 614 S of Middle Creek unit); **Hanging Rock** (SR 72, 2 m N of Dungannon); to Apple Orchard Falls at **North Creek** (SR 614 S of Natural Bridge); the **Pines** (15 m NE of New Castle); around **Scott-Wise Lake** (7 m S of Tacoma); **White Rocks** (18 m E of Pearisburg via SR 635, 613); also a few tough trails **(3)** in lesser used area near Wytheville. Among prettiest areas are interpretive trail **(2)** to waterfalls at **Cascades** (4 m E of Pembroke) and nearby **Mountain Lake Scenic Area** (SR 613 S of Kire); trails **(1)** to **Glenwood Furnace** ruins (S of Natural Bridge) and fish hatcheries at Paint Bank. At S end of forest is **Natural Tunnel State Park** (2 m N of Clinchport via US 23, then ½ m E on SR 871), scenic area with trail through 850-ft tunnel and a 20-minute trail along the crater rim **(2)**; summer historical museum; picnicking.

State parks with water sports, camping, picnicking: **Fairy Stone** (17 m SE on US 220, 20 m S on SR 40), nature center, nature trail **(1)**, interpretive trail to abandoned iron mine **(1)**; fairy stones (staurolites) at S end; park borders **Philpott Lake**, with public recreation area; **1.**

WILLIAMSBURG: Colonial   Williamsburg   Information   Center (Colonial Pkwy & SR 132), information on the nation's most extraordinary restoration, 1-m long and ½-m wide; grounds (traffic banned 8-6) are free; tickets at various price levels provide a choice of bldgs, exhibits, events, and include bus service. More than 80 original bldgs are restored; many others reconstructed on original sites; dozens are fully furnished and house exhibits; 100 acres of period gardens and greens; interpretive programs; most bldgs open daily 9-5. Carter's Grove Plantation (8 m SE on US 60), magnificent mansion on James River (Mar.-Nov. daily; adm). **Colonial Parkway,** 25-m long, links Colonial Williamsburg with Jamestown (10 m SW) and Yorktown (15 m NE); overlooks, historic markers, picnicking; free. At **Jamestown, Colonial National Historic Park Visitor Center** (daily exc Dec. 25) offers exhibits, audiovisual programs, guided tours on site of first permanent English settlement in the New World; only foundations remain; cemetery, church, monuments, Confederate earthworks, interpretive signs on 5-m drive or wilderness trail; nearby Glasshouse with colonial glassmaking demonstrations; **1. Jamestown Festival Park** (adj) is a state-administered re-creation of early Jamestown with wattle-and-daub structures, pavilions with historic displays, Indian ceremonial building, replicas of the ships on which settlers arrived; special events; picnicking; daily exc Jan. 1, Dec. 25; adm, **1.** At **Yorktown, Visitor Center** has historical exhibits on the city and the siege, audiovisual programs, booklets for self-guiding tour (daily exc Dec. 25; free); observation deck.

WINCHESTER: Chamber of Commerce (29 S Cameron St.), maps of historic sites including Washington's Office (Cork & Braddock Sts.).

Shenandoah National Park runs 80 m S from Front Royal and is bisected by the spectacular 105-m-long **Skyline Drive** (posted with mile markers starting with 0 at Front Royal); visitor centers at **Dickey Ridge** (mile 4.6), open Apr.-Oct. daily, and at **Byrd** (mile 51.1), open Apr.-Oct. daily plus winter weekends and hols; naturalist-led walks, other activities. **Appalachian Trail** runs 95 m, paralleling Skyline Drive, which offers easy access; information from Potomac Appalachian Trail Club (1718 N St. NW, Washington D.C. 20026). Other trails: **Matthews Arm** (mile 22.3) nature trail **(1); Thornton Gap** (mile 31.5) trail to Marys Rock **(2);** 1½-m round-trip **(2) Little Stony Man Trail** (mile 39.1); **Skyland** (mile 41.7), Stony Man Nature Trail **(1); Whiteoak Canyon** (mile 42.6), 5-m round-trip trail to falls **(2, 3); Hawksbill Gap** (mile 45.6), trails up 4049-ft Hawksbill Mtn **(2, 3)**, conducted hikes in summer; **Upper Hawksbill** (mile 46.7) is 2-m round-trip to summit **(2,3); Dark Hollow** (mile 50.5), 1½-m round-trip to falls **(2); Big Meadows** (mile 51), swamp nature trail **(1)**, access to trails to Lewis Falls, Black Rock, Dark Hollow falls **(2); South River** (mile 62.9) has 2½-m round-trip trail to falls **(2); Rockytop** (mile 78.2), trails **(2); Loft Mtn** (mile 79.8), short nature trail **(1)**. Information: Supt., Luray 22835.

WASHINGTON

ABERDEEN-HOQUIAM: Samuel Benn Park (E 9th & N "I" St.), rose gardens, paths, picnicking; **1.** Beautiful beaches for water sports, clamming, beachcombing **(1): Olympic Beaches** (12 m W to SR 109), between Ocean Shores and Moclips, with camping at Ocean City State Park (1½ m S of Ocean City); **Twin Harbor Beaches** (18 m SW on SR 105), between Westport and N Cove, with camping at state parks Westhaven (N of Westport) and Twin Harbors (3 m N of Westport).

ANACORTES: Walks (1) at public beaches with camping, picnicking here, at Oak Harbor, and at other towns on Fidalgo and Whidbey islands; **La Conner** (10 m E on SR 20, then S), old fishing village; **Whidbey Island Historic District** at Coupeville (25 m S on SR 20), information at Chamber of Commerce (Front St.). Picnicking, camping, swimming at state parks: **Deception Pass** (9 m S on SR 20), 2337 acres, beautiful site with cliffs, clamming, lake, salmon rearing station, nature trail, hiking; **Ft. Casey** (28 m S on SR 20), 1890s post, interpretive exhibits (Apr.-Sept. daily) at old lighthouse; **S Whidbey** (9 m S of Ft. Casey off SR 525), 85 acres, trails; **1,2.** Good views and trails **(1,2)** in wooded, 480-acre **Little Mtn** (26 m S on I-5 on Blackburn St. W in Mt. Vernon). **San Juan Islands,** 172 islands reached by Washington State Ferries (write Pier 52, Seattle 98104) from Anacortes; largest is Orcas, with 4934-acre Moran State Park for swimming, camping, picnicking, nature trail, other trails, overlook from Mt. Constitution; **San Juan Island** has National Historic Park (commemorating settlement of boundary dispute with Canada) with picnicking and interpretive centers (summers) at American Camp and English Camp, office (daily exc Jan. 1, Dec. 25), University of Washington Marine laboratories (summers); a dozen other islands have state park facilities—those with best walks are Doe, James, Jones, Matia, Stuart, Sucia, Turn; **1, 2.**

BELLINGHAM: Many fine parks include **Cornwall** (Cornwall Ave. & Illinois St.) and **Fairhaven** (Chuckanut Dr., S end of town) with rose gardens, picnicking; **Sehome Hill** (25th St.), wonderful views, picnicking; **Bloedel Donovan** (4 m E on Lake Whatcom) with beach; **1.** State parks with swimming, clamming, camping, picnicking: 2000-acre **Larrabee** (7 m S on SR 11), reached via beautiful drive along Chuckanut Bay, good hiking; **Birch Bay** (13 m NW off I-5), 172 acres, trails; **Bayview** (20 m S via SR 11, 537), 24 acres; **Rockport** (SR 20 E of Concrete), 457 acres; **1, 2. International Peace Arch** (24 m NW on I-5), landscaped with flowers; **1.**

North Cascades National Park (Supt., Sedro Woolley 98284), an incredibly beautiful 1053 sq m of alpine scenery with 300 glaciers, deep canyons, jagged peaks, mtn lakes, streams; maps, information, permits for mtn climbing and backcountry hiking from hq in **Sedro Woolley** (weekdays), Interagency Information Station at **Concrete** (daily in summer, weekends in fall), ranger station in **Marblemount** (daily all yr). Of 4 units, least accessible and developed are N and S Units, best for mtn climbing and backcountry hiking **(3).** **N Unit** is reached on trails from Mt. Baker Forest—from Mt. Baker Hwy (SR 542) camps, trails **(3)** loop around Copper Mtn area or cut across N Unit via Whatcom Pass to Ross Lake; from Baker Lake (N of Concrete), trail **(2)** along Baker River. **S. Unit** (E of Marblemount), is reached by 25-m Cascade River Rd. which ends at 3-m trail **(2)** to Cascade Pass; trail may be continued **(1)** SE to Lake Chelan, to spurs W along Flat Creek or to Glacier teak Wilderness, to spurs NE along Maple Creek, to Thunder Creek Trail via Park Creek Pass to Ross Lake; also on Cascade River Rd. are trails **(2,3)** to Found, Hidden, and Monogram (with spur to Lookout Mtn) lakes, with Marble Creek and Mineral Park campgrounds good bases. Most developed unit is **Ross Lake National Recreation Area** (NW of Marblemount on SR 20, the N Cascades Hwy): **Newhalem** is hq for Seattle City Light's Skagit operation (tours by advance reservation; write City Light Bldg, 1015 3rd Ave., Seattle 98104); Goodell Creek camp and picnic area with naturalist programs in summer; Trail of the Cedars (starts at Skagit River suspension bridge) through ancient cedars **(1)**; 4-m uphill trail to Thornton Lakes **(2)**; 7.5-m uphill trail to Pyramid Lake **(3)**; nearby Gorge Dam has lovely Rock Gardens and ladder Creek Falls via suspension bridge **(1, 2). Diablo Lake** has incline railway; Colonial Creek camp and picnic area, naturalist programs in summer; overlook to hanging glaciers; Thunder Creek Trail **(1, 2)** may be continued 25 m **(3)** to Lake Chelan; other trails **(1, 2). Ross Lake** is reached by boat or by trails such as 3.5-m Diablo Lake Trail **(2)** or 8-m Panther Creek Trail **(3)**; campsites reachable by trail or boat (Hozomeen, at N end, also reached by road from Hope, Canada). Trail **(2,3)** along E shore of lake follows shore to divide at Lightning Creek for Desolation Peak or inland curve to Hozomeen camp; spurs **(3)** off Lightning Creek to Okanogan Forest; Devils Dome Trail **(3)** loops from lake shore via Crater Mtn to SR 20 (E of Ruby Creek). Trail **(2, 3)** on W shore follows lake a short distance and then turns inland along Big Beaver Creek through Beaver Pass—here Little Beaver Trail **(3)** goes E to lake shore (boat access only) or trail may be taken W to Granite Mtn area of Mt. Baker forest. **Lake Chelan National Recreation Area** information at Stehekin District Office in Chelan; open daily), at N end of Lake Chelan, is reached by boat (daily, late spring to early fall; limited schedule early spring & late fall; no boats Jan.-mid-Feb) or float plane; Visitor Center (daily all yr); summer naturalist programs; summer shuttle-bus service up the valley; float trips, pack trips; guided tours; campsites along the Stehekin River are good bases for hikes; Pacific Crest Trail (3) cuts across main valley; good trails (1-3) along Lake Chelan, through Stehekin River valley and side valleys; Agnes, Company, Devore Creek trails (2,3) to Glacier Peak Wilderness; trails (2,3) from E and N of Lake Chelan connect to extensive trail system (3) in Okanogan Forest and S Unit of Cascade Park.

COLVILLE: Walks (1, 2) at fish hatchery; lookout on 5774-ft Old Dominion (E on SR 20 then N); **Little Pend Oreille Wildlife Refuge** (E on SR 20, then S); **Douglas Falls Park** (NE); old mining camps, including **Leadpoint** (30 m N on road beyond Deer Lake).

Colville National Forest trail maps from Federal Bldg, zip 98114, or ranger stations), 944,000 acres; rolling, timbered mtns rise 4-5000 ft in W, 6-7000 ft in E; pleasant green valleys; many lakes, streams. **Little Pend Oreille River** (E on US 20) has chain of 6 lakes connected by channels; camping, picnicking, trails (1, 2) at Gillette, Leo, Thomas lakes, also at Twin Lakes (N off SR 20). Pend Oreille River has been tamed by dams; Boundary Dam (on SR 31 near Canadian border) has Vista House overlook, tours of underground powerhouse facilities (daily), Pee Wee Falls, Gardner Cave (open when ranger is on duty); state and federal camping, picnicking, water sport sites, trails (1-3) are at Boundary Dam, Sullivan Lake and Metaline Falls (NE of Ione), Box Canyon Dam (N of Ione off SR 21), Browns Lake (SE of Ione off SR 20) with nearby fish hatchery at Cusick, and on river near Idaho line. **Indian Rock Caves,** on Kalispel Indian Reservation (off SR 20 at Usk, across river, then N), one large cave 100 ft above road, smaller caves E; **2,3.** Trails (1,2) from campsites along **Sheep Creek** (W of Northport), with waterfalls (steep trails to pool at bottom, 2), nearby Elbow and Pierre lakes; picnicking at Pepoon Lake, partway up 4253-ft Flagstaff Mtn (2). Hiking (2,3) from camp at **Boulder Creek Pass** (E of Curlew). Trails (1-3) along **Sherman Creek** (W of Colville on SR 20) include climb to lookout on Columbia Mtn.

Coulee Dam National Recreation Area (see Grand Coulee) has information station at Kettle Falls (10 m W on US 395) with maps.

GRAND COULEE: Coulee Dam National Recreation Area, created by Grand Coulee and other dams along the Columbia River, offers hundreds of miles of shoreline with state and federal sites for camping, picnicking, swimming, boating; some sites reachable only by water; some sites have no drinking water; in semiarid W section walking (1) is easy at grassy developed sites and open terraces (few trees), and buttes (2); marked trails (1-3) and more attractive walks are along the mountainous, forested N arm of the Columbia (see Colville). **Grand Coulee Dam Center** (near jct SR 155, 174) provides information, self-guiding tours of plant, exhibits, taped narration (daily exc Dec. 25); observation areas (best is Crown Pt. on SR 174).

Banks Lake (S on SR 155) is a 29-m-long storage reservoir in scenic canyon; camping, water sports, hiking (1-3) at Steamboat Rock State Park (8 m S on SR 155); walks (1, 2) along lake shore; Dry Falls Dam at S end (near Coulee City). **Sun Lakes State Park** (4-6 m S of Coulee City on SR 17), 4000 acres, camping, picnicking, water sports; trails (1-3); interpretive center (spring-fall, Tues.-Sun.; free) explains Dry Falls, 400-ft cliffs of Channelled Scablands carved into lava plateau by Columbia River; **Lake Lenore Caves** (10 m S of Dry Falls on SR 17) reached by footpaths (2) from parking ares. **Summer Falls State Park** (11 m SE of Coulee City), picnicking, trails (1,2), spectacular falls.

KENNEWICK-PASCO-RICHLAND: Tri-Cities Visitor & Convention Bureau (222 W Kennewick Ave., zip 99336), information, maps. Columbia River has been dammed by McNary Dam (30 m S on SR 14) to form **Lake Wallula**, with public parks.

Snake River has several dams: **Ice Harbor Lock & Dam** (13 m NE of Pasco off SR 124), self-guiding tours of powerhouse, fish ladders; Corps of Engineers water sports, camping, picnicking on E & W shores. **Lower Monumental Dam** (just N), similar facilities; visitor center; fish-viewing rooms, self-guiding tours; **Marmes Rock Shelter** (N shore); **Palouse Falls** and **Lyons Ferry** state parks (N shore off SR 261), 1282 acres, camping, picnicking, trails (1,2), 198-ft falls over basalt cliff in deep gorge. **Little Goose Dam** (off SR 261), view, fish-viewing room. **Juniper Forest** (27 m NE on Kahlotus Rd. to Snake River; 6 m W via Blackman Ridge & Rypzinski Rds), large stand of Western Juniper among sand dunes; wildflowers; 2.

LONG BEACH: Scenic, hard-sand beach stretches 28 m N along peninsula; on bay side is **Willapa Bay National Wildlife Refuge.** Picnicking, walks (1,2) at state parks **Ft. Canby** (7 m S on SR 103), 1666 acres overlooking mouth of Columbia River, water sports, camping; **Ft. Columbia** (11 m SE on US 101), 591 acres, several bldgs, interpretive center (late May-early Sept. daily; sm adm).

OLYMPIA: Walks (1, 2) at: **Capitol Group** (Capitol Way, 11-14th Aves.), 35-acre landscaped park on lake with government bldgs, fountain, flower beds, sunken garden, Japanese cherry trees, greenhouse; **Capitol Lake,** water sports, picnicking, trails, salmon run (begins mid-Aug.) at dam; **Priest Pt. Park** (Bay Dr.), wooded area overlooking Budd Inlet, picnicking, trails; **Olympia Marina** (Ft of Washington St.) and other dock walks; salmon runs (mid-Aug.-Oct.) at **Tumwater Falls Park** (S off I-5), 15 acres with picnicking on Deschutes River; **Millersylvania State Park** (10 m S off I-5), 835 acres with swimming, camping, picnicking, nature trail, other trails; **oyster beds** in Mud, Oyster, Big Skookum, Little Skookum Bays. **Ft. Lewis** (11 m E on I-5), active Army post, has lakes, streams, forests on 87,000 acres; daily in daylight; free; **1, 2**. **Hood Canal** (starts 41 m N on US 101) has sandy beaches, forest glades **(1, 2)** with access to national forest trails **(2, 3)**; state parks with water sports, camping, picnicking are 57-acre **Potlatch** (41 m N), 1-acre **Pleasant Harbor** (2 m S of Brinnon), 424-acre **Dosewallips** (at Brinnon) with river trail to forest and Olympic National Park.

OMAK: E Omak Park (SR 155), 70 acres, camping, picnicking, sports; **1**. State parks with picnicking, camping, water sports: **Conconully** (17 m NW), 43 acres on reservoir **(1)**; S are remains of gold rush town of Ruby. **Pearrygin Lake** (33 m NW on SR 20), 578 acres, trails **(1-3)**; nearby Winthrop is partially restored mining town; fish hatchery. **Osoyoos Lake** (38 m N on US 97), trails **(1-3)**; on lake partially in Canada; walking also along Similkameen River and W to camping and trails **(1-3)** at BLM sites on Palmer and Chopaka Lakes. **Alta Lake** (32 m S off US 97), 177 acres, trails **(1, 2)**. **Ft. Okanogan** (27 m S on US 97), 47-acre state historic site, interpretive center on fur trade (May-Sept. daily; free); **(1, 2)**.
    Okanogan National Forest (P.O. Box 950. Okanogan 98840), 1½-million acres W and NE of town; glaciers, snowcapped peaks, alpine meadows. **Pacific Crest Trail** begins near Castle Peak at the Canadian border and runs via mountain crests and ridges 2313 m (not all well marked or completed) to the Mexican border (information: Pacific Crest Club, P.O. Box 1907, Santa Ana, CA 92702). **Pasayten Wilderness** (between SR 20 and Canadian border), 520,000 acres, jagged pinnacles (good mtn climbing), glaciated valleys; access in S to Pacific Crest Trail and 7488-ft Slate Peak (wonderful views) from SR 20 NW of Mazama to camps Chancellor (30 m), Harts Pass (18 m), Meadows (17 m), Rattlesnake (9 m); access on E from camps N of Winthrop—Lake Creek (21 m), Andrews Creek (23 m), Thirtymile (30 m)—or W of Loomis from Long Swamp (23 m) or Daisy (16 m) camps; access on W from N Cascades Ntl Park; **2, 3**. Tough trails **(2-3)** at **Lone Fir** and **Klipchuck** (20 m NW of Winthrop off SR 20), **Cutthroat** (21 m NW of Winthrop off SR 20). Trails **(1-3)** at **Early Winters** (16 m NW of Winthrop off SR 20), **Memorial** (7 m N of Winthrop); **Tiffany Spring** and **Thirtymile Meadows** (22 & 30 m NW of Conconully off US 97); **Alder** and **Salmon Meadows** (5 & 9 m NW of Conconully off US 97); **Hidden** (15 m E of Twisp); **War Creek, South Creek, Roads End** camps (14, 22, 25 m W of Twisp). Trails **(1-3)** W of Tonasket at **Aeneas Spring** (10 m W of Aeneas), **W Fork Sanpoil** (6 m SE

of Aeneas), **Upper Beaver Lake** (10 m W of Aeneas), **W Fork Sanpoil** (6 m SE of Aeneas), **Upper Beaver Lake** (13 m N of Wauconda).

PORT ANGELES: Olympic National Park, 1400-sq-m wilderness with 60 glaciers on rugged mtns rising to 7965 ft at Mt Olympus; alpine wild-flowers; beautiful 60-m coast with beaches, rocky headlands; ex-traordinary, lush rain forest; lovely small lakes; **Port Angeles Visitor Center** and hq (Park Ave. & Race St. zip 98362) provides exhibits, guided walks and naturalist programs at many locations, trail maps (daily exc Jan. 1, Thnks, Dec. 25); information also at **Storm King Visitor Center** (on US 101, 21 m SW of Port Angeles) at Lake Crescent, open summers, and **Hoh Rain Forest Visitor Center** (14 m S of Forks on US 101, 19 m E), open all yr; 600 miles of trails; some roads and facilities close in winter. **Nature trails** and other easy trails (**1, 2**) are at main camping centers—Port Angeles Visitor Center, Heart O'the Hills entrance and Hurricane Hill (S), Elwha (SW), Lake Crescent, Soleduck Hot Springs (S of Lake Crescent), Hoh Rain Forest, Queets River (SW), Lake Quinault (SW), Staircase at Lake Cushman (SE). **E trail system** is mostly **3,** through rugged mtns in-cluding glaciers S at Mt. Anderson; access from parking area at Ob-struction Pt. (S of Hurricane Hill) or campsites at Deer Park, Gray Wolf River, Dosewallips, Staircase; NW of Dosewallips, and through long route S and W of Mt. Anderson, trails connect to central trail system. **Central trail system** runs S from Elwha, E of Mt Olympus, to Lake Quinault; S of Mt Olympus connections can be made to Queets River area or Enchanted Valley of Quinault River; most approach trails are **2,** becoming **3** due to length and interior climbs. **W trail system** is unique, through moss-draped vegetation of rain forests, in Hoh River (with parallel trail just N), Queets River, and Quinault River valleys; trails (**1, 2**) connect to interior systems (**3**). **Mt Olympus (3)** is reached from Hoh or Soleduck; Soleduck has pret-ty trails (**2**) to Waterfalls and Seven Lakes Basin, trails (**3**) to Elwha and Lake Crescent via Happy Lake Ridge system. Spectacular beach walks are at: **Kalaloch,** camping, 9 short trails off hwy to beaches, all different (**1, 2**); **Mora-Rialto** (off US 101, N of Forks), with camping, road and trails (**1-3**) to other beaches; **LaPush Indian Village. Ozette Lake** (off US 101 at Sappho), camping, 3.3-m Indian Village Nature Trail (**2**), other trails (**2,3**). **Bogchiel State Park** (6 m S of Forks on US 101), 119 acres, trails (**1,2**), swimming, camping, picnicking.

  Olympic National Forest (Supervisor, Federal Bldg, Olympia 98501) almost surrounds Olympic Ntl Park; 622,000 acres; lush rain forest (W), lakes, lakes, streams, 6-7000-ft peaks, towering trees, seacoast; beautiful interpretive trail (**1**) among giant trees of **Big Tree Grove** in rain forest near Falls Creek campground (E of Lake Quinault), other trails (**1, 2**); at-tractive walks (**2**) at **Campbell Tree Grove** (23 m NE of Humptulips) and **Wynoochee** dam (with visitor center) and lake (43 m N of Montesano),

Brown Creek (22 m NW of Shelton). **In E mtns,** trails and mtn climbs (**2, 3**) at Hamma Hamma and Lena Creek camps, 2-m trail (**2**) to Lena Lake; trails (**2, 3**) at Collins, Steelhead, Elkhorn camps (8, 9.5, 11 m NW of Brinnon); scenic trails (**1-3**) at Falls View, Rainbow, Big Quilcene camps (4, 5, 7 m SW of Quilcene), near Mt. Walker observation site; rocky Seal Rock Beach (off US 101, 2 m N of Brinnon), camping, picnicking, oyster gathering on saltwater Hood Canal; trails (**2, 3**) at Dungeness Forks and Slab camps (13 & 17 m SW of Sequim), on streams.

State parks with picnicking, swimming, clamming, camping, walks (**1, 2**): **Sequim Bay** (20 m SE on US 101), 89 acres, trails; state salmon hatchery 5 m N at Dungeness, near state swimming and clamming area. **Old Ft. Townsend** (10 m N of Discovery Bay on SR 113), 376 acres, and **Ft. Worden** (4 m N), 338 acres, with historic markers. **Ft. Flagler** (10 m NE of Chimacum on Marrowstone Pt.), 794 acres, remains of gun batteries; historic marker.

National Fish Hatchery (2 m S of Quilcene on US 101, then W), salmon tanks, rare albino trout, taped narration; daily; free; **1**.

SEATTLE: Seattle & Kings Co. Convention & Visitors Bureau (185 7th Ave., zip 98101), information (daily exc hols); in summer, information booths are open in Pioneer Square and Seattle Center. Best source for hiking information and publications is **Sierra Club** (4534½ University Way NE). Walking (**1**): **Pioneer Square** Historic District (Alaska Way S to 3rd Ave. S, Cherry to S King Sts.), Victorian section with cobblestone streets, boutiques and cafes in renovated bldgs; Bill Speidel's **Underground Tours** (601 1st Ave., zip 98104), interesting 2-hr guided tour of 5-block area of the original mill town, now underground; **International Settlement** (5-8th Aves, off E Yesler Way), oriental section; **Gold Rush Strip** (Pier 50 at Yesler Way to Pier 60 at Union St.), renovated waterfront with Washington State Ferries (Pier 52) and excursion boats, aquarium (Pier 56), shops, restaurants; **Pike Place Public Market** (W of 1st Ave, Stewart to Pike Sts.); **Seattle Center** (5th Ave. N between Mercer St. & Denny Way), 74 acres, International Fountain, Space Needle (revolving restaurant, observation deck; adm), art and science museums, international bazaar, museums of firefighting and aircraft, craft center, theaters, concert halls, amusement park in park setting, other facilities. Visitor Center of **University of Washington** (University Way NE & NE Campus Pkwy) provides information on art, natural history, textile, library collections; Arboretum (S of campus on Lake Washington Blvd), 250 acres, 4-acre Japanese garden (Apr.-Oct. daily; weekends rest of yr; closed hols; sm adm); azaleas and rhododendrons (Apr.-June), other blooms most of yr (daily; free). **Volunteer Park** (15th Ave E & E Prospect St.), gardens, conservatory, observation deck with fine views, Seattle Art Museum (Tues.-Sun.; closed some hols; free) with extraordinary collections and grounds with animal figures that once lined paths to tombs of Chinese emperors. **Admiral Way,** view of waterfront; **Alki Beach Park** (59th Ave SW & Alki Ave SW), swimming beach, monument, lighthouse; **Schmitz Park** (Admiral Way SW & SW Stevens St.), virgin forest, trails; **Lincoln Park** (Fauntleroy Ave. SW & SW Rose St.), beach, swimming pools, trails; **Seward Park** (peninsula off Lake Washington Blvd S), swimming beach, Japanese arch, fish ponds, paths. **Elliott Bay** piers; **Lake Union** with houseboats, boatyards, **Northway Seaport** (Waterway 19, Northlake Way), marine exhibits; **Lake Washington Canal,** Shilshole Bay Marina (7001 Seaview Ave. NW), Fishermen's Terminal (winter home of Alaska fleet); **Woodland Park** (N 50-59th Sts. on Phinney Ave. N), fine zoo, children's zoo, International Test Rose Gardens; **Green Lake** (N 65-72nd Sts. on Aurora Ave.), beaches, pier, picnicking, lakeside walk; **Carkeek Park** (NW 110th St.), beach, picnicking on Puget Sound; **Golden Gardens Park** (Seaview Ave.), beach, picnicking.

 King Co. Parks (W 226 King Co. Courthouse, zip 98104), 5000 acres, offer extensive sports and swimming facilities, classes, special programs; many offer walks (1) at lakes (such as Lake Wilderness, SE 248th & 224th SE) or saltwater beaches (such as Seahurst, SW 144th off Ambaum Ave.); those with attractive paths (1) include **Eastgate** (Newport Way & 145th SE), **Edith Moulton** (108th NE near NE 140th), **Hamlin** (NE 160th & 15th NE), **Luther Burbank** (84th Ave N Mercer I), **Marymoor** (6046 W Lake Sammamish Pkwy NE); **Tolt Pipeline Trail (1, 2)** runs 12 m from Duvall (on SR 203 NW) NW to Blyth Park.

 State parks with swimming, camping, picnicking: **Lake Sammamish** (18 m SE on I-90), 432 acres, trails **(1,2)**. **Lake Easton** (69 m SE on I-90), 141 acres, trails **(1,2)** continue into national forest **(2,3)**. **Federation Forest State Park** (30 m S on SR 169 to Enumclaw, 17 m E on SR 410), 610 acres of virgin timber; Montgomery Interpretive Center with ecology displays; guided nature walks; booklets for self-guiding trails; part of pioneer Naches Trail; picnicking; **1.**

 Mt. Baker-Snoqualmie National Forest (Supervisor, 2nd Ave. Bldg, Seattle 98101), 2½-million acres of superb Cascade Mtn scenery stretching N from Mt. Rainier to Canadian border; glaciers, beautifuly alpine lakes, giant Douglas firs. In N, 10,778-ft **Mt. Baker** (E of Bellingham) is a dormant volcano that still emits fumes; hiking and mtn climbs **(2, 3)** from Austin Pass picnic area (23 m E of Glacier on SR 542) or from several campgrounds (along SR 542, 2–22 m E of Glacier); lovely trails **(2, 3)** also from Baker Lake and other camp and picnic sites N of Concrete (17–25 m N on Baker River Rd.). Camps near **Marblemount**—Bacon Creek (5 m N), Marble Creek (9 m E), Mineral Park (17 m SE)—have trails **(2, 3)** connecting to N Cascades Ntl Park. **Glacier Peak Wilderness** (NE of Seattle), ½-million acres, rises from wildflower valleys to barren alpine peaks with glaciers, beautiful lakes; Pacific Crest Trail cuts through S portion; access (3) in N from Mineral Park camp, N Cascades Ntl Park, Lake Chelan Ntl Recreation Area; from S & E, Wenatchee Ntl Forest; from W, Buck Creek, Downey Creek, Sulphur Creek (24, 30, 32 m E of Darrington), Owl Creek and Sloan Creek (20 & 26 m SE of Darrington), all with additional trails (2,3). **Mountain Loop Hwy** (NE of Everett via SR 92 to Granite Falls, Silverton, Darrington, Arlington) has excellent trails (1-3) to 5-6800-ft mtns and lakes from more than a dozen camp and picnic areas along this pretty river route. Scenic trails with rugged peaks rising above green forests and stony, rushing waters from camp and picnic sites at **Troublesome Creek** (12 m NE of Index); **Deception Falls** and **Tye Canyon** (10 m E of Skykomish), with access to Pacific Crest Trail N & S of US 2 at Stevens Pass; **Foss River** (7 m SE of Skykomish). **Snoqualmie Pass** (23m SE of N Bend on I-90) has access to Pacific Crest Trail N and S, nature trail (1,2) at Asahel Curtis picnic area, trails and rockhounding (1-3) at Denny Creek, Commonwealth (rock climbing), and other nearby campgrounds. **Corral Pass** (37m SE of Enumclaw off SR 410) has camping, rockhounding, trails (1-3). On **Naches River** (NW of Yakima on SR 410), a beautiful valley surrounded by mtns over 6000 ft, trails (1-3) are at Boulder Cave, Crow Creek, Jungle Creek, and S at pretty Granite Lake and Deep Creek. In **Tieton River** valley (W of Yakima via US 12), with beautiful Rimrock Lake, good trails (1-3) are at Hause Creek, East Pt., Crane Park, Lost Lake, Russell Creek (W end of Rimrock Lake), Soda Springs (mtn climbing base).

SPOKANE: Chamber of Commerce (W 1020 Riverside, zip 99210), information. Walks (1) at **Havermale** and **Cannon Islands** (in Spokane River) near Spokane Falls; **Manito Park** (Grand Blvd & 18th Ave), gardens, fountain, lagoon, ponds, greenhouse, Japanese gardens; **Cliff Park** (13th Ave. & Grove St.), city view; **Coeur d'Alene Park** (2nd Ave.), native trees; **Finch Arboretum** (3404 Woodland off Sunset Blvds), 67 acres with rhododendron gardens.

TACOMA: Chamber of Commerce (752 Broadway, zip 98401), information on museums, historic bldgs, scenic drives, city parks (Wright, 6th Ave. & Yakima St., has lovely arboretum and conservatory of tropical trees). **Point Defiance Park** (4 m N at end of Pearl St.) contains re-created bldgs of Old Ft. Nisqually, museum (Tues.-Sun; closed hols; free); Camp Six, reconstructed logging camp (daily; free); Job Carr House, first home in Tacoma (daily; free); aquarium (daily; sm adm), zoo (daily; free), farm zoo (summer); children's storybook forest (June-Sept. daily; sm adm); 637 acres also has splendid flower gardens, Puget Sound beach, picnicking. State parks with picnicking, camping, swimming, beach walks (1): **Dash Point** (just N of city line on SR 509), 290 acres, and **Saltwater** (9 m N of Dash Pt. on SR 509), 88 acres; **Kopachuck** (4 m NW on SR 16 to Gig Harbor, 5 m W), 104 acres; **Penrose Point** (10 m NW on SR 16, 10 m S off SR 302 near Lakebay), 146 acres.

Mt. Rainier National Park (hq, Longmire 98397), 14, 410-ft snowcapped volcanic peak surrounded by 40 glaciers in 378-sq-m park; 34 waterfalls; over 60 lakes; meadows of alpine wildflowers (July-Aug.). Accessible from all entrances is stunning 90-m **Wonderland Trail** (2,3) circling Mt. Rainier, crossing meadows, streams, forests; maximum elevation 6500 ft at Panhandle Gap (E); entire loop takes a week to 10 days, but short walks possible at many points; more than 200 m of side trails connect to it; trail guides for sale. Visitor Centers (exhibits, naturalist programs, guided walks), open all yr: **Longmire** (61 m E of Tacoma on SR 706 via Nisqually entrance), camping, picnicking; interpretive .5-m Trail of the Shadows (1) circles meadow; steep 3.5-m trail (2) for overlook from 5955-ft Eagle Peak; 1½-m trail to falls (2) continues in 7-m loop along Rampart Ridge (3); 4-m self-guiding Kautz Mudflow Trail (2, 3) to Wonderland Trail, Mirror Lakes; other trails (2, 3) nearby. **Paradise** (E of Paradise), picnicking; climbing school, guided climbs; self-guiding trails (2) to Nisqually Vista (1 m), Ice Caves (3 m); trails (2, 3) to overlooks, glaciers (Stevens and Paradise are most accessible), lakes, 6562-ft Pinnacle Peak, 10,000-ft Camp Muir, Mt. Rainier summit (register with ranger first). Visitor Centers open summers only: **Ohanapecosh** (68 m W of Yakima via US 12, SR 123), camping; excellent hiking center; 2-m round-trip loop (2) along swift Ohanapecosh River to Silver Falls; short loop (1) Trail of the Patriarchs; steep trails nearby (2, 3) to Shriner Peak overlook (4 m), Cowlitz Divide (4 m), Three Lakes and Cascade Crest (6 m); summer-only W Side Rd. to overlooks, trails (2, 3). **Sunrise** (78 m from Tacoma via SR 410), camping, picnicking; .7-m self-guiding Emmons Vista trail (2); many short (½-4 m) trails (1, 2) to overlooks, lakes, glacial moraine; long trails (2, 3) to glacier basin, lakes, Northern Loop to natural bridge and Ipsut Creek, Huckleberry Creek (to national forest on N). Other entrances open summer only: **Carbon River** (40 m from Tacoma via SR 165) to Ipsut Creek campground; trails (1-3) to Green Lake, Spray Park, 5939-ft Tolmie Peak, others. **Tipsoo Lake** (65 m from Yakima via SR 410) picnic area; access trail to Pacific Crest (3); Chinook Creek trail (3) W to Kotsuck Creek and Owyhigh Lakes or S to Stevens Canyon entrance; nearby trails to Crystal Lake (2, 3).

VANCOUVER: Ft. Vancouver National Historic Site (E Evergreen Blvd.), 1825 post established by Hudson's Bay Co. is being authentically reconstructed; Visitor Center exhibits, audiovisual programs; daily exc Jan. 1, Thnks, Dec. 25; free; **1.** Historic bldgs nearby include Ulysses S. Grant Museum (1106 E Evergreen Blvd), Covington House (4303 Main St.), Clark Co. Historical Museum (1511 Main St.); **1.** State parks with camping, picnicking, swimming: **Beacon Rock** (32 m E on SR 14), 4093 acres, 840-ft monolith landmark, many trails **(1-3)**; **Paradise Pt.** (19 m N off I-5), 70 acres **(1)**.

Gifford Pinchot National Forest (PO. Box 449, zip 98660) extends NE to Mt. Rainier Ntl Park; 1.3-million acres, many lakes; 4-5000-ft peaks in W rise to 6-12,000-ft in E; Pacific Crest Trail along E boundary. Walks **(1,2)** and forest nursery on attractive **Wind River,** with Govt. Mineral Springs (19 m NE of Carson) or Crest (30 m N of Carson) campgrounds good bases; trails **(1, 2)** at **Kalama Spring** (12 m N of Cougar on SR 503); at stunning **Spirit Lake** (46 m E of Castle Rock via SR 504), nature trail, other trails **(1-3)**, several campgrounds (some 1½-7 m by trail from the lake plus mtn climbing at Mt. St. Helens 3½-m S of the lake); trails **(1, 2)** at **Blue Lake Creek** (16 m SE of Randle off US 12) picnic area; trails **(2, 3)** at **Wobbly Lake** camp (36 m SE of Randle off US 12); **Big Creek** (4 m SE of Ashford off SR 706) has camping, trails **(1, 2)**. **Goat Rocks Wilderness** (S & E of US 12, W of Yakima), 82,000 acres with rock formations, peaks to 8201 ft, wildflower meadows; Pacific Crest Trail **(3)** runs N-S; easy access **(2)** from Walupt Lake or Chambers Lake (S) or Packwood Lake (W) campgrounds to interconnecting trail system; other access **(3)** from US 12, Takima Indian Reservation. **Mt. Adams Wilderness** (S of Goat Rocks), 42,000 acres, has trails (including Pacific Crest) circling 12,307-ft Mt. Adams; easiest access is from campgrounds at Cold Springs, Morrison Creek, Timberline to beautiful wildflower area at Bird Creek Meadows **(2)**, Ridge of Wonders lava flow area **(2,3)**, trail **(3)** along E boundary, mtn climbing **(3)**; access **(2-3)** from camps at Council Lake (W) and Killen Creek (N) to W trail system and mtn climbing. **Cispus Environmental Center** (at Randle), state-run, 45 acres, has self-guiding trails **(1,2)**; closed many weekends.

WENATCHEE: Ohme Gardens (4 m N near jct US 2, 97), 9 acres on promontory with natural rock formations, waterfalls, pools, alpine plants, overviews; early Apr.-late Oct. daily; adm; **1,2**.

Wenatchee National Forest (P.O. Box 811, zip 98801), 1½-million acres of varied terrain from semiarid hills (S) to Pacific Crest glaciers, lakes, whitewater rivers. In the N, 555-m-long **Lake Chelan,** a fiord-lake between precipitous mtns, has beaches in town of Chelan plus hiking **(1, 2)**, water sports, camping, picnicking at **Lake Chelan State Park** (9 m W of Chelan off US 97), but the lake is more beautiful farther N; just beyond the state park some campgrounds are reachable on dirt roads, but beyond these the camps are reachable only by boat or seaplane and, in some cases, trails: good trails at Grouse Mtn (27 m NW), Prince Creek (35 m), Refrigerator Harbor (41 m), Lucerne (41 m), Domke Lake (2½ m S of Lucerne by trail), Holden (12 m W of Lucerne) with rockhounding and beautiful trail to Glacier Peak Wilderness. From **Entiat** (via US 97), campgrounds with trails **(1-3)** at beautiful Silver Falls (31 m); North Fork (33 m); lovely Halfway Spring (34 m); Cottonwood (39 m) and Big Hill (40 m) with rockhounding. From **Leavenworth** (NW via SR 209), camps with good trails (**1-3**) include Grouse Creek (26 m), Rock Creek (29 & 31 m); Atkinson Flat (35 m), rockhounding; Grasshopper Meadows and White River Falls (36 m), access to Glacier Peak Wilderness; and Alpine Meadow, Maple Creek, Phelps Creek (37-39 m) with rockhounding. From Leavenworth (NW VIA SR 207), trails (**1-3**) are at lovely, quiet **Lake Wenatchee** (with water sports, camping at state park) and Wenatchee River (part of the Wild & Scenic system), surrounded by Glacier Peak and other rugged mtns; good camps for walks are scenic Glacier View (on lake), Soda Springs and Riverview (8 m W of the lake), Lake Creek (13 m W of lake) and Little Wenatchee Ford (18 m W of lake) with rockhounding in beautiful area. **Swiftwater** picnic area (7 m NW of Leavenworth off US 2) is pretty, nature trail (**1**); trails (**2**) at Chiwaukum Creek (11 m NW of Leavenworth off US 2). Beautiful **Icicle Creek** (W of Leavenworth off US 2) has national fish hatchery and trails (**1-3**) at Eightmile (8 m), rockhounding; Bridge Creek (9 m), rockhounding, mtn climbs; Johnny Creek (12 m); Ida Creek (15 m); Chatter Creek (17 m), rockhounding. **Sand Creek** picnic area (8 m S of Cashmere off US 2), has rockhounding, trails (**1, 2**). From **Ellensburg** (NW via US 97), Lion Rock Springs (21 m, then E) is a beautiful campsite with views, rockhounding, trails (**1, 2**); easy trails (**1, 2**) at Mineral Springs and Baker (25 m), at Swauk (28 m) with rockhounding; Beverly (26 m), on Teanaway River, scenic, trails (**2**). **Cle Elum Lake** (11 m NW of Cle Elum off SR 903) has easy trails (**1, 2**) at campsites, with rockhounding on lovely streams and tougher hikes (including access to Pacific Crest Trail) from campgrounds N of lake; **Lake Kachess** (26 m NW of Cle Elum off US 10), camping, picnicking, nature trail (**1**), other scenic trails (**2, 3**).

YAKIMA: Franklin Park (Tieton Dr. & S 21 St.), museum, replicas of pioneer bldgs; **1.**

State parks with picnicking: **Yakima** (3 m E on SR 24), 211 acres, camping; **1. Ft. Simcoe** (15 m S on US 97 to Toppensih, 28 m W on SR 220), 200 acres; restored bldgs of historic fort; interpretive center (Apr.-Aug., Tues.-Sun.); trails (**1, 2**). **Olmstead Place** (30 m N on I-82, 3 m E on I-90, S on Squaw Creek Trail Rd.), 19th-C farm homestead, interpretive displays (Apr.-Nov., Tues.-Sun; sm adm); **1,2. Ginkgo Petrified Forest** (28 m E of Ellensburg via I-90 to Vantage), 7635 acres; petrified trees include prehistoric ginkgo; interpretive center; petroglyphs; interpretive trails (**1, 2**). **Wanapum** (S of Ginkgo on SR 243), 451 acres at Wanapum Dam on Columbia River; water sports, camping; dam (closed Nov.-mid-Apr.) has self-guiding tours, historic exhibits, fish-viewing rooms (May-Sept.); Colockum Caves (Apr.-Oct.) reached by boat.

WEST VIRGINIA

BECKLEY: New River Park (N Oakwood Ave.) has tours of Beckley Exhibition Coal Mine (May-Sept; adm), picnicking; **Lake Stephens** (8 m W on SR 3), swimming, camping; **Plum Orchard** (11 m NW off US 21), 2500-acre public hunting area, lake, camping allowed; **1, 2.** State parks with picnicking: **Twin Falls** (25 m SW on SR 16, 54; then W), 3780 acres, summer pool, pioneer homestead, trails **(1, 2)**; **Castle Rock** (W at Pineville), trail up a rock formation for views **(2).** **Grandview** (5 m SE on US 19, 5 m NE), 878 acres with sweeping views of New River Gorge, rhododendron gardens, scenic trails **(2, 3).** **Babcock** (29 m NE on US 19), 3637 acres in New River Gorge, waterfalls, camping, summer pool, trails **(1-3)** with scenic overlooks. **Bluestone Lake** (21 m SE on SR 3), Corps of Engineer impoundments with camping, picnicking, water sports on E shore (off SR 12); on NW shore is **Bluestone State Park** (off SR 20), 5000 acres with camping, picnicking, overlooks, scenic trails **(1-3)**; SW, at Bluestone River Gorge, is **Pipestem Resort State Park** (off SR 20), many facilities, camping, swimming, beautiful trails **(1-3).**

CLARKSBURG: Lowndes Hill (S 2nd St.) has remains of Civil War earthworks, observation tower (daily; free); **1. Salem College** (12 m W off US 50), pioneer exhibits in 20 restored log cabins re-creating Ft. New Salem (daily exc academic hols; sm adm); **1. Watters Smith Memorial State Park** (9 m SE off US 19), 278-acre, 18th-C pioneer homestead; visitor center exhibits; creek and wood walks; **1. Jackson's Mill State 4-H Camp** (20 m SE off US 19) has exhibits on area and Stonewall Jackson in museum (late spring-early fall), formal garden; free; **1. Tygart Lake** (11 m E on US 50, then SE), Corps of Engineers project with camping, water sports, dam tours, observation deck **(1)**; on E shore is **Tygart Lake State Park,** 1376 acres, swimming, camping, picnicking **(1)**; N on Tygart River is **Valley Falls** (SR 6), scenic 1034-acre picnic site **(1, 2)**; on W shore is 1000-acre public hunting area **(2)**; S of lake in **Arden** area (off US 119), the river banks bloom with wildflowers in spring **(1, 2)**; S of lake at **Valley Furnace** (SR 38), furnace ruins, picnicking **(1).**

HARPERS FERRY: Harpers Ferry National Historical Park preserves 1500 acres of historic town, site of John Brown's raid, at lovely gap where Shenandoah and Potomac rivers meet; visitor center (daily exc Jan. 1,

Dec. 25; free) exhibits, audiovisual program, maps for walking tours; many bldgs are furnished or have exhibits; picnicking; hillside views from **Jefferson Rock Trail (2)**, **Lockwood House**, **Harper Cemetery (2)**; **Loudoun Heights Trail** (S across Shenandoah off US 340) connects **(2)** to Appalachian Trail; **Maryland Heights Blue-blazed Trail** (W of park via US 340 across Shenandoah and Potomac rivers to Sandy Hook, then E to parking area) is 3½ hour walk on fortified heights, overlooks, interpretive signs **(2)**, map at visitor center.

Berkeley Springs (11 m W on US 340, 41 m N on SR 9), oldest spa in the nation; warm springs, swimming pool in state-owned **Berkeley Springs Park** (town center); **Castle**, a 19th-C stone structure, is on hill above springs **(2)**; wonderful overlook from **Prospect Peak** (on SR 9); **Cacapon State Park** (10 m S off US 522), 6115 acres, swimming lake, camping, picnicking, trails **(1, 2)**, naturalist-led walks; **Sleepy Creek** (15 m SE off US 522) is a 20,000-acre public hunting ground, camping, lake, 70 m of lovely mtn trails **(2, 3)**; valleys in this area bloom with wildflowers in spring.

MONONGAHELA NATIONAL FOREST: Visitor Information Service & hq in Elkins (zip 26241); 824,000 acres in beautiful Allegheny Mountains from N of Elkins S almost to White Sulphur Springs; mtns (4862-ft Spruce Knob is highest in state) rise steeply from narrow valleys; thick stands of timber, balds, areas of Arctic-like vegetation; 1900 m of lovely streams and rivers; limestone caves, rock formations; wildflowers; best walking areas include: **Blackwater Falls State Park** (2 m W of Davis off SR 32), 1688 acres with 60-ft amber-colored falls, deep river canyon; camping, picnicking; naturalist-led walks; rim and valley trails **(1-3)**. **Canaan Valley State Park** (7 m S of Davis on SR 32), 6000-acre ski area, camping overlooks, trails **(1-3)** to forest trails. **Dolly Sods Scenic Area** (15 m W of Petersburg), 10,000 acres of upland bogs, treeless plains, is reached from Red Creek campground; trails **(1-3)** 1½-7-m long interconnect for longer hikes. **Fernow Experimental Forest** (SE of Parsons), interpretive trail **(1)**. **Spruce Knob-Seneca Rocks National Recreation Area,** spectacular 100,000-acre preserve in 2 units (29 & 36 m E of Elkins on US 33) with recreation sites. **Seneca Rocks** unit (N) has rock climbing, caves, rock formations, 23-m N Mtn Trail along ridge over 3000 ft (several access trails) plus shorter trails near campgrounds and along streams **(1-3)**; **Spruce Knob** unit (S) has beautiful trail past waterfalls that follows Seneca Creek for 11 m (several short spurs), several climbs to mtn tops, other trails 2–10-m long **(1-3)**. **Bowden National Fish Hatchery** (10 m E of Elkins on US 33), visitor center (May-Oct. daily), outdoor tanks (all yr); free. **Otter Creek Wilderness** (12 m E of Elkins on US 33, then N), 18,000 acres of high, forested plateau; bogs, rhododendron; reached from Alpena Gap camp; 11-m trail along Otter Creek, 13-m trail along mtn ridge; many short trails (1-5 m) off these; **1-3**. **Cheat Bridge Scenic Area** (31 m S of

Elkins on US 250 to Cheat Bridge), stands of red spruce, balsam fir, waterfalls, lovely riversl toughest trail is 16-m along ridgetops (above 3500 ft) between Cheat Bridge and Glady (SE of Elkins); easier trails run in the valleys along beautiful Laurel Fork or along Greenbrier River (S to Seneca State Forest); many short trails intersect these; **1-3**. **Seneca State Forest** (just S), 11,686 acres, camping, picnicking, lake, lovely trails along Greenbrier River, to mtn peaks **(1-3)**; state trout hatchery (18 m S near Edray), daily **(1)**. **Cranberry Mtn Visitor Center** (20 m E of Richwood on SR 39) has information (June-Sept.) on unusual botanical area, Cranberry Glades, where orchids, cranberries, carnivorous plants, rare vegetation grow in bogs like those of the Arctic; boardwalk through open glades and forest **(1)**; 150-m of interconnecting trails and old roads allow walks **(1-3)** of any length; 18-m Pocahontas Trail from visitor center to 4426-ft Blue Knob, trails along pretty Cranberry River and other creeks and rivers, ridgetop trails, mtn climbs, are a few choices. **Watoga State Park** (1 m N of Hillsboro on US 219, then SE), 10,000 acres in high mtns, lake, swimming, camping, picnicking, naturalist, arboretum, trails **(1-3)**.

MORGANTOWN: W Virginia University has 3 campuses, with museums, 75-acre arboretum with wildflower trails **(1, 2)**, 7500-acre forest with naturalist programs and trails **(1, 2)**; **(1)**. **Mont Chateau State Park** (8 m E on SR 73), 42 acres with swimming and sports facilities, adj **Coopers Rock State Forest** (10 m E on SR 73), 12,747 acres, lake, camping, picnicking, scenic trails **(1-3)** to historic sites, views of Cheat River Gorge.

PETERSBURG: State fish hatchery (SW); **1**. **Lost River State Park** (31 m NE on SR 55, 13 m S on SR 259), 3680 acres in outstanding mtn scenery; museum; summer pool, many activities, naturalist, miles of lovely trails **(1-3)**.

WHEELING: Oglebay Park (N of city on SR 88), outstanding 1500-acre municipal facility; zoo; boating lake; garden center, greenhouses, arboretum; naturalist-led walks; sports; museum, art gallery; special events; **1**. **Wheeling Park** (5 m E on US 40), 406 acres, small zoo, picnicking, sports; **1**. **Tomlinson Run State Park** (34 m N off SR 2 on SR 8), 1399 acres, swimming pool, lake, 4 ponds, trails **(1, 2)**.

WHITE SULPHUR SPRINGS: Walks **(1)** at **Oldest Living Things** (2 m W), rare ancient plants; national fish hatchery (US 60) with visitor center (daily; free). **Greenbrier State Forest** (2 m W on US 60, S on Harts Run Rd), 5062 acres, camping, picnicking, pool, trails, **(1-3)** along Greenbrier River, in mtns. Droop Mtn Battlefield State Park (10 m W on I-64, 26 m N on US 219), 288-acre Civil War site, lookout tower, picnicking, trails; nearby 107-acre Beartown state picnic site with rock formations; **1, 2**.

WISCONSIN

ASHLAND: Beach with camping, picnicking in **Prentice Park** (W end of town); **1. Copper Falls State Park** (23 m SE on SR 13 to Mellen, 3 m NE on SR 169), beautiful 1796-acre forest, rocky gorges, waterfalls, observation tower, camping, picnicking, lake swimming; trails **(1, 2)**. **Potato River Falls** (21 m E on US 2, 4 m S on SR 169 near Gurney); **1.**

Apostle Islands National Lakeshore (Supt., 1972 Centennial Dr., Bayfield 54814) consists of 11-m mainland lakeshore (35 m NW on SR 13 to **Little Sand Bay**)—with Visitor Center, picnicking, boat shuttle to island campsites—and 20 lake Superior islands (N & E of Bayfield Peninsula) ranging from 3-acre Gull Island to 10,000-acre Stockton Island; **Bayfield** (20 m N on SR 13) has Visitor Center, island excursion trips and boat service (city dock), campground (on lake N of city); **Red Cliff Indian Reservation** (23 m N on SR 13) has boat service to islands, camping at Red Cliff and Raspberry Bay, lakeside walks, museum. **Madeline Island** (ferries Apr-Dec. from Bayfield) is not owned by NPS; museum of several bldgs with exhibits on fur trade and logging (mid-May-mid-Sept. daily; sm adm); water sports, camping, picnicking at **Big Bay State Park, Big Bay Town Park; 1, 2.**

BARABOO: Circus World Museum (426 Water St.), 15-acre complex, once circus winter quarters; magnificent collections, demonstrations; spring-fall daily, adm; **1. Wisconsin Dells** (10 m NW on US 12), stunning area of rock formations on Wisconsin River; camping, picnicking just N at **Rocky Arbor State Park;** trails on state land E along river toward Portage; **1,2.** State parks with camping, picnicking: **Mirror Lake** (5 m N off US 12), 2000 acres, swimming lake, trails **(1, 2); Devil's Lake** (3 m S on SR 123), 5000 stunning acres, spring-fed lake rimmed with dramatic rock formations and cliffs; part of Ice Age National Scientific Reserve; glaciation explained at nature center; swimming beaches; Indian mounds; trails **(1-3).**

CHIPPEWA FALLS: Irvine Park (N on SR 124) has zoo, picnicking, camping; **1.** State parks with camping, picnicking, water sports: **Lake Wissota** (5 m E on N shore of lake) 1000 acres, walks **(1)** through woods, prairie marsh; nearby trails **(2)** on Yellow River (E) or public hunting grounds (N). **Brunet Island** (24 m N on SR 178), 580 acres **(1) Chippewa Moraine Unit** (14 m N on US 53, 6 m N on SR 40), part of Ice Age National Scientific Reserve; 300 kettlehole lakes and pools; many trails **(1,2).**

DOOR COUNTY: Chamber of Commerce (Green Bay Rd., Sturgeon Bay 54235) provides information; miles of sand beach and wooded walks, attractive towns with fishing piers: **Sturgeon Bay** has: 40-acre Sunset Park; wildlife sanctuary; Potawatomi State Park (on Sturgeon Bay), 1126 acres, camping, picnicking, wooded trails, observation tower; Ahnapee Trail, old railroad grade, 15 m S to Algona; lighthouse **(1)** at Coast Guard station (4 m E on Lake Michigan); LaSalle Co. Park (on Lake Michigan), picnicking, monuments; The Farm (5 m N on SR 57), pioneer homestead (summer; adm); Cave Point Co. Park (10 m NE on SR 57, Clark Lake Rd.) caves in cliffs, picnicking; **1, 2. Baileys Harbor,** water sports and picnicking at Kangaroo Lake (S), Ridge's Sanctuary (N), privately owned flower preserve; Egg Harbor lookout tower (Co. G); **1. Peninsula State Park** (SR 42 at Ephraim), 3670 acres, lighthouse museum (summers; sm adm); swimming, camping, picnicking; observation tower, caves; trails; cliffs; **1-3. Ellison Bay** with Death's Door, a bluff at Gills Rock with legends of Indian deaths and shipwrecks; Newport State Park, 1991 acres, with beach on Lake Michigan, picnicking, wooded trails; **1, 2. Washington Island** (reached by ferry from Ellison Bay), site of Icelandic settlement, has summer museum, parks, scenic shore, **1, 2. Rock Island State Park** (reached by boat from Gills Rock), 783 acres, bldgs in Icelandic style, swimming, camping, picnicking, walks; **1, 2.**

LA CROSSE: On the Mississippi, Black, and La Crosse rivers; **Grandad Bluff** (E on Main St.), panoramic views, picnica; **Myrick Park** (La Crosse St.), zoo (spring-fall), picnics; **Riverside Park** (Main St.), landscaped, river views, picnics; **Goose Island Park** (7 m S on SR 35, W on Co. G 1), camping on river; national **fish hatchery** (14 m S on SR 35 at Genoa); **1, 2.** State parks on Mississippi with camping, picnicking, water sports: **Perrot** (8 m N on US 53, 9 m W on SR 93), 1392 acres at historic heights; **Merrick** (13 m N on US 53, 26 m W on SR 35), 324 acres, with trails to adj hunting area; **1,2. Wildcat Mtn State Park** (38 m E on SR 33), 2907 acres on Kickapoo River; camping, picnicking; lookout towers; many scenic trails; **1, 2. Elroy-Sparta Trail** (1-3) runs 32 m along a former rail route from park off I-90 (22 m E at jct SR 71) to Elroy; flat trail for bikers or walkers; 3 tunnels; picnic and camp sites at Sparta, Norwalk, wilton, Kendall. **Arcadia** (40 m NW via US 54, SR 93) has mineral springs, trout hatchery, deer park, recreation park; **1.**

MADISON: Chamber of Commerce (615 E Washington Ave.), map for tour of historic bldgs in town, information on trails in many public hunting areas in vicinity (especially N near Portage). **Capitol Park** is landscaped on peninsula between lakes Mendota and Monona; **Univ. of Wisconsin** (S shore of Lake Mendota) offers maps of beautiful campus from Memorial Union. (N Park & Langdon Sts.) and wooded walks including **Picnic Point; U.S. Forest Products Laboratory** (university Ave. & Walnut St.) is open weekdays (closed hols; free); city park on S shore of **Lake Monona; Lake Wingra** has zoo and bathing beach in Henry Vilas Park (500 S Randall Ave.), Indian mounds on campus of Edgewood College (855 Woodrow St.), extensive plantings; **Univ. of Wisconsin Arboretum** (1207 Seminole Hwy.), 1240 acres of woodlands and marshes, open all yr; **Jackson School Forest** (502 Caromar Dr.), 300 acres, open all yr; **Cherokee Marsh** outdoor education area (write Supt. of Parks, 704 E Garham St., zip 53703); **Nevin Fish Hatchery** (S on Fish Hatchery Rd.); **1. MacKenzie Environmental Center** (23 m N on I-90, 94; 5 m E on Co. CS beyond Pognette), 250 acres, arboretum, museum, small zoo; Apr.-Oct. daily; weekdays in winter; closed some hols; free; **1. Cross Plains** (13 m W on US 14), unit of Ice Age National Scientific Reserve; trails, **2. Little Norway** (18 m W off US 18, 151), historical complex with Norwegian-style bldgs, church, exhibits (May-late Oct. daily; adm). **Swiss Historical Village** (23 m SW on SR 69 to 6th Ave. & 7th St. in New Glarus), complex of historic bldgs, exhibits on Swiss immigrants (May-Oct. daily; adm.). **New Glarus-Brodhead Trail** runs 23 m SE along old railroad grade. **Mineral Point** (37 m W on US 18, 151; 9 m S on US 151), settled by Cornish miners; **Pendarvis-Cornish Restorations** (114 Shake Rag St.), complex of Cornish miners' homes, is open May-Oct. daily (adm); Chamber of Commerce has maps for other historical sites; **First Capitol** (museum open May-Sept. daily; free) and **Belmont Mound** with observation tower are historic sites with picnicking (13 m S of Mineral Point on US 151 to Belmont, 3 m NW).

Sierra Club (444 W Main St., zip 53703) sponsors hikes.

MANITOWOC: Chamber of Commerce (Box 603, ZIP 54220), information on many lakes and streams for Manitowoc-Two Rivers area. City parks include **Silver Creek** (S on 10th St.) on Lake Michigan, and **Lincoln** (1200 N 8th St.) with zoo; **Submariners Memorial** (9th St. at river) and Maritime Museum (809 S 8th St.); **Neshotah Park** (6 m N on Lake Shore Dr. in Two Rivers) has swimming, picnicking on Lake Michigan; **Point Beach State Forest** (11 m N off SR 42), 2770 acres of Lake Michigan beach, camping, picnicking, wooded trails, dunes; **Point Beach Power Plant** (15 m N on SR 42 at Two Creeks), information center, observation tower, nature trails (daily Apr.-Oct.; weekends rest of yr; free); **Two Creeks Buried Forest,** Unit of Ice Age National Scientific Reserve, is also here (on SR 42); **1.**

MARINETTE: Chamber of Commerce (601 Marinette Ave.) provides maps for public lands, waterfalls in area; city park (Carney Ave.) with camping, picnicking; lakeside walks; public lands with trails are S on

Green Bay and NW (19 m W on SR 64, N on US 141) to NW of Beaver, Lake Noquebay, Amberg (NW on Pike River, SW), Pembine (E on Co. Z and NE to Long Slide Falls), falls at Niagara; 1,2.

MILWAUKEE: Convention & Visitors Bureau (828 N Broadway), information on historic sites; museums including Milwaukee Co. Historical Center (910 N 3rd St.), Milwaukee Public Museum (800 W Wells St.); remarkable system of county parks (directory may be bought from Milwaukee Co. Park Commission, Rm 301, Courthouse, Zip 53233). Much of the Lake Michigan waterfront has been landscaped along **Lake Dr.** (SR 32); from the Art Center, Lincoln Memorial Dr. runs N with **Juneau, McKinley,** and **Lake** parks, **Shorewood Park** (at SR 190), and **Big Bay** and **Klode** parks on Whitefish Bay; S from Russell Ave. are **S Lake Shore, Sheridan, Warnimont,** and **Grant** parks; from Grant Park, a green belt follows the banks of **Oak Creek** inland (access off Rawson & Drexel Aves., Puetz & Ryan Rds.). **Kosciuszko, Pulaski, Jackson,** and **McCarty** parks follow creek from 6th St. W to Beloit Rd. **Kern, Estabrook, Lincoln,** and **Kletzch** parks follow waterways from Green Bay and Hampton Aves. N to Hope Rd. and W to Teutonia Ave. The longest green belt is in the W, following **Little Menomonee River** (from Granville Rd.) S along SR 100 to the 184-acre zoo (1000 W Blue Mound Rd.), with parks spurs following waterways E and W; in the SW, parks follow **Root River** from Greenfield Park (Lincoln Ave. & 124th St.) to Root River Pkwy. and Loomis Rd., with a few scattered park areas to the S. All have paths and trails (1,2), most have picnicking. Special areas include- **Mitchell Park** (S Layton Blvd. at W Pierce St.) with exceptional conservatory; **Whitnall Park** (S 92nd St. & Whitnall Park Dr.) with Alfred Boerner Botanical Gardens, formal gardens, exotic plants, marshland, nature center; 1,2.

 Kettle Moraine State Forest is in 2 units, both with camping, picnicking, water sports, observation towers; **S unit** (28 m SW via SR 15, 99), 15,000 wooded acres, Whitewater Lake, trails; **N unit** (50 m N off US 45), part of Ice Age National Scientific Reserve, 26,000 acres with scenic drive, interpretive programs, 2 lakes, trails, Old Wade House State Park (N end in Greenbush) with historic bldgs and exhibits (May-Oct.; adm), 1,2. Smaller units of the Ice Age reserve are **Campbellsport Drumlin** (6 m W of Kettle Moraine N unit via SR 67 between Co. V and Co. Y) and **Sheboygan Marsh** (6 m N of Kettle Moraine N unit via Co. A to Elkhart Lake, then W), an extensive marshland extending into county park and public hunting areas; 2.

 Other walks (1,2): **Vernon Marsh** (20 m SW on SR 59, 4 m S on SR 83, E on Frog Alley Rd.), on Fox River; **Frame Park** (10 m W on SR 59 to Waukesha, N on SR 164), on Fox River, gardens; **Oak Ridge Demonstration Farm** (22 m W on US 18 to Dousman), 100 acres, interpretive programs, guided tours only; **Riveredge Nature Center** (22 m N on US 141,

8 m NW on SR 33 to Newburg), 250-acre sanctuary on river (closed Aug.).

State parks with picnicking: **Harrington Beach** (35 m N off US 141), 634 acres on Lake Michigan, swimming, trails (1); **Lizard Mound** (33 m N via US 45, SR 144), 31 acres, Indian mounds, interpretive markers (1); **Pike Lake** (20 m N on US 45, 3 m W on SR 60), 580 acres, lake swimming, camping, trails (1); **Cushing** (27 m W off I-94), 10-acre historic site on stream (1), nearby observation tower, fish hatchery, public park on Pewaukee Lake; **Aztalan** (51 m W on I-94, S on SR 89), 143-acres, Indian mounds, restored stockade (1), nearby public lands with trails, federal fish hatchery at Lake Mills (1).

OSHKOSH: Paine Art Center & Arboretum (1410 Algoma Blvd.), Tudor-style manor with fine collections on 15-acre landscaped grounds (Tues.-Sun. in summer; some afternoons rest of yr; free); **1. Menominee Park** is on Lake Winnebago; swimming, picnicking, small zoo (free); **1.** Lakes **Winneconne** and **Poygan** (NW off SR 110 or 21) are surrounded by public lands with trails; **1,2.**

PARK FALLS: Public lands NW on N **Fork Flambeau River, Turtle Flambeau Flowage. Flambeau River State Forest** (4 m S on SR 13, 13 m W on SR 70), 86,000 acres, swimming, camping, picnicking, lakes, evergreen forest trails **(1,2). Park Falls-Tuscobia Trail** runs 72 m SW on an old railroad grade via Chequamegon National Forest, Ojibwa State Park (4 m S on SR 13, 40 m W on SR 70) with camping and picnicking, Chetac and Red Cedar Lakes (at Birchwood) to just N of Rice Lake; **2,3.**

Chequamegon National Forest (Supervisor, Park Falls 54552), 838,000 acres in units NW, S, E of town; 400 tree-rimmed lakes; 460 m of streams; Flambeau, Chippewa, other canoeing rivers; swimming; many camp and picnic sites; 70 m of trails plus miles of logging roads; visitor center W of Ino (US 2). **North Country Trail** cuts W across center of forest from Wayside (W of Mellen entrance) via campsites at Lake Three and Beaver Lake, to Lake Owen (S of Drummond); here it turns NW via many pretty lakes and Delta fire lookout to Lake Ruth (S of Iron River); **1-3.** Other trails: **Mt. Valhalla** campsite (W of Washburn) N to Washburn fire lookout, S to Twin Lakes Camp and Long Lake; **2. Wanoka Lake** camp (W of Ino on US 2) has trails **(1,2)** to nearby lakes; nearby are Moquah Natural Area (NE), Moquah Barrens Wildlife Area (N), Moquah (NE) and Iron River (NW) fire lookouts; **2. Perch Lake** camp (N of Drummond) has trails **(1,2)** to many nearby lakes, access to North Country Trail. Also near Drummond are walks (1) at **Pigeon Lake** Nature Trail (W), **Bearsdale Springs** red pine area (SW), **Virgin Pine** Trail (E), interpretive trail at **Lake Owen** (S), interpretive trail at **Namekagon Lake** (SE). **Mineral Lake** camp (W of Mellen) trails **(1,2)** include lookout, access to North Country Trail, nearby lakes, and Black Granite Quarry (E toward Mellen). Camp at **Day Lake** (N of Clam Lake) has trails **(1,2)** to many nearby lakes, lookout. **Chippewa River** and **Moose Lake** camps (SW of Clam Lake), waterside trails **(1,2)**, lookouts **(2)**, Indian battle site **(1)** at Moose Lake. Forest unit **E of Park Falls** (via SR 182) has trails **(1,2)** at many lakes and Doering Tract Primitive Area; Flambeau trails (parking on SR 70 near Fifield fire lookout) run S via lakes and Squaw Creek Wildlife Area, or N via Smith Rapids to lake area **(1-3)**; Riley Lake Wildlife Area and Schmuland Waterfowl Area are E and S of Sailor Lake camp; Memorial Grove interpretive trail (E of Fifield on SR 70) is SE on Pike Lake **(1)**. Forest unit **NW of Medford** has picnic and camp sites at Mondeaux Flowage, with auto tour, interpretive trails **(1)** at dam and at Spearhead Pt., waterfowl area (NW), other trails **(2)**; camping and trails **(1,2)** also at Chequamegon Waters Reservoir, with Beaver Creek Waterfowl Area (S end); trails **(1,2)**, camping at Kathryn Lake area.

PRAIRIE DU CHIEN: Villa Louis (521 N Villa Louis Rd.) lavish 19th-C mansion, museum, on extensive grounds (May-Oct. daily; adm); **1.** Tours **(2)** at **Eagle Cave** (26 m farther E on SR 60), 300 acres, picnic areas, nature trails, swimming, camping (tours daily in summer, weekends rest of yr; closed some hols; adm). Along **Wisconsin River** from Kickapoo Caverns E to Spring Green are many public hunting areas with trails; **1,2.** State parks with camping, picnicking: **Wyalusing** (7 m SE on US 18; W on Co. C, X), 2596 acres of canyons and valleys at confluence of Mississippi and Wisconsin rivers; waterfalls, springs, caves; beautiful trails **(1-3)**. **Nelson Dewey** (35 m S via US 18, SR 35, 133) contains Stonefield, 19th-C village of more than 20 bldgs, museum, exhibits, demonstrations (May-Oct. daily; adm): trails **(1,2)** on 591 acres.

RACINE: Racine Zoological Park (1½ m N on Main St.), on Lake Michigan, picnicking, swimming, zoo (daily; free); extensive park system with walks on **Lake Michigan** and **Root River; 1. Hawthorne Hollow** Arboretum & Wildlife Sanctuary (7 m S on SR 31, W on Co. E at Somers), 40 acres (inquire for hrs; not open daily); **1.**

RHINELANDER: Chamber of Commerce (City Hall, Stevens & Pelham Sts, Zip 54501), maps for extensive recreation areas surrounding city. **Pioneer Park** (US 8) has Rhinelander Logging Museum with bldgs, locomotive, other exhibits (spring-early fall; free). **Trees for Tomorrow** (28 m N on SR 17 in Eagle River), demonstration forest with nature trail (daily; free); **1. Warbonnet Zoo** (10 m S of Minocqua on US 51) is open spring-fall (adm); **1. Consolidated Papers, Inc.** (PR Dept., Box 50, Wisconsin Rapids 54494) will send information on hiking on its lands; 11-m self-guiding auto tour of forest management (starts 14 m E on US 8 to jct US 45 just E of Monico), runs N through plantations, swamp, to just N of Co. C on US 45 (open daily in summer; free; short walks possible; 1).

Nicolet National Forest (Supervisor, Federal Bldg, Zip 54501), beautiful 650,000 acres from Michigan line (S along SR 139, 32) to Mountain (information station, trout rearing station, lake, camping); evergreen forests, cedar-spruce swamps; white water Wolf River, gentler Pine, Popple, Wisconsin, Peshtigo, Oconto rivers; many lovely lakes with swimming, camping, picnicking, walks, opportunities for scenic walks (1,2) on self-guiding auto tours including 53-m Oconto River (from Mountain), 21-m Peshtigo River (N of Laona), 5-m Alvin Creek (SW of Alvin). Good trails in these recreation areas: Lac Vieux Desert (E of Land O'Lakes), headwaters of Wisconsin River, trails (1,2) here and to lakes (S) and Military Creek area (SE); Franklin Lake (E of Eagle River on SR 70), 1-m Butternut Lake interpretive trail, 45 m of trails at lakes and in Kimball Creek Area (E & S), evergreen plantations (S); Alvin Creek (E of Franklin Lake), 17 m of trails (1,2), scenic overlooks, red pine plantations, deer yards; Lost Lake (E of Tipler off SR 70), forest trail (1), Purdue University forestry camp, access to 11 m of trail (1,2) in Riley Lake Area (NE); Long Lake (S of Tipler on SR 139), sawmill, overlook, nearby pine plantations (1,2). At Laona are lakes, a sawmill, summer train ride (adm) to Camp Five logging complex, scenic view from 1951-ft Sugar Bush Hill (W), sawmill at Cavour (N), extensive trails (1,2) around lakes and in forests, trails (1,2) on Peshtigo River (NE), 30 m of trails (1,2) in Catwillow Creek area (E), 5 m in Colburn Creek Area (SE); small logging museum, trails (1,2) S at Wabeno. At Lakewood, ranger station provides maps for extensive lake region with many trails (1,2), Cathedral of Pines (W), trout rearing stations (NE and SW), overlooks, seed orchard (SW); trails from Boot Lake camp W to Jones Spring and Popple Ridge areas extend S to Boulder Lake (interpretive trail); trails NW to Ada Lake camp and lookout.

American Legion State Forest (N on SR 47), 47,500 acres; water sports, camping, picnicking on Bearskin, Tomahawk, other lakes; fish hatchery (E of Woodruff) with aquariums open spring-fall (free); Northern Highland State Forest (27 m NW on SR 47, N on US 51), 144,000 acres adj American Legion Forest, with similar facilities on more than a dozen pretty lakes; zoo at Boulder Junction (adm) open spring-fall; 1,2.

Walks also from state waysides along lakes and Wisconsin River (SW on US 51, 8 via Tomahawk); scenic SR 17 (S) through Prairie River Dells and Harrison Hills has much public land along the route; 1,2.

ST. CROIX FALLS: St. Croix National Scenic Riverway (Box 579, St. Croix Falls 54024), under development, is accessible N of town from roads off SR 87, 48, Co. F into St. Croix River State Forest (camp and canoe-launch sites); extensive pine barrens with many trails (2); information station open in summer on SR 70 W of Grantsburg. **Interstate State Park** (W off US 8), 1118 acres on the river; outstanding scenic gorge; state fish hatchery; water sports, camping, picnicking; trails (**1-3**) to potholes, other volcanic rock formations.

SHAWANO: Shawano Lake (2 m E on SR 22), camping; **Wolf River** (Riverside Dr. N), swimming; **1**. Waterfalls at **Wolf River** (8 m N on SR 47 to jct SR 55), being developed as National Scenic Riverway; river S (along SR 187) has public land on shores with trails; **1,2**. **New London** (30 m S on SR 22, US 45) has 6 parks, wildlife refuge, nature trails; **1,2**. **Menominee Indian Reservation** (hq 20 m N on SR 47 at Neopit) is developing forest, 82 lakes, 300 m of streams for recreation; many trails (**1,2**).

SHEBOYGAN: Walks (**1**) at: **Indian Mound Park** (S 9th St. & Panther Ave.), 18 mounds, burials; all yr; free. **Terry Andrae-Kohler State Park** (4 m S), 750 acres on Lake Michigan, camping, picnicking.

SUPERIOR: Walks (**1**) at: **Wisconsin Point**, peninsula in Lake Superior, swimming, picnicking; **Billings Park** (W end of 21st St.), swimming, picnicking, lagoons, pretty; boat launching ramps and ore **docks** (off US 2, 53) with whaleback freighter *Metero*. State park camping, picnicking, walks (**1,2**): **Pattison** (15 m S on SR 35), 1368 acres of woodland, swimming beach; 1½-m nature trail (**1**) on lake; trails (**2**) to 31-ft Little Manitou Falls, 165-ft Big Manitou Falls and river gorge. **Amnicon Falls** (5 m SE on US 2), stream (**2**). **Lucius Woods** (25 m S on US 53), 39 acres on swimming lake; nearby 20,000-acre Solon Springs Upland Bird Sanctuary (**1,2**); Mosinee Paper Corp. lands (contact district forest ranger in Solon Springs) open for hiking, camping, picnicking. **Brule River State Forest** (21 m SE on US 2), 34,000 acres along Brule River from Lake Superior shore S (to just NE of Solon Springs), swimming, camping, picnicking; smaller S section on river E of Gorden; **1,2**.

TOMAH: Mill Bluff State Park (7 m E off US 12), camping, picnicking, swimming on 247 acres of Ice Age National Scientific Reserve; towering rocky buttes rise from flat plain; **1, 2**.

WISCONSIN RAPIDS: Walks (**1,2**) at: **Griffith State Forest Nursery** (3 m S on SR 13), open May-Sept. weekdays exc hols (free); **Roche-A Cri State Park** (25 m S on SR 13), camping, picnicking. Impoundments on **Wisconsin River** S of town for Petenwell and Castle Rock Flowages provide water sports. **Consolidated Papers Forest Tour** (5 m NE on Co. U) through forest and marsh on Wisconsin River.

WYOMING

CASPER: Chamber of Commerce Visitor Center (500 N Center St.), information on historic sites, recreation areas; parks include **N Casper** (N on K St.), on N Platte River, **Garden Creek** (S off SR 220), **Yesness** (S on Poplar St.), **Valley Hills** (S off Mariposa Blvd.)—all with picnicking, walks (1)—and **Casper Mtn** (10 m S) with 3 parks, waterfalls, camping, picnicking, trails (1-3). **Old Fort Casper Museum** (3 m W on W 13th St. & Ft. Casper Rd.), restored frontier fort; exhibits; park adj; mid-May-mid-Sept. daily; free; **1. Fish hatchery** (10 m W), open daily; **1. Oregon Trail** (SW via SR 220) is marked with graves and interpretive signs including Sweetwater Stage Station (46 m); Independence Rock (50 m), with more than 50,000 names carved on it; Devil's Gate (55 m), gorge through Rattlesnake Mtns, frontier ranch bldgs; **1, 2. Petrified Forest** (18 m SW on SR 220, 17 m S off SR 487), trunks and fragments; **1-3. Shirley Mtn** (18 m SW on SR 220, 30 m S off SR 4 & 7), summit reached via 17-m dirt road; camping, hiking (1-3) in historic mining area; June-Oct.; free.

CODY: Buffalo Bill Historical Center (Sheridan Ave. & 8th St.) has art museum, museum of Plains Indians, Cody artifacts (May-Sept. daily; adm); **Buffalo Bill Village** (Sheridan Ave. & 16th Sts.) re-created Western town (summers; possibly spring or fall hrs; adm to some bldgs); **1. Buffalo Bill Reservoir** (W on US 14, 16, 20), camping, picnicking, at Buffalo Bill State Park (N shore); walks (1, 2) on reservoir and along S Fork Shoshone River, overlooks, old mine sites (E), cave (E); seasonal roads surrounding reservoir lead to trailheads in national forest (2,3). **Rattlesnake Mtn** (6 m NW), camping, trails (1-3), views on BLM land. **Carter Mtn** (31 m S on SR 120, 15 m W), view camping, trails (1-3).

 Shoshone National Forest (P.O. Box 961, zip 82414), 2.4-million acres of superlative scenery, most preserved as wilderness; good mtn climbing, many rough trails; it is possible to hike from Popo Agie Primitive Area to Montana. **Beartooth Hwy** (US 212; see also Mont.), one of most scenic routes in the nation, is closed in winter; Island Lake and Beartooth Lake campgrounds, and other lakes N off the hwy, have easy (1, 2) lakeside trails that become rugged (3) as they go N; trails (2, 3) N to lakes and mtns along Muddy Creek and from Lake Creek and Crazy Creek camps; S off hwy near Beartooth Pass are lake trails (2), tough trails (3) through 9-10,000-ft mtns to Clarks Fork Canyon; Clarks Fork also accessible along

SR 296 (between Lake Creek campground and Cody), with campsites, easy trails (1), swamp and creek trails (2, 3), trail along Clarks Fork (2, 3) from S of Hunter Peak camp that may be continued (3) to Beartooth Pass area trails, access to N Absaroka Wilderness (3). **N Absaroka Wilderness,** 350,000 acres of rugged terrain with peaks to 12,000 ft, many miles of trail (mostly 3); access on W from Yellowstone National Park; access on N (to trails going W) from US 212 (S of Fox Creek camp) and SR 296 (near Crandall ranger station); access on E from Sunlight Creek and Dead Indian camps (on SR 296); access on S from Wapiti Valley and via primitive roads from Cody and Buffalo Bill Reservoir. **Wapiti Valley** (along US 14, 16, 20 W of Cody), stunning canyon separating N and S Absaroka Wildernesses; rock formations; many campsites, lodges, easy trails (1, 2); at W end, beautiful Pahaska-Sunlight Trail (starts 2, then 3), follows Shoeshone river Fork N to N Absaroka Wilderness, with spurs W along creeks to Yellowstone park; trail (2) along Grinnell Creek and other creeks; between Eagle Creek camp and Chimney Rock, trails go S along Eagle, Kitty, and Fishhawk creeks (start 2, then 3) to S Absaroka Wilderness; near Fire Memorial is Natural Bridge Trail (2, 3) S to Blackwater Natural Bridge, spur to 11,715-ft Clayton Mtn (3); Elk Fork campground has trail (2, then 3) S along creek to wilderness. **S Absaroka Wilderness,** 480,000 acres with 12,000-ft peaks, is remote country bounded on W by Teton Wilderness (3), on S by Stratified Primitive Area (3); access on N from Wapiti Valley; a road SW of Cody along S Fork of Shoshone River provides trails W at Ishawooa Hill (3), Ishawooa Mesa (3), Deer Creek (2, 3), and S Fork ranger station with S Fork Trail (starts 2, then 3) running S to Stratified Primitive Area and Boulder Basin Trail (starts 2, then 3) going E through Boulder Basin to extensive trail system in Greybull River area (also reachable by several primitive roads W and SW of Greybull). **Stratified Primitive Area,** 200,000 acres, has scattered small lakes, buttes, mtns; virtually all trails follow creeks, with rockhounding and petrified wood in gravel bars; access on W from Teton Wilderness (3); from S Absaroka Wilderness, trails (3) include S Fork Trail (W) and several spurs from Greybull River trail (E); easiest access (2) is to Frontier Creek and Wiggins Fork trails from Double Cabin campground (N of dubois), reachable by road or trail; several primitive roads N of Dubois also offer trailheads (2, 3); on E, long trails (3) enter along the Wood and Wind rivers. **Glacier Primitive Area,** 180,000 acres, is the most rugged section of forest; living glaciers; lakes; bounded on W by Continental Divide and Bridger Wilderness; best entry is on N, via Torrey Lake (starts 2, then 3), which leads to main N-S trail (3) running to Gannett Peak; from Dubois, primitive roads and then trails join this (3); other scattered trails (3) enter from the E along creeks (SE of Dubois along US 26, 287); tough trail (3) in S from Bridger forest. **Popo Agie Primitive Area,** 70,000 acres, is accessible via long trails

(3) on NE from Wind River (closest) or E from Lander; beautiful jagged mtns, deep canyons, many lakes; trails intersect and continue into surrounding forests.

GUERNSEY: This was the first stop W of Ft. Laramie for pioneers on the Oregon Trail; among historic sites with interpretive signs are **Register Rock** (US 26), where emigrants carved their names; **Oregon Trail Ruts** (S off US 26), worn as deep as 5 ft in sandstone; **Emigrants Washtub** (E), a natural pool; information at Oregon Trail Museum (mid-Apr.-early Sept.) in **Guernsey State Park** (3 m N off SR 270), swimming, camping, picnicking on reservoir with high bluffs on N Platte River. Ft. Laramie National Historic Site (25 m E on US 26, SW on SR 160), more than 20 well-preserved bldgs on plains at jct of Laramie and N Platte rivers; visitor center exhibits; living history programs in summer; daily exc Jan. 1, Dec. 25; free; **1.** Ghost towns include **Hartville** (5 m N on SR 270); **Fairbanks-** (near Sunrise; 5½ m N on SR 270); **Jireh** (38 m N on SR 270, then W on US 18, 20), with nearby **Silver Cliff; 2.**

JACKSON: Town Square, ornamented with elkhorns and lined with Western shops **(1). National Elk Refuge** (E & N of town), 23,500 acres with exhibition pasture (daily all year); **National Fish Hatchery** (1 m N of Elk Refuge), daily; **1.**

    Grand Teton National Park (4 m N on US 26, 89, 187), 40-m-long range of peaks (13,770-ft Grand Teton the highest) soaring abruptly out of sagebrush flats and reflected in morainal lakes; most facilities (lodges, campsites, horse rental, water sports) are on the flats; 200-m trail system into the mtns (trail maps, mountaineering school, guides, and shelters available); climbers and off-trail hikers must register. **Moose Visitor Center** (daily exc Dec. 25) has information, fur-trade museum; visitor centers at **Jenny Lake** (8 m N) and **Colter Bay** (24 m N) are open seasonally, also with good exhibits. Good trails: N of **Moose,** 2-m trails **(2)** to Taggart or Bradley Lake (can be combined in 5-m round-trip hike); from N of **Bradley Lake,** trails climb 2500 ft W to Surprise or Amphitheatre lakes **(2-3)** or go N **(2)** to Jenny Lake; from S of **Taggart Lake** a trail **(2, 3)** follows Beaver Creek S to Phelps Lake, Death Canyon (spur to Teton Peaks), Open Canyon, Granite Canyon, Teton Village, and into surrounding national forest—this extensive system can also be reached off road S of Moose, from Teton Village, or from Coal Creek campground near Teton Pass; walks **(1)** at **Menor-Nobie Historic District** (on Snake River) and at **Cunningham Cabin Historic Exhibit** (12 m N on US 26, 89, 187); climb **(2)** to 7688-ft **Blacktail Butte** (S of hq off pkwy) for excellent view. At **Jenny Lake,** ¼-m nature trail **(1);** 6.6-m trail around lake **(2);** W of lake, a trail ½-m to **Hidden Falls** and climb to overlook **(2)** may be continued up Cascade Canyon N 6 m to Lake Solitude or S to Teton peaks **(3);** N of lake, 3.5-m loop (2) of **String Lake,** with 3-m spur (2) N along Leigh Lake that continues .7-m farther to Bearpaw Lake or a spur (2, 3) W in Indian Paintbrush Canyon 4½ m to Holly Lake and 2½ m more to Lake Solitude (meeting trail from Jenny Lake); S of lake, short trails climb W 2500 ft to Amphitheatre or Surprise lakes, or connect S to Bradley Lake. At **Colter Bay,** 1½-m nature trail (1) from Colter Bay Marina over causeway to pretty island in Jackson Lake; from Colter Bay or Jackson Lodge, 8.8-m loop (2) of lovely **Hermitage Point,** a peninsula in Jackson Lake; from lodge, trails (1, 2) circle **Emma Matilda Lake** with overlooks and spurs to Two Ocean Lake; S of lodge, trail (2) to **Signal Mtn;** trails (2, 3) follow **Arizona, Pilgrim,** and **Pacific** creeks (all off US 89, 287 between Buffalo entrance and Fonda Pt.) into Teton Wilderness; from ranger station at **Wilcox Pt.** (NW shore of Jackson Lake), trails (2, 3) loop through Webb Canyon, Owl Creek, other creeks, with spurs W and N into national forests.

Bridger-Teton National Forest (hq in Kemmerer, Wy 83101), 3,400,000 acres of magnificent scenery surrounding town; extends N to Yellowstone National Park (access trails), E to Shoshone National Forest (many connecting trails), borders Grand Teton National Park (access trails), S (on US 89) to beyond Smoot, SE (E off US 187) to S Pass City (SR 28); many miles of trail; rock climbing. **Teton Wilderness** (S of Yellowstone Park), 563,500 acres of high plateaus, coniferous forests, wide valleys and meadows (including Yellowstone River Valley), steep canyons along Continental Divide, scattered lakes; 400 m of trail interconnect to reach virtually all areas; good access from: Snake River campsite area (US 89, 287 between Yellowstone and Grand Teton parks) with swimming at nearby hot springs (1-3); Grand Teton Park (2, 3); stunning campsites E of Moran (off US 26, 287), with other trails S (2, 3), NE to Breccia Cliffs area (3), N to lovely falls (2) on S Fork of Buffalo River. **Gros Ventre Slide Geological Area** (8 m NE of Jackson on US 89, then 10 m E on Gros Ventre Rd.), overlook and interpretive trail (1) at site where mountainside slid into the valley, damming the river into a lake; **Red Hills** aand other camps (E of slide area) are good bases for trails (2, 3) E along creeks off this road; trails (2) via Gros Ventre River and Crystal Creek connect S (3) to those in Gros Ventre Mtns. **Hoback River Canyon** (along US 189, 187 SE of Jackson) has trails (2,3) along creeks N and S of river, campsites; N on road along Granite Creek are campsites, hot springs (small pool for swimming), many trails (1-3) into Gros Ventre Mtns. Beautiful **Snake River's** "Grand Canyon" (NE of Alpine Junction on US 26, 89) has many campsites with trails (1-3) going N into Targhee Forest and S into Bridger Forest. **Grey's River** (SE of Alpine Junction), also scenic; many campsites with trails (1-3); some trails (mostly 2) follow creeks, but others (mostly 3) follow ridges many miles S throughout this entire section of forest to Hams Fork campground at S end. **Swift Creek** camp (E of Afton) has trails along creeks (2), to ridges (3), and to lovely canyon with Periodic Spring (2) which turns itself on and off every 18 minutes in summer. Campsites at **Middle Piney Lake** (W OF Marbleton) have lake (1), creek (2), ridge (3) trails; the **Lander Cut-off of the Oregon Trail** (marked with graves and plaques from S Pass to Ft. Hall in Idaho) enters the forest S of here (it passes N of Marbleton, then W along S Piney Creek), via Snider Basin ranger station, goes W to Smiths Fork ranger station, then turns N toward Afton. **Green River** area (NW of Pinedale), scenic, warm springs, waterfalls, historic sites, camping, walks (1), trails (2); Bridger Wilderness is easily accessible from beautiful trails (1, 2) around Lower Green River Lake, with longer trails (3) into wilderness from Upper Green River Lake. A BLM campground outside the forest (17 m N of Pinedale on US 187) gives access to Green River farther S; 1, 2. **Bridger Wilderness** (E of Pinedale), 383,000 acres of rugged landscape in Wind River Range, 1300 lakes, largest glaciers outside of Alaska (including Mammoth Glacier), mtns that include 13,804-ft Gannett Peak; Continental Divide on E boundary (trails cross in S to Popo Agie Primitive Area, 3); 600 m on interconnecting trails are mostly 3, but easy walks (1) and trails (2) are at **New Fork Lakes** (NW of Pinedale), **Fremont Lake** area (N of Pinedale) with Elkhart Park and nearby lakes, **Boulder Lake** (E of Pinedale), all with campgrounds; **Big Sandy** camp (SE of Pinedale off SR 353) also has wilderness access (2, 3); also mtn climbing.

LARAMIE: University of Wyoming (9-15th, Ivinson to Lewis Sts.) is beautifully landscaped, flower beds, botanic gardens (free), museums (free), stock farm (W end of city across Laramie River); 1.

Medicine Bow National Forest (hq in Laramie, zip 82070), 1-million acres in beautiful Medicine Bow Mtns, many fishing streams; visitor information center at **Centennial** (30 m W on SR 130) is start of 30-m scenic drive through **Snowy Range Lake Region;** many camp and picnic sites here have interconnecting trails (1, 2) plus climbs (3) including 12,013-ft Medicine Bow Peak; Brush Creek Trail (2) may be continued (3) over 6 m W; trail (2) S from Silver Lake camp along French Creek; trail N (mostly 2) 8 m via Sheep and Sand lakes to Deep Creek camp and then N to Crater Lake (2) or N along Deep Creek (2,3) to Arlington; trail S (mostly 2) from Libby Flats may be continued (3) 11 m to Holmes campground (N of Keystone). Forest roads in the **Keystone area** have trailheads for the many creeks—Savage Run and Mullen (NW), Muddy (SE), Devil's Gate and Douglas (SW). **Lake Owen** (S of Albany) and **Miller Lake** area (at Foxpark off SR 230) have camping, picnicking, trails at lakes, along creeks, to mtn peaks (1-3). **Jack Creek Camp** (40 m S of Rawlins via SR 71) has a tough climb (3) via lakes to 11,004-ft Bridger Peak on Continental Divide (trail may be continued to Battle Pass); Battle Pass (13 m SW of Encampment on SR 70) is also trailhead for hikes (2, 3) along creeks SW

(Battle Creek and Haskins Creek camps are good bases) that are more easily reached (2) from camps near Sandstone ranger station (NE of Savery). **Encampment River Trail** (S of Encampment) starts 2 but may be continued more than 20 m; it ends on primitive road to lookout on 10,979-ft Blackhall Mtn (off SR 230, E of Riverside); other creek trails (1, 2) also reached off SR 230 (SE of Riverside). **Sherman Mtns Unit** (11 m E off I-80), a rocky, wooded area with streams, waterfalls, has short trails (1, 2) at camp and picnic grounds plus climbs (1,2) at camp and picnic grounds plus climbs (2,3) to 9053-ft Pole Mtn from Tie City camp or Wallis picnic site; rockhounding (1), trails (2), rock climbing (3) among rock formations at **Vedauwoo** camp and picnic area.

RAWLINS: Ruins of **Ft. Fred Steele** (15 m E off I-80); **1. Saratoga Hot Springs State Park** (20 m E on I-80, 21 m S on SR 130), small park, picnicking, swimming in mineral water pool; nearby fish hatchery and public access areas on N Platte River; **1. Bennett Park** (22 m SE of Saratoga via SR 130, 203), via dirt road, BLM camping, picnicking, hiking (1-3). **Grand Encampment Mining District** (20 m E on I-80, 28 m S on SR 130, 10 m S off SR 230) contains ghost town of Encampment (1) with preserved bldgs, museum (late spring-fall daily; sm adm); 7 other ghost towns and many mining remains nearby (1, 2); BLM campsite on Encampment River, with trails (1-3), is 2 m S via primitive road.

RIVERTON: Surrounded by **Wind River Indian Reservation,** with hq in historic bldgs of former Ft. Washakie; nearby swimming in mineral springs; museum and historic mission at Ethete; trails (2, 3) to mtn lakes. **Castle Garden Pictograph Site** (25 m E on Gas Hills Rd.), picnicking; **1, 2. Sinks Canyon State Park** (24 m S on SR 789 to Lander, 10 m SW on SR 131), where fork of Popo Agie River disappears into a cave and reappears as a spring pool; visitor center; camping; nature trails (1, 2), overlooks, hiking trails (2, 3).

ROCK SPRINGS: Flaming Gorge National Recreation Area (see Utah) is accessible SW (off I-80 via SR 373) to E shore or from visitor information station at Green River (15 m W on I-80, S on SR 530) to W shore; camping; walking (1, 2) on dirt or primitive roads on either shore, with trailless hiking and climbing (2, 3) in some areas; especially beautiful is Firehole Canyon area (E shore), with camping.

SHERIDAN: Bradford Brinton Memorial Ranch (7 m S on US 87, 5 m SW on SR 334), ranchouse with Western art; carriage barn; mid-May-early Sept. daily; free; **1. Ft. Phil Kearney Site** (22 m S off US 87) with monument to Fetterman massacre; interpretive signs; **1. Buffalo Chamber of Commerce** (35 m S on US 87 & 55 N Main St., Buffalo) offers booklets for self-guiding tours of historic sites and ranches; guided car caravan tours in summer. **Bighorn National Forest** (hq in Sheridan, zip 82801), 1-million acres W of town; striking mtns rise abruptly out of Great Plains to peaks over 13,000 ft; 300 lakes; 137,000-acre **Cloud Peak Wilderness** is at 8500-13,000-ft elevations along the rugged divide of Big Horn Range; many miles of fine trails include: **Medicine Wheel** (W of Burgess Junction on US 14A), on 9956-ft Medicine Wheel Mtn, a mysterious circle made of stones in prehistoric times; other stone constructions nearby; reached by short trail (**2**) from road; nearby are Fire Springs Falls (nature trail), picnic area, historic sites, Porcupine campground with trail (**2, 3**) NE along Little Bighorn River with spur to Burgess Junction trails. **Burgess Junction** (jct US 14, 14A) has ranger station, camping, picnicking; trail (**2, 3**) NW to Little Bighorn River has spurs; trail (**2, 3**) NE to Tongue Canyon; trails (**1,2**) at nearby Prune Creek, Sibley Lake. **Woodrock** campground area (S of Burgess Junction off US 14) has extensive trail system (**1-3**) including Wolf Creek, Black and Lookout Mtns, Duncan Lake; trails SE to Big Goose area may be continued into Cloud Peak Wilderness. **Granite Creek,** Shell Creek, Post Creek (S of Woodrock camp on US 14) have camp and picnic areas, trails (**1, 2**); waterfalls; trails (**3**) N to rugged divide of Big Horn Mtns. **Big Goose** tranger station (SW of Sheridan via SR 335) is a pretty lake area with camp and picnic grounds, easy trails (**1, 2**); extensive trail system includes trails (**2, 3**) SW and S into Cloud Peak Wilderness (also accessible via roads and trails W off US 87 between Sheridan and Buffalo). **Hunter** ranger station (W of Buffalo on US 16), with nearby camp and picnic grounds, has many easy trails (**1, 2**) plus extensive trail system (**2, 3**); good access into Cloud Peak Wilderness W (**2, 3**) to jewel-like lakes including Lake Solitude, NW (**3**) to lakes, 13,165-ft Cloud Peak, 13,014-ft Blacktooth Mtn; also lower overlooks such as Hunter Mesa (**2**). **Crazy Woman** campground (S of Hunter ranger station on US 16) has several creek trails (**2**), mtn climbing (**3**); Sheep Mtn lookout reachable by trail (**3**) or road. Beautiful **Tensleep Creek** Canyon (NE of Ten Sleep on US 16) has many camp and picnic sites on creek and on nearby Meadow Lark Lake; short lake, creek, overlook trails (**1, 2**); long trails (**2, 3**) N include hikes to Lake Solitude area of Cloud Peak **Wilderness** and to Paint Rock Creek; wilderness area also reachable from **Cold Springs** campground or camps at **Paint Rock Lakes** ranger station (both accessible via seasonal road from Hyattville).

SUNDANCE: Sundance Commercial Club (zip 82729) provides information on recreation; N are the Black Hills; S are Thunder Basin National Grasslands, with big game, fossil deposits (another section is NW at Weston); directions to ghost towns of Mineral Hill and Welcome from Crook Co. Museum (in courthouse, open weekdays). **Black Hills National Forest** (see S. Dakota) has campsites NW on forest road, trails

(2) along creeks and in low Bear Lodge Mtns, lookout on Warren Peak; unit E has streams, small lakes, Cement Ridge lookout (2, 3); 6313-ft Inyan Kara Mtn (S) is a tiny unit preserving the landmark on which Gen. Custer carved his name (2, 3). **Keyhole State Park** (14 m W on I-90, 8 m NW), on reservoir on Belle Fourche River, camping, picnicking, swimming (1, 2). **Devil's Tower National Monument** (29 m NW on SR 24), 1280-ft landmark above grasslands is a molten rock intrusion covered with many-hued lichens that glow in certain lights; visitor center (May-Oct. daily); campfire programs in summer; booklet for 1¼-m self-guiding Tower Trail (1), circling base; 2¾-m Red Beds Trail also circles tower (); 1½-m Joyner Ridge trail to N (2); 1½-m Valley View trail to S (2); exhibits at prairie dog colony; camping; picnicking; skilled climbers who have proper equipment may ascend the tower (3).

THERMOPOLIS: Hot Springs State Park (E of river on US 20), surrounds large hot springs; mineral cones and terraces; bathhouse; indoor and outdoor pools; camping; picnicking; **1. Wind River Canyon** (S along US 20), has interesting formations; **Boysen State Park** (20 m S on US 20), on huge reservoir, has swimming beaches, camping, picnicking (1). **Castle Garden** (33 m N on US 20 to Worland, 18 m E on US 16, 6 m S), colorful badlands with striking formations, Rainbow Canyon; walking (1-3).

YELLOWSTONE NATIONAL PARK: Mammoth Hot Springs Visitor Center (5 m S of Gardiner, Mont., from N Entrance) is open all yr; E (W of Cody), S (N of Jackson) and W (E of Yellowstone) entrances plus interior roads are open, weather permitting, May-Oct.; NE entrance (W of Cooke City) is usually open June-mid-Oct.; 6 other visitor centers, accommodations, campgrounds, and other facilities are generally open mid-June-Labor Day or later; information from Supt. (zip 82190). Grand Loop Road forms a figure-8 through the park center, linking all entrances, facilities, most trailheads, other attractions. Visitor Centers provide excellent exhibits and publications; schedules of naturalist-led walks, other activities.

The 1000-m trail system varies from paved paths to backcountry hikes into adj national forests; **Mammoth Hot Springs**, self-guiding boardwalks (1,2) to beautifully hued travertine terraces, flowing springs; trails (3) across Gallatin Range; nearby trails (1-3) to other formations, waterfalls, Appolinaris Spring, Grizzly Lake, Mt. Holmes, Obsidian Cliff. **Norris Geyser Basin** (21 m S), 2-m self-guided boardwalk and trail (1, 2) through exciting area with hundreds of geysers and hot springs; trail (2, 3) to lakes and canyon area; museum; nearby wildlife meadows, Gibbon Geyser Basin (2) with violent and colorful springs, Artist Paint Pots with vivid-hued bubbling mud springs (1, 2), steep 1-m trail to Monument Geyser Basin (2) thermal activities and waterfalls in dark-walled Gibbon

Canyon **Madison Junction** (14 m SW of Norris), beautiful, placed Madison River; boardwalk to lovely Terrace Springs (1); climb to 2000-ft overlook on Purple Mtn (2); Firehole Canyon with cascades against black lava rock, wildflowers (1,2); ½-m boardwalk (1); boardwalk (2) to Grand Prismatic, largest hot spring, other thermal features; Biscuit Basin with beautiful Sapphire Pool and geysers (1, 2), 1-m trail (2) to Mystic Falls, trail (3) across Continental Divide. **Old Faithful** (16 m S of Madison), with boardwalk and trails (1, 2) among erupting geysers, stunning pools (including Emerald); trail (2) to overlook and Solitary geyser; Kepler Cascades (1) with trail (3) over Continental Divide; 7½-m trail (2, 3) to stunning Shoshone Lake and its geyser basin and beyond; Craig Pass trail (3) via Shoshone Lake and beyond; beautiful lakes and dense forests in this area. **West Thumb** (17 m SE of Old Faithful) and Grant Visitor Center have museum, beautiful small geyser basin (2), Lewis River Falls and Lewis Lake (1), spectacular Moose Falls (2); trails (2, 3) go W toward Shoshone Lake, Old Faithful; trails (3) go E to Mt. Sheridan, Heart Lake, and continue out of park or along S and E shores of Yellowstone Lake to Steamboat Pt. near Fishing Bridge. **Bridge Bay** and **Fishing Bridge** (34 m NE of W Thumb) are on NW shore of Yellowstone Lake; museum; walks **1, 2**; trails (3) go E to E Entrance and NE to NE Entrance into beautiful Alpine scenery of Absaroka Range, hidden lakes, overlooks (short stretches on these trails are **2**); trail (2, 3) N toward Canyon; N are dark mud geysers, most with pungent odors, many with awesome sound effects, some brightly colored (1,2), and sagebrush flats and meadows favored by big game and waterfowl. **Canyon** is in park center (26 m N of Fishing Bridge, 19 m E of Norris, 31 m S of Tower), at the stunning yellow canyon for which the park was named; trails here are wonderful; on N and S rims of Grand Canyon of the Yellowstone, paved trails (1) give spectacular views of waterfalls among most beautiful in the nation; other short trails (2) drop below the rims for closer views of falls and wildlife area; 3-m, 1400-ft climb to Observation Point (2,3) on N rim for an outstanding view; 1½-m, strenuous (2,3) Uncle Tom Trail (S rim) is also worth the effort; many other trails (2,3) go down and along the canyon; trail follows the river S, as it changes from raging to placid, through Hayden Valley meadows to Yellowstone Lake (start is **2**, full length is **3**); trail W (2) via beautiful lakes (3-9-m) goes to Norris (3); trail E (3) to Wapiti Lake (18 m) continues to NE and E entrances; trail SW to Fountain Paint Pot (3). **Tower** (29 m E of Mammoth Hot Springs), pine forests, extinct hot springs, petrified tree, waterfalls (1,2); all-day hikes (3) S to petrified forests of Specimen Ridge (ranger-conducted hikes sometimes offered, **2**); lovely trails in Lamar River Valley (2) S to E Entrance (3); several trails along Yellowstone River, Slough Creek, other nearby creeks are **2** but continue for miles in backcountry (3).